THE Ayn Rand LETTER®

VOLUMES 1–4
1971–1976

Published by the Ayn Rand Institute
6 Hutton Centre Drive, Suite 600, Santa Ana, CA 92707

ISBN 1-56114-147-X
Library of Congress Catalog Card Number: 90-61904

13 12 11 10 9 8 7

Printed in the United States of America

The following is Ayn Rand's handwritten, edited manuscript of the opening and closing passages of Atlas Shrugged.

September 2, 1946

I "The Calendar"

"Who is John Galt?"

The light was ebbing, and Eddie Willers could not distinguish the bum's face. The bum had said it simply, without expression. But from the sunset far at the end of the street, yellow glints caught his eyes, and the eyes looked straight at Eddie Willers, mocking and still; as if the question had been addressed to the causeless uneasiness within him.

„Why did you say that?" Eddie Willers asked sharply.

„Why does anybody say it?"

The sound of mockery was unmistakeable in the drawling, indifferent voice. The bum leaned against the side of the doorway; a wedge of broken glass behind him reflected the metal yellow of the sky.

„Why does it bother you?" he added.

„It doesn't," snapped Eddie Willers.

There was only a void of darkness and rock, but the darkness was hiding the ruins of a continent: the roofless homes, the rusting tractors, the lightless streets, the abandoned rail. But far in the distance, on the edge of the earth, a small flame was waving in the wind, the defiant and stubborn flame of Wyatt's Torch, twisting, being torn and regaining its hold, not to be uprooted or extinguished. It seemed to be calling and waiting for the words John Galt was now to pronounce.

"The road is cleared," said Galt. "We are going back to the world."

He raised his hand and over the desolate earth he traced in space the sign of the dollar.

Ayn Rand

The End

March 20, 1957

TABLE OF CONTENTS

VOLUME III

Vol. 1, No. 1 October 11, 1971

CREDIBILITY AND POLARIZATION

Intellectual confusion is the hallmark of the twentieth century, induced by those whose task is to provide enlightenment: by modern intellectuals.

One of their methods is the destruction of language - and, therefore, of thought and, therefore, of communication - by means of anti-concepts. An anti-concept is an unnecessary and rationally unusable term designed to replace and obliterate some legitimate concept. The use of anti-concepts gives the listeners a sense of *approximate* understanding. But in the realm of cognition, nothing is as bad as the approximate. If, loaded with too many approximations, you find yourself giving up the attempt to understand today's world, check your premises and the words you are hearing. To understand what one hears and reads today requires a special translation.

Now to introduce myself, in this context. Philosophically, I am an advocate of reason. Practically, my task is to demonstrate that man needs philosophy in order to discover the proper way to live on earth. Journalistically, part of my task is to serve as a translator by identifying, whenever necessary, the meaning of the worst anti-concepts in our cultural smog. Colloquially, in this respect, call me a bromide-buster.

One of today's fashionable anti-concepts is "polarization." Its meaning is not very clear, except that it is something bad - undesirable, socially destructive, evil - something that would split the country into irreconcilable camps and conflicts. It is used mainly in political issues and serves as a kind of "argument from intimidation": it replaces a discussion of the merits (the truth or falsehood) of a given idea by the menacing accusation that such an idea would "polarize" the country - which is supposed to make one's opponents retreat, protesting that they didn't mean it. Mean - what?

"Polarization" is a term borrowed from physics; a dictionary defines "polarity" as: "the presence or manifestation of two opposite or contrasting principles or tendencies." (*Random House Dictionary*, 1966.)

Transplanted from the realm of physics to the realm of social issues, this term means a situation in which men hold "opposite or contrasting" views or ideas (*principles*), and goals or values (*tendencies*). When used as a pejorative term, this means that men should not differ in their views, ideas, goals and values, that such differences are evil, that *men must not disagree*.

This notion is propagated by the same intellectuals who denounce conformity, decry the status quo, clamor for change, and proclaim that the right to dissent includes the right to implement it by physical force.

But - the anti-polarizers might protest - they do not object to all disagreements: the key term in the above definition is "principles"; which is true. It is principles - fundamental principles - that they are struggling to eliminate from public discussion. It is a clash of fundamental principles that the term "polarization" is intended to hide and to avert. Fundamental principles, they feel, must be accepted uncritically - on faith, by "instinct," by implication, by emotional commitment - and must never be named or questioned. No, they do not mind dissent and differences - such differences as between St. Peter and St. Paul, or Auguste Comte and Karl Marx, or Senator Muskie and Senator Kennedy. But do not dare bring up the differences between Aristotle and Marcuse, or Adam Smith and J.M. Keynes, or George Washington and Richard M. Nixon. This would polarize the country, they cry. And it sure would.

The most timid, frightened, conservative defenders of the status quo - of the intellectual status quo - are today's liberals (the leaders of the conservatives never ventured into the realm of the intellect). What they dread to discover is the fact that the intellectual status quo they inherited is bankrupt, that they have no ideological base to stand on and no capacity to construct one. Brought up on the philosophy of Pragmatism, they have been taught that principles are unprovable, impractical or non-existent - which has destroyed their ability to integrate ideas, to deal with abstractions, and to see beyond the range of the immediate moment. Abstractions, they claim, are "simplistic" (another anti-concept); myopia is sophisticated. "Don't polarize!" and "Don't rock the boat!" are expressions of the same kind of panic.

It is doubtful - even in the midst of today's intellectual decadence - that one could get away with declaring explicitly: "Let us abolish all debate on fundamental principles!" (though some men have tried it). If, however, one declares: "Don't let us polarize," and suggests a vague image of warring camps ready to fight (with no mention of the fight's object), one has a chance to silence the mentally weary. The use of "polarization" as a pejorative term means: the suppression of fundamental principles. Such is the pattern of the function of anti-concepts.

The leaders of today's intellectuals are probably aware of the fact that the injunction to avoid polarization means that unity - a nation's unity - must be given priority over reason, logic and truth, which is a fundamental principle of collectivism. But the rank-and-file intellectuals are not aware of it: it is too abstract a conclusion. Like children and savages, they believe that human wishes are omnipotent, that everything would be all right if only we'd all agree on it, and that anything can be solved by cooperation, negotiation and compromise.

This has been the ruling doctrine in our political, academic and intellectual life for the last fifty years or longer, with no noteworthy dissenters but one: reality.

The ideal of "consensus" did not work. It did not lead to social harmony among men, or security or confidence or unity or mutual understanding and good will. It has led us to a general sense of hostility, of fear, uncertainty, lethargy, bitterness, cynicism, and a growing mistrust of everyone by everyone.

The same intellectuals who advocate non-polarization, are now deploring the "credibility gap." They do not realize that the latter is the unavoidable consequence of the former.

If clear-cut principles, unequivocal definitions and inflexible goals are barred from public discussion, then a speaker or writer has to struggle to hide his meaning (if any) under coils of meaningless generalities and safely popular bromides. Regardless of whether his message is good or bad, true or false, he cannot state it openly, but must smuggle it into his audience's subconscious by means of the same unfocused, deceptive, evasive verbiage. He must strive to be misunderstood in the greatest number of ways by the greatest number of people: this is the only way to keep up the pretense of unity.

If, in such conditions, people are urged to cooperate, negotiate or compromise, how are they to do it? How can they cooperate, if their common goal is not named explicitly? How can they negotiate, if the intentions of the various men or groups involved are not revealed? How can they know, when they compromise, whether they have made a reasonable deal or sold out their future? Since there is no way to do it - since concrete problems cannot even be grasped, let alone judged or solved, without reference to abstract principles - men begin to regard social relationships not as a matter of dealing with one another, but of putting something over on one another. And the worst of it is not that this policy turns the men who act in good faith into easy prey for the frauds and the manipulators. The worst of it is the genuine misunderstandings between honest men who take the loose verbiage to mean two opposite things. If there is a surer way to breed mistrust and bitterness, I do not know of it.

In politics, the intellectuals profess their desire "to make democracy work" and their devotion to the will of the people as expressed by vote. How are people to choose or trust their representatives in an age of non-polarizing language? A parliamentary system stands or falls on the quality - the precision - of public communication (and its precondition: the freedom of public information). A program, platform, promise, or forecast of the future cannot be offered except in terms of explicitly defined principles - and such principles are the people's only means of ascertaining whether a candidate has kept his word or not. In the last decades, people have become cynically accustomed to ignoring the empty catch phrases of campaign oratory and to voting on the basis of implications. But this does not work - as has been demonstrated definitively by Mr. Nixon, who made a U-turn on a dime (or on a paper dollar), discarding overnight every approximate principle he was approximately believed to stand for. (I shall discuss Mr. Nixon's performance in a subsequent Letter.) Whatever our politicians now talk about, they had better not talk about reviving anyone's "faith in the democratic process" or about credibility.

In the absence of intellectual polarization, we are witnessing the growth of the ugliest kind of divisiveness or existential polarization, if you will: pressure-group warfare. The country is splitting into dozens of blind, deaf, but screaming camps, each drawn together not by loyalty to an idea, but by the accident of race, age, sex, religious creed, or the frantic whim of a given moment - not by values held in common, but by a common hatred of some other group - not by choice, but by terror.

When men abandon principles (i.e., their conceptual faculty), two of the major results are: individually, the inability to project the future; socially, the impossibility of communication. Trapped in a maze of immediate problems, with no means of grasping the context, causes, consequences or solutions, men seek a way out by ganging up on one another, which means: by accepting brute physical force as the ultimate arbiter of disputes. A shrunken, range-of-the-moment mentality sees other men as the immediate cause of its troubles; it can see no further; forcing its demands on others is the only answer it can grasp. But these others, acting on the same non-principle, gang up to retaliate and to force _their_ demands, which leads _their_ intended victims to gang up, and so on. Who is the ultimate victim? The smallest minority on earth: the individual - which means: every man qua man.

Is there a solution? Yes. In its present state, what this country needs above all is the clarifying, reassuring, confidence-and-credibility-inspiring guidance of fundamental principles - i.e., in modern parlance, _intellectual polarization_.

This would bring to our cultural atmosphere an all-but-forgotten quality: honesty, with its corollary, clarity. It would establish the minimum requirement of civilized discourse: that the proponents of ideas strive to make themselves understood and lay all their cards on the table (including their axioms). It would leave no significant audience or influence to those who specialize in the unintelligible, or preach blatant contradictions, or proclaim ends with total unconcern for means, or hold fundamental principles they would not dare name openly, or disseminate anti-concepts. It would enable men to know their own stand and that of their adversaries. It would enable them to make conscious choices and to take the consequences - or to change their course, when proved wrong. What they would regain is the power to understand, to consider, to judge - and to communicate with one another. What they would lose is the sense of suffocating in a smog of impotent bewilderment.

What if men disagree, you ask? No open disagreement can be as destructive as the secret, nameless, virulent hostility now splintering this country.

But isn't unity desirable, you ask? Unity is a consequence, not a primary. The unity of a lynch mob, of Nazi storm troopers or of the Soviet press is not desirable. Only fundamental principles, rationally validated, clearly understood and voluntarily accepted, can create a desirable kind of unity among men.

But such principles cannot be defined, you say? Check your premises and those of the speakers who told you so. There is a science whose task is to discover and define fundamental principles. It is the forgotten, neglected, subverted and currently disgraced base of all the other sciences: philosophy.

Ayn Rand

The Ayn Rand Letter, published fortnightly by The Ayn Rand Letter, Inc., 183 Madison Avenue, New York, N.Y. 10016.

Contributing Editor: **Leonard Peikoff**; Subscription Director: **Elayne Kalberman**; Production Manager: **Barbara Weiss.**

Vol. 1, No. 2 October 25, 1971

"THE MORATORIUM ON BRAINS"

> "Hell, what it comes down to is that we can manage to exist as and where we are, but we can't afford to move! So we've got to stand still. We've got to stand still. We've got to make those bastards stand still!"

If you have read Atlas Shrugged, you know the meaning - and the relevance - of this quotation. If you have not, I suggest that you read the first sequence of Chapter VI, Part II. It will give you some idea of the political motives, philosophical goals, psychological mechanisms, intellectual stature, and moral dignity behind an event such as the wage-price freeze of August 15, 1971. But please do not think that that sequence is literary naturalism, a journalistic report on the conference at Camp David on August 13-14, with the names changed to protect the guilty. It was published fourteen years ago.

If one knows the principles behind a given policy, one can predict the direction it will take and the ultimate results. Besides, the progression of this particular policy has been repeated in country after country, with consequences that no one but a modern newsman could take as news.

The special twist, in the case of Mr. Nixon, is that his counterparts on the road to statism in other countries were not elected to office on the implicit promise to save the country from a statist trend. In spite of the usual pragmatist evasions, it was clear to his supporters and enemies alike that he was elected as a champion - or semi-champion - of free enterprise. If one needs factual proof of the danger of implicit promises, unnamed hopes, undeclared principles - i.e., of the futility and impracticality of playing it short-range - Mr. Nixon is the proof. He is an immortal refutation of Pragmatism.

The worst thing one can say about Mr. Nixon is that he is sincere. A clever demagogue would not believe that one can protect a country's freedom by establishing the foundation, the principle and the precedent of a totalitarian dictatorship. Mr. Nixon, apparently, does.

It used to be widely believed that the election of a semi-conservative (a "moderate") is a way of gaining time and delaying the statist advance. President Eisenhower proved the opposite; President Nixon proved it conclusively. Their policies have not delayed, but helped and accelerated the march to statism. A major reason is the silencing and destruction of the opposition. If Mr. Nixon's program had been proposed by a liberal Democrat, the Republicans would have screamed their heads off - either on some remnant of principle or, at least, on the grounds of narrow party interests. But when total economic controls are imposed by a Republican President - in the name of preserving free enterprise -

who, among today's politicians, is going to protest and in the name of what?

Mr. Nixon's lip service to free enterprise is the most offensive aspect of his performance. It is adding insult to injury - if one considers his estimate of the people's intelligence. But this is an objective conclusion, i.e., a conclusion based on judging statements by their relation to facts. It is not Mr. Nixon's viewpoint: he does not see it as lip service, he means it. As a pragmatist, he believes that anything is "free enterprise" if we believe it is, and nothing is "dictatorship" if we don't use that name. To him, apparently, _voluntary enslavement_ is neither a contradiction in terms nor the vilest form of self-abasing pretense; it is the central concept, the theme, the hope and the plea of his new economic policy.

"I am today ordering a freeze on all prices and wages throughout the United States for a period of ninety days," declared Mr. Nixon in the briefest paragraph of his speech on August 15 - thus paralyzing the initiative, extinguishing the prospects, wiping out the plans, abrogating the contracts, obliterating the personal choice, judgment and control over his own life of every individual in this country. A country in which a government official has the power to do this, is _not_ a free country.

"It is temporary," he explained, two paragraphs later. "To put the strong vigorous American economy into a permanent strait jacket would lock in unfairness; it would stifle the expansion of our free-enterprise system..." How is a _temporary_ strait jacket going to foster expansion? No answer - unless you take the following as an implicit answer: if a man could manage to put on a strait jacket all by himself, it would not hamper his freedom of movement. But he can't, you say? Mr. Nixon thinks that a nation can. "I am relying on the voluntary cooperation of all Americans..." he declared in the next paragraph. "Working together, we will break the back of inflation, and we will do it without the mandatory wage and price controls that crush economic and personal freedom."

This means: if you don't move, if you stand still, your freedom will not be crushed.

("'Say,' asked Kinnan, 'how is the emergency to end if everything is to stand still?' 'Don't be theoretical,' said Mouch impatiently. 'We've got to deal with the situation of the moment.'" This is from the above-mentioned conference in _Atlas Shrugged_.)

Counting, apparently, on the concrete-bound mentality of pragmatists, Mr. Nixon tried to reassure the country by asserting that dictatorial power is not dictatorial power if it is not embodied in the physical shape of a swarm of men. "While the wage-price freeze will be backed by Government sanctions, if necessary, it will not be accompanied by the establishment of a huge price-control bureaucracy." This is worse than control by bureaucracy, and this is the meaning Mr. Nixon attaches to the term "voluntary": control by fear.

Either in the belief that his audience was asleep, or as a final seal on the fact that words do not mean anything to anyone any longer, Mr. Nixon permitted himself the following: "Freedom brought America where it is today and freedom is the road to the future for America" - in an address asking Congress to help him abolish the last of it. (September 9.)

The purpose of the freeze, Mr. Nixon kept repeating, is to stop inflation. But what is the cause of inflation? There is only one cause, as the science of economics and the history of wrecked economies have demonstrated time and time again: the expansion of the money supply to finance government spending. Mr. Nixon almost admitted as much. "We have paid out nearly $150-billion in foreign aid, economic and military, over the past twenty-five years," he explained in his speech to Congress.

If you are now asked to "tighten your belt," to forgo a raise you had counted on and earned, to lower your expectations and your standard of living, to accept a bleak future with no advance or improvement in sight, remember that foreign aid is the drain down which your work, your hope and your freedom have been poured. (There were other, domestic drains in the past twenty-five years, such as the welfare-state programs. Now the U.S. dollar, like a rubber check, is bouncing, marked: "Account overdrawn.")

Mr. Nixon did not condemn the policy of his predecessors. "We have done this," he declared in the same speech, "because we are America, and America is a good and a generous nation." Sentimentality is embarrassing, even in cheap popular songs that use some such line as "because you're you." But to hear that sort of explanation in regard to a national tragedy, goes painfully beyond embarrassment.

That line, however, is a clue to the deeper cause of the disaster.

Unlike his counterparts in other lands, Mr. Nixon had no scapegoat to blame for our troubles. He merely hinted darkly at some undefined "international money speculators" who are somehow responsible for it all. (Which raises the question of how did the makers of our foreign policy leave this country's fate at the mercy of such "speculators" and of any moment's panic.) But look for the deeper cause.

You can see its claw-prints all over Mr. Nixon's speeches - the rusty claw in a marshmallow glove, which is the insignia of altruism. No one could hope to get away with those speeches, or with the policy they proclaimed, or with the decades of suicidal policies that led to it, if it were not for the magic power of the call to self-sacrifice - not the power of people's belief in it (nobody believes in it), but worse: the power of people's fear to admit that they don't.

Mr. Nixon set the tone and example of that fear, apparently to reassure any moral cannibals, foreign or domestic, who have become used to human sacrifices: "The time has come to be ourselves again - still compassionate, pouring out our wealth to all of those in need around the world, when we can. Still with a sense of responsibility toward others in the world, still ready to help those who need help." This - at a time of national financial disaster. (Speech to the Knights of Columbus, August 17.)

"But the United States of America, at this time in history, must maintain the strength in the free world" - Because we have the right to exist? No - "to provide the help that others aren't able to provide for themselves." (Ibid.)

"What's happening to the willingness for self-sacrifice that enabled us to build a great nation, to the moral code that made self-reliance a part of the American character, to the competitive spirit that made it possible for us to lead the world?" (Labor Day speech, September 6.)

The proper answer is: You're happening, Mr. President - and a long, long line of men who taught you these notions.

But Mr. Nixon's philosophical ancestors knew better than to offer a combination of this kind and worked very hard to undercut man's *self-reliance*. They knew that self-reliance is the antithesis of self-sacrifice. Self-reliance is a product of self-esteem, and a man of self-esteem does not regard himself as a sacrificial animal; the man who does, has nothing to rely on. It's either-or.

To preach self-reliance in the context of a government edict tying men hand and foot, would be sadistic cruelty, if anyone took it seriously. But most people do not even hear it; they accept it by conditioned reflex.

As to the notion of "competitive spirit," it is an interesting clue to Mr. Nixon's dilemma: he was obviously struggling to whip up a crusade, and a crusade requires something strong, uplifting, inspiring, but the concept he needed - since he was calling for productivity - is taboo in the altruist code: *personal ambition*. So he picked a ludicrous substitute, a nonessential which is shameful if and when it serves as a *primary* motive: competitiveness. Competition is a by-product of productive work, *not* its goal. A creative man is motivated by the desire to achieve, *not* by the desire to beat others. And with whom does Mr. Nixon want us to compete? With those same foreign countries we are supposed to serve self-sacrificially? Or are we asked to help them get on their feet in order to punch them in the jaw as soon as they stand up - as, for instance, West Germany and Japan?

But even this image of an envy-ridden, "competitive" second-hander as a national ideal is better than the following catalog of inspirational goals: "We need a healthy and productive economy in order to achieve the great goals to which we all are so firmly committed: To help those who cannot help themselves. To feed the hungry. To provide better health care for the sick. To provide better education for our children. To provide more fully for the aged. To restore and renew our natural environment, and to provide more and better jobs and more and greater opportunity for all of our people." (Address to Congress.)

Who is missing from this hospital litany? The men who are missing from all of Mr. Nixon's speeches, policies and concerns, the men whose existence, character and *needs* are never mentioned or acknowledged: the men who are expected to provide it all. The men who do not join an "aristocracy of pull," do not seek favors, do not function by permission, do not bargain with government boards, and do not co-operate at the point of a gun: the men of creative ability, of intelligence, integrity and ambition - the Atlases who have been shrugging and vanishing for many decades (by psychological necessity, not by conscious choice).

I shall discuss the public reaction, Phase Two and what we may now expect of the future - in my next Letter.

Ayn Rand

The Ayn Rand Letter, published fortnightly by The Ayn Rand Letter, Inc., 183 Madison Avenue, New York, N.Y. 10016.
Contributing Editor: **Leonard Peikoff**; Subscription Director: **Elayne Kalberman**; Production Manager: **Barbara Weiss.**

Vol. 1, No. 3 November 8, 1971

"THE MORATORIUM ON BRAINS"

Part II

The public reaction to the wage-price freeze was a significant indication of this country's intellectual state.

The general public's response was, predominantly, approval. It could not be claimed that this indicates popular approval of statism: few people would understand the meaning - and the necessary consequences - of the freeze, particularly when a chorus of bipartisan voices assures them that freedom is not endangered. But what the popular reaction does indicate is the preamble to statism: ignorance, helplessness, confusion, despair. People sense that the country cannot go on in its present state much longer - and feel blindly that somebody ought to "do something" about it. The danger is the "do something," i.e., the uncritical reliance on action, *any* action, in order to be pulled out of the growing chaos, the hysterical screaming, and the gray, silent crumbling wrought by the spreading quicksands of a mixed economy.

The reaction of the country's political leaders was just as ominous, but less innocent.

Discussing the views of what it describes as "a host of distinguished grandstand quarterbacks" in Washington, a story in the *New York Times* (September 5) indicates general approval of the freeze, then reports on answers to some questions. "'Should the freeze be followed by a full-scale program of wage-price control, with the issuance of daily regulations on everything from the price of pickles to the wages of household servants?' *The answer was an almost universal no.* No witness before Congress favored it. The President has long been appalled by the idea." (Emphasis mine.)

I do not know what convolutions of Jamesian-Keynesian fog enable those national leaders to evade the knowledge that the course they have chosen leads of necessity to full-scale controls. But I do believe that most of them do *not* want a totalitarian economy - and this is one tragic aspect of today's situation: we are being pushed to destruction not by avowed enemies, but by reluctant destroyers.

It is Pragmatism that permits them to hope to avoid, somehow, the consequences of their own policies, to find a loophole in the law of causality, to have their freedom and eat it, too. Later, when they are trapped by the consequences they refused to consider, they will call for controls and more controls, crying that they didn't mean it and couldn't help it. This is the way it happened in other countries.

As to the reaction of the major economic groups, it was American industry that welcomed the freeze, and labor that did not. Labor, in fact, was the only significant group that opposed Mr. Nixon's edict with properly righteous defiance - and obtained some (temporary) concessions.

According to the _Times_ (August 17): "Many [businessmen] hailed particularly the psychological lift they anticipated from the 'decisive' program to tackle basic economic problems." "This series of moves 'lanced the boil of pessimism,'" said one of them. "'An important aspect of [Nixon's] program is the elimination of uncertainty,'" said another, believe it or not. It is the government's arbitrary, unpredictable, unanswerable power that he hailed as a cure for _uncertainty_ (and this right after Mr. Nixon's series of sudden reversals).

In regard to the future "review" board, George Meany "has made plain labor's preference - even insistence - on a tripartite structure [i.e., equal numbers of union, industry and "public" representatives]. Industry leaders have given equally strong - though much less public - notice that they would prefer an all-Government board." (The _Times_, September 6.)

As a group, businessmen have been withdrawing for decades from the ideological battlefield, disarmed by the deadly combination of altruism and Pragmatism. Their public policy has consisted in appeasing, compromising and apologizing: appeasing their crudest, loudest antagonists; compromising with any attack, any lie, any insult; apologizing for their own existence. Abandoning the field of ideas to their enemies, they have been relying on lobbying, i.e., on private manipulations, on pull, on seeking momentary favors from government officials. Today, the last group one can expect to fight for capitalism is the capitalists.

Organized labor has been much more sensitive to the danger of government power and much more aware of ideological issues. Its spokesmen have fought the government in proper, morally confident terms whenever they saw a threat to their rights. (To name a few examples of such occasions: the attempt at labor conscription in World War II, the issue of U.S. contributions to the Soviet-dominated International Labor Organization, President Kennedy's attempt to impose guidelines in the steel crisis of 1962.) Labor's concern was aroused only in defense of _its_ rights; still, whoever defends his own rights defends the rights of all. But labor was pursuing a contradictory policy, which could not be maintained for long. In many issues - notably in its support of welfare-state legislation - labor violated the rights of others and fertilized the growth of the government's power. And, today, labor is in line to become the next major victim of advancing statism.

It was business, not labor, that initiated the policy of government intervention in the economy (as long ago as the nineteenth century) - and business was the first victim. Labor adopted the same policy and will meet the same fate. He who lives by a legalized sword, will perish by a legalized sword.

Today's freeze is obviously directed against labor. The "wage-price spiral," which is merely a consequence of inflation, is being blamed as its cause, thus deflecting the blame from the real culprit: the government. But the government's guilt is hidden by the esoteric intricacies of the national budget and of international finance - which the public cannot be expected to understand - while the disaster of nationwide strikes is directly perceivable by everyone and gives plausibility to the public's growing resentment of labor unions.

Furthermore, the theoretical (partly Marxist) foundation of labor's confidence has withered away. Organized labor is not the "exploited" underdog any longer, it is a prosperous middle class, systematically attacked and undercut by the _Lumpenproletariat_: the intellectuals of the New Left. In economic fact, organized labor is not responsible for the inflationary spiral, but - since labor is backed by compulsory unionization - it _is_ responsible for unemployment. Thus there is an unidentified ground for the public's resentment, which the statists are exploiting to their own advantage and which labor's once courageous theoreticians dare not face - just as the advocates of governmental favors to business did not (and do not) dare face the contradictions of _their_ case.

Now, we have reached the logical climax of a mixed economy: the stage at which the unlimited power of the government is the only ideological constant in the tangled, switching theoretical equipment of all social groups. The manifestations of the tangle are all around us. Mr. Nixon believes that as long as he tries to protect industry's profits, he is protecting free enterprise. Businessmen hail the freeze because they believe that this particular administration is more sympathetic to their interests than to labor's (with no thought of what will happen to them at the hands of another administration, a year or, at most, five years from now). And labor, in the person of George Meany, declares that the freeze is "a form of socialism for big business" (which is true), then proceeds to demand a freeze on profits, while demanding more social benefits and more jobs. (To be financed and provided by what and by whom? Blank out.)

There is a name for a system of "socialism for big business": it is called _fascism_. I have stated repeatedly that the trend in this country is toward a fascist system with communist slogans. But what all of today's pressure groups are busy evading is the fact that neither business nor labor nor anyone else, except the ruling clique, gains anything under fascism or communism or any form of statism - that all become victims of an impartial, egalitarian destruction.

By what is probably a curious coincidence, Mr. Nixon called the freeze a "new economic policy," and the press has accepted the name, along with the abbreviation "N.E.P." These were the names of the Soviet policy introduced by Lenin in 1921, after a period of strict military communism. The significant difference is this: in Russia, the original N.E.P. and its later variants, prompted by economic crises, consisted in lifting some controls and allowing the citizens a modicum of freedom, in order to revive some degree of productivity (after which the controls were clamped down again, until the next crisis). In the U.S., the N.E.P., prompted by an economic crisis, consists in imposing controls on the remnants of freedom. In this respect, the Soviet rulers seem to have a better understanding of economics.

The American people's precarious acceptance of the freeze rests on a single, false premise: that the government knows what it is doing. A great deal of evasion is required not to notice the open admissions to the contrary: Mr. Nixon, his associates, the commentators, the press have been speaking of bold experimentation, of imagination, of improvisation, of "flexibility." In this pragmatist laboratory, _we_ are the guinea pigs. And while the people hope that the government will "do something," the government hopes that the people will "do something" somehow to make the unworkable work.

The program announced as "Phase Two" confirms the fact that the government has no program. The _Times_ (October 9) describes it as follows: "Faced with contrary pressures from special interest groups for a Phase Two wage-price program tailored to differing desires, President Nixon is seeking to resolve the conflicts by giving all sides a little something to cheer about....Mr. Nixon came up with a tripartite board on pay, a public commission on prices and rents, and a Government council over both groups _along with built-in uncertainty as to which group will exercise greater authority_. 'It's ingenious,' declared a lobbyist for one segment of the nation's banking community....And one official of the Cost of Living Council, acknowledging White House efforts to satisfy everyone, observed succinctly, 'Smart man, that President.'" (Emphasis mine.)

These boards have been given an unlimited and undefined power over the entire economy - without any standards, principles or rules to guide their edicts. Their edicts, we are told, are to be fair (i.e., just) and flexible (i.e., arbitrary), which is a contradiction in terms. There is only one standard of justice in the field of economics: the verdict of a free market. No other standard can be or has ever been defined. In the absence of a standard, these boards can be guided by nothing but chance, pull and whim, regardless of the personal character or intentions of their members. Non-objective law is a virulently destructive social phenomenon. But this is worse than non-objective law: it is non-objective personal power without any pretense at formal law. These boards represent the institutionalizing of rule by fear and favor.

"It is a grave error to suppose that a dictatorship rules a nation by means of strict, rigid laws which are obeyed and enforced with rigorous, military precision. Such a rule would be evil, but almost bearable; men could endure the harshest edicts, provided these edicts were known, specific and stable; it is not the known that breaks men's spirits, but the unpredictable. A dictatorship has to be capricious; it has to rule by means of the unexpected, the incomprehensible, the wantonly irrational; it has to deal not in death, but in _sudden_ death; a state of chronic uncertainty is what men are psychologically unable to bear." (From my article "Antitrust: The Rule of Unreason," _The Objectivist Newsletter_, February 1962.)

No, I do not believe that Mr. Nixon wants to be a dictator. But if you throw a noose around a man's (or a nation's) throat and keep tightening it, it makes no difference whether you want to be a murderer or not.

In view of the fact that Mr. Nixon's whole structure, along with all of its underlying policies, maneuvering, manipulations, deceptions and anti-ideology, rests on a single hope: a rise in the country's productivity, it is grimly ironic that this structure cuts off and paralyzes the men it needs most: the men who raise a country's productivity. There is no pressure group to represent the men of intelligence, the nonconformists, the originators, the innovators - and yet it is against their brains that any freezing program is directed.

Nothing can raise a country's productivity except technology, and technology is the final product of a complex of sciences (including philosophy), each of them kept alive and moving by the achievements of a few independent minds. Such minds do not function on the expediency of the moment. The better the mind, the longer the range. Scientists, inventors, discoverers work and plan in terms of decades. To a pragmatist or a politician, ten years is the unknowable; to a great mind pursuing a great achievement, it is just one step. The steadfast confidence required for such work is based on certainty, not the certainty of guaranteed success, but the certainty of one's freedom to take calculated - and calculable - risks. Can you see such a mind venturing out on such a road, with the knowledge that a single sentence broadcast over the air without warning can stop him dead at any moment? Can you see him pleading with a board for permission to continue? Can you see him entering the game of pressure politics and wriggling his way through a maze of boards with built-in uncertainty in their functions? If not, then you know what this country will lose and what incalculable loss it has sustained already - in the form of a traumatic shock of helpless discouragement sustained by a young mind on hearing Mr. Nixon's freezing bombshell, a young mind that could have become a skyrocket lighting the world, but will never be heard from or seen. And we will never know how many hopes, half-formed plans, and half-grasped visions died in lesser men that night, along with the best within them.

Oh yes, there are men who will adjust. But they are not the kind that raise a country's productivity. For a preview, take a look at the public characters (their private characters are often different) of two groups of men who live under non-objective law: businessmen under the rule of antitrust legislation, and broadcasters under the rule of the FCC. If you observe their timidity, their uncertainty, their gray conformity, their stale superficiality, their lack of life, of fire, of color, of self-assertive ambition, you can see the image of what will become our national character under Mr. Nixon's new economic policy.

Favors are not a substitute for rights, and fear is not an incentive to ambition. Fear makes people shrink in moral and mental stature, and draw away from action. It is precisely this kind of shrinking - he calls it "self-sacrifice" - that Mr. Nixon expects. Even though distorted by a mixed economy, the essential demands of legitimate economic groups are not arbitrary: a businessman cannot run his business at a loss, a worker cannot continue working if he cannot meet his expenses. What is Mr. Nixon demanding of them? Renunciation - the shrinking of their ambition to grow and of their standard of living. Fear and controls can accomplish this. But ask yourself what this will do to the growth of productivity.

Mr. Nixon's immediate intention is clear and, probably, deliberate: he has set up a choice of scapegoats. First, the blame for the coming disasters will be placed on one board or another, or on their various members, or on the groups they represent. Then, the blame will be placed on the victims, i.e., the people, and on freedom. Observe Mr. Nixon's insistent pleas for the people's "voluntary" cooperation. "But Government with all of its powers does not hold the key to the success of a people. That key, my fellow Americans, is in your hands....whether we hold fast to the strength that makes peace and freedom possible in this world or lose our grip - all that depends on you." (Speech of August 15.)

The next phase is to declare that people's greed, selfishness and lack of faith have defeated the bold experiment - that "voluntarism" and freedom were given a chance, but failed - and, therefore, that stronger measures are necessary. The rest is history - the kind of bloodily, monotonously repeated history that men are still refusing to learn from.

No one can predict how long this process will take, or what twists, delays, disguises and momentary illusions of safety will prolong it, or how much the resilient vitality and persevering energy of the American people will be able to stand. It may be a year, it may be longer, but such is the end of the trail we are following (if we continue to follow it).

The symptoms to expect are: a general spread of physical and spiritual shoddiness, in people, in professional services, in industrial products - shortages - black markets - corruption - favor-peddling - "temporary" controls and more "temporary" controls - and, possibly, a runaway inflation.

Space does not permit me a fuller discussion of what such a system does to men's psychology. But I suggest that you read - or reread - the last sequence of Chapter VII, Part II of <u>Atlas Shrugged</u>. It will show you the effects - and the causes - of a national freeze better than I can do it here. Privately, I call that passage "the damnation sequence." The chapter is called "The Moratorium on Brains."

A question I am constantly asked today is whether I still hold any hope for this country's future. The answer is: yes - but I will discuss my reasons in my next Letter.

Ayn Rand

The Ayn Rand Letter, published fortnightly by The Ayn Rand Letter, Inc., 183 Madison Avenue, New York, N.Y. 10016.
Contributing Editor: **Leonard Peikoff**; Subscription Director: **Elayne Kalberman**; Production Manager: **Barbara Weiss.**

Vol. 1, No. 4 November 22, 1971

DON'T LET IT GO

In order to form a hypothesis about the future of an individual, one must consider three elements: his present course of action, his conscious convictions, and his sense of life. The same elements must be considered in forming a hypothesis about the future of a nation.

A sense of life is a pre-conceptual equivalent of metaphysics, an emotional, subconsciously integrated appraisal of man and of existence. It represents an individual's unidentified philosophy (which can be identified - and corrected, if necessary); it affects his choice of values and his emotional responses, influences his actions, and, frequently, clashes with his conscious convictions. (For a detailed discussion, see "Philosophy and Sense of Life" in my book _The Romantic Manifesto_.)

A nation, like an individual, has a sense of life, which is expressed not in its formal culture, but in its "life style" - in the kinds of actions and attitudes which people take for granted and believe to be self-evident, but which are produced by complex evaluations involving a fundamental view of man's nature.

A "nation" is not a mystic or supernatural entity: it is a large number of individuals who live in the same geographical locality under the same political system. A nation's culture is the sum of the intellectual achievements of individual men, which their fellow-citizens have accepted in whole or in part, and which have influenced the nation's way of life. Since a culture is a complex battleground of different ideas and influences, to speak of a "culture" is to speak only of the _dominant_ ideas, always allowing for the existence of dissenters and exceptions.

(The dominance of certain ideas is not necessarily determined by the number of their adherents: it may be determined by majority acceptance, or by the greater activity and persistence of a given faction, or by default, i.e., the failure of the opposition, or - when a country is free - by a combination of persistence and truth. In any case, ideas and the resultant culture are the product and active concern of a minority. Who constitutes this minority? Whoever chooses to be concerned.)

Similarly, the concept of a nation's sense of life does not mean that every member of a given nation shares it, but only that a dominant majority shares its essentials in various degrees. In this matter, however, the dominance is numerical: while most men may be indifferent to cultural-ideological trends, no man can escape the process of subconscious integration which forms his sense of life.

A nation's sense of life is formed by every individual child's early impressions of the world around him: of the ideas he is taught (which he may or may not accept) and of the way of acting he observes and evaluates (which he may evaluate correctly or not). And although there are exceptions at both ends of the psychological spectrum - men whose sense of life is better (truer philosophically) or worse than that of their fellow-citizens - the majority develop the essentials of the same subconscious philosophy. This is the source of what we observe as "national characteristics."

A nation's political trends are the equivalent of a man's course of action and are determined by its culture. A nation's culture is the equivalent of a man's conscious convictions. Just as an individual's sense of life can clash with his conscious convictions, hampering or defeating his actions, so a nation's sense of life can clash with its culture, hampering or defeating its political course. Just as an individual's sense of life can be better or worse than his conscious convictions, so can a nation's. And just as an individual who has never translated his sense of life into conscious convictions is in terrible danger - no matter how good his subconscious values - so is a nation.

This is the position of America today.

If America is to be saved from destruction - specifically, from dictatorship - she will be saved by her sense of life.

As to the two other elements that determine a nation's future, one (our political trend) is speeding straight to disaster, the other (culture) is virtually nonexistent. The political trend is pure statism and is moving toward a totalitarian dictatorship at a speed which, in any other country, would have reached that goal long ago. The culture is worse than nonexistent: it is operating below zero, i.e., performing the opposite of its function. A culture provides a nation's intellectual leadership, its ideas, its education, its moral code. Today, the concerted effort of our cultural "Establishment" is directed at the obliteration of man's rational faculty. Hysterical voices are proclaiming the impotence of reason, extolling the "superior power" of irrationality, fostering the rule of incoherent emotions, attacking science, glorifying the stupor of drugged hippies, delivering apologias for the use of brute force, urging mankind's return to a life of rolling in primeval muck, with grunts and groans as means of communication, physical sensations as means of inspiration, and a club as means of argumentation.

This country, with its magnificent scientific and technological power, is left in the vacuum of a pre-intellectual era, like the wandering hordes of the Dark Ages - or in the position of an adolescent before he has fully learned to conceptualize. But an adolescent has his sense of life to guide his choices. So has this country.

What is the specifically American sense of life?

A sense of life is so complex an integration that the best way to identify it is by means of concrete examples and by contrast with the manifestations of a different sense of life.

The emotional keynote of most Europeans is the feeling that man belongs to the State, as a property to be used and disposed of, in compliance with his natural, metaphysically determined fate. A typical European may disapprove of a given State and may rebel, seeking to establish what he regards as a better one, like a slave who might seek a better master to serve - but the idea that he is the sovereign and the government is his servant, has no emotional reality in his consciousness. He regards service to the State as an ultimate moral sanction, as an honor, and if you told him that his life is an end in itself, he would feel insulted or rejected or lost. Generations brought up on statist philosophy and acting accordingly, have implanted this in his mind from the earliest, formative years of his childhood.

A typical American can never fully grasp that kind of feeling. An American is an independent entity. The popular expression of protest against "being pushed around," is emotionally unintelligible to Europeans, who believe that to be pushed around is their natural condition. Emotionally, an American has no concept of service (or of servitude) to anyone. Even if he enlists in the Army and hears it called "service to his country," his feeling is that of a generous aristocrat who chose to do a dangerous task. A European soldier feels that he is doing his duty.

"Isn't my money as good as the next fellow's?" used to be a popular American expression. It would not be popular in Europe: a fortune, to be good, must be old and derived by special favor from the State; to a European, money earned by personal effort is vulgar, crude or somehow disreputable.

Americans admire achievement; they know what it takes. Europeans regard achievement with cynical suspicion and envy. Envy is not a widespread emotion in America (not yet); it is an overwhelmingly dominant emotion in Europe.

When Americans feel respect for their public figures, it is the respect of equals; they feel that a government official is a human being, just as they are, who has chosen this particular line of work and has earned a certain distinction. They call celebrities by their first names, they refer to Presidents by their initials (like "F.D.R." or "J.F.K."), not as insolence or egalitarian pretentiousness, but in token of affection. The custom of addressing a person as "Herr Doktor Doktor Schmidt" would be impossible in America. In England, the freest country of Europe, the achievement of a scientist, a businessman or a movie star is not regarded as fully real until he has been clunked on the head with the State's sword and declared to be a knight.

There are practical consequences of these two different attitudes.

An American economist told me the following story. He was sent to England by an American industrial concern, to investigate its European branch: in spite of the latest equipment and techniques, the productivity of the branch in England kept lagging far behind that of the parent-factory in the U.S. He found the cause: a rigidly circumscribed mentality, a kind of psychological caste system, on all the echelons of British labor and management. As he explained it: in America, if a machine breaks down, a worker volunteers to fix it, and usually does; in England, work stops and people wait for the appropriate department to summon the appropriate engineer. It is not a matter of laziness, but of a profoundly ingrained feeling that one must keep one's place, do one's prescribed duty, and never venture beyond it. It does not occur to the British worker that he is free to assume responsibility for anything beyond the limits of his particular job. Initiative is an "instinctive" (i.e., automatized) American characteristic; in an American consciousness, it occupies the place which, in a European one, is occupied by obedience.

As to the differences in the social atmosphere, here is an example. An elderly European woman, a research biochemist from Switzerland, on a visit to New York, told me that she wanted to buy some things at the five-and-ten. Since she could barely speak English, I offered to go with her; she hesitated, looking astonished and disturbed, then asked: "But wouldn't that embarrass you?" I couldn't understand what she meant: "Embarrass - how?" "Well," she explained, "you are a famous person, and what if somebody sees you in the five-and-ten?" I laughed. She explained to me that in Switzerland, by unwritten law, there are different stores for different classes of people, and that she, as a professional, has to shop in certain stores, even though her salary is modest, that better goods at lower prices are available in the workingmen's stores, but she would lose social status if she were seen shopping there. Can you conceive of living in an atmosphere of that kind? (We did go to the five-and-ten.)

A European, on any social level, lives emotionally in a world made by others (he never knows clearly by whom), and seeks or accepts his place in it. The American attitude is best expressed by a line from a poem: "The world began when I was born and the world is mine to win." ("The Westerner" by Badger Clark.)

Years ago, at a party in Hollywood, I met Eve Curie, a distinguished Frenchwoman, the daughter of Marie Curie. Eve Curie was a best-selling author of non-fiction books and, politically, a liberal; at the time, she was on a lecture tour of the United States. She stressed her astonishment at American audiences. "They are so happy," she kept repeating, "so _happy_..." She was saying it without disapproval and without admiration, with only the faintest touch of amusement; but her astonishment was genuine. "People are not like that in Europe...Everybody is happy in America - except the intellectuals. Oh, the intellectuals are unhappy everywhere."

This incident has remained in my mind because she had named, unwittingly, the nature of the breach between the American people and the intellectuals. The culture of a worn, crumbling Europe - with its mysticism, its lethargic resignation, its cult of suffering, its notion that misery and impotence are man's fate on earth, and that unhappiness is the hallmark of a sensitive spirit - of what use could it be to a country like America?

It was a European who discovered America, but it was Americans who were the first nation to discover this earth and man's proper place on it, and man's potential for happiness, and the world which is man's to win. What they failed to discover is the words to name their achievement, the concepts to identify it, the principles to guide it, i.e., the appropriate philosophy and its consequence: an _American_ culture.

(To be continued.)

Ayn Rand

The Ayn Rand Letter, published fortnightly by The Ayn Rand Letter, Inc., 183 Madison Avenue, New York, N.Y. 10016.
Contributing Editor: **Leonard Peikoff**; Subscription Director: **Elayne Kalberman**; Production Manager: **Barbara Weiss.**

Vol. 1, No. 5 December 6, 1971

DON'T LET IT GO

Part II

America has never had an original culture, i.e., a body of ideas derived from her philosophical (Aristotelian) base and expressing her profound difference from all other countries in history.

American intellectuals were Europe's passive dependents and poor relatives almost from the beginning. They lived on Europe's drying crumbs and discarded fashions, including even such hand-me-downs as Freud and Wittgenstein. America's sole contribution to philosophy - Pragmatism - was a bad recycling of Kantian-Hegelian premises.

America's best minds went into science, technology, industry - and reached incomparable heights of achievement. Why did they neglect the field of ideas? Because it represented Augean stables of a kind no joyously active man would care to enter. America's childhood coincided with the rise of Kant's influence in European philosophy and the consequent disintegration of European culture. America was in the position of an eager, precocious child left in the care of a scruffy, senile, decadent guardian. The child had good reason to play hooky.

An adolescent can ride on his sense of life for a while. But by the time he grows up, he must translate it into conceptual knowledge and conscious convictions, or he will be in deep trouble. A sense of life is not a substitute for explicit knowledge. Values which one cannot identify, but merely senses implicitly, are not in one's control. One cannot tell what they depend on or require, what course of action is needed to gain and/or keep them. One can lose or betray them without knowing it. For close to a century, this has been America's tragic predicament. Today, the American people is like a sleepwalking giant torn by profound conflicts. (When I speak of "the American people," in this context, I mean every group, including scientists and businessmen - except the intellectuals, i.e., those whose professions deal with the humanities. The intellectuals are a country's guardians.)

Americans are the most reality-oriented people on earth. Their outstanding characteristic is the childhood form of reasoning: common sense. It is their only protection. But common sense is not enough where theoretical knowledge is required: it can make simple, concrete-bound connections - it cannot integrate complex issues, or deal with wide abstractions, or forecast the future.

For example, consider the statist trend in this country. The doctrine of collectivism has never been submitted explicitly to the American voters; if it had been, it would have sustained a landslide defeat (as the various socialist parties have demonstrated). But the Welfare State was put over on Americans piecemeal, by degrees, under cover of some undefined "Americanism" - culminating in the absurdity of a President's declaration that America owes its greatness to "the willingness for self-sacrifice." People sense that something has gone wrong; they cannot grasp what or when. This is the penalty they pay for remaining a silent (and deaf) majority.

Americans are anti-intellectual (with good grounds, in view of current specimens), yet they have a profound respect for knowledge and education (which is being shaken now). They are self-confident, trusting, generous, enormously benevolent and innocent. "...that celebrated American 'innocence' [is] a quality which in philosophical terms is simply an ignorance of how questionable a being man really is and which strikes the European as alien..." declares an existentialist (William Barrett, _Irrational Man_). The word "questionable" is a euphemism for miserable, guilty, impotent, groveling, evil - which is the European view of man. Europeans do believe in Original Sin, i.e., in man's innate depravity; Americans do not. Americans see man as a value - as clean, free, creative, rational. But the American view of man has not been expressed or upheld _in philosophical terms_ (not since the time of our first Founding Father, Aristotle; see his description of the "magnanimous man").

Barrett continues: "Sartre recounts a conversation he had with an American while visiting in this country. The American insisted that all international problems could be solved if men would just get together and be rational; Sartre disagreed and after a while discussion between them became impossible. 'I believe in the existence of evil,' says Sartre, 'and he does not.'" This, again, is a euphemism: it is not merely the existence but the _power_ of evil that Europeans believe in. Americans do not believe in the power of evil and do not understand its nature. The first part of their attitude is (philosophically) true, but the second makes them vulnerable. On the day when Americans grasp the cause of evil's impotence - its mindless, fear-ridden, envy-eaten smallness - they will be free of all the man-hating manipulators of history, foreign and domestic.

So far, America's protection has been a factor best expressed by a saying attributed to con men: "You can't cheat an honest man." The innocence and common sense of the American people have wrecked the plans, the devious notions, the tricky strategies, the ideological traps borrowed by the intellectuals from the European statists, who devised them to fool and rule Europe's impotent masses. There have never been any "masses" in America: the poorest American is an individual and, subconsciously, an individualist. Marxism, which has conquered our universities, is a dismal failure as far as the people are concerned: Americans cannot be sold on any sort of class war; American workers do not see themselves as a "proletariat," but are among the proudest of property owners. It is professors and businessmen who advocate cooperation with Soviet Russia - American labor unions do not.

The enormous propaganda effort to make Americans fear fascism but not communism, has failed: Americans hate them both. The terrible hoax of the United Nations has failed. Americans were never enthusiastic about that institution, but they gave it the benefit of the doubt for too long. The current polls, however, indicate that the majority have turned against the U.N. (better late than never).

The latest assault on human life - the ecology crusade - will probably end in defeat for its ideological leadership: Americans will enthusiastically clean their streets, their rivers, their backyards, but when it comes to giving up progress, technology, the automobile, and their standard of living, Americans will prove that the man-haters "ain't seen nothing yet."

The sense-of-life emotion which, in Europe, makes people uncertain, malleable and easy to rule, is unknown in America: fundamental guilt. No one, so far, has been able to infect America with that contemptible feeling (and I doubt that anyone ever will). Americans cannot begin to grasp the kind of corruption implied and demanded by that feeling.

But an honest man can cheat himself. His trusting innocence can lead him to swallow sugar-coated poisons - the deadliest of which is altruism. Americans accept it - not for what it is, not as a vicious doctrine of self-immolation - but in the spirit of a strong, confident man's overgenerous desire to relieve the suffering of others, whose character he does not understand. When such a man awakens to the betrayal of his trust - to the fact that his generosity has brought him within reach of a permanent harness which is about to be slipped on him by his sundry beneficiaries - the consequences are unpredictable.

There are two ways of destroying a country: dictatorship or chaos, i.e., immediate rigor mortis or the longer agony of the collapse of all civilized institutions and the breakup of a nation into roving armed gangs fighting and looting one another, until some one Attila conquers the rest. This means: chaos as a prelude to tyranny - as was the case in Western Europe in the Dark Ages, or in the three hundred years preceding the Romanoff dynasty in Russia, or under the war lords regime in China.

A European is disarmed in the face of a dictatorship: he may hate it, but he feels that he is wrong and, metaphysically, the State is right. An American would rebel to the bottom of his soul. But this is all that his sense of life can do for him: it cannot solve his problems.

Only one thing is certain: a dictatorship cannot take hold in America today. This country, as yet, cannot be ruled - but it can explode. It can blow up into the helpless rage and blind violence of a civil war. It cannot be cowed into submission, passivity, malevolence, resignation. It cannot be "pushed around." Defiance, not obedience, is the American's answer to overbearing authority. The nation that ran an underground railroad to help human beings escape from slavery, or began drinking on principle in the face of Prohibition, will not say "Yes, sir," to the enforcers of ration coupons and cereal prices. Not yet.

If America drags on in her present state for a few more generations (which is unlikely), dictatorship will become possible. A sense of life is not a permanent endowment. The characteristically American one is being eroded daily all around us. Large numbers of Americans have lost it (or have never developed it) and are collapsing to the psychological level of Europe's worst rabble.

This is prevalent among the two groups that are the main supporters of the statist trend: the very rich and the very poor - the first, because they want to rule; the second, because they want to be ruled. (The leaders of the trend are the intellectuals, who want to do both.) But this country has never had an unearned, hereditary "elite." America is still the country of self-made men, which means: the country of the middle class - the most productive and exploited group in any modern society.

The academia-jet set coalition is attempting to tame the American character by the deliberate breeding of helplessness and resignation - in those incubators of lethargy known as "Progressive" schools, which are dedicated to the task of crippling a child's mind by arresting his cognitive development. (See "The Comprachicos" in my book The New Left: The Anti-Industrial Revolution.) It appears, however, that the "progressive" rich will be the first victims of their own social theories: it is the children of the well-to-do who emerge from expensive nursery schools and colleges as hippies, and destroy the remnants of their paralyzed brains by means of drugs.

The middle class has created an antidote which is perhaps the most hopeful movement of recent years: the spontaneous, unorganized, grass-roots revival of the Montessori system of education - a system aimed at the development of a child's cognitive, i.e., rational, faculty. But that is a long-range prospect.

At present, even so dismal a figure as President Nixon is a hopeful sign - precisely because he is so dismal. If any other country were in as desperately precarious a state of confusion as ours, a dozen flamboyant Führers would have sprung up overnight to take it over. It is to America's credit that no such Führer has appeared, and if any did, it is doubtful that he would have a chance.

Can this country achieve a peaceful rebirth in the foreseeable future? By all precedents, it is not likely. But America is an unprecedented phenomenon. In the past, American perseverance became, on occasion, too long-bearing a patience. But when Americans turned, *they turned*. What may happen to the Welfare State is what happened to the Prohibition Amendment.

Is there enough of the American sense of life left in people - under the constant pressure of the cultural-political efforts to obliterate it? It is impossible to tell. But those of us who hold it, must fight for it. We have no alternative: we cannot surrender this country to a zero - to men whose battle cry is mindlessness.

We cannot fight against collectivism, unless we fight against its moral base: altruism. We cannot fight against altruism, unless we fight against its epistemological base: irrationalism. We cannot fight *against* anything, unless we fight *for* something - and what we must fight for is the supremacy of reason, and a view of man as a rational being.

These are philosophical issues. The philosophy we need is a conceptual equivalent of America's sense of life. To propagate it, would require the hardest intellectual battle. But isn't that a magnificent goal to fight for?

Ayn Rand

The Ayn Rand Letter, published fortnightly by The Ayn Rand Letter, Inc., 201 East 34th Street, New York, N.Y. 10016.

Contributing Editor: **Leonard Peikoff**; Subscription Director: **Elayne Kalberman**; Production Manager: **Barbara Weiss.**

Vol. 1, No. 6 December 20, 1971

THE DISFRANCHISEMENT OF THE RIGHT

The campaign to defeat the nomination of William H. Rehnquist to the Supreme Court, is a microcosm of our culture: it reveals the tactics of modern intellectuals, their moral stature - and what permits them to get away with it.

The campaign is also an object lesson for those who do not see the connection of philosophy to practical politics. It demonstrates the function of fundamental principles by displaying the consequences of their obliteration.

I am not acquainted with Mr. Rehnquist, and my knowledge of his ideas is confined to the current news stories. I agree with some, though not all, of his statements. In discussing public figures, one can speak only on the basis of the presently available evidence. As of this writing, the evidence indicates that Mr. Rehnquist is a man of unusual professional competence, and that his political views are "rightist."

(Since, today, there are no clear definitions of political terms, I use the word "rightist" to denote the views of those who are predominantly in favor of individual freedom and capitalism - and the word "leftist" to denote the views of those who are predominantly in favor of government controls and socialism. As to the middle or "center," I take it to mean "zero," i.e., no dominant position, i.e., a pendulum swinging from side to side, moment by moment.)

For about half a century, the intellectuals, most of whom are leftist, have been struggling to achieve a spatial situation which is geometrically impossible: a political field consisting of a middle and a left-of-middle, with no right-of-middle. They came close to succeeding. Their success was made possible by the non-philosophical attitude of most rightists, who surrendered the intellect to the leftists, accepted their basic premises, and mouthed empty slogans in answer to deadly political principles - or: who accepted a wholesaler's warehouse of tainted meat, then haggled over the price and cut of the chops at the corner grocery store.

This permitted the intellectuals to play the game of "window dressing," i.e., to preach political tolerance or impartiality and to practice it, on suitable occasions, by featuring the weakest, most befuddled champion of capitalism as a representative of the right. (Which led people to the conclusion: "If *this* is the best that can be said for the right, then the leftist position must be true.")

Professional competence and personal integrity have been generally regarded as the criteria for judging a nominee to the Supreme Court. These are not ideal criteria: they are open to various interpretations and have not been observed very strictly in the past. The intellectuals of the left found ways to stretch them for or against a nominee, depending on his political views, yet managed to preserve a semblance of political impartiality. Now, however, they have come up against a phenomenon they did not expect to exist: a rightist whose competence and integrity are unimpeachable, and who is an intellectual (in the legitimate sense of the word).

The best exposition of the reasons behind the anti-Rehnquist campaign, was given by Tom Wicker in The New York Times (November 11, 1971): "The Rehnquist matter is not even like that of Lewis Powell, whom Mr. Nixon has also named to the Court. Mr. Powell is a pillar of the Southern establishment...he is 64 years old and his tenure on the Court will be limited by that; he is not expected by most observers to become a powerful leader within the Court. Mr. Rehnquist is a horse of a very different color. At 47, he can look forward to a long and active tenure on the bench. Moreover, his record is that of a hard-working and vigorous champion of conservative political causes...Persons in and out of the Administration who know his work credit him with superior intellect and skill in the law. Thus Mr. Rehnquist on the Court is altogether likely to become a driving force for the principles he espouses. There are those who believe that as the years go along he will be a more formidable leader than Chief Justice Burger in the conservative wing of the Court..."

This means that the vaunted tolerance, the respect for differences of opinion, the fairness toward nonconformity, the protection of the right to dissent - so loudly advocated by the left - are to be extended only to ineffectual adversaries, but not to those who are a serious threat. It amounts to the declaration: "We'll play with you, boys, so long as you don't have a chance to win."

I seldom agree with Mr. Wicker, but he had the honesty to say that to reject Mr. Rehnquist's nomination solely on the basis of his political views "is dangerous business. It presumes some kind of rightful political orthodoxy; it would tend to politicize the courts according to the temporary political coloration of Congress; it could punish some individuals for their ideas and frighten others out of having any." (Which, in today's context, is unanswerably true.)

But Mr. Wicker's fellow-liberals stuck to their usual tactics and reverted to their catch phrases of the 1960s. The champions of dissent began shouting that Mr. Rehnquist is "out of the mainstream of American thought." (If being in a "mainstream of thought" is not conformity, what is?) They went further back than that: the smear campaign they staged belongs to the 1930s - only it is cruder and more shameful than the efforts of the past.

Under the guise of examining Mr. Rehnquist's philosophy, the liberals on the Senate Judiciary Committee questioned him about his views on such subjects as: (a) school busing, (b) the rights of criminals, and (c) the government's electronic surveillance of men suspected of criminal or subversive activities. These, I submit, are not philosophical questions: these are concrete applications of philosophical principles. To evaluate Mr. Rehnquist's philosophy, they should have asked him to state his views on: (a) racism, (b) individual rights, (c) the proper functions of government - which would have established the meaning of the concretes they were discussing.

Instead, they proceeded to denounce, not Mr. Rehnquist's views, but their own interpretations of his views - with the dogmatic, authoritarian irrationality of religious Inquisitors on a heresy hunt, or of demagogues. Anyone who disapproves of busing, they declared, is an enemy of minorities; anyone who holds that the police must be enabled to protect the rights of law-abiding citizens, is hostile to the concept of rights; anyone who holds that the proper function of the government is to protect the country from the initiators of force, foreign or domestic, is an enemy of freedom and an advocate of statism. (Observe the philosophical switch: it is the "rights" of criminals that they were discussing as the paradigm case of the rights of man.)

"Mr. Rehnquist's record reveals a dangerous hostility to the great principles of individual freedom under the Bill of Rights and equal justice for all people," declared the minority report of four liberals on the Senate Judiciary Committee.

The technique of the Big Lie is a well-known phenomenon. But not enough attention has been paid to a similar technique, which may be called the "Big Projection": it consists in ascribing to your adversary the evil of which _you_ are guilty. Soviet Russia accusing the United States of "imperialism," is an example of such Projection. So is the spectacle of four leftists (i.e., statists) accusing a rightist (i.e., an advocate of free enterprise) of "hostility to individual freedom."

To the credit of the Senate Judiciary Committee, which approved Rehnquist's nomination by a vote of 12 to 4, the majority report declared that the charges against him were "totally unfounded."

What was the evidence on which the liberals based their charges?

The main issue, apparently, was the allegation that he had once been a member of a group called "Arizonans for America." Mr. Rehnquist denied it. According to the _Times_ (November 23): "Senator Birch Bayh, Democrat of Indiana, had specifically raised the membership question on the basis of information compiled by Mrs. Frank Brookes of Phoenix, who died earlier this year. Mrs. Brookes, who attended many meetings sponsored by right-wing groups and took notes, had listed Mr. Rehnquist, who lived here, as a member of Arizonans for America in 1958 and For America in 1960."

What do we know about Mrs. Brookes or her veracity? Here is the only evidence offered in the story: "Several women who helped Mrs. Brookes compile this record... say she worked with painstaking care to be accurate in listing names of persons who participated in the meetings or other activities of their organizations. Mrs. Guy A. Reem, former membership chairman for Arizonans for America, said that actually the group had had no membership list as such. But she said that it had had a mailing list, and that Mr. Rehnquist had been on this."

Have you ever tried to get off a mailing list? Until recently, it was practically impossible. Mailing lists of every conceivable kind are compiled and sold, and there is no way of knowing why or how your name came to be included. (This practice is harmless, however, since you are free to ignore the mailings.) But to regard the presence of a man's name on a mailing list as an indication, or a _proof_, of the nature of his political views is so grotesquely absurd that no one could discuss it seriously - if it were not for the fact that this sort of argument is offered to the _U.S. Senate_.

A responsible person cares about the objectivity of his reputation. If he is going to be judged, not by facts, but by the nature of the circulars he receives in the mail - if his financial status is judged by investment solicitations, his future plans by travel folders, his health by insurance brochures, and his ideas by the magazines he did not subscribe to - what becomes of his reputation?

But - the Times story goes on - two members of the Arizona group "recalled hearing Mr. Rehnquist speak to the group in a panel discussion on the income tax in 1958." This is more vicious an attempt than the mailing list bit. This is an insidious kind of intimidation: it equates a speaker's views with those of the discussion's sponsors. A man of integrity is conscientiously precise about the nature of his views on any subject. If his views are going to be judged, not by his own statements, but by the views of those who invite him to speak - if, in today's orgy of contradictions, when most people do not know their own political ideas from moment to moment, a speaker is to be held responsible for the present and future ideas of any organization he addresses - then his only alternative is to accept no speaking engagements. If so, what happens to our freedom of speech?

Such tactics would be outrageous regardless of the nature of the groups involved, even if the groups were actually disreputable. But consider the nature of the two Arizona groups mentioned. The Times describes them as follows: "The organizations opposed the United Nations, foreign aid, foreign trade, international treaties, recognition of Communist countries, Federal aid to education and the Federal income tax." Are these crimes? Are these ideas so evil that, at the faintest suspicion of any contact with them, a man becomes a pariah, a second-class citizen barred from high public office?

It is obvious that those organizations were merely primitive patriotic groups. Most of their ideas as listed above are valid. Personally, I have little sympathy with such groups because they do not know how to uphold their ideas intellectually, because they rush unarmed and unprepared into a deadly battle and do more harm than good to the rightist cause. But this is a different matter. What is relevant here is only the fact that the present smear campaign is attempting once more to snatch an official sanction - the sanction of the U.S. Senate - for the notion that patriotism (primitive or otherwise) is a forbidden, subversive doctrine.

Now observe the full display of a double standard.

The Communist Party openly advocates the overthrow of the government by force and violence, but an individual member, who knew it when he joined the party, is not presumed to share this view, unless it is proved that he personally advocated it. Yet a rightist is presumed to share the views of an organization on the basis of a mailing list or a panel discussion.

Leftists who associate with groups that preach and engage in riots, looting, bombing, killing, suffer no social penalty for such association. Yet a rightist is threatened with public opprobrium for a suspicion of an unproved association with a group that opposes the income tax and the U.N.

Women's Lib joins a common front with lesbians and prostitutes, but its individual members are treated as respectable women. Yet a rightist is regarded as disreputable because the leader of an organization he may have addressed, later joined the John Birch Society.

The worst issue of all - from the standpoint of the leftists' own premises - is Mrs. Brookes' lists.

In the 1940s and '50s, some rightist groups compiled lists of persons who were members of organizations classified by the U.S. Attorney General as subversive. These lists allegedly led to the blacklisting of some persons in the movie and radio industries. The screaming fury of the leftists' protests was louder than on any other issue. It was not the inaccuracy of the lists that they objected to - as far as is known, the lists were accurate - but _the practice of private political surveillance_. They screamed that the rightist groups were "vigilantes," that the practice violated the civil rights of the victims, that it bred suspicion, hatred, fear. ("Don't be a self-appointed spy on your neighbors," was the line, "leave surveillance to the government.") Some of the alleged victims filed lawsuits against the compilers of the lists, and won heavy financial damages.

If we accept the leftists' premise, then by what right did Mrs. Brookes compile _her_ lists? What is the social meaning and moral nature of _her_ activity - particularly in view of the fact that her sources were not actual membership records? What is the moral status of those who introduce such material into the deliberations of the U.S. Senate - and attempt, on such basis, to deny to a man, not a movie job, but a seat on the Supreme Court?

And more: today, the leftists are objecting to government surveillance of suspected criminals and subversives, on the grounds that some methods, such as wiretapping, violate a suspect's civil rights - and they are objecting to all forms of government surveillance of political organizations. A news story in the _Times_ (November 17) states: "The Supreme Court has agreed to consider if citizens can go to court to block Army intelligence agents from conducting surveillance of civilian political activities." A lower court had ruled that "individuals and groups that claim to have been spied upon by Army agents are entitled to a trial to determine if there has been a 'chilling effect' upon free expression." The purpose of the suit is: "to stop the Army from spying upon civilian political matters and to force the Army to destroy records of its past surveillance which were said to have been stored in computers."

If so, why are there no voices demanding that Mrs. Brookes' records be destroyed?

(Parenthetically, to untangle the principles involved: since private citizens have political freedom, which includes the right of free expression, free association, and any form of _non-violent_ (i.e., non-criminal) political activity, they have the right to observe the political activities of others. Both Mrs. Brookes and the rightist groups of the '40s-'50s had the right to compile political lists - provided they could prove the _truth_ of their allegations. As to governmental surveillance, it is the _duty_ of the government to protect the country from criminals and enemy agents, i.e., subversives, which includes the necessity of spying. Such surveillance, if conducted under objectively defined rules of evidence, does not endanger a citizen's rights, because the government cannot prosecute or punish him for his political ideas or activities. But it can and should prosecute him if he is proved to be the agent of a foreign government - which is a military, not an ideological, matter. A foreign government has no civil rights inside a country, only legally granted privileges; subversion is not one of them.)

As to the issue of a "chilling effect upon free expression," who is kidding whom? It is an established fact that Soviet Russia is conducting an ideological war against the free or semi-free world, and that Russian agents infiltrate the political organizations of other countries. In such circumstances, how can a private citizen complain about being "chilled" by the surveillance of his own country's government? If he is innocent, it should be much more "chilling" to him that he might be manipulated by foreign agents, spies and saboteurs, with his government offering him no protection. If he wants to take that chance, he has to expect to be "chilled" - because the rest of us feel a stronger "chill" at the prospect of

Russian agents fishing around for nuclear secrets.

But if we must consider such a problem as the "chilling effect upon free expression," then what about the terrorization under which the rightists in this country have had to live for decades? What about the torrents of smears, misrepresentations, defamation, abuse poured by the intellectuals on any defender of capitalism? There are many people who are afraid to speak out against today's "mainstream" because they know that their views will be misrepresented. There are college students who are afraid to express disagreement with leftist professors, because they know that their grades will suffer. No one has looked into the systematic intimidation of such few rightist professors as still exist. And not many voices were raised in protest against the college goons' attacks on the persons and the works (the manuscripts) of rightist professors.

And if now the leftists are struggling to make it known, from a rostrum such as the U.S. Senate, that any sort of association with people who hold rightist views, will mark a man for life - that if he addresses such people, he will be penalized thirteen years later for *their* ideas - what will *this* do to the rightists' freedom of expression and association? Would you call it a "chill" - or a total freeze?

It is by means of such outrageous violations of his civil rights that the leftists are now attacking William H. Rehnquist for his "hostility" to civil rights.

Those intellectuals who favor a "peaceful" establishment of socialism mean, apparently, that it is not to be established by force, but by fraud - by the stealthy, gradual disfranchisement of its opponents.

Accepting the leftists' own terms for a moment, ask yourself: *What* are the rightists? If they are a majority, then the leftists are fascists opposing the will of the people. If the rightists are a minority, then they have a right to be represented on the Supreme Court (and everywhere else, including college faculties) - as much right as the Poor, the Black, the Young, or the Women. (And if such pressure-group divisions are evil, which they are, then question the premises of those who propagate them.)

At this writing, Mr. Rehnquist's nomination is about to be voted on by the Senate - and the present reports indicate that he will be confirmed. I hope so.

I am fully aware of the fact that man possesses volition, that his ideas may change, and that Mr. Rehnquist, like any other candidate for public office, may prove to be a disappointment to his supporters. But the issue is wider than Mr. Rehnquist: it is an issue of preserving the full rights of the rightists. It is a matter of principle.

Ayn Rand

The Ayn Rand Letter, published fortnightly by The Ayn Rand Letter, Inc., 183 Madison Avenue, New York, N.Y. 10016.
Contributing Editor: **Leonard Peikoff**; Subscription Director: **Elayne Kalberman**; Production Manager: **Barbara Weiss.**

Vol. 1, No. 7 January 3, 1972

"WHAT CAN ONE DO?"

This question is frequently asked by people who are concerned about the state of today's world and want to correct it. More often than not, it is asked in a form that indicates the cause of their helplessness: "What can one person do?"

I was in the process of preparing this article when I received a letter from a reader who presents the problem (and the error) still more eloquently: "How can an individual propagate your philosophy on a scale large enough to effect the immense changes which must be made in every walk of American life in order to create the kind of ideal country which you picture?"

If this is the way the question is posed, the answer is: he can't. No one can change a country single-handed. So the first question to ask is: why do people approach the problem this way?

Suppose you were a doctor in the midst of an epidemic. You would not ask: "How can one doctor treat millions of patients and restore the whole country to perfect health?" You would know, whether you were alone or part of an organized medical campaign, that you have to treat as many people as you can reach, according to the best of your ability, and that nothing else is possible.

It is a remnant of mystic philosophy - specifically, of the mind-body split - that makes people approach intellectual issues in a manner they would not use to deal with physical problems. They would not seek to stop an epidemic overnight, or to build a skyscraper single-handed. Nor would they refrain from renovating their own crumbling house, on the grounds that they are unable to rebuild the entire city. But in the realm of man's consciousness, the realm of ideas, they still tend to regard knowledge as irrelevant, and they expect to perform instantaneous miracles, somehow - or they paralyze themselves by projecting an impossible goal.

(The reader whose letter I quoted was doing the right things, but felt that some wider scale of action was required. Many others merely ask the question, but do nothing.)

If you are seriously interested in fighting for a better world, begin by identifying the nature of the problem. The battle is primarily intellectual (philosophical), not political. Politics is the last consequence, the practical implementation, of the fundamental (metaphysical-epistemological-ethical) ideas that dominate a given nation's culture. You cannot fight or change the consequences without fighting and changing the cause; nor can you attempt any practical implementation without knowing what you want to implement.

In an intellectual battle, you do not need to convert everyone. History is made by minorities - or, more precisely, history is made by intellectual movements, which are created by minorities. Who belongs to these minorities? Anyone who is able and willing actively to concern himself with intellectual issues. Here, it is not quantity, but quality that counts (the quality - and consistency - of the ideas one is advocating).

An intellectual movement does not start with organized action. Whom would one organize? A philosophical battle is a battle for men's minds, not an attempt to enlist blind followers. Ideas can be propagated only by men who understand them. An organized movement has to be preceded by an educational campaign, which requires trained - self-trained - teachers (self-trained in the sense that a philosopher can offer you the material of knowledge, but it is your own mind that has to absorb it). Such training is the first requirement for being a doctor during an ideological epidemic - and the precondition of any attempt to "change the world."

"The immense changes which must be made in every walk of American life" cannot be made singly, piecemeal or "retail," so to speak; an army of crusaders would not be enough to do it. But the factor that underlies and determines every aspect of human life is philosophy; teach men the right philosophy - and their own minds will do the rest. Philosophy is the wholesaler in human affairs.

Man cannot exist without some form of philosophy, i.e., some comprehensive view of life. Most men are not intellectual innovators, but they are receptive to ideas, are able to judge them critically and to choose the right course, when and if it is offered. There are also a great many men who are indifferent to ideas and to anything beyond the concrete-bound range of the immediate moment; such men accept subconsciously whatever is offered by the culture of their time, and swing blindly with any chance current. They are merely social ballast - be they day laborers or company presidents - and, by their own choice, irrelevant to the fate of the world.

Today, most people are acutely aware of our cultural-ideological vacuum; they are anxious, confused, and groping for answers. Are you able to enlighten them?

Can you answer their questions? Can you offer them a consistent case? Do you know how to correct their errors? Are you immune from the fallout of the constant barrage aimed at the destruction of reason - and can you provide others with antimissile missiles? A political battle is merely a skirmish fought with muskets; a philosophical battle is a nuclear war.

If you want to influence a country's intellectual trend, the first step is to bring order to your own ideas and integrate them into a consistent case, to the best of your knowledge and ability. This does not mean memorizing and reciting slogans and principles, Objectivist or otherwise: knowledge necessarily includes the ability to apply abstract principles to concrete problems, to recognize the principles in specific issues, to demonstrate them, and to advocate a consistent course of action. This does not require omniscience or omnipotence; it is the subconscious expectation of automatic omniscience in oneself and in others that defeats many would-be crusaders (and serves as an excuse for doing nothing). What is required is honesty - intellectual honesty, which consists in knowing what one does know, constantly expanding one's knowledge, and never evading or failing to correct a contradiction. This means: the development of an active mind as a permanent attribute.

When or if your convictions are in your conscious, orderly control, you will be able to communicate them to others. This does not mean that you must make philosophical speeches when unnecessary and inappropriate. You need philosophy to back you up and give you a consistent case when you deal with or discuss specific issues.

If you like condensations (provided you bear in mind their full meaning), I will say: when you ask "What can one do?" - the answer is "SPEAK" (provided you know what you are saying).

A few suggestions: do not wait for a national audience. Speak on any scale open to you, large or small - to your friends, your associates, your professional organizations, or any legitimate public forum. You can never tell when your words will reach the right mind at the right time. You will see no immediate results - but it is of such activities that public opinion is made.

Do not pass up a chance to express your views on important issues. Write letters to the editors of newspapers and magazines, to TV and radio commentators and, above all, to your Congressmen (who depend on their constituents). If your letters are brief and rational (rather than incoherently emotional), they will have more influence than you suspect.

The opportunities to speak are all around you. I suggest that you make the following experiment: take an ideological "inventory" of one week, i.e., note how many times people utter the wrong political, social and _moral_ notions as if these were self-evident truths, with _your_ silent sanction. Then make it a habit to object to such remarks - no, not to make lengthy speeches, which are seldom appropriate, but merely to say: "I don't agree." (And be prepared to explain why, if the speaker wants to know.) This is one of the best ways to stop the spread of vicious bromides. (If the speaker is innocent, it will help him; if he is not, it will undercut his confidence the next time.) Most particularly, _do not keep silent_ when your own ideas and values are being attacked.

Do not "proselytize" indiscriminately, i.e., do not force discussions or arguments on those who are not interested or not willing to argue. It is not your job to save everyone's soul. If you do the things which are in your power, you will not feel guilty about not doing - "somehow" - the things which are not.

Above all, do not join the wrong _ideological_ groups or movements, in order to "do something." By "ideological" (in this context), I mean groups or movements proclaiming some vaguely generalized, undefined (and, usually, contradictory) _political_ goals. (E.g., the Conservative Party, that subordinates reason to faith, and substitutes theocracy for capitalism; or the "libertarian" hippies, who subordinate reason to whims, and substitute anarchism for capitalism.) To join such groups means to reverse the philosophical hierarchy and to sell out fundamental principles for the sake of some superficial political action which is bound to fail. It means that you help the defeat of _your_ ideas and the victory of your enemies. (For a discussion of the reasons, see "The Anatomy of Compromise" in my book _Capitalism: The Unknown Ideal_.)

The only groups one may properly join today are _ad hoc_ committees, i.e., groups organized to achieve a single, specific, clearly defined goal, on which men of differing views can agree. In such cases, no one may attempt to ascribe _his_ views to the entire membership, or to use the group to serve some hidden ideological purpose (and _this_ has to be watched very, very vigilantly).

I am omitting the most important contribution to an intellectual movement - writing - because this discussion is addressed to men of every profession. Books, essays, articles are a movement's permanent fuel, but it is worse than futile to attempt to become a writer solely for the sake of a "cause." Writing, like any other work, is a profession and must be approached as such.

It is a mistake to think that an intellectual movement requires some special duty or self-sacrificial effort on your part. It requires something much more difficult: a profound conviction that ideas are important to you and to your own life. If you integrate that conviction to every aspect of your life, you will find many opportunities to enlighten others.

The reader whose letter I quoted, indicates the proper pattern of action: "As a teacher of astronomy, for several years, I have been actively engaged in demonstrating the power of reason and the absolutism of reality to my students...I have also made an effort to introduce your works to my associates, following their reading with discussion when possible; and have made it a point to insist on the use of reason in all of my personal dealings."

These are some of the right things to do, as often and as widely as possible.

But that reader's question implied a search for some shortcut in the form of an organized movement. No shortcut is possible.

It is too late for a movement of people who hold a conventional mixture of contradictory philosophical notions. It is too early for a movement of people dedicated to a philosophy of reason. But it is never too late or too early to propagate the right ideas - except under a dictatorship.

If a dictatorship ever comes to this country, it will be by the default of those who keep silent. We are still free enough to speak. Do we have time? No one can tell. But time is on our side - because we have an indestructible weapon and an invincible ally (if we learn how to use them): reason and reality.

Ayn Rand

OBJECTIVIST CALENDAR

(Under this heading, we shall announce, from time to time, events or activities that may be of interest to the readers of this Letter.)

* Tapes of Dr. Leonard Peikoff's twelve-lecture course, Modern Philosophy: Kant to the Present, are still available, to groups of ten persons or more, on a rental basis. (This course, first offered in the Fall of 1970, concludes with two lectures on the philosophy of Objectivism.) There has been a change of address: Inquiries should be mailed to Susan Ludel, c/o TV Guide, 1290 Avenue of the Americas, New York, N.Y. 10019.

* We have been asked to announce that full-color reproductions of Portrait of Ayn Rand by Ilona, and Diminishing Returns by Frank O'Connor, are available from Sures Art Enterprises, Ltd. The portrait appears (in black and white) on the jackets of many of Miss Rand's books. Diminishing Returns is a fantasy that features a puppet in a sunlit landscape, juggling bright Christmas tree balls. For illustrated brochures, write to SAE, Ltd., P.O. Box 207, Silver Spring, Md. 20907.

B.W.

The Ayn Rand Letter, published fortnightly by The Ayn Rand Letter, Inc., 201 East 34th Street, New York, N.Y. 10016.

Contributing Editor: **Leonard Peikoff**; Subscription Director: **Elayne Kalberman**; Production Manager: **Barbara Weiss.**

Vol. 1, No. 8 January 17, 1972

THE STIMULUS...

There are occasions when a worthless, insignificant book acquires significance as a scrap of litmus paper exposing a culture's intellectual state. Such a book is Beyond Freedom and Dignity by B.F. Skinner.

"Skinner is the most influential of living American psychologists..." says Time magazine (September 20, 1971). "Skinner has remained a highly influential figure among U.S. college students for well over a decade," says Newsweek (September 20, 1971). "Burrhus Frederic Skinner is the most influential psychologist alive today, and he is second only to Freud as the most important psychologist of all time. This, at least, is the feeling of 56 percent of the members of the American Psychological Association, who were polled on the question. And it should be reason enough to make Dr. Skinner's new book, Beyond Freedom and Dignity, one of the most important happenings in 20th century psychology," says Science News (August 7, 1971).

One cannot evaluate the cultural significance of such statements until one identifies the nature of their object.

The book itself is like Boris Karloff's embodiment of Frankenstein's monster: a corpse patched with nuts, bolts and screws from the junkyard of philosophy (Pragmatism, Social Darwinism, Positivism, Linguistic Analysis, with some nails by Hume, threads by Russell, and glue by the New York Post). The book's voice, like Karloff's, is an emission of inarticulate, moaning growls - directed at a special enemy: "Autonomous Man."

"Autonomous Man" is the term used by Mr. Skinner to denote man's consciousness in all those aspects which distinguish it from the sensory level of an animal's consciousness - specifically: reason, mind, values, concepts, thought, judgment, volition, purpose, memory, independence, self-esteem. These, he asserts, do not exist; they are an illusion, a myth, a "prescientific" superstition. His term may be taken to include everything we call "man's inner world," except that Mr. Skinner would never allow such an expression; whenever he has to refer to man's inner world, he says: "Inside your skin."

"Inside his skin," man is totally determined by his environment (and by his genetic endowment, which was determined by his ancestors' environment), Mr. Skinner asserts, and totally malleable. By controlling the environment, "behavioral technologists" could - and should - control men inside out. If people were brought to give up individual autonomy and to join Mr. Skinner in proclaiming: "To man *qua* man we readily say good riddance," (p. 201) the behavioral technologists would create a new species and a perfect world. This is the book's thesis.

One expects that an assertion of this kind would be supported by some demonstration or indication of the methods these technologists will use in order to manipulate those non-autonomous bipeds. Curiously enough, there is no such indication in the book. I may be flattering Mr. Skinner, but it occurred to me that perhaps _the book itself_ was intended to be a demonstration of the methods he envisions.

There are certain conditions which the book requires of its readers: (a) Being out of focus. (b) Skimming. (c) Self-doubt. (d) The premise, when confronted with outrageous absurdity: "I don't get it, but he must have reasons for saying it."

These conditions will bring the reader to miss the main ingredients of the book's epistemological method, which are: 1. Equivocation. 2. Substituting metaphors for proof, and examples for definitions. 3. Setting up and knocking down straw men. 4. Mentioning a given notion as controversial, following it up with two or three pages of irrelevant small talk, then mentioning it again and treating it as if it had been proved. 5. Raising valid questions (to indicate that the author is aware of them) and, by the same technique, leaving them unanswered. 6. Overtalking and overloading the reader's consciousness with overelaborate discussions of trivia, then smuggling in enormous essentials without discussion, as if they were incontrovertible. 7. Assuming an authoritarian tone to enunciate dogmatic absolutes - and the more dubious the absolute, the more authoritarian the tone. 8. Providing a brief summary at the end of each chapter, which summary includes, as if they had been proved, notions not included or barely mentioned in the chapter's text.

All of this (and more) is done grossly, crudely, obviously, which leaves the book pockmarked with gaping craters of contradictions, like a moon landscape and as lifelessly dull.

In _Atlas Shrugged_, I discussed two variants of mysticism: the mystics of spirit and the mystics of muscle, "those who believe in consciousness without existence and those who believe in existence without consciousness. Both demand the surrender of your mind, one to their revelations, the other to their reflexes." I said that their aims are alike: "in matter - the enslavement of man's body, in spirit - the destruction of his mind."

Mr. Skinner is a mystic of muscle - so extreme, complete, all-out a mystic of muscle that one could not use him in fiction: he sounds like a caricature.

At the start of his book, what he demands of his readers is: _faith_. "In what follows, these issues are discussed 'from a scientific point of view,' but this does not mean that the reader will need to know the details of a scientific analysis of behavior. A mere interpretation will suffice....The instances of behavior cited in what follows are not offered as 'proof' of the interpretation. The proof is to be found in the basic analysis. The principles used in interpreting the instances have a plausibility which would be lacking in principles drawn entirely from casual observation." (Pp. 22-23.)

This means: the proof of Mr. Skinner's theory is inaccessible to the laymen, who must take him on faith, substituting "plausibility" for logic: if his "interpretation" sounds plausible, it means that he has valid ("non-casual") reasons for expounding it. This is offered as _scientific_ epistemology.

(It must be noted that Mr. Skinner's interpretations of the "scientific analysis of behavior" are rejected by a great many experts initiated into its higher mysteries, not only by psychiatrists and by psychologists of different schools, but even by his own fellow-behaviorists.)

As a cover against criticism, Mr. Skinner resorts to the mystics' usual scapegoat: language. "The text will often seem inconsistent. English, like all languages, is full of prescientific terms...but the issues are important to the nonspecialist and need to be discussed in a nontechnical fashion." (Pp. 23-24.) The mystics of spirit accuse language of being "materialistic"; Mr. Skinner accuses it of being "mentalistic." Both regard their own theories as ineffable, i.e., incommunicable in language.

Many psychologists are envious of the prestige - and the achievements - of the physical sciences, which they try not to emulate, but to imitate. Mr. Skinner is archetypical in this respect: he is passionately intent on being accepted as a "scientist" and complains that only "Autonomous Man" stands in the way of such acceptance (which, I am sure, is true). Mr. Skinner points out scornfully that primitive men, who were unable to see the difference between living beings and inanimate objects, ascribed the objects' motions to conscious gods or demons, and that science could not begin until this belief was discarded. In the name of science, Mr. Skinner switches defiantly to the other side of the same basic coin: accepting the belief that consciousness is supernatural, he refuses to accept the existence of man's mind.

All human behavior, he asserts, is the product of a process called "operant conditioning" - and all the functions we ascribe to "Autonomous Man" are performed by a single agent called a "reinforcer." In view of the omnipotence ascribed to this agent throughout the book, a definition would have been very helpful, but here is all we get: "When a bit of behavior is followed by a certain kind of consequence, it is more likely to occur again, and a consequence having this effect is called a reinforcer. Food, for example, is a reinforcer to a hungry organism; anything the organism does that is followed by the receipt of food is more likely to be done again whenever the organism is hungry....Negative reinforcers are called aversive in the sense that they are the things organisms 'turn away from.'" (P. 27.)

If you assume this means that a "reinforcer" is something which causes pleasure or pain, you will be wrong, because, on page 107, Mr. Skinner declares: "There is no important causal connection between the reinforcing effect of a stimulus and the feelings to which it gives rise....What is maximized or minimized, or what is ultimately good or bad, are things, not feelings, and men work to achieve them or to avoid them not because of the way they feel but because they are positive or negative reinforcers." Then by what means or process do these "reinforcers" affect man's actions? In the whole of the book, no answer is given.

The only social difference between positive and negative "reinforcers" is the fact that the latter provoke "counterattack" or rebellion, and the former do not. Both are means of controlling man's behavior. "Productive labor, for example, was once the result of punishment: the slave worked to avoid the consequences of not working. Wages exemplify a different principle: a person is paid when he behaves in a given way so that he will continue to behave in that way." (P. 32.)

From this bit of package-dealing, context-dropping, and definition-by-nonessentials, Mr. Skinner slides to the assertion that slave-driving and wage-paying are both "techniques of control," then to the gigantic equivocation which underlies most of the others in his book: that every human relationship, every instance of men dealing with one another, is a form of control. You are "controlled" by the grocer across the street, because if he were not there, you would shop elsewhere. You are controlled by the person who praises you (praise is a "positive reinforcer"), and by the person who blames you (blame is an "aversive reinforcer"), etc., etc., etc.

Here Mr. Skinner revives the ancient saw to the effect that volition is an illusion, because one is not free if one has reasons for one's actions - and that true volition would consist in acting on whim, a causeless, unaccountable, inexplicable whim exercised in a vacuum, free of any contact with reality.

From this, Mr. Skinner's next step is easy: political freedom, he declares, necessitates the use of "aversive reinforcers," i.e., punishment for evil behavior. Since you are not free anyway, but controlled by everyone at all times, why not let specialists control you in a scientific way and design for you a world consisting of nothing but "positive reinforcers"?

What kind of world would that be? Here, Mr. Skinner seems to make a "Freudian slip": he is surprisingly explicit. "...it should be possible to design a world in which behavior likely to be punished seldom or never occurs. We try to design such a world for those who cannot solve the problem of punishment for themselves, such as babies, retardates, or psychotics, and if it could be done for everyone, much time and energy would be saved." (P. 66.)

"...there is no reason," he declares, "why progress toward a world in which people may be automatically good should be impeded." (P. 67.) No reason at all - provided you are willing to view yourself as a baby, a retardate or a psychotic.

"Dignity" is Mr. Skinner's odd choice of a designation for what is normally called "*moral worth*" - and he disposes of it by asserting that it consists in gaining the admiration of other people. Through a peculiar jumble of examples, which includes unrequited love, heroic deeds, and scientific (i.e., *intellectual*) achievements, Mr. Skinner labors to convince us that: "...we are likely to admire behavior more as we understand it less," (p. 53) and: "...the behavior we admire is the behavior we cannot yet explain." (P. 58.) It is mere vanity, he asserts, that makes our heroes cling to "dignity" and resist "scientific" analysis, because, once their achievements are explained, they will deserve no greater admiration - and *no greater credit* - than anyone else.

This last is the core, essence and purpose of his jumbled argument; the rest of the verbiage is merely a haphazard cover. There is a kind of veiled, subterranean intensity in Mr. Skinner's tired prose whenever he stresses the point that *men should be given no credit for their virtues or their achievements*. The behavior of a creative genius (my expression, not Mr. Skinner's) is determined by "contingencies of reinforcement," just like the behavior of a criminal, and neither of them can help it, and neither should be admired or blamed. Unlike other modern determinists, Mr. Skinner is not concerned primarily with the elimination of blame, but with the elimination of credit.

This sort of concern is almost self-explanatory. But I did find it surprising that Mr. Skinner includes achievement among the roots of *moral worth* (of "dignity"). He and I are probably the only two theoreticians who understand - from opposite moral poles - how much depends on this issue.

(To be continued.)

Ayn Rand

The Ayn Rand Letter, published fortnightly by The Ayn Rand Letter, Inc., 201 East 34th Street, New York, N.Y. 10016.

Contributing Editor: **Leonard Peikoff**; Subscription Director: **Elayne Kalberman**; Production Manager: **Barbara Weiss.**

Vol. 1, No. 9 January 31, 1972

THE STIMULUS...

Part II

In reason, one would expect that so thorough a determinist as Mr. Skinner would not deal with questions of morality; but his abolition of reason frees him from concern with contradictions. Beyond Freedom and Dignity is a normative tract, prescribing the actions men ought to take (even though they have no volition), and the motives and beliefs they ought to adopt (even though there are no such things).

From the casual observation that "ethos and mores refer to the customary practices of a group," (pp. 112-113) Mr. Skinner slides to the assertion that morality is exclusively social, that moral principles are inculcated through socially designed contingencies of reinforcement "under which a person is induced to behave for the good of others," (p. 112) - then to the notion, smuggled in as an undiscussed absolute, that morality is behavior for the good of others - and then to the following remarkable passage: "The value or validity of the reinforcers used by other people and by organized agencies may be questioned: 'Why should I seek the admiration or avoid the censure of my fellow men?' 'What can my government - or any government - really do to me?' 'Can a church actually determine whether I am to be eternally damned or blessed?' 'What is so wonderful about money - do I need all the things it buys?' 'Why should I study the things set forth in a college catalogue?' In short, 'Why should I behave "for the good of others"?'" (Pp. 117-118.)

Yes, read that quotation over again. I had to, before I realized what Mr. Skinner means: he means that the asking of such questions is a violation of the good of others, because it challenges socially inculcated principles of behavior (so that even the pursuit of money or of a college education represents, not one's own good, but the good of others). And wider: all principles of long-range action, moral or practical, represent the good of others, because all principles are a social product.

This is supported by the statements immediately following the above quotation: "When the control exercised by others is thus evaded or destroyed, only the personal reinforcers are left. The individual turns to immediate gratification, possibly through sex or drugs." (P. 118.) Just as altruism is the primeval moral code of all mystics, of spirit or muscle, so this view of an individual's self-interest is their primordial cliché. But Mr. Skinner adds some epistemological "explanations" of his own.

Man, he asserts, is aware of nothing but the immediate moment: he has no capacity to form abstractions, to act by intention, to project the future. "Behavior is shaped and maintained by its consequences," (p. 18) and: "Behavior cannot really be affected by anything which follows it, but if a 'consequence' is immediate, it may overlap the behavior." (P. 120.) Evolution, he asserts, did the rest. "The process of operant conditioning presumably evolved when those organisms which were more sensitively affected by the consequences of their behavior were better able to adjust to the environment and survive." (P. 120.) What is this "sensitivity" and through what organ or faculty does it operate? No answer.

Claiming that man's first discoveries (such as banking a fire) were purely accidental (pp. 121-122), Mr. Skinner concludes that other men learned, somehow, to imitate those lucky practices. "One advantage in being a social animal is that one need not discover practices for oneself." (P. 122.) As to the time-range of man's awareness, Mr. Skinner asserts: "Probably no one plants in the spring simply because he then harvests in the fall. Planting would not be adaptive or 'reasonable' if there were no connection with a harvest, but one plants in the spring because of more immediate contingencies, most of them arranged by the social environment." (P. 122.) How is this done by a social environment consisting of men who are unable to think long-range? No answer.

The phenomenon of language is a problem to a mystic of muscle. Mr. Skinner gets around it semantically, by calling it "verbal behavior." "Verbal behavior presumably arose under contingencies involving practical social interactions..." (P. 122.) How? No answer. "Verbal behavior" is a means of controlling men, because words, somehow, become associated with physical "reinforcers." To be exact, one cannot use the word "words" in Mr. Skinner's context: it is sounds or marks on paper that acquire an associational link with the omnipotent "reinforcers" and stick inside a man's skin, forming "a repertoire of verbal behavior." This would require an incredible feat of memorizing. But Mr. Skinner denies the existence of memory - he calls it "storage" and declares: "Evolutionary and environmental histories change an organism, but they are not stored within it." (Pp. 195-196.) His view of the nature of language, therefore, is as simple as the views of black-magic practitioners: verbal incantations have a mystic power to effect physical changes in a living organism.

"The verbal community" (i.e., society), Mr. Skinner asserts, is the source and cause of man's self-awareness and introspection. How? This time, an answer is given: "It [the verbal community] asks such questions as: What did you do yesterday? What are you doing now? What will you do tomorrow? Why did you do that? Do you really want to do that? How do you feel about that? The answers help people to adjust to each other effectively. And it is because such questions are asked that a person responds to himself and his behavior in the special way called knowing or being aware. _Without the help of a verbal community all behavior would be unconscious. Consciousness is a social product._" (P. 192; emphasis added.) But how did such questions occur to men who were incapable of discovering introspection? No answer.

Apparently to appease man's defenders, Mr. Skinner offers the following: "In shifting control from autonomous man to the observable environment we do not leave an empty organism. A great deal goes on inside the skin, and physiology will eventually tell us more about it." (P. 195.) This means: No, man is not empty, he is a solid piece of meat.

Inexorably, like all mystics, Mr. Skinner reverts to a mystic dualism - to an equivalent of the mind-body split, which becomes a body-bodies split. In Mr. Skinner's version, it is not a conflict between God and the Devil, but between man's two conditioners: social environment and genetic endowment. The conflict takes place inside man's skin, in the form of _two selves_. "A self is a repertoire of behavior appropriate to a given set of contingencies." (P. 199.) The conflict, therefore, is between two repertoires. "The controlling self (the conscience or superego) is of social origin, but the controlled self is more likely to be the product of genetic susceptibilities to reinforcement (the id, or the Old Adam). The controlling self generally represents the interests of others, the controlled self the interests of the individual." (P. 199.)

Where have we heard this before, and for how many "prescientific" millennia?

Mr. Skinner's voice is loud and clear when he declares: "To be for oneself is to be almost nothing." (P. 123.) As proof, he revives another ancient saw: the capacity of the human species to transmit knowledge deprives man of any claim to individuality (or to individual achievement) because he has to start by learning from others. "The great individualists so often cited to show the value of personal freedom have owed their successes to earlier social environments. The involuntary individualism of a Robinson Crusoe and the voluntary individualism of a Henry David Thoreau show obvious debts to society. If Crusoe had reached the island as a baby, and if Thoreau had grown up unattended on the shores of Walden Pond, their stories would have been different. We must all begin as babies, and no degree of self-determination, self-sufficiency, or self-reliance will make us individuals in any sense beyond that of single members of the human species." (Pp. 123-124.)

This means: we all begin as babies and remain in that state; since a baby is not self-sufficient, neither is an adult; nothing has happened in-between. Observe also the same method of setting up a straw man that was used in regard to volition: setting it up outside of reality. E.g., in order to be an individual, Thomas A. Edison would have had to appear in the jungle by parthenogenesis, as an infant without human parents, then rediscover, all by himself, the entire course of the science of physics, from the first fire to the electric light bulb. Since no one has done this, there is no such thing as individualism.

From a foundation of this kind, Mr. Skinner proceeds to seek "justice or fairness" or a "reasonable balance" in the "exchange between the individual and his social environment." (P. 124.) But, he announces, such questions "cannot be answered simply by pointing to what is personally good or what is good for others. There is another kind of value to which we must now turn." (P. 125.)

Now we come to the payoff.

A mystic code of morality demanding self-sacrifice cannot be promulgated or propagated without a supreme ruler that becomes the collector of the sacrificing. Traditionally, there have been two such collectors: either God or society. The collector had to be inaccessible to mankind at large, and his authority had to be revealed only through an elite of special intermediaries, variously called "high priests," "commissars," "Gauleiters," etc. Mr. Skinner follows the same pattern, but he has a new collector and supreme ruler to hoist: the culture.

A culture, he explains, is "the customs, the customary behaviors of a people." (P. 127.) "A culture, like a species, is selected by its adaptation to an environment: to the extent that it helps its members to get what they need and avoid what is dangerous, it helps them to survive and transmit the culture. The two kinds of evolution are closely interwoven. The same people transmit both a culture and a genetic endowment - though in very different ways and for different parts of their lives." (P. 129.) "A culture is not the product of a creative 'group mind' or the expression of a 'general will.'...A culture evolves when new practices further the survival of those who practice them." (Pp. 133-134.) Thus we owe our survival to the culture. Therefore, Mr. Skinner announces, to the two values discussed - personal good and the good of others - "we must now add a third, the good of the culture." (P. 134.)

What is the good of a culture? Survival. Whose survival? Its own. A culture is an end in itself. "When it has become clear that a culture may survive or perish, some of its members may begin to act to promote its survival." (P. 134.) Which members? By what means are they able to grasp such a goal? No answer.

Mr. Skinner stresses repeatedly that the survival of a culture is a value different from, and superior to, the survival of its members, of oneself or of others - a value one ought to live and die for. Why? Mr. Skinner is suddenly explicit: "None of this will explain what we might call a pure concern for the survival of a culture, but we do not really need an explanation....The simple fact is that a culture which *for any reason* induces its members to work for its survival, or for the survival of some of its practices, is more likely to survive. Survival is the only value according to which a culture is eventually to be judged, and any practice that furthers survival has survival value by definition." (P. 136.) *Whose* survival? No answer. Mr. Skinner lets it ride on an equivocation of this kind.

If survival "is the only value according to which a culture is eventually to be judged," then the Nazi culture, which lasted twelve years, had a certain degree of value - the Soviet culture, which has lasted fifty-five years, has a higher value - the feudal culture of the Middle Ages, which lasted five centuries, had a still higher value - but the highest value of all must be ascribed to the culture of ancient Egypt, which, with no variations or motion of any kind, lasted *unchanged* for thirty centuries.

A "culture," in Mr. Skinner's own terms, is not a thing, not an idea, not even people, but a collection of *practices*, a "behavior," a disembodied behavior that supersedes those who behave - i.e., a way of acting to which the actors must be sacrificed. This is *mysticism* of a kind that makes God or society seem sensibly realistic rulers by comparison. It is also *conservatism* of a metaphysical kind that makes political conservatism seem innocuously childish. It demands that we live, work and die not for ourselves or for others, but for the sake of preserving and transmitting to yet unborn generations and in perpetuity the way we dress, the way we ride the subway, the way we get drunk, the way we deal with baseball or religion or economics, etc.

Thus Mr. Skinner, the arch-materialist, ends up as a worshiper of disembodied motion - and the arch-revolutionary, as a guardian of the status quo, *any* status quo.

In order to be induced to sacrifice for the good of the culture, the victims are promised "deferred advantages" (*indeterminately* deferred). "But what is its [an economic system's] answer to the question: 'Why should I be concerned about the survival of a particular kind of economic system?' The only honest answer to that kind of question seems to be this: 'There is no good reason why you should be concerned, but if your culture has not convinced you that there is, so much the worse for your culture.'" (P. 137.) This means: in order to survive, a culture must convince its members that there *is* a good reason to be concerned with its survival, even though there is none.

This is *Social Darwinism* of a kind that Herbert Spencer would not dream of. The nearest approach to an exponent in practice was Adolf Hitler who "reinforced" his followers by demanding sacrifices for the survival of the German *Kultur*.

But Mr. Skinner envisions a grander scale. He advocates "a single culture for all mankind," which, he admits, is difficult to explain to the sacrificial victims. "We can nevertheless point to many reasons why people should now be concerned for the good of all mankind. The great problems of the world today are all global....But pointing to consequences is not enough. We [who?] must arrange contingencies under which consequences have an effect." (Pp. 137-138.) This "arranger of contingencies" is to be a single totalitarian world state, serving the survival of a single culture, ruling every cell of every man's brain and every moment of his life.

What are the "great problems" this state would solve? What are the "terrifying possibilities" from which we must be saved - at the price of giving up our freedom, dignity, reason, mind, values, self-esteem? Mr. Skinner answers: "Overpopulation, the depletion of resources, the pollution of the environment, and the possibility of a nuclear holocaust - these are the not-so-remote consequences of present courses of action." (P. 138.)

If lightning struck Mount Sinai, and Moses appeared on the mountaintop, carrying sacred tablets, and silenced the lost, frightened, desperate throng below in order to read a revelation of divine wisdom, and read a third-rate editorial from a random tabloid - the dramatic, intellectual and moral effect would be similar (except that Moses was less pretentious).

Mr. Skinner's book falls to pieces in its final chapters. The author's "verbal behavior" becomes so erratic that he sounds as if he has lost all interest in his subject. Tangled in contradictions, equivocations and non sequiturs, he seems to stumble wearily in circles, seizing any rationalization at random - not to defend his thesis, but to attack his critics, throwing feeble little jabs, projecting an odd kind of stale, lethargic, perfunctory malice, almost a "reflex-malice." He sounds like a man filling empty pages with something, anything, in order to circumvent the accumulated weight of unanswered questions - or like a man who resents being questioned.

Who will be the "designers" of his proposed global culture and the rulers of mankind? He answers unequivocally: the "technologists of behavior." What qualifies them for such a job? They are "scientists." What is science? In the whole of the book, no definition is given, as if the term were a self-evident, mystically hallowed primary.

Since man, according to Mr. Skinner, is biologically unable to project a time span of three months - from spring planting to fall harvest - how are these technologists able to see the course and plan the future of a global culture? No answer. What sort of men are they? The closest approach to an answer is: "those who have been induced by their culture to act to further its survival..." (P. 180.)

It is futile to ask by what means and through what agencies the culture (i.e., the <u>behavior</u>) of birdbrained creatures can accomplish such a feat, because here we are obviously dealing with a standard requirement of mysticism: Mr. Skinner is establishing an opportunity for the high priesthood to "hear voices" - not the voice of God or of the people, but the voice of the culture <u>inducing</u> them to act. But the culture "induces" a great many people to different courses of action, including the people who paint prophecies of doom on rocks by the side of highways. How are the culture-designers (and the rest of us) to know that theirs is the true voice of the culture? No answer. One must assume that they <u>feel</u> it.

Now we come to the grand cashing-in on the book's basic equivocation. Mr. Skinner keeps stressing that mankind needs "more controls, not less"; in a polemical passage, he quotes his critics asking: "Who is to control?" - and answers them as follows: "The relation between the controller and the controlled is reciprocal. The scientist in the laboratory, studying the behavior of a pigeon, designs contingencies and observes their effects. His apparatus exerts a conspicuous control on the pigeon, but we must not overlook the control exerted by the pigeon. The behavior of the pigeon has determined the design of the apparatus and the procedures in which it is used. Some such reciprocal control is characteristic of all science....[Here I omit one sentence, which is an unconscionable misuse of a famous statement.] The scientist who designs a cyclotron is under the control of the particles he is studying. The behavior with which a parent controls his child, either aversively or through positive reinforcement, is shaped and maintained by the child's responses. A psychotherapist changes the behavior of his patient in ways which have been shaped and maintained by his success in changing that behavior. A government or religion prescribes and imposes sanctions selected by their effectiveness in controlling citizen or communicant. An employer induces his employees to work industriously and carefully with wage systems determined by their effects on behavior. The classroom practices of the teacher are shaped and maintained by the effects on his students. In a very real sense, then, the slave controls the slave driver, the child the parent, the patient the therapist, the citizen the government, the communicant the priest, the employee the employer, and the student the teacher." (P. 169.)

To this, I shall add just one more example: the victim controls the torturer, because if the victim screams very loudly at a particular method of torture, this is the method the torturer will select to use.

The above quotation is sufficient to convey the book's intellectual stature, the logic of its arguments, and the validity of its thesis.

As far as one can judge the book's purpose, the establishment of a dictatorship does not seem to be Mr. Skinner's _personal_ ambition. If it were, he would have been more clever about it. His goal seems to be: 1. to clear the way for a dictatorship by eliminating its enemies; 2. to see how much he can get away with.

The book's motive power is hatred of man's mind and virtue (with everything they entail: reason, achievement, independence, enjoyment, moral pride, self-esteem) - so intense and consuming a hatred that it consumes itself, and what we read is only its gray ashes, with feeble, snickering obscenities (such as the title) as a few last, smoking, stinking coals. To destroy "Autonomous Man" - to strike at him, to punch, to stab, to jab, and, if all else fails, to spit at him - is the book's apparent purpose, and it is precisely the long-range, _cultural_ consequences that the author does not seem to give a damn about.

The passages dealing with the Global State are so rambling, incoherent and diffuse, that they sound, not like a plan, but like a daydream - the kind of daydream Mr. Skinner, apparently, finds "reinforcing." But he remains unoriginal even in his fantasy: borrowing Plato's notion of a philosopher-king, Mr. Skinner fancies a world ruled by a psychologist-king - in terms which sound as if a small-time manipulator were tempted by the image of a big shot.

If only we would abolish "Autonomous Man" - Mr. Skinner declares with a kind of growling wistfulness - we would be able to turn "from the miraculous to the natural, from the _inaccessible_ to the _manipulable_." (P. 201; emphasis added.) This, I submit, is the secret behind the book - and behind the modern intellectuals' response to it (which I will discuss in my next Letter).

In _Les Misérables_, describing the development of an independent young man, Victor Hugo wrote: "...and he blesses God for having given him these two riches which many of the rich are lacking: work, which gives him freedom, and thought, which gives him dignity."

I doubt that B.F. Skinner ever did or could read Victor Hugo - he wouldn't know what it's all about - but it is not a mere coincidence that made him choose the title of his book. Victor Hugo knew the two essentials that man's life requires. B.F. Skinner knows the two essentials that have to be destroyed if man qua man is to be destroyed.

Ayn Rand

The Ayn Rand Letter, published fortnightly by The Ayn Rand Letter, Inc., 183 Madison Avenue, New York, N.Y. 10016.
Contributing Editor: **Leonard Peikoff**; Subscription Director: **Elayne Kalberman**; Production Manager: **Barbara Weiss.**

Vol. 1, No. 10 February 14, 1972

...AND THE RESPONSE

"The attention lavished on Harvard psychologist B.F. Skinner and his new book has been nothing short of remarkable," states The New York Times Book Review (October 24, 1971), in a special box on its front page. After citing a long list of Mr. Skinner's press interviews and television appearances, the statement continues: "The American Psychological Association gave him its annual award in September and hailed him as 'a pioneer in psychological research, leader in theory, master in technology, who has revolutionized the study of behavior in our time. A superlative scholar, scientist, teacher and writer.'"

Dear Reader: please keep my last two Letters in sight and in mind (or B.F. Skinner's book, Beyond Freedom and Dignity, if you care to check the accuracy of my report) while you read this present Letter.

Bear in mind the fact that the above testimonial was given to a theoretician whose theory consists in proclaiming that man is a mindless automaton - to a technologist whose technology consists in urging people to accept totalitarian control - to a scholar who substitutes the oldest of old wives' tales for a knowledge of philosophy - to a scientist who commits the kinds of logical fallacies for which a freshman would be flunked.

It would be unfair to assume that that testimonial represents the intellectual level of the entire psychological profession. Obviously, it does not - and we all know how such testimonials (or resolutions or protests) are put over by a special clique on a busy, confused, indifferent majority. But which is worse: a profession that actually subscribes to that testimonial - or a profession that does not, yet permits this sort of thing to be issued in its name? I think the latter is worse. Manipulators, such as Mr. Skinner's clique, do not seek to persuade, but to put something over on people. The fact that Mr. Skinner got away with the mere title of the book (let alone its thesis) indicates that the cultural field is empty, that no serious opposition is to be expected, that anything goes.

To be exact, I would say: not quite anything and not quite yet, but the cultural prognosis is pretty bleak. Mr. Skinner's trial balloon has been punctured by many different people, including some able sharpshooters, but if he studies the shreds, he will notice that only buckshot was used. The book deserves no heavier ammunition; its thesis does.

With a few exceptions, the superlatives hailing the book's importance came from press agents or blurb writers, not from reviewers. Most of the reviews were mixed or negative. As a whole, they conveyed an odd feeling, not the violence of a storm, but the sadness of a steady drizzle, as if exhausted men were still unable to accept the evil brazenly offered to them for appraisal, but unable without knowing why, their reasons long since forgotten, moved by some remnant of decency as by a faint echo from a very distant past. What deserved a scream of indignation, was received with a sigh.

The two best - i.e., thoroughly unfavorable - reviews appear in _The New Republic_ and _The New York Review of Books_. The rest of them attack Mr. Skinner, but concede his case. They accept him as an exponent of reason and science - and seize the opportunity to damn reason and science.

The review in _The New Republic_ (October 16, 1971) is quietly firm and civilized. Its primary target is Mr. Skinner's - and behaviorism's - view of man, which it describes as "psychology without a psyche." As an example of its approach: Skinner's argument "goes like this: physics used to attribute human characteristics to physical objects (such as growing more jubilant as they approached their natural places); only when it stopped doing this did scientific progress follow. Would not scientific progress follow in psychology if we could stop attributing human characteristics to human beings? He does not, naturally, put it quite in those terms, but I have given the structural essence of the matter." As an example of its appraisal of other aspects: "...the argumentation is often sloppy, the sensibility often philistine, the language often eccentric." As an apparent rebuke for Mr. Skinner's expression "inside man's skin": "And something inside my skull is reluctant to accept the simple, unproblematic world that Skinner offers, not just because it doesn't like it but because it thinks it all wrong for people whose skulls contain similarly complex apparatus." In all the reviews I read, this is the only passage that defends _intelligence_.

A cautious little piece in the _Saturday Review_ (October 9, 1971) praises the book for the following: "First of all, Dr. Skinner pays admirable attention to social problems...Skinner's sharp critique of punishment as largely ineffectual control is pertinent to the pressing question of prisons." In the context of the profound philosophical fundamentals that Mr. Skinner challenges, this sort of comment cannot even be classified as journalistic or range-of-the-moment: this is range-of-the-split-second. After which, the reviewer proceeds gently to blame Mr. Skinner for "his lust to objectivize everything." This, he complains, destroys the "mystery of man." Therefore, he concludes placatingly: "Another dream of reason has ended as a nightmare of an eminent psychologist, in this case perhaps the most influential of living American psychologists. But was it a good dream to begin with? Was it even an especially rational one? [I.e.: Is it rational to use reason?] We all know some of the devastating results of following the old imperative to control and subdue nature outside man, of adopting the dictum of Skinner's spiritual forebear, Francis Bacon, that 'knowledge is power.' Are we about to try the same experiment with 'manipulable man'?" This means that Mr. Skinner is a man of reason and a great scientist, whose theory would lead us to triumphs as brilliant as those achieved by the physical sciences, but we must not try it. The reviewer concludes sweetly: "Thus only if the views of this book are for the most part rejected will it really have a good effect on the social environment." (I suppose, on prison reform.) This sort of mealy-mouthed insult is unfair to any book, even Mr. Skinner's.

The review in _Psychotherapy & Social Science Review_ (January 1972) is of a much higher caliber. It blasts many aspects of Mr. Skinner's notions, competently and effectively - then blasts itself by the following indications of its own viewpoint: "But what in individual terms may be a struggle between narcissism and object-love, between indulgence in self and love of others, in societal terms becomes a struggle between anarchy and overcontrol. It is hard to know what the remedy should be." The reviewer mentions "the vicissitudes of the personal and social super ego" - and "the slowly accumulating evidence that man will _always_ have to struggle with his dual and decisive nature" (which consists of the capacity to think and to feel). He concludes: "But to pursue the last path, to attempt to turn pure instinct into pure reason is to fly in the face of the ambivalent nature of man..." (This means that Mr. Skinner is an advocate or representative of pure reason.) And: "Perhaps to be able to face these unresolvable dilemmas and painful paradoxes without recourse to either impotence _or_ grandiosity may finally deserve the name of dignity." If behaviorism declares, through Mr. Skinner: "I can resolve anything (somehow)," and its major rival school of psychology, Freudianism, advises: "Resign yourself to unresolvable dilemmas," behaviorism will win.

The review in The Atlantic (October 1971) is a peculiar mixture. The reviewer (properly) condemns Mr. Skinner for his "love of power over others." He attacks Mr. Skinner on a crucial issue: the destruction of language and, therefore, of judgment. But observe the following statement: "Let us be clear: it is not the sublime dumbness of mysticism [?!] toward which Skinner's idealism [?] moves. It is rather closer to the societies of 1984 and their Newspeak - the atrophy of consciousness through the shriveling of language." In his best paragraph, the reviewer states that Skinner's "own gospel of environmental determinism is one of the most serious threats conceivable to human survival. By eroding the sense of responsibility, it licenses people to shift the blame from themselves to 'the system.' It provides universal exoneration for atrocity after atrocity, or for compliance after compliance. It works to increase the amount of evil in the world." This is eminently true. But a few paragraphs earlier the reviewer said: "Determinism may be true, false, or both. But whatever it is, if it is used as Skinner uses it, the doom of conscious life is announced." How else can determinism "be used"? If a man cannot help what he does, how can he be held responsible for it? And if a given idea could be "true, false, or both" (at the same time and in the same respect), what sort of conscious life would be possible?

The mystery of that reviewer's stand is solved in his last paragraph: "Skinner believes that we can survive only if we allow a gigantic simplification of life. By that he means - he must finally mean - the atrophy of consciousness. He does not think that introspective, complex, self-doubting, self-torturing, self-indulgent, dissident, wordy people are efficient. He can set things up, he is sure, so that fewer such people occur. Does he not see that only silly geese lay golden eggs?" This means: Mr. Skinner represents reason, order, efficiency, but it is the emotion-ridden, contradiction-riddled, self-confessedly silly and sloppy souls who give value or meaning to life.

The review in The New Leader (January 10, 1972) is cruder and more open. It declares: "'The reasonable man,' Shaw said, 'tries to adapt himself to the world' (certainly the behaviorist's approach), 'the unreasonable one persists in trying to adapt the world to himself. Therefore all progress depends on the unreasonable man.'" Also: "And behaviorism is still, thank God, a science, not a technology." Also: "History, no less than behavioristic experiments, proves that man is innately selfish. The manipulation of mankind is unacceptable not because man is a noble being, but precisely because he is not. Those with power have always used it for their own ends, and there is no reason to suppose that their selfish preoccupations will diminish." (This means, one must assume, that the totalitarian control and manipulation of noble, selfless beings by noble, selfless beings would be all right.)

Then there is a batch of small-fry reviews which echo similar sentiments or no sentiments at all, make feeble objections, carefully miss the point, and do not commit themselves to anything. An astonishing one is a piece in Science News (August 7, 1971), which seems to be written by a teen-ager and makes a remarkable statement. Mr. Skinner's new book, it announces, may be one of the most important of the century: "Not only because it represents the summation of the Harvard psychologist's behavioristic approach to psychology, but because it goes beyond psychology into philosophy. And because Dr. Skinner's philosophy will probably be insulting to a great many people." Further, this particular expert declares that "Dr. Skinner makes [his] arguments logically and rationally..."

After a collection of this kind, it is a relief to read the essay in The New York Review of Books (December 30, 1971), entitled "The Case Against B.F. Skinner." The essay is neither apologetic nor sentimental. It is bright and forceful. It is a demolition job. What it demolishes is Mr. Skinner's scientific pretensions - and, to this extent, it is a defense of science.

"His [Skinner's] speculations are devoid of scientific content and do not even hint at general outlines of a possible science of human behavior." In regard to Skinner's claims: "Claims...must be evaluated according to the evidence presented for them. In the present instance, this is a simple task, since no evidence is presented...In fact, the question of evidence is beside the point, since the claims dissolve into triviality or incoherence under analysis."

The reviewer employs one of the best methods of dealing with a false theory: he takes it literally. "If Skinner's thesis is false, then there is no point in his having written the book or our reading it. But if his thesis is true, then there is also no point in his having written the book or our reading it. For the only point could be to modify behavior, and behavior, according to the thesis, is entirely controlled by arrangement of reinforcers. Therefore reading the book can modify behavior only if it is a reinforcer, that is, if reading the book will increase the probability of the behavior that led to reading the book (assuming an appropriate state of deprivation). At this point, we seem to be reduced to gibberish."

There are many other notable passages in that review. But its author is Noam Chomsky who, philosophically, is a Cartesian linguist advocating a theory to the effect that man's mental processes are determined by innate ideas - and who, politically, belongs to the New Left.

I shall reserve for my next Letter the two significant reviews that appeared in _The New York Times_. But the picture of our cultural devastation is clear. There are no defenders of _reason_ - in the country that was created not by historical accident, but by philosophical design. There are no defenders of _freedom_ - in what had once been the only moral social system on earth. There are no defenders of man's _mind_ - in the world's greatest scientific-technological civilization. All that is left is a battle between the mystics of spirit and the mystics of muscle - between men guided by their _feelings_ and men guided by their _reflexes_.

We are passengers on a plane flying at tremendous speed. One of these days, we will discover that its cockpit is empty.

(To be continued.)

Ayn Rand

OBJECTIVIST CALENDAR

On Saturday, March 4 (5:30 P.M.), Ayn Rand will appear on "Speaking Freely," an hour-long interview program, on NBC-TV in New York City. For the date and hour in other cities, please check with your local NBC-TV station.

B.W.

The Ayn Rand Letter, published fortnightly by The Ayn Rand Letter, Inc., 183 Madison Avenue, New York, N.Y. 10016.

Contributing Editor: **Leonard Peikoff**; Subscription Director: **Elayne Kalberman**; Production Manager: **Barbara Weiss.**

Vol. 1, No. 11 February 28, 1972

...AND THE RESPONSE

Part II

Newspapers do not create a culture, they are its product. They are transmission belts that carry ideas from the universities to the general public. The New York Times is one of the most influential newspapers in this country and a good indicator of our cultural trends. It published two reviews of Mr. Skinner's book, which - in different ways - are the most objectionable ones of the lot.

"There is just no gainsaying the profound importance of B.F. Skinner's new book, 'Beyond Freedom and Dignity.' If you plan to read only one book this year, this is probably the one you should choose." This is the opening of the review in the daily Times (September 22, 1971) - the only essentially favorable review I have found.

"Dr. Skinner's message is hard to take," the reviewer claims, but warns that "it cannot be dismissed so frivolously..." Then, without protective evasions, he summarizes accurately the brutal essentials of Mr. Skinner's thesis, and declares: "All of which is logically unassailable..." (Emphasis added.) Attempting, apparently, to resist the thesis, he states that "one tries reviewing the traditional criticisms of behaviorism. But even here, Skinner is not nearly so vulnerable as he once seemed. For he has confronted his many critics with telling counterarguments....To those who call his program totalitarian, he replies that 'the relation between the controller and the controlled is reciprocal'..." This refers to the passage on page 169 of Mr. Skinner's book, which is quoted on pages 5-6 of my Letter of January 31. Please reread it in order to judge whether that is a "telling counterargument."

"No, none of the familiar objections to behaviorism will suffice to demolish 'Beyond Freedom and Dignity,'" the reviewer sighs. "...the book remains logically tenable. I don't like it, which is to say that it doesn't reinforce me in the manner to which I am accustomed." To make a concession of this kind is to confess that one has no grounds for one's convictions, and that one is not aware of one's own mental processes. The concession is followed by an odd statement: "But for the moment the only retort that I can think of is that conceived by Dostoyevsky's 'underground man' - to 'deliberately go mad to prove' that all behavior cannot be predicted or controlled. But such a response might not prove very useful to me or the culture....So we may indeed be trapped in a Skinnerian maze." What is odd here is the fact that the quotation from Dostoyevsky's "underground man" is not a retort the reviewer thought of spontaneously: this very quotation is discussed by Mr. Skinner on pages 164-165 of his book and is, properly, dismissed.

At first glance, the review creates the impression that it was written by an earnest intellectual who struggled desperately against the necessity of accepting a totalitarian state, but failed to find counterarguments and gave in, reluctantly, to the power of unanswerable logic. After one has read the book, one asks: Is that the reviewer's case? Or is it the case of a man eager to convince us that Mr. Skinner's thesis is unanswerable?

The review in The New York Times Book Review (October 24, 1971) is different. It is unfavorable. It declares that Skinner has a secret motive (a "hidden agenda") which is unknown to him, but known to the reviewer. "The actual text of Skinner's new book reveals a man desperately in search of some way to preserve the old-fashioned virtues associated with 19th-century individualism in a world where self-reliance no longer makes sense." Which virtues? Hard work, believe it or not. "First, behavior control appears to him a way to get people hard at work again in an age where indolence is rife." If hard work is the essential characteristic of individualism, then the Nazi and Soviet forced labor camps are examples of individualism unmatched in the nineteenth or any other century. But there is no discussion or advocacy of "hard work" in Mr. Skinner's book, and nothing to justify the allegation that this is his *first* concern.

"This hidden agenda can first be detected in the way Skinner talks about controlling behavior. All his attention is centered on situations where one person is being controlled; he employs such phrases as 'a person's behavior' or 'operant conditioning of the subject.' He seldom refers to different controls for different kinds of social groups." Even Mr. Skinner does not deserve a reviewer of this kind. Many people are unable to deal with metaphysical questions, but this one is militantly aggressive about it. He is so rabid a collectivist that he will not tolerate any concern with the individual, even for the purpose of destroying him. He does not see that if his own beliefs are to be put into practice, it is Mr. Skinner who is laying the necessary foundation.

If a doctor stated that man needs food, and were criticized as follows: "Which man does he mean, Smith or Jones? Different men need different foods. And he hasn't said anything about the poor, the black, the young, and the women" - the Skedunk Gazette would not publish it. Yet this type of mentality is published on the front page of The New York Times Book Review. If you think I am exaggerating, judge the following. The reviewer picks on a passage in which Mr. Skinner attempts to teach us behaviorist language by describing a young man's emotional states in behaviorist terms - e.g., Mr. Skinner translates "he feels uneasy or anxious" into "his behavior frequently has unavoidable aversive consequences which have emotional effects." The reviewer's comment: "But Professor, there's a war on! Why aren't you talking about the social cause of his behavior? Why do you treat him as if he lives in a vacuum?"

Mr. Skinner is not only too individualistic, the reviewer claims, but also *too rational*. "While Heisenberg contemplated the unpredictable behavior of matter, Skinner insists that we must find unambiguous facts about human behavior; the difference is between wanting to explore the world as it is and wanting to possess knowledge. The possession of knowledge, of hard facts you can act on, is an echo of 19th-century positivistic science, just as Skinner's beliefs are an echo of that century's small-town society."

If "the possession of knowledge" is unattainable, what do you acquire when you "explore the world as it is" - and why do you explore it? What is a "soft" fact? What do you act on, when you cannot act on knowledge or facts? (That review may be an example of such action.) But I shall borrow a phrase from Noam Chomsky's essay, and say that these are questions "which I happily leave to others to decode."

The daily Times reviewer may be taken as typical of the present - a frightened liberal trying to convince us (and himself) that Mr. Skinner's totalitarian state is the wave of the future. But the Sunday Times reviewer is the future - the future of Mr. Skinner's theories, their successful product and embodiment, who has been molded by the "contingencies of reinforcement" in our universities, who sees reason, individualism and "autonomy" as incontrovertibly nonexistent, sees no point in arguing about them, sees nothing beyond the range of the immediate moment, regards Mr. Skinner as old-fashioned, and goes on from there. If you have read The Fountainhead, you will understand the relationship: he is the Gus Webb to Mr. Skinner's Ellsworth Toohey.

The Times chose the publication of Beyond Freedom and Dignity as an occasion to go beyond B.F. Skinner. A different push in the same direction was provided by Time magazine. The headline on its cover (September 20, 1971) announced: "B.F. Skinner Says: WE CAN'T AFFORD FREEDOM" - not a very original statement, but regarded, apparently, as important or valuable enough to justify placing Mr. Skinner's picture on the cover, and giving him a lengthy story. The story, however, is flattering only in its length; otherwise, it is noncommittal and empty, playing both sides of the fence in the "safe" modern manner, i.e., praising Mr. Skinner, and insulting him by quoting his enemies.

If you wonder what motives could bring Mr. Skinner to his theories, what frustration could lead him to so profound a hatred of mankind, and who would be his first victims, the Time story offers three passages that provide eloquent clues. The first is a quotation from Mr. Skinner's novel Walden Two. The speaker, Time explains, "is T.E. Frazier, a character in Walden Two and the fictional founder of the utopian community described in that novel. He is also an alter ego of the author..." The quotation: "I've had only one idea in my life - a true idée fixe. To put it as bluntly as possible - the idea of having my own way. 'Control!' expresses it. The control of human behavior. In my early experimental days it was a frenzied, selfish desire to dominate. I remember the rage I used to feel when a prediction went awry. I could have shouted at the subjects of my experiments, 'Behave, damn you! Behave as you ought!'"

The second passage deals with Mr. Skinner's youth. In his college days, he wrote short stories and "sent three of them to Robert Frost, who praised them warmly. That encouragement convinced Fred Skinner that he should become a writer. The decision, he says, was 'disastrous.'...In his own words, he 'failed as a writer' because he 'had nothing important to say.'"

The third passage is about Twin Oaks, a real-life commune founded on a farm in Virginia, and "governed by Skinner's laws of social engineering." "Private property is forbidden, except for such things as books and clothing...No one is allowed to boast of individual accomplishments...What is considered appropriate behavior - cooperating, showing affection, turning the other cheek and working diligently - is, on the other hand, applauded, or 'reinforced,' by the group." "The favorite sports are 'cooperation volleyball' and skinny-dipping in the South Anna River - false modesty is another of the sins that are not reinforced - and there is plenty of folk singing and dancing." In regard to the consequences: "After starting with only $35,000, Twin Oaks, four years later, still finds survival a struggle. The farm brings more emotional than monetary rewards; members would find it cheaper to work at other jobs and buy their food at the market....Beyond economics, there are serious psychological problems at Twin Oaks, and few members have stayed very long. [Emotional rewards?] Turnover last year was close to 70%. The ones who leave first, in fact, are often the most competent members, who still expect special recognition for their talents. 'Competent people are hard to get along with,' says Richard Stutsman, one of Twin Oaks' trained psychologists. 'They tend to make demands, not requests. We cannot afford to reinforce ultimatum behavior, although we recognize our need for their competence....' When they leave, the community not only loses their skills but also sacrifices a potential rise in its standard of living."

For my comments on this, see Atlas Shrugged.

The cultural establishment has pushed Beyond Freedom and Dignity to the best-seller lists. The most dangerous part of its potential impact - particularly on young readers - is not that the book is convincing or eloquent, but that it is so bad. If it were less crudely irrational and inept, a reader could give the benefit of the doubt to those who were taken in by some trickily complex arguments. But if so evil a thesis as the advocacy of totalitarian dictatorship is offered in such illogical, unconvincing terms, yet is acclaimed as "important," what is one to think of the intellectual and moral state of our culture? A rational reader may become paralyzed - not by fear, fear is not his psychological danger - but by disgust, contempt, discouragement and, ultimately, withdrawal from the realm of the intellect (which, perhaps, is Mr. Skinner's hope).

But before you draw the "malevolent-universe" conclusion that falsehood always wins over truth, or that men prefer irrationality to reason, and dictatorship to freedom (and, therefore, "What's the use?") - consider the following. Human Events (January 15, 1972) reports that "the National Institutes of Mental Health had granted $283,000 to Dr. B.F. Skinner..." which, apparently, financed the writing of his book. The New Republic (January 28, 1972) gives some details: the Skinner grant "was one of 20 Senior Research Career Awards, that is, plums for scientific leaders in 'mental health' across the board rather than a unique grant....The particular award was made for the purpose of 'integrating and consolidating' Skinner's findings and 'considering the application of the science of behavior to the problems of society' [!]..."

This is the way an "establishment" is formed and placed beyond the reach of dissent. What chance would a beginner, a nonconformist, an opponent of behaviorism, have against the entrenched power of a clique supported by government funds? This is not a free marketplace of ideas any longer. Evil, falsehood, irrationality are not winning in free competition with virtue, truth, reason. Today's culture is ruled by intellectual pressure groups which have become intellectual monopolies backed, like all monopolies, by the government's gun and the money of the victims.

(The solution, of course, is not to censor research projects, but to abolish all government subsidies in the field of the social sciences and, eventually, in all fields. But this is a different subject, which I shall discuss at a later date.)

The significance of B.F. Skinner's book lies in its eloquent demonstration of the results of philosophical collapse and governmental power: when the intellectual default of the victims permits the dead hand of the government to get a strangle hold on the field of ideas, a nation will necessarily be pushed beyond freedom and dignity.

Ayn Rand

The Ayn Rand Letter, published fortnightly by The Ayn Rand Letter, Inc., 183 Madison Avenue, New York, N.Y. 10016.
Contributing Editor: **Leonard Peikoff**; Subscription Director: **Elayne Kalberman**; Production Manager: **Barbara Weiss.**

Vol. 1, No. 12 March 13, 1972

TAX-CREDITS FOR EDUCATION

Politically, the goal of today's dominant trend is statism. Philosophically, the goal is the obliteration of reason; psychologically, it is the erosion of ambition.

The political goal presupposes the two others. The human characteristic required by statism is *docility*, which is the product of hopelessness and intellectual stagnation. Thinking men cannot be ruled; ambitious men do not stagnate.

"Ambition" means the systematic pursuit of achievement and of constant improvement in respect to one's goal. Like the word "selfishness," and for the same reasons, the word "ambition" has been perverted to mean only the pursuit of dubious or evil goals, such as the pursuit of power; this left no concept to designate the pursuit of actual values. But "ambition" as such is a neutral concept: the evaluation of a given ambition as moral or immoral depends on the nature of the goal. A great scientist or a great artist is the most passionately ambitious of men. A demagogue seeking political power is ambitious. So is a social climber seeking "prestige." So is a modest laborer who works conscientiously to acquire a home of his own. The common denominator is the drive to improve the conditions of one's existence, however broadly or narrowly conceived. ("Improvement" is a moral term and depends on one's standard of values. An ambition guided by an irrational standard does not, *in fact*, lead to improvement, but to self-destruction.)

An economic "freeze" is intended to paralyze ambition (and its root: the active mind). A freeze is an order not to act, not to grow, not to improve. It is a demand to sacrifice one's future. But - since an essential characteristic of life is motion - when men do not move forward, they move back; the demand to stop cannot stop and becomes a demand to sacrifice one's present.

The Nixon Administration did not even take the trouble to delay or disguise this process. After all the mawkish pleas to "hold the line" against inflation - to forgo, "temporarily," higher profits or higher wages or a higher standard of living - the Administration is now proposing *higher taxes*. This means that our standard of living is not to stand still, but to collapse under a huge new tax burden, a so-called "value-added tax" (which is a complex form of national sales tax).

To add insult to injury, this tax is intended to finance not some sudden national emergency, but public education.

Of all the government undertakings, none has failed so disastrously as public education. The scope, the depth, and the evidence of this failure are observable all around us. To name three of its obvious symptoms: drug addiction among the young (which is an attempt to escape the unbearable state of a mind unable to cope with existence) - functional illiteracy (the inability of the average high-school or college graduate to speak English, i.e., to speak or write coherently) - student violence (which means that students have not learned what savages know to some minimal extent: the impracticality and immorality of resorting to physical force).

In the face of such evidence, one would expect the government's performance in the field of education to be questioned, at the least. Instead, the government is demanding more money - at a time of national economic crisis - to continue spreading the wreckage wider and wider. (Observe, incidentally, the consistency with which moral principles work out in politics: when need, not achievement, is the standard of value, success at a given assignment is penalized, and failure rewarded. E.g., NASA's success in landing a man on the moon was followed by cuts in Congressional appropriations for the space program; the growing failures of the educational establishment are followed by the appropriation of larger and larger sums.)

There is, however, a practical alternative. If the countless individuals who are eager to "do something" in politics, and the countless groups who profess concern over the growth of statism, really wish to accomplish something of value, the coming debate on the new tax to support education offers them a chance. (It is also a chance for any honest politician, of either party, who seeks a worthy issue to crusade for at election time.) It is an opportunity to unite many people of different viewpoints in an ad hoc movement for a specifically defined goal.

The goal is: tax-credits for education.

The idea is not entirely new. (I was advocating it ten years ago.) Different versions of it were periodically proposed in Congress, but were defeated in committee. (In 1964, one of the proposal's notable supporters was Senator Ribicoff.) The evidence of the desperate need for such a program has never been as clear as it is at present.

The essentials of the idea (in my version) are as follows: an individual citizen would be given tax-credits for the money he spends on education, whether his own education, his children's, or any person's he wants to put through a bona-fide school of his own choice (including primary, secondary and higher education).

The upper limits of what he may spend on any one person would be equal to what it costs the government to provide a student with a comparable education (if there is a computer big enough to calculate it, including all the costs involved, local, state and federal, the government loans, scholarships, subsidies, etc.).

If a young person's parents are too poor to pay for his education or to pay income taxes, and if he cannot find a private sponsor to finance him, the public schools would still be available to him, as they are at present - with the likelihood that these schools would be greatly improved by the relief of the pressure of overcrowding, and by the influence of a broad variety of private schools.

I want to stress that I am _not_ an advocate of public (i.e., government-operated) schools, that I am _not_ an advocate of the income tax, and that I am _not_ an advocate of the government's "right" to expropriate a citizen's money or to control his spending through tax-incentives. None of these phenomena would exist in a free economy. But we are living in a disastrously mixed economy, which cannot be freed overnight. And, in today's context, the above proposal would be a step in the right direction, a measure to avert an immediate catastrophe.

It would accomplish the following: instead of becoming a crushing new tax burden at a time when the country is staggering under the present one, the costs of education would be borne directly by those who now pay them indirectly - by individual citizens. (The public schools would remain in existence and would be financed out of general tax revenues.) Parents would still have to pay for education, but they would have a choice: either to send their children to free public schools and pay their taxes in full - or to pay tuition to a private school, with money saved from their taxes.

It would give private schools a chance to survive (which they do not have at present). It would bring their tuition fees within the reach of the majority of people (today, only the well-to-do can afford them). It would break up the government's stranglehold, decentralize education, and open it to competition - as well as to a free marketplace of ideas.

It would eliminate the huge educational bureaucracy of the government (which is now growing with the speed of a terminal cancer) and reduce it to a reasonable size. The amount of money this would save is literally inconceivable to the average citizen. To give just one example: it was estimated that the Job Corps spent $9,210 to $13,000 per year per enrollee; at some camps, the figure reached $22,000, and even $39,205. At private residential schools giving vocational training, the costs ranged from $2,300 to $2,600 per student per year. (Shirley Scheibla, _Poverty Is Where the Money Is_, New Rochelle, N.Y., Arlington House, 1968.)

Let the school teachers and college professors remember these figures. Theirs is one of the lowest paid professions today, yet most of them are supporters of the status quo. Let them realize that it is not the poverty of their students, but the enrichment of the bureaucracy, that is responsible for their plight - and what a competitive market would do in regard to the financial value of their services.

At present, the biggest spender of government funds, the largest recipient of tax money in the national budget, is not the Department of Defense, but the Department of Health, Education and Welfare. It is clear why the government must hold a monopoly on national defense. But no one - except a full-fledged communist or fascist - would advocate a government monopoly on education. Yet such a monopoly is what we are, in fact, approaching - and taxation is the main cause of the trend.

Private universities are being ground out of existence between two modern disasters, both products of government policies: the erosion of private contributions (eaten away by taxes), and rising costs (brought about by inflation, which is caused by government spending). State universities with nominal or free tuition are another factor destroying the chances of the private universities' survival. No private concern can compete with a government institution for any length of time, and the injustice involved is obvious: it is a competition in which one contestant has unlimited funds, part of them taken from the other, and in which one contestant is forced to obey the rules arbitrarily set by the other. If any private schools survive, they will survive in name only (which is the typical policy of a fascist state): they are all but hogtied by the government already. The current attempts to assist private universities with federal funds will complete the job. If "the power to tax is the power to destroy," the power to disburse government funds is the power to rule.

Now consider the nature of today's tax policies in regard to the educational needs of young people.

While millions of dollars are being spent by the government on attempts to educate young people most of whom have no ability and/or no desire to get an education, what happens to the young man who has both? If he is poor, he has to work his way through school - a terrible process that takes eight years or longer for a four-year course, consuming his youth and becoming progressively harder, in view of rising costs and shrinking opportunities of employment. (Scholarships are a drop in the bucket, nor are they always granted fairly.) Yet out of his meager income, he has to pay taxes - not only the hidden ones in the cost of everything he buys, but income taxes as well. Thus while he is allowed no deductions for the costs of his own education, he is paying for the free education of the youths enrolled in government projects.

To seek education in such circumstances requires an unusual strength of character, an unusual independence, ambition and long-range vision. The young people who do it are, potentially, the best of the nation; they are its future; they do not need help, only a fair chance, which they are denied. Many of them are broken by the struggle and driven to give up. But, wherever they go, their taxes still pay for the education and "rehabilitation" efforts which allegedly strive (but fail) to develop in stuporous hippies the qualities of character which they, the victims, had once possessed.

If a young man does not, or cannot afford to, go to college, but goes to work instead, to earn his living, he will soon discover - if he is an actively interested, conscientious, ambitious worker - that he needs education to rise to a better job. The tax laws allow him deductions only if the schooling is demanded by his employer as a condition of keeping his job - not if he seeks special training on his own initiative. What does this do to his self-confidence or his sense of control over his own future? Yet, in the government's job-training programs, the lethargic recipients are not merely given free training, but are paid for attending the courses. It is inequities of this kind that make Mr. Nixon's exhortations to "self-reliance" sound so ludicrously and cruelly hypocritical.

All over the country, self-respecting and self-supporting young couples are carrying a double financial burden: paying constantly rising taxes for the support of schools to which they cannot in conscience send their own children. The private revival of Montessori schools demonstrates the plight of conscientious young parents on a nationwide scale. Aware of the ravages of "Progressive" education in public schools, such parents send their children to private schools (or join to build such schools), which few of them can afford. It is a heavy sacrifice for most of them, at a time when they are struggling to achieve some degree of professional and financial security. They are given no tax-relief for such expenses, which places private schools outside the reach of the hard-working, respectable lower middle class.

The same injustice is perpetrated against the parents who send their children to parochial schools. As you surely know, I am not an advocate of religion or of religious education; but the double burden of a forced necessity to pay for the support of secular schools is a violation of the parents' right to religious freedom. The parochial schools are collapsing financially, for the same reasons and under the same pressures as the private universities - and the current controversy over the support of parochial schools illustrates the nature of the issue. On the one hand, it is certainly improper and unconstitutional to use public funds for the support of religious schools. On the other hand, it is unjust that the children of religious taxpayers are denied the special advantages granted to the children of nonreligious ones. You may take it as a general rule: whenever an issue leads to an unresolvable conflict, you will find, at its root, the violation of someone's rights.

These are only a few of the problems that tax-credits for education would solve.

The opposition to such a program would be horrendous and would come from an entrenched pressure group: the educational establishment. But this is the time to raise the question of a "conflict of interests." Public officials who have connections with private sources of income that involve government matters - as, for instance, with a company seeking government contracts - are regarded as suspect, unless they break the connection. By the same token, a bureaucrat whose source of income is a government job (an unnecessary job, more often than not) should be regarded as suspect, when and if he opposes a program that threatens the source of his income.

Some people would oppose the program on the grounds that it will foster the development of different educational theories and methods in the various private schools. The answer to them is that that precisely is one of the program's goals - that differences, not regimented uniformity, are essential to the progress of a free country - and that equality before the law, _not_ egalitarianism, is one of this country's fundamental principles.

Let us take the educational establishment at their word and hold them to it: that their goal is to provide education, _not_ to control the intellectual life of this country.

Ayn Rand

OBJECTIVIST CALENDAR

We have been asked to announce that on Saturday, March 25, Dr. George Reisman will speak in Silver Spring, Maryland. Time: 8:30 P.M. Place: University Towers (Party Room), 1111 University Blvd. W. Subject: "Capitalism: The Cure for Racism." For further information, contact Dr. Edwin A. Locke, 6100 Westchester Park Dr., Apt. 1418, College Park, Md. 20740; phone: (301) 474-8857 (evenings).

B.W.

The Ayn Rand Letter, published fortnightly by The Ayn Rand Letter, Inc., 183 Madison Avenue, New York, N.Y. 10016.

Contributing Editor: **Leonard Peikoff**; Subscription Director: **Elayne Kalberman**; Production Manager: **Barbara Weiss.**

Vol. 1, No. 13 March 27, 1972

THE SHANGHAI GESTURE

When President Nixon announced his decision to visit China, there were grounds to reserve judgment on the meaning of his policy.

So long as the United States recognizes and deals with Soviet Russia (a thoroughly immoral policy), there is no reason not to deal with China, which is much less of a threat to the civilized world. China, potentially, could serve as a "great wall" against Russia. (Now, however, this is not likely to happen.)

For the last ten years or longer, there has been a kind of muted, soft-sell propaganda going on in this country, to the following effect: we must not be too hostile to Russia, China is the real menace and the real revolutionary, Russia is becoming "moderate" or close to "capitalistic," World War III will be fought between America and China - and we will need Russia's help to save us. This line was not pushed too hard, it went on in occasional small puffs (in obscure books, in speeches by undistinguished professors, in casual remarks, in articles on other subjects), but it went on steadily, with remarkable uniformity and no apparent cause, like a series of cheap little trial balloons - and it had all the earmarks of the typical Soviet propaganda campaign.

Observe that it became fashionable in a certain kind of semiliberal demimonde to hold up China, not Russia, as the communist menace - in detective stories, in movies, in the sort of fiction that approaches big issues with small courage. Observe that most activists of the New Left make it a point to stress that they are _equally_ opposed to Soviet Russia and capitalistic America, and that their source of inspiration is not Stalin, but Mao.

Russia was the only winner of and profiteer on World War II - which she won not by military might (as demonstrated by the fact that she was twice defeated by Finland), but through victory over Roosevelt and Churchill at Yalta. It is obvious why Russia's rulers would dream of and gradually seek another war: they hope that America would deliver Asia into their power, as she helped to deliver Europe. (For a discussion of why dictatorships must resort to military aggression, see "The Roots of War" in my book _Capitalism: The Unknown Ideal_.) A third world war, with America once again in the role of Russia's ally, would drain the last of America's power and complete Russia's conquest of the world.

If such a war ever came, it would be incalculably better for America to help China rather than Russia. But such a war does not have to come.

If the breach between Russia and China is genuine, as it seems to be at the moment, a rapprochement with China would be the wisest step an American President could take to avert a world war. Since international politics is what it has always been among statist regimes, only more viciously so - a "balance of power" game - he would have to play one potential aggressor against the other and thus save the rest of the world. But a policeman (or a peace-protector) playing with criminals has to be a giant if he is not to be outwitted by them in a game at which they are expert. For instance, America might be led to build up China's economic and military power, only to see the two criminals pull a sudden switch, join forces, and attack us. A sudden Russia-China alliance is not as unlikely as the Hitler-Stalin pact was in its time. It would take a giant to prevent a future catastrophe - a giant who knows clearly, firmly and precisely what he is doing, where he is going, what is the nature of the enemy, and what are the best interests of the United States of America.

Mr. Nixon is no giant.

If there were grounds to give him the benefit of the doubt, his performance has undercut them and removed all doubts. Whatever his policy, if any, he will not be able to carry it out.

It was not necessary for him to visit China in person. A less flamboyant manner of establishing communications with China would have been sufficient to serve notice on Russia that she is not to regard the United States as her international mercenary army. But these are specific details of diplomatic procedure, which the public is not always in a position to judge. The television spectacular of Mr. Nixon's visit, however, was staged for the public and was submitted to the public's judgment.

The television spectacle was as colorful as an old-fashioned Grauman's Chinese Theater prologue in Hollywood, as vulgar, as phony, and much more dangerous. It was dangerous on three counts: 1. morally, it was confusing and embarrassing for the American viewer; 2. politically, it was doing the work of China's propagandists; 3. psychologically, it was a disastrous confession of weakness, publicly displayed in the presence of adversaries whose power rests on detecting and expertly manipulating just such human weaknesses.

1. Morally, it was impossible to watch all those gracious ceremonies, benevolent smiles, lengthy handshakes, cordial speeches - and hold in mind the actual nature of Red China. One kept alternating between two feelings: the kind of unreality and childish amusement one feels at a circus - and the shock of returning to reality, the reality of China's terror, starvation, torture chambers, mass slaughter. I kept thinking of the thousands of men who try to escape from China by swimming many miles, under the gunfire of patrol boats, to reach freedom in Hong Kong. What about them? - I kept thinking, whenever somebody uttered one of those ringing speeches about universal peace and love for mankind - isn't there anyone to defend them? The shock came from the realization that the smiling figure in the midst of the ghastly pretense on the TV screen was the President of the United States.

2. Politically, both sides kept hiding behind the hypocritical device of proclaiming their good will toward <u>the people</u> of the opposite country, as apart from its political system. But there was this difference: to the American people, particularly to the naive and the gullible, the Chinese government's declaration of good will might bring pleasure or reassurance; to the Chinese people, the American government's declaration of good will would bring despair. It is America that all the enslaved peoples of the world look up to as the symbol of freedom and as their

last hope. For the Chinese to see an American President drinking toasts to their jailers is so cruel a blow that, in the name of humanity, no one should ever permit himself to deliver it.

What the American people think, does matter in international politics and does matter to Mr. Nixon. (He is accused by the Democrats of staging that show as part of his election campaign, which is probably true.) What the Chinese people think, does not matter to their rulers and cannot affect the world or even their own country: they are chained and helpless. So while Chou En-lai was courting the American people, all that Mr. Nixon was courting was Chou En-lai.

It is vitally important to China's rulers to give the American people the impression that Chinese communists are "good guys," not monsters, that they are gracious, benevolent and civilized - an impression which years of propaganda would not achieve, but which was achieved for them in one week, courtesy of an American President. China's popular impression of the American government is of no consequence: if all of the Chinese people were to fall in love with Mr. Nixon (which is highly unlikely), they would still be forced to chant curses against "American imperialist dogs," then keep silent for a week, then chant the curses again. No one is as much in love with America as the Russian people. What good does it do them - or us?

Both the American and the Chinese officials recited declarations to the effect that they have political "differences" (which were left unnamed), but that they would set the differences aside and confine themselves to a quest for things they have in common. Nevertheless, the Chinese invited Mr. Nixon to attend the performance of a revolutionary ballet - in which a pajamas-clad ballerina, representing a girl-guerrilla, jerked acrobatically across the stage, through a jerking corps de ballet in proletarian costumes, seeking a way to fight her enemy (the capitalist system), and ended up brandishing a huge wooden rifle. Via satellite-relayed television, the world saw an American President applauding this.

If the roles were reversed, and the Chinese officials, visiting Washington, were invited to attend an opera based, say, on *The Manchurian Candidate*, would anyone take it as an expression of our respect for them? I do not believe that they would attend. But they knew, I guess, what they were doing in Peking, and what type of man they were dealing with, because it was Mr. Nixon who, in parting, chose to quote from a revolutionary poem by Mao Tse-tung. Chou En-lai did not quote from the Declaration of Independence.

If anyone wonders how the Chinese government is to explain Mr. Nixon's visit, to its allies and to the world at large, the explanation would be simple (and not entirely false): the visit, they would say, proves the invincible power of communism, since its capitalistic enemies are obliged to curry its favor. And *that* is the impression which the television version of The Shanghai Gesture would make on an impartial observer. The Chinese officials were much more dignified than Mr. Nixon. He did not have to smile so often nor in such an ingratiating manner. He did not have to act like a beggar, and worse: a beggar who had nothing to beg for.

3. Psychologically, the disaster of the entire spectacle was that Mr. Nixon seemed to *enjoy* it. He was like a man taken in by his own press releases: he projected simultaneously that he was playing a well-rehearsed role and that he was seeing himself as a great peacemaker, a man of destiny - of a selfless, sentimental, unassuming, all-loving destiny. Besides, he projected that he was flattered to pieces - the worst thing to be, considering the character and perceptiveness of his hosts.

It is widely believed that Franklin D. Roosevelt was flattered by Stalin into the Yalta surrender. Whatever his other qualities, Franklin D. Roosevelt was a man of stronger character than Richard M. Nixon.

Mr. Nixon, apparently, was traumatized by the alleged success of his so-called "kitchen debate" with Khrushchev, and has been trying to repeat it ever since. His performance in that innocuous little "debate" had the same qualities: a mild, friendly, almost obsequious suggestion of disagreement with Khrushchev's gross, bombastic, offensive pronouncements. I do not know what anyone would regard as successful in that encounter, unless it is the fact that Khrushchev condescended to speak to Mr. Nixon at all.

There is another, deeper reason why President Nixon is bound to fail in foreign policy, a reason he shares with President Johnson. Both of them are expert politicians who reached the Presidency not through popular appeal, but through skillful manipulation of other politicians, in Congress or in local party machines. A man's habitual method of dealing with other men becomes automatized in his mind and seldom changes. Both President Johnson and President Nixon seem to believe that personal, man-to-man, behind-the-scenes maneuvers can solve anything, and both feel confident of their ability to manipulate people - to soothe, to reassure, to flatter, to charm, to convince, to deceive.

But international politics is not a smoke-filled backroom, a party caucus, or a Congressional committee. The tactics, the methods, and the stakes involved are not the same. It is not like promising a new dam to a senator from Iowa in exchange for his vote for a bill to provide school lunches - or like half-promising the same government contract to five different people in unmentioned, but understood, exchange for a campaign contribution. The trickiest American manipulators are crude, naive and innocent compared to their European or Asian counterparts. "Horse traders" is the usual epithet describing American politicians; the foreign ones are <u>death-traders</u>.

Mr. Nixon has already agreed to one such trade - thus signaling his Chinese adversaries that his accommodating flexibility will offer them no problem in the deadly game he has ventured to play. I can only hope that this trade will not become one of the darkest spots on America's record. Its outward form is the U.S.-Chinese Communiqué. Its name is Taiwan.

I shall discuss it in my next Letter.

(To be continued.)

Ayn Rand

The Ayn Rand Letter, published fortnightly by The Ayn Rand Letter, Inc., 183 Madison Avenue, New York, N.Y. 10016.

Contributing Editor: **Leonard Peikoff**; Subscription Director: **Elayne Kalberman**; Production Manager: **Barbara Weiss.**

Vol. 1, No. 14 April 10, 1972

THE SHANGHAI GESTURE

Part II

The first major consequence of Mr. Nixon's announcement that he intended to visit China, was the obscenity perpetrated at the U.N.

It is futile to express indignation about the U.N. or even to discuss it. In the presence of a certain level of depravity, indignation - which has a moral base - is inappropriate. When an institution reaches the degree of corruption, brazen cynicism and dishonor demonstrated by the U.N. in its shameful history, to discuss it at length is to imply that its members and supporters may possibly be making an innocent error about its nature - which is no longer possible. There is no margin for error about a monstrosity that was created for the alleged purpose of preventing wars by uniting the world against any aggressor, but proceeded to unite it against any victim of aggression. The expulsion of a charter member, the Republic of China - an action forbidden by the U.N.'s own Charter - was a "moment of truth," a naked display of the United Nations' soul.

What was Red China's qualification for membership in the U.N.? The fact that her government seized power by force, and has maintained it for twenty-two years by terror. What disqualified Nationalist China? The fact that she was a friend of the United States.

It was against the United States that all those beneficiaries of our foreign aid were voting at the U.N. It was hatred of the United States and the pleasure of spitting in our face that they were celebrating, as well as their liberation from morality - with savages, appropriately, doing jungle dances in the aisles.

Any junior clerk in the diplomatic service would know that this was such a resounding demonstration of the bankruptcy of our foreign policy that some fundamental checking of its premises was required. What did Mr. Nixon do? He merely wiped his face. Then he proceeded to help reinstate the foreign aid which Congress - in a rare and proper burst of outraged national honor - had abolished.

After which - and after his many previous declarations that one must "negotiate from strength, not from weakness" - Mr. Nixon departed for China.

The results of his journey were to be expected. But it was difficult to believe that they would be as openly evil as they are.

An appropriate introduction to an analysis of the U.S.-Chinese Communiqué, is a brief passage from Henry A. Kissinger's news conference in Shanghai (*The New York Times*, February 28, 1972):

"Q. Did Chairman Mao participate? Did his participation go to the detailed substance of the matter or was it largely philosophical and general?

"A. I don't believe that it would be appropriate for me to go into detail about that conversation with Chairman Mao....But it was not just a vague philosophical discussion."

This is a succinct example of the view held by most Americans today: that philosophy is just a collection of vague generalities and has no practical significance. This is not the view held by the Chinese rulers. Observe the consequences of both attitudes in the joint Communiqué.

"There are essential differences between China and the United States in their social systems and foreign policies," declares a section to which both sides subscribed. These differences are not identified; they were left, presumably, to the two sections in which each side speaks for itself and states its own position.

The U.S. section begins by declaring: "Peace in Asia and peace in the world requires efforts both to reduce immediate tensions and to eliminate the basic causes of conflict." Since these basic causes are left unnamed, which country or government on earth would not subscribe to that declaration?

Foggy generalities of this kind fill the rest of the U.S. section. It contains no statement that is distinctively American, no mention of what America stands for, and *not a single reference to any principle of the American social system*.

The closest approach to it is the following: "The United States supports individual freedom and social progress for all the peoples of the world, free of outside pressure or intervention." The words "individual freedom" might sound right, but read that sentence again. Does it mean the freedom of an individual man - or the freedom of "an individual people"? If the first, then to what do the words "social progress" refer? If the second, then does the U.S. regard "peoples," not men, as the basic units of political theory and concern? (But political theory is a *philosophical* issue.)

You can read it either way, because this is the only sentence that contains the word "individual." The word "rights" does not appear at all (except in a phrase about "the right of the peoples of South Asia to shape their own future in peace..."). The words "individual rights" - the one and only unmistakably American concept, the basic principle and badge of honor of the United States of America - are neither mentioned nor implied. Such is the method by which our President tries to make our social system acceptable to the bloody thugs who rule a dictatorship.

"Countries should treat each other with mutual respect," the section continues, "and be willing to compete peacefully, letting performance be the ultimate judge." Leaving aside the bad grammar of this last, *who* is to judge the performance of _what_? Judgment requires a standard of value, which is a _philosophical_ issue. If the standard is power, i.e., the total subjugation of a people, then China wins the competition. If the standard is production, abundance, progress (and the well-being of individual citizens), then the United States has won long ago. Does Mr. Nixon actually believe that the totalitarian rulers do not know it? If he does, then by what performance does he expect the United States to prove it and to convince them?

A declaration of willingness to be judged by one's performance rests on the premise of _objectivity_ - so profoundly _philosophical_ and, today, unfashionable a concept that Mr. Nixon could not possibly be willing to uphold it. If he were, one would have to ask: what would he accept as proof of the fact that objectivity is a concept which communist rulers are struggling to obliterate? They have been proving it over and over again.

According to Mr. Kissinger's statement at the news conference in Shanghai, the U.S. section of the Communiqué was composed piecemeal "as we put together the various paragraphs that were supplied to us on our side by various individuals." If so, then I would venture to bet that at least one sentence was written by Mr. Nixon himself; it has the inimitable style of his performances at home and abroad: "No country should claim infallibility and each country should be prepared to re-examine its own attitudes for the common good."

Whose "common good"? The world's? Mankind's? Or America's and China's combined? Good - by what standard? The "good" is a moral, i.e., a _philosophical_, concept. According to a rational morality, the President of a country has no right to pursue any goal except the legitimate interests - the _good_ - of his own country; he has no right to sacrifice his country to a game of international altruism. According to the altruist morality, he must do just that. Those who do not understand the evil of altruism in domestic policy, should ponder this example of it in foreign policy, on a broad, international scale.

And those who regard _humility_ as a virtue, should ask themselves whether it is becoming to the President of a great country when he deals with its enemies. Of all the possible variants, Pragmatist humility is the worst: the silly reference to "infallibility" is embarrassingly awful in that context. This is an epistemological, i.e., a _philosophical_, issue. Infallibility is not a precondition of knowing what one does know, of firmness in one's convictions, and of loyalty to one's values. Since Mr. Nixon's Chinese adversaries have made it amply clear that they do not intend ever "to re-examine their own attitudes," the declaration served notice on them that Mr. Nixon does, that _he_ is prepared to re-examine, to reverse - or to betray - anything.

By contrast, observe the firmness, the decisiveness, the morally confident tone of the Chinese section of the Communiqué - and consider the nature of the strength which a _philosophy_ (i.e., a set of fundamental principles integrating one's view of life) gives men in practical action (even when it is one of the most vicious philosophies on record).

The Chinese section begins by declaring: "Wherever there is oppression, there is resistance. Countries want independence, nations want liberation and the people want revolution - this has become the irresistible trend of history."

This is a miniature manifesto, taking an uncompromising position on a fundamental issue and proclaiming the doom of the United States. The position is false, but it acquires, in this context, the persuasive power of truth, because there is nothing in the U.S. statement to contradict it.

It is generally known that by the word "oppression" the communists mean economic freedom - and by the word "liberation," a totalitarian dictatorship. Did anything in the U.S. section claim otherwise?

The Chinese section continues: "The Chinese side stated that it firmly supports the struggles of all oppressed people and nations for freedom and liberation and that the people of all countries have the right to choose their social systems according to their own wishes..."

The second part of this sentence is not merely left uncontested, but is explicitly supported by the U.S. section. Yet a "wish" is not an ultimate justification of human action, particularly not of political action. No people and no country has the _right_ to choose a system of slavery: there can be no such thing as the right to violate rights. But this principle cannot be upheld by men who, lacking the courage to uphold the rights of the individual, have long since switched the advocacy of _rights_ to the collectivist notion of a tribal "right to self-determination."

(Once this switch is granted _philosophically_, and rights are regarded as belonging to groups, not to individuals, such issues as the absence of free elections and the rulers' contempt for a people's actual wishes become trivial debates over who does or does not represent the people. The communists have an arsenal of arguments to justify the seizure of power by force in pursuit of the people's "right" to unlimited rule - including the claim that only the poor, the sick, and the communists are people.)

As to the first part of the above-quoted sentence, it is an open declaration of war on the United States, an assertion of China's intent to support a "people's revolution" in this country. The Chinese were safe in declaring it: they knew that the U.S. side had no intellectual ammunition against it, no _philosophical_ ground to stand on.

A man (or a nation) who is not loyal to his values, cannot be loyal to his friends; if he does not uphold his own interests, he will not uphold theirs. A selfless man - or an altruistic nation that has been sacrificing itself on an international altar for over fifty years - will not hesitate to sacrifice others.

The Chinese took full advantage of that - as I shall discuss in my next Letter.

(To be continued.)

Ayn Rand

The Ayn Rand Letter, published fortnightly by The Ayn Rand Letter, Inc., 183 Madison Avenue, New York, N.Y. 10016.
Contributing Editor: **Leonard Peikoff**; Subscription Director: **Elayne Kalberman**; Production Manager: **Barbara Weiss.**

Vol. 1, No. 15 April 24, 1972

<u>THE SHANGHAI GESTURE</u>

Part III

Here is the ultimate price of altruism - in the form of a special section of the U.S.-Chinese Communiqué:

China declares: "...the government of the People's Republic of China is the sole legal government of China; Taiwan is a province of China...the liberation of Taiwan is China's internal affair in which no other country has the right to interfere; and all U.S. forces and military installations must be withdrawn from Taiwan...."

The U.S. answers: "The United States acknowledges that all Chinese on either side of the Taiwan Strait maintain there is but one China and that Taiwan is a part of China. The United States Government does not challenge that position. It reaffirms its interest in a peaceful settlement of the Taiwan question by the Chinese themselves. With this prospect in mind, it affirms the ultimate objective of the withdrawal of all U.S. forces and military installations from Taiwan. In the meantime, it will progressively reduce its forces and military installations on Taiwan as the tension in the area diminishes."

What is a "peaceful" settlement between an armed, bloodthirsty, totalitarian State of 800 million people and a tiny sanctuary of 14 million people, including a 2 million minority of refugees from the mainland? What can this minority negotiate? What is there to "settle," except their life or death? Can anyone doubt the kind of unthinkable horror that would be unleashed on Taiwan if it were surrendered to Red China?

The United States has a <u>treaty</u> to protect Taiwan. A treaty is more than "an interest," it is an <u>obligation</u>. But while the Chinese permit themselves to dictate the foreign policy of the U.S. - by declaring what the U.S. forces "<u>must</u>" do (regardless of obligations) - the U.S. side carefully fails to mention the treaty. And more: the U.S. side bends backward to assure the Chinese that its "ultimate objective" is to obey them and withdraw all its forces from Taiwan (an "objective" never announced before). The slender reservation of setting no date for the withdrawal is undercut by the promise that our forces, "in the meantime," will be progressively reduced "as the tension in the area diminishes."

In <u>what</u> area? <u>Whose</u> tension? How is "tension" to be gauged - and by whom? Under what tension does this now place the people on Taiwan? How would you like to live with the threat of a massacre hanging over you by such a contemptibly precarious semantic thread?

When Mr. Kissinger was asked, at the news conference in Shanghai, why the U.S.

government did not "affirm its treaty commitment to Taiwan," he answered that this issue is "an extraordinarily difficult one to discuss on the territory of a country with which we do not maintain formal diplomatic relations..." If this is a matter of etiquette, it did not restrain the Chinese. If it is more, then did an American President make an official statement under foreign censorship? For China, Mr. Kissinger added, the issue of Taiwan "is a matter of profound principle." Isn't it for us?

The United States bears a large part of the responsibility for the victory of communism in China: it was U.S. pressure that forced the Nationalists into the compromise of accepting a "coalition government" that included communists - which was the beginning of the end, as it had been wherever it was tried. The treaty to protect Taiwan was an inadequate atonement for so monstrous an error (assuming it was merely an error). If this were the only reason, we would still be morally obliged to protect the victims. But this is not the only reason.

The Republic of China on Taiwan is a mixed economy, like the rest of the semi-free world, but it is free enough to have become, in the past twenty-two years, one of the world's outstanding examples of economic progress and prosperity. Think of how hard and how courageously those two million Chinese refugees had to work for such an achievement. Of all the various refugee groups that escaped from the mass slaughter conducted by totalitarian regimes in their native lands, only two - the Chinese Nationalists and the Israelis - had a chance not to vanish into the resigned futility of "ethnic" memories, rituals and prayers, and have built a new life for themselves against tremendous odds. Are we - the United States of America, the country that had proudly stood as an asylum for victims of tyranny - are we to betray men of that caliber and deliver them into the hands of their executioners?

If we are, then what sort of obscene mockery is our foreign-aid program? What is the purpose of all the billions poured into the undeveloped countries, under the pious slogan of helping them to help themselves? Here is a country - the Republic of China - that took us at our word and our honor, that struggled and worked and rose to stand on its own feet, as a beacon of civilization on the edge of an enormous continent swallowed by primordial brutality. If we desert Taiwan, then what are we doing in the rest of the world? Or are we helping to fatten victims for the slaughter? Are we urging undeveloped people to develop in order to give the communist hordes a prosperous country to plunder? Are we declaring to the newly independent nations that if they establish a pestilential tribal-socialist community, they will be safe, but not if they achieve any sort of respect for individual rights or any part of capitalism and freedom? If that is our policy, then what are we doing in Vietnam?

We have heard three successive Presidents tell us that our national self-interest is involved in the war in Vietnam. Why? No clear answer was ever given, except the pious platitude that we must protect freedom anywhere in the world. Are we to protect the freedom of South Vietnam, but not of Taiwan?

We have sacrificed thousands of American lives, and billions of dollars, to protect a primitive people who never had freedom, do not seek it, and, apparently, do not want it. Are we about to betray and abandon a cultivated, civilized people who represent the best of China and the last of its once great culture - a people who do know freedom, have paid an enormous price for it, and are willing to die rather than lose it?

We have been told that we are fighting for South Vietnam's "right to self-determination" through "free, democratic elections." Are we to leave the fate of Taiwan to be settled "by the Chinese themselves"? In "free, democratic elections" and on the principle of "one man, one vote"? By a ratio of 800 to 2? We, who are supposed to be defenders of the rights of minorities?

We have been told that the purpose of the war in Vietnam is to prevent a communist conquest of Asia - to "contain communism." Will the preservation of South Vietnam "contain" it, but the preservation of Taiwan will not? Will the fall of jungle villages unleash the communist conquest - but the surrender of a rich, civilized island, with an intelligently anticommunist people, will not?

We all remember those large, earnest close-ups of President Nixon in his earlier television appearances, and the piously, prissily self-righteous tone of his voice telling us that the protection of South Vietnam is a matter of our national honor. But we never had a treaty to protect South Vietnam. We have one to protect Taiwan. What will the abrogation of that treaty do to our national honor?

We cannot let down our friends in Asia - Mr. Nixon kept saying about Vietnam - we cannot betray the faith of the people who trusted us, we cannot undercut their confidence. "We must save face," was, in effect, the meaning of Mr. Nixon's pleas. What will be left of our face - in Asia or anywhere else - if we betray Taiwan?

No, this is not an appeal for another senseless, altruistic war, this time to defend Taiwan. Taiwan can take care of itself, if we do not turn deserter. It is not a policeman's gun, but his <u>firmness</u> that keeps peace in a neighborhood and protects it from gangsters. Our token military presence has kept Taiwan peacefully safe for twenty-two years. Our withdrawal could precipitate a war involving the entire Pacific. (Does anyone remember the consequences of the Allies' withdrawal from the Sudetenland and the Ruhr?) And whatever our view of Nationalist China, we do not have the right to bargain its lives away as pawns in secret negotiations for some undisclosed policy of our own.

What did Mr. Nixon obtain in exchange for a trade he had no right to make? Nothing - judging by the spirit and content of the Communiqué. There was nothing that China could offer us. She is too primitive, too poor, too weak to be much of a market for our products - and she needs our help to build up her hopelessly stagnant economy. It is China that needs us, not vice versa. Yet it is we who made shameful - and potentially disastrous - concessions. As to the only possible interest in common, there is a single paragraph in the joint section of the Communiqué that might be directed against Russia: "Neither should seek hegemony in the Asia-Pacific region and each is opposed to the efforts by any other country or group of countries to establish such hegemony..." This is so vague that it can be interpreted and reinterpreted by anyone at any time in any manner whatever - while the deal in regard to Taiwan is explicit and clear.

Yet it is China that is threatened directly and needs our help against Russia. It is China that dreads encirclement and the prospect of a two-front war. An American statesman could have obtained a great deal in exchange for a pledge of mere neutrality, which is all China could hope for. But there were no American statesmen on the trip to Peking, only pragmatists. Now, in view of the results, China knows that she will encounter no resistance, that she can play us for all we're worth, and switch sides any time she wishes.

In defense of Mr. Nixon's policy, some commentators claim that China, too, made concessions. What concessions? <u>She agreed to talk to us</u>.(!) So much for the practical power of wealth and arms against the "impractical" power of <u>philosophy</u>.

Observe the steadfast loyalty and support that Soviet Russia offers to any budding tumor of communism anywhere on earth. Then observe the shrinking range, the frantic pace, and the international effects created by our pragmatist flux. Without warning, Mr. Nixon announced a "new economic policy," thus delivering a sudden blow to the economy of two allies whose security and confidence he needed most: West Germany and Japan - the two that have achieved the greatest degree of recovery and economic progress. If they - as well as Israel - are now pushed into "exploring" the possibility of "closer ties" with Soviet Russia, is it Russia's power that pushed them?

Without warning, Mr. Nixon announced his intention to visit China. It was followed, the next day, by gushing assurances to the two stunned victims - Japan and Taiwan - that the U.S. would stand by its friends and commitments. After which, Mr. Nixon sells Taiwan down the river - after which, Washington officials assure us that he did not say what he said, that the treaty stands. This sort of thing does not work any longer even in a campaign platform aimed at the least perceptive voters. Credibility gap? *This* is a credibility abyss - among nations armed with nuclear weapons.

Such policies used to be called "unprincipled" and "opportunism." They are now hailed, by liberal commentators, as "flexibility" and "Pragmatism." The worst deception spread by Pragmatism is the notion that it is practical.

An editorial in *The New York Times* (February 28, 1972) tried, characteristically, to defend the Communiqué by saying: "The official outlines of the two nations' ideological positions are remarkable for their moderation. They seemed designed largely to reassure each of the negotiators' own people that fundamental principles have not been bartered away." This may be true of the Chinese side: China's communist minority would have reason to feel reassured by and proud of their leaders' uncompromising firmness. But the U.S. side? Where did anyone find any fundamental principles in the U.S. section of the Communiqué? What are America's fundamental principles? Peace at any price? Double-crossing of allies? Appeasement of enemies? Tribal "self-determination"? Pragmatist chicanery and universal self-sacrifice, combined? Is there anyone who felt reassured or inspired by the American part of that Communiqué?

And what is America's self-image? It used to be a stern Uncle Sam; or a fearless, confident, straight-shooting cowboy; or a somberly dignified Indian; or a self-made, self-reliant, enterprising businessman. Has it now become an international social worker, cooing baby talk and wagging her finger at armed gangs, urging them to remember that they are not infallible?

But - like charity - courage, consistency, integrity have to begin at home. Foreign policy is merely a consequence of domestic policy. The cynicism of the Communiqué is shocking, but it is only a reflection of the moral-intellectual shambles made of this country. It shows us what we are now doing to others, but we began by doing it to ourselves. We are the victims of self-inflicted bacteriological warfare: altruism is the bacteria of amorality, Pragmatism is the bacteria of impotence.

"When men reduce their virtues to the approximate, then evil acquires the force of an absolute, when loyalty to an unyielding purpose is dropped by the virtuous, it's picked up by scoundrels - and you get the indecent spectacle of a cringing, bargaining, traitorous good and a self-righteously uncompromising evil." (*Atlas Shrugged*.)

Ayn Rand

The Ayn Rand Letter, published fortnightly by The Ayn Rand Letter, Inc., 183 Madison Avenue, New York, N.Y. 10016.

Contributing Editor: **Leonard Peikoff**; Subscription Director: **Elayne Kalberman**; Production Manager: **Barbara Weiss.**

Vol. 1, No. 16 May 8, 1972

THE ESTABLISHING OF AN ESTABLISHMENT

Staleness is the dominant characteristic of today's culture - and, at first glance, it may appear to be a puzzling phenomenon.

There is an air of impoverished drabness, of tired routine, of stagnant monotony in all our cultural activities - from stage and screen, to literature and the arts, to the allegedly intellectual publications and discussions. There is nothing to see or to hear. Everything produces the effect of déjà vu or déjà entendu. How long since you have read anything startling, different, fresh, unexpected?

Intellectually, people are wearing paste jewelry copied from paste jewelry by artisans who have never seen the original gems. Originality is a forgotten experience. The latest fads are withering at birth. The substitutes for daring and vitality - such as the screeching hippies - are mere camouflage, like too much make-up on the lined face of an aging slut.

The symptoms of today's cultural disease are: conformity, with nothing to conform to - timidity, expressed in a self-shrinking concern with trivia - a kind of obsequious anxiety to please the unknown standards of some nonexistent authority - and a pall of fear without object. Psychologically, this is the cultural atmosphere of a society living under censorship.

But there is no censorship in the United States.

I have said that the fundamental cause of a culture's disintegration is the collapse of philosophy, which leaves men without intellectual guidance. But this is the _fundamental_ cause; its consequences are not always direct or obvious, and its working may raise many questions. By what intermediary processes does this cause affect men's lives? Does it work only by psychological means, from within, or is it assisted, from without, by practical, existential measures? When philosophy collapses, why are there no thinkers to step into the vacuum and rebuild a system of thought on a new foundation? Since there was no philosophical unanimity, why did the collapse of falsehoods paralyze the men who had never believed them? Why do the falsehoods linger on, unchallenged - like a cloud of dust over the rubble? Philosophy affects education, and a false philosophy can cripple men's minds in childhood; but it cannot cripple them all, nor does it cripple most men irreparably - so what becomes of those who manage to survive? Why are they not heard from? What - except physical force - can silence active minds?

The answer to this last question is: nothing. Only the use of physical force can protect falsehoods from challenge and perpetuate them. Only the intrusion of force into the realm of the intellect - i.e., only the action of a government - can silence an entire nation. But then how does the cultural wreckage maintain its power over the United States? There is no governmental repression or suppression of ideas in this country.

As a mixed economy, we are chained by an enormous tangle of government controls; but, it is argued, they affect our incomes, not our minds. Such a distinction is not tenable; a chained aspect of a man's - or a nation's - activity will gradually and necessarily affect the rest. But it is true that the government, so far, has made no overt move to repress or control the intellectual life of this country. Anyone is still free to say, write and publish anything he pleases. Yet men keep silent - while their culture is perishing from an entrenched, institutionalized epidemic of mediocrity. It is not possible that mankind's intellectual stature has shrunk to this extent. And it is not possible that all talent has vanished suddenly from this country and this earth.

If you find it puzzling, the premise to check is the idea that governmental repression is the only way a government can destroy the intellectual life of a country. It is not. There is another way: *governmental encouragement*.

Governmental encouragement does not order men to believe that the false is true: it merely makes them indifferent to the issue of truth or falsehood.

Bearing this preface in mind, let us consider an example of the methods, processes and results of that policy.

In December 1971, Representative Cornelius E. Gallagher (D.-N.J.) declared in the House that "the National Institute of Mental Health has granted to Dr. B.F. Skinner the sum of $283,000 for the purpose of writing 'Beyond Freedom and Dignity.'" On further inquiry, he discovered that "this merely represents the tip of the iceberg." (*Congressional Record*, December 15, 1971, H12623.)

Human Events (January 15, 1972) summarized his findings as follows: "When Gallagher sought information about the Skinner grant and the scope and amount of government spending in the behavioral research field, the General Accounting Office reported back that the task was virtually impossible. Agency officials stated that there were tens of thousands of behavioral research projects being financed by government agencies. A preliminary check turned up 70,000 grants and contracts at the Department of Health, Education and Welfare and 10,000 within the Manpower Administration of the Labor Department. Thousands of additional behavioral projects, costing millions of dollars, also are being financed by the Defense Department, National Aeronautics and Space Administration, and the Atomic Energy Commission, according to the General Accounting Office's survey."

In his speech to the House, Representative Gallagher declared: "The Congress has authorized and appropriated every single dollar in these grants and contracts yet, for the most part, we are unaware of how they are being spent." And further: "...the Federal grant and contract system has inextricably intertwined colleges and universities with moneys authorized and appropriated by the Congress. I mean to imply no suggestion of a lessening of academic freedom in the Nation, but I do suggest that the Congress should at the very least be fully informed and, if need be, have the tools and expertise at our own disposal to counter antidemocratic thoughts launched with Federal funds." (*Cong. Rec.*, H12624.)

Mr. Gallagher stated that he believes in Dr. Skinner's right to advocate his ideas. "But what I question is whether he should be subsidized by the Federal Government [-] especially since, in my judgment, he is advancing ideas which threaten the future of our system of government by denigrating the American traditions of individualism, human dignity, and self-reliance." (Ibid., H12623.)

If Mr. Gallagher were a consistent supporter of the American traditions he describes in the second half of his sentence, he would have stopped after its first half. But, apparently, he was not aware of the contradiction, because his solution was a proposal to create "a Select Committee on Privacy, Human Values, and Democratic Institutions....designed to deal specifically with the type of threats to our Constitution, our Congress, and our constituents which are contained in the thoughts of B.F. Skinner." (Ibid., H12624.)

Nothing could be as dangerous a threat to our institutions as a proposal to establish a government committee to deal with "antidemocratic thoughts" or B.F. Skinner's thoughts or anyone's thoughts. The liberal New Republic was quick to sense the danger and to protest (January 28, 1972). But, not questioning the propriety of government grants, it merely expounded the other side of the same contradiction: it objected to the notion of the government determining which ideas are right or acceptable and thus establishing a kind of intellectual orthodoxy.

Yet both contentions are true: it is viciously improper for the government to subsidize the enemies of our political system; it is also viciously improper for the government to assume the role of an ideological arbiter. But neither Representative Gallagher nor The New Republic chose to see the answer: that those evils are inherent in the vicious impropriety of the government subsidizing ideas. Both chose to ignore the fact that any intrusion of government into the field of ideas, for or against anyone, withers intellectual freedom and creates an official orthodoxy, a privileged elite. Today, it is called an "Establishment."

Ironically enough, it is The New Republic that offered an indication of the mechanics by which an Establishment gets established - apparently, without realizing the social implications of its own argument. Objecting to Gallagher's contention that a deliberate policy may be favoring the behaviorist school of psychology, The New Republic stated: "The Gallagher account did not note that the Skinner grant was one of 20 Senior Research Career Awards, that is, plums for scientific leaders in 'mental health' across the board rather than a unique grant. No new awards of this kind have been made by NIMH since 1964, but 18 of them, which were originally for five years, have been renewed. Skinner's was renewed in 1969, so his $283,000 amounts to $28,300 a year ending in 1974....Skinner has continued to teach roughly one seminar a year at Harvard since 1964...In other words his Harvard salary will be paid by the feds until [1974], a bonanza perhaps more rewarding to Harvard than to him, since he could command at least as large a salary...in a number of other places."

Consider the desperate financial plight of private universities, then ask yourself what a "bonanza" of this kind will do to them. It is generally known that most universities now depend on government research projects as one of their major sources of income. The government grants to those "Senior" researchers establish every recipient as an unofficially official power. It is his influence - his ideas, his theories, his preferences in faculty hiring - that will come to dominate the school, in a silent, unadmitted way. What debt-ridden college administrator would dare antagonize the carrier of the bonanza?

Now observe that these grants were given to senior researchers, that they were "plums" - as The New Republic calls them coyly and cynically - for "scientific leaders." How would Washington bureaucrats - or Congressmen, for that matter - know which scientist to encourage, particularly in so controversial a field as social science? The safest method is to choose men who have achieved some sort of reputation. Whether their reputation is deserved or not, whether their achievements are valid or not, whether they rose by merit, pull, publicity or accident, are questions which the awarders do not and cannot consider. When personal judgment is inoperative (or forbidden), men's first concern is not how to choose, but how to justify their choice. This will necessarily prompt committee members, bureaucrats and politicians to gravitate toward "prestigious names." The result is to help establish those already established - i.e., to entrench the status quo.

The worst part of it is the fact that this method of selection is not confined to the cowardly or the corrupt, that the *honest* official is obliged to use it. The method is forced on him by the terms of the situation. To pass an informed, independent judgment on the value of every applicant or project in every field of science, an official would have to be a universal scholar. If he consults "experts" in the field, the dilemma remains: either he has to be a scholar who knows which experts to consult - or he has to surrender his judgment to men trained by the very professors he is supposed to judge. The awarding of grants to famous "leaders," therefore, appears to him as the only fair policy - on the premise that "somebody made them famous, somebody knows, even if I don't."

(If the officials attempted to by-pass the "leaders" and give grants to promising beginners, the injustice and irrationality of the situation would be so much worse that most of them have the good sense not to attempt it. If universal scholarship is required to judge the value of the actual in every field, nothing short of omniscience would be required to judge the value of the potential - as various privately sponsored contests to discover future talent, even in limited fields, have amply demonstrated.)

Furthermore, the terms of the situation actually forbid an honest official to use his own judgment. He is supposed to be "impartial" and "fair" - while considering awards in the social sciences. An official who does not have some knowledge and some convictions in *this* field, has no moral right to be a public official. Yet the kind of "fairness" demanded of him means that he must suspend, ignore or evade his own convictions (these would be challenged as "prejudices" or "censorship") and proceed to dispose of large sums of public money, with incalculable consequences for the future of the country - without judging the nature of the recipients' ideas, i.e., without using any judgment whatever.

The awarders may hide behind the notion that, in choosing recognized "leaders," they are acting "democratically" and rewarding men chosen by the public. But there is no "democracy" in this field. Science and the mind do not work by vote or by consensus. The best-known is not necessarily the best (nor is the least-known, for that matter). Since no rational standards are applicable, the awarders' method leads to concern with personalities, not ideas; pull, not merit; "prestige," not truth. The result is: rule by press agents.

(To be continued.)

Ayn Rand

The Ayn Rand Letter, published fortnightly by The Ayn Rand Letter, Inc., 201 East 34th Street, New York, N.Y. 10016.
Contributing Editor: **Leonard Peikoff**; Subscription Director: **Elayne Kalberman**; Production Manager: **Barbara Weiss.**

Vol. 1, No. 17 May 22, 1972

THE ESTABLISHING OF AN ESTABLISHMENT

Part II

The profiteers of government grants are usually among the loudest protesters against "the tyranny of money": science and the culture, they cry, must be liberated from the arbitrary private power of the rich. But there is this difference: the rich can neither buy an entire nation nor force one single individual. If a rich man chooses to support cultural activities, he can do so only on a very limited scale, and he bears the consequences of his actions. If he does not use his judgment, but merely indulges his irrational whims, he achieves the opposite of his intention: his projects and his protégés are ignored or despised in their professions, and no amount of money will buy him any influence over the culture. Like vanity publishing, his venture remains a private waste without any wider significance. The culture is protected from him by three invincible elements: choice, variety, competition. If he loses his money in foolish ventures, he hurts no one but himself. And, above all: the money he spends is his own; it is not extorted by force from unwilling victims.

The fundamental evil of government grants is the fact that men are forced to pay for the support of ideas diametrically opposed to their own. This is a profound violation of an individual's integrity and conscience. It is viciously wrong to take the money of rational men for the support of B.F. Skinner - or vice versa. The Constitution forbids a governmental establishment of religion, properly regarding it as a violation of individual rights. Since a man's beliefs are protected from the intrusion of force, the same principle should protect his reasoned convictions and forbid governmental establishments in the field of thought.

Socially, the most destructive consequences of tyranny are spread by an indeterminate, unofficial class of rulers: the officials' favorites. In the histories of absolute monarchies, it was the king's favorites who perpetrated the worst iniquities. Even an absolute monarch was restrained, to some minimal extent, by the necessity to pretend to maintain some semblance of justice, in order to protect his image from the people's indignation. But the recipients of his arbitrary, capricious favor held all the privileges of power without any of the restraints. It was among the scrambling, conniving, bootlicking, backstabbing climbers of a royal court that the worst exponents of power for power's sake were to be found. This holds true in any political system that leaves an opportunity open to them: in an absolute monarchy, in a totalitarian dictatorship, in a mixed economy.

Today, what we see in this country's intellectual field is one of the worst manifestations of political power: rule by favorites, by the unofficially privileged - by private groups with governmental power, but without governmental responsibility. They are shifting, switching groups, often feuding among themselves, but united against outsiders; they are scrambling to catch momentary favors, their precise status unknown to their members, their rivals, or their particular patrons among the hundreds of Congressmen and the thousands of bureaucrats - who are now bewildered and intimidated by these Frankensteinian creations. As in any other game devoid of objective rules, success and power in this one depend on barkers (press agents) and bluff.

Private cliques have always existed in the intellectual field, particularly in the arts, but they used to serve as checks and balances on one another, so that a nonconformist could enter the field and rise without the help of a clique. Today, the cliques are consolidated into an Establishment.

The term "Establishment" was not generally used or heard in this country until about a decade ago. The term originated in Great Britain, where it was applied to the upper-class families which traditionally preempted certain fields of activity. The British aristocracy is a politically created caste - an institution abolished and forbidden by the political system of the United States. The origin of an aristocracy is the king's power to confer on a chosen individual the privilege of receiving an unearned income from the involuntary servitude of the inhabitants of a given district.

Now, the same policy is operating in the United States - only the privileges are granted not in perpetuity, but in a lump sum for a limited time, and the involuntary servitude is imposed not on a group of serfs in a specific territory, but on all the citizens of the country. This does not change the nature of the policy or its consequences.

Observe the character of our intellectual Establishment. It is about a hundred years behind the times. It holds as dogma the basic premises fashionable at the turn of the century: the mysticism of Kant, the collectivism of Marx, the altruism of street-corner evangelists. Two world wars, three monstrous dictatorships - in Soviet Russia, Nazi Germany, Red China - plus every lesser variant of devastating socialist experimentation in a global spread of brutality and despair, have not prompted modern intellectuals to question or revise their dogma. They still think that it is daring, idealistic and unconventional to denounce the rich. They still believe that money is the root of all evil - except government money, which is the solution to all problems. The intellectual Establishment is frozen on the level of those elderly "leaders" who were prominent when the system of governmental "encouragement" took hold. By controlling the schools, the "leaders" perpetuated their dogma and gradually silenced the opposition.

Dissent still exists among the intellectuals, but it is a nit-picking dissent over trivia, which never challenges fundamental premises. This sort of dissent is permitted even in the Catholic Church, so long as it does not challenge the dogma - or in the "self-criticism" sessions of Soviet institutions, so long as it does not challenge the tenets of communism. A disagreement that does not challenge fundamentals serves only to reinforce them. It is particularly in this respect that the collapse of philosophy and the growth of government power work together to entrench the Establishment.

Rule by unofficially privileged private groups spreads a special kind of fear, like a slow poison injected into the culture. It is not fear of a specific ruler, but of the unknown power of anonymous cliques, which grows into a chronic fear of unknowable enemies. Most people do not hold any firm convictions on fundamental issues; today, people are more confused and uncertain than ever - yet the system demands of them a heroic kind of integrity, which they do not possess: they are destroyed by means of fundamental issues which they are unable to recognize in seemingly inconsequential concretes. Many men are capable of dying on the barricades for a big issue, but few - very few - are able to resist the gray suction of small, unheralded, day-by-day surrenders. Few want to start trouble, make enemies, risk their position and, perhaps, their livelihood over such issues as a colleague's objectionable abstract notions (which should be opposed, but are not), or the vaguely improper demands of a faculty clique (which should be resisted, but are not), or the independent attitude of a talented instructor (who should be hired, but is not). If a man senses that he ought to speak up, he is stopped by the routine "Who am I to know?" of modern skepticism - to which another, paralyzing clause is added in his mind: "Whom would I displease?"

Most men are quick to sense whether truth does or does not matter to their superiors. The atmosphere of cautious respect for the recipients of undeserved grants awarded by a mysterious governmental power, rapidly spreads the conviction that truth does not matter because merit does not matter, that something takes precedence over both. (And the issue of grants is only one of the countless ways in which the same arbitrary power intrudes into men's lives.) From the cynical notion: "Who cares about justice?" a man descends to: "Who cares about truth?" and then to: "Who cares?" Thus most men succumb to an intangible corruption, and sell their souls on the installment plan - by making small compromises, by cutting small corners - until nothing is left of their minds except the fear.

In business, the rise of the welfare state froze the status quo, perpetuating the power of the big corporations of the pre-income-tax era, placing them beyond the competition of the tax-strangled newcomers. A similar process took place in the welfare state of the intellect. The results, in both fields, are the same.

If you talk to a typical business executive or college dean or magazine editor, you can observe his special, modern quality: a kind of flowing or skipping evasiveness that drips or bounces automatically off any fundamental issue, a gently noncommittal blandness, an ingrained cautiousness toward everything, as if an inner tape recorder were whispering: "Play it safe, don't antagonize - whom? - anybody."

Whom would these men fear most, psychologically - and least, existentially? The brilliant loner - the beginner, the young man of potential genius and innocently ruthless integrity, whose only weapons are talent and truth. They reject him "instinctively," saying that "he doesn't belong" (to what?), sensing that he would put them on the spot by raising issues they prefer not to face. He might get past their protective barriers, once in a while, but he is handicapped by his virtues - in a system rigged against intelligence and integrity.

We shall never know how many precociously perceptive youths sensed the evil around them, before they were old enough to find an antidote - and gave up, in helplessly indignant bewilderment; or how many gave in, stultifying their minds.

We do not know how many young innovators may exist today and struggle to be heard - but we will not hear of them because the Establishment would prefer not to recognize their existence and not to take any cognizance of their ideas.

So long as a society does not take the ultimate step into the abyss by establishing censorship, some men of ability will always succeed in breaking through. But the price - in effort, struggle and endurance - is such that only exceptional men can afford it. Today, originality, integrity, independence have become a road to martyrdom, which only the most dedicated will choose, knowing that the alternative is much worse. A society that sets up these conditions as the price of achievement, is in deep trouble.

The following is for the consideration of those "humanitarian" Congressmen (and their constituents) who think that a few public "plums" tossed to some old professors won't hurt anyone: it is the moral character of decent average men that has no chance under the rule of entrenched mediocrity. The genius can and will fight to the last. The average man cannot and does not.

In *Atlas Shrugged*, I discussed the "pyramid of ability" in the realm of economics. There is another kind of social pyramid. The genius who fights "every form of tyranny over the mind of man" is fighting a battle for which lesser men do not have the strength, but on which their freedom, their dignity, and their integrity depend. It is the pyramid of moral endurance.

Ayn Rand

OBJECTIVIST CALENDAR

Starting on May 25, the tape lectures of Leonard Peikoff's course, *Modern Philosophy: Kant to the Present*, will be given in Nuernberg, West Germany. For further information, contact Gerald Salchert, Elsa - Brandstroemstr. 6, Nuernberg, West Germany; phone: 0911-61 31 89 (evenings).

We have been asked to announce that on Friday, June 23, Dr. George Reisman will give a lecture in New York City. Time: 7:30 P.M. Place: Biltmore Hotel (Bowman Room), Madison Ave. and 43rd St. Subject: "Capitalism: The Cure for Racism." Advance reservations are available. For further information, contact Dr. Reisman at (212) 684-0006 (9 A.M.-3 P.M.) or (212) 628-2017 (8-10 P.M.).

B.W.

The Ayn Rand Letter, published fortnightly by The Ayn Rand Letter, Inc., 183 Madison Avenue, New York, N.Y. 10016.

Contributing Editor: **Leonard Peikoff**; Subscription Director: **Elayne Kalberman**; Production Manager: **Barbara Weiss.**

Vol. 1, No. 18 June 5, 1972

"FAIRNESS DOCTRINE" FOR EDUCATION

The "Fairness Doctrine" is a messy little makeshift of the mixed economy, and a poor substitute for freedom of speech. It has, however, served as a minimal retarder of the collectivist trend: it has prevented the Establishment's total takeover of the airwaves. For this reason - as a temporary measure in a grave national emergency - the fairness doctrine should now be invoked in behalf of education.

The doctrine is a typical product of the socialist sentimentality that dreams of combining government ownership with intellectual freedom. As applied to television and radio broadcasting, the fairness doctrine demands that equal opportunity be given to all sides of a controversial issue - on the grounds of the notion that "the people owns the airwaves" and, therefore, all factions of "the people" should have equal access to their communal property.

The trouble with the fairness doctrine is that it cannot be applied fairly. Like any ideological product of the mixed economy, it is a vague, indefinable approximation and, therefore, an instrument of pressure-group warfare. Who determines which issues are controversial? Who chooses the representatives of the different sides in a given controversy? If there are too many conflicting viewpoints, which are to be given a voice and which are to be kept silent? Who *is* "the people" and who *is not*?

It is clear that the individual's views are barred altogether and that the "fairness" is extended only to groups. The formula employed by the television stations in New York declares that they recognize their obligation to provide equal time to "*significant* opposing viewpoints." Who determines which viewpoint is "significant"? Is the standard qualitative or quantitative? It is obviously this last, as one may observe in practice: whenever an answer is given to a TV editorial, it is given by a representative of some group involved in the debated subject.

The fairness doctrine (as well as the myth of public ownership) is based on the favorite illusion of the mushy socialists, i.e., those who want to combine force and freedom, as distinguished from the bloody socialists, i.e., the communists and fascists. That illusion is the belief that the people ("the masses") would be essentially unanimous, that dissenting groups would be rare and easily accommodated, that a monolithic majority-will would prevail, and that any injustice done would be done only to recalcitrant individuals, who, in socialist theory, do not count anyway. (For a discussion of why the airwaves should be private property, see "The Property Status of Airwaves" in my book *Capitalism: The Unknown Ideal*.)

In practice, the fairness doctrine has led to the precarious rule of a "centrist" attitude: of timidity, compromise and fear (with the "center" slithering slowly, inexorably to the left) - i.e., control by the Establishment, limited only by the remnants of a tradition of freedom: by lip service to "impartiality," by fear of being caught at too obvious an "unfairness," and by the practice of "window dressing," which consists in some occasional moments of air time tossed to some representatives of extreme and actually significant opposing viewpoints. Such a policy, by its very nature, is temporary. Nevertheless, this "window dressing" is the last chance that the advocates of freedom have, as far as the airwaves are concerned.

There is no equivalent of the fairness doctrine in the field which is much more important to a nation's future than its airwaves - the field which determines a country's intellectual trends, i.e., the dominant ideas in people's minds, in the culture, in the Establishment, in the press and, ultimately, on the air: the field of higher education.

So long as higher education was provided predominantly by private colleges and universities, no problem of unfairness existed. A private school has the right to teach any ideas of its owners' choice, and to exclude all opposing ideas; but it has no power to force such exclusion on the rest of the country. The opponents have the right to establish schools of their own and to teach their ideas or a wider spectrum of viewpoints, if they so choose. The competition of the free marketplace of ideas does the rest, determining every school's success or failure - which, historically, was the course of the development of the great private universities. But the growth of government power, of state universities, and of taxation brought the private universities under a growing control by and dependence on the government. (See my Letters of March 13, May 8 and May 22.) The current bill providing Federal "aid" to higher education will make the control and dependence all but total, thus establishing a governmental monopoly on education.

The most ominously crucial question now hanging over this country's future is: _what_ will our universities teach at our expense and without our consent? What ideas will be propagated or excluded? (This question applies to all public and semi-public institutions of learning. By "semi-public" I mean those formerly private institutions which are to be supported in part by public funds and controlled in full by the government.)

The government has no right to set itself up as the arbiter of ideas and, therefore, its establishments - the public and semi-public schools - have no right to teach a single viewpoint, excluding all others. They have no right to serve the beliefs of any one group of citizens, leaving others ignored and silenced. They have no right to impose inequality on the citizens who bear equally the burden of supporting them.

As in the case of governmental grants to science, it is viciously wrong to force an individual to pay for the teaching of ideas diametrically opposed to his own; it is a profound violation of his rights. The violation becomes monstrous if _his_ ideas are excluded from such public teaching: this means that he is forced to pay for the propagation of that which he regards as false and evil, and for the suppression of that which he regards as true and good. If there is a viler form of injustice, I challenge any resident of Washington, D.C., to name it.

Yet _this_ is the form of injustice committed by the present policy of an overwhelming majority of our public and semi-public universities.

There is a widespread impression that television and the press are biased and slanted to the left. But they are models of impartiality and fairness compared to the ferocious intolerance, the bias, the prejudices, the distortions, the savage obscurantism now running riot in most of our institutions of higher learning - in regard to matters deeper than mere politics. With rare exceptions, each of the various departments and disciplines is ruled by its own particular clique that gets in and virtually excludes the teaching of any theory or viewpoint other than its own. If a private school permits this, it has the right to do so; a public or semi-public school has not.

Controversy is the hallmark of our age; there is no subject, particularly in the humanities, which is not regarded in fundamentally different ways by many different schools of thought. (This is not to say that all of them are valid, but merely to observe that they exist.) Yet most university departments, particularly in the leading universities, offer a single viewpoint (camouflaged by minor variations) and maintain their monopoly by the simple means of evasion: by ignoring anything that does not fit their viewpoint, by pretending that no others exist, and by reducing dissent to trivia, thus leaving fundamentals unchallenged.

Most of today's philosophy departments are dominated by Linguistic Analysis (the unsuccessful product of crossbreeding between philosophy and grammar, a union whose offspring is less viable than a mule), with some remnants of its immediate progenitors, Pragmatism and Logical Positivism, still clinging to its bandwagon. The more "broad-minded" departments include an opposition - the other side of the same Kantian coin, Existentialism. (One side claims that philosophy is grammar, the other that philosophy is feelings.)

Psychology departments have a sprinkling of Freudians, but are dominated by Behaviorism, whose leader is B.F. Skinner. (Here the controversy is between the claim that man is moved by innate ideas, and the claim that he has no ideas at all.)

Economics departments are dominated by Marxism, which is taken straight or on the rocks, in the form of Keynesianism.

What the political science departments and the business administration schools are dominated by is best illustrated by the following example: in a distinguished, Ivy League university, a dean of the School of Business recently suggested that it be renamed "School of Management," explaining that profit-making is unpopular with students and that most of them want to work for non-profit institutions, such as government or charities.

Sociology departments are dominated by the fact that no one has ever defined what sociology is.

English departments are dominated by *The New York Times Book Review*.

I do not know the state of the various departments in the physical sciences, but we have seen an indication of it: the "scientific" writings of the ecologists.

As a result of today's educational policies, the majority of college graduates are virtually illiterate, in the literal and the wider sense of the word. They do not necessarily accept their teachers' views, but they do not know that any other views exist or have ever existed. There are philosophy majors who graduate without having taken a single course on Aristotle (except as part of general surveys). There are economics majors who have no idea of what capitalism is or was, theoretically or historically, and not the faintest notion of the mechanism of a free market. There are literature majors who have never heard of Victor Hugo (but have acquired a full vocabulary of four-letter words).

So long as there were variations among university departments in the choice of their dominant prejudices - and so long as there were some distinguished survivors of an earlier, freer view of education - non-conformists had some chance. But with the spread of "unpolarized" unity and Federal "encouragement" - the spread of the same gray, heavy-footed, deaf-dumb-and-blind, hysterically stagnant dogma - that chance is vanishing. It is becoming increasingly harder for an independent mind to get or keep a job on a university faculty - or for the independent mind of a student to remain independent.

This is the logical result of generations of post-Kantian statist philosophy and of the vicious circle which it set up: as philosophy degenerates into irrationalism, it promotes the growth of government power, which, in turn, promotes the degeneration of philosophy.

It is a paradox of our age of skepticism - with its proliferation of bromides to the effect that "Man can be certain of nothing," "Reality is unknowable," "There are no hard facts or hard knowledge - everything is soft [except the point of a gun]" - that the overbearing dogmatism of university departments would make a medieval enforcer of religious dogma squirm with envy. It is a paradox but not a contradiction, because it is the necessary consequence - and purpose - of skepticism, which disarms its opponents by declaring: "How can you be sure?" and thus enables its leaders to propound absolutes at whim.

It is this kind of intellectual atmosphere and these types of cynical, bigoted, envy-ridden, decadent cliques that the Federal Government now proposes to support with public funds, and with the piously reiterated assurance that the profiteering institutions will retain their full freedom to teach whatever they please, that there will be "no strings attached."

Well, there is one string which all the opponents of the intellectual status quo now have the right to expect and demand: the fairness doctrine.

(To be continued.)

Ayn Rand

OBJECTIVIST CALENDAR

I am very happy to announce that the motion picture rights to Atlas Shrugged have been bought by Albert S. Ruddy. Mr. Ruddy is Hollywood's top producer, who - in the face of enormous opposition - made the sensationally successful film The Godfather.

For almost fifteen years, I had refused to sell Atlas Shrugged except on condition that I would have the right of approval of the film script, a right which Hollywood does not grant to authors. Mr. Ruddy had the courage (and the respect for Atlas Shrugged) to break the precedent and agree to my condition. Work on the film will begin at once. If all those concerned do their best - as we intend to - the cultural consequences will be incalculable.

Thank you for the fact that you will want, I know, to celebrate this event - the biggest news this Calendar can offer you.

Ayn Rand

The Ayn Rand Letter, published fortnightly by The Ayn Rand Letter, Inc., 201 East 34th Street, New York, N.Y. 10016.

Contributing Editor: **Leonard Peikoff**; Subscription Director: **Elayne Kalberman**; Production Manager: **Barbara Weiss.**

Vol. 1, No. 19 June 19, 1972

"FAIRNESS DOCTRINE" FOR EDUCATION

Part II

If the public allegedly owns universities, as it allegedly owns the airwaves, then for all the same reasons _no specific ideology can be permitted to hold a monopoly in any department of any public or semi-public university_. In all such institutions, every "significant viewpoint" must be given representation. (By "ideology," in this context, I mean a system of ideas derived from a theoretical base or frame of reference.)

The same considerations that led to the fairness doctrine in broadcasting, apply to educational institutions, only more crucially, more urgently, more desperately so, because much more is involved than some ephemeral electronic sounds or images, because the mind of the young and the future of human knowledge are at stake.

Would this doctrine work in regard to universities? It would work as well - and as badly - as it has worked in broadcasting. It would work not as a motor of freedom, but as a brake on total regimentation. It would not achieve actual fairness, impartiality or objectivity. But it would act as a temporary impediment to intellectual monopolies, a retarder of the Establishment's takeover, a breach in the mental lethargy of the status quo, and, occasionally, an opening for a brilliant dissenter who would know how to make it count.

Remember that _dissenters_, in today's academic world, are not the advocates of mysticism-altruism-collectivism, who are the dominant cliques, the representatives of the entrenched status quo. The dissenters are the advocates of reason-individualism-capitalism. (If there are universities somewhere that bar the teaching of overtly vicious theories, such as communism, the advocates of these theories would be entitled to the protection of the fairness doctrine, so long as the university received government funds - because there are taxpaying citizens who are communists. The protection would apply to the right to teach ideas - _not_ to criminal actions, such as campus riots or any form of physical violence.)

Since the fairness doctrine cannot be defined objectively, its application to specific cases would depend in large part on subjective interpretations, which would often be arbitrary and, at best, approximate. But there is no such approximation in the universities of Soviet Russia, as there was not in the universities of Nazi Germany. The purpose of the approximation is to preserve, to keep alive in men's minds, the principle of intellectual freedom - until the time when it can be implemented fully once more, in free, i.e., private, universities.

The main function of the fairness doctrine would be a switch of the burden of fear, from the victim to the entrenched gang - and a switch of moral right, from the entrenched gang to the victim. A dissenter would not have to be in the position of a martyr facing the power of a vast Establishment with all the interlockings of unknowable cliques, with the mysterious lines of secret pull leading to omnipotent governmental authorities. He would have the protection of a recognized *right*. On the other hand, the Establishment's hatchet men would have to be cautious, knowing that there is a limitation (at least, in principle) on the irresponsible power granted by the use of public funds "with no strings attached."

But the fight for the fairness doctrine would require intellectual clarity, objectivity, and good, i.e., contextual, judgment - because the elements to consider are extremely complex. For instance, the concept of "equal time" would not be entirely relevant: an hour in the class of an able professor can undo the harm done by a semester in the classes of the incompetent ones. And it would be impossible to burden the students with courses on every viewpoint in every subject.

There is no precise way to determine which professors' viewpoints are the appropriate opposites of which - particularly in the midst of today's prevalent eclecticism. The policy of lip service to impartiality and of window dressing is practiced in many schools; and the eclecticism in some of the smaller colleges is such that no specific viewpoint can be discerned at all. It is the cases of extremes, of ideological unity on the faculty and monopolistic monotony in teaching - particularly in the leading universities (which set the trends for all the rest) - that require protest by an informed public opinion, by the dissenting faculty members, and by the main victims: the students.

Intellectual diversity and ideological opposites can be determined only in terms of essentials - but it is an essential of modern philosophy to deny the existence or validity of essentials (which are called "oversimplification"). The result is that some advocates of a guaranteed minimum income are regarded as defenders of capitalism, advocates of theories of innate ideas are regarded as champions of reason, the tribal conformity of hippies is regarded as an expression of individualism, etc. And most college students have lost or never developed the ability to think in terms of essentials.

But - as in the case of political election campaigns, in which essentials are evaded more stringently than in modern universities - everyone knows implicitly which side he is for or against, though no public voices care to identify the issues explicitly. The consistency of such politicians' or professors' followers is remarkable for men who claim man's inability to distinguish essentials. (Which is one clue to the motives of the advocates of the "non-simplified," i.e., concrete-bound, approach.)

The ability explicitly to identify the essentials of any subject he studies, is the first requirement of a student who would want to fight for the fairness doctrine. Then, if he sees that he is offered only one viewpoint on a given *fundamental* issue - and knows that other "significant" viewpoints exist - he can protest, on the grounds of his right to know and to make an informed choice.

"Significance," in this context, should be gauged by one of two standards:

the degree of historical influence achieved by a given theory or, if the theory is contemporary, its value in providing original answers to fundamental questions. As in the case of broadcasting, it would be impossible to present every individual's viewpoint. But if the great historical schools of thought were presented, the fairness doctrine would achieve its purpose (or perform its "trustbusting" function, if you will): the breakup of that one-sided indoctrination which is the hallmark of government-controlled schools.

In all fields that the government enters (outside of its proper sphere), two motives - one vicious, the other virtuous - produce the same results. In the case of schools, the vicious motive is power-lust, which prompts a teacher or an educational bureaucrat to indoctrinate students with a single viewpoint (of the kind that disarms them mentally, stunts their critical faculty, and conditions them to the passive acceptance of memorized dogma). The virtuous motive is a teacher's integrity: a man of integrity has firm convictions about what he regards as true; he teaches according to his convictions, and he does not propagate or support the theories which he regards as false (though he is able to present them objectively, when necessary). Such a teacher would be invaluable in a private university; but in a government-controlled school, his monopolistic position makes him as tyrannical an indoctrinator as the power-luster. (The solution is not what the opponents of any firm convictions suggest: that the honest teacher turn into a flexible pragmatist who'll switch his ideas from moment to moment, or into a skeptical pig who'll eat anything.) The consequences of any attempt to rule or _to support_ intellectual activities by means of force will be evil, regardless of motives. (This does not mean that dissent is essential to intellectual freedom; the _possibility_ of dissent, is.)

Who would enforce the fairness doctrine in education? Not the executive branch of the government, which is the distributor of the funds and has a vested interest in uniformity, i.e., conformity. The doctrine has to be invoked and upheld by private individuals and groups. This is another opportunity for those who wish to take practical action against the growth of statism. This issue could become the goal of an ad hoc movement, uniting all men of good will, appealing (in the name of intellectual justice) to whatever element of nineteenth-century liberalism still exists in the minds of academic liberals - as distinguished from the Marcusians, who openly propose to drive all dissenters off the university faculties. (Is the Marcusians' goal to be achieved at public expense and with government support?)

If a fairness movement enlisted the talents of some intelligent young lawyers, it could conceivably find support in the courts of law, which are still supposed to protect an individual's civil rights. The legal precedent for a fairness doctrine is to be found in the field of broadcasting. The practical implementation, i.e., the challenge to the Establishment in specific cases, is up to the voluntary effort, the dedication, and the persuasiveness of individuals.

It must be remembered firmly that a fairness doctrine is not a string on the universities' freedom, but a string on the government's power to distribute public funds. That power has already demonstrated its potential for fantastically evil and blatantly unconstitutional control over the universities. Under threat of withholding government funds and contracts, the Department of Health, Education and Welfare is now imposing racial and sexual quotas on university faculties, demanding that some unspecified number of teachers consist of ethnic minority-members and women. To add insult to injury, HEW insists that this is not a demand for quotas, nor a demand to place racial considerations above merit, but a demand for "proof" that a university (e.g., Columbia) has made an effort "to find" teachers of equal merit among those groups. Try and prove it. Try and prove that you have "searched." Try to measure and prove the various applicants' merit - when no precise, objective standards of comparison are given or known. The result is that almost any female or minority-member is given preference over anyone else. The consequence is a growing anxiety about their future among young teachers who are male and do not belong to an ethnic minority: they are now the victims of the most obscenely vicious discrimination - obscene, because perpetrated in the name of fighting discrimination.

If the rights of various physiological minorities are so loudly claimed today, what about the rights of intellectual minorities?

I have said that the fairness doctrine is a product of the mixed economy. The whole precarious structure of a mixed economy, in its transition from freedom to totalitarian statism, rests on the power of pressure groups. But pressure-group warfare is a game that two (or more) ideological sides can play as well as one. The disadvantage of the statists is the fact that up to the last minute (and even beyond it) they have to play under cover of the slogans of individual rights and freedom. The advocates of freedom can beat them at their own game - by taking them at their word, but playing it straight. The time is right for it. The Establishment is not very popular at present, neither politically nor intellectually, neither with the country at large nor with many of its own members. A movement of the serious students and of the better teachers, defending the rights of intellectual minorities and demanding a fairness doctrine for education, would have a good chance to grow and to succeed. But taking part in such a movement would be much more difficult and demanding (and rewarding) than chanting slogans and dancing ring-around-a-rosy on some campus lawn.

If student minorities have succeeded in demanding that they be given courses on such subjects as Zen Buddhism, guerrilla warfare, Swahili, and astrology, then an intellectual student minority can succeed in demanding courses on, for instance, Aristotle in philosophy, von Mises in economics, Montessori in education, Hugo in literature. At the very least, such courses would save the students' mind; potentially, they would save the culture.

No, the fairness doctrine would not reform the universities' faculties and administrations. There would be a great deal of hypocrisy, of compromising, of cheating, of hiring weak advocates to teach the unfashionable theories, of "tokenism," of window dressing.

But think of what one window can do for a sealed, airless, lightless room.

Ayn Rand

The Ayn Rand Letter, published fortnightly by The Ayn Rand Letter, Inc., 201 East 34th Street, New York, N.Y. 10016.
Contributing Editor: **Leonard Peikoff**; Subscription Director: **Elayne Kalberman**; Production Manager: **Barbara Weiss.**

Vol. 1, No. 20 July 3, 1972

THE DEAD END

There were three casualties in the Democratic Presidential primaries this year: the notion of rule by consensus, the notion of safety in the middle of the road, and Pragmatism. (This last is the root; the two others are its consequences.)

President Johnson was the climax of the policy of rule by consensus - and he fell as a martyr to the principle that principles are unnecessary. It took only four years to carry him from a popular landslide to so great an unpopularity that he could not venture to face the voters again. Rule by consensus is the practice of the belief that a country splintered into pressure groups can be run indefinitely by an expert contortionist-juggler, who would encourage the pressure groups, multiply them, and play them against one another, in the name of balancing their demands and reaching a consensus of compromises, by means of distributing favors and burdens at whim, on the expediency of the moment.

This policy rested on some implicit premises and the strict precondition that they must never be named: 1. that any group demand is as valid as any other and is to be weighed according to the group's numbers, regardless of justice or rights; 2. that individual rights are obsolete; 3. that the lives and property of the citizens belong to the government, as a common pool to be ladled out for the purchase of the next election; 4. that the people are too dumb to understand, so that neither the expropriated victims nor the expropriating profiteers would "go to extremes" and upset the game.

Sooner or later, somebody had to cash in on it and make those premises explicit. Senator George McGovern did.

President Nixon opened the way for him (just as another "conservative," President Hoover, opened the way for the welfare-state policies of President Roosevelt). As a true pragmatist, Mr. Nixon saw nothing wrong in proposing to save capitalism by providing everyone with a guaranteed minimum income. But, with the usual circumlocutions, he evaded the full moral-legal meaning of his proposal. Mr. McGovern did not.

Mr. McGovern announced that he proposes "a redistribution of wealth." That term has been bandied about for some time by the intellectual Establishment, as a dreamily sloppy metaphor. Mr. McGovern adopted it as an explicit political program.

If a man proposes to redistribute wealth, he means explicitly and necessarily that the wealth is his to distribute. If he proposes it in the name of the government, then the wealth belongs to the government; if in the name of society, then it belongs to society. No one, to my knowledge, did or could define a difference between that proposal and the basic principle of communism. It might be said, perhaps, that communism is more practical and less cruel, at least in theory: a communist government takes over an entire economy and forbids men to act, but assumes the responsibility of providing for their livelihood. Mr. McGovern's proposal is closer to the theory of fascism: it leaves to individual men the responsibility of production and of struggling for existence, but lets the government assume the power to dispose of anything they produce.

No one, to my knowledge, has asked him the only relevant question: By what right?

(To ask that question, a man would have to uphold individual rights, which means that he would have to discover that individual rights are incompatible with altruism, which means that he would have to reject altruism all the way down, down to its roots. Most men profess to see no connection between altruism and politics. So it is curious, psychologically, to observe the extent of their fear - which is now approaching panic - at the necessity of facing the issue and challenging the altruist creed.)

Since the notion of rule by consensus had replaced individual rights with the untenable fiction of "group rights," there was nothing to prevent Mr. McGovern from discarding "group rights" and aligning himself with the demands of just one group at the expense of all others: the *Lumpenproletariat* of body or spirit, i.e., those who do not work, i.e., most of the very poor and the very rich.

Mr. McGovern proposes to slice off the top, the near-top, and the middle of the economic pyramid, thus cutting off the future, the ambition, the energy, and the hope of every individual in this country, except those on public or parental welfare. As far as can be calculated from Mr. McGovern's switching, contradictory statements, the expropriation would apply to the "wealth" of anyone earning more than $20,000 a year for a family of four.

This proposal is not aimed at the very rich, because it would not expropriate what one owns already, but only what one *earns*. The very rich are a very small minority and most of them, today, are not producers, but heirs of the second and third generation; many of them are in the vanguard of Mr. McGovern's supporters (and backers). They could be taxed 100% of their income and still live for the rest of their days in a luxury which the rest of the nation would be forbidden to equal or approach. The McGovern plan would stop everyone on whatever level he has happened to reach and forbid him to rise. It would freeze the nation into economic castes and destroy one of this country's best features, the hallmark of economic freedom: upward mobility. Observe that the plan is beginning to be referred to, not as "redistribution of wealth," but as "redistribution of *income*" - which makes it clear that it is not the "ability to pay," but the ability to earn, that will be crushed under an unspeakable mortgage.

A nation's productive - and moral, and intellectual - top is the middle class. It is a broad reservoir of energy, it is a country's motor and lifeblood, which feeds the rest. The common denominator of its members, on their various levels of ability, is: independence. The upper classes are merely a nation's past; the middle class is its future.

It is against this class - and its symbol: the self-made man - that the McGovern proposal is directed.

For a man with a family, an income of $20,000 a year is not luxury, but merely a state of precarious comfort, in view of today's government-created inflation. If this is all a man can hope to earn, he will not work very hard or for very long. Human effort, insofar as it is human, is goal-directed. No worker, on any level of ability, can stand an endless routine of toil with no goal in sight, no hope of progress, improvement or achievement. Those who become adjusted to it - like the robots of totalitarian states or of primitive cultures - do not produce much more than their own barest sustenance. What, then, would become of the men on welfare? Who would provide them with their guaranteed incomes?

And who, on an income of $20,000 a year, would be able to invest - and thus to finance, not the growth, but the mere maintenance of industry? Who would provide jobs for those willing and able to work? There is a silly current expression that describes a capitalist economy as a "trickling down of wealth." Wait till you see what a trickling down of paralysis would do.

It is an indication of the state of today's culture that Mr. McGovern's plan is being criticized, not on the grounds of moral or political principles, but on the grounds of his faulty figures. His critics are not saying: "This is too evil," but only: "This is too expensive." (So much for the humanitarian motives of the welfare statists.)

But even that level of criticism has revealed a morally shameful fact. Having, apparently, little or no respect for human rights and lives, Mr. McGovern permitted himself to slapdash his program in such a manner that economists have been demonstrating the gross inaccuracy of his figures in regard to the costs of his plan, clearly implying either deceit or fantastic irresponsibility on his part. Mr. McGovern's answer was a series of evasive, contradictory statements, including the assertion that his specific proposal was merely an "experimental" idea. Whose guinea pigs are we? What state have we reached if a politician may permit himself to experiment in such a manner with the personal, individual work, property, ambition, goals and life of every one of us?

There are other indications of Mr. McGovern's character. For instance, while promising a national expropriation of wealth to his followers, Mr. McGovern had an ad published in The Wall Street Journal, in which he attempted to reassure businessmen by declaring that he, as President, would not be able to enact confiscatory tax legislation, since only Congress holds the power to do so. How is that for the neatest trick of the decade? Yet this is the candidate now publicized as a man of integrity.

I shall not discuss Mr. McGovern's foreign policy. It is regarded as bad form to cast doubt on the sincerity of a candidate's motives (a rule of etiquette with which I agree, as far as "psychologizing" is concerned). But I wish some political Master of Protocol would tell us how to assess an obscenity such as a proposal for the unilateral disarmament of the United States - and would suggest some possible explanation, other than treasonable irresponsibility or a staggering degree of stupidity.

A more charitable assessment is not helped by Mr. McGovern's statements. He has declared on television that there has been too much fear of communism, that the real danger to an American citizen at night in the city streets is the crime wave, not communism. A concrete-bound, small-town housewife may, perhaps, think in that manner. But a Presidential candidate?

The liberal Establishment and its pragmatist commentators seem to be bewildered by Mr. McGovern's success in the primaries. They had regarded him as a negligible contender, who had no chance because: a. he is an extremist, and the country wants the middle of the road; b. he has no "charisma," and the people's choice of a President is determined by his charm on the television screen. With their road blasted straight through the middle, they are now reaching for equally serious explanations, such as the claim that Mr. McGovern owes his victories to a handful of college goons.

Since pragmatists deny the validity of principles and the power of ideas, it is not within their capacity to grasp that Mr. McGovern owes his victories to the Messrs. Humphrey, Muskie, Lindsay, etc.

"In any _conflict_ between two men (or two groups) who hold the _same_ basic principles, it is the more consistent one who wins....The inconsistent person will endorse and propagate the same ideas as his adversary, but in a weaker, diluted form - and thus will sanction, assist, and hasten his adversary's victory, creating in the minds of their disputed following the impression of his adversary's greater honesty and courage, while discrediting himself by an aura of evasion and cowardice."

This is a pretty accurate description of what happened in the Democratic primaries of 1972 - except that I wrote it in 1964 ("The Anatomy of Compromise" in _Capitalism: The Unknown Ideal_).

Since there were no _fundamental_ differences among the candidates, those in the middle of the road paved it with altruist-statist generalities and evasions, thus enabling Mr. McGovern to march forward as the consistent representative of their unadmitted notions, the practical implementer of their undefined promises, the fearless dispeller of the murky fog they had left behind. Time and again, in televised interviews, voters explained their rejection of various candidates by saying helplessly, almost pleadingly: "I don't know what he stands for." This referred most often to Senator Muskie, who was the best exponent of the status quo and managed to convey, no matter what he said, that he was saying nothing.

It is the status quo that got the worst beating - and even the Establishment commentators admit it - the hopeless, aimless, corrupt, mealy-mouthed and violence-ridden status quo of the consensus-centrist-pragmatist policies. People are sick of lies, evasions, uncertainty, broken promises, switching stands, inexplicable contradictions, chronic emergencies, and the inexorable reality of the fact that, under all the grandiose slogans, things are growing worse and worse. People know that the country cannot go on like this much longer. But since they do not know which direction it ought to take - since neither the politicians nor the commentators nor the professors nor the intellectual leaders will tell them - people have reached the only conclusion open to the helplessly frustrated: "Anything is better than this!" They have expressed it by voting almost indiscriminately against the middle - by voting for two "extremists" who seemed to be the strongest opponents of the status quo: Senator McGovern and Governor George C. Wallace.

The commentators regard these two as opposites - as the extremes of left and right - and are shocked by the extent of Mr. Wallace's popularity. Mr. McGovern is the consistent representative of the New Left. But can one call Mr. Wallace a representative of the right? Yes - symbolically and journalistically. No - in fact, if by "right" one means capitalism. Mr. Wallace is a "conservative," which means a statist; and a "populist," which means an old-fashioned, anti-intellectual, non-ideological collectivist. He can match any liberal in attacks on the rich and in appeals to the "little fellows." He is behind the times: he sounds like a New Dealer of the 1930s. But he has the courage to attack some of the modern outrages which the Establishment protects by uncritical silence: welfare, busing, foreign aid, the U.N., the appeasement of Soviet Russia. People are relieved to hear these attacks, which are long overdue.

Perhaps the most pathetic and significant aspect of the primaries was the large number of voters (as shown in newspaper and television polls) who voted for McGovern and named Wallace as their second choice, or vice versa. In terms of their concrete proposals and professed intentions, these two candidates sound like opposites. But the voters are not listening to concretes (or to promises) any longer: they are looking primarily for a man they can trust. They saw two significant characteristics which these two candidates had in common: both denounced the status quo - and both projected moral self-confidence (at least, in manner), i.e., the confidence of being *morally* right.

It is *this* quality that people respond to in political candidates, not their "charm," their "personality," or their photogenic profiles (as witness, Mr. Lindsay). Mr. McGovern and Mr. Wallace are signally lacking in such characteristics. But both of them project moral self-confidence. And this is the secret of the mysterious, allegedly indefinable "charisma" projected by some persons on the television screen. The source of this quality is an uncompromising commitment to a broadly consistent set of ideas (a set which may be true or false).

This quality is not a substitute for ideas, but their consequence and their transmitter. A tragic example of its absence was provided by the Humphrey-McGovern television debates, during the California primary. As far as content was concerned, Mr. Humphrey won hands down: he had all the arguments and he reduced Mr. McGovern to blatant evasions, particularly on the issue of the expropriation of wealth. But Mr. McGovern was calm, firm, confident - while Mr. Humphrey was emotional, aggressive and garrulously inarticulate. As a result, Mr. McGovern, while evading, sounded as if he were rational and honest - while Mr. Humphrey, while uttering the truth, sounded as if he were putting something over on the audience.

It is only in the absence of logical arguments, however, that this quality becomes decisive. Those who doubt that voters can be influenced by ideas or by logic, should note the following: before the debates, the polls gave Mr. McGovern a 20% lead over Mr. Humphrey; in the actual primary, that lead was reduced to 5.5%, which commentators ascribe to the debates. Mr. Humphrey resorted to logic too late and only partially. But this is what a logical argument - even a badly presented one - can do. The tragedy is that no political candidate is fully able or willing to believe it.

At this writing, I do not know whether Mr. McGovern will win the nomination or not. If he does, it will be by courtesy (and default) of his opponents. In either case, the Democratic Party has gone past the middle and reached the dead end of the welfare-state road, which it has spent forty years denying: expropriation and confiscation.

The ominous question is: what will President Nixon do to fight a program of this kind? Will he choose to float above the battle? Will he repeat Mr. Muskie's mistake of trying to coast on his current percentage of popularity and thus lose it? Will he cling to the discredited, nationally rejected policy of pragmatist consensus and compromise? Will he evade the issue? Will he fail to tell a desperate nation the full truth about the nature of the McGovern proposal? Will he assume the gentle, smiling, ingratiating, apologetic manner which makes one feel that he is deceiving us, even when he is stating some incontrovertible truth?

If anyone can get George McGovern elected President of the United States, it will be Richard M. Nixon.

Ayn Rand

The Ayn Rand Letter, published fortnightly by The Ayn Rand Letter, Inc., 183 Madison Avenue, New York, N.Y. 10016.
Contributing Editor: **Leonard Peikoff**; Subscription Director: **Elayne Kalberman**; Production Manager: **Barbara Weiss.**

Vol. 1, No. 21 July 17, 1972

REPRESENTATION WITHOUT AUTHORIZATION

The theory of representative government rests on the principle that man is a rational being, i.e., that he is able to perceive the facts of reality, to evaluate them, to form rational judgments, to make his own choices, and to bear responsibility for the course of his life.

Politically, this principle is implemented by a man's right to choose his own agents, i.e., those whom he authorizes to represent him in the government of his country. To represent him, in this context, means to represent his views in terms of political principles. Thus the government of a free country derives its "just powers from the consent of the governed." (For the basis of this discussion, see "Man's Rights" and "The Nature of Government" in Capitalism: The Unknown Ideal.)

As a corroboration of the link between man's rational faculty and a representative form of government, observe that those who are demonstrably (or physiologically) incapable of rational judgment cannot exercise the right to vote. (Voting is a derivative, not a fundamental, right; it is derived from the right to life, as a political implementation of the requirements of a rational being's survival.) Children do not vote, because they have not acquired the knowledge necessary to form a rational judgment on political issues; neither do the feeble-minded or the insane, who have lost or never developed their rational faculty. (The possession of a rational faculty does not guarantee that a man will use it, only that he is _able_ to use it and is, therefore, responsible for his actions.)

The mentally unprepared or incapacitated are unable personally to exercise their rights - e.g., the right to acquire property or to assume contractual obligations - and the protection of their rights is delegated to their parents or to legally appointed guardians, who act in their name. The right to vote, however, is nontransferable. The father of twelve minors does not acquire the right to cast twelve votes in addition to his own; neither does the keeper of an insane asylum.

Philosophically, the theory of representative government is in profound conflict with the dominant schools of modern philosophy, which deny the efficacy or existence of reason and of volition. Dictatorship and determinism are reciprocally reinforcing corollaries: if one seeks to enslave men, one has to destroy their reliance on the validity of their own judgments and choices - if one believes that reason and volition are impotent, one has to accept the rule of force.

Ever since Kant, the dominant method of modern philosophers has been to fight issues not by open intellectual presentation, but by corruption - the corruption into its opposite of any concept which they dared not oppose explicitly. Just as Kant corrupted the concept "reason" to mean a mystic faculty pertaining to another dimension, so his theoretical and practical descendants have been employing his technique on an ever growing scale and shrinking subjects. Thus "freedom," in today's jargon, means obedience to a totalitarian ruler - "security" is dependence on the whims of the government - "individuality" is conformity to the life-style of a pack - a Putsch to seize dictatorial power is a "War of Liberation" - the "Right to Life" is the right of the unborn to sacrifice the living - and "love of this earth" consists in making it impossible for men to live on it.

It is fairly easy to corrupt the concept of representative government in a country that has had no experience of it: people are offered the flattering paraphernalia of ballot boxes, but only one party to vote for. It is more difficult in a country whose history began with free elections. For half a century (or longer), the collectivist intellectuals have been corrupting our two major political parties to make them merge into one by making them indistinguishable - while the commentators ignored the country's discontent and pretended that no opposition existed. But this did not work: instead of merging, both parties are now breaking up into irreconcilable factions. In the meantime, the collectivists have come out with a new corruption of the concept of political representation, more grotesque than the rest of their notions.

It is expressed in the demand that various statistical quotas be imposed on this country, in order to "represent" various kinds of people.

It has never been made clear what the term "represent" means in this context. Represent - where and by whom? At first, the demands were voiced in regard to private or semiprivate activities, but in fields vulnerable to political pressure - e.g., the demands for racial quotas in the student enrollment and on the faculties of schools, or in the employment practices of government-controlled industries, such as television. Then the demands grew louder and more directly political, seeking "representation" in Cabinet posts and even on the Supreme Court. The current rules for the Democratic Party's choice of convention delegates implemented these demands and brought them straight into the field of political elections.

It is, therefore, time to examine the meaning of the quota doctrine.

The notion of racial quotas is so obviously an expression of racism that no lengthy discussion is necessary. If a young man is barred from a school or a job because the quota for his particular race has been filled, he is barred by reason of his race. Telling him that those admitted are his "representatives," is adding insult to injury. To demand such quotas in the name of fighting racial discrimination, is an obscene mockery.

But observe that the demands for "representation" by quotas are not confined to minorities and are not made exclusively on the grounds of race. The same demands are presented on behalf of a majority: women - on the grounds of age: the young - and on the grounds of economics: the poor.

Now observe the common denominator of these groups. The basis of their grouping and of the quotas they advocate is not intellectual, but _physiological_. (In the case of poverty, it is physical: an absence of material means.)

This is the sort of doctrine with which today's intellectuals, particularly the academic crowd, would feel profoundly at home - most of them emotionally and subconsciously, and a few of them with full, conscious awareness of all the implications.

This doctrine - a product of determinism - assumes that physiology is the determining factor in human life and that the interests of all the members of a given physiological group are identical. Yet it is obvious that an intelligent, efficient career woman has more interests in common with men than with a sloppy housewife who joins Women's Lib and refuses to cook her husband's dinner. A successful, self-made black businessman has more interests in common with white businessmen than with a black mugger. A rational young student, seeking knowledge, has more interests in common with old professors than with drugged young "Jesus Freaks."

The quota doctrine assumes that all members of a given physiological group are identical and interchangeable - not merely in the eyes of other people, but in their own eyes and minds. Assuming a total merging of the self with the group, the doctrine holds that it makes no difference to a man whether _he_ or his "representative" is admitted to a school, gets a job, or makes a decision. This particular notion is widely believed by the student activists, who clamor for participation in running universities and other institutions, declaring: "We want to have a say about the things that affect our lives" - the "say" consisting in casting one vote out of thousands for some little campus politician, while surrendering the only "say" they have the right to demand: the say about _their own_ lives.

It is obvious why the quota doctrine appeals to modern intellectuals: it eliminates the responsibility of thought, judgment and choice. Just follow your group leaders - it advises - they are physiologically predestined to protect you and take care of you. To most of them, this promises the comfort of lethargy, and to a few - a road to power.

If and to the extent that the quota doctrine is taken seriously, it can lead to the abolition of actual political elections, which would be replaced by a system guaranteeing that every sort of group - except one - will be "represented" in the government. There are already suggestions for labor "representation," and special demands by groups laying the groundwork for welfare-recipients' "representation," for "gay representation," for the "representation" of the fetus, etc. The one kind of group to be excepted and excluded is a group brought together by _ideas_. There is to be no _ideological_ representation - or differentiation.

(A precedent for this sort of electoral policy is offered by Soviet Russia. Ethnic, or physiological, diversity is welcomed and fostered in Russia [unless some group displeases the authorities]. The Soviet Union is broken up into a number of racially different states, each with its own language, folk songs, commemorative postage stamps, and U.N. representation. This flatters the enslaved and is of no danger to the rulers. But ideological diversity is not to be mentioned or dreamed about, under penalty of death.)

As one more example of the connection between reason and freedom, observe that the quota doctrine relegates people to the status of children or of the mentally incompetent, with appointed guardians in place of genuine representatives. No individual choice, no personal authorization to represent him, is required on the part of the citizen - physiology provides the authorization.

The advantages to the leaders of the pressure-group racket, are obvious. As to the followers, they would have to reach that hopeless, brutalized state in which people accept as flattery the assertion that the Pharaoh's pyramids or the palaces of Versailles, of Berchtesgaden, of the Kremlin are erected to "represent" _their_, the people's, glory.

I do not believe that the collectivists can get away with it in America. But any suggestion of the quota doctrine is too much for this country - and, today, we are hearing and seeing more than a suggestion. The introduction of that doctrine into the Democratic Party's rules of delegate selection is not merely a future and potential, but a present and actual, violation of a citizen's individual rights.

The violation lies in the _statistical_ method of apportioning the quotas. They are apportioned, not on the basis of a given organization's membership, but on the basis of the number of persons of a certain physiological type who live in a given district or in the country at large. Thus 50% of a delegation "represents" women (_all_ women), 10% "represents" blacks (_all_ blacks), etc. This means that an individual woman or an individual black - who has never heard of these delegates, may not agree with their views, may not even be a Democrat - is counted as one of the delegate's constituents, without voting, consent, or authorization on her or his part.

An individual's right to choose his own representatives or agents is recognized in the material realm, but, apparently, not in the ideological one. If some stranger sold you the Brooklyn Bridge or the Empire State Building, he would be arrested for fraud, because he had no authorization to act as agent for the owners of the bridge or the building. Yet the quota advocates regard you as a unit of meat and appoint themselves your "representatives" in so vast, complex and controversial a field as political elections.

No organization has the right to speak for or to act in the name of anyone but its own members. No organization may be taken as an agent for an individual without his personal knowledge and consent.

If "taxation without representation is slavery," then representation without authorization is slavery embellished with fraud.

Ayn Rand

The Ayn Rand Letter, published fortnightly by The Ayn Rand Letter, Inc., 183 Madison Avenue, New York, N.Y. 10016.

Contributing Editor: **Leonard Peikoff;** Subscription Director: **Elayne Kalberman;** Production Manager: **Barbara Weiss.**

Vol. 1, No. 22 July 31, 1972

A PREVIEW

The Democratic National Convention was an eloquent dramatization of the role of philosophy in politics. It performed the task of good fiction: to select the essentials of an abstract issue and present them in action.

One may object to the term "good fiction" by pointing out that that Convention was lifeless, uninspiring, devoid of any serious ideological conflict or discussion, and excruciatingly boring. But this is in the nature of the philosophy - and of the tactics - it was dramatizing.

Modern cynicism has made it fashionable to call a forecast based on scientific theory, a "scenario." The word is more applicable to today's political programs. It is, therefore, appropriate to say that the Convention was an advance "trailer" or preview of what its particular scenario would do if shot on a national scale.

In spite of the overstressed, Madison-Avenue-style declarations that this was a new, open kind of convention, a fresh start, the dawn of the New Politics - the atmosphere was not that of a birth, but of a wake. The Convention was not open: its result was set before the delegates arrived; in a broader sense, it was set forty years ago (or longer). The Convention's main business was the silent ending of a patricidal war - between semi-tamed, awed young barbarians and decadent, hostile, cynically sentimental old politicians disarmed by the unadmitted knowledge that the barbarians were their sons. What the scared young hordes took over was an empire gutted long ago.

There were no ideological grounds on which Senator McGovern's opponents could fight him: he had merely brought their own political philosophy to its ultimate logical conclusions. So while those opponents were "doing their thing," i.e., maneuvering over the apportionment of delegates, scrambling in technicalities to defeat California's rule of "winner take all," they surrendered the essentials of the Party Platform - the campaign's ideological manifesto - to the rule of "winner take all."

The Platform is tailored to the McGovern program in content, but not in form. In form, it is like a contract drawn up by a shyster who intends to put over as much as possible on the careless signatories and is counting on them to skim the thing quickly, recognize the familiar sugary phrases, and miss the ground glass sprinkled through the sugar.

"We believe in the rights of citizens," the Platform declares, "to achieve to the limit of their talents and energies. [Who would object to that?] We are determined to remove barriers that limit citizens because they are black, brown, young or women; because they never had the chance to gain an education; because there was no possibility of being anything but what they were."

Observe the package deal you are asked to accept. Its gimmick is the inclusion of the "young" in what looks like a list of victims of race prejudice (with Women's Lib thrown in). Considering this country's cult of youth, what barriers are there against the young? - unless a refusal to give the young a ruling voice over things of which they have no knowledge is to be regarded as a prejudice. If the "barriers" imposed by ignorance must be removed, then untrained men (or women) must be given jobs as surgeons, airplane pilots, nuclear physicists, university presidents, or Justices of the Supreme Court - on the premise that an objection to ignorance is bigotry. Whom would this protect? Anyone to whom you may object on intellectual grounds.

No, that declaration does not mean that those who "never had the chance" should be given an education. Its purpose is not political, but metaphysical; what it is selling is not school programs, but _determinism_ - the obliteration of the concept of volition, the tenet that men have "no possibility of being anything but what they are." Whom would this vindicate? The blacks or browns? No. Anyone to whom you may object on _moral_ grounds. (I call this to the special attention of those "practical" men who are busy counting delegates or dividends, and cannot imagine what such things as metaphysics or volition have to do with political platforms.)

As to the main issue - the McGovern plan for the redistribution of wealth - the Platform does not present it, but smuggles it in. "Full employment - a guaranteed job for all - is the primary economic objective of the Democratic party....*We are determined to make economic security a matter of right.* [Emphasis added.] This means a job with decent pay and good working conditions for everyone willing and able to work and an adequate income for those unable to work. It means abolition of the present welfare system."

Since the things man needs for survival have to be produced, and nature does not guarantee the success of any human endeavor, there is not and cannot be any such thing as a _guaranteed economic security_. The employer who gives you a job, has no guarantee that his business will remain in existence, that his customers will continue to buy his products or services. The customers have no guarantee that they will always be able and willing to trade with him, no guarantee of what their needs, choices and incomes will be in the future. If you retire to a self-sustaining farm, you have no guarantee to protect you from what a flood or a hurricane might do to your land and your crops. If you surrender everything to the government and give it total power to plan the whole economy, this will not guarantee your economic security, but it _will_ guarantee the descent of the entire nation to a level of miserable poverty - as the practical results of every totalitarian economy, communist or fascist, have demonstrated.

Morally, the promise of an impossible "right" to economic security is an infamous attempt to abrogate the concept of rights. It can and does mean only one thing: a promise to enslave the men who produce, for the benefit of those who don't. "If some men are entitled _by right_ to the products of the work of others, it means that those others are deprived of rights and condemned to slave labor." ("Man's Rights" in _Capitalism: The Unknown Ideal_.) There can be no such thing as the right to enslave, i.e., the right to destroy rights.

In short-range terms, that promise rests on the hope that America is so rich and productive a nation that by the time both producers and parasites perish, the rulers will have enjoyed their exercise of power and will be safely dead. But America's free, creative energy would accelerate, not retard, the collapse. Peasants can be forced into a semi-adjustment to serfdom; an industrial civilization cannot.

The motive behind such programs is the same as the motive of all the exponents of power-lust, all the theorists of the absolute state, throughout history: the desire to obtain by force a prestige they were unable to obtain by achievement, the desire for an unearned living in exchange for their unwanted services, and, above all, the desire to gratify the emotion of envy.

"Millions of jobs - real jobs, not make-work - need to be provided. Public service employment must be greatly expanded in order to make the Government the employer of last resort and guarantee a job for all." If these are to be "real jobs," i.e., jobs for which there is an economic justification, private employers would provide them. If these are to be jobs "of last resort," they necessarily have to be make-work.

In private industry, it takes an investment of thousands of dollars to create one job. Since the government is not a producer (only a collector) of wealth, whose money will enable it to provide make-work on such a large scale? Yours, of course. Since the government's undertakings will not be commercial, i.e., will not produce any goods or bring any profits, who will subsidize it in its role of "employer" and for how long? You, of course - for the rest of your life.

What will you get in return for your money? The kinds of services that you do not need, or do not want, or cannot use - and, above all, cannot afford. Here is another package deal: "Cleaning up our air and water will take skills and people in large numbers. In the school, the police department, the welfare agency [which was to be abolished?] or the recreation program, there are new careers to be developed to help insure that social services reach the people for whom they are intended. It may cost more, at least initially, to create decent jobs than to perpetuate the hand-out system of present welfare. But the return - in new public facilities and services, in the dignity of bringing a paycheck home and in the taxes that will come back in [from whom and to whom?] - far outweighs the cost of the investment."

Suppose that you are a self-respecting, self-supporting couple, struggling desperately to carry your own weight. Half your paycheck (or more) is gone in taxes, open and hidden. But the former welfare recipient next door proudly brings to his home a paycheck earned in his new career of ecological bird watcher. Confronted by the rising price of meat, you are struggling with the problem of how to provide proper nutrition for your children. But the social workers at the welfare agency are giving free lessons in Spanish cooking and community dancing to their former clients. You could not afford a proper lock, and your house has been burglarized. But the "new career" policeman - trained in smelling people at "encounter therapy" sessions - who comes in answer to your call, gives you a lecture on loving and understanding the burglar's psychology. You cannot afford to buy a car - but public transportation is available, to places you don't want to go. You cannot afford a vacation - but public parks are open to you, if you can see the trees for the hippies. Your child needs a serious operation; you want the best, most expensive surgeon - who does not work under any form of Medicare - and you cannot afford his services, because there is no such thing as savings any longer. But a "recreation program" is being offered on the corner of your street, with drugged young bums doing folk dances and screeching unintelligible curses against the selfishness of the rich.

It has been said that college professors and students represent the core of McGovern supporters. Do you see their fingerprints all over the Democratic Party Platform? Who else would long for such programs, and who else would profit?

If one skims through the Platform, one might misunderstand it to mean that all the former welfare recipients, except the disabled, would be put to work. To grasp fully that the Platform's objective is not the relief of poverty, but the fostering of parasitism, one should note the following brief paragraph slipped in among the others: "President Nixon's welfare reform, H.R. 1 and its various amendments, is not humane and does not meet the social and economic objectives that we believe in, and it should be defeated. It perpetuates the coercion of forced work requirements."

This means that the guaranteed-income recipients will have a choice as to whether they want to work, but you will have no choice as to whether you want to support them. It means that the necessity to work (which is imposed on man by nature) is coercion - but the expropriation of your earned income by the government, and your forced descent into meager subsistence, are not.

The rest of the issues covered in the Platform are enmeshed in vaguer and drippier generalities than the paragraphs quoted above, with the collectivist fangs showing through the syrup once in a while. For example: the hint of a program of forced resettlement "to promote a balance of population," on the grounds that: "Problems of overgrowth are not caused so much by land scarcity as by the wrong distribution of people..." (the idea of a "redistribution of people" is left implicit) - the official establishment of quotas "in all branches of the Federal Government to achieve an equitable ratio of women and men" - the creation of a full system of socialized medicine, "including preventive medicine, mental and emotional disorders," etc. The fog of evasions gets heavier and heavier - and Mr. McGovern's promise to cut military spending down to the level of unilateral disarmament, becomes a promise to "reduce military spending, where consistent with national security." (Who is to judge this? Mr. McGovern?)

The method employed throughout the Democratic Party Platform is the equivalent of the method that would produce the following hypothetical contract:

"Recognizing that love makes the world go 'round, that love is superior to grubby materialism, that need takes precedence over greed, the Party of the First Part hereby declares its special love for you, the Party of the Second Part, in acknowledgment of which, and of other good and valuable considerations, it shall give you absolutely free a brand new automobile, which retails at a price of $1,800, but which shall be yours free - think of it, Free! - with absolutely no payment, inconvenience or obligation on your part, simply as a matter of your natural right. In return, the Party of the Second Part shall, every Friday, turn his paycheck over to the Party of the First Part, who shall return it promptly after deducting a minimal service charge plus other small expenses - such as the construction of roads, bridges, tunnels, the research to discover a nonpolluting fuel, the removal of billboards that mar the natural beauty of the countryside, the rehabilitation of drunken drivers, etc. - all of which are absolutely essential to the driving of an automobile. This may seem expensive, at least initially, but the return - in new public facilities and services, in the dignity of not having to bring your paycheck home, and in the taxes you will have nothing to pay with - far outweighs the cost of the investment."

You would not sign such a contract in your home, office or place of work, at any time. Do not sign it in a voting booth in November.

(To be continued.)

Ayn Rand

The Ayn Rand Letter, published fortnightly by The Ayn Rand Letter, Inc., 183 Madison Avenue, New York, N.Y. 10016.

Contributing Editor: **Leonard Peikoff**; Subscription Director: **Elayne Kalberman**; Production Manager: **Barbara Weiss.**

Vol. 1, No. 23 August 14, 1972

A PREVIEW

Part II

What made the Democratic Party accept so shameful a document as its present Platform? The accumulated sum and trend of its past platforms. So long as the statist-altruist-pragmatist doctrine of the welfare state remained unchallenged, there was no other place to go.

Morally and economically, the welfare state creates an ever accelerating downward pull. Morally, the chance to satisfy demands by force spreads the demands wider and wider, with less and less pretense at justification. Economically, the forced demands of one group create hardships for all others, thus producing an inextricable mixture of actual victims and plain parasites. Since need, not achievement, is held as the criterion of rewards, the government necessarily keeps sacrificing the more productive groups to the less productive, gradually chaining the top level of the economy, then the next level, then the next. (How else are unachieved rewards to be provided?)

There are two kinds of *need* involved in this process: the need of the group making demands, which is openly proclaimed and serves as cover for another need, which is never mentioned - the need of the power-seekers, who require a group of dependent favor-recipients in order to rise to power. Altruism feeds the first need, statism feeds the second, Pragmatism blinds everyone - including victims and profiteers - not merely to the deadly nature of the process, but even to the fact that a process is going on.

Historically, the first group that served as the object of the welfare statists' concern was industrial labor. This lent a certain superficial plausibility (if not justification) to their crusades: they did not ask for handouts, but for "just" compensation to men engaged in *productive work* (with legalized force as the standard of justice). The coalition that built the base of the welfare state, under the name of the "New Deal," consisted of statist intellectuals, the more ambitious ("progressive") politicians, and industrial labor. The first two groups were the "benefactors" and achieved their ends; the last served as means.

But once compulsory unionization became established beyond the challenge of either major party, the relationship changed. Organized labor *did not need the politicians any longer* - it was the politicians who now needed organized labor's support. To the credit of American labor leaders, they understood the crucial importance of preserving some degree of independence from the government's power. They understood this issue much better than did the representatives of business. Ever since the passage of antitrust legislation, in 1890, businessmen were in the government's potentially total power; as a group, they offered no resistance; instead of fighting, they paid protection money to the politicians of both parties at election time, assuming the permanent role of stealthy favor-seekers. Labor leaders knew better. From as far back as the Roosevelt Administration, they stood on guard against any extension of government power over organized labor - and thus maintained, for the past four decades, its position as the largest, comparatively independent group, delaying the growth of statism and protecting the remnants of this country's economic freedom.

But organized labor was trapped in a contradiction which could not be maintained forever. Holding its economic power by legislative force, it wanted to arrest the growth of statism at *that* level - just as businessmen had wanted to retain the pro-business controls of the mid-nineteenth century and allow them to grow no further. Both groups, in different ways, were asking for the impossible: for the preservation of a cancer that had to be cut out or grow.

The artificially high wages forced on the economy by compulsory unionism imposed economic hardships on other groups - particularly on non-union workers and on unskilled labor, which was being squeezed gradually out of the market. Today's widespread unemployment is the result of organized labor's privileges and of allied measures, such as minimum wage laws. For years, the unions supported these measures and sundry welfare legislation, apparently in the belief that the costs would be paid by taxes imposed on the rich. The growth of inflation has shown that the major victim of government spending and of taxation is the middle class. Organized labor is part of the middle class - and the actual value of labor's forced "social gains" is now being wiped out.

During the past decades, while the precariously mixed economy of the country was going down, the intellectual pressure of the academic world was going up: it demanded an ever greater extension of government power - i.e., of force - as the solution to all problems. But ambitious politicians were unable to find a "power base" - i.e., some new group of potential favor-recipients whose "needs" they could champion as a means of rising to power. There were random attempts to create artificial pressure groups by promises of economic advantages which would be provided by the enslavement of the professions - e.g., the promise of socialized medicine to the "senior citizens," of universal college education to the junior citizens, even of free legal services to the criminals. But these were small drops in the big power bucket.

The real turning point came when the welfare statists switched from economics to physiology: they began to seek a new power base in deliberately fostered racism, the racism of minority groups, then in the hatreds and inferiority complexes of women, of "the young," etc. The significant aspect of this switch was the severing of economic rewards from productive work. Physiology replaced the conditions of employment as the basis of social claims. The demands were no longer for "just compensation," but just for compensation, with no work required.

So long as the power-seekers clung to the basic premises of the welfare state, holding need as the criterion of rewards, logic forced them, step by step, to champion the interests of the less and less productive groups, until they reached the ultimate dead end of turning from the role of champions of "honest toil" to the role of champions of open parasitism, parasitism on principle, parasitism as a "right" (with their famous slogan turning into: "Who does not toil, shall eat those who do"). In a country wrecked by forty years of their policies, they had no other place to turn, no other group to tempt by promises of unearned rewards into the trap of grateful docility.

When a demand for a guaranteed and unearned income is presented to society at large, it is presented to every productive group and person in the country. Which group offers the richest prospects for legalized looting? Not business, which is all but milked dry, as demonstrated by our falling behind the industrial development of other semi-free countries. Which group, today, is politically the most powerful, and legally the most privileged? Against whom is this new movement directed? Against organized labor.

The New Left signifies the breach between the statist intellectuals and the working class; it represents the intellectuals' rejection of Marxist theory (which failed them in this country). The American workers are too independent, too highly skilled, too confident to become a revolutionary proletariat obediently serving the power-lust of every stray assistant professor.

When they discovered that they could not rule the workers, that the prosperously self-supporting cannot be ruled, that helplessly dependent hordes are needed to fuel the absolute state, the intellectuals attacked the source of America's prosperity: technology. They are no longer out to fight the "greed" of industrialists, but to demolish industry. The ecological movement is directed against labor as much as or more than against business; the ecologists' avowed intention to lower the general standard of living, is a deadly threat to labor, not to the owners of inherited fortunes; the delays and sabotage of new industrial ventures hit the unemployed harder than the investors.

The barefoot hippies who demand the right to eat without working - the rhapsodies to the "beauty of the untouched wilderness" - the war on labor-saving devices - the demands for a return to grubby "earthiness" and primitive toil - the dazed stupor, the hysterical screaming, the drugged mindlessness, the cheap, tawdry, phony exhibitionism of "self-expression," the whole "artsy-craftsy" atmosphere - do not belong in an industrial civilization nor in the world of skilled, disciplined industrial workers.

The group that did not belong at the Democratic National Convention was organized labor.

Whether labor's grim-faced, bewildered representatives and their brash, smirking juvenile antagonists knew it consciously or not, both sides sensed it. The average labor leaders were probably aware of nothing more than a vague uneasiness. But the best and wisest among them (some of whom were not present) knew that labor was being maneuvered into the pen of the stockyards as the State's next milch cow and sacrificial victim. They knew that labor had nothing to gain from that Convention but some new chains. The subsequent refusal of George Meany and the A.F.L.-C.I.O. leadership to support McGovern's candidacy, does credit to their intellectual and moral stature.

The men at the Convention who knew nothing and grasped nothing - because they could not permit themselves to grasp it - were the defeated candidates, the deposed leaders of the Democratic Party. When Hubert Humphrey withdrew from the race, he was tragically sincere in his determination to support his Party's choice - but it was the out-of-context sincerity of a man who clings to party loyalty as to the only remnant of his shattered universe. During the primaries, he expressed bitter astonishment at the fact that he had a better, more liberal record than McGovern, as a champion of labor and of civil rights, yet his former supporters were deserting him. He was obviously unable to understand that he had spent a lifetime preparing the way for McGovern's victory, and that he was losing not in spite of his record, but because of it.

Like many men of the New Deal generation, the old leaders of the welfare statists, such as Humphrey or Muskie, did not consciously want to destroy the capitalist system. They merely wanted to keep on modifying it indefinitely, without expecting any adverse consequences. As pragmatists, they scrambled for one single, concrete "reform" of the moment (then for another), in the tacit hope that the rest of the economy would remain unchanged. But it did not. A mixed economy has to reach the day when it faces a final crossroad: either the private sector regains its freedom and starts rebuilding - or it gives up and lets the absolute state take over the shambles. The old leaders of the Democratic Party did not have the courage to turn to the first - nor the baseness to accept the second.

It is significant that the Party was taken over, not by some brilliant new leader, but by an old, plodding, conventional, undistinguished politician, who was more hostile and less scrupulous than his colleagues. They had nothing to offer the country, but were, perhaps, too fastidious to invade it as the head - the figurehead - of the New Left. George McGovern did not mind. The combination of his gray, dull, repression-eaten, streetcorner-preacher personality and the sloppy, unbridled, psychedelic, streetcorner-hoodlum character of his young followers, was one of the most instructive aspects of the televised spectacle offered by the Democratic National Convention.

In spite of the commentators' bewildered tributes to the supposed efficiency and discipline of McGovern's "organization," what came across on the television screen was the exact opposite: the spectacle of disorganized motion, of a shapeless horde pulled in various directions by countless crosscurrents, caught in a situation way above its depth - like a mob invading an abandoned fortress, running through its empty rooms, struggling frantically, humbly and resentfully to guess what the former occupants used them for.

The presence of an "organization" was noticeable only in the achievement of a single purpose: to take over - with no thought or plan for what came next (which indicates the leaders' motives). The crudeness of the *Putsch* was obvious: the "new politicians," particularly the younger ones - oozing insolence, smugness, hysterical rush, and big-executive postures - were intent on shoving the "old guard" out in order to demonstrate who's boss. Then - after they had obtained McGovern's nomination and every other tactical victory they wanted from a crowd of their semi-domesticated hippies - they turned to the old guard with innocent, ingratiating, frightened smiles, pleading for unity. One could almost hear the words: "We're really nice, friendly, regular fellows - if you toe the line. Now help, damn you!"

The petty jealousies, the mean little rivalries, the sneaky deceits, the cheap manipulations, the touchy egos, the jockeying for status, the scramble for power - and for ten minutes of free nationwide television time - were sparking and fuming all over the assembly of the crusaders who had promised to fight for openness, integrity and selfless brotherlove.

Who will now run the Democratic Party? No one and anyone. Is McGovern the leader or the captive of the hippies? Both and neither. Relying on the premises of the old politics, McGovern projected the assumption that he owns his following, can take it for granted, and can now extend his reach further. But the hippies lost no time in throwing their weight about, just to make it clear who owns whom. And *this* is the situation McGovern now proposes to carry from the Convention floor to a national arena.

The statists have miscalculated: the non-productive, the seekers of the unearned, are not a power base. Politicians may cash in - for a while - on a warfare among productive groups, setting business against labor, and labor against farmers, etc. But groups outside the economy - the non-producers, non-workers, non-contributors - have nothing to offer, and nothing to fight for. Looting is not a goal, beyond the range of a night or a week. The statists' last hope, the helplessly dependent, are just that: helplessly dependent - and lack the concept that holds a movement or a society together: tomorrow. There is a difference between a people and a mob, between a revolution and a riot. The power base that McGovern now teeters on is only a pile of buckshot to be scattered under his first step.

The defeated old leaders seemed to sense it. "*This* is a third party," said a television commentator. They sensed that, too - but they were unable fully to grasp that, within the span of four days, the Democratic Party had been replaced by so negligible an adversary.

The most pathetic and terrible moment of the Convention was its finale: the smiles on the faces of the defeated candidates when they lined up, on the podium, at McGovern's side, raising and waving their clasped hands in token of unity and victory, clinging to one another, desperately trying to believe, for a moment, what none of them believed. Senator Henry M. Jackson was the only one who had the good grace not to smile.

(To be continued.)

Ayn Rand

OBJECTIVIST CALENDAR

Beginning Thursday, September 14, Leonard Peikoff will offer a new twelve-lecture course: *Founders of Western Philosophy: Thales to Hume*.

The lectures present the ideas of the philosophers who shaped Western civilization, the meaning and practical consequences of these ideas, their unidentified influence on the minds of modern men - and a critical analysis, which will provide a defense against many of today's prevalent intellectual fallacies. The course concludes with a lecture on the Objectivist answer to selected philosophic problems.

Founders of Western Philosophy will be given every week, on Thursday evening at 7:30 P.M., from September 14 to December 14 (excluding October 26 and November 23), at the Hilton Hotel, 6th Ave. at 53rd St., New York City. Tuition is $60; registration is limited to 250 students. Brochures, including registration forms, are being sent to *The Ayn Rand Letter* subscribers in the New York City area. For further information, write to Dr. Peikoff at 315 W. 91st St., New York, N.Y. 10024.

In other cities, tapes of the lectures will be made available, to groups of ten persons or more, on a rental basis; inquiries should be addressed to Susan Ludel, c/o *TV Guide*, 1290 6th Ave., New York, N.Y. 10019. (Inquiries concerning *Modern Philosophy: Kant to the Present*, the other course in Dr. Peikoff's series on the history of philosophy, should also be addressed to Miss Ludel.)

B.W.

The Ayn Rand Letter, published fortnightly by The Ayn Rand Letter, Inc., 201 East 34th Street, New York, N.Y. 10016.
Contributing Editor: **Leonard Peikoff**; Subscription Director: **Elayne Kalberman**; Production Manager: **Barbara Weiss.**

Vol. 1, No. 24 August 28, 1972

A PREVIEW

Part III

There was one significant factor in the grotesque spectacle of the Democratic National Convention: McGovern's candidacy is a declaration of war on the American people by America's intellectuals.

Artificial pressure groups of drifters, publicity-chasers, and handout-seekers are not a political power base. The only social group behind (and ahead of) McGovern is the intellectuals. They are a group that holds a unique prerogative: the potential of being either the most productive or the most parasitical of all social groups.

The intellectuals serve as guides, as trend-setters, as the transmission belts or middlemen between philosophy and the culture. If they adopt a philosophy of reason - if their goal is the development of man's rational faculty and the pursuit of knowledge - they are a society's most productive and most powerful group, because their work provides the base and the integration of all other human activities. If the intellectuals are dominated by a philosophy of irrationalism, they become a society's unemployed and unemployable.

From the early nineteenth century on, American intellectuals - with very rare exceptions - were the humbly obedient followers of European philosophy, which had entered its age of decadence. Accepting its fundamentals, they were unable to deal with or even to grasp the nature of this country. Kant's irrationalism, Schopenhauer's pessimism, Mill's epistemological agnosticism, Hegel's worship of the absolute state were doctrines appropriate to a continent liberated from one form of tyranny and looking for another. Accustomed by tradition to exist under the protection and by the favor of some royal patron, European intellectuals were looking for a new, omnipotent master. There was no such opportunity in America.

The illiterate immigrants who came here looking for work, were not afraid to compete on a free market; the intellectuals were terrified by the free marketplace of ideas. Imbued with the notion that reason is impotent, they were not equipped to regard ideas as a value; ideas, to them, were means of deception and manipulation; a free country did not offer much of a market for such skills. Their terror was not economic, but metaphysical: this country contradicted their deepest assumptions. They felt as if they were in exile on another planet, like self-made refugees longing for a lost homeland.

Hence the unprecedented phenomenon of a society's intellectuals spitting defamations and a virulent hatred at their own country - now going so far as to proclaim moral sympathy with the enemy in an armed conflict. This kind of ferocious reverse-chauvinism comes from the panic of men unable and unwilling to accept the reality of the fact that a country such as theirs - a free, prosperous, brilliantly successful country, a living refutation of Kant, Hegel, etc. - is possible.

The breach between the American people and the intellectuals has been growing wider for years. The people were left without guidance, voice or conceptual understanding, with nothing but their common sense to protect them. The welfare state was not born by popular demand. It was an artificial, European (Bismarckian) contraption, grafted onto this country. It took all of the intellectuals' skill at deception to put it over on a generous, naively innocent people, who are barely beginning to understand its nature. The conflict is now approaching a climax.

The intellectuals' longing for an absolute state, which they would both obey and rule, is the modern expression of a court-favorite's policy: to bow and scrape before the ruler in public, to manipulate him behind the scenes in private, and to take out one's self-contempt on an awed populace that accepts any authority.

The grotesque inappropriateness of such a policy in America is almost self-evident; if it is not, the Democratic National Convention has made it so.

Observe the Convention's synthetic character. It was stacked against the people by means of a quota system that gave preference (and numerical advantage) to some groups over others - specifically, to the groups known to agree with the manipulators' views. Thereafter, the leaders' proclamations that this is a grass-roots movement sounded like the patronizing condescension of a British lady slumming with a basket of groceries. The intellectuals' attempted "populism" - expressed in such stage effects as the hippies' studiedly "informal" clothing and "folksy" chanting, or the Indian chief, in full regalia, making an announcement in an Indian dialect - has as much to do with the American people as the vaudevillians doing Cossack dances in a Russian restaurant have to do with the Russian people.

An element of second-handedness permeates the whole movement. McGovern's candidacy was no one's first choice. The first leader of the leftist attempt to take over the Democratic Party, in 1968, was Eugene McCarthy, a much more intellectual figure; he was followed by Robert Kennedy, who was stronger and more colorful. When George McGovern followed their lead and me-too-ed himself into that Presidential race, no one paid any attention to him. This year, he came forward as the only candidate available to the intellectuals, as the bargain-basement remnant of a fire sale, which the unemployed McCarthy-Kennedy staffs could afford. He was an ambitious man looking for some program - any program - to ride on; they were looking for a docile figurehead.

(The selection of the Democratic candidate for the Vice Presidency had the same hand-me-down quality. The choice and the subsequent dumping of Eagleton were a sickening demonstration of irresponsibility - and it would have been no better if he had been kept on the ticket. The final choice - R. Sargent Shriver, an aging, loud-mouthed professional altruist, who earned no distinction at the head of such disreputable projects as the Peace Corps and the War on Poverty - has nothing to his credit but the position of an in-law of the Kennedy family, on which he has been riding for years. Besides, he was the seventh choice of the kingmakers, after six others had turned them down.)

McGovern's candidacy demonstrates the truth of the warning given to careless shoppers: a bargain is a very costly purchase.

There is an old fable to the effect that a mountain was struggling to give birth to something - and, as the awed populace watched, expecting some unknown terror, after a gigantic struggle of storms, thunder, lightning, and earthshaking convulsions, the mountain gave birth to a mouse. This is an appropriate description of the context and the quality of McGovern's acceptance speech at the Democratic National Convention.

After two centuries of gigantic philosophical struggle - of noumenal Kantian earthquakes to annihilate man's reason - of dialectic Hegelian convulsions to obliterate his freedom - of treachery, deceit, manipulation, and global wars - of bloody sacrifices, and ringing promises of dedication to a better world, to loftier ideals, to purer honesty, to fresher thinking, to revolutionary change, to a new life - the standard-bearer of the intellectuals delivered a speech in which he declared that Richard Nixon is "the fundamental issue of this campaign."

No, not irrationality versus reason, not collectivism versus individualism, not altruism versus egoism, not even the redistribution of wealth or unilateral disarmament or the war in Vietnam - just Richard Nixon.

For many years, I had watched Republican candidates start out as uncompromising champions of free enterprise, then throw it all away and lose the election in a disgracefully mealy-mouthed, fence-straddling, cliché-ridden acceptance speech - e.g., Wendell L. Willkie and Thomas E. Dewey. Now, I had the bitter satisfaction of hearing a Democratic candidate outdo them all.

McGovern's speech was a flat, trite, uninspired and uninspiring combination of two elements: intellectually, the generalities of a cautious demagogue - emotionally, the banalities of a small-town evangelist. With the significant exception of a few passages, such as a promise to end the war in Vietnam by immediate surrender, any politician could have delivered that speech (though some of them have better ghost-writers).

The manner of delivery matched the content. The openness, the firmness, the tone of moral self-confidence that McGovern projected in the primaries, were gone. Instead, a nervous, resentful, frozen-faced man was reciting a prepared lesson, like a rancorously unfocused student. And the characteristic he had previously managed to hide, came flooding the television screen: hostility - an enormous, fundamental hostility as a dominant overtone.

About one-third of the speech, its opening, was devoted to a litany of acknowledgments and of overtures to his antagonists - in the manner of a Hollywood producer who, after stabbing people in the back, tries to appease them by placing their names on an endless list of screen credits. "My old and treasured friend and neighbor, Hubert Humphrey; that gracious and good man from Maine, Ed Muskie...George Wallace... whose courage in the face of pain and adversity is the mark of a man of boundless will." As to the acknowledgments: McGovern's political organization "gives dramatic proof to the power of love and to a faith that can move mountains." (They'll need it.)

The only time McGovern seemed to come to life was when he opened the ideological part of his speech by declaring Richard Nixon to be "the fundamental issue." There was a sudden brief sparkle in his eyes. It was a sparkle of pure malice. He quoted with relish Nixon's statement of ten years ago, made on the occasion of Nixon's defeat and retirement from politics. Whatever Nixon's faults, the courage of his unprecedented political comeback deserves respect. It takes the meanness of an unusually small soul to crack cheap jokes about it.

The rest of the speech sounded as if McGovern were running, not against Nixon, but against Lyndon Johnson and all his Democratic predecessors. "This is also the time to turn away from excessive preoccupation overseas to rebuilding our own nation....for 30 years we have been so absorbed with fear and danger from abroad that we have permitted our own house to fall into disarray." Who made "isolationism" - i.e., concern with the interests of our own nation - a pejorative term? Which Party created the bipartisan foreign policy that has been followed for the past thirty years?

"America cannot exist with most of our people working and paying taxes to support too many others mired in the demeaning, bureaucratic welfare system." Who created the welfare system? Which Party kept raising taxes and pouring money down the drain of larger and larger hordes of bureaucrats? Has McGovern forgotten the War on Poverty? (Surely his latest running mate ought to remember it.) Does he expect a President who inherited the Augean stables to clean them up in four years - while Congress, controlled by the Party that created them, keeps adding to the accumulations of . . . welfare schemes faster than they can be cleaned? And would the tax burden on the working people be diminished if the welfare parasites were placed in the non-demeaning position of holding a first mortgage - a guaranteed income - on the earnings of the workers?

In this first manifesto of the candidate who promised to redistribute wealth, that slogan and the words "guaranteed income" were never mentioned. They were switched into the promise of a guaranteed job. "This job guarantee will and must depend upon a reinvigorated private economy [?!], freed at last from the uncertainties and burdens of war. But it is our commitment that whatever employment the private sector does not provide, the Federal Government will either stimulate, or provide itself. [How? Somehow.] Whatever it takes, this country is going back to work." It will take everything you own, and still would fail. Work is not created by edict. See the experiences of other countries.

If an appeal to the worst in people could be called wistful, there was a kind of wistfulness in McGovern's attempts to disinter the rabble-rousing appeals of the New Deal era by blaming the rich for all of the country's problems. But there is a difference between crying: "They rob the people!" and crying: "They don't pay enough taxes!" The grandiose slogans of the New Deal era - such as "Princes of Privilege" and "Malefactors of Great Wealth" - had a certain plausibility for the ignorant, who could be led to believe that the rich grow rich by charging arbitrarily high prices and paying arbitrarily low wages. But McGovern's modernized version of the rich as scapegoats, with their "malefaction" consisting in "tax loopholes," is a ludicrous substitute: under today's general burden of taxation, people are more likely to feel sympathy for such "malefactors" rather than righteous indignation. Only a very limited mentality could still think that a heavier burden on the rich would relieve the burden on the poor (the experience of too many years has shown otherwise), or believe that tax loopholes are the cause of this country's troubles.

On the crucial issue of unilateral disarmament, the only reassurance McGovern offered was: "...I give you my sacred pledge that if I become President of the United States, America will keep its defenses alert and fully sufficient to meet any danger." The value and meaning of this pledge were made clear a few paragraphs later: "National security includes schools for our children as well as silos for our missiles, the health of our families as much as the size of our bombs, the safety of our streets and the condition of our cities and not just the engines of war. And if we some day choke on the pollution of our own air, there will be little consolation in leaving behind a dying continent ringed with steel."

And if some day a living but disarmed continent is overrun by Soviet thugs - who have declared their intention to do so, and have demonstrated it on other continents - there will be little consolation in leaving to them the best schools, the healthiest families, the safest streets, the cleanest cities, and the purest air achievable on earth.

Ask a soldier who has seen combat duty, whether "the health of his family" would help him if the size of his bombs proved inadequate. When you deal with the threat of force, nothing can answer it but armed force. When a bloody aggressor is loose in the world, a threatened nation must subordinate all expenditures to the requirements of national defense, which is the first and foremost duty of its government; only when defense is secure, can one begin to live or breathe. To simper, in the context of the possibility of a nuclear war, about schoolhouses for the kiddies, or free aspirin for Grandma, or new housing projects for Mom and Pop, or clean air for the birdies - to attempt to confuse and deceive the people by so cheap a collection of irrelevancies and so deadly a package deal - is such a ghastly performance that, for the honor of American history, I hope McGovern is merely stupid.

But this was not the worst passage in his speech. The worst came last - and it was directed at American history.

It was introduced by a measly little paragraph, of no great significance except as a cowardly attempt to straddle the fence between the intellectuals' hatred of America and the people's patriotism: "We are not content with things as they are. We reject the view of those who say: 'America - love it or leave it.' We reply: 'Let us change it so we can love it the more.'" (I do not know whether that last sentence necessarily has to turn your stomach; it turned mine.)

This was followed by: "And this is the time. It is the time for this land to become again a witness to the world for what is noble and just in human affairs. It is the time to live more with faith and less with fear...So join with me in this campaign, lend me your strength and your support, give me your voice - and together, we will call America home to <u>the founding ideals that nourished us in the beginning</u>." (Emphasis added.)

I do not know what level of contempt for truth, for history, for ideals, and for the American people one has to reach in order to utter that statement in that context. Perhaps the answer lies in a different question: What level of contempt for his own professed convictions does a man have to reach in order to declare that his goal is to return to the very ideals which his crusade is designed to destroy?

<u>America's founding ideal was the principle of individual rights</u>. Nothing more - and nothing less. The rest - everything that America achieved, everything she became, everything "noble and just," and heroic, and great, and unprecedented in human history - was the logical consequence of fidelity to that one principle. The first consequence was the principle of political freedom, i.e., an individual's freedom from physical compulsion, coercion or interference by the government. The next was the economic implementation of political freedom: the system of capitalism.

To claim that America's "founding ideals" were a totalitarian state in which man's life, work and property belong to the government, which may dispose of them as it pleases - a collectivist-altruist chain gang, in which some men labor to provide an unearned guaranteed income for others - is either a brazen attempt at the biggest Big Lie, or else the consequence of a profound conviction that nobody pays any attention to what one is saying.

In the concluding litany of the speech, McGovern introduced his campaign slogan: "Come home, America." Which home? The welfare home of the free and the white-flag home of the brave? Since the slogan did not refer to any recognizable home, it connoted only an abject acceptance of the slogan of the worst rabble in foreign countries: "Yankee, go home!"

"Come home," said McGovern, "to the affirmation that we have a dream."

"Dream," like "imagination," is a very dubious kind of attribute or compliment. Its value or disvalue depends on its relation to reality. Two kinds of dreams are observable in American history. One was the dream of men who came here seeking an opportunity to exercise their creative ability in full, unrestricted freedom; they were the men who built this country. The other was the dream of men who came here believing that America's streets were paved with gold and that a fortune was to be theirs without effort. _They_ are the men whose spokesman is George McGovern.

The silent, unadmitted, underground conflict between these two types of men has been growing for two centuries. Now it is in the open. The Democratic Convention has declared which side it chooses to uphold. That speech was its voice, and this is the meaning of what it is now offering the country.

To the great credit of the American people, the polls taken immediately after the Democratic Convention showed a significant drop in McGovern's popularity and a significant rise in Nixon's. At this writing, Nixon leads by the enormous figure of 26%.

I am not an admirer of President Nixon, as my readers know. But I urge every able-minded voter, of any race, creed, color, age, sex, or political party, to vote for Nixon - as a matter of national emergency. This is no longer an issue of choosing the lesser of two commensurate evils. The choice is between a flawed candidate representing Western civilization - and the perfect candidate of its primordial enemies.

If there were some campaign organization called "Anti-Nixonites for Nixon," it would name my position.

The worst thing said about Nixon is that he cannot be trusted, which is true: he cannot be trusted to save this country. But one thing is certain: McGovern _can_ be trusted to destroy it.

Ayn Rand

OBJECTIVIST CALENDAR

On Sunday, October 22, Ayn Rand will give a talk at The Ford Hall Forum in Boston. Time: 8 P.M. Place: Jordan Hall, 30 Gainsboro St. (Title not yet chosen.)

We have been asked to announce that Phillip J. Smith is offering an acting workshop, open to beginning and intermediate students. The workshop will run for 14 weeks beginning Tuesday, September 19. For further information, call Mr. Smith at (212) 724-1117 or write him at 315 W. 91st St., New York, N.Y. 10024.

Reminder: On Thursday, September 14, Leonard Peikoff will begin his course on _Founders of Western Philosophy: Thales to Hume_. Time: 7:30 P.M. Place: Hilton Hotel, 6th Ave. at 53rd St., New York City.

B.W.

The Ayn Rand Letter, published fortnightly by The Ayn Rand Letter, Inc., 201 East 34th Street, New York, N.Y. 10016.

Contributing Editor: **Leonard Peikoff**; Subscription Director: **Elayne Kalberman**; Production Manager: **Barbara Weiss.**

Vol. 1, No. 25 September 11, 1972

AN OPEN LETTER TO BORIS SPASSKY

Dear Comrade Spassky:

I have been watching with great interest your world chess championship match with Bobby Fischer. I am not a chess enthusiast or even a player, and know only the rudiments of the game. I am a novelist-philosopher by profession.

But I watched some of your games, reproduced play by play on television, and found them to be a fascinating demonstration of the enormous complexity of thought and planning required of a chess player - a demonstration of how many considerations he has to bear in mind, how many factors to integrate, how many contingencies to be prepared for, how far ahead to see and plan. It was obvious that you and your opponent had to have an unusual intellectual capacity.

Then I was struck by the realization that the game itself and the players' exercise of mental virtuosity are made possible by the metaphysical absolutism of the reality with which they deal. The game is ruled by the Law of Identity and its corollary, the Law of Causality. Each piece is what it is: a queen is a queen, a bishop is a bishop - and the actions each can perform are determined by its nature: a queen can move any distance in any open line, straight or diagonal, a bishop cannot; a rook can move from one side of the board to the other, a pawn cannot; etc. Their identities and the rules of their movements are immutable - and this enables the player's mind to devise a complex, long-range strategy, so that the game depends on nothing but the power of his (and his opponent's) ingenuity.

This led me to some questions that I should like to ask you.

1. Would you be able to play if, at a crucial moment - when, after hours of brain-wrenching effort, you had succeeded in cornering your opponent - an unknown, arbitrary power suddenly changed the rules of the game in his favor, allowing, say, his bishops to move like queens? You would not be able to continue? Yet out in the living world, this is the law of your country - and this is the condition in which your countrymen are expected, not to play, but to live.

2. Would you be able to play if the rules of chess were updated to conform to a dialectic reality, in which opposites merge - so that, at a crucial moment, your queen turned suddenly from White to Black, becoming the queen of your opponent, and then turned Gray, belonging to both of you? You would not be able to continue? Yet in the living world, this is the view of reality your countrymen are taught to accept, to absorb, and to live by.

3. Would you be able to play if you had to play by teamwork - i.e., if you were forbidden to think or act alone and had to play not with a group of advisers, but with

a team that determined your every move by vote? Since, as champion, you would be the best mind among them, how much time and effort would you have to spend persuading the team that your strategy is the best? Would you be likely to succeed? And what would you do if some pragmatist, range-of-the-moment mentalities voted to grab an opponent's knight at the price of a checkmate to you three moves later? You would not be able to continue? Yet in the living world, this is the theoretical ideal of your country, and this is the method by which it proposes to deal (someday) with scientific research, industrial production, and every other kind of activity required for man's survival.

4. Would you be able to play if the cumbersome mechanism of teamwork were streamlined, and your moves were dictated simply by a man standing behind you, with a gun pressed to your back - a man who would not explain or argue, his gun being his only argument and sole qualification? You would not be able to start, let alone continue, playing? Yet in the living world, this is the practical policy under which men live - and die - in your country.

5. Would you be able to play - or to enjoy the professional understanding, interest and acclaim of an International Chess Federation - if the rules of the game were splintered, and you played by "proletarian" rules while your opponent played by "bourgeois" rules? Would you say that such "polyrulism" is more preposterous than polylogism? Yet in the living world, your country professes to seek global harmony and understanding, while proclaiming that she follows "proletarian" logic and that others follow "bourgeois" logic, or "Aryan" logic, or "third-world" logic, etc.

6. Would you be able to play if the rules of the game remained as they are at present, with one exception: that the pawns were declared to be the most valuable and non-expendable pieces (since they may symbolize the masses) which had to be protected at the price of sacrificing the more efficacious pieces (the individuals)? You might claim a draw on the answer to this one - since it is not only your country, but the whole living world that accepts this sort of rule in morality.

7. Would you care to play, if the rules of the game remained unchanged, but the distribution of rewards were altered in accordance with egalitarian principles: if the prizes, the honors, the fame were given not to the winner, but to the loser - if winning were regarded as a symptom of selfishness, and the winner were penalized for the crime of possessing a superior intelligence, the penalty consisting in suspension for a year, in order to give others a chance? Would you and your opponent try playing not to win, but to lose? What would this do to your mind?

You do not have to answer me, Comrade. You are not free to speak or even to think of such questions - and I know the answers. No, you would not be able to play under any of the conditions listed above. It is to escape this category of phenomena that you fled into the world of chess.

Oh yes, Comrade, chess is an escape - an escape from reality. It is an "out," a kind of "make-work" for a man of higher than average intelligence who was afraid to live, but could not leave his mind unemployed and devoted it to a placebo - thus surrendering to others the living world he had rejected as too hard to understand.

Please do not take this to mean that I object to games as such: games are an important part of man's life, they provide a necessary rest, and chess may do so for men who live under the constant pressure of purposeful work. Besides, some games - such as sports contests, for instance - offer us an opportunity to see certain human skills developed to a level of perfection. But what would you think of a world champion runner who, in real life, moved about in a wheelchair? Or of a champion high jumper who crawled about on all fours? You, the chess professionals, are taken as exponents of the most precious of human skills: intellectual power - yet that power deserts you beyond the confines of the sixty-four squares of a chessboard, leaving you confused, anxious, and helplessly unfocused. Because, you see, the chessboard is not a training ground, but a substitute for reality.

A gifted, precocious youth often finds himself bewildered by the world: it is people that he cannot understand, it is their inexplicable, contradictory, messy behavior that frightens him. The enemy he rightly senses, but does not choose to fight, is human irrationality. He withdraws, gives up, and runs, looking for some sanctuary where his mind would be appreciated - and he falls into the booby trap of chess.

You, the chess professionals, live in a special world - a safe, protected, orderly world, in which all the great, fundamental principles of existence are so firmly established and obeyed that you do not even have to be aware of them. (They are the principles involved in my seven questions.) You do not know that these principles are the preconditions of your game - and you do not have to recognize them when you encounter them, or their breach, in reality. In your world, you do not have to be concerned with them: all you have to do is think.

The process of thinking is man's basic means of survival. The pleasure of performing this process successfully - of experiencing the efficacy of one's own mind - is the most profound pleasure possible to men, and it is their deepest need, on any level of intelligence, great or small. So one can understand what attracts you to chess: you believe that you have found a world in which all irrelevant obstacles have been eliminated, and nothing matters but the pure, triumphant exercise of your mind's power. But have you, Comrade?

Unlike algebra, chess does not represent the abstraction - the basic pattern - of mental effort; it represents the opposite: it focuses mental effort on a set of concretes, and demands such complex calculations that a mind has no room for anything else. By creating an illusion of action and struggle, chess reduces the professional player's mind to an uncritical, unvaluing passivity toward life. Chess removes the motor of intellectual effort - the question "What for?" - and leaves a somewhat frightening phenomenon: intellectual effort devoid of purpose.

If - for any number of reasons, psychological or existential - a man comes to believe that the living world is closed to him, that he has nothing to seek or to achieve, that no action is possible, then chess becomes his antidote, the means of drugging his own rebellious mind that refuses fully to believe it and to stand still. This, Comrade, is the reason why chess has always been so popular in your country, before and since its present regime - and why there have not been many American masters. You see, in this country, men are still free to act.

Because the rulers of your country have proclaimed this championship match to be an ideological issue, a contest between Russia and America, I am rooting for Bobby to win - and so are all my friends. The reason why this match has aroused an unprecedented interest in our country is the longstanding frustration and indignation of the American people at your country's policy of attacks, provocations, and hooligan insolence - and at our own government's overtolerant, overcourteous patience. There is a widespread desire in our country to see Soviet Russia beaten in any way, shape or form, and - since we are all sick and tired of the global clashes among the faceless, anonymous masses of collectives - the almost medieval drama of two individual knights fighting the battle of good against evil, appeals to us symbolically. (But this, of course, is only a symbol; you are not necessarily the voluntary defender of evil - for all we know, you might be as much its victim as the rest of the world.)

Bobby Fischer's behavior, however, mars the symbolism - but it is a clear example of the clash between a chess expert's mind, and reality. This confident, disciplined, obviously brilliant player falls to pieces when he has to deal with the real world. He throws tantrums like a child, breaks agreements, makes arbitrary demands, and indulges in the kind of whim-worship one touch of which in the playing of chess would disqualify him for a high-school tournament. Thus he brings to the real world the very evil that made him escape it: irrationality. A man who is afraid to sign a letter, who fears any firm commitment, who seeks the guidance of the arbitrary edicts of a mystic sect in order to learn how to live his life - is not a great, confident mind, but a tragically helpless victim, torn by acute anxiety and, perhaps, by a sense of treason to what might have been a great potential.

But, you may wish to say, the principles of reason are not applicable beyond the limit of a chessboard, they are merely a human invention, they are impotent against the chaos outside, they have no chance in the real world. If this were true, none of us would have survived nor even been born, because the human species would have perished long ago. If, under irrational rules, like the ones I listed above, men could not even play a game, how could they live? It is not reason, but irrationality that is a human invention - or, rather, a default.

Nature (reality) is just as absolutist as chess, and her rules (laws) are just as immutable (more so) - but her rules and their applications are much, much more complex, and have to be discovered by man. And just as a man may memorize the rules of chess, but has to use his own mind in order to apply them, i.e., in order to play well - so each man has to use his own mind in order to apply the rules of nature, i.e., in order to live successfully. A long time ago, the grandmaster of all grandmasters gave us the basic principles of the method by which one discovers the rules of nature and of life. His name was Aristotle.

Would you have wanted to escape into chess, if you lived in a society based on Aristotelian principles? It would be a country where the rules were objective, firm and clear, where you could use the power of your mind to its fullest extent, on any scale you wished, where you would gain rewards for your achievements, and men who chose to be irrational would not have the power to stop you nor to harm anyone but themselves. Such a social system could not be devised, you say? But it *was* devised, and it came close to full existence - only, the mentalities whose level was playing jacks or craps, the men with the gun and their witch doctors, did not want mankind to know it. It was called *Capitalism*.

But on this issue, Comrade, you may claim a draw: your country does not know the meaning of that word - and, today, most people in our country do not know it, either.

Sincerely,

Ayn Rand

OBJECTIVIST CALENDAR

Starting on October 6, the tape lectures of Leonard Peikoff's course, *Modern Philosophy: Kant to the Present*, will be given in Phoenix, Arizona. For further information, contact Dennis Wilson at (602) 956-7678 (evenings).

B.W.

The Ayn Rand Letter, published fortnightly by The Ayn Rand Letter, Inc., 183 Madison Avenue, New York, N.Y. 10016.

Contributing Editor: **Leonard Peikoff**; Subscription Director: **Elayne Kalberman**; Production Manager: **Barbara Weiss.**

Vol. 1, No. 26 September 25, 1972

HOW TO READ (AND NOT TO WRITE)

"He was doling his sentences out with cautious slowness, balancing himself between word and intonation to hit the right degree of semi-clarity. He wanted her to understand, but he did not want her to understand fully, explicitly, down to the root - since the essence of that modern language, which he had learned to speak expertly, was never to let oneself or others understand anything down to the root." (Atlas Shrugged.)

Today, this is the dominant method of communication in public speaking and writing, particularly on the subject of politics. A recent editorial in The New York Times is a valuable specimen of that method - an unusually clear example of the art of unclarity.

"The Fourth of July is a good time to remind ourselves that there is urgent necessity for the nation's intellectual and political leaders to provide moral guidance at a time when so many people feel that the nation has lost its way..." said the Times, concluding an editorial, on July 4, 1972.

This statement is incontrovertibly true, and one would be tempted to say "amen" - but the rest of the editorial is a remarkable example of the reasons why the nation has lost its way (though not in the sense the editorial intended).

The most important issue confronting us today, the editorial declares, is "how to prevent powerful special interests from frustrating the democratic process." No definitions are given, but the context suggests that "special interests" means pressure groups. This is not exactly a fundamental issue, but this is what the editorial regards as an urgent problem. To solve a problem, one must identify and correct or eliminate its causes; therefore, one would expect the editorial writer to mention what caused the emergence of pressure groups. But he does not. He treats the subject as if pressure groups were facts of nature or irreducible primaries.

It is interesting to wonder what went on in that writer's mind in the space between two paragraphs - because the editorial continues by attacking those who might name the unnamed causes he did not find it necessary to mention:

"That issue is so difficult to solve because all the clear, simple extremes are unworkable. Given modern industrial technologies, this country cannot go back to the highly atomistic, competitive model of the early nineteenth century - even if it were willing to accept the workings of the marketplace as the arbiter of all social values and outcomes. But the experience of totalitarian and democratic societies alike suggests that mere substitution of the power of big government for that of big business and the marketplace is no solution."

As an exercise in intellectual precision, see how many things you can list as wrong in that one little paragraph. I shall indicate some of them (omitting the paragraph's first sentence, which I shall take up later).

If a euphemism is an inoffensive way of identifying an offensive fact, then "highly atomistic, competitive model" is an anti-euphemism, i.e., an offensive way of identifying an inoffensive (or great and noble) fact - in this case, capitalism. "Competitive" is a definition by nonessentials; "atomistic" is worse. Capitalism involves competition as one of its proper consequences, not as its essential or defining attribute. "Atomistic" is usually intended to imply "scattered, broken up, disintegrated." Capitalism is the system that made productive cooperation possible among men, on a large scale - a _voluntary_ cooperation that raised everyone's standard of living - as the nineteenth century has demonstrated. So "atomistic" is an anti-euphemism, standing for "free, independent, individualistic." If the editorial's sentence were intended to be fully understood, it would read: "this country cannot go back to the free, individualistic, private-property system of capitalism."

Now why would "modern industrial technologies" make a return to capitalism impossible? No answer is given. It is fashionable to treat technology as a dark mystery, as a kind of black magic beyond the layman's power to understand - so the phrase is just thrown in, as an ineffable threat. But observe that modern industrial technology is a product of capitalism and, today, of the private sector of the U.S. economy, which is still the freest economy on earth - observe the abysmal failure of the world's most controlled economy, Soviet Russia, to approach America's technological achievements - observe the correlation, in all the mixed economies, between the degree of a country's freedom and the degree of its technological development - and you will have grounds to suspect that that phrase was thrown in to prevent you from realizing that modern industrial technology (if it is to survive) makes statism, not capitalism, impossible.

The clause: "...even if it [this country] were willing to accept the workings of the marketplace as the arbiter of all social values and outcomes," is an attack on a straw man. No advocate of capitalism ever held the workings of the marketplace as the arbiter of _all_ social values and outcomes - only of the _economic_ ones, i.e., those pertaining to production and trade. In a free marketplace, these values and outcomes are determined by a free, general, "democratic" vote - by the sales, purchases and choices of every individual. And - as one indication of the fact that, under capitalism, there are social values outside the power of the marketplace - each individual votes only on those matters which he is qualified to judge: on his own preferences, interests and needs. The paramount social value he has no power to encroach upon is: the rights of others. He cannot substitute his vote and judgment for theirs; he cannot declare himself to be "the voice of the people" and leave the people disenfranchised.

Is this what our country would be unwilling to accept?

The last sentence of the quoted paragraph resorts to the shabby old gimmick of equating opposites by substituting nonessentials for their essential characteristics. In this case, the defacing acid, obliterating differences, is the attribute of "bigness." If a reader is to be made to feel that businessmen and dictators are interchangeably equal villains, he must be pushed to forget that a _big_ productive genius, e.g., Henry Ford, Sr., and a _big_ killer, e.g., Stalin, are not the same thing - and that the difference between a totalitarian and a free society does not consist in substituting Stalin for Henry Ford, Sr. (For a discussion of the difference between economic and political power, see "America's Persecuted Minority: Big Business" in my book _Capitalism: The Unknown Ideal_.)

When the baser kind of politician resorts to that gimmick, he is counting on the ugliest emotion of lesser people: envy - and if they confuse "bigness" with "greatness," it serves his purpose. But why would a reputable newspaper do it?

The editorial's next paragraph gives a clue to the answer: "The crucial task facing the United States and other democratic societies is to find workable answers between the extremes - to limit concentrations of corporate power without undermining the efficiency of business; to permit the market to allocate resources insofar as possible - but also to use adequate resources to achieve socially desirable purposes in response to the democratically exercised choices of the society."

Who is to _permit_ the market to allocate resources? Whose resources? What are "socially desirable purposes"? Who desires them - and at whose expense? Since the greatest, the fundamental, factor ("resource") of production is human intelligence, is it to be disposed of by the "choices of the society"?

No explicit answers are given. But observe the workings of the unnamed in the above quotation. The two "extremes" are capitalism (i.e., freedom) and totalitarianism (i.e., dictatorship). The "workable answers" are to be sought in the middle, in a combination of these two. Observe the method suggested. Business efficiency must not be undermined (which is an implicit admission that this efficiency depends on freedom) - but government must control the development and limit the growth of business. The market must be kept free "insofar as possible" - but if "society" desires some particular "purpose," freedom becomes impossible. Which of the two "extremes" is violated and which is given priority in this suggested method?

So it turns out that the editorial writer is advocating the very thing which he falsely ascribed to capitalism: he is suggesting that the marketplace _should be made_ "the arbiter of all social values and outcomes" - not, however, the clean, _economic_ marketplace, but the corrupt, _political_ one. (An intrusion of political power, i.e., of force, into the market is corrupt and corrupting, since it introduces an opportunity for legalized looting.) He is using the word "democratic" in its original meaning, i.e., unlimited majority rule, and he is urging us to accept a social system in which one's work, one's property, one's mind, and one's life are at the mercy of any gang that may muster the vote of a majority at any moment for any purpose.

If _this_ is a society's system, no power on earth can prevent men from ganging up on one another in self-defense - i.e., from forming _pressure groups_.

"There is no magic formula for reconciling those aims," the editorial continues. "Instead, this nation and all others can only seek to diffuse power by such measures as more effectively employing the antitrust laws..." etc.

After raising so momentous a problem as the attempt to mix freedom and dictatorship (an attempt which has brought us where we are today) - after demonstrating (between the lines) that these two extremes cannot mix and that there is, indeed, no magic formula for reconciling opposites or for having your cake and eating it, too - the editorial proceeds to suggest such remedies as: the miserably false, decrepit notion of persecutions by antitrust laws; a "sense of mission" in regulatory agencies; "new types of regulatory institutions" on the order of "public-interest crusaders" with an "'ombudsman' role both within and outside government" (i.e., the most vicious of pressure groups: quasi-governmental private groups); the abolition of "the illegal financing of political campaigns by great corporations or labor unions"; etc., etc. (with not a word about how to "diffuse" the other power in that mixture, the power of the government).

This is offered as _moral_ guidance for a nation that has lost its way.

If I were using that editorial for an actual test of reading comprehension, I would give A+ to anyone who would discover why the word "moral" is introduced at the conclusion of a piece that does not discuss morality. If you look past the modern verbiage, you will find, smuggled between the lines, the thing which the editorial writer wants you "to understand, but not to understand fully, explicitly, down to the root": _altruism_. It is not any practical considerations, not "modern industrial technologies," or "the workings of the marketplace," or economics, or politics, or reality, that make it impossible for us to return to capitalism - to freedom, progress, abundance - it is the altruist moral code, which the editorial is struggling to preserve in the form of "socially desirable purposes" that supersede individual rights. The "workable answer" it exhorts us to seek, is how to combine capitalism with the creed of self-sacrifice. Brother, it can't be done. I have been saying it for years. You may take it now from the horse's mouth - from an editorial written, apparently, in the horse's unguarded moment.

It is futile to bemoan this country's moral decadence or blame politicians for the "credibility gap" - if this is the kind of guidance the nation is given by its intellectual leaders. Credibility? It is almost a miracle that the nation has managed to preserve some unconquerable element of decency and common sense, instead of collapsing altogether into a sewer of amoral, anti-intellectual cynicism and skepticism - under a cultural barrage of that kind.

Politicians are not the cause of a culture's trend, only its consequence. They get their notions from the cultural atmosphere, particularly from newspapers, magazines and TV commentaries; they speak as these media teach them to speak. Who teaches the media?

And now we come down to the root: of all our institutions, it is the universities that are primarily responsible for this country losing its way - and of all the university departments, it is the departments of philosophy.

If you want to see what makes things such as that editorial possible, you will find the hoofprints of Pragmatism in two key sentences: "That issue is so difficult to solve because all the clear, simple extremes are unworkable," and: "There is no magic formula for reconciling those aims."

By "clear, simple extremes," modern intellectuals mean any rational theory, any consistent system, any conceptual integration, any precise definition, any firm principle. Pragmatists do not mean that no such theory, system or principle has yet been discovered (and that we should look for one), but that none is possible. Epistemologically, their dogmatic agnosticism holds, as an absolute, that _a principle is false because it is a principle_ - that conceptual integration (i.e., thinking) is impractical or "simplistic" - that an idea which is clear and simple is necessarily "extreme and unworkable." Along with Kant, their philosophic forefather, the pragmatists claim, in effect: "If you perceive it, it cannot be real," and: "If you conceive of it, it cannot be true."

What, then, is left to man? The sensation, the wish, the whim, the range and the concrete of the moment. Since no solution to any problem is possible, anyone's suggestion, guess or edict is as valid as anyone else's - provided it is narrow enough.

To give you an example: if a building were threatened with collapse and you declared that the crumbling foundation has to be rebuilt, a pragmatist would answer that your solution is too abstract, extreme, unprovable, and that immediate priority must be given to the need of putting ornaments on the balcony railings, because it would make the tenants feel better.

There was a time when a man would not utter arguments of this sort, for fear of being rightly considered a fool. Today, Pragmatism has not merely given him permission to do it and liberated him from the necessity of thought, but has elevated his mental default into an intellectual virtue, has given him the right to dismiss thinkers (or construction engineers) as naive, and has endowed him with that typically modern quality: the arrogance of the concrete-bound, who takes pride in not seeing the forest fire, or the forest, or the trees, while he is studying one inch of bark on a rotted tree stump.

Like all of Kant's progeny, modern philosophy has a single goal: the defeat of reason. The degree to which such philosophers succeed is the degree to which men and nations lose their way in a deepening night of insolvable problems.

The human products of that philosophy - on all levels of today's society - are the crude skeptics and another, more offensive breed: the professional "seeker of truth," who hopes to God he'll never find it.

If you meet one of those (and they are ubiquitous), you will find the answer to his problems - and to the dilemmas of modern philosophy - in another passage from Atlas Shrugged: "Do you cry that you find no answers? By what means did you hope to find them? You reject your tool of perception - your mind - then complain that the universe is a mystery. You discard your key, then wail that all doors are locked against you. You start out in pursuit of the irrational, then damn existence for making no sense."

Ayn Rand

OBJECTIVIST CALENDAR

Starting on October 1, the tape lectures of Leonard Peikoff's course, Modern Philosophy: Kant to the Present, will be given in Boston. For further information, contact Erich Veyhl at (617) 495-3248 (days) or (617) 492-4219 (evenings).

In mid-October, the office of The Ayn Rand Letter will move to a new address: 183 Madison Avenue (40 East 34th Street), New York, N.Y. 10016.

The title of Ayn Rand's talk at The Ford Hall Forum in Boston, on October 22, will be: "A Nation's Unity."

B.W.

The Ayn Rand Letter, published fortnightly by The Ayn Rand Letter, Inc., 183 Madison Avenue, New York, N.Y. 10016.

Contributing Editor: **Leonard Peikoff**; Subscription Director: **Elayne Kalberman**; Production Manager: **Barbara Weiss.**

Vol. II, No. 1 October 9, 1972

A NATION'S UNITY

Every four years, at about this time, we begin to hear louder and louder appeals for national unity. We hear them between Presidential elections as well - particularly when something is about to be put over on us - though they are uttered in a more perfunctory manner.

Observe, however, that in recent years it has become fashionable to disparage unity, between elections, and to praise dissent as a kind of moral or patriotic duty. But the pattern of a Presidential election remains the same: first, there is a campaign in which the candidates denounce each other and seem to appeal to some sort of unstated principles; then, when the election is over, the appeals become, in effect: now let's forget all about principles - national unity comes first.

This is, therefore, an appropriate time to examine the issue of national unity and to ask certain questions: Is such unity necessary? Is it possible? What makes it possible? What is the alternative? What are the consequences? The present election campaign offers many clues to the answers.

As in the case of many other errors or evils, today's appeals for national unity are based on a perverted element of truth. It is true that, in order to exist as a nation, the large number of men who live in the same geographical area and deal with one another, must agree on some fundamental principle(s). And more: any two men who choose to deal with each other must have some sort of basic agreement, at least for the duration of their joint action. If you joined forces with another man in order to lift a heavy boulder, and you strained to lift it while he strained to push it down, nothing would come of both your efforts but failure, frustration, and - if the issue were important enough to both of you - the recourse to blows and mutual extermination.

The fact that in case of disagreement men can resort to physical force, i.e., to human destruction, is the reason why every human association is based on some sort of agreement, which is implemented by certain rules of conduct. An agreement, in this context, does not necessarily mean a common purpose: you may make an agreement with a neighbor that you will not attack him so long as he does not attack you - and if both of you abide by it, you are free to go your own ways and, perhaps, never see each other again. The fundamental agreement which is required of a nation is _an agreement on the rules of peaceful coexistence_. A territory inhabited by men engaged in perpetual conflicts, chronic fighting, physical violence, and general hatred of all for all, is not a nation nor a country, but a bloody mess. Internal peace and some sort of harmony are the precondition of the existence of a nation.

The big questions, however, are: Peace - at what price? Harmony - on what terms? Agreement - about what? And more: Can such terms and agreements be chosen arbitrarily? Can men choose any terms and make them work simply by wishing them to do so? Or are there objective factors which necessitate certain principles of human association, and defeat all others? In sum, the fundamental social question is: What principles should men agree upon in order to live and deal with one another?

The best way to answer questions of this kind is to start not with an enormous, floating abstraction, such as "society as a whole," but with one member of society, the one you know best: yourself. Ask yourself: What rules of conduct would you be able and willing to accept in order to deal with your neighbors?

Let us say you are a young man who knows that he must work in order to support his life. You have a good job, a small family, and a home in the suburbs. Since you do not intend to stagnate, you maintain a certain financial and intellectual balance between the present and the future; you budget your money and your time: your money, to provide for your present needs and to improve your standard of living, e.g., to pay off the mortgage on your home - your time, to do your present job well and to study in order to qualify for a better one. You like some of your neighbors, and you dislike others, but you are not afraid of any of them: they are not a threat to you, nor you to them.

This is the normal pattern of your life and you take it for granted, as if it were a fact of nature. But it is not. It took thousands and thousands of years to achieve it. Let us see what it depends on.

Suppose this country's political system was changed: it was decided that the affairs of each community are to be determined at a monthly meeting of all its citizens, by a general, democratic vote, and that the rule of the majority is absolute, without limits or appeal. It would mean that you could be thrown out of your home and out of the community - if the majority so voted. It would mean that you could be sentenced to die - if, not liking your manners or your _ideas_, the majority so voted. This is not fantasy. This was the social system of many Greek city-states: pure democracy, unlimited majority rule. Would you agree to accept it in the name of communal unity?

No? Then would you agree to accept it on a much larger scale and by remote control?

Suppose it was decided (but never announced openly and explicitly) that the nation holds the absolute power of a Greek city-state. But since one cannot convene an entire nation to a monthly meeting, the people are compressed into groups representing various interests - and the government acts as arbiter and ruler, who listens to their clashing demands and enforces the will of those it deems to be representative of the public interest. These groups are not elected, they are formed informally, "spontaneously," "democratically," anyone is free to form them - and to clamor demands for anything.

How will you adjust to it? First, there is a business lobby, but you don't mind it, it helps your boss. Then, there is a labor lobby, but you don't mind it, it helps _you_. Then, there is a farm lobby, but you don't notice it, it's too remote from your activities. Then, a neighbor on the next block forms a group demanding better roads - and two blocks further, a woman forms a group demanding better schools. Another group demands free lunches for all schoolchildren - and a rival group demands free textbooks. Your windows are smashed, one night, by the group of the local juvenile delinquent, or "problem-adolescent": they shout "nonnegotiable demands," which you cannot quite untangle, but you gather it has something to do with "Youth Power." The residents of the local Old Folks' Home form a group, demanding "Senior-Citizen Power." The old-maid file-clerk at the office, whom you can't stand because she can't keep the files straight, is given a promotion - with the help of a group that demands the "Liberation of Women." You have no time to keep track of it all, you notice only that your taxes keep rising and rising - and your money keeps buying less and less.

You are late getting to the office, one morning, because the local welfare-recipients' group lies stretched out across the highway, demanding a yearly income greater than half of yours; you slam on the brakes just in time to avoid running over the group's leader, a lady known as "Fatso," who has twelve children and no visible husband. You had planned to have three children, but you decide to wait a little for that third one - you cannot afford him. A long-haired young man forms a group to forbid anyone to have more than two children - and a short-haired young woman forms a group to forbid abortions and the use of contraceptives. There's a group that demands the display of sexual intercourse on the screen, and another group that demands censorship of all movies above the intellectual level of a six-year-old - so you give up going to the movies.

You fall behind in your mortgage payments, but your property taxes keep rising and rising. You consider giving up your house and renting one in a new development, five miles away. But the local bird-watcher's group is suing the developer, demanding that the land he cleared be turned into a public park. Your boss has promised you a promotion, the job of managing the new branch factory he is planning to build in your district. But he does not build it: the lady who used to head the local poetry club, now has a group that demands the preservation of the beautiful swamp he was going to fill.

Then an educational group decrees that you cannot send your children to the local school, which so much of your property taxes has gone to pay for, so your children are bused to a distant town - a daily trip of two hours going there and another two hours coming back. This, you are told, will achieve racial integration. You had never thought of it before, but you become race conscious and try to untangle your own ancestry. You find it so mixed that you cannot qualify for any of the groups into which your community is splitting: the Afro-Americans, the Chicano-Americans, the Italo-Americans, the Jewish-Americans, the Irish-Americans, etc. And you - you are just a mongrel American, a title of which you would have been proud at one time, but which is becoming dangerous. If you lose your job, there will be no preferential quota to help you get another one, and no way of knowing how many "ethnic" applicants will be pushed ahead of you; there will be no preferential quota for your son's admission to a college, when the time comes. You are alone, unprotected, defenseless - and the only reason you know that you are living in a human society and not on a desert island is the fact that your taxes keep rising and rising.

How do you adjust, to whom, and to what? The first thing to go is your future. You can barely keep up with your current expenses. You have no way to plan ahead: if you try to save, you do not know which demands of which groups will eat up your savings in the form of new taxes and higher prices. Why study to develop your skills? You do not know whether you will ever get a better job, or what new obstacles will spring up overnight, or whether there will be anyone left to hire you. You used to plan your course in terms of years; the range of your concern shrinks to one year, then to one month, and then to next payday: you can see nothing beyond but a black void.

Strange things happen to a man without a future. You begin to act like the type of man you had once despised: you become sloppy at your job, you can barely summon the effort just to get by; you get drunk too often; you buy a luxurious lawn mower, which you have no time to use - and you quarrel with your wife over the expensive cut of lamb chops she bought for dinner. And when you hear a seedy lecturer, at a group meeting, declare that the Horatio Alger stories are a myth, that a man cannot rise by individual effort and ability, you applaud defiantly and belligerently.

Oh yes, you have joined a group; you have joined several groups. You do not know exactly what they stand for, but they talk of community action and mutual protection, and they denounce other groups, you do not know clearly which ones or why. You had tried to get it clear, but gave up. Every time you read a newspaper or listen to the snarling voices on television, things grow murkier.

You do not know by what steps your attitude toward your neighbors has changed. You have begun to watch them suspiciously. Whenever you see two of them in a heated discussion, or observe several cars parked in front of a house, you feel a touch of anxiety: you do not know what they might be up to, what new group might be formed, and what it will do to you. You learn to feel fear. You are afraid of your neighbors - of any human being. You are afraid to speak. You smile, and you agree with everyone you meet. You are afraid to think. One day, you discover that what you feel for men is hatred.

In rare moments, you wonder what has happened to your neighbors. They were decent people once - you remember vaguely - they did not act like wild packs scrambling to get at one another's throats (and pockets). You do not know how many of them are wondering the same thing about you. You know only that there was a time when the local bird watcher and the "problem-adolescent" and the poetry-club ladies and Ms. Fatso were of no danger to anyone, but now they are. Why were they better in the past? If someone answered: "*Because they did not have a gun*" - you would not understand it.

You have come to believe that people are no good and that force is the only practical way to deal with them, since reason - they all tell you - has failed. You cannot cope with the enormous complexity of an entire nation's problems; you have no way of knowing, you conclude, who is right or wrong - so let some groups force others and re-establish order. No one has explained to you that the Golden Rule applies to politics: if certain conditions of social existence are unacceptable and unbearable to *you*, you cannot expect others to accept them and make them work - and what these conditions do to you, they do to "society as a whole."

Do *you* agree to accept a social system of this kind?

It is, of course, the system under which we are living today, but which we have never chosen. It is important to consider it now because, in the coming Presidential election, one of the candidates is asking us to agree and - in the name of national unity - explicitly to accept the principle that our lives belong to the State.

(To be continued.)

Ayn Rand

OBJECTIVIST CALENDAR

The following starting dates have been scheduled for the tape lectures of Leonard Peikoff's course, *Founders of Western Philosophy: Thales to Hume*. Lafayette, Ind., Nov. 4 (contact Ken MacKenzie, 317-463-3646); Hartford, Conn., Nov. 7 (Brian Bambrough, 203-549-5840); Washington, D.C., Nov. 15 (Betty Clifford, 301-585-7703, eves.); Winnipeg, Canada, Nov. 16 (Ellen Moore, 205-253-1630).

B.W.

The Ayn Rand Letter, published fortnightly by The Ayn Rand Letter, Inc., 183 Madison Avenue, New York, N.Y. 10016.

Contributing Editor: **Leonard Peikoff**; Subscription Director: **Elayne Kalberman**; Production Manager: **Barbara Weiss.**

Vol. II, No. 2 October 23, 1972

A NATION'S UNITY

Part II

Among many other issues which he exemplifies, George McGovern offers us a clear example of the fact that, paradoxically enough, statism is incompatible with national unity - if by "unity" we mean men's peaceful coexistence.

Supposing, for a moment, that one wanted to "unite" with McGovern and support his programs - which McGovern and which programs would one join, since both keep switching every few weeks? It is bad enough if a President changes his policies while in office, as Mr. Nixon did. But a man who cannot hold a steady set of convictions for the three months of an election campaign, makes Mr. Nixon look like the Rock of Gibraltar.

At the moment, McGovern is trying to justify himself by declaring, in television advertisements, that a man should not be afraid to change his mind. True enough - but not as a chronic policy; and not if he is a Presidential candidate who demands an unprecedented power: the total power to dispose of our incomes and, therefore, of our lives. Yes, he is free to change his mind, but what does this do to the minds of his followers? Obviously, what he expects of them is not the agreement, the unity, that comes from reasoned convictions, but *faith* in him, i.e., unthinking obedience.

This is a simple example of the connection between man's mind and his rights. Those who refuse to recognize individual rights are necessarily obliged to seek to destroy individual intelligence. How else would they obtain unthinking obedience? The goose-stepping automatons of Nazi Germany and Soviet Russia are not the exponents of a nation's unity, but of a nation's death.

There are two crucial problems in human relationships, and the issue of national unity depends on their proper solution: the factor of force and the factor of time. The first involves the realm of criminals and despots; the second involves the realm of man's mind.

As a being of rational - i.e., *conceptual* - consciousness, man is unable to live like an animal, on the range of the immediate moment. He is unable to live exclusively in the present. Some projection of the future - no matter how primitive - is a necessity of his mental and physical survival. (If you point to the hippies, with their "*Now*" slogans, as evidence to the contrary, I shall claim them as evidence to support my contention: observe their epidemic of drug addiction, which is an attempt to escape from an unbearable mental state.)

Man lives by means of projecting the future, i.e., projecting goals and taking the actions necessary to achieve them. This is a process enacted in time, and it requires the conviction that the goal will remain achievable. If a primitive savage spends days or months hewing a stone weapon, it is because he knows that he needs it to hunt with. If a primitive settler spends most of the year tilling the soil and planting, it is because he knows that it is necessary in order to collect a harvest. Both know that their success is not guaranteed, that some calamity of nature may defeat their efforts. But they know that they can learn to deal with nature, and that nature gives them a chance to get the products of their hunting or planting.

What men do not know - and have not learned fully to this day - is whether they will be able to <u>keep</u> their products once they get them.

The problem of human predators is as old as recorded history, or older. When men learned to hunt or to plant, some men learned to avoid that effort: to seize the products of others by <u>force</u>. The early forms of human associations, such as primitive tribes, were prompted in large part by the need for self-protection against the attacks of human enemies, with the tribal ruler as the chief warrior. How to organize protection against the use of force was - and is - man's fundamental social problem. What has to be protected is man's time - time free from forcible interference with the process of production (and of its goal, consumption). Without self-protection, men would be unable to produce - or to survive.

The need for organized protection against force is the root of the need for a government. In the history of Western civilization, the period known as the Dark Ages, after the fall of the Roman Empire, was a period when Western Europe existed without any social organization beyond chance local groupings clustered around small villages, large castles, and remnants of various traditions - swept periodically by massive barbarian invasions, warring robber bands, and sundry local looters. It was as close to a state of pure anarchy as men could come. The feudal system grew out of the need for organized protection. The system, in essence, consisted in the peasants swearing allegiance to a lord, who claimed ownership of the land and a percentage of their harvest in exchange for his duty to protect them against military attacks.

This system brought some semblance of order, but no protection and no peace. Disarmed men were left in the total power of an armed ruler, who had his own military gang and who robbed them as ruthlessly as, but more systematically than, any foreign invader. The history of the Middle Ages is a series of internal and external wars: there were various lords struggling to enlarge their domains, foreign lords struggling to subjugate neighboring lands, and bloody, hopeless uprisings of desperate peasants, bloodily suppressed. It was also the longest period of stagnation - intellectually and productively - in Europe's history.

The Renaissance was the great rebirth intellectually, but not politically. Still seeking order and unity, men attempted to solve the problem of feudal tyranny by replacing many small tyrants with a single big one. This was the birth of modern absolute monarchies. The rule of force continued, externally and internally. Externally, it took the form of perpetual wars among various monarchs seeking to conquer the kingdoms of other monarchs. Internally, bloody terror as a way of life was moved, in effect, to society's upper levels. This is not to say that the people as a whole were exempt: the people were crushed in the serfdom of hopeless toil and helpless obedience. But those who declare, today, that force is the only way to deal with men (with the unstated footnote that they, the speakers, would be safe in the position of rulers), ought to take a careful look at the history of absolute monarchies - and of modern dictatorships as well. Under the rule of force, it is the rulers who are in greatest danger, who live - and die - in permanent terror. The court intrigues, the plots and counterplots, the coups d'état, the known executions and secret assassinations are a matter of record. So are the purges of Party leaders and their cliques, in Nazi Germany and Soviet Russia. National unity? Peace and harmony among men?

If the history of animals were recorded, the most ferocious species would not equal the carnage perpetrated by men when they choose force as their means of dealing with one another.

It is in this context - from the perspective of the bloody millennia of mankind's history - that I want you to look at the birth of a miracle: the United States of America. If it is ever proper for men to kneel, we should kneel when we read the Declaration of Independence.

The concept of individual rights is so prodigious a feat of political thinking that few men grasp it fully - and two hundred years have not been enough for other countries to understand it. But this is the concept to which we owe our lives - the concept which made it possible for us to bring into reality everything of value that any of us did or will achieve or experience.

This is the key - and the only key - to the problem of national unity. If men seek peaceful coexistence, they must accept the principle that every man has rights which other men may not infringe - that he has the right to exist for his own sake and to pursue his own happiness - that he is an end in himself, not the means to the ends of others, not of *any* others, big or small, strong or weak, neither as cannon fodder nor as unrewarded drone toiling to support the Feudal Lord, or the King, or the Emperor, or the children of welfare recipients.

I shall not repeat here what rights are, how to define them, and how to implement them. (I refer you to my book *Capitalism: The Unknown Ideal*.) I shall merely remind you that the only rule of conduct men must accept - if they wish to achieve peaceful coexistence - is the rule that none may *initiate* the use of physical force against others. The rest is a matter of consistent implementation - the first step of which is to delegate to the government the right to use force in retaliation, and *only in retaliation*. (This is necessary in order to take the homicidal power, force, out of the reach of human whims and human irrationality, and place it under the control of *objective* laws.)

Benevolence is incompatible with fear. It is only when a man knows that his neighbors have no power forcibly to interfere with his life, that he can feel benevolence toward them, and they toward him - as the history of the American people has demonstrated. The freest people on earth was the most benevolent and the most generous - fearlessly and innocently too generous. Since agreement on the principle of individual rights does not impose any official dogma and does not violate anyone's convictions, the greatest variety of views and ideas could coexist peacefully in the same country without threatening anyone. If two men disagreed, they were free not to deal with each other, and neither could force his choices on the other. Incidentally, this applied even to the man who refuses to respect individual rights, i.e., the criminal: if he chose to initiate the use of force, he was answered on the terms *he* had chosen, i.e., by force.

Individual rights is the only proper principle of human coexistence, because it rests on man's nature, i.e., the nature and requirements of a conceptual consciousness. Man gains enormous values from dealing with other men; living in a human society is his proper way of life - but only on certain conditions. Man is not a lone wolf and he is not a social animal. He is a *contractual* animal. He has to plan his life long-range, make his own choices, and deal with other men by voluntary agreement (and he has to be able to rely on their observance of the agreements they entered).

National unity, like love, is not a primary, but a consequence and must come voluntarily or not at all. Just as one cannot order a child to love his mother, and if one does, one will make him hate her - so one cannot order or urge a nation to unite. When a politician's demands for unity violate your convictions, when he claims that unity supersedes your judgment, when he urges you to support policies which you oppose, to participate in actions you regard as evil, to join your own destroyers, or to leap into a sacrificial furnace - all in the name of national unity - then pretense, hypocrisy, corruption, hatred, and national disintegration will be the only results.

It is the last remnants of the principle of individual rights - and, therefore, any remnants of national unity - that George McGovern is avowedly out to destroy.

While some of his followers were demanding an unearned annual income of $6,500 for welfare recipients, McGovern was advocating a proposal (which he was later obliged to change) that all income above $12,000 a year be expropriated. This meant that the best, the ablest, the most hard-working, the most productive Americans would be left with less than double the income - and standard of living - of welfare recipients. Such a proposal is the confession of a mentality totally devoid of the concept of individual rights (and of justice).

As to his concept of national unity, it was McGovern who rewrote the Democratic Convention rules, which enabled his boys to stack the delegations by means of preferential quotas given to some minority pressure groups - not all pressure groups, only those that agreed with his views. He was helped by the ideological weakness of the other candidates, and by a gang of sundry young manipulators, power-lusters and hippies, who publicized themselves as a "grass-roots movement." He seized the nomination by crudely, ruthlessly "divisive" tactics, denouncing, insulting and shoving aside all the established factions of the Democratic Party. Then, when he found that his grass roots turned out to be weed roots, that the country was not responding to his campaign, he came begging his own victims to help him - in the name of party unity. It is hard to say who lacked integrity more shamefully: McGovern - or Humphrey, Muskie, and even sad little Eagleton, who were dragged out to campaign for a man they had good reason to despise.

This is the kind of unity McGovern hopes to extort from the nation.

(To be continued.)

Ayn Rand

OBJECTIVIST CALENDAR

A symposium on tax reform appears in the October 21 issue of Saturday Review; Ayn Rand is one of the contributors to this symposium.

Starting on November 13, the tape lectures of Leonard Peikoff's course, Founders of Western Philosophy: Thales to Hume, will be given in Lake Oswego, Oreg. For further information, contact Joyce Hoberg Lee at (503) 636-4268.

B.W.

The Ayn Rand Letter, published fortnightly by The Ayn Rand Letter, Inc., 183 Madison Avenue, New York, N.Y. 10016.

Contributing Editor: **Leonard Peikoff**; Subscription Director: **Elayne Kalberman**; Production Manager: **Barbara Weiss.**

Vol. II, No. 3 November 6, 1972

A NATION'S UNITY

Part III

As a political candidate, George McGovern is a fiction-like concretization of certain abstractions: he is the perfect embodiment of the soul of modern American intellectuals. (This is not to say that he is an intellectual; but neither are they.)

It is not an attractive soul, and he projects too many of its essential characteristics: pretentiousness, uncertainty, inconsistency; borrowed notions and, therefore, contempt for ideas; a vacuum of values and feeling, hidden under the tritest sentimentality; a patronizing attitude toward the people; a seething hostility; and, above all, an enormous distance from reality.

I offer in evidence the fact that a campaign which had been announced as a crusade for momentous issues, for revolutionary change, for reestablishing integrity and credibility in government - a crusade in the name of "New Politics," led by a candidate publicized as an "idealist" - started at the bottom of the old politics and went on down. No issues were raised or discussed, except for a few evasive snatches. We have heard nothing but personal denunciations, insults, attacks, and irresponsible smears. (A smear is an accusation without particulars or proof - such as the claim that the Nixon Administration is "the most corrupt in our history.") A campaign dedicated to "love" has dissolved into shrieks of hatred, and the worst kind of rabble-rousing: the attempt to arouse hatred for the rich. Is this the road to national unity?

But McGovern has miscalculated. There is no rabble in America - only the synthetic rabble imagined by the intellectuals and manufactured by the universities (out of a small percentage of students). The intellectuals' - and McGovern's - view of the people is a measure of their distance from reality. They do not see a modern nation: they see a nation of helpless peasants and cruel, overbearing masters - and they long to play the role of overbearing, but kindly masters. They have perceived nothing in the last two hundred years. (This is an example of philosophically induced blindness: the philosophy still guiding modern intellectuals is of the pre-French-Revolution era. Their souls are still in Europe. They have missed the achievements of two great men: Aristotle and Christopher Columbus.)

The patronizing attitude which regards the people as "the masses" - as helpless, whining, begging masses that plead for handouts from a benevolent ruler and wait for his permission to drag the rich to the guillotine - is so dated that it would not work even in modern Europe. To preach that view in America is grotesque.

The American people, including the poorest, have never regarded themselves as humble mendicants waiting to be helped. Nor have they ever resented the rich and the successful; to most Americans, the successful are not objects of envy and hatred, but of inspiration. An American worker, properly, identifies with his boss, the industrialist, rather than with a welfare recipient. And, I would venture to guess, so do many welfare recipients - excepting the group organizers or the professional bums who see welfare as a way of life.

Americans are men of action; they do not indulge in self-pity, and they do not accept passive resignation to suffering. In the face of hardships or misfortunes, their automatic response is to act, to fight, to solve the problem - an attitude for which they are so frequently condemned by the mystics of the intellectual "elite" of European barrooms and basements. To confront Americans with the patronizing "kindness" of a combined social worker and small-time Lord of the Manor, is such an impertinence that a landslide defeat is the least McGovern deserves for it.

Here is a recent example of McGovern's view of the people and of national unity - as reported by The New York Times (October 21, 1972). McGovern stated: "Let's face it. This election is more than a contest between George McGovern and Richard Nixon. It is a fundamental struggle between the little people of America and the big rich of America, between the average working man or woman and a powerful elite." I read this to my husband and said: "There are no little people in America." He answered: "Well... there's George McGovern..."

It is obvious that McGovern had counted on hatred - on deliberately stimulated class hatred and hatred for Richard Nixon - to unite the nation. It is revulsion against George McGovern that is uniting it now. Americans do not want any masters-rulers, kindly or otherwise.

Nor do they want any "redistribution of wealth." Americans are a future-oriented people. It was not the socialistic rich, it was the workers who protested angrily against McGovern's proposal to expropriate inheritances. Men who may never save more than a few thousand dollars to leave to their children, rebelled against the notion of forbidding multimillion-dollar legacies. Do you think that this is optimistic self-delusion? No, it is hard-headed realism. Americans know the importance of having all doors and all roads kept open to them.

McGovern and his intellectual supporters are obviously stunned and bewildered. They do not know which way to turn or how to explain the people's attitude. It seems incredible, but apparently they really thought that the people would follow them - which shows what degree of isolation from reality they had reached in their tight little cliques, their "in-groups," their esoteric fads, their private establishments, their unintelligible sign language. After years of talking only to those who agreed with them, they came to believe that no one else existed and are now in a state of shock.

A very revealing article by James Reston appeared in the Times (September 10, 1972) under the title: "What Kind of People Are We?"

"Candidates for the Presidency make certain assumptions about the condition of the nation and the world, and particularly about what kind of people we are, and what we think, or at least what we will swallow."

The Administration assumes - Mr. Reston points out bitterly - that "a majority of the people are fairly well off" and are opposed to McGovern's programs. "...it would be difficult to prove that the President has misjudged the popular mood. 'Welfare,' which used to be a symbol of America's compassion, is now regarded by many not only as an administrative mess, which it is, but almost as a racket in which money is taken from the people who work to support the people who won't work." Which is precisely what it is. What else can it be? Mr. Reston doesn't say.

And further: "Indifference to the massacre of human life [in Vietnam], provided it is not American lives, is not exactly the ideal that set the American nation apart as the most unselfish and compassionate society in history, but so far in this election there has been remarkably little response to Mr. McGovern's arguments that we should end the war, reform the tax structure, redistribute the wealth, reconcile the races and the generations and cut the defense budget - and do all these things because unity and justice at home are essential to the spiritual and physical security of the nation."

This is an unusually clear demonstration of the reason why altruism is incompatible with individual rights, with justice, and with national unity. Altruism demands sacrificial victims. What sort of unity can one establish between victims and executioners? What sort of unity does Mr. Reston envision? He demands that we unite on a program to "end the war" - by surrender; to "reform the tax structure" - by guaranteeing unearned incomes for some people at the expense of others; to "redistribute the wealth" - by confiscation; to "reconcile the races and the generations" - by preferential quotas; to "cut the defense budget" - by relying on the good will of Soviet Russia. Such is the nature - and the loathsome evil - of altruism, which is now on public display in the form of a program that an unconscionable candidate has had the effrontery to offer to the American people. An obscure Balkan nation would not accept it. A pack of cornered rats would not accept it. But the altruists believed that the American people would.

Mr. Reston is wrong when he declares that "there has been remarkably little response to Mr. McGovern's arguments" (unless by "response" he means "agreement"). The response - as shown by the polls - has been overwhelming; it represents the American people's rejection of totalitarianism the first time they got a clear smell of it.

"It would be unfair and even silly to indict the character of a whole people on the basis of the evidence in this campaign," says Mr. Reston - and proceeds to do it. Or rather, he struggles not to accept the fact that the American people could reject altruism, clearly implying that if they did, he would indict them. "The people," he declares, "can't see his [McGovern's] ideals and his proposals for his blunders. Maybe they long for the unity and justice and change he wants..." He then blames McGovern for having failed to present his "ideals" effectively, with the implication that if the people had understood those "ideals," they would have leaped joyously into a global sacrificial furnace.

"Nevertheless," he declares, "the main question remains. Even if he argued his ideals effectively, would the American people in their present mood respond?" He is not too certain. I am. No human beings can accept altruism fully and consciously - i.e., accept the role of sacrificial animals - the American people least of all. Their response to McGovern's program is a magnificent assertion of independence and self-esteem.

It is obvious that altruism is the intellectuals' only hope and their only weapon - a rusted, blunted, bloody weapon. It is embarrassing to hear the maudlin sentimentality of all those skeptics and cynics when they attempt to deal with values. Here is another sample from the Times (October 4, 1972). According to William V. Shannon, George McGovern has shown "a candid, un-neurotic friendly personality," and is "an experienced politician moving in the mainstream of the country's liberal tradition." After trying lamely to justify McGovern's switches and compromises, Mr. Shannon declares:

"But in any event a political leader's programs are not like a builder's blueprints. Rather, they are signposts on the road he hopes the country will travel. Through all the partisan smoke and clamor, Mr. McGovern's signposts are perfectly clear. He would lead the way to an America of peace, compassion and concern - for the hungry child and the ailing old persons, for the overtaxed fed-up worker on the assembly line and the hard-pressed small farmer, for the malnourished Indian on the forgotten reservation and the unseen war orphan in a distant land."

What about compassion and concern for those who seek happiness in life? When will they have time for it? But an altruist wouldn't know what I'm talking about.

In another aspect of his statement, however, Mr. Shannon hints at a valid point. It is true that political programs today are not like blueprints, but more like signposts. In a mixed economy, dominated by the philosophy of Pragmatism, a political candidate does not dare proclaim clear-cut principles; he has to pay lip service to the notions of every pressure group and to the opposite of his own convictions, if any. This means that we, the voters, have to learn the art of lip reading and make a choice, in effect, between two hypocrites - by means of the signposts that indicate the nature of their hypocrisy, as well as the road they actually want us to travel. This is not a procedure conducive to national unity, but, at present, we have no other.

By that criterion, both Mr. Nixon and Mr. McGovern are hypocrites. Both have paid tributes to Americanism (i.e., free enterprise) and to altruistic statism. But here is the difference between them: Mr. Nixon, though not a champion of free enterprise, yearns in that direction, and does not mean his tributes to altruistic statism. Mr. McGovern does not mean his tributes to Americanism.

In an alternative of this kind, there is only one choice for those who value individual rights. As you know, I am not an admirer of Mr. Nixon - but whatever his flaws, they are nothing when compared to his adversary's "perfectly clear signposts." It is _against statism_ that we have to vote. It is statism that has to be defeated - and defeated resoundingly.

The American people, apparently, understand this. Left without any guidance, any intellectual leadership, any conceptual understanding, on the basis of nothing but their sense of life, they knew when to say "_No_" loudly and clearly. Now, more than ever, after this election, they will need the help of every honest, articulate person to translate their knowledge into firm, consistent, conceptual terms - because their sense of life is a magnificent foundation, but not a sufficient weapon to save the country. Now, more than ever, they will need a new philosophy.

A year ago, I was being asked whether I held any hope for the future of this country. I gave my answer, under the title "Don't Let It Go," in the November 22 and December 6, 1971, issues of this _Letter_. I would like you to read my answer or reread it now. It dealt with the sense of life of the American people. In the present campaign, the American people have confirmed and surpassed my best hopes.

If I were religious, which I am not, I would say: "God bless America." I am saying it, anyway.

Ayn Rand

The Ayn Rand Letter, published fortnightly by The Ayn Rand Letter, Inc., 183 Madison Avenue, New York, N.Y. 10016.
Contributing Editor: **Leonard Peikoff**; Subscription Director: **Elayne Kalberman**; Production Manager: **Barbara Weiss.**

Vol. II, No. 4 November 20, 1972

THE AMERICAN SPIRIT

I would like to start this Letter by saying "Good morning" - even though I know that it is premature. It may take a long time before we learn whether the event of November 7 was a beautiful morning or the last glow of a beautiful sunset. It is up to men's volition, i.e., up to every one of us, to determine which it will be - depending on the course we take. But, in either case, it was beautiful.

In my last Letter, I asked you to read or reread "Don't Let It Go" (in the November 22-December 6, 1971 issues of this Letter). It was a discussion of the American people's sense of life and its fundamentally independent, individualistic nature. At the end of that discussion, I wrote: "Is there enough of the American sense of life left in people - under the constant pressure of the cultural-political efforts to obliterate it? It is impossible to tell."

I did not expect that we would be told a year later - and in such an unmistakable, resounding, magnificently affirmative manner. The election was a triumph of the American sense of life, a demonstration of its survival.

A year ago, I wrote: "There have never been any 'masses' in America: the poorest American is an individual and, subconsciously, an individualist. Marxism, which has conquered our universities, is a dismal failure as far as the people are concerned: Americans cannot be sold on any sort of class war..." And: "The doctrine of collectivism has never been submitted explicitly to the American voters; if it had been, it would have sustained a landslide defeat..." It has.

The election was set up almost like an event in good fiction or like a scientific experiment, i.e., in a manner which eliminated all the irrelevant, lesser factors so that a single, fundamental issue would be unmistakably clear. The landslide was not a matter of personal popularity: Nixon is not a popular President. It was not a matter of personal "charisma": neither candidate has it. It was not a matter of the voters' approval of Nixon's policies: these are so contradictory that approval on some issues necessitates disapproval on others. It was not a matter of "centrist" sympathies or of support for the status quo: the people's growing confusion, anxiety, and dissatisfaction with the status quo were apparent in the primaries and for some years past. It was not a matter of current or specific (i.e., lesser) practical issues: with a Presidential landslide of such magnitude, the Congressional elections showed virtually no change, no trend in favor of the Republicans or against the Democrats - since neither party's Congressional candidates offered anything more than the usual mixture of contradictory attitudes, out-of-context proposals, and firm stands on shaky questions.

It was a matter of a single, fundamental issue: the imperative necessity to defeat George McGovern, i.e., statism.

For once, people had an opportunity to vote on an abstract principle and on a long-range issue - though they were guided not by full, conscious knowledge, but by their sense of life. In a way, McGovern deserves a grim kind of negative credit: he did make the issue clear - even though he spent the entire campaign struggling to evade, disguise and deny it. But a sense of life is impervious to sophistry - it responds only to essentials. What people grasped was not merely the explicit content of McGovern's program, but the emotional vibrations he projected; not merely his gross defiance of individual rights, but the fact that he seemed unaware of there being anything there to defy - as demonstrated by his casual proposals to redistribute wealth, to limit income, to bribe the entire nation with thousand-dollar handouts, and to disarm unilaterally. People saw the obscene spectacle of altruism's essence: sacrifice and surrender. It was dramatized in the form of an economic and military program that represented one huge giveaway: of the nation's wealth - to those who had not earned it; of the nation - to North Vietnam, i.e., to Soviet Russia. (When, in the midst of such a spectacle, its chief protagonist began to whine about the people's callous indifference to "spying," "bugging," and the infringement of _his_ civil rights, the nightmare became a farce.)

One great value achieved by the election is the fact that it has demonstrated what no poll, survey, or theoretical deduction could have established with certainty: that the American people's sense of life has not been destroyed by almost a century of subterranean war against it - that it has not been affected by the intellectual-moral collapse engulfing the rest of the world - that the Americans' errors may permit mounts of wreckage to accumulate, seemingly burying their spirit, but when the chips are down, it will break through and proclaim to the world that this is still the country of freedom and self-esteem.

No, this is not a guarantee of the future nor a safe substitute for philosophy. But the thrilling experience on the night of November 7 was the rare sight of human beings acting like human beings, on a large scale, the spontaneous, unplanned, uncontrolled and uncontrollable rebellion sweeping forty-nine states, gathering a major or a significantly enlarged number of voters from every group, class, race and type of people, uniting them all - for Nixon? who cares about Nixon in such a context? - in a defiant "No!" flung at the face of the altruist-collectivist creed. Americans are still revolutionaries - in _their_ original meaning of the word.

It is significant that McGovern's popularity crashed immediately after the Democratic National Convention and never recovered. That Convention dramatized everything that is choking this country with helpless anger and indignation: the mawkish slogans and the cynical manipulations; the sentimentality and the power-lust; the flaunting of brazenly self-righteous irrationality; the preferential quotas for minorities, disfranchising the majority; "the Poor, the Black, the Young and the Women" in their professional costumes - the whole "counter-culture," as they call it (though "anti-culture" would be more appropriate). It was against _this_ that people were voting - not merely against an outrageous political program, but against the cultural outrage which is both its cause and its consequence (since culture and politics are always two mutually reinforcing manifestations of the same philosophy).

Another value achieved by the election is the fact that it has demonstrated how small - how miserably small - and impotent a minority had been posturing for decades as the standard-bearer of the culture, the voice of the people, the wave of the future.

McGovern's following consisted predominantly of two groups: the college people and the welfare recipients - i.e., those who are presumed to be the epitome of the intellect, and those who are the most helplessly ignorant. The latter can be absolved of blame, to a large extent: many of them are victims of a mixed economy, and they are not in a position to know what is a national economy, what keeps it going, and why the expropriation of a millionaire's profits would condemn _them_ to starve. But what is the intellectual, scholarly and moral stature of the college professors?

Since the majority of college students (but not of the working young) voted for McGovern and statism, the biggest question raised by the election is: What are they being taught in our universities? Does a college education consist in reducing a student's mind to the level of the lowest illiterates? These are rhetorical questions on my part: you know my answers. But the election has demonstrated the urgency of this issue so eloquently that the questions are now hanging over the country like a banner strung from coast to coast. Anyone who now pretends not to see it, had better drop the pretense of being concerned with politics, with public life, with cultural development, and with the future of this country.

The election has demonstrated that the breach between the people and the intellectuals is an abyss. This does not mean that the intellectuals have to accept the views of the majority - but it does mean that they should drop the fraud of posturing as the spokesmen, the servants, or the champions of the people. It is a costly fraud for the country - and the guiltiest men are not those who perpetrate it, but those who fall for it, particularly the politicians and the businessmen.

The proper task of the intellectuals is left undone: the mood of the people is ignored, the state of the nation is unidentified, the country's real problems are evaded, and blanketed in silence - while the intellectuals are busy manufacturing artificial problems and blowing them up with an astonishing unanimity. Their synthetic, waxworks "revolutionaries" - the activists of the New Left - are an example, with all of the consequent violence, the campus riots, the sit-ins, the demonstrations, the demands, the looting, the arson, the bloodshed, all of it publicized as a national movement of the young, and all of it staged by a minuscule gang that does not have the wits to think a day ahead nor the numbers to elect a dogcatcher.

"Madison Avenue" is one of the intellectuals' favorite pejorative terms to express their contempt for the advertising and public-relations techniques used by businessmen to sell unworthy products or policies. The joke is on the intellectuals: the alleged leftist trend of the past decade was a super-Madison-Avenue concoction - but George McGovern fell for it, and the campaign debacle was the product of people who had been taken in by their own P.R. men.

It would be one small blessing achieved by the election if the young activists were now to stop yelling: "Power to the People!" - since the people has just clobbered them with it. But they won't; they are impervious to reality.

So is their intellectual leadership. The election's moment of truth was the public disclosure of the fact that the leftist trend has neither quantity at the bottom nor quality at the top. The reaction of the liberal press to the election's results was a feeble, blind, stubbornly superficial rehash of the usual liberal dogma, but with a strong undercurrent of hatred, formerly hidden, now breaking out into the open. The liberal consensus claims that McGovern was defeated: a. because the country is too prosperous; b. because McGovern was too "idealistic"; c. because people want a rest or a slower tempo of "change" (not that people reject their kind of change, only that they want it in smaller doses); d. because people are cynically indifferent to public "corruption" and to the violation of individual rights (the Watergate affair, they claim, is such a violation; the McGovern program is not); e. because (this one is only peripheral, like a kind of paranoia-by-proxy) the basic, but secret, motive behind the landslide was racism.

The extent of these liberals'-collectivists'-populists' hatred for the people is startling. The majority "implicitly opted for the reality of their own affluence...the general feeling among most Americans [is] that 'we never had it so good'..." (The New

York Times, November 8, 1972.) Nixon's "genius lay in appealing to the worst in us, to selfishness and meanness..." (The Times, November 6.) A majority of the voters "care more about keeping taxes down and keeping the blacks out than they do about the poor who have been left behind." (The Times, November 5.) Nixon "represents some of the uglier instincts of the American character....He stood for deceit, evasiveness, corruption, and criminality; and still the people chose him..." (New York Post, November 10.) "The people, as always, voted their fears, their pitiful hopes and their meanest prejudices ....People feel more comfortable with Nixon, a Michigan professor wrote to The Times the other day. 'They feel more at home in the presence of self-serving power, corruption, lying, callousness and hokum.'" (The Post, November 8.)

The darkest shadow hanging over America's future is the intellectual vacuum filled, by default, with voices of that kind.

It is hard to tell what Nixon's policies will be, and - within the usual range of a mixed-economy Executive - it is almost irrelevant. Political power can destroy a culture; it cannot heal, save or rebuild it. We may hope that Nixon might gain time for the nation, by granting some relief (i.e., removing a few chains) to the private sector of the economy and by arresting the growth of the public sector. But, in view of his record, we cannot be certain. There is, however, one promise of his 1968 campaign - perhaps, the most important one - which he *has* kept: the appointment to the Supreme Court of men who respect the Constitution. It is still too early to tell the exact nature of these men's views and the direction they will choose to take. But if they live up to their enormous responsibility, we may forgive Mr. Nixon a great many of his defaults: the Supreme Court is the last remnant of a *philosophical* influence in this country.

No, the election has not solved all problems. It has merely brought them out into the open, but it is still a question whether men will choose to see them. The election has averted America's immediate collapse, and it has demonstrated the fundamental healthiness of the American people. But the problem of this country's future is cultural-ideological. The people's rebellion against statism was an expression of their sense of life. A nation's sense of life is activated by crucial emergencies or obvious threats of disaster; it cannot discern subtler forms of danger. It cannot protect the people against accepting the same collectivist program gradually, step by unobtrusive step, as they accepted the growth of the Welfare State. Without conscious knowledge and intellectual guidance, their desperate swing to the right will prove futile and will lead to nothing but some blind alley, such as George C. Wallace's party. The people have certainly rejected the left (i.e., statism); but they have no idea of what the right (i.e., capitalism) is or how to get there.

To paraphrase a passage from *Atlas Shrugged*: "They had defeated McGovern today; they had cheered American achievement. But tomorrow they would vote for some smoother Senator, and clamor for new handouts, while the country collapsed about their heads. They would do it, because they would be told to forget, as a sin, that which had made them cheer American achievement."

This sort of telling has already begun; in fact, it is being howled all around us. What are the American people being accused of? Of being prosperous, of being successful, of being self-supporting, of being *selfish*.

The thing most loudly revealed by the election, yet not mentioned by anyone, is the nature of America's fundamental enemy: *altruism*.

During the campaign, the press reported many interviews with average voters, whose answers foretold the landslide and clearly stated its reasons. "Bob Owen, a twenty-eight-year-old salesman from Pleasanton, California, gave the New York Times the answer most of us would give McGovern: 'I spent long, hard hours going to school and getting where I am,' he said. 'My income is just above the mean now, and I don't want to be pulled back to the mean. I don't want them to redistribute my wealth.'" (Al Capp, Saturday Review, October 21.)

"...Norman Dreznin, a lamp-store owner [in Brooklyn] and long-time Democrat... [said:] 'You know what I think? I think McGovern's just another one of those phony liberals - the 15-year-olds, the Left, those people at the Democratic convention. I'll say this about liberals. Whatever we do, and we do plenty, those liberals always slap us in the face.'" (The Times, November 3.)

"John E. Hazuda Sr., a 42-year-old boilermaker [in Pennsylvania], has always voted for the Democratic Presidential candidate. This Election Day he is going to vote for President Nixon....he is proud of the material comforts he has been able to provide for his family with his labor and determined that those comforts will not be taken from him ....Mr. Hazuda works very hard. He gets up at 5:30 every weekday morning to drive 60 miles to a construction project in Ohio...But he drives to work in a white-and-green 1972 Oldsmobile....Having worked hard and provided well for his family, which includes four children and 'my first grandchild on the way,' Mr. Hazuda sees no reason why the government should help out 'people who are too lazy to go out and make a living.'...'I just don't see anything wrong with this country,' he asserted. 'It is still the land of the free. There are no limits to what you could do or how much money you could make. What could be fairer?'...President Nixon, he feels sure, will not take away what he got with his back. About Mr. McGovern he is not so sure." (The Times, November 6.)

This is what the intellectuals deplore, denounce and damn as evil, as "selfish... mean...ugly...corrupt": men's pride in their achievement, men's self-reliance, men's refusal to lie down as sacrificial animals.

It is not the "idle rich" that the altruists are denouncing now, it is not the "tycoons of big business" or the "wolves of Wall Street" - it is plain, average laborers who manage to earn a decent living "with their backs." It is no longer a matter of reproaching men for their yachts and Rolls Royces - the altruists are now reproaching them for driving to work in an Oldsmobile. It is no longer an issue of "taking a little from the rich, they'll never miss it" - it is an issue of forcing a man, after a lifetime of effort, back into the hopeless poverty of the gutter. (Do you hear me, President Nixon?)

And this is called "idealism" - this is called a doctrine of compassion, of concern, of love for men.

At present, the workers still have the courage of self-assertion, and the self-esteem to uphold their own rights - a courage and self-esteem lost by businessmen long ago. The workers retain their moral confidence because their achievement is modest, and we are still close to the time when they were regarded as the "little people," whose rights were not to be questioned. Furthermore, the workers perceive their achievements directly - in the sense that they are aware of every hour of effort that paid for every piece of furniture in their homes - and the monstrous injustice of expropriation is inescapably clear to them. It is an awareness which businessmen - who work much harder, whose achievement is much greater, who make the workers' achievements possible - have allowed to be battered out of them.

But the workers are not the "little people" any longer: the altruists have found someone littler. So the workers are next in line for the sacrificial altar, and the battering has started. And if, by some miracle, today's welfare recipients were lifted one step above the slums, they would be next in line - in the name of "compassion" for the immeasurably less fortunate populace of the globe. That, too, has started. Such is the nature of altruism.

"Let all live for all. Let all sacrifice and none profit. Let all suffer and none enjoy. Let progress stop. Let all stagnate. There's equality in stagnation," said Ellsworth Toohey in The Fountainhead.

Those who did not (or did not care to) understand me theoretically, can see the essence of altruism concretized in this election. Let those who managed to evade the unspeakable injustices perpetrated against men of genius, now try to evade and justify the injustice of expropriating an average worker's car.

The danger to the future of this country is the fact that the people do not know the nature of their own motives and feelings: they do not know that the motive of their landslide vote was moral and idealistic - not merely "practical," as they are now being told on all sides - and that it represented man's highest morality and noblest idealism.

This is what the American people now need to be taught. This is the task of the New Intellectuals, wherever they exist. If America is to be saved, it has to be set free of the doctrine of altruism. If you are afraid to fight altruism, give up: no lesser battle will do. The country of George Washington cannot survive on the creed of George McGovern.

Do not let anyone whine that things are hopeless. The election has demonstrated that it is not too late, that the people are ready to hear the voice of reason - and that so much is still possible.

Ayn Rand

OBJECTIVIST CALENDAR

Night of January 16th, Ayn Rand's courtroom drama, is scheduled for off-Broadway production in 1973 - with the opening set tentatively for January or February. The producers are Phillip J. Smith and Kay Nolte Smith. This will be the first New York production of Miss Rand's definitive version of the play (published by New American Library in 1968). The opening date and theater are to be announced later.

The following starting dates have been scheduled for the tape lectures of Leonard Peikoff's course, Founders of Western Philosophy: Thales to Hume. Hartford, Conn., November 28 (a new starting date; contact Brian Bambrough, 203-549-5840, eves.); Syracuse, N.Y., December 1 (Stephen Goldman, 315-476-0420, 5-7 P.M.).

We have been asked to announce that on Monday, December 4, Dr. George Reisman will give a lecture at Columbia University. Time: 7:30 P.M. Place: Ferris Booth Hall (Schiff Room), Broadway and 114th Street. Subject: "Capitalism: The Cure for Racism." Open to the public. For further information, contact Barbara Filler at (212) 280-3281 (days) or (212) 662-1027 (eves.).

B.W.

The Ayn Rand Letter, published fortnightly by The Ayn Rand Letter, Inc., 183 Madison Avenue, New York, N.Y. 10016.

Contributing Editor: **Leonard Peikoff**; Subscription Director: **Elayne Kalberman**; Production Manager: **Barbara Weiss.**

Vol. II, No. 5 December 4, 1972

In this issue of my Letter, I take great pleasure in introducing to you a guest correspondent: Dr. Leonard Peikoff. Dr. Peikoff is Associate Professor of Philosophy at the Polytechnic Institute of Brooklyn, and Contributing Editor of this publication.

The following is an excerpt from his forthcoming book, The Ominous Parallels, to be published by Weybright & Talley, Inc.

The book is a study of the relationship between Nazism and contemporary America. It asks (and answers) the question: What is required to turn a country into a totalitarian dictatorship, how did the Nazis accomplish it, and is it happening here?

Contrary to most of the other writers on this subject, Dr. Peikoff holds that the roots of German Nazism lie not in existential crises, but in ideas - in a centuries-long philosophic development that nurtured the Nazi mentality and disarmed the rest of the country. He holds that, with certain exceptions, the fundamental philosophic principles that led to the rise of Nazism in Germany are operating in contemporary America; that, as a result, America is moving, by default, toward the establishment of a totalitarian dictatorship (specifically of a Nazi type); and that America now stands at an ominous crossroads.

The earlier chapters of the book discuss the essentials of the Nazi politics (totalitarian collectivism, of a racist/nationalist variety) and of the Nazi epistemology (irrationalism and mysticism, in the form of a mixture of religious dogmatism, pragmatist relativism, and social subjectivism). The present excerpt is from a chapter dealing with the Nazi ethics: altruism, in the form of the doctrine that the highest ethical value is the welfare of the group (the race or nation), and the highest virtue is the selfless performance of one's duty to the group, i.e., a life of self-sacrificial service to others. Dr. Peikoff traces the philosophic sources of altruism, showing the unbroken line of development that led to the crucial modern turning point: Kant, and on to Lenin, Mussolini and Hitler.

The present excerpt concludes that chapter's presentation of the Nazi ethics. It deals with the amoralist consequences of the altruist morality. In view of the fact that altruism is now a direct and immediate threat to this country, and that we have just escaped from a close call (though by a wide margin), I think that the following analysis will be of special interest - and relevance - to the readers of this Letter. (We have omitted the footnote references for quoted material; these will appear in the book.)

I shall not comment on Dr. Peikoff's brilliant philosophic ability and perceptiveness. Since, in accordance with Objectivist principles, I prefer not to assert, but to prove, I shall merely offer his work in evidence.

If, as a consequence of the leftists' misrepresentations, you find it hard to believe that Hitler - and every other Nazi leader - was a fervent and explicit advocate of altruism, I shall give you one quotation from Mein Kampf, which appears among the many thoroughly documented facts in the earlier part of Dr. Peikoff's chapter on the Nazi ethics:

"This self-sacrificing will to give one's personal labor and if necessary one's own life for others is most strongly developed in the Aryan. The Aryan is not greatest in his mental qualities as such, but in the extent of his willingness to put all his abilities in the service of the community.... The basic attitude from which such [fulfillment of duty] arises, we call - to distinguish it from egoism and selfishness - idealism. By this we understand only the individual's capacity to make sacrifices for the community, for his fellow men."

Judge for yourself - from the following presentation - the moral consequences of this kind of "idealism."

Ayn Rand

ALTRUISM, PRAGMATISM AND BRUTALITY

By Leonard Peikoff

The ethical spokesmen of the Nazis do not merely issue generalized exhortations to dutiful, Aryan-benefiting self-sacrifice; they accept and flaunt, as official elements of their ideology, every significant moral consequence of the altruist ethics.

The Nazis accept - in a racialized version - Hegel's distinctive contribution to the ethics of altruism: the doctrine that the group is not only the proper beneficiary of man's actions, but also the creator of morality, the definitive ethical lawgiver. The source of ethical principles, according to Nazism, and the final judge in all questions of moral truth, is: the feelings - the non-rational, "will"-generated feelings - of the Aryan race (or the Volk). "Right," declared Alfred Rosenberg to the Academy of German Law, "is that which Aryan people find right; wrong is that which they reject." Nazi philosophy, he states, "declares that the racially determined national soul is the measure of all of our thoughts, of our aspirations and actions, the final standard wherewith to judge all values."

The view that the group's feelings are the creator of *moral* truth, is the doctrine of social subjectivism applied to the realm of ethics. In the pre-Kantian era, subjectivism in ethics was restricted to philosophic skeptics; in the post-Kantian era, however, it has dominated the field - in part, because of the widespread, nineteenth-century advocacy of feeling as superior to reason; in part, because of the decay of the traditional supernaturalism, with its divine-commandment approach to ethics; above all, because of the pervasive, neo-mystic, altruist insistence on the sentiments of the group as the unchallengeable ethical standard.

The Nazis (and Fascists) simply follow this post-Kantian trend. The corollary of their avowed subjectivism in epistemology combined with their fervent altruism in morality, is an equally fervent *ethical subjectivism*....

Qua racial subjectivist, the Nazi holds that morality - every system of morality, every code of virtues and values - is a product of the racial instinct (or national character) of a given people; he holds that ethical ideas, like all others, are devoid of objectivity, that there is no such thing as "*the* truth" in ethics, but only "our truth," i.e., truth for a particular group.

Thus, for the Nazis, there are many moralities, each valid for some men and invalid for the others. Each racial (or national) group has, by its nature, its own distinctive patterns of behavior based on its own distinctive ethical feelings, so that, in the same circumstances, the course of action that is moral for one group may be immoral for the others.

Therefore, the Nazis claim, no alien can criticize any Nazi action, or submit it to the judgment of an impartial, universally applicable code of morality. Anything is right - right for Germans - if the Volk decrees it. As the source of right, the Volk - like the God of the medieval Christian voluntarists - antecedes moral principles and is not to be limited by them.

Nor is it to be limited even by its own previous moral declarations. The main line of Greek philosophy had held that the facts of reality demand immutable principles in the realm of human conduct. The main line of Christian philosophy had held that God is immutable, and so are His commandments. The main line of post-Kantian philosophy, however, swept any such viewpoint aside: the moderns recognized that their new moral legislator, the group, is eminently mutable - and that a mutable authority cannot generate an immutable code. If it is the decrees of society that create morality, they concluded, then morality is subject to perpetual alteration; there can be no moral principles outside the prerogative of society to modify or repeal. The Volk, therefore, must be free to change its mind on any moral question; if it does, what was morally right prior to the change thereby becomes morally wrong.

Accordingly, the Nazis repudiate any unchanging code of values, *any* fixed, unyielding theory of the nature of good and evil, virtue and vice. No ethical principles, they maintain, their own included, are permanently valid; there are *no moral absolutes*; morality is flexible, adaptable, relative.

The Nazi relativism in ethics is reinforced by another aspect of the

Nazi ideology: their acceptance of the epistemology of pragmatism.

According to pragmatism, the rules governing every branch of knowledge apply equally to ethics: the standard of truth, in morality as in science, is expediency. On this view, ethical ideas, like all others, are provisional tools designed to serve men's purposes in a constantly changing world. Ethical ideas, like all others, are to be judged not by reference to the "unknowable" facts of reality (or to "preconceived" theory or to "dead" abstraction), but by the standard of "practical" success. It follows that any particular ethical idea is to be accepted only so long as it continues to promote the sort of consequences desired by its advocates, i.e., only so long as it continues to "work" successfully. Ethics is mutable; what is right (or good) today, may be wrong (or evil) tomorrow; virtue and vice - like truth and falsehood - are not "rigid," but relative. Again, by a somewhat different route, there are no moral absolutes.

Qua pragmatist, the Nazi, therefore, takes pride in being ethically "flexible"; he flaunts the fact that his "will" is not bound or restricted by a system of unswerving principles; for him, "Thou shalt not kill [or commit mass murder]" has the same status as "Twice two makes four": both are valid only so long as they are useful. Qua pragmatist, the Nazi repudiates the concept of principles, moral or otherwise; he does not want principles, he wants results: "...the sole earthly criterion of whether an enterprise is right or wrong," says Hitler, "is its success." "Important is not what is right," says Goebbels, "but what wins."

Shunning absolutes as they do, most philosophical pragmatists refuse to endorse egoism or altruism in explicit terms; they refuse to define or endorse any systematic code of values. We must not, they say, attempt to decide moral questions abstractly or in advance, but must judge actions piecemeal, by "practical" results. By itself, however, this is a contentless approach to morality. To say that an action "works" is only to say that it is a successful means to some end(s) - which raises two questions for those who invoke such "working" as a standard of moral judgment: what end - and whose end? Pragmatism fails on principle to answer either: by itself, as a distinctive ethical theory, it does not tell men how an action must work to qualify as "practical," i.e., what goals it must achieve - nor for whom it must work, i.e., which men are to profit from it. It leaves its central concept - "practicality" - empty of specific meaning, defining neither value-standard nor beneficiary.

To apply their approach at all, therefore, pragmatists have been compelled, in spite of their strictures against "rigidity," to accept some view of man's proper goals, and some view of the proper beneficiary of man's actions. In the typical case, the pragmatist accepts these views without acknowledging them; he accepts them largely by implication, by a process of osmosis, eclectically absorbing the cultural deposits left by the value theories of other, non-pragmatist moralists - and protesting all the while the futility of these moralists' theories.

Some pragmatists have absorbed from their surroundings an egoist predisposition (of a subjectivist sort), holding that the right is that which "works" for a particular individual, i.e., that which enables him to achieve his own, personal goals, whatever they may be. But, in the light of modern philosophy's Kantian-Hegelian trend (of which pragmatism itself is an offshoot), it is not astonishing that the great majority of pragmatists - in Europe and in America - should have absorbed, and been shaped by, an antithetical predisposition. The right, these men have declared, is that which "works" _for society_, that which achieves public purposes, not private ones, that which promotes the welfare of the community. On this view, it is the moral duty of the pragmatic individual to subordinate his own personal desires in order to serve his fellows - i.e., it is his duty to live just as altruist theory would have him live.

The content of pragmatist morality, in any version, is never original; it is always a reflection of established ethical trends. In its dominant, social version, pragmatism is simply a _form of altruism_ - an avowedly relativist, "practical" form.

The Nazis are social pragmatists. Qua altruists, they declare: Sacrifice yourself to serve the Volk. Qua pragmatists, they declare: The right is whatever works to achieve the ends of the Volk. Both viewpoints enjoin the same basic code of conduct, and the famous Nazi slogan, "Right is what is good for the German people," can be taken, interchangeably, as a statement of either.

Failing to understand the relationship among the various elements of the Nazi ethics; failing to grasp in what way the Nazi subjectivism, pragmatism and relativism in ethics are derivatives of the morality of altruism; looking out of context at isolated Nazi declarations and actions - many observers are unable to identify the nature of the Nazi ethical mentality, or to define its essence.

Some, observing the intensity of the altruist element, conclude that the Nazis are essentially a party of burning moral idealists, i.e., of fanatic, crusading apostles of the spirit of self-sacrificial duty to the community. The great majority, however, disagree with this interpretation; observing the subjectivist-pragmatist-relativist element of the Nazi ethics, they conclude that the Nazis are essentially a gang of ethical "realists," i.e., of cynical, Machiavellian amoralists, who regard their arbitrary desires and the gospel of unprincipled expediency as their only guide, and who are contemptuous of ideals and of moral law.

This debate is superfluous and wholly artificial. In essential terms, _both_ of these views are correct - because these two elements of the Nazi mentality are not antithetical; they are distinguishable but harmonious aspects of one unified creed: the worship of the group.

In their Nazi form, the difference between the two elements is a matter of emphasis, in the nature of a division of labor. The altruist element lays down the foundation and the basic approach of the Nazi ethics - i.e., its ultimate end: the welfare of a specific group; and its primary virtue: self-sacrifice in that group's behalf. As a single abstract formulation, however, the principle of altruism is not a complete code of ethics: it does not state what constitutes the welfare of the group, nor by what standards such welfare is to be gauged, nor by what kinds of sacrifices on what kinds of occasions it is to be achieved - i.e., the altruist element, considered by itself, leaves open the specific means by which it is to be put into practice.

At this point, the subjectivist-pragmatist-relativist derivatives of altruism take over and declare: The welfare of the group is anything it (or its spokesman) decrees, anything that satisfies its desires - what it decrees at present, it may revoke in the future - the sacrifices that work today, may fail tomorrow - there are no moral absolutes - no options may ever be foreclosed - anything goes. In essence: altruism sets the end - subjectivism-pragmatism-relativism gives a blank check to any means to that end; the one injects the note of fervent commitment to duty - the other, the note of unprincipled, Machiavellian *Realpolitik*.

In the one capacity, the Nazi exudes the aura of an "idealist" - in the other, of an amoralist. But the truth is that the Nazis appeal to the particular nature of their end to derive and justify the practical means they use. The truth - the full truth about the Nazi ethical mentality - is the union of the two: the "idealism" defines the good abstractly, as the Nazis conceive it, the amoralism makes it possible to translate the abstraction into specific courses of action - i.e., the "idealism" validates and sanctions the amoralism, the amoralism administers and carries out the "idealism."

In their formulations of these two elements, as one might expect, the Nazis characteristically utter clashing contradictions: sacrifice is an absolute duty - there are no absolutes; Nazism is the true morality - there is no truth; the Nazi is the only virtuous man - down with conscience, the Party must be practical; etc. But this sort of clash is entirely on the surface; it does not affect the essence of the Nazi viewpoint. The clash amounts to the following. The Nazi "idealism" declares: There are no moral principles to protect the individual, we can sacrifice anyone we choose - because we are acting in the name of the only fundamental moral principle, the welfare of the group. The Nazi amoralism declares: There are no moral principles to protect the individual, we can sacrifice anyone we choose - because the group we represent is above moral principles.

The actions, in both cases, are the same. So is the essential, operative moral philosophy.

(To be continued.)

OBJECTIVIST CALENDAR

The following starting dates have been scheduled for the tape lectures of Leonard Peikoff's course, *Founders of Western Philosophy: Thales to Hume*. Denver, Colorado, January 11 (contact Robert Gifford, 303-377-0372); Nuernberg, West Germany, January 11 (Gerald Salchert, Elsa-Brandstroemstr. 6, Nuernberg; phone: 0911-61-31-89, evenings).

B.W.

The Ayn Rand Letter, published fortnightly by The Ayn Rand Letter, Inc., 183 Madison Avenue, New York, N.Y. 10016.

Contributing Editor: **Leonard Peikoff**; Subscription Director: **Elayne Kalberman**; Production Manager: **Barbara Weiss.**

Vol. II, No. 6 December 18, 1972

ALTRUISM, PRAGMATISM AND BRUTALITY

Part II

By Leonard Peikoff

Just as, in epistemology, there is no ultimate contradiction between religious dogmatism and skeptical pragmatism, so, in ethics, there is no ultimate contradiction between altruist "idealism" and subjectivist-pragmatist-relativist amoralism. And just as, in the Nazi epistemology, the practical purpose of each element is the same, so it is in the Nazi ethics: to obliterate the possibility of intellectual independence, and thereby ensure unquestioning obedience to the Führer.

On what moral grounds, even in the privacy of his own mind, could a man, accepting the Nazi ethics, object to or resist any decree - no matter how brutal or monstrous - issued to him by the spokesman and embodiment of the Volk? On the grounds that the decree destroys his personal values - his goals, ambitions, happiness, life? Qua altruist, he has been trained to the view that he must learn to sacrifice for the sake of others. On the grounds that the decree visits suffering, expropriation and death upon other men, who are innocent? Qua altruist, he has been trained to the view that they must learn to sacrifice for the sake of others. On the grounds that the decree violates his conscience, his independent moral judgment? Qua social subjectivist, he has been trained to the view that moral judgment is not his prerogative, but society's. On the grounds that the decree violates his principles? Qua pragmatist, he has been trained to the view that whatever works, as judged by the Führer, is right. On the grounds that the decree commands an absolute evil, which must be fought to the death? Qua relativist, he has been trained to the view that there are no absolutes.

The true Nazi, the man who has been philosophically prepared by all these doctrines, understands his function: he is not to express himself, but to do his duty; not to uphold his desires, but to sacrifice them; not to raise moral questions, but to accept the answers given by others; not to cling unyieldingly to moral principles, but to adapt himself to the ever changing voice of the collective as it determines the purpose of his life and every means to that purpose. In the field of morality, the Nazi's primary obligation is to renounce - renounce his self, in the full, literal sense of the term: his values, in the name of society; his judgment, in the name of authority; his convictions, in the name of flexibility.

The Nazi metaphysics and epistemology preach mind-sacrifice, thereby removing facts and thought (reality and reason) from the Führer's path. The Nazi ethics completes the job: by preaching *self*-sacrifice, it removes morality from his path. The result is the destruction, on every level, of the possibility of individual self-assertion. The graduate of the Nazi epistemology asks: "Who am I to know?"; his counterpart in ethics asks: "Who am I to know what is right?" Both answer: "No man is an island. The Führer knows best."

S.S. Captain Josef Kramer, a long-time exterminator of human beings at Auschwitz, Dachau, and other camps, was asked at the Nuremberg trials what his feelings were on a certain day in August 1943, when he had personally stripped and then gassed eighty women at the Natzweiler camp. He replied: "I had no feelings in carrying out these things because I had received an order to kill the eighty inmates in the way I already told you. *That, by the way, was the way I was trained.*"

If one fully understands this answer of Josef Kramer, in a manner that Kramer himself perhaps did not, if one understands "the way he was trained" - trained on the deepest of all levels, at the very core of his person, i.e., trained *philosophically* - one need look no further for the answer to the secret of the mystery of Nazism. What other practical result could anyone expect from a man, or a culture, shaped to its roots by every imaginable variant of the soul-killing ideas of centuries of mind-killing, *ego*-killing philosophy?

The mental attitude of Josef Kramer represents the primary virtue of the true Nazi, the one absolute of his anti-absolutist mentality, the ultimate commandment of the ethics of self-subordination to the group: to obey, to obey without reservations, to obey the group or its leader - and, therefore, not merely to slaughter, but to slaughter unfeelingly, unthinkingly, *indifferently*.

"We will never forget," declared Hitler to an assembly of 50,000 young Germans in 1935, "that the sum total of all virtues and all strength can be effective only when it is subservient to one will and one command....Nothing is possible unless one will commands, a will which has to be obeyed by others, beginning at the top and ending only at the very bottom....We must train our people so that whenever someone has been appointed to command, the others will recognize it as their duty to obey him."

"I have no conscience," said Goering, discussing the Reichstag fire with Himmler, Frick and others. "My conscience is Adolf Hitler."

As to the men who do have a conscience, the men who refuse (in any one case or across the board) to obey Hitler's commands - there is, according to the official Nazi ideology, only one proper method by which to deal with them, whether they be German or non-German, anti-Nazi or uncommitted or apolitical. The advocacy of this method as a formal ethical theory, is the capstone of the Nazi morality, the last of its central tenets, the most obvious (and least understood) expression of the Nazi ethical mentality.

The method is: compulsion, violence, ravishment, i.e., *physical force* - in any of its degrees from fist-backed threat to wholesale extermination.

When the Nazis glorify the Aryan as the exponent of "strength" or "power," which they never tire of doing, they do not refer to intellectual independence or unyielding integrity or personal wealth (all three are antisocial evils, in their view); they mean literal, brute strength - the power of destruction, of muscles, mobs and guns - the power effectively to wield physical force, massive force against masses of men. "...on earth and in the universe force alone is decisive," said Hitler in 1928. "Whatever goal man has reached is due to his originality plus his brutality." "The fundamental motif through all the centuries," said Hitler in 1926, "has been the principle that force and power are the determining factors....Only force rules."

As his practice testified, Hitler meant these utterances; they do not express a temporary, fluctuating policy, but a permanent, philosophical view of human life - a view in regard to which, beyond cavil, Hitler was "sincere." What are the roots of such a brute-worshiping mentality, and of the enthusiastic approval it evoked among Nazis and Nazi-sympathizers of every description?

The roots lie in the Nazi epistemology and in the Nazi ethics. There are only two fundamental methods by which men can deal with one another: by reason or by force, by intellectual persuasion or by physical coercion, by directing to an opponent's brain an argument - or a bullet. Activists who believe that reason is impotent, the intellect irrelevant, theory useless, ideas futile, will feel, of necessity, that their only chance to achieve their ends in the face of men who disagree, is by the resort to force. Logic is weakness, they feel, but violence is omnipotent; talk is effete, but a battalion backed by the _Wehrmacht_ is irresistible; argumentation is merely a parlor game, unless the appropriate engines of death are introduced by the S.S. into the rules. The Nazi ethics completes the job of brute-worship: altruism gives to the use of force a _moral sanction_, making it not only an unavoidable recourse, but also a positive virtue, not only an expression of practicality, but also of militant righteousness.

Some unphilosophical, eclectic altruists, invoking such concepts as "inalienable rights," "personal freedom," "private choice," have claimed that service to others, though morally obligatory, should not be compulsory. The committed, philosophical altruists, however, are consistent: recognizing that such concepts represent an individualist approach to ethics and that this is incompatible with the altruist morality, they declare that there is nothing wrong with compulsion in a good cause - that the use of force to counteract selfishness is ethically justified - and more: that it is ethically _mandatory_.

Every man, they argue, is morally the property of others - of those others it is his lifelong duty to serve; as such, he has no moral right to invest the major part of his time and energy in his own private concerns. If he attempts it, if he refuses voluntarily to make the requisite sacrifices, he is by that fact harming others, i.e., depriving them of what is morally theirs - he is violating men's rights, i.e., the right of others to his service - he is a moral delinquent, and it is an assertion of morality if others forcibly intervene to extract from him the fulfillment of his altruist obligations, on which he is attempting to default. Justice, they conclude, "social justice," _demands_ the initiation of force against the non-sacrificial individual; it demands that others put a stop to his evil. Thus has moral fervor been joined to the rule of physical force, raising it from a criminal tactic to a governing principle of human relationships. (The consistent, religious advocates of self-sacrifice accept the same viewpoint, but stress God, not the group, as the entity to whom man belongs, and whose moral commandments must be enforced.)

Human nature, according to most of the anti-egoists in Western history, is tainted with an irredeemable selfishness; men refuse voluntarily to do what is right, i.e., to sacrifice. The alternative confronting men, they conclude, is the establishment of agencies of compulsion, directed by those who are more insightful and selfless than the common herd - or the atrophy and extinction of the good as an operative factor in human life. The threat of force, according to this view, is the factor which gives potency to idealism; to renounce that threat is to renounce morality, by rendering it ineffective in man's existence. "He who will not hear God's word when it is spoken with kindness," summarizes Luther, "must listen to the headsman when he comes with his axe." "History," declared Hitler in 1923, "proves: He who has not the strength - him the 'right in itself' profits not a whit."

Once, says the Fascist philosopher Mario Palmieri wistfully (and incorrectly), men were eager to sacrifice themselves. But no longer: "Gone is forever the time when it was possible to find a way to the heart of man through his devotion to higher things than his personal affairs; gone is the time when it was possible to appeal to the mystic side of his nature through a religious commandment; gone, finally, is the time when it was possible to illuminate the reasoning powers of his mind with the light of ideals whose existence and whose reason of being cannot be proved through the powers of reason. All that remains is an appeal to force, to compulsion; intellectual as well as physical, an appeal to what lies outside of man, to what he fears and with what he must of necessity abide."

If a man is moral, says Hitler, he will submit of his own choice to the edicts of those exponents of "strength" to whom he owes his service. Idealism, he writes, "alone leads men to voluntary recognition of the privilege of force and strength, and thus makes them into a dust particle of that order which shapes and forms the whole universe." But when men - and/or nations - do not choose freely to become such dust particles, then: "...what is refused amicably, it is up to the fist to take."

Qua altruist, the Nazi uses his fist - at home and abroad - in the name of his ideals; qua amoralist, he scorns ideals - and, at home and abroad, uses the other fist. Qua amoralist, the Nazi reflects the mainstream of traditional ethical skepticism. Denying the existence of any rational, objective or absolute moral principles, such skeptics have characteristically scoffed at morality, holding that it is simply a social rationalization to conceal the standard which is actually operative in human affairs, the one which men _must_ recognize, like it or not: force. Justice or "right," said the Greek Sophist Thrasymachus in a famous formulation, "means simply what serves the interest of the stronger party..." (i.e., might makes right). There is, said Hitler, no such thing as objective justice: "Justice is a means of ruling. Justice is the codified practice of ruling."

The Nazi advocacy of amoralism, however, is only a derivative of other elements - ethical and epistemological. In essence, it is a dual Nazi worship: of unreason and of human sacrifice, that unleashes - at home and abroad, in dictatorship domestically and in war internationally - the advocacy and the rule of brutality.

Nor is this pattern distinctive to the Nazi movement. The same cause has produced the same effect throughout Western history, no matter how superficially varied the forms of each - whether men call their particular brand of unreason "ecstatic union with the Idea of the Good," or "Divine revelation," or "dialectic logic," or "Aryan instinct" - whether they demand sacrifice in the name of the World of Forms, or of God, or of the economic class, or of the master nation - whether the tyrannized, brutalized subjects submit to a philosopher king, or a medieval inquisitor, or an "agent of the World Spirit," or the dictatorship of the proletariat, or the Gauleiters and the Gestapo - whether the subjects are commanded to emulate the militarist conditions of Sparta, or commanded to launch a Crusade against the infidel, or the next stage in the bloody evolution of the Absolute, or the next war of "people's liberation," or the next war for *Lebensraum* and racial purification.

Most of these men and movements claim that their advocacy of force is only temporary; violence, they say, is necessary now, but, in another dimension - in a non-material reality, in the millenium, at infinity, in the classless society - men will live freely, in harmonious peace, and coercion will be forever banished. None, however, explains how (apart from death) his Utopia is to be reached, or how its harmony will be possible, given the premises of unreason and human sacrifice which all endorse as a permanent (not temporary) feature of their philosophies. On this issue, the Nazis are simply more brazen and explicit than the rest: they do not apologize for preaching openly what the others practice but attempt to evade, extenuate or minimize. The Nazis take the skeleton in the closet of centuries and rattle it boastfully. Force, they declare, will *always* be necessary, since it is in the nature of human life (which is true, if one accepts their concept of human life).

In this respect, as in so many others, Nazism is the final, most consistent expression of the irrationalist-altruist tradition in Western philosophy. The consequence of *undisguised* irrationalism and *undisguised* passion for man's sacrifice, is the *undisguised* lust to rule men by physical force.

"Force," said Hitler in a characteristically superficial statement, "is the first law." The truth is that it is *last*, not first; it is the ultimate, culminating consequence of a long chain of theorists, academicians, premises and centuries. First, philosophers had to destroy the faculty which discovers the good, and the standards which define it - i.e., reason and morality. Only then could the primordial brute arise amid the skyscrapers and factories of modern civilization and, all obstacles removed, proceed unhampered about his blood-drenched business.

"Providence," declared Hitler in an uncharacteristically philosophical statement to Rauschning, "has ordained that I should be the greatest liberator of humanity. I am freeing men from the restraints of an intelligence that has taken charge; from the dirty and degrading self-mortifications of a chimera called conscience and morality, and from the demands of a freedom and independence which only a very few can bear." Here he offers, if not the proper evaluation, then at least the correct order and the essentials of the Nazi philosophy, in epistemology, in ethics, in politics. If intelligence, morality and freedom are "restraints," then Hitler *was* a "liberator." After he had removed them, men, released from bondage, were left with a single problem and a single terror: the kind of life, and the deaths, that follow inexorably upon the removal of these "restraints."

POSTSCRIPT

The growth of the same philosophic doctrines in contemporary American culture is discussed in later chapters of Dr. Peikoff's forthcoming book, *The Ominous Parallels*. The events of our immediate present confirm his thesis and, specifically, the fact that our culture is dominated by the fusion of the same elements: altruism-pragmatism-brute force.

Observe the shrill, militant proclamations of altruistic slogans filling our cultural atmosphere, and the proliferation of government projects which are automatically whitewashed by altruistic "ideals," and which are acclaimed by the intellectuals as if altruism were an absolute requiring no proof and permitting no challenge. Observe the simultaneous advocacy of pragmatism by the same public voices, and the references to "flexibility" as a virtue. Observe the claims that acts of brute physical force are justified if perpetrated in the name of an altruistic cause - and that the drugged, bloody perpetrators are "idealists."

Observe also that, contrary to Marxist explanations, this is not an economic, but an intellectual movement - that the "idealists" did not emerge from the slums, but from college campuses.

The above excerpt from Dr. Peikoff's book was written long before this year's Presidential election, but the accuracy of his philosophic analysis clarifies many aspects of that event. Most commentators were baffled by the crudely pragmatic maneuvering of the New Left "idealists" at the Democratic Convention; but, as Dr. Peikoff demonstrates, their pragmatism was necessitated by their altruism.

The fact that biologically defined pressure groups, making outrageous demands, were treated with "compassion," but ordinary workingmen, fighting to protect their livelihood and rights, were denounced as "selfish" - is not baffling if one understands the relationship of altruism to social subjectivism. The fact that McGovern reversed his stand every other day, and that he ran the dirtiest campaign on record, spitting malice, hatred, defamations at his adversaries, yet is now touted as an "idealist" who was "too pure" to win in the dirty game of politics - is not astonishing if one understands the philosophic ooze that produces certain kinds of mentalities wherever and whenever it accumulates on the banks of a culture's mainstream.

The same philosophy will lead to the same results in any country - if left unchallenged. The philosophic doctrines that led to Nazism in Germany are generating the same intellectual, cultural and political consequences in America. These are the ominous parallels of Dr. Peikoff's book.

Ayn Rand

OBJECTIVIST CALENDAR

The following starting dates have been scheduled for the tape lectures of Leonard Peikoff's course, Founders of Western Philosophy: Thales to Hume. Lansing, Mich., January 14 (contact Ron Walker, 517-337-1636, evenings); Cleveland, Ohio, January 14 (Lesley Dunn, 216-423-3147, evenings).

B.W.

The Ayn Rand Letter, published fortnightly by The Ayn Rand Letter, Inc., 183 Madison Avenue, New York, N.Y. 10016.

Contributing Editor: **Leonard Peikoff**; Subscription Director: **Elayne Kalberman**; Production Manager: **Barbara Weiss.**

Vol. II, No. 7 January 1, 1973

"TO DREAM THE NON-COMMERCIAL DREAM"

Have you ever wondered about the mentality of those who advocate government financing of intellectual and artistic pursuits, in the name of intellectual independence and creative freedom?

Their goal, they claim, is to liberate men's mind from material concerns or economic pressures. The necessity to earn a living in a free marketplace, they claim, is demeaning and corrupting. In their language, the word "commercial" is a pejorative term, an antonym of "intellectual." Only the security of government support, they claim, can release the full power of the intellect.

The contradictions in this viewpoint are so obvious that it seems impossible for anyone to miss seeing them. Nothing is less secure than a position of dependence on the arbitrary power of politicians dispensing favors. The fate of thinkers, scientists and artists whose livelihood depends on the government - any government in any age, at the courts of absolute monarchs or in modern dictatorships or in mixed economies - is too well known to leave anyone in "idealistic" doubt. So are the fear, the intrigues, the rigid censorship, and the abject bootlicking in which and with which the recipients of governmental favors have to live moment by precarious moment. How can today's intellectuals fail to know it?

Some of them are motivated by power-lust and long for political careers in the roles of manipulators or "powers behind the thrones." But these, as a rule, advocate some form of government control over the intellectual professions, in the hope of maneuvering themselves or their cliques into the posts of professional "czars"; they do not plead for economic security and do not talk too much about intellectual freedom. What is the motive of those who do? What prompts the rank and file of the intellectual professions, who are loudly, touchily, belligerently championing such things as the First Amendment, civil liberties, academic freedom, etc., and, simultaneously, are pleading with the government for financial support? What can they hope for?

A significant answer may be found in a very enlightening article which appeared in *The New York Times* (July 29, 1972): "Another Channel" by Lester Markel, the retired Sunday Editor of the *Times*.

The article discusses the current troubles of public television: the chronic and growing financial plight of this non-commercial venture. The issue has aroused the intellectuals' angrily anxious concern ever since President Nixon vetoed a bill appropriating 65 million dollars for public television, which Congress had passed.

"The Government has been engaged in an unholy crusade against public television..." the article declares. "[The Administration's] attacks aroused neither the general public nor the Congress because of the feeling that public television is a dispensable institution. It isn't, but it has not shown that it isn't."

What makes public television indispensable? Mr. Markel does not say; he merely indicates that its purpose is "to fill the large gaps left by commercial television." What gaps? "It can reach an audience commercial television considers economically unfeasible." What audience? Mr. Markel states only that it is (either actually or potentially) an "audience of 10 or 15 million listeners" and that they are very "intent." What does this audience want? "In the cultural and entertainment areas [public television] can do much imaginative and experimental work."

But it is "the area of public affairs" that Mr. Markel regards as most important. "Genuine democracy depends ultimately on an informed opinion; American opinion is insufficiently or wrongly informed; this means that those whose duty it is to enlighten the citizenry are not doing their jobs." In the news area, commercial television "shirks the assignment because the undertaking is unprofitable; entertainment pays off, information doesn't. And public television has failed to fill the gap; it has not provided public affairs programming of consequence and immediacy."

If "information doesn't pay off," it means that the public doesn't want to listen to it. If so, then what will be accomplished by broadcasts which people do not hear? Will "genuine democracy" be served by the "informed opinion" of 10 or 15 million people, i.e., less than ten percent of a population of 210 million, whose taxes have to pay for it? No answer is given, except for the statement (at the end of the article) that "the size of informed minority can be significantly increased - and that would be a long forward stride in the democratic process."

"In general, the shortcoming of public television can be attributed to lack of independence, of money, of inspiration and of perspective. The first two lacks can be remedied only if the Government, executive and Congress, are pressured into action by public demand." What public? The 10 or 15 million? Do they represent or are they the public? No answer is given, but, in the context of today's pressure-group demands, the answer is obvious.

"That demand will not come unless public television supplies the two other ingredients - imagination and balance." And then, astonishingly, Mr. Markel proceeds to list the present flaws of public television, more correctly and succinctly than its enemies have done. "...for the most part, public television caters to the elite and preaches to the converted. In the effort to be different, programs have often been only eccentric or ineffectively experimental; they have been marked by an amateur rather than a professional touch...Moreover and most seriously, the attacks on the score of bias have been justified in numerous instances; for example, many of the programs of station WNET [in New York City] have had a distinctly leftist coloration...The sledding for public television has been made harder also because of clashes and power duels in the system, notably between left- and right-wing outfits and over the issue of central versus local power."

All this is eminently true; it has always been true of any government-sponsored "cultural" establishment. It is not a matter of personalities: a man of integrity and impeccable taste will not preserve either in such an establishment.

It is not the free market, but government patronage that corrupts. The corruption is inherent in the status of a privileged political elite - i.e., an elite selected by favor and maintained by force. If a member of that elite has no particular convictions, his performance will be bad; if he has, it will be worse. His convictions, his vanity, and his quest for "prestige" will blend inextricably into a driving motive to ram _his_ ideas down the throats of the country and of his disarmed opponents, who are forced to pay for his support. Thus, whether for "idealistic" or for the lowest kinds of motives, the "power duels" among the members of the elite will continue.

As to the quality of their work, a "professional touch" is achieved by the element of _objectivity_ - by objective standards of value, of performance, of taste - which is a necessity for an artist seeking the voluntary support of an audience. Men liberated from that necessity and guided by whims can be nothing but amateurs.

On the basis of his own observations, one would expect Mr. Markel to conclude that public television is a useless, hopeless and evil institution. But he springs another surprise on his readers.

"If public TV is to have a future," he declares, "it must evolve a new philosophy and a new approach. It must clear its head and clean its house." What philosophy, what approach, what is to be cleared or cleaned and in what way, is not indicated, beyond the statement that "the coverage of public affairs must be greatly improved," and the advice to emulate the B.B.C. And on the basis of these floating platitudes, Mr. Markel comes out with the one paragraph for which all the rest serves merely as verbal window dressing:

"In such ways public TV can win popular support and so achieve both independence and economic relief (the two are linked). As long as it is dependent for funding on Congress, and therefore on politics, public TV will not be free. _The only solution is an excise tax, possibly a levy on sets as in Britain_." (Emphasis added.)

Get this straight: public TV is to be liberated from politics by the non-political (!) means of a tax imposed on the people for the exclusive benefit, use and disposal of the men in public TV.

Even the welfare recipients who stage demonstrations have more decency than that: they, at least, present demands to Congress - they do not seek a direct lien on their neighbors' pockets.

Congress is a body of representatives chosen by the people; if public TV is _public_, on whom should its funding - and its control - depend if not on the public's representatives? Yet it is Congress that Mr. Markel's proposal seeks to by-pass.

Yes, Congress is a fluid, flexible institution, unpredictable in its policies, subject to the fluctuating views of the electorate - as it has to be, in a free country (where its power is limited by a Constitution), or in the sort of "genuine democracy" that liberals of Mr. Markel's kind are constantly touting. Yes, to depend on the switching moods of momentary majorities is as precarious as to build on quicksand - which is one of the reasons why intellectual pursuits must be kept outside the reach of government power. Yes, "independence and economic relief [i.e., the security of one's financial means] are linked," and there can be no independence when the means to achieve one's goals depend, not on mutual trade, but on unilateral favor - which is one of the reasons why independence is the corollary of a free economy and cannot be achieved anywhere else.

But Mr. Markel wants to eat his cake and have it, too. He advocates public service without public responsibility; a blank check on public funds without public accounting; the "security" of a public income without public control.

Who, in such a setup, would determine the policies of public TV? Who would choose its managers and performers, the recipients of public money? Who would judge the value of its programs - and by what standard? Who would establish what is "imagination" and "balance"? Who would determine what is biased and what is not - what is informative and what is not - what sort of information is needed by the public and what sort is not - what is "imaginative" and what is "eccentric" - and whether a symbolic study of space, time and sex in the subconscious of a fruit fly is effectively or ineffectively "experimental"?

If, under the vague control of a loose, haphazard, too easily tolerant Congressional supervision, public TV has done as badly as it has - and as Mr. Markel describes - what can lead one to expect that it would turn into an assembly of genius, of great thinkers, unbiased commentators, and brilliantly original artists, if unlimited funds were placed at its disposal, with no supervision, no rules, no strings attached? No group of people has so great a faith in the power of money as those who are socialistically inclined.

It is useless to raise moral questions in regard to a moral obscenity such as the proposal to *force* people to support public TV - which means: to take from people, by force, the money they had to work for, and give it to sundry intellectual connivers in exchange for a nebulous non-product which people cannot use, would not want to use, and would hate if they tried it (but which is allegedly desired by 10 million college hippies who do not propose to pay for anything they desire). Consider the issue of pay-TV (for which only those who want it, would pay): the same types of mentalities who oppose pay-TV, for fear that it might eventually deprive the poor of the free commercial programs they now enjoy, do not hesitate to support the imposition of a tax on the television sets of the poor, in order to make them pay for programs they would not see.

In my *Letter* on "The Establishing of an Establishment" (May 22, 1972), which discussed government grants to the social sciences, I wrote: "The origin of an aristocracy is the king's power to confer on a chosen individual the privilege of receiving an unearned income from the involuntary servitude of the inhabitants of a given district. Now, the same policy is operating in the United States - only the privileges are granted not in perpetuity, but in a lump sum for a limited time, and the involuntary servitude is imposed not on a group of serfs in a specific territory, but on all the citizens of the country."

I overestimated the moral stature and underestimated the ambition of modern intellectuals. Their goal is not the position of a temporary elite, but the establishment of a full-fledged aristocracy in perpetuity (with the succession determined not by birth, but by self-perpetuating professional guilds) - an aristocracy which, once established, would no longer be subject to public choice, approval or control, an aristocracy independent of the government, except for the government's obligation to send out internal revenue agents to collect from the country at large the private tax imposed by the aristocrats.

This is the secret dream of those advocates of "genuine democracy" who regard the free market as insecure and the necessity to earn a living as an impediment, who long for liberation from material concerns, and who are not afraid to exchange the "tyranny" of a private employer for the terrible chains of a government's control. They do not intend to be under government control; they would be exempt; the government would guarantee their income, collect it, deliver it, and ask no questions; they would achieve liberation from material concerns, by the only means it can ever be attempted: by the slave labor of others.

There is a limit to everything, even to the human capacity for evasion. No man could face others and declare that he intends to force them to support him for no reason whatever, just because he wants it, for his own "selfish" sake. He needs to justify his intention, not merely in their eyes, but, above all, in his own. There is only one doctrine that can pass for a justification: altruism.

Observe that such men are impassioned advocates of altruistic ideals, of collectivism, brother-love, social service, and self-sacrificial dedication to the good of others. They are not hypocrites; in their own way, they are "sincere"; they have to be. They need to believe that their work serves others, whether those others like it or not, and that the good of others is their only motivation; they do believe it - passionately, fiercely, militantly - in the sense in which a belief is distinguishable from a conviction: in the form of an emotion impervious to reality.

It makes no difference whether they embraced altruism as a means to their ulterior motives or the motives grew out of their altruistic creed. The two elements are mutually reinforcing, and neither is given a conscious identification in their minds. The same lack of self-esteem that would make a man accept and desire the position of being supported by the forced labor of others, would make him accept, and regard as noble, the doctrine demanding his self-immolation.

In this special sense, the advocates of every vicious, irrational doctrine are "sincere" and believe what they preach, though their belief is somewhat different and deeper than the faith they demand of their victims (if "depth," in this case, is to be measured by distance from reality). The victims are commanded to believe and to take the blame if they permit their faith to be shaken by facts that contradict it. The leaders are free (up to a point) to face the facts of their own performance, to lie, to cheat, to rob, to kill - so long as they hold, as an inviolate absolute, the belief that they are the vehicles of a higher truth which justifies, somehow, any action they might commit; this grants them the kind of malleable, non-absolute reality which is their basic goal.

For the victims of altruism, doubt is paralyzed by guilt; for the leaders, altruism removes the necessity of doubt, i.e., of thought.

In the case of some liberals' clamor for public TV, nothing more may be involved than some hack's desire to see his epic produced at public expense. But that hack's psychology - his belief - is part of a continuum that leads to Robespierre or Hitler or Stalin.

Let me give you an illustration of such belief. When Khrushchev visited the United States, in 1959, he was interviewed on various television news programs, usually through the voice of a translator; but on one occasion his answers were broadcast in Russian (with the English translation following). He was asked about the grounds of his faith in the ultimate triumph of world communism. And suddenly this cynical old brute - this Big Boss, feared by the whole world, known in Russia as "the Butcher of the Ukraine" for the mass slaughter that raised him to prominence - began to recite the credo of dialectic materialism in the exact words and tone in which I had heard it recited at exams, in my college days, by students at the University of Leningrad. He had the same uninflected, monotonous tone of a memorized lesson, the same automatic progression of sounds rather than meaning, the same earnest, dutiful, desperate hope that the sacred formulas would come out correctly. But in the face and eyes of a large television close-up, there was a shade more intensity than in the faces of the poor little college robots, more superstitious awe, and less comprehension: it was the face of a man performing a magic ritual on which his life depends. This man, I thought, believes it; he is compelled to believe it; he does not know what it means - but he knows that if this string of sounds were taken away from him, he would be left to face something more frightening than death.

Such is the nature, the pattern, and the ultimate exponent of those who have faith - and a vested interest - in altruism.

Ayn Rand

OBJECTIVIST CALENDAR

Starting on February 8, the tape lectures of Leonard Peikoff's course, *Modern Philosophy: Kant to the Present*, will be given in New York City. Dr. Peikoff will deliver the opening lecture in person. For further information, write to Susan Day, 15 Park Avenue, New York, N.Y. 10016, or telephone her at (212) 889-1627 (eves.).

The following starting dates have been scheduled for the tape lectures of Leonard Peikoff's course, *Founders of Western Philosophy: Thales to Hume*. Boston, February 7 (contact Joel Franck, 617-623-3684); San Francisco, February 11 (Michael Kitz-Miller, 415-839-6898 or Stephanie Staab, 415-451-2094).

We have been asked to announce that a full-color reproduction of *The Kingdom of Earth*, a painting by Joan Mitchell Blumenthal, is available from Sures Art Enterprises, Ltd. *The Kingdom of Earth* features a city of skyscrapers and towers seen at sunset. For illustrated brochure, write to SAE, Ltd., P.O. Box 207, Silver Spring, Md. 20907.

B.W.

The Ayn Rand Letter, published fortnightly by The Ayn Rand Letter, Inc., 183 Madison Avenue, New York, N.Y. 10016.

Contributing Editor: **Leonard Peikoff**; Subscription Director: **Elayne Kalberman**; Production Manager: **Barbara Weiss.**

Vol. II, No. 8 January 15, 1973

EPITAPH FOR A CULTURE

"A sense of loss pervades the space community on the day after Apollo. It is the bewilderment that comes from having achieved 'the impossible dream' - a frequently used phrase here - and now being left with nothing but memories and a gnawing feeling that all the effort was not really appreciated."

This is the opening paragraph of a news story in The New York Times (December 21, 1972), sent from Houston on December 20, the day after the splashdown of Apollo 17, which marked the end of the Apollo program. It is an interesting story in that it is written by a good reporter who, by presenting the facts, offers, inadvertently, a profound indictment of today's culture.

In regard to great events, objectivity is possible to good reporters, but neutrality is not. It is obvious that that reporter feels sympathy for the men of the Apollo program and shares their bewilderment. It is obvious also that he feels admiration for their achievements - and, at a certain point, proceeds to repress it, right there, on paper, before the reader's eyes.

The story, entitled "Meaning of Apollo: The Future Will Decide," is an attempt to answer the question: "After 11 years and an expenditure of $25-billion, after nine spaceships have flown to the moon and 12 men have walked its surface, what has it all meant?"

"It may be the greatest achievement of the century....It may be a major 'turning point' in history...But it may never be possible for the people who willed this glorious adventure to know what they have wrought. Such is the inevitable frustration of those who attempt truly great things." He is wrong on this point. Those who achieve truly great things *know* what they have achieved, which makes their social position harder to bear: it is the lack of appreciation that they are unable to understand.

The story quotes one tribute - introducing it as "Perhaps the most satisfying assessment for the 400,000 people who toiled on Apollo at its peak..." - a statement made by, of all people, Arthur Schlesinger, Jr.: "The 20th century will be remembered, when all else about it is forgotten, as the century in which man first burst his terrestrial bonds and began the exploration of space." This seems to be a minority opinion, however, at least as far as the material quoted in the story is concerned.

"The critics of Apollo, and there have been many, believe it was an evasion of earthly responsibility. They usually share the sentiments of the late Max Born, the Nobel laureate who said, 'Space travel is a triumph of intellect, but a tragic failure of reason.' They view Apollo as America's pyramids, a folly of national vanity, or as technology's Chartres, a symbol of the machine's new dominion over man and reason."

Don't ask me what they mean by the word "reason" - ask Immanuel Kant.

"Even though there are no immediate plans for return trips to the moon or for manned voyages to the planets, who knows how the awareness of such a capability will affect man's image of himself?"

Some people seem to know - and are struggling frantically to kill that image. The reporter indicates their kind of reaction. The first photographs of the whole earth, he states, which were brought by Apollo 8, made people feel that "the earth was a small and fragile sphere." I do not personally know anyone who felt that way, but it has certainly been a stressed, pushed, well-press-agented sentiment, then and since.

Whose purpose and motives would it serve? Well, Dr. René Dubos, a microbiologist at the Rockefeller University (and an influential leader of the ecological crusade), says that this sentiment "may be Apollo's greatest contribution and could lead to a 'new theology of the earth.' It was no coincidence, he says, that the ecology movement gathered real force at the time of Apollo."

Two paragraphs later, the story presents the three truest, most perceptive, most philosophical - and, in regard to the essence of today's culture, most horrifying - paragraphs I have ever read in a newspaper:

> "Another reason for some confusion over Apollo's significance could be that, in one sense, the program was out of step with the times. For all its vaunted technology, it was somewhat old-fashioned, a reflection of America past more than of America present.
>
> "Apollo was an expression of faith in the value of scientific discovery in a time of reaction against science, even against rationality. Apollo was an act of can-do optimism, of a belief in progress, in a time of reigning pessimism.
>
> "Apollo was the work of a dedicated team, pursuing a well-defined goal, in a time of bitter confusion of national purpose. Apollo was, moreover, a success rising above so much failure."

If you want to know the difference between me and many other people, it is this: the moment I grasped that such was the essence of the culture, I would be on the barricades, fighting for man's highest value: his mind - against the whole world, if necessary (as I am doing). And I would not be able fully to grasp the answer to the question: How can anyone accept such a culture in passive resignation? (Forgive me for talking about myself at this point and in this context: I have no other way to express my appraisal.)

Oddly enough, the story gives a clue to that answer. The very next paragraph is an act of repression displayed in public, the act of a mind slamming the door on a blinding vision, on itself, and on the best within it: "But these are complex contradictions better left to the historians of another time" - which is an impersonal substitute for the sentence: "Who am I to know?"

What is left after such an abdication? Within the two-and-a-half inches of newsprint concluding the story, we are offered the sight of a phenomenon much broader than the problem of that particular reporter: the birth of a hopeless longing in a human mind, of a limp, quiet, wistful aspiration and a static pain - the noninflammable ashes left by the renunciation of something man may not renounce:

"Perhaps a better measure of Apollo will come from some future Homer, who will be able to thrill generations with tales of those frail little vessels out on the black sea of space and of those men in strange white suits stepping tentatively among the boulders and craters of the moon....In those legends of Tranquility Base and Neil A. Armstrong, of the beauty of the earth as seen from space, may lie the inspiration for even greater deeds both in space and on earth."

If that future Homer came today, that reporter would no longer be able to hear him.

I remember wondering, at the age of about ten, why adults admired virtue and heroism in literature, yet never sought to bring them into their own lives. In this respect, I have never grown up. But I felt an enormous sadness, when I began to understand such lives.

For my estimate of the meaning of Apollo (and of its enemies), I refer you to my article "Apollo 11," in the September 1969 issue of <u>The Objectivist</u>. I shall quote one relevant passage, pertaining to the launching of Apollo 11, which I had attended: "For once, if only for seven minutes, the worst among those who saw it had to feel - not 'How small is man by the side of the Grand Canyon!' - but 'How great is man and how safe is nature when he conquers it!' That we had seen a demonstration of man at his best, no one could doubt... And no one could doubt that we had seen an achievement of man in his capacity as a rational being..."

Apparently, Dr. Dubos's followers and I perceived the same implications in the same event. The difference - the death or life difference - lies in our respective estimates of these implications.

I have been saying for years that the goal of modern philosophy is the destruction of reason, and that today's culture is motivated by hatred of man. Now, you can hear it admitted - not in esoteric, academic publications, nor in the tone of a shocking discovery, but in the matter-of-fact, taken-for-granted, reportorial voice of a newspaper story.

Referring to that story's three crucial paragraphs, ask yourself whether men may permit themselves to evade the conclusions that scream from between the lines. If the Apollo program was "out of step with the times," then what sort of hell is our time, and where are our steps leading us? If Apollo was "somewhat old-fashioned," then what is the meaning of today's fashions? If Apollo was "a reflection of America past more than of America present," then America past was incalculably superior to America present: it had created a better way of living, it knew some truths which we have lost and which, if we value our lives, we should rush to recover.

"Apollo was an expression of faith in the value of scientific discovery" ("faith in science" is a post-Kantian contradiction in terms: "confidence" is the proper word) - while ours is "a time of reaction against science, even against rationality." If so, then that reaction should have been blasted out of any honest mind by the blast that lifted Apollo 11 - which was a spectacular proof of the power of science and rationality.

"Apollo was an act of can-do optimism, of a belief in progress" ("can-do" is a timid substitute for "self-confidence") - while ours is "a time of reigning pessimism." If so, then self-confident optimism and the conviction that progress is possible to man, have been justified and validated more resoundingly than anyone could ask for. And the same event has shown us the precondition of self-confidence, optimism and progress, like skywriting left in the wake of those rockets: rationality. There is no necessity or justification for men to suffer in stagnant hopelessness. If pessimism is reigning over our time, who enthroned it and isn't it time to stage a revolution against its reign?

"Apollo was, moreover, a success rising above so much failure." Is _this_ a reason for being confused over and indifferent to Apollo's significance? _Innocent_ failure makes an honest mind check its premises, seek further knowledge, and seize upon the sight of a triumphant success as upon a life line - in order to gain courage, inspiration, and a lead to the secret that made it possible.

But all these conclusions presuppose an honest (i.e., rational) mind, an authentic good will toward men, an unbreached dedication to the pursuit of truth, and an eager desire to discover the proper way for man to live on earth. What if a person lacks these qualifications? If he does, the result will be the mentality represented by the "critics of Apollo."

If repeated failures make some men stick blindly to the same course, and damn success as evil - while proclaiming that they are moved by love for mankind - it is their motive that must be questioned.

In various disguises, the motive has been the same throughout history: hatred of man's mind - and, therefore, of man - and, therefore, of life - and, therefore, of any success, happiness or value man may achieve in life. The motive is hatred of the good for being the good. (See my article "The Age of Envy," in _The Objectivist_, July-August 1971.)

The publicly visible symptom of this hatred is the desire to infect man with a _metaphysical_ inferiority complex - to hold up to him a loathsome self-image, to keep him small, to keep him guilty. The invisible part of it is the desire to break man's spirit. The greatest threat to such a goal is any glimpse of man the hero, which the victims might catch. And nothing could offer mankind so direct, dramatic and stunning an image of man the hero, on such a globally visible scale, as Apollo's feat has done.

For ages, it was religion that had done the job of keeping man small - by comparing him to the immensity of alleged supernatural powers. Its secular equivalents implemented the same intention by comparing him to the size of the Grand Canyon. When science enabled man to lift his head, when he began to gain control of the earth, and the Grand Canyon ploy wore out, the haters' contingents swooped down upon the task of minimizing his achievement by shrinking the stature of the earth - which, they declared, "was a small and fragile sphere." No, it was no coincidence that "the ecology movement gathered real force at the time of Apollo" - or that Dr. René Dubos is dreaming of a new *theology*.

Most people do not share the views of Apollo's critics. The popular reaction to Apollo 11 was a significant demonstration of the breach between the American people and the intellectuals. But, in this issue, the people are helpless: they respond to Apollo's greatness, they admire it, they long for the values it represents - but they are not aware of their reasons in clear, conscious terms. They cannot express, uphold or fight for what they know only in the form of nameless emotions, and they will give up - as the *Times* reporter gave up. A culture is made - or destroyed - by its articulate voices.

That reporter could have enlightened people - but he, too, is a victim. He said more, with deeper theoretical perceptiveness, than most newsmen do today. But without the help of philosophy, he was unable to be certain of his own convictions - so he passed the buck to future historians and bowed to the will of "our times." *Who* makes our time what it is? *Who* makes any times or any culture? Philosophers. What did they teach that reporter in college? What are they teaching today?

Suppose you heard a man make the following speech: "I ignore the great achievement I have just witnessed - because the age of achievement is past. This achievement is a feat of science - but science is futile. This achievement is a triumph of rationality - but reason is impotent. This achievement is the product of self-confidence and of man's capacity for progress - but man is a weak, evil, miserable creature, born to be depraved and helpless. This achievement is the product of a dedicated team, pursuing a well-defined goal - but voluntary cooperation is impossible to men, goals are unattainable, and definitions are superfluous (or arbitrary). This achievement is a glorious success rising above a swamp of failure, but man, by his nature, is doomed to fail - and anyone who says otherwise, is a hater of mankind!" If you heard this, you would run - or you would fight. Yet this is the speech which modern philosophy has been making for well over a century - and this is the speech you have been hearing for years, from two-bit intellectuals and fifty-grand-a-year professors, who are in control of today's culture.

A culture that tolerates such leadership is doomed. That reporter's story is its appropriate epitaph. If a future historian were to say: "This was the age when men traveled to another celestial body for the first time, but their contemporaries did not acclaim their achievement - some, because they knew it was great; the rest, because greatness did not matter to them any longer" - this would be the most damning obituary on the soul of our times.

As to the men of Apollo, this would add another measure of heroism (the status of being an exception) to their heroic achievement - like a salute from a great distance, some sense of which may, perhaps, reach them in their present loneliness: they are used to great distances.

Ayn Rand

OBJECTIVIST CALENDAR

Starting on February 18, the tape lectures of Leonard Peikoff's course, Founders of Western Philosophy: Thales to Hume, will be given in Wellesley, Mass. For further information, contact Susan Winokur at (617) 235-9640.

Ayn Rand's courtroom drama, Night of January 16th, will open February 22 at the McAlpin Rooftop Theatre (34th St. and 6th Ave.). The play will be presented under its original title, Penthouse Legend. The producers are Phillip and Kay Smith; Mr. Smith will direct. There will be 10 preview performances, beginning February 13. All ticket sales will be handled by the box office of the theatre. A brochure with ticket information will be sent to our readers in the New York-Washington-Boston areas.

B.W.

AUTHOR'S NOTE

Many of my readers have been asking, in regard to helping the fight against today's intellectual trends: "What can I do?" Well, here is one opportunity - in the field of the arts. If the production of Penthouse Legend is successful, it may become a breakthrough: the start of a Romantic movement in the theatre.

As you know, we cannot count on a single good review from present-day critics. Word-of-mouth is the play's best chance. Therefore, if you wish to help, come to see the play - come to the previews if possible, because the first two weeks are crucial to a play's run. Then, if you like it, please tell as many people as possible.

I do not have to tell you about the play's script: you have probably read it or can read it in book form. But what I can tell you is that it is being produced in the right spirit and style, with an excellent cast under a brilliant director.

A.R.

The Ayn Rand Letter, published fortnightly by The Ayn Rand Letter, Inc., 183 Madison Avenue, New York, N.Y. 10016.

Contributing Editor: **Leonard Peikoff**; Subscription Director: **Elayne Kalberman**; Production Manager: **Barbara Weiss.**

Vol. II, No. 9 January 29, 1973

AN UNTITLED LETTER

The most appropriate title for this discussion would be "I told you so." But since that would be in somewhat dubious taste, I shall leave this Letter untitled.

In Atlas Shrugged, and in many subsequent articles, I said that the advocates of mysticism are motivated not by a quest for truth, but by hatred for man's mind; that the advocates of altruism are motivated not by compassion for suffering, but by hatred for man's life; that the advocates of collectivism are motivated not by a desire for men's happiness, but by hatred for man; that their three doctrines come from the same root and blend into a single passion: hatred of the good for being the good; and that the focus of that hatred, the target of its passionate fury, is the man of ability.

Those who thought that I was exaggerating have seen event after event confirm my diagnosis. Reality has been providing me with references and footnotes, including explicit admissions by the advocates of those doctrines. The admissions are becoming progressively louder and clearer.

The major ideological campaigns of the mystic-altruist-collectivist axis are usually preceded by trial balloons that test the public reaction to an attack on certain fundamental principles. Today, a new kind of intellectual balloon is beginning to bubble in the popular press - testing the climate for a large-scale attack intended to obliterate the concept of justice.

The new balloons acquire the mark of a campaign by carrying, like little identification tags, the code words: "A New Justice." This does not mean that the campaign is consciously directed by some mysterious powers. It is a conspiracy, not of men, but of basic premises - and the power directing it is logic: if, at the desperate stage of a losing battle, some men point to a road logically necessitated by their basic premises, those who share the premises will rush to follow.

Since my capacity for intellectual slumming is limited, I do not know who originated this campaign at this particular time (its philosophical roots are ancient). The first instance that came to my attention was a brief news item over a year ago. Dr. Jan Tinbergen from the Netherlands, who had received a Nobel Prize in Economic Science, spoke at an international conference in New York City and suggested "that there be a tax on personal capabilities. 'A modest first step might be a special tax on persons with high academic scores,' he said." We reprinted this item in the "Horror File" of The Objectivist (June 1971). The reaction of my friends, when they read it, was an incredulously indignant amusement, with remarks such as: "He's crazy!"

But it is not amusing any longer when a news item in The New York Times (January 2, 1973) announces that Pope Paul VI "issued a call today for a 'new justice.' True justice recognizes that all men are in substance equal, the Pontiff said....'The littler, the poorer, the more suffering, the more defenseless, even the lower a man has fallen, the more he deserves to be assisted, raised up, cared for, and honored. We learn this from the Gospel.'"

Observe the package deal: to be "little," "poor," "suffering," "defenseless" is not necessarily to be immoral (it depends on the cause of these conditions). But "even the lower a man has fallen" implies, in this context, not misfortune but immorality. Are we asked to absorb the notion that the lower a man's vices, the more concern he deserves - and the more honor? Another package deal: to be "assisted," "raised up," "cared for" obviously does not apply to those who are great, rich, happy or strong; they do not need it. But - "to be honored"? They are the men who would have to do the assisting, the raising up, the caring for - but they do not deserve to be honored? They deserve less honor than the man who is saved by their virtues and values?

In Atlas Shrugged, exposing the meaning of altruism, John Galt says: "What passkey admits you to the moral elite? The passkey is lack of value. Whatever the value involved, it is your lack of it that gives you a claim upon those who don't lack it. ...To demand rewards for your virtue is selfish and immoral; it is your lack of virtue that transforms your demand into a moral right."

What is an abstract ethical suggestion in the Pope's message, becomes specific and political in a brief piece that appeared in the Times on January 20, 1973 - "The New Inequality" by Peregrine Worsthorne, a columnist for The Sunday Telegraph of London. In addition to altruism, which is its base, this piece was made possible by two premises: 1. the refusal to recognize the difference between mind and force (i.e., between economic and political power); and 2. the refusal to recognize the difference between existence and consciousness (i.e., between the metaphysical and the man-made). Those who ignore or evade the crucial importance of these distinctions, will find Mr. Peregrine Worsthorne ready to welcome them at the end of their road.

There was a time, Mr. Worsthorne begins, when "gross hereditary inequalities of wealth, status and power were universally accepted as a divinely ordained fact of life." He is speaking of feudalism and of the British caste system. But modern man, he says, "finds this awfully difficult to understand. To him it seems absolutely axiomatic that each individual ought to be allowed to make his grade according to merit, regardless of the accident of birth. All positions of power, wealth and status should be open to talent. To the extent that this ideal is achieved a society is deemed to be just."

If you think that this is a proclamation of individualism, think twice. Modern liberals, Mr. Worsthorne continues, "have tended to believe it to be fair enough that the man of merit should be on top and the man without merit should be underneath." On top - of what? Underneath - what? Mr. Worsthorne doesn't say. Judging by the rest of the piece, his answer would be: on top of anything - political power, self-made wealth, scientific achievement, artistic genius, the status of earned respect or of a government-granted title of nobility - anything anyone may ever want or envy.

The current social "malaise," he explains, is caused by "the increasing evidence that this assumption [about a just society] should be challenged. The ideal of a meritocracy no longer commands such universal assent."

"Meritocracy" is an old anti-concept and one of the most contemptible package deals. By means of nothing more than its last five letters, that word obliterates the difference between mind and force: it equates the men of ability with political rulers, and the power of their creative achievements with political power. There is no difference, the word suggests, between freedom and tyranny: an "aristocracy" is tyranny by a politically established elite, a "democracy" is tyranny by the majority - and when a government protects individual rights, the result is tyranny by talent or "merit" (and since "to merit" means "to deserve," a free society is ruled by the tyranny of justice).

Mr. Worsthorne makes the most of it. His further package dealing becomes easier and cruder. "It used to be considered manifestly unjust that a child should be given an enormous head-start in life simply because he was the son of an earl, or a member of the landed gentry. But what about a child today born of affluent, educated parents whose family life gets him off to a head-start in the educational ladder? Is he not the beneficiary of a form of hereditary privilege no less unjust than that enjoyed by the aristocracy?"

What about Thomas Edison, the Wright brothers, Commodore Vanderbilt, Henry Ford, Sr. or, in politics, Abraham Lincoln, and <u>their</u> "enormous head-start in life"? On the other hand, what about the Park Avenue hippies or the drug-eaten children of college-bred intellectuals and multimillionaires?

Mr. Worsthorne, it seems, had counted on "universal public education" to level things down, but it has disappointed him. "Family life," he declares, "is more important than school life in determining brain power...Educational qualifications are today what armorial quarterings were in feudal times. Yet access to them is almost as unfairly determined by accidents of birth as was access to the nobility." This, he says, defeats "any genuine faith in equality of opportunity" - and "accounts for the current populist clamor to do away with educational distinctions such as exams and diplomas, since they are seen as the latest form of privilege which, in a sense, they are."

This means that if a young student (named, say, Thomas Hendricks), after days and nights of conscientious study, proves that he knows the subject of medicine, and passes an exam, he is given an arbitrary privilege, an unfair advantage over a young student (named Lee Hunsacker) who spent his time in a drugged daze, listening to rock music. And if Hendricks gets a diploma and a job in a hospital, while Hunsacker does not, Hunsacker will scream that he could not help it and that he never had a chance. Volitional effort? There is no such thing. Brain power? It's determined by family life - and he couldn't help it if Mom and Pop did not condition him to be willing to study. He is <u>entitled</u> to a job in a hospital, and a <u>just</u> society would guarantee it to him. The fate of the patients? He's as good as any other fellow - "all men are in substance equal" - and the only difference between him and the privileged bastards is a diploma granted as unfairly as armorial quarterings! Equal opportunity? Don't make him laugh!

Socialists, Mr. Worsthorne remarks, have used "the ideal of equality of opportunity" as "a way of moving in the right, that is to say the Left, direction." They regarded it as "the thin end of the egalitarian wedge."

Then, suddenly, Mr. Worsthorne starts dispensing advice to the Right - which the Left has always insisted on doing (and with good reason: any "rightist" who accepts it, deserves it). His advice, as usual, involves a threat and counts on fear. "But there is a problem here for the Right quite as much as for the Left. It seems to me certain that there will be a growing awareness in the coming decades of the unfairness of existing society, of the new forms of arbitrary allocation of power, status and privilege. Resentment will build up against the new meritocracy just as it built up against the old aristocracy and plutocracy."

The Right, he claims, must "devise new ways of disarming this resentment, without so curbing the high-flyers, so penalizing excellence, or so imposing uniformity as to destroy the spirit of a free and dynamic society." Observe that he permits himself to grasp and cynically to admit that such an issue as <u>the penalizing of excellence</u> is involved, but he regards it as the Right's concern, not his own - and he does not object to penalizing virtue for being virtue, provided the penalties do not go to extremes. This - in an article written as an appeal for justice.

Mr. Worsthorne has a solution to offer to the Right - and here comes the full flowering of altruism's essence and purpose, spreading out its petals like a hideous jungle plant, the kind that traps insects and eats them. The purpose is not to burn sacrificial victims, but to have them leap into the furnaces of their own free will: "What will be required of the new meritocracy is a formidably revived and re-animated spirit of _noblesse oblige_, rooted in the recognition that they _are_ immensely privileged and must, as a class, behave accordingly, being prepared to pay a far higher social price, in terms of taxation, in terms of service, for the privilege of exercising their talents."

Who granted them "the privilege of exercising their talents"? Those who have no talent. To _whom_ must they "pay a higher social price"? To those who have no social value to offer. _Who_ will impose taxation on their productive work? Those who have produced nothing. _Whom_ do they have to serve? Those who would be unable to survive without them.

"Did you want to know who is John Galt? I am the first man of ability who refused to regard it as guilt. I am the first man who would not do penance for my virtues or let them be used as the tools of my destruction. I am the first man who would not suffer martyrdom at the hands of those who wished me to perish for the privilege of keeping them alive." (_Atlas Shrugged_.)

"This [the 'social price'] is not an easy idea for a meritocracy to accept," Mr. Worsthorne concludes. "They like to think that they deserve their privileges, having won them by their own efforts. But this is an illusion, or at any rate a half truth. The other half of the truth is that they are terribly lucky and if their luck is not to run out they must be prepared to pay much more for their good fortune than they had hoped or even feared."

I submit that any man who ascribes success to "luck" has never achieved anything and has no inkling of the relentless effort which achievement requires. I submit that a successful man who ascribes his own (legitimate) success in part to luck, is either a modest, concrete-bound represser who does not understand the issue - or an appeaser who tries to mollify the resentment of envious mediocrities. (For the nature of such resentment, see my article "The Age of Envy" in _The Objectivist_, July-August 1971.)

Envy is a widespread sentiment in Europe, not in America. Most Americans admire success: they know what it takes. They believe that one must pay for one's sins, not for one's virtues - and the monstrous notion of paying ransoms for good fortune would not occur to them, nor would they take it seriously.

Resentment against "meritocracy"? Our last Presidential election was a spectacular demonstration of America's loyalty to achievement (on any level) - and of resentment against those egalitarian intellectuals who are trying to smuggle this country into a new caste system proposed by their British mentors: a _mediocracy_.

(To be continued.)

Ayn Rand

The Ayn Rand Letter, published fortnightly by The Ayn Rand Letter, Inc., 183 Madison Avenue, New York, N.Y. 10016.

Contributing Editor: **Leonard Peikoff**; Subscription Director: **Elayne Kalberman**; Production Manager: **Barbara Weiss.**

Vol. II, No. 10 February 12, 1973

AN UNTITLED LETTER

Part II

Politically, statism breeds a swarm of "little Caesars," who are motivated by power-lust. Culturally, statism breeds still lower a species: a swarm of "little Neros," who sing odes to depravity while the lives of their forced audiences go up in smoke.

I have said repeatedly that American intellectuals, with rare exceptions, are the slavish dependents and followers of Europe's intellectual trends. The notion of a cultural aristocracy established and financed by the government is so grotesque in this country that one wonders how an article such as Mr. Peregrine Worsthorne's got published here. Can you see any group or class in America posturing about in the "spirit of *noblesse oblige*"? Can you see Americans bowing to, say, Sir Burrhus Frederic (Skinner) or Dame Jane (Fonda), thanking them for their charitable contributions? Yet this is the goal of Britain's little Neros - and of their American followers. I refer you to my *Letter* of January 1, 1973, "To Dream the Non-Commercial Dream," for a discussion of why such "aristocrats" would have a vested interest in altruism and why they would be eager to pay a social price "for the privilege of exercising their talents."

If, by "meritocracy," Mr. Worsthorne means a government-picked elite (for instance, the B.B.C.), then it is true that such an elite owes its privileges to luck (and pull) more than to merit. If he means the men of ability who demonstrate their merit in the free marketplace (of ideas or of material goods), then his notions are worse than false. Package-dealing is essential to the selling of such notions. Mr. Worsthorne's technique consists in making no distinction between these two kinds of "merit" - which means: in seeing no difference between Homer and Nero.

An article such as Mr. Worsthorne's (and its various equivalents) would not appear in a newspaper, without some heavy academic-philosophical base. Newspapers are not published by or for theoretical innovators. Journalists do not venture to propagate an outrageous theory unless they know that they can refer to some "reputable" source able, they hope, to explain the inexplicable and defend the indefensible. An enormous amount of unconscionable nonsense comes out of the academic world each year; most of it is stillborn. But when echoes of a specific work begin to spurt in the popular press, they acquire significance as an advance warning - as an indication of the fact that some group(s) has a practical interest in shooting these particular bubbles into the country's cultural arteries.

In the case of the new egalitarianism, an academic source does exist. It may not be the first book of that kind, but it is the one noticeably touted at present. It is *A Theory of Justice* by John Rawls, Professor of Philosophy at Harvard University.

The New York Times Book Review (December 3, 1972) lists it among "Five Significant Books of 1972" and explains: "Although it was published in 1971, it was not widely reviewed until 1972, because critics needed time to get a grip on its complexities. In fact, it may not be properly understood until it has been studied for years..." The Book Review itself did not review it until July 16, 1972, at which time it published a front-page review written by Marshall Cohen, Professor of Philosophy at The City University of New York. The fact that the timing of that review coincided with the period of George McGovern's campaign may or may not be purely coincidental.

Let me say that I have not read and do not intend to read that book. But since one cannot judge a book by its reviews, please regard the following discussion as the review of a review. Mr. Cohen's remarks deserve attention in their own right.

According to the review, Rawls "is not an equalitarian, for he allows that inequalities of wealth, power and authority may be just. He argues, however, that these inequalities are just only when they can reasonably be expected to work out to the advantage of those who are worst off. The expenses incurred [by whom?] in training a doctor, like the rewards that encourage better performance from an entrepreneur, are permissible only if eliminating them, or reducing them further, would leave the worst off worse off still. If, however, permitting such inequalities contributes to improving the health or raising the material standards of those who are least advantaged, the inequalities are justified. But they are justified only to that extent - never as rewards for 'merit,' never as the just deserts of those who are born with greater natural advantages or into more favorable social circumstances."

I assume that this is an accurate summary of Mr. Rawls's thesis. The Book Review's plug of December 3 offers corroboration: "The talented or socially advantaged person hasn't earned anything: 'Those who have been favored by nature, whoever they are,' he [Rawls] writes, 'may gain from their good fortune only on terms that improve the situation of those who have lost out.'"

("...it is the parasites who are the moral justification for the existence of the producers, but the existence of the parasites is an end in itself..." John Galt, analyzing altruism, in Atlas Shrugged.)

Certain evils are protected by their own magnitude: there are people who, reading that quotation from Rawls, would not believe that it means what it says, but it does. It is not against social institutions that Mr. Rawls (and Mr. Cohen) rebels, but against the existence of human talent - not against political privileges, but against reality - not against governmental favors, but against nature (against "those who have been favored by nature," as if such a term as "favor" were applicable here) - not against social injustice, but against metaphysical "injustice," against the fact that some men are born with better brains and make better use of them than others are and do.

The new "theory of justice" demands that men counteract the "injustice" of nature by instituting the most obscenely unthinkable injustice among men: deprive "those favored by nature" (i.e., the talented, the intelligent, the creative) of the right to the rewards they produce (i.e., the right to life) - and grant to the incompetent, the stupid, the slothful a right to the effortless enjoyment of the rewards they could not produce, could not imagine, and would not know what to do with.

Mr. Cohen would object to my formulation. "It is important to understand," he writes, "that according to Rawls it is neither just nor unjust that men are born with differing natural abilities into differing social positions. These are simply natural facts. [True, but if so, what is the purpose of the next sentence?] To be sure, no one deserves his greater natural capacity or merits a more favorable starting point in society. The natural and social 'lottery' is arbitrary from a moral point of view.

But it does not follow, as the equalitarian supposes, that we should eliminate these differences. There is another way to deal with them. As we have seen, they can be put to work for the benefit of all and, in particular, for the benefit of those who are worst off." If a natural fact is neither just nor unjust, by what mental leap does it become a moral problem and an issue of justice? Why should those "favored by nature" be made to atone for what is not an injustice and is not of their making?

Mr. Cohen does not explain. He continues: "What justice requires, then, is that natural chance and social fortune be treated as a collective resource and put to work for the common good. Justice does not require equality, but it does require that men share one another's fate." This is the conclusion that required reading a 607-page book and taking a year "to get a grip on its complexities." That this is regarded as a new theory, raises the question of where Mr. Rawls's readers and admirers have been for the last two thousand years. There is more than this to the book, but let us pause at this point for a moment.

Observe that Mr. Cohen's (and the egalitarians') view of man is literally the view of a children's fairy tale - the notion that man, before birth, is some sort of indeterminate thing, an entity without identity, something like a shapeless chunk of human clay, and that fairy godmothers proceed to grant or deny him various attributes ("favors"): intelligence, talent, beauty, rich parents, etc. These attributes are handed out "arbitrarily" (this word is preposterously inapplicable to the processes of nature), it is a "lottery" among pre-embryonic non-entities, and - the supposedly adult mentalities conclude - since a winner could not possibly have "deserved" his "good fortune," a man does not deserve or earn anything after birth, as a human being, because he acts by means of "undeserved," "unmerited," "unearned" attributes. Implication: to earn something means to choose and earn your personal attributes before you exist.

Stuff of that kind has a certain value: it is a psychological confession projecting the enormity of that envy and hatred for the man of ability which are the root of all altruistic theories. By preaching the basest variant of the old altruist tripe, Mr. Rawls's book reveals altruism's ultimate meaning - which may be regarded as an ethical innovation. But A Theory of Justice is not primarily a book on ethics: it is a treatise on politics. And, believe it or not, it might be taken by some people as a way to save capitalism - since Mr. Rawls allegedly offers a "new" moral justification for the existence of social inequalities. It is fascinating to observe against whom Mr. Rawls's polemic is directed: against the utilitarians.

Virtually all the defenders of capitalism, from the nineteenth century to the present, accept the ethics of utilitarianism (with its slogan "The greatest happiness of the greatest number") as their moral base and justification - evading the appalling contradiction between capitalism and the altruist-collectivist nature of the utilitarian ethics. Mr. Cohen points out that utilitarianism is incompatible with justice, because it endorses the sacrifice of minorities to the interests of the majority. (I said this in 1946 - see my old pamphlet Textbook of Americanism.) If the alleged defenders of capitalism insist on clinging to altruism, Mr. Rawls is the retribution they have long since deserved: with far greater consistency than theirs, he substitutes a new standard of ethics for their old, utilitarian one: "The greatest happiness for the least deserving."

His main purpose, however, is to revive, as a moral-political base, the theory of social contract, which utilitarianism had replaced. In the opinion of John Rawls, writes Mr. Cohen, "the social contract theory of Rousseau and Kant" (wouldn't you know it?) provides an alternative to utilitarianism.

Mr. Cohen proceeds to offer a summary of the way Mr. Rawls would proceed to establish a "social contract." Men would be placed in what he calls the "original position" - which is not a state of nature, but "a hypothetical situation that can be entered into at any time." Justice would be ensured "by requiring that the principles which are to govern society be chosen behind a 'veil of ignorance.' This veil prevents those who occupy the 'original position' from knowing their own natural abilities or their own positions in the social order. What they do not know they cannot turn to their own advantage; this ignorance guarantees that their choice will be fair. And since everyone in the 'original position' is assumed to be rational [?!], everyone will be convinced by the same arguments [??!!]. In the social contract tradition the choice of political principles is unanimous." No, Mr. Cohen does not explain or define what that "original position" is - probably, with good reason. As he goes on, he seems to hint that that "hypothetical situation" is the state of the pre-embryonic human clay.

"Rawls argues that given the uncertainties that characterize the 'original position' (men do not know whether they are well- or ill-endowed, rich or poor) and given the fateful nature of the choice to be made (these are the principles by which they will live) rational men would choose according to the 'maximin' rule of game theory. This rule defines a conservative strategy - in making a choice among alternatives, we should choose that alternative whose worst possible outcome is superior to the worst possible outcome of the others." And thus, men would "rationally" choose to accept Mr. Rawls's ethical-political principles.

Regardless of any Rube Goldberg complexities erected to arrive at that conclusion, I submit that it is impossible for men to make any choice on the basis of ignorance, i.e., using ignorance as a criterion: if men do not know their own identities, they will not be able to grasp such things as "principles to live by," "alternatives" or what is a good, bad or worst "possible outcome." Since in order to be "fair" they must not know what is to their own advantage, how would they be able to know which is the least advantageous (the "worst possible") outcome?

As to the "maximin" rule of choice, I can annul Mr. Rawls's social contract, which requires _unanimity_, by saying that in long-range issues I choose that alternative whose _best_ possible outcome is superior to the _best_ possible outcome of the others. "You seek escape from pain. We seek the achievement of happiness. You exist for the sake of avoiding punishment. We exist for the sake of earning rewards. Threats will not make us function; fear is not our incentive. It is not death that we wish to avoid, but life that we wish to live." (_Atlas Shrugged_.)

(To be continued.)

Ayn Rand

OBJECTIVIST CALENDAR

The following starting dates have been scheduled for the tape lectures of Leonard Peikoff's courses. _Founders of Western Philosophy: Thales to Hume_. Toronto, March 6 (contact Edmund West, 416-927-6450, eves.); Rochester, N.Y., March 11 (Harry Ladne, 716-244-0873, eves.); Chicago, March 27 (Dr. Douglas Mayfield, 312-787-9836, eves.); Atlanta, April 2 (Dr. Bonar Newton, 404-351-9096).

Modern Philosophy: Kant to the Present. Syracuse, N.Y., March 9 (Stephen Goldman, 315-476-0420, eves.); Cleveland, April 15 (Lesley Dunn, 216-423-3147, eves.).

B.W.

The Ayn Rand Letter, published fortnightly by The Ayn Rand Letter, Inc., 183 Madison Avenue, New York, N.Y. 10016.

Contributing Editor: **Leonard Peikoff**; Subscription Director: **Elayne Kalberman**; Production Manager: **Barbara Weiss.**

Vol. II, No. 11 February 26, 1973

AN UNTITLED LETTER

Part III

Mr. Cohen is not in full agreement with Mr. Rawls. He seems to think that Mr. Rawls is not egalitarian enough: "...one would like to be clearer about the sorts of inequalities that are in fact justified in order to 'encourage' better performance. And is it in fact legitimate for Rawls to exclude considerations of what he calls envy from the calculations that are made in the 'original position'? It is arguable that including them would lead to the choice of more egalitarian principles." Does this mean that pre-embryos without attributes are able to experience envy of other pre-embryos without attributes? Does this mean that a just society must grind its best members down to the level of its worst, in order to pander to envy?

I am inclined to guess that the answer is affirmative, because Mr. Cohen continues as follows: "However that may be I, for one, am inclined to argue that once an adequate social minimum has been reached, justice requires the elimination of many economic and social inequalities, even if their elimination inhibits a further raising of the minimum." Is this motivated by the desire to uplift the weak or to degrade the strong - to help the incompetent or to destroy the able? Is this the voice of love or of hatred - of compassion or of envy?

What value would be gained by such a cerebrocidal atrocity? "I ought to forgo some economic benefits," says Mr. Cohen, "if doing so will reduce the evils of social distance, strengthen communal ties, and enhance the possibilities for a fuller participation in the common life." Whose life? In common with whom? On whose standard of value: the folks' next door? - the corner louts'? - the hippies'? - the drug addicts'?

"Dagny...I had seen...what it was that I had to fight for...I had to save you...not to let you stumble the years of your life away, struggling on through a poisoned fog...struggling to find, at the end of your road, not the towers of a city, but a fat, soggy, mindless cripple performing his enjoyment of life by means of swallowing the gin your life had gone to pay for!" (Atlas Shrugged.)

Mr. Cohen mentions that Mr. Rawls rejects "the perfectionistic doctrines of Aristotle." (Wouldn't you know that?) Mr. Rawls, by the way, is an American, educated in American universities, but he completed his education in Great Britain, at Oxford, on a Fulbright Fellowship.

What is the cause of today's egalitarian trend? For over two hundred years,

Europe's predominantly altruist-collectivist intellectuals had claimed to be the voice of the people - the champions of the downtrodden, disinherited masses and of unlimited majority rule. "Majority" was the omnipotent word of the intellectuals' theology. "Majority will" and "majority welfare" were their moral base and political goal which - they claimed - permitted, vindicated and justified anything. With varying degrees of consistency, this belief was shared by most of Europe's social thinkers, from Marx to Bentham to John Stuart Mill (whose *On Liberty* is the most pernicious piece of collectivism ever adopted by suicidal defenders of liberty).

In mid-twentieth century, the intellectuals were traumatized by seeing their axiomatic bedrock disintegrate into thin ice. The concept of "majority will" collapsed when they saw that the majority was not with them and did not share their "ideals." The concept of "majority welfare" collapsed when they discovered - through the experiences of communist Russia, Nazi Germany, welfare-state England, and sundry lesser socialist regimes - that only their hated adversary, the free, selfish, individualistic system of capitalism, is able to benefit the majority of the people (in fact, *all* of the people).

Some intellectuals began to stumble toward the Right - a bankrupt Right, which had nothing to offer. Some gave up, turning to drugs and astrology. The vanguard - stripped of cover, of respect, of credibility, and of safely popular bromides - began to reveal their hidden motives in the open glare of verbalized theory.

The cult of the "majority" has come to an end among the altruist-collectivists. They are not declaring any longer: "Why shouldn't a minuscule elite of geniuses and millionaires be sacrificed to the broad masses of mankind?" - they are declaring that the broad masses of mankind should be sacrificed to a minuscule elite, not of gods, kings or heroes, but of congenital incompetents. They are not declaring that greedy capitalists are exploiting and stifling men of talent - they are declaring that men of talent should not be permitted to function. They are not declaring that capitalism is impeding technological progress - they are declaring that technological progress should be retarded or abolished. They are not deriding the promise of "pie in the sky" - they are demanding that pie on earth be forbidden. They are not promising to raise men's standard of living - they are proclaiming that it should be lowered. They are not seeking to redistribute wealth - they are seeking to wipe it out. What, then, remains of their former creed? Only one constant: *sacrifice* - which they are now preaching openly in the form they had always endorsed secretly: sacrifice for the sake of sacrifice.

"It is not your wealth that they're after. Theirs is a conspiracy against the mind, which means: against life and man." (*Atlas Shrugged*.)

Anyone who proposes to reduce mankind to the level of its lowest specimens, cannot claim benevolence as his motive. Anyone who proposes to deprive men of aspiration, ambition or hope, and sentence them to stagnation for life, cannot claim compassion as his motive. Anyone who proposes to forbid men's progress beyond the limit accessible to a cripple, cannot claim love for men as his motive. Anyone who proposes to forbid to a genius any achievement which is not of value to a moron, cannot claim *any* motive but envy and hatred.

Observe that it has never been possible to preach an evil notion on the basis of reason, of facts, of this earth. The advocates of man-destroying theories have always had to step outside reality, to seek a mystic base or sanction. Just as religionists had to invoke the myth of Adam's sin, in order to propagate the notion of man's prenatal guilt - just as Kant had to rely on a noumenal world in order to destroy the world that exists - just as Hegel had to call on the Absolute Idea, and Marx had to call on Hegel - so today, on the grubby scale of our shrinking culture, those who want to deprive man of his right to life, are proclaiming the rights of the fetus, and those who want to deny all rights to the man of ability, are demanding that he atone for what he did not earn before he was a fetus and for nature's prenatal unfairness to the Mongolian idiot next door.

Observe also that an honest theoretician does not try to present his ideas in the guise of their opposites. But Kant's philosophy is presented as "pure reason" - altruism is presented as a doctrine of "love" - communism is presented as "liberation" - and egalitarianism is presented as "justice."

"Justice is the recognition of the fact that you cannot fake the character of men as you cannot fake the character of nature...that every man must be judged for what he *is* and treated accordingly...that to place any other concern higher than justice is to devaluate your moral currency and defraud the good in favor of the evil...and that the bottom of the pit at the end of that road, the act of moral bankruptcy, is to punish men for their virtues and reward them for their vices..." (*Atlas Shrugged*.)

Mr. Rawls's book is entitled *A Theory of Justice*, and yet, curiously enough, Mr. Cohen never mentions Mr. Rawls's definition of "justice" - which, I suspect, may not be Mr. Cohen's fault.

In *Atlas Shrugged*, in the sequence dealing with the tunnel catastrophe, I list the train passengers who were philosophically responsible for it, in hierarchical order, from the less guilty to the guiltiest. The last one on that list is a humanitarian who had said: "The men of ability? I do not care what or if they are made to suffer. They must be penalized in order to support the incompetent. Frankly, I do not care whether this is just or not. I take pride in not caring to grant any justice to the able, where mercy to the needy is concerned." Today, a "scientific" volume of 607 pages is devoted to claiming that *this* constitutes justice.

In *Capitalism: The Unknown Ideal*, I wrote: "The moral justification of capitalism lies in the fact that it is the only system consonant with man's rational nature, that it protects man's survival *qua* man, and that its ruling principle is: *justice*." If capitalism and its moral-metaphysical base, man's rational nature, are to be destroyed, then it is the concept of justice that has to be destroyed. Apparently, the egalitarians understand this; the utilitarian defenders of capitalism do not.

Is *A Theory of Justice* likely to be widely read? No. Is it likely to be influential? Yes - precisely for that reason.

If you wonder how so grotesquely irrational a philosophy as Kant's came to dominate Western culture, you are now witnessing an attempt to repeat that process. Mr. Rawls is a disciple of Kant - philosophically and psycho-epistemologically. Kant originated the technique required to sell irrational notions to the men of a skeptical, cynical age who have formally rejected mysticism without grasping the rudiments of rationality. The technique is as follows: if you want to propagate an outrageously evil idea (based on traditionally accepted doctrines), your conclusion must be brazenly clear, but your proof unintelligible. Your proof must be so tangled a mess that it will paralyze a reader's critical faculty - a mess of evasions, equivocations, obfuscations, circumlocutions, non sequiturs, endless sentences leading nowhere, irrelevant side issues, clauses, sub-clauses and sub-sub-clauses, a meticulously lengthy proving of the obvious, and big chunks of the arbitrary thrown in as self-evident, erudite references to sciences, to pseudo-sciences, to the never-to-be-sciences, to the untraceable and the unprovable - all of it resting on a zero: the *absence* of definitions. I offer in evidence the *Critique of Pure Reason*.

Mr. Cohen gives some indications that such is the style of Mr. Rawls's book. E.g.: "...the boldness and simplicity of Rawls's formulations depend on a *considered*, but questionable, looseness in his understanding of some fundamental political concepts." (Emphasis added.) "Considered" means "deliberate."

Like any overt school of mysticism, a movement seeking to achieve a vicious goal has to invoke the higher mysteries of an incomprehensible authority. An unread and unreadable book serves this purpose. It does not count on men's intelligence, but on their weaknesses, pretensions and fears. It is not a tool of enlightenment, but of intellectual intimidation. It is not aimed at the reader's understanding, but at his inferiority complex.

An intelligent man will reject such a book with contemptuous indignation, refusing to waste his time on untangling what he perceives to be gibberish - which is part of the book's technique: the man able to refute its arguments, will not (unless he has the endurance of an elephant and the patience of a martyr). A young man of average intelligence - particularly a student of philosophy or of political science - under a barrage of authoritative pronouncements acclaiming the book as "scholarly," "significant," "profound," will take the blame for his failure to understand. More often than not, he will assume that the book's theory has been scientifically proved and that he alone is unable to grasp it; anxious, above all, to hide his inability, he will profess agreement, and the less his understanding, the louder his agreement - while the rest of the class are going through the same mental process. Most of them will accept the book's doctrine, reluctantly and uneasily, and lose their intellectual integrity, condemning themselves to a chronic fog of approximation, uncertainty, self-doubt. Some will give up the intellect (particularly philosophy) and turn belligerently into "pragmatic," anti-intellectual Babbitts. A few will see through the game and scramble eagerly for the driver's seat on the bandwagon, grasping the possibilities of a road to the mentally unearned.

Within a few years of the book's publication, commentators will begin to fill libraries with works analyzing, "clarifying" and interpreting its mysteries. Their notions will spread all over the academic map, ranging from the appeasers, who will try to soften the book's meaning - to the glamorizers, who will ascribe to it nothing worse than their own pet inanities - to the compromisers, who will try to reconcile its theory with its exact opposite - to the avant-garde, who will spell out and demand the acceptance of its logical consequences. The contradictory, antithetical nature of such interpretations will be ascribed to the book's profundity - particularly by those who function on the motto: "If I don't understand it, it's deep." The students will believe that the professors know the proof of the book's theory, the professors will believe that the commentators know it, the commentators will believe that the author knows it - and the author will be alone to know that no proof exists and that none was offered.

Within a generation, the number of commentaries will have grown to such proportions that the original book will be accepted as a subject of philosophical specialization, requiring a lifetime of study - and any refutation of the book's theory will be ignored or rejected, if unaccompanied by a full discussion of the theories of all the commentators, a task which no one will be able to undertake.

This is the process by which Kant and Hegel acquired their dominance. Many professors of philosophy today have no idea of what Kant actually said. And no one has ever read Hegel (even though many have looked at every word on his every page).

This process has already begun in regard to Mr. Rawls's book, in the form of such manifestations as Mr. Peregrine Worsthorne's "The New Inequality." But the process is being forced by P.R. techniques; it is being pushed artificially and in the wrong direction: toward the popular press and the man in the street, who, in this country, is the least likely prospect for the role of sucker. Furthermore, Mr. Rawls is not in Kant's league: he is a politically oriented lightweight, who has scrambled together the worst of the old philosophic traditions, adding nothing new. His two outstanding points of similarity to Kant are: the method - and the motive.

The danger lies in the cultural similarity of Kant's time and ours. An age ruled by skepticism and cynicism can be swayed by anyone, even Mr. Rawls. There is no intellectual opposition to anything today - as there was none to Kant. Kant's opponents were men who shared all his fundamental premises (particularly altruism and mysticism), and merely engaged in nit-picking, thus hastening his victory. Today, the utilitarians, the religionists, and sundry other "conservatives" share all of Mr. Rawls's fundamental premises (particularly altruism). If his book does not make them see the nature of altruism and its logical consequences, if it does not make them realize that altruism is the destroyer of man (and of reason, justice, morality, civilization), then nothing will. When and if they get Mr. Rawls's world, they will have deserved it. So will the "practical" men whose lard-encrusted souls feel that ideas are innocuous playthings to be left to impractical intellectuals, and that any idea can be circumvented by making a deal with the government.

But it is only by default - by intellectual default - that theories such as Kant's or Rawls's can win. An intransigent, _rational_ opposition could have stopped Kant in his time. Rawls is easier to defeat - particularly in this country, which is the living monument to a diametrically opposite philosophy (he would have had a better chance in Europe). If there is any spirit of rebellion on American campuses (and elsewhere), _here_ is an evil to rebel against, to rebel _intellectually_, righteously, intransigently: any hint, touch, smell, or trial balloon of _A Theory of Justice_ and of the egalitarian movement.

If rational men do not rebel, the egalitarians will succeed. Succeed in establishing a world of shoddy equality and brotherly stagnation? No - but this is not their purpose. Just as Kant's purpose was to corrupt and paralyze man's mind, so the egalitarians' purpose is to shackle and paralyze the men of ability (even at the price of destroying the world).

If you wish to know the actual motive behind the egalitarians' theories - behind all their maudlin slogans, mawkish pleas, and ponderous volumes of verbal rat-traps - if you wish to grasp the enormity of the smallness of spirit for the sake of which they seek to immolate mankind, it can be presented in a few lines:

"'When a man thinks he's good - _that's_ when he's rotten. Pride is the worst of all sins, no matter what he's done.'

"'But if a man knows that what he's done is good?'

"'Then he ought to apologize for it.'

"'To whom?'

"'To those who haven't done it.'" (_Atlas Shrugged_.)

Ayn Rand

OBJECTIVIST CALENDAR

We have been asked to announce that on Monday, March 26, Dr. George Reisman will give a lecture at the University of Maryland at College Park. Time: 4 P.M. Subject: "Capitalism: The Cure for Racism." For further information, contact Dr. Edwin Locke at (301) 474-8857 (eves. until 10 P.M. and wkends.).

B.W.

The Ayn Rand Letter, published fortnightly by The Ayn Rand Letter, Inc., 183 Madison Avenue, New York, N.Y. 10016.
Contributing Editor: **Leonard Peikoff**; Subscription Director: **Elayne Kalberman**; Production Manager: **Barbara Weiss.**

Vol. II, No. 12 March 12, 1973

THE METAPHYSICAL VERSUS THE MAN-MADE

"God grant me the serenity to accept things I cannot change, courage to change things I can, and wisdom to know the difference."

This remarkable statement is attributed to a theologian with whose ideas I disagree in every fundamental respect: Reinhold Niebuhr. But - omitting the form of a prayer, i.e., the implication that one's mental-emotional states are a gift from God - that statement is profoundly true, as a summary and a guideline: it names the mental attitude which a rational man must seek to achieve. The statement is beautiful in its eloquent simplicity; but the achievement of that attitude involves philosophy's deepest metaphysical-moral issues.

I was startled to learn that that statement has been adopted as a prayer by Alcoholics Anonymous, which is not exactly a philosophical organization. In view of the fact that today's social-psychological theories stress emotional, not intellectual, needs and frustrations as the cause of human suffering (e.g., the lack of "love"), it is astonishing that that organization has discovered that such a prayer is relevant to the problems of alcoholics - that the misery of confusion on those issues has devastating consequences and is one of the factors driving men to drink, i.e., to seek escape from reality. This is just one more example of the way in which philosophy rules the lives of men who have never heard or cared to hear about it.

Most men spend their lives in futile rebellion against things they cannot change, in passive resignation to things they can, and - never attempting to learn the difference - in chronic guilt and self-doubt on both counts.

Observe what philosophical premises are implicit in that advice and are required for an attempt to live up to it. If there are things that man can change, it means that he possesses the power of choice, i.e., the faculty of volition. If he does not possess it, he can change nothing, including his own actions and characteristics, such as courage or lack of it. If there are things that man cannot change, it means that there are things that cannot be affected by his actions and are not open to his choice. This leads to the basic metaphysical issue that lies at the root of any system of philosophy: <u>the primacy of existence</u> or <u>the primacy of consciousness</u>.

The primacy of existence (of reality) is the axiom that existence exists, i.e., that the universe exists independent of consciousness (of <u>any</u> consciousness), that things are what they are, that they possess a specific nature, an <u>identity</u>. The epistemological corollary is the axiom that consciousness is the faculty of perceiving that which exists - and that man gains knowledge of reality by looking outward. The rejection of these axioms represents a reversal: the primacy of consciousness - the notion that the universe has no independent existence, that it is the product of a consciousness (either human or divine or both). The epistemological corollary is the notion that man gains knowledge of reality by looking inward (either at his own consciousness or at the revelations it receives from another, superior consciousness).

The source of this reversal is the inability or unwillingness fully to grasp the difference between one's inner state and the outer world, i.e., between the perceiver and the perceived (thus blending consciousness and existence into one indeterminate package-deal). This crucial distinction is not given to man automatically; it has to be learned. It is implicit in any awareness, but it has to be grasped conceptually and held as an absolute. As far as can be observed, infants and savages do not grasp it (they may, perhaps, have some rudimentary glimmer of it). Very few men ever choose to grasp it and fully to accept it. The majority keep swinging from side to side, implicitly recognizing the primacy of existence in some cases and denying it in others, adopting a kind of hit-or-miss, rule-of-thumb epistemological agnosticism, through ignorance and/or by intention - the result of which is the shrinking of their intellectual range, i.e., of their capacity to deal with abstractions. And although few people today believe that the singing of mystic incantations will bring rain, most people still regard as valid an argument such as: "If there is no God, who created the universe?"

To grasp the axiom that existence exists, means to grasp the fact that nature, i.e., the universe as a whole, cannot be created or annihilated, that it cannot come into or go out of existence. Whether its basic constituent elements are atoms, or subatomic particles, or some yet undiscovered forms of energy, it is not ruled by a consciousness or by will or by chance, but by the law of identity. All the countless forms, motions, combinations and dissolutions of elements within the universe - from a floating speck of dust to the formation of a galaxy to the emergence of life - are caused and determined by the identities of the elements involved. Nature is the <u>metaphysically given</u> - i.e., the nature of nature is outside the power of any volition.

Man's volition is an attribute of his consciousness (of his rational faculty) and consists in the choice to perceive existence or to evade it. To perceive existence, to discover the characteristics or properties (the identities) of the things that exist, means to discover and accept the metaphysically given. Only on the basis of this knowledge is man able to learn how the things given in nature can be rearranged to serve his needs (which is his method of survival).

The power to rearrange the combinations of natural elements is the only creative power man possesses. It is an enormous and glorious power - and it is the only meaning of the concept "creative." "Creation" does not (and metaphysically cannot) mean the power to bring something into existence out of nothing. "Creation" means the power to bring into existence an arrangement (or combination or integration) of natural elements that had not existed before. (This is true of any human product, scientific or esthetic: man's imagination is nothing more than the ability to rearrange the things he has observed in reality.) The best and briefest identification of man's power in regard to nature is Francis Bacon's "Nature, to be commanded, must be obeyed." In this context, "to be commanded" means to be made to serve man's purposes; "to be obeyed" means that they cannot be served unless man discovers the properties of natural elements and uses them accordingly.

For example, two hundred years ago, men would have said that it is impossible to hear a human voice at a distance of 238,000 miles. It is as impossible today as it was then. But if we are able to hear an astronaut's voice coming from the moon, it is by means of the science of electronics, which discovered certain natural phenomena and enabled men to build the kind of equipment that picks up the vibrations of that voice, transmits them, and reproduces them on earth. Without this knowledge and this equipment, centuries of wishing, praying, screaming and foot-stamping would not make a man's voice heard at the distance of ten miles.

Today, this is (implicitly) understood and (more or less) accepted in regard to the physical sciences (hence their progress). It is neither understood nor accepted - and is, in fact, vociferously denied - in regard to the humanities, the sciences dealing with man (hence their stagnant barbarism). Almost unanimously, man is regarded as an _unnatural_ phenomenon: either as a _supernatural_ entity, whose mystic (divine) endowment, the mind ("soul"), is above nature - or as a _subnatural_ entity, whose mystic (demoniacal) endowment, the mind, is an enemy of nature ("ecology"). The purpose of all such theories is to exempt man from the law of identity.

But man exists and his mind exists. Both are part of nature, both possess a specific identity. The attribute of volition does not contradict the fact of identity, just as the existence of living organisms does not contradict the existence of inanimate matter. Living organisms possess the power of self-initiated motion, which inanimate matter does not possess; man's consciousness possesses the power of self-initiated motion in the realm of cognition (thinking), which the consciousnesses of other living species do not possess. But just as animals are able to move only in accordance with the nature of their bodies, so man is able to initiate and direct his mental action only in accordance with the nature (the _identity_) of his consciousness. His volition is limited to his cognitive processes; he has the power to identify (and to conceive of rearranging) the elements of reality, but not the power to alter them. He has the power to use his cognitive faculty as its nature requires, but not the power to alter it nor to escape the consequences of its misuse. He has the power to suspend, evade, corrupt or subvert his perception of reality, but not the power to escape the existential and psychological disasters that follow. (The use or misuse of his cognitive faculty determines a man's choice of values, which determine his emotions and his character. It is in this sense that man is a being of self-made soul.)

Man's faculty of volition as such is not a contradiction of nature, but it opens the way for a host of contradictions - when and if men do not grasp _the crucial difference between the metaphysically given and any object, institution, procedure, or rule of conduct made by man._

It is the metaphysically given that must be accepted: it cannot be changed. It is the man-made that must never be accepted uncritically: it must be judged, then accepted or rejected and changed when necessary. Man is not omniscient or infallible: he can make innocent errors through lack of knowledge, or he can lie, cheat and fake. The man-made may be a product of genius, perceptiveness, ingenuity - or it may be a product of stupidity, deception, malice, evil. One man may be right and everyone else wrong, or vice versa (or any numerical division in between). Nature does not give man any automatic guarantee of the truth of his judgments (and _this_ is a metaphysically given fact, which must be accepted). Who, then, is to judge? Each man, to the best of his ability and honesty. What is his standard of judgment? _The metaphysically given._

The metaphysically given cannot be true or false, it simply _is_ - and man determines the truth or falsehood of his judgments by whether they correspond to or contradict the facts of reality. The metaphysically given cannot be right or wrong - it is the standard of right or wrong, by which a (rational) man judges his goals, his values, his choices. The metaphysically given is, was, will be, and had to be. Nothing made by man _had to be_: it was made by choice.

To rebel against the metaphysically given is to engage in a futile attempt to negate existence. To accept the man-made as beyond challenge is to engage in a successful attempt to negate one's own consciousness. Serenity comes from the ability to say "Yes" to existence. Courage comes from the ability to say "No" to the wrong choices made by others.

Any natural phenomenon, i.e., any event which occurs without human participation, is the metaphysically given, and could not have occurred differently or failed to occur; any phenomenon involving human action is the man-made, and could have been different. For example, a flood occurring in an uninhabited land, is the metaphysically given; a dam built to contain the flood water, is the man-made; if the builders miscalculate and the dam breaks, the disaster is metaphysical in its origin, but intensified by man in its consequences. To correct the situation, men must obey nature by studying the causes and potentialities of the flood, then command nature by building better flood controls.

But to declare that all of man's efforts to improve the conditions of his existence are futile, to declare that nature is unknowable because we cannot prove that there will be a flood next year, even though there has been one every year in memory, to declare that human knowledge is an illusion because the original dam builders were certain that the dam would hold, but it did not - is to drive men back to the primordial confusion on the relationship of consciousness to existence, and thus to rob men of serenity and courage (as well as of many other things). Yet this is what modern philosophy has been declaring for two hundred years or longer.

Observe that the philosophical system based on the axiom of the primacy of existence (i.e., on recognizing the absolutism of reality) led to the recognition of man's identity and rights. But the philosophical systems based on the primacy of consciousness (i.e., on the seemingly megalomaniacal notion that nature is whatever man wants it to be) lead to the view that man possesses no identity, that he is infinitely flexible, malleable, usable and disposable. Ask yourself why.

(To be continued.)

Ayn Rand

OBJECTIVIST CALENDAR

We have been asked to announce that on Tuesday, May 8, Professor George Walsh will give a lecture on "John Rawls's Theory of Justice: A New Ethics for the Welfare State," at Cornell University, under the auspices of Cornell Radicals for Capitalism. Time: 8 P.M. Place: Ives Hall, Room 114. Open to the public; admission free.

Please note the following change of address. Effective immediately, all correspondence regarding Dr. Leonard Peikoff's tape courses on the history of philosophy should be sent to Susan Ludel, 120 East 34th St., New York, N.Y. 10016.

B.W.

The Ayn Rand Letter, published fortnightly by The Ayn Rand Letter, Inc., 183 Madison Avenue, New York, N.Y. 10016.

Contributing Editor: **Leonard Peikoff**; Subscription Director: **Elayne Kalberman**; Production Manager: **Barbara Weiss.**

Vol. II, No. 13 March 26, 1973

THE METAPHYSICAL VERSUS THE MAN-MADE

Part II

A major part of the philosophers' attack on man's mind is devoted to attempts to obliterate the difference between the metaphysically given and the man-made. The confusion on this issue started as an ancient error (to which even Aristotle contributed in some of his Platonist aspects); but today it is running deliberately and inexcusably wild.

A typical package-deal, used by professors of philosophy, runs as follows: to prove the assertion that there is no such thing as "necessity" in the universe, a professor declares that just as this country did not _have to_ have fifty states, there could have been forty-eight or fifty-two - so the solar system did not _have to_ have nine planets, there could have been seven or eleven. It is not sufficient, he declares, to prove that something _is_, one must also prove that it _had to be_ - and since nothing had to be, nothing is certain and anything goes.

The technique of undercutting man's mind consists in palming off the man-made as if it were the metaphysically given, then ascribing to nature the concepts that refer only to men's lack of knowledge, such as "chance" or "contingency," then reversing the two elements of the package-deal. From the assertion: "Man is unpredictable, therefore nature is unpredictable," the argument goes to: "Nature possesses volition, man does not - nature is free, man is ruled by unknowable forces - nature is not to be conquered, man is."

Most people believe that an issue of this kind is empty academic talk, of no practical significance to anyone - which blinds them to its consequences in their own lives. If one were to tell them that the package-deal made of this issue is part of the nagging uncertainty, the quiet hopelessness, the gray despair of their daily inner state, they would deny it: they would not recognize it introspectively. But the inability to introspect is one of the consequences of this package-deal.

Most men have no knowledge of the nature or the functioning of a human consciousness and, consequently, no knowledge of what is or is not possible to them, what one can or cannot demand of oneself and of others, what is or is not one's fault. On the implicit premise that consciousness has no identity, men alternate between the feeling that they possess some sort of omnipotent power over their consciousness and can abuse it with impunity ("It doesn't matter, it's only in my mind") - and the feeling that they have no choice, no control, that the content of consciousness is innately predetermined, that they are victims of the impenetrable mystery inside their own skulls, prisoners of an unknowable enemy, helpless automatons driven by inexplicable emotions ("I can't help it, that's the way I am").

Many men are crippled by the influence of this uncertainty. When such a man considers a goal or desire he wants to achieve, the first question in his mind is: "Can _I_ do it?" - not: "What is required to do it?" His question means: "Do I have the innate ability?" For example: "I want to be a composer more than anything else on earth, but I have no idea of how it's done. Do I have that mysterious gift which will do it for me, somehow?" He has never heard of a premise such as the primacy of consciousness, but that is the premise moving him as he embarks on a hopeless search through the dark labyrinth of his consciousness (hopeless, because without reference to existence, nothing can be learned about one's consciousness).

If he does not give up his desire right then, he stumbles uncertainly to attempt to achieve it. Any small success augments his anxiety: he does not know what caused it and whether he can repeat it. Any small failure is a crushing blow: he takes it as proof that he lacks the mystic endowment. When he makes a mistake, he does not ask himself: "What do I need to learn?" - he asks: "What's wrong with me?" He waits for an automatic and omnipotent inspiration, which never comes. He spends years on a cheerless struggle, with his eyes focused inward, on the growing, leering monster of self-doubt, while existence drifts by, unseen, on the periphery of his mental vision. Eventually, he gives up.

Substitute for "composer" any other profession, goal or desire - to be a scientist, a businessman, a reporter or a headwaiter, to get rich, to find friends, to lose weight - and the pattern remains the same. Some of the pattern's victims are phonies, but not all. It is impossible to tell what amount of authentic intelligence, particularly in the arts, has been hampered, stunted or crushed by the myth of "innate endowment."

Unable to determine what they can or cannot change, some men attempt to "rewrite reality," i.e., to alter the nature of the metaphysically given. Some dream of a universe in which man experiences nothing but happiness - no pain, no frustration, no illness - and wonder why they lose the desire to improve their life on earth. Some feel that they would be brave, honest, ambitious in a world where everyone automatically shared these virtues - but not in the world as it is. Some dread the thought of eventual death - and never undertake the task of living. Some grant omniscience to the passage of time and regard tradition as the equivalent of nature: if people have believed an idea for centuries, they feel, it must be true. Some grant omnipotence and the status of the metaphysically given, not even to people's ideas, but to people's _feelings_, and pander to the irrationality of others, to their blind emotions (such as prejudices, superstitions, envy), regardless of the truth or falsehood of the issues involved - on the premise that "It doesn't matter whether this is true if people _feel_ that it's true."

Some men switch to others (who were helpless in the matter) the blame for their own actions; some men, who were helpless in the matter, accept the blame for the actions of others. Some feel guilty because they do not know what they have no way of knowing. Some feel guilty for not having known yesterday what they have learned today. Some feel guilty for not being able to convert the whole world to their own ideas effortlessly and overnight.

The question of how to deal with nature is partially understood, at least by some people; but the question of how to deal with men and how to judge them is still in the state of a primeval jungle. It is man's faculty of volition that sets him apart (even in the eyes of those who deny the existence of that faculty), and makes men regard themselves and others as unintelligible, unknowable, exempt from the law of identity.

But nothing is exempt from the law of identity. A man-made product did not have to exist, but, once made, it *does* exist. A man's actions did not have to be performed, but, once performed, they are *facts* of reality. The same is true of a man's character: he did not have to make the choices he made, but, once he has formed his character, it is a *fact*, and it is his personal *identity*. (Man's volition gives him great, but not unlimited, latitude to change his character; if he does, the change becomes a *fact*.)

Things of human origin (whether physical or psychological) may be designated as "man-made facts" - as distinguished from the metaphysically given facts. A skyscraper is a man-made fact, a mountain is a metaphysically given fact. One can alter a skyscraper or blow it up (just as one can alter or blow up a mountain), but so long as it exists, one cannot pretend that it is not there or that it is not what it is. The same principle applies to men's actions and characters. A man does not have to be a worthless scoundrel, but so long as he chooses to be, he *is* a worthless scoundrel and must be treated accordingly; to treat him otherwise is to contradict a *fact*. A man does not have to be a heroic achiever; but so long as he chooses to be, he *is* a heroic achiever and must be treated accordingly; to treat him otherwise is to contradict a *fact*. Men did not have to build a skyscraper; but, once they did, it is worse than a contradiction to regard a skyscraper as a mountain, as a metaphysically given fact which, on this view, "just happened to happen."

The faculty of volition gives man a special status in two crucial respects: 1. unlike the metaphysically given, man's products, whether material or intellectual, are not to be accepted uncritically - and 2. by *its metaphysically given nature*, a man's volition is outside the power of other men. What the unalterable basic constituents are to nature, the attribute of a volitional consciousness is to the entity "man." Nothing can force a man to think. Others may offer him incentives or impediments, rewards or punishments, they may destroy his brain by drugs or by the blow of a club, but they cannot order his mind to function: *this* is in his exclusive, sovereign power. Man is neither to be obeyed nor to be commanded.

What has to be "obeyed" is man's metaphysically given nature - in the sense in which one "obeys" the nature of all existents; this means, in man's case, that one must recognize the fact that his mind is not to be "commanded" in any sense, including the sense applicable to the rest of nature. Natural objects can be reshaped to serve men's goals and are to be regarded as means to men's ends, but man himself cannot and is not.

In regard to nature, "to accept what I cannot change" means to accept the metaphysically given; "to change what I can" means to strive to rearrange the given by acquiring knowledge - as science and technology (e.g., medicine) are doing; "to know the difference" means to know that one cannot rebel against nature and, when no action is possible, one must accept nature serenely.

In regard to man, "to accept" does not mean _to agree_, and "to change" does not mean _to force_. What one must accept is the fact that the minds of other men are not in one's power, as one's own mind is not in theirs; one must accept their right to make their own choices, and one must agree or disagree, accept or reject, join or oppose them, as one's mind dictates. The only means of "changing" men is the same as the means of "changing" nature: knowledge - which, in regard to men, is to be used as a process of _persuasion_, when and if their minds are active; when they are not, one must leave them to the consequences of their own errors. "To know the difference" means that one must never accept man-made evils (there are no others) in silent resignation, one must never submit to them voluntarily - and even if one is imprisoned in some ghastly dictatorship's jail, where no action is possible, serenity comes from the knowledge that one does _not_ accept it.

To deal with men by force is as impractical as to deal with nature by persuasion - which is the policy of savages, who rule men by force and plead with nature by prayers, incantations and bribes (sacrifices). It does not work and has not worked in any human society in history. Yet this is the policy to which modern philosophers are urging mankind to revert - as they have reverted to the notion of the primacy of consciousness. They urge a passive, mystic, "ecological" submission to nature - and the rule of brute force for men.

The philosophers' denial of the law of identity permits them to evade man's identity and the requirements of his survival. It permits them to evade the fact that man cannot survive for long in a state of nature, that reason is his tool of survival, that he survives by means of man-made products, and that the source of man-made products is man's _intelligence_. Intelligence is the ability to grasp the facts of reality and to deal with them long-range (i.e., conceptually). On the axiom of the primacy of existence, intelligence is man's most precious attribute. But it has no place in a society ruled by the primacy of consciousness: it is such a society's deadliest enemy.

Today, intelligence is neither recognized nor rewarded, but is being systematically extinguished in a growing flood of brazenly flaunted irrationality. As just one example of the extent to which today's culture is dominated by the primacy of consciousness, observe the following: in politics, people hold a ruthless, absolutist, either-or attitude toward elections, they expect a man either to win or not and are concerned only with the winner, ignoring the loser altogether (even though, in some cases, the loser was right) - while in economics, in the realm of production, they evade the absolutism of reality, of the fact that a man either produces or not, and destroy the winners in favor of the losers. To them, men's decisions are an absolute; reality's demands are not.

The climax of that trend, the ultimate cashing-in on the package-deal of the metaphysical and the man-made, is the egalitarian movement and its philosophical manifesto, John Rawls's _A Theory of Justice_. This obscenely evil theory proposes to subordinate man's nature and mind to the desires (including the envy), not merely of the lowest human specimens, but of the lowest non-existents - to the emotions these would have felt before they were born - and requires that men make lifelong choices on the premise that they are all equally devoid of brains. The fact that a brain cannot project an alteration of its own nature and power, that a genius cannot project himself into the state of a moron, and vice versa, that the needs and desires of a genius and a moron are not identical, that a genius reduced to the existential level of a moron would perish in unspeakable agony, and a moron raised to the existential level of a genius would paint graffiti on the sides of a computer, then die of starvation - all this does not enter the skulls of men who have dispensed with the law of identity (and, therefore, with reality), who demand "equal results" regardless of unequal causes, and who propose to alter metaphysical facts by the power of whims and guns.

This is being preached, touted and demanded today. There can be no intellectual - or moral - neutrality on such an issue. The moral cowards who try to evade it by pleading ignorance, confusion or helplessness, who keep silent and avoid the battle, yet feel a growing sense of guilty terror over the question of what they can or cannot change, are paving the way for the egalitarians' atrocities, and will end up like the derelicts whom Alcoholics Anonymous is struggling to help.

The least that any decent man can do today is to fight that book's doctrine - to fight it intransigently on _moral_ grounds. A proposal to annihilate intelligence by slow torture cannot be treated as a difference of civilized opinion.

If any man feels that the world is too complex and its evil is too big to cope with, let him remember that it is too big to drown in a glass of whiskey.

Ayn Rand

The following is a letter from a reader. I am reprinting it here because it is excellent, both in its argument and in its spirit.

A.R.

Dear Miss Rand,

In regard to your Feb. 12th _Letter_, it occurred to me that Mr. Rawls is even wrong on his own terms; _i.e._, on the basis of "maximin" his conclusion about the best society does not follow.

He assumes that the "worst case" is to be born a paraplegic in a society that abandons paraplegics. But this is not the worst case. The worst case is to be born a genius in the kind of world Mr. Rawls wants. To be an abandoned paraplegic is better than to be a crushed genius. The fate of the Hunchback of Notre Dame is pitiable, but Galileo's fate is terrifying.

I wonder at the hugeness of Mr. Rawls' "oversight." Could it be that even in the "original position" his "ignorance" is not complete? Perhaps he feels he _knows_ that while he might well have been born paralyzed..., he could _never_ have been born a Galileo. I'm serious.

Best regards,

T.W.C., Jr.
Watertown, Mass.

The Ayn Rand Letter, published fortnightly by The Ayn Rand Letter, Inc., 183 Madison Avenue, New York, N.Y. 10016.
Contributing Editor: **Leonard Peikoff;** Subscription Director: **Elayne Kalberman;** Production Manager: **Barbara Weiss.**

Vol. II, No. 14 April 9, 1973

BROTHERS, YOU ASKED FOR IT!

I had hoped to write a Letter, someday, entitled "Why I will not write about Watergate" - and explain that I do not take part in lynchings. But the issue has grown beyond the level of party politics, and is acquiring a deeper meaning - like an unfocused illustration for a certain philosophical text, which is worth considering in full focus.

Curiously enough, in spite of the enormous coverage given to the Watergate affair by the press, it is impossible to untangle facts from allegations, events from comments, proof from rumors, truth from innuendo. No one can follow the case coherently - which, perhaps, is the goal of this type of news coverage. So far, the only things that can be taken as (probably) facts are the actions admitted by the accused.

The bugging of the Democratic headquarters is a sordid, but not very important, offense. Spying on the opposite party and planting spies in its organization (or hiring hecklers to disrupt the opponents' meetings) is such an old trick and has been practiced for so long by both major parties that it is not sufficient to provoke nationwide concern and indignation - particularly, unilateral indignation. One of the worst forms of injustice is to condemn the accused when the accusers are guilty of the same crimes: it serves to whitewash the accusers. Bugging is reprehensible, but it is not the worst offense of today's politicians of both parties - and what they do to one another is of small significance compared to what most of them do to the country.

The break-in and theft or copying of documents at the office of Daniel Ellsberg's former psychiatrist is worse: it is a violation of the rights of private citizens - even though Ellsberg himself was on trial for theft.

The worst of the things admitted so far is the forgery of a letter, on stationery stolen from Senator Muskie's campaign offices, which was mailed to voters in the Florida Presidential primary last year: giving the impression that it came from Senator Muskie, the letter accused two other Democratic candidates of sexual misconduct. This is so sickening an approach to political campaigning that it is truly shocking that its perpetrators should have been employed by anyone employed by the White House.

Morally, the Watergate break-in, by itself, was petty larceny; the attempts to cover it up transformed it into a felony. But here, the fog is so thick that nothing can be judged with certainty - so far.

President Nixon's television speech on the matter (April 30) made things worse. The speech was godawful. Whether he did or did not know about all the dirty business, the tone of the speech made one suspect anything and anybody. This was not the time to speak "from the heart." It was not the time to plead, to appease, to placate. What was needed was firmness, clarity, and moral certainty. These were glaringly absent. What, exactly, is the meaning of accepting the "responsibility," but not the blame? If his chief aides were innocent, as he asserted, one would expect the boss to stand by them (until and unless they were proved guilty). One would also expect some explanation of the events and some clue to the motives of the participants, some better clue than a reference to their "zeal." Zeal - for what? No answer. No explanations were offered. It is likely that there were none to offer.

The most puzzling aspect of the Watergate break-in is its senselessness. The unanswered question is: Why? What did the burglars find? What did they _hope_ to find? As David Brinkley pointed out in a recent broadcast, there was nothing for them to learn that anyone in Washington could not have learned by normal means. In the screaming avalanche of press commentaries, no plausible motives have been ascribed to those men; the most frequently touted assertion is that they were seeking to perpetuate their own or Nixon's power by destroying the Constitution and the country's freedom - which is ludicrous, considering the avowed political convictions of the accusers. So the question remained unanswered.

But three columns on the Op-Ed page of _The New York Times_ of May 6, 1973, give a clue to the answer and to the whole story - the whole _psychological_ story. They do it unintentionally, by implication, between the lines - or rather, between the columns that appear accidentally on the same page.

The first column, "Pragmatism and Zeal" by Tom Wicker, declares that "the Watergate corruption is qualitatively different" from the scandals of the past. "Without memorable exception, most political corruption has concerned itself with money - payoffs, bribes and kickbacks for crooked or dubious services rendered, or simple theft of the taxpayers' dollars...No charge has yet been made that any part of the vast sums involved in the Watergate case were simply pocketed by larcenous men....It does not appear that any of the principals had the usual grafter's motive of enriching himself...The motive underlying Watergate was to insure the re-election of the President and the retention of power of those around him....In their cold pragmatism, some Nixon men apparently saw neither right nor wrong but concentrated on their goal, regardless of right or wrong."

The second column, "'The Use of Adversity'" by James Reston, echoes the same sentiments (or vice versa). "The problem [of Watergate] is the assumption that chiseling pays, that dishonesty is the best policy, that loyalty to the President is the same as loyalty to the Republic, and that if the President's objectives or ends are good and honorable, his men can use any means to support him, including discrediting, bugging, burglarizing or vilifying his opponents." Then Mr. Reston expresses the hope that Watergate may "make us wonder whether expediency and pragmatism, divorced from right and wrong, are worthy of the American republic, and even whether they work."

Pragmatism _wedded_ to "right and wrong" (i.e., to morality) is a philosophical contradiction in terms, as bad a contradiction as, for instance, an attempt to preach an atheism wedded to God. Morality is a code of principles; Pragmatism denies the validity of any principles, moral or epistemological. Pragmatism holds expediency as the only criterion of human values and actions. Truth or falsehood, it claims, cannot be known in advance of action: truth is "that which works" in a particular situation. According to this standard, the only way the Watergate burglars could know that they were doing wrong in their particular situation, was by getting caught.

Mr. Reston knows this. He is a pragmatist - not an ignorant one, but a skillfully intellectual one - judging by his columns of the past. He has praised President Nixon explicitly for Nixon's "pragmatism" and "flexibility" - on such occasions as the wage-price freeze or the rapprochement with Red China. Does this mean that when "the President's objectives or ends" meet with Mr. Reston's approval, the President "can use any means" to achieve them, including reversing himself, breaking promises, betraying friends, allies, and the voters who put him in power? I do not know Mr. Reston's answer. But a pragmatist would have to answer: "Why, yes. That's different. Everybody knows that dogmatic adherence to a rigid ideology is old-fashioned and impractical." An ideology is a set of principles.

Mr. Reston and Mr. Wicker are not the worst spokesmen of the liberal establishment; they are among the best. Politically, they would be called "moderate," and they have always been generously tolerant or compassionately sympathetic toward the Left. Yet a touch of gloating hatred for the political Right breaks through in their columns - in the form of an attempt to involve half the nation (or more) in a broad ideological smear. As follows:

Wicker: "Some of these men seemed to have believed that Mr. Nixon's re-election, his and their retention of power, the carrying out of their public purposes, were such overriding necessities that any expedient was justified. Patriotism, the national security, law and order, the work ethic, reorganization of the Federal Government - only Mr. Nixon and they could adequately provide these and other great values; liberals, doves and the like would damage or destroy them, and that could not be allowed whatever the cost."

Reston: "Nothing has hurt the President and his closest aides in the White House more than their assumption of moral superiority, their lectures on patriotism and defending the flag, which they carry in their buttonholes - all this followed by disclosures that the root assumptions of fair play and decency in the American system were being corrupted by self-righteous manipulators, managers, hucksters and burglars working out of the White House."

If this is how the liberals are cashing in on Watergate, isn't there anyone to defend that nameless, voiceless, unrepresented side which is never identified, but merely symbolized by "patriotism and the flag"? Yes. The third column on that page.

A few months ago, I said to a friend who knows Washington well, that somebody should tell Nixon that he is letting the country down - that, in line with his spectacular election victory, he ought to give people some heartening news, some fresh, clear, intellectual policy of an inspirational kind. "Oh, don't say that!" my friend cried. "If he heard it, he would give us Billy Graham!"

The third column, spread out in the center of the Op-Ed page, like a bridge linking Reston's column on one side and Wicker's on the other, is "Watergate and Its Lessons of Morality" - by Billy Graham.

"We live," says Mr. Graham, "in a society that is too often dominated by selfish interests and expediency. The time is overdue for Americans to engage in some deep soul-searching about the underpinnings of our society and our goals as a nation....No, it is not too late, but time is rapidly running out if American democracy based on Judeo-Christian tradition is to survive. First, we need a national and pervasive awakening that includes repentance for our individual and corporate sins....Let's face it - we need supernatural help! American leaders were driven to God for help at crisis periods such as the Revolutionary War, the Constitutional Convention, and the Civil War!...[The media] could render constructive service to the nation at this critical moment of history if they joined hands with the churches and synagogues and used their vast powers to fan the dying embers of the moral and spiritual life of the nation....Watergate can teach us that we need to take the law of Moses and the Sermon on the Mount seriously....The moral laws expressed in these two great documents could form the moral guidelines for every American."

In view of an intellectual spokesman or defender of this kind, do you wonder why the political Right loses every battle - and why the Left can batter rightists with impunity? Mr. Graham is not the worst of his kind. Other representatives of the Right may have a more sophisticated literary style, but, philosophically, they have nothing more to offer than the passage quoted above.

Thus, in the microcosm of a single newspaper page, you can see the reasons of America's tragedy - and of Watergate. The ideas expressed in these three columns are, jointly, the spiritual roots of the Watergate mentality.

The men involved in the Watergate conspiracy (and in its ramifications) are, for the most part, younger than those three columnists. They are the products of the same universities - which have been dominated by Pragmatism for generations; the influence of Pragmatism (and of its allies) was growing stronger, while the voices of any rational opposition were dying away. Mr. Reston had the benefit of the last echoes of a civilized past, to dilute and temper his Pragmatism. The Watergate boys did not. With nothing but such voices as Mr. Graham's to offer a counterinfluence, these boys were molded by the universities. They were too intelligent not to grasp the momentary advantages of Pragmatism, but not intelligent enough to think independently; they were too ambitious to be "impractical," but not ambitious enough to think long-range. They became pragmatists - but pure, undiluted, unexpurgated pragmatists, pragmatists to the letter and all the way down. One could almost call them "honest pragmatists," if this were not such an ambiguous term.

As a rule, it is an accident whether the smart young intellectual wheeler-dealers emitted by the colleges turn to the Left or to the Right. More often than not, those who turn to the Right do so because the Left is overcrowded and they see less competition for opportunities to climb, on the intellectually arid rocks of the Right. It is not a matter of political principles. What principles? Pragmatism has taught them that there are no such things.

But the big dilemma for all the pragmatists of the Right, is: what are they to fight and by what means, if principles are inoperative? Politics is a field in which one deals with ideas and it requires the ability to argue, to discuss, to persuade. What does one do in politics if one has discarded the whole realm of ideas? One fights _men_.

(To be continued.)

Ayn Rand

P.S. This _Letter_ was written later than the date that appears on its heading. I apologize for my delay.

The Ayn Rand Letter, published fortnightly by The Ayn Rand Letter, Inc., 183 Madison Avenue, New York, N.Y. 10016.

Contributing Editor: **Leonard Peikoff**; Subscription Director: **Elayne Kalberman**; Production Manager: **Barbara Weiss.**

Vol. II, No. 15 April 23, 1973

BROTHERS, YOU ASKED FOR IT!

Part II

The concrete-bound pragmatist mentality cannot fight for an abstract goal. It cannot fight *for* anything in the realm of ideas, only *against* something. To fight *for*, means to struggle to bring something into existence, which requires the power of abstraction; to fight *against*, means to oppose something which is there already. But even to fight against an existing idea requires the promulgation of ideas. What can one find as a substitute, which is there already and which - one has been taught - is unaffected by ideas? *Men*.

For many years past, the ideological policy and argumentation of most of the political Right has been one solid *ad hominem*. Republican candidates me-too'd the Democrats, adding only the claim that they, the Republicans, would do the job better, because they were better, kindlier, more experienced, or more folksy *men* (thus losing election after election). The crusade of Senator Joseph McCarthy was not fighting communism, but *communists*; it consisted merely in a campaign of party-card hunting. General Motors did not fight Ralph Nader on the issues, but hired investigators to spy on him, hoping to find material for a *personal* exposé (and failed). The John Birch Society ascribes all the disasters of the modern world to a conspiracy of evil *men*.

Since, according to Pragmatism's standards, it is futile to think beyond the range of the moment (of the "particular situation"), the pragmatists of the Right do not see a political job as a means to the achievement of some long-range, ideological end. To them, getting the job is the end. (E.g., if one of them aspired to the job of President, his ultimate goal would be "to be President" - with a blank thereafter.) They seek power, because that is what one is supposed to seek in politics, with no idea of "What for?" Their particular goal is not power for power's sake - this requires an ideology, even though an evil one - but *power without purpose*. Their ambition is not to change, enslave or rule the country - this requires large-scale calculations - but merely to sit in a big office, rule a staff of secretaries, and grant or deny favors to the biggest industrialists, who come begging, hat in hand. (The reward of this sort of ambition is an occasional secret thought: "Imagine poor little me, from the back streets of Podunk, refusing to see the president of International Amalgamated Gas & Oil!")

Perhaps the most damning thing I have read in connection with Watergate, is the following (*The New York Times*, May 1, 1973): "Mr. Haldeman built the Nixon staff and, when he fell, it seemed to fall with him....He looked upon himself not as an 'issues' man but as a technician and organizer, and the young men he hired and promoted met the same qualifications." At a time like the present, with the country (and the world) facing life-or-death issues, the men involved in top policy-making decisions were indifferent to issues. If so, what would their technique consist in, what would they be organizing and to what end?

Such "technicians" would know that one is supposed to fight, at election time. What would be a pragmatist's idea of a fight? Ideas - he has been taught - are impractical, it is only immediate events that count; what is true today, may not be true tomorrow; rigid values are childish, cynical "flexibility" is mature. People - he has concluded - don't think; people are not interested in ideas, only in scandal, they do not care about the good, only about some sensational exposé of somebody's evil.

Thus the younger, more impatient pragmatists would come to believe that bugging, spying, burglary, in pursuit of somebody's scandalous personal secrets, are more effective than years of speechmaking about "issues." Pragmatism is a philosophy of action, of the "now." The mentality of the activists of the Left, becomes, on the Right, the mentality of the Watergate conspirators.

This is why the moral indignation of the liberals sounds so artificial and hollow. Mr. Reston and Mr. Wicker are casting stones at their own philosophical brothers - at the children of the colleges they have praised, of the teachers they have supported, of the intellectual establishment for which they speak. True, any philosophy can be distorted by unscrupulous men. But the Watergate boys did not distort the philosophy of Pragmatism: consciously or not, they acted in accordance with its essence, they applied it faithfully and literally - and they demonstrated, in a pure, extreme, fiction-like manner, what it means to practice Pragmatism literally.

If it should be asked: but why do the liberal pragmatists succeed on the same philosophy? - the answer is: because they are not pure pragmatists; they have (or had) a long-range goal, and they claim a moral base, which the rightists cannot use. Altruism is compatible with any collectivist philosophy; it is incompatible with capitalism. Even the feeblest semi-advocates of "reformed" semi-capitalism are dimly aware of this conflict; the majority of the rightists accept altruism as the unchallengeable moral code - and are unable to reconcile it with their political views. No man and no group can have or inspire confidence without a moral base. Hence the timidity, the evasiveness, the anti-intellectuality of the Right - and the loud, aggressive moralizing of the Left. While the Right cringes, apologizes, and mumbles about "techniques" and "practicality" - the Left proposes monstrously inhuman programs (e.g., egalitarianism) in the name of the altruist code, and hears no sound of moral protest.

If the pragmatists of the Right were to reject Pragmatism and, following Billy Graham's advice, were to turn to the moral code of the Judeo-Christian tradition, it is altruism that they would have to "take seriously" and try to practice consistently. This would reenact the whole sorry history of altruism, in the minds of individual men - and would carry them straight into the camp of Mr. Reston and Mr. Wicker, into the liberal establishment and further left beyond it.

The liberal pragmatists are not very successful any longer: their goal, the Welfare State, is only a precarious way station in the march of altruism and collectivism. The liberals are not fighting for anything today, they are merely fighting against the remnants of capitalism - and they are losing ground to the more consistent altruists-collectivists, whom they appease, placate and fear: the New Left.

The moral credibility of the liberal establishment is gone. Observe their ferocious, hysterical, lynch-mob fury over the issue of Watergate. Their excesses are too much even for some liberals - for instance, Senator William Proxmire, who had the decency to say on the floor of the Senate that "the press was engaged in a campaign of 'McCarthyistic destruction' of the President that represented 'the press at its worst.'" (The Times, May 9, 1973.) He said that "'when former White House counsel John Dean is reported throughout this country to have privately told grand jury investigators that the President was directly involved in a Watergate cover-up, President Nixon is being tried, sentenced and executed by rumor and allegation.'"

The same treatment is accorded, not only to the President, but to the whole White House staff, the whole executive branch of the government, the entire American system, and wider: the more than half of the nation to whom "patriotism and the flag" are not terms of opprobrium or derision.

All the iniquities which were (falsely) ascribed to "McCarthyism" are now being practiced by the press in a nationwide orgy: _character assassination_, by unidentified witnesses ("reliable sources"), whom the victims have no chance to question or to answer - _guilt by association_, branding anyone who received a telephone call from the White House staff as a suspect in undefined crimes - _intimidation_, aimed at instilling in people the fear of supporting any group or person on the Right - smears, innuendos, malicious rumors, the hinted, the unnamed, the unspecified, the unproved, etc. There is no excuse for this type of journalism, even if all the accused were later proved to be guilty - just as there is no excuse for a lynching, even when the victim is guilty.

What is the actual motive behind this unprecedented explosion of hatred, and against whom is it actually directed? It is directed against the American people - it is the intellectuals' revenge for the landslide that rejected their leadership. It is an attempt to defeat the people and circumvent the election, not by a _coup d'état_, but by a _coup de plume_ - not by the armed force of some military clique, but by the howls of a cynical, amoral, manipulated press. Manipulated by whom? By the liberal establishment. (But censorship or government control of the press is not the answer. If the Right does not know how to fight intellectually, it is getting what it deserves.)

There is no way of knowing, at present, who is ultimately guilty in the Watergate case, but the liberal establishment and its child, the press, have proved themselves guilty on a charge which they have touchily, indignantly denied: bias - and an outrageous double standard.

Every alleged protection of civil rights, which they had invoked on behalf of the Left, has now been blown sky-high, as if none had ever existed. They had clamored that crimes motivated by political ideas are not to be treated as crimes - in the cases of Ellsberg, the Berrigan brothers, the "Chicago Seven," the various Black Panthers, etc. If so, why are the Watergate conspirators treated as criminals? I refer you to Tom Wicker's column, quoted earlier, for a clear statement of the fact that the Watergate conspirators were not motivated by "the usual grafter's motive" of financial gain, but solely by _their_ political ideas. (I do not agree with the notion that political motives excuse crimes - on _any_ political side.)

The liberals and the press have described as "idealistic" and demanded compassion for the college rebels and the activists of the New Left, whose crimes included mob violence, robbery, vandalism, destruction, arson, bombing and murder. If so, why no compassion for men guilty of eavesdropping? In case after case, the convicted criminals of the Left have received suspended or minimal sentences. The men who pleaded guilty in the Watergate case were given maximum sentences. The issue of "pre-trial publicity" has been invoked repeatedly by defendants of the Left (and even by plain criminals), with their attorneys demanding a change of venue or a dismissal, on the grounds that adverse remarks in the press made it impossible for the accused to obtain "a fair trial" in their hometowns. _Where_ would the Watergate defendants obtain a fair trial today?

The liberals and the press raise an outcry about any suspected "conflict of interests," when it involves an official who owns ten shares of some company's stock; his integrity, they claim, cannot be trusted. What about the integrity - and the veracity - of an attorney who steals his clients' documents, then bargains about immunity in exchange for his testimony against his clients?

If it is illegal to spy on a political organization and leak its secrets to its opponents, has anything been done to discover and prosecute those who leak to the press the content of secret grand-jury testimony?

And if the press is now boasting about its fearless pursuit of truth, its dedication to the people's "right to know," its dogged devotion to the uncovering of secret corruption, what was it doing a few years ago? President Johnson is alleged to have ordered a million-dollar payment to Bobby Baker, in exchange for silence about the fact that the corruption (at which Baker was caught) involved the highest level of government officials. Did any crusading journalists pursue that story? Did any dedicated seekers of the truth attempt to break through the cover-up of Chappaquiddick? And - if the fate of the entire nation is the criterion of journalistic concern - did anyone demand or pursue an investigation of the frauds in the Presidential election of 1960?

This last is, perhaps, the darkest moral stain on the record of the man who covered it up: Richard Nixon. Stewart Alsop tells the story in Newsweek (May 21, 1973): after he had conceded the election to Kennedy, Mr. Nixon "got a number of telephone calls from major supporters urging him to contest the election, on the ground that it had been stolen. More important, he got word from J. Edgar Hoover, an old ally, that the FBI had clear proof of massive vote stealing in Illinois, Texas and elsewhere." Mr. Nixon decided not to contest the election. "He might win the Presidency by demanding a recount, he said, but only at the price of chaos and bitterness, and 'I would not want the Presidency on those terms.'"

This story, if true, is a gruesome example of the murderously evil nature of altruism. (Mr. Alsop, however, cites it with approval.) By sacrificing himself and his ambition for the sake of the country, it is the country that Mr. Nixon sacrificed. By accepting an injustice, it is justice that he sacrificed. By forgiving a fraud of that magnitude, it is the Constitution that he sacrificed: he turned the country over to a man who, perhaps, in legal and moral fact, was not its President. How much of America's history would have been different if the disasters of the Kennedy and Johnson administrations had been averted? For one thing, the men who died in Vietnam would have been alive today. For another, the country would not have reached the brink of economic bankruptcy. Other consequences are incalculable. This was the way reality paid Mr. Nixon for his altruism (and lack of moral courage).

But here is the ultimate payoff (the Times, May 19, 1973): "The designation of Archibald Cox as special prosecutor for the Watergate imbroglio is a belated if hopeful start on the awesome task of restoring public confidence in the Administration's return to the rule of law....There must be some wry memories at the White House today of the new prosecutor when he was full-time leader of the Kennedy brain-trust for the 1960 election victory over Richard M. Nixon."

Ayn Rand

(This Letter was written later than the date that appears on its heading.)

The Ayn Rand Letter, published fortnightly by The Ayn Rand Letter, Inc., 183 Madison Avenue, New York, N.Y. 10016.
Contributing Editor: **Leonard Peikoff**; Subscription Director: **Elayne Kalberman**; Production Manager: **Barbara Weiss.**

Vol. II, No. 16 May 7, 1973

THE MISSING LINK

I shall begin by giving you four examples and asking you to identify what psychological element they have in common.

1. I once knew a businessman in a large Midwestern city, who was an unusually hard-working, active, energetic person. He had built a small business of his own and risen from poverty to affluence. He was the adviser and protector of an enormous conglomeration of relatives, friends, and friends of friends, who ran to him, not merely for loans, but for help with problems of any kind. He was in his late thirties, but acted as a sort of tribal patriarch.

It was hard to tell whether he enjoyed or resented his role; he seemed to take it for granted, as a kind of metaphysical duty: he had probably never thought of questioning it. He did enjoy acting as a small big shot, however, and doing favors for people, about which he was very generous. He had, apparently, some marginal connections with his particular district's political machine and he loved obtaining for his friends the sort of favors that were unobtainable without special pull, such as extra ration coupons (in World War II) or the fixing of traffic tickets. The concept of "friends" had some peculiar significance to him. He watched their _intentions_ like a hypochondriac watches his health - in a manner that projected a touchy suspiciousness and a fierce loyalty to some unwritten moral code.

Politically, he tended to be a conservative, and was usually complaining about this country's trends. One day, he launched into a passionate denunciation of the liberals, the government, the unfairness to businessmen, the arbitrary power of political machines. "Do you know how powerful they are?" he asked bitterly, and proceeded to tell me that he had tried to run for some minuscule city office, but "they" had ordered him to withdraw his candidacy "or else," and he had complied.

I said that such problems would always exist so long as government controls existed, and that the only solution was a system of full, laissez-faire capitalism, under which no groups could acquire economic privileges or special pull, so that everyone would have to stand on his own. "That's impossible!" he snapped; his voice was peculiarly tense, abrupt, defensive, as if he were slamming a mental door on some barely glimpsed fact; the voice conveyed fear. I did not pursue the subject: I had grasped a psychological issue that was new to me.

2. A well-known lady novelist once wrote an essay on the nature of fiction. Adopting an extreme Naturalist position, she declared: "The distinctive mark of

the novel is its concern with the actual world, the world of fact..." And by "fact," she meant the immediately available facts - "the empiric element in experience." "The novel does not permit occurrences outside the order of nature - miracles....You remember how in The Brothers Karamazov when Father Zossima dies, his faction (most of the sympathetic characters in the book) expects a miracle: that his body will stay sweet and fresh because he died 'in the odor of sanctity.' But instead he begins to stink. The stink of Father Zossima is the natural, generic smell of the novel. By the same law, a novel cannot be laid in the future, since the future, until it happens, is outside the order of nature..."

She declared that "the novel's characteristic tone is one of gossip and tittletattle....Here is another criterion: if the breath of scandal has not touched it, the book is not a novel....The scandals of a village or a province, the scandals of a nation or of the high seas feed on facts and breed speculation. But it is of the essence of a scandal that it be finite...It is impossible, except for theologians, to conceive of a world-wide scandal or a universe-wide scandal; the proof of this is the way people have settled down to living with nuclear fission, radiation poisoning, hydrogen bombs, satellites, and space rockets." Why facts of this kind should be regarded as the province of theology, she did not explain. "Yet these 'scandals,' in the theological sense, of the large world and the universe have dwarfed the finite scandals of the village and the province..."

She then proceeded to explain what she regards as "the dilemma of the novelist": we forget or ignore the events of the modern world, "because their special quality is to stagger belief." But if we think of them, "our daily life becomes incredible to us....The coexistence of the great world and us, when contemplated, appears impossible." From this, she drew a conclusion: since the novelist is motivated by his love of truth, "ordinary common truth recognizable to everyone," the novel is "of all forms the least adapted to encompass the modern world, whose leading characteristic is irreality. And that, so far as I can understand, is why the novel is dying."

3. The following story was told to me by an American businessman. In his youth, he took a job as efficiency-expert adviser to the manager of a factory in South America. The factory was using U.S. machines, but was getting only 45% of the machines' potential productivity. Observing the low wage scale, he concluded that the men were given no incentive to work - and suggested the introduction of pay by piecework. The elderly manager told him, with a skeptical smile, that this would be futile, but agreed to try it.

In the first three weeks of the new plan, productivity soared. In the fourth week, no one showed up for work: virtually the entire labor force vanished - and did not come back until a week later. Having earned a month's wages in three weeks, the workers saw no reason to work that extra week; they had no desire to earn more than they had been earning. No arguments could persuade them; the plan was discontinued.

4. A professor of philosophy once invited me to address his class on ethics; they were studying the subject of "justice," and he asked me to present the Objectivist view of justice. The format he proposed was a fifteen-minute presentation, followed by a question period. I pointed out to him that it would be very difficult to present, in fifteen minutes, the basis of the Objectivist ethics and thus give the reasons for my definition of justice. "Oh, you don't have

to give the reasons," he said, "just present your views." (I did not comply.)

The circumstances and the people in these four examples are different; the type of mentality they display is the same. This mentality is self-made, but many different factors can contribute to its formation. These factors may be social, as in the case of the South American workers - or personal, as in the case of the lady novelist - or both, as in the case of the Midwestern businessman. As to the professor of philosophy, the modern trend of his profession is the factor responsible for all the rest.

These cases are examples of the anti-conceptual mentality.

The main characteristic of this mentality is a special kind of passivity: not passivity as such and not across-the-board, but passivity beyond a certain limit. It is a mentality which decided, at a certain point of development, that it knows enough and does not care to look further. What does it accept as "enough"? The immediately given, directly perceivable concretes of its background - "the empiric element in experience."

To grasp and deal with such concretes, a human being needs a certain degree of conceptual development, a process which the brain of an animal cannot perform. But after the initial feat of learning to speak, a child can perform this process almost automatically, by memorization and imitation. The anti-conceptual mentality stops on this level of development - on the first levels of abstractions, which identify perceptual material consisting predominantly of physical objects - and does not choose to take the next, crucial, fully volitional step: the higher levels of abstraction from abstractions, which cannot be learned by imitation. (See my book Introduction to Objectivist Epistemology.) Such a mind can grasp the scandals of a village or a province or (at secondhand) a nation; it cannot grasp the concepts of "world" or "universe" - or the fact that their events are not "scandals."

The anti-conceptual mentality takes most things as irreducible primaries and regards them as "self-evident." It treats concepts as if they were (memorized) percepts; it treats abstractions as if they were perceptual concretes. To such a mentality, everything is the given: the passage of time, the four seasons, the institution of marriage, the weather, the breeding of children, a flood, a fire, an earthquake, a revolution, a book are phenomena of the same order. The distinction between the metaphysical and the man-made is not merely unknown to this mentality, it is incommunicable.

The two cardinal questions, the prime movers of a human mind - "Why?" and "What for?" - are alien to an anti-conceptual mentality. If asked, they elicit nothing beyond the conventionally accepted answers. The answers are usually some equivalent of "Such is life" or "One is supposed to." Whose life? Blank out. Supposed - by whom? Blank out.

The absence of concern with the "Why?" eliminates the concept of causality and cuts off the past. The absence of concern with the "What for?" eliminates long-range purpose and cuts off the future. Thus only the present is fully real to an anti-conceptual mentality. Something of the past remains with it, in the form of stagnant bits of a random chronicle, like a kind of small talk of memory, without goal or meaning. But the future is a blank; the future cannot be grasped perceptually.

In this respect, paradoxically enough, the hidebound traditionalist and the modern college activist are two sides of the same psycho-epistemological coin. The first seeks to escape the terror of an unknowable future by seeking safety in the alleged wisdom of the past. ("What was good enough for my father, is good enough for me!") The second seeks to escape the terror of an unintelligible past by screaming his way into an indefinable future. ("If it's not good for my father, it's good enough for me!") And, paradoxically enough, neither of them is able to live in the present - because man's life span is a continuum whose only integrator is his _conceptual_ faculty.

In the brain of an anti-conceptual person, the process of integration is largely replaced by a process of association. What his subconscious stores and automatizes is not ideas, but an indiscriminate accumulation of sundry concretes, random facts, and unidentified feelings, piled into unlabeled mental file folders. This works, up to a certain point - i.e., so long as such a person deals with other persons whose folders are stuffed similarly, and thus no search through the entire filing system is ever required. Within such limits, the person can be active and willing to work hard - like the Midwestern businessman, who exercised a great deal of initiative and ingenuity, within the limits set by his particular city district - like the lady novelist, who wrote many books, within the terms set by her college teachers - like the professor of philosophy, who spent his time analyzing results, without bothering about their causes.

A person of this mentality may uphold some abstract principles or profess some intellectual convictions (without remembering where or how he picked them up). But if one asks him what he means by a given idea, he will not be able to answer. If one asks him the _reasons_ of his convictions, one will discover that they are a thin, fragile film floating over a vacuum, like an oil slick in empty space - and one will be shocked by the number of questions it had never occurred to him to ask.

This kind of psycho-epistemology works so long as no part of it is challenged. But all hell breaks loose when it is - because what is threatened then is not a particular idea, but that mind's whole structure. The hell ranges from fear to resentment to stubborn evasion to hostility to panic to malice to hatred.

The best illustration of an anti-conceptual mentality is a small incident in a novel published years ago, whose title, unfortunately, I do not remember. A commonplace kind of blonde goes out on a date with a college boy; when she is asked later whether she had a good time, she answers: "No. He was awfully boring. He never said anything I ever heard before."

(To be continued.)

Ayn Rand

The Ayn Rand Letter, published fortnightly by The Ayn Rand Letter, Inc., 183 Madison Avenue, New York, N.Y. 10016.

Contributing Editor: **Leonard Peikoff**; Subscription Director: **Elayne Kalberman**; Production Manager: **Barbara Weiss.**

Vol. II, No. 17 May 21, 1973

THE MISSING LINK

Part II

The concrete-bound, anti-conceptual mentality can cope only with men who are bound by the same concretes - by the same kind of "finite" world. To this mentality, it means a world in which men do not have to deal with abstract principles: principles are replaced by memorized rules of behavior, which are accepted uncritically as the given. What is "finite" in such a world is not its extension, but the degree of mental effort required of its inhabitants. When they say "finite," they mean "perceptual."

Within the limits of their rules (which are usually called "traditions"), the inhabitants of such worlds are free to function - i.e., to deal with concretes without worrying about consequences, to deal with results without bothering about causes, to deal with "facts" as discrete phenomena, unhampered by the "intangibles" of theory - and to feel safe. Safe from what? Consciously, they would answer: "Safe from outsiders." Actually, the answer is: safe from the necessity of dealing with fundamental principles (and, consequently, safe from full responsibility for one's own life).

It is the fundamentals of philosophy (particularly, of ethics) that an anti-conceptual person dreads above all else. To understand and to apply them requires a long conceptual chain, which he has made his mind incapable of holding beyond the first, rudimentary links. If his professed beliefs - i.e., the rules and slogans of his group - are challenged, he feels his consciousness dissolving in fog. Hence, his fear of outsiders. The word "outsiders," to him, means the whole wide world beyond the confines of his village or town or gang - the world of all those people who do not live by his "rules." He does not know why he feels that outsiders are a deadly threat to him and why they fill him with helpless terror. The threat is not existential, but psycho-epistemological: to deal with them requires that he rise above his "rules" to the level of abstract principles. He would die rather than attempt it.

"Protection from outsiders" is the benefit he seeks in clinging to his group. What the group demands in return is obedience to its rules, which he is eager to obey: those rules <u>are</u> his protection - from the dreaded realm of abstract thought. By whom are those rules established? In theory, by tradition. In fact, by those who happen to be the leaders of his group; the way it stands in his mind is: by those who know the mysteries he does not have to know.

Thus, his survival depends on the substitution of <u>men</u> for ideas - and on the subordination of the metaphysical to the man-made. The metaphysical is beyond his grasp - laws of nature cannot be grasped perceptually - but man-made rules are absolutes that protect him from the unknowable, psychologically and existentially. The group comes to his rescue if he gets into trouble - and he does not have to <u>earn</u> their help, it is given to him automatically, it is not at the precarious mercy of his own virtues, flaws or errors, it is his by grace of the fact that he belongs to the group.

As an example of the principle that the rational is the moral, observe that the anti-conceptual is the profoundly anti-moral. The basic commandment of all such groups, which takes precedence over any other rules, is: <u>loyalty to the group</u> - not to ideas, but to people; not to the group's beliefs, which are minimal and chiefly ritualistic, but to the group's members and leaders. Whether a given member is right or wrong, the others must protect him from outsiders; whether he is innocent or guilty, the others must stand by him against outsiders; whether he is competent or not, the others must employ him or trade with him in preference to outsiders. Thus a physical qualification - the accident of birth in a given village or tribe - takes precedence over morality and justice. (But the physical is only the most frequently apparent and superficial qualification, since such groups reject the nonconforming children of their own members. The actual qualification is psycho-epistemological: men bound by the same concretes.)

Primitive tribes are an obvious example of the anti-conceptual mentality - perhaps, with some justification: savages, like children, are on the pre-conceptual level of development. Their later counterparts, however, demonstrate that this mentality is not the product of ignorance (nor is it caused by lack of intelligence): it is self-made, i.e., self-arrested. It has resisted the rise of civilization and has manifested itself in countless forms throughout history. Its symptom is always an attempt to circumvent reality by substituting men for ideas, the man-made for the metaphysical, favors for rights, special pull for merit - i.e., an attempt to reduce man's life to a small backyard (or rat hole) exempt from the absolutism of reason. (The driving motive of these attempts is deeper than power-lust: the rulers of such groups seek protection from reality as anxiously as the followers.)

Racism is an obvious manifestation of the anti-conceptual mentality. So is xenophobia - the fear or hatred of foreigners ("outsiders"). So is any caste system, which prescribes a man's status (i.e., assigns him to a tribe) according to his birth; a caste system is perpetuated by a special kind of snobbishness (i.e., group loyalty) not merely among the aristocrats, but, perhaps more fiercely, among the commoners or even the serfs, who like to "know their place" and to guard it jealously against the outsiders from above or from below. So is guild socialism. So is any kind of ancestor worship or of family "solidarity" (the family including uncles, aunts and third cousins). So is any criminal gang.

Tribalism (which is the best name to give to all the group manifestations of the anti-conceptual mentality) is a dominant element in Europe, as a reciprocally reinforcing cause and result of Europe's long history of caste systems, of national and local (provincial) chauvinism, of rule by brute force and endless, bloody wars. As an example, observe the Balkan nations, which are perennially bent upon exterminating one another over minuscule differences of tradition or language. Tribalism had no place in the United States - until recent decades. It could not take root here, its imported seedlings were withering away and turning to slag in the melting pot whose fire was fed by two inexhaustible sources of energy: individual rights and objective law; these two were the only protection man needed.

The remnants of European tribalism, imported by the more timid immigrants, took the innocuous form of "ethnic" neighborhoods in cities, each neighborhood offering its own customs, traditional festivals, old-country restaurants, and words in its native language on battered store-signs. Those signs were battered, because the men who clung to the tribal rule of giving trade priorities to fellow-tribesmen, remained in the backwaters of impoverished neighborhoods, while the torrent of productive energy that placed merit above tribe, swept past them, carrying away the best of their children.

There was no harm in such backwaters, so long as no one was forced to remain in them. The pressure of enlightenment by example was undercutting the group loyalty of the most stubbornly anti-conceptual mentalities, urging them to venture out into the great world where no man is an "outsider" (or all men are, as far as special privileges are concerned).

The disintegration of philosophy reversed this trend. Tribalism is a product of fear, and fear is the dominant emotion of any person, culture or society that rejects man's power of survival: reason. As philosophy slithered into the primitive swamp of irrationalism, men were driven - existentially and psychologically - into its primordial corollary: tribalism. Existentially, the rise of the Welfare State broke up the country into pressure groups, each fighting for special privileges at the expense of the others - so that an individual unaffiliated with any group became fair game for tribal predators. Psychologically, Pragmatism lobotomized the country's intellectuals: John Dewey's theory of "Progressive" education (which has dominated the schools for close to half a century), established a method of crippling a child's conceptual faculty and replacing cognition with "social adjustment." It was and is a systematic attempt to manufacture tribal mentalities. (See my article "The Comprachicos" in _The New Left: The Anti-Industrial Revolution_.)

Observe that today's resurgence of tribalism is not a product of the lower classes - of the poor, the helpless, the ignorant - but of the intellectuals, the college-educated "elitists" (which is a purely tribalistic term). Observe the proliferation of grotesque herds or gangs - hippies, yippies, beatniks, peaceniks, Women's Libs, Gay Libs, Jesus Freaks, Earth Children - which are not tribes, but shifting aggregates of people desperately seeking tribal "protection."

The common denominator of all such gangs is the belief in motion (mass demonstrations), not action - in chanting, not arguing - in demanding, not achieving - in feeling, not thinking - in denouncing "outsiders," not in pursuing values - in focusing only on the "now," the "today" without a "tomorrow" - in seeking to return to "nature," to "the earth," to the mud, to physical labor, i.e., to all the things which a _perceptual_ mentality is able to handle. You don't see advocates of reason and science clogging a street in the belief that using their bodies to stop traffic, will solve any problem.

Most of those embryonic tribal gangs are leftist or collectivist. But, as a demonstration of the fact that the cause of tribalism is deeper than politics, there are tribalists still further removed from reality, who claim to be rightists. They are champions of individualism, they claim, which they define as the right to form one's own gang and use physical force against others - and they intend to preserve capitalism, they claim, by replacing it with anarchism (establishing "private" or "competing" governments, i.e., tribal rule). The common denominator of such individualists is the desire to escape from objectivity (objectivity requires a very long conceptual chain and very abstract principles), to act on whim, and to deal with men rather than with ideas - i.e., with the men of their own gang bound by the same concretes.

These rightists' distance from reality may be gauged by the fact that they are unable to recognize the actual examples of their ideals in practice. One such example is the Mafia. The Mafia (or "family") is a "private government," with subjects who chose to join it voluntarily, with a rigid set of rules rigidly, efficiently and bloodily enforced, a "government" that undertakes to protect you from "outsiders" and to enforce your immediate interests - at the price of your selling your soul, i.e., of your total obedience to any "favor" it may demand. Another example of a "government" without territorial sovereignty is offered by the Palestinian guerrillas, who have no country of their own, but who engage in terroristic attacks and slaughter of "outsiders" anywhere on earth.

The activist manifestations of modern tribalism, of Left or "Right," are crude extremes. It is the subtler manifestations of the anti-conceptual mentality that are more tragic and harder to deal with. These are the "mixed economies" of the spirit - the men torn inwardly between tribal emotions and scattered fragments of thought - the products of modern education who do not like the nature of what they feel, but have never learned to think.

The Watergate affair offers an example, on both political sides. On the Left, there is the press, whose biased unanimity would be the envy of any dictator's censorship bureau. But that unanimity is voluntary and it is not the product of a conspiracy - it is the product of the notion that one must "belong," one must be "in," one must swim with the mainstream, one must take one's cue from "those who know." Occasionally, some newsman's voice cries out in protest, pleading for fairness, then vanishes. No man can be blind to reality all of the time; but modern men do not know how to maintain the continuity of their sight.

(In the intellectual professions, tribalism takes the form of cliques. Today, there is only one clique, because there is only one kind of philosophy in the educational establishment. The clashes and rivalries of factions scrambling for power within a clique are ferocious, as they are within any tribe, but the clique or the tribe presents a united front against "outsiders" - in this case, against the rightists.)

On the Right, there are the men involved in Watergate, who offer the pathetically horrible spectacle of what happens when men with basically tribal (pragmatist) premises find no tribe to join, yet attempt to practice tribal loyalty - i.e., to substitute a group for principles, or men for ideas.

With no ideology to guide them, those boys had to feel that fighting the "outsiders" by any kind of means was the proper and practical thing to do. Each of them acted as the others were acting, each assumed that the others knew what they were doing (or that some higher authorities knew it), none questioned anything. It was the desperate voice of tribalism that we heard when one of them confessed that he was willing to commit perjury rather than have his superiors think that he was not a "team player."

But there was no "team" or tribe. A tribe has firm rules, and it stands by those who observe them. This horde had firm rules of procedure (of who sends memos to whom), but no rules in regard to substance. As at a Progressive nursery school's fantasy-playing time, the boys were sent out into the arena with a single commandment: "Do something!" They did.

Then they found themselves alone, with no tribe to protect them, abandoned by those trusted leaders who knew the mysteries they did not have to know. They found their immediate superiors scrambling frantically to pass the buck to them and to one another, each struggling to frame the others and to save himself by the loudest "singing." What else was there for those pragmatists to do? Loyalty can be maintained in only one of two ways: by terrorism - or by dedication to ideas. But if those Republicans had been united by ideas, they would not have been a quasi-tribe - they would have been a rational human association.

This is the crucial difference between an association and a tribe. Just as a proper society is ruled by laws, not by men, so a proper association is united by ideas, not by men, and its members are loyal to the ideas, not to the group. It is eminently reasonable that men should seek to associate with those who share their convictions and values. It is impossible to deal or even to communicate with men whose ideas are fundamentally opposed to one's own (and one should be free not to deal with them). All proper associations are formed or joined by individual choice and on conscious, intellectual grounds (philosophical, political, professional, etc.) - not by the physiological or geographical accident of birth, and not on the ground of tradition. When men are united by ideas, i.e., by explicit principles, there is no room for favors, whims, or arbitrary power: the principles serve as an *objective* criterion for determining actions and for *judging* men, whether leaders or members.

This requires a high degree of conceptual development and independence, which the anti-conceptual mentality is desperately struggling to avoid. But this is the only way men can work together justly, benevolently - and *safely*. There is no way for men to survive on the perceptual level of consciousness.

I am not a student of the theory of evolution and, therefore, I am neither its supporter nor its opponent. But a certain hypothesis has haunted me for years; I want to stress that it is only a hypothesis. There is an enormous breach of continuity between man and all the other living species. The difference lies in the nature of man's consciousness, in its distinctive characteristic: his conceptual faculty. It is as if, after aeons of physiological development, the evolutionary process altered its course, and the higher stages of development focused primarily on the consciousness of living species, not their bodies. But the development of a man's consciousness is volitional: no matter what the innate degree of his intelligence, he must develop it, he must learn how to use it, he must become a human being by choice. What if he does not choose to? Then he becomes a transitional phenomenon - a desperate creature that struggles frantically against his own nature, longing for the effortless "safety" of an animal's consciousness, which he cannot recapture, and rebelling against a human consciousness, which he is afraid to achieve.

For years, scientists have been looking for a "missing link" between man and animals. Perhaps that missing link is the anti-conceptual mentality.

Ayn Rand

The Ayn Rand Letter, published fortnightly by The Ayn Rand Letter, Inc., 183 Madison Avenue, New York, N.Y. 10016.
Contributing Editor: **Leonard Peikoff**; Subscription Director: **Elayne Kalberman**; Production Manager: **Barbara Weiss.**

Vol. II, No. 18 June 4, 1973

SELFISHNESS WITHOUT A SELF

In my last two Letters, I discussed the anti-conceptual mentality and its social (tribal) manifestations. All tribalists are anti-conceptual in various degrees, but not all anti-conceptual mentalities are tribalists. Some are lone wolves (stressing that species' most predatory characteristics).

The majority of such wolves are frustrated tribalists, i.e., persons rejected by the tribe (or by the people of their immediate environment): they are too unreliable to abide by conventional rules, and too crudely manipulative to compete for tribal power. Since a perceptual mentality cannot provide a man with a way of survival, such a person, left to his own devices, becomes a kind of intellectual hobo, roaming about as an eclectic second-hander or brainpicker, snatching bits of ideas at random, switching them at whim, with only one constant in his behavior: the drifting from group to group, the need to cling to people, any sort of people, and to manipulate them.

Whatever theoretical constructs he may be able to spin and juggle in various fields, it is the field of ethics that fills him with the deepest sense of terror and of his own impotence. Ethics is a conceptual discipline; loyalty to a code of values requires the ability to grasp abstract principles and to apply them to concrete situations and actions (even on the most primitive level of practicing some rudimentary moral commandments). The tribal lone wolf has no firsthand grasp of values. He senses that this is a lack he must conceal at any price - and that this issue, for him, is the hardest one to fake. The whims that guide him and switch from moment to moment or from year to year, cannot help him to conceive of an inner state of lifelong dedication to one's chosen values. His whims condition him to the opposite: they automatize his avoidance of any permanent commitment to anything or anyone. Without personal values, a man can have no sense of right or wrong. The tribal lone wolf is an amoralist all the way down.

The clearest symptom by which one can recognize this type of person, is his total inability to judge himself, his actions, or his work by any sort of standard. The normal pattern of self-appraisal requires a reference to some abstract value or virtue - e.g., "I am good because I am rational," "I am good because I am honest," even the second-hander's notion of "I am good because people like me." Regardless of whether the value-standards involved are true or false, these examples imply the recognition of an essential moral principle: that one's own value has to be earned.

The amoralist's implicit pattern of self-appraisal (which he seldom identifies or admits) is: "I am good because it's me."

Beyond the age of about three to five (i.e., beyond the perceptual level of mental development), this is not an expression of pride or self-esteem, but of the opposite: of a vacuum - of a stagnant, arrested mentality confessing its impotence to achieve any personal value or virtue.

Do not confuse this pattern with psychological subjectivism. A psychological subjectivist is unable fully to identify his values or to prove their objective validity, but he may be profoundly consistent and loyal to them in practice (though with terrible psycho-epistemological difficulty). The amoralist does not hold subjective values; he does not hold _any_ values. The implicit pattern of all his estimates is: "It's good because _I_ like it" - "It's right because _I_ did it" - "It's true because _I_ want it to be true." What is the "I" in these statements? A physical hulk driven by chronic anxiety.

The frequently encountered examples of this pattern are: the writer who rehashes some ancient bromides and feels that his work is new, because _he_ wrote it - the non-objective artist who feels that his smears are superior to those made by a monkey's tail, because _he_ made them - the businessman who hires mediocrities because _he_ likes them - the political "idealist" who claims that racism is good if practiced by a minority (of _his_ choice), but evil if practiced by a majority - and any advocate of any sort of double standard.

But even such shoddy substitutes for morality are only a pretense: the amoralist does not believe that "I am good because it's _me_." That implicit policy is his protection against his deepest, never-to-be-identified conviction: "_I am no good through and through_."

Love is a response to values. The amoralist's actual self-appraisal is revealed in his abnormal need to be loved (but not in the rational sense of the word) - to be "loved for himself," i.e., _causelessly_. James Taggart reveals the nature of such a need: "I don't want to be loved _for_ anything. I want to be loved for myself - not for anything I do or have or say or think. For myself - not for my body or mind or words or works or actions." (_Atlas Shrugged_.) When his wife asks: "But then...what _is_ yourself?" he has no answer.

As a real-life example: Years ago, I knew an older woman who was a writer and very intelligent, but inclined toward mysticism, embittered, hostile, lonely, and very unhappy. Her views of love and friendship were similar to James Taggart's. At the time of the publication of _The Fountainhead_, I told her that I was very grateful to Archibald Ogden, the editor who had threatened to resign if his employers did not publish it. She listened with a peculiar kind of skeptical or disapproving look, then said: "You don't have to feel grateful to him. He did not do it for _you_. He did it to further his own career, because he thought it was a good book." I was truly appalled. I asked: "Do you mean that his action would be better - and that I should prefer it - if he thought it was a worthless book, but fought for its publication out of _charity_ to me?" She would not answer and changed the subject. I was unable to get any explanation out of her. It took me many years to begin to understand.

A similar phenomenon, which had puzzled me for a long time, can be observed in politics. Commentators often exhort some politician to place the interests of the country above his own (or his party's) and to compromise with his opponents - and such exhortations are not addressed to petty grafters, but to reputable men. What does this mean? If the politician is convinced that his ideas are right, it is the country that he would betray by compromising. If he is convinced that his opponents' ideas are wrong, it is the country that he would be harming. If he is not certain of either, then he should check his views for his own sake, not merely the country's - because the truth or falsehood of his ideas should be of the utmost _personal_ interest to him.

But these considerations presuppose a conceptual consciousness that takes ideas seriously - i.e., that derives its views from principles derived from reality. A perceptual consciousness is unable to believe that ideas can be of _personal_ importance to anyone; it regards ideas as a matter of arbitrary choice, as means to some immediate ends. On this view, a man does not seek to be elected to a public office in order to carry out certain policies - he advocates certain policies in order to be elected. If so, then why on earth should he want to be elected? Perceptual mentalities never ask such a question: the concept of a long-range goal is outside their limits. (There are a great many politicians and a great many commentators of that type - and since that mentality is taken for granted as proper and normal, what does this indicate about the intellectual state of today's culture?)

If a man subordinates ideas and principles to his "personal interests," what are his personal interests and by what means does he determine them? Consider the senseless, selfless drudgery to which a politician condemns himself if the goal of his work - the proper administration of the country - is of no personal interest to him (or a lawyer, if justice is of no personal interest to him; or a writer, if the objective value of his books is of no personal interest to him, as the woman I quoted was suggesting). But a perceptual mentality is incapable of generating values or goals, and has to pick them secondhand, as the given, then go through the expected motions. (Not all such men are tribal lone wolves - some are faithful, bewildered tribalists out of their psycho-epistemological depth - but all are anti-conceptual mentalities.)

With all of his emphasis on "himself" (and on being "loved for himself"), the tribal lone wolf has no self and no personal interests, only momentary whims. He is aware of his own immediate sensations and of very little else. Observe that whenever he ventures to speak of spiritual (i.e., intellectual) values - of the things he personally loves or admires - one is shocked by the triteness, the vulgarity, the borrowed trashiness of what comes out of him.

A tribal lone wolf feels that his "self" is dissociated from his actions, his work, his pursuits, his ideas. All these, he feels, are things that some outside power - society or reality or the material universe - has somehow forced on him. His real "self," he feels, is some ineffable entity devoid of attributes. One thing is true: his "self" _is_ ineffable, i.e., non-existent. A man's self is his mind - the faculty that perceives reality, forms judgments, chooses values. To a tribal lone wolf, "reality" is a meaningless term; his metaphysics consists in the chronic feeling that life, somehow, is a conspiracy of people and things against _him_, and he will walk over piles of corpses - in order to assert himself? no - in order to hide (or fill) the nagging inner vacuum left by his aborted self.

The grim joke on mankind is the fact that _he_ is held up as a symbol of _selfishness_. This encourages him in his depredations: it gives him the hope of success in faking a stature he knows to be beyond his power. Selfishness is a profoundly philosophical, _conceptual_ achievement. Anyone who holds a tribal lone wolf as an image of selfishness, is merely confessing the perceptual nature of his own mental functioning.

Yet the tribalists keep proclaiming that morality is an exclusively social phenomenon and that adherence to a tribe - any tribe - is the only way to keep men moral. But the docile members of a tribe are no better than their rejected wolfish brother and fully as amoral: their standard is "We're good because it's _us_."

The abdication and shriveling of the self is a salient characteristic of all perceptual mentalities, tribalist or lone-wolfish. All of them dread self-reliance; all of them dread the responsibilities which only a self (i.e., a conceptual consciousness) can perform, and they seek escape from the two activities which an actually selfish man would defend with his life: judgment and choice. They fear reason (which is exercised volitionally) and trust their emotions (which are automatic) - they prefer relatives (an accident of birth) to friends (a matter of choice) - they prefer the tribe (the given) to outsiders (the new) - they prefer commandments (the memorized) to principles (the understood) - they welcome every theory of determinism, every notion that permits them to cry: "I couldn't help it!"

It is obvious why the morality of altruism is a tribal phenomenon. Prehistorical men were physically unable to survive without clinging to a tribe for leadership and protection against other tribes. The cause of altruism's perpetuation into civilized eras is not physical, but psycho-epistemological: the men of self-arrested, perceptual mentality are unable to survive without tribal leadership and "protection" against reality. The doctrine of self-sacrifice does not offend them: they have no sense of self or of personal value - they do not know what it is that they are asked to sacrifice - they have no firsthand inkling of such things as intellectual integrity, love of truth, personally chosen values, or a passionate dedication to an idea. When they hear injunctions against "selfishness," they believe that what they must renounce is the brute, mindless whim-worship of a tribal lone wolf. But their leaders - the theoreticians of altruism - know better. Immanuel Kant knew it; John Dewey knew it; B.F. Skinner knows it; John Rawls knows it. Observe that it is not the mindless brute, but reason, intelligence, ability, merit, self-confidence, self-esteem that they are out to destroy.

Today, we are seeing a ghastly spectacle: a magnificent scientific civilization dominated by the morality of prehistorical savagery. The phenomenon that makes it possible is the split psycho-epistemology of "compartmentalized" minds. Its best example are men who escape into the physical sciences (or technology or industry or business), hoping to find protection from human irrationality, and abandoning the field of ideas to the enemies of reason. Such refugees include some of mankind's best brains. But no such refuge is possible. These men, who perform feats of conceptual integration and rational thinking in their work, become helplessly anti-conceptual in all the other aspects of their lives, particularly in human relationships and in social issues. (E.g., compare Einstein's scientific achievement to his political views.)

Man's progress requires specialization. But a division-of-labor society cannot survive without a rational philosophy - without a firm base of fundamental principles whose task is to train a human mind to be human, i.e., conceptual.

Ayn Rand

The Ayn Rand Letter, published fortnightly by The Ayn Rand Letter, Inc., 183 Madison Avenue, New York, N.Y. 10016.
Contributing Editor: **Leonard Peikoff**; Subscription Director: **Elayne Kalberman**; Production Manager: **Barbara Weiss.**

Vol. II, No. 19 June 18, 1973

THE PRINCIPALS...

Television has a peculiar power to reveal the essence of a man's character. One learns more from a televised image than from a face-to-face encounter; an act that may work in a drawing room is magnified and stripped away, leaving the man naked. The camera seems to photograph, not men's faces, but their souls. It is a wonderful invader of psychological privacy, more potent than a lie detector. Most politicians should run from a TV camera, invoking the Fifth Amendment.

Whatever other truth the televised Senate hearings on Watergate may disclose or obfuscate, there is one truth which they have resoundingly succeeded in disclosing: the characters of men representing a good cross section of both political parties. We had a chance to see, under the luminous microscope of a television camera, the kind of men who run this country's government. "Government," to most people, is a big, vague, floating abstraction; the hearings concretized it. The question I would like to ask the viewers who stuck it out to the end of the first phase, is: Do you feel respect for the men on either side of the long committee table?

The witnesses' side gave us a sample of the executive branch of the government. We were shown a hierarchical progression of the White House (and reelection committee) staff, which displayed an interesting paradox: with some exceptions, the progression went from lower to higher administratively, but in reverse psychologically.

First, we saw the hopeless little pragmatists of the lower echelons, who were climbers with no peak to reach, idealists with no ideals to uphold, and tribalists with no tribe to protect them. (See my *Letter* of May 21, 1973.) They had been willing blindly to trust their superiors, in the belief that those superiors knew the philosophical base and moral principles guiding their activities, which they, the underlings, did not have to know. Now observe what knowledge (and character) was revealed by their superiors.

Jeb Stuart Magruder, deputy director of the Committee to Re-elect the President, seemed to assume a soft, pleasant manner on the witness stand; but the TV camera revealed that his softness was genuine, inside and out. His act did not jell: he projected contriteness and brashness, pleading and glibness, remorse and resentment, and an incurably juvenile superficiality. He was a thoroughly conventional young man, molded - without any inner resistance - by *modern* conventions.

An old-fashioned code of honor demanded that a captain be last to leave a sinking ship. Magruder reversed that code: he leaped off the ship, with a life belt of perjury - abandoning, not only the seven burglars who had acted under his authorization, but the rest of his staff as well, hoping that they would all go down in silence. Then, struck with bewildered indignation at the possibility that his superiors might abandon him, he decided to "sing."

Magruder had been in active command of a national election campaign, yet the startling aspect of his performance on the witness stand was the total absence of any ideological concerns - the crude inability to grasp political issues, principles or implications. He admitted that his activities had been illegal, but explained them by placing the blame on the fact that leftist demonstrators were getting away with illegal activities. A man of principle would be justified in feeling moral indignation at the demonstrators - so long as he did not sink to their level. But Magruder did - and he opposed them, not on principle, but on personal grounds. He described his motive as: "...there was that feeling of resentment and of frustration at being unable to deal with issues on a legal basis."

This gave Senator Ervin a springboard for one of his most vicious bursts of oratory. "I came up here during Joe McCarthy days when Joe McCarthy saw a communist hiding under every rose bush," he thundered, "and I have been here fighting the no-knock laws and preventive detention laws and indiscriminate bugging by people who've found subversives hiding under every bed. In this nation, we have had a very unfortunate fear. And this fear went to the extent of deploring the exercise of personal rights for those who wanted to assemble and petition the Government for redress of grievances....Now, I think that all grew out of this complement of fear, did it not, the whole Watergate incident?"

To ridicule the recognition of the clear and present danger posed by subversives, as paranoid "fear," is worse than demagoguery. When bombings, arson and murder are running loose on college campuses and city streets, it should be clear to anyone that the subversives have crawled out from under beds and rose bushes. But it was not clear to Magruder. "I think from my own personal standpoint, I did lose some respect for the legal process simply because I did not see it working as I had hoped it would when I came here," answered Magruder, blithely deaf to the horrendous implications of Ervin's speech.

Fred D. Thompson, the perceptive minority counsel (Republican), tried to bail Magruder out and counteract Ervin's unconscionable statement, by asking: "Were you concerned about legitimate demonstrations, or were there more serious things going on in the country at that time? Up until that time had there been bombings of public buildings, for example?" In an almost patronizing tone of voice, Magruder answered: "Well I think it goes much deeper than that, not only were there bombings of public buildings, we had death threats against Mr. Mitchell's life. We had continuous demonstrations in front of our headquarters." The tone of voice said, in effect: "Public bombings, hell! They threatened us!"

Mr. Thompson tried again, obviously struggling to impart some political stature to a sulking juvenile: "Had there been a series of break-ins of F.B.I. offices, for example?" "Yes, sir, many." "Was it your opinion at the time there were plans afoot to make some attempt to overthrow the Government by illegal and improper means?" "I would not go so far as to say overthrow the Government," Magruder answered scornfully, and went on in a tone of disclosing something much more important: "I think we had some concern about them overthrowing our convention as they did the Democratic party convention in 1968." Mr. Thompson gave up.

Former Secretary Maurice H. Stans, director of the campaign's finance committee, disclaimed any concern with ideological issues, as a matter of right. His job, he declared, was only to raise money for the campaign, not to know how the money was spent nor what was the content, policy or strategy of the campaigning. For these, he passed the buck to the director of the re-election committee, former Attorney General John N. Mitchell.

Mr. Mitchell was an old pro; his calm, self-confident manner was a relief to see after a procession of cringing penitents; by contrast, he imparted some dignity to the proceedings. But ideological issues were not his specialty; he was, he implied, an executive, not a theoretician. The TV camera suggested - by some almost imperceptible shadings of his facial expressions - that he was, perhaps, more dedicated to his political convictions than any of his younger, sloppier predecessors on the witness stand. But what these convictions were, he firmly avoided saying. He named his devotion to Richard Nixon as his only political motive. Listening to him, one felt that some of the things he said were true and some were not, but which was which no one would ever be able to tell.

John W. Dean 3d., Counsel to the President, interrupted the progression of witnesses, with its inversely rising-falling lines: the psychological line crashed to the bottom and stayed there for the duration of his testimony. Dean's face, with its rodent-like jaw structure, was almost unbearable to watch. It is probable that he does not look quite so sordidly contemptible in person; but the television camera reveals too much.

Dean's testimony was based on the calculation that it would take years of effort to untangle all his evasions, contradictions, half-truths, and gaping holes - an effort no one would care to waste. In answering questions, he used the technique of giving an overabundance of unverifiable details, or repeating long, memorized passages in identical words, or launching into such a web of irrelevant side issues that the question was lost and remained unanswered.

Three things stood out in his testimony: 1. According to the facts of his own story, his role in the cover-up consisted, not in investigating or containing the scandal, but in deliberately involving as many prominent members and associates of the Nixon Administration as possible (for a purpose one can easily guess). 2. Only the pure malice of a defeated manipulator can explain his ultimatum that he would not resign unless Haldeman and Ehrlichman were also forced to resign. 3. As a general rule, whenever a man refuses to put his words in writing, one may be certain that he has been lying. When Dean was asked by Mr. Nixon to prepare a <u>written</u> report on Watergate, he would not comply; he ran to the prosecutor, instead (knowing, apparently, that the jig was up). This alone should be sufficient to impeach Dean's credibility.

But all these are merely details, of no importance compared to one overriding fact: John Dean is a lawyer who bargained for his own immunity in exchange for the confidential documents he stole from his former clients. Nothing else need be known - or considered - about him. That this should be accepted and passed over in silence by a Senate committee - a committee whose alleged purpose (and rhetorical theme) was to protect the right of <u>privacy</u>, to deplore this country's <u>moral</u> deterioration, to seek a rebirth of public <u>morality</u> - that Dean should be given a respectful, almost friendly treatment by such a committee, will contribute more to this country's demoralization than any grafters or wiretappers ever could. <u>This</u> - more than all the other manifestations of a cynical double standard - can destroy the last of people's confidence in anyone's appeals to decency, morality and justice.

Neither the young witnesses nor the public could expect any ideological guidance from John Dean: the concept of "political ideas" is irrelevant in his case. But Ehrlichman and Haldeman were at the top of the executive pyramid; if anyone knew the philosophical base, the goals and the ideals of the political battle, these two would be expected to know and to give some indication - some defense of a party subjected to such an uncontested battering.

John D. Ehrlichman was regarded as the "issues" man, i.e., the ideologue of the White House. A tall, muscular, somewhat beefy figure, he lounged in the witness chair and answered questions by turn too placidly or too defiantly, in the arrogant manner of a man faking self-confidence. How can one tell it was faked? A self-confident man does not sneer; there was a chronic sneer in the corners of Ehrlichman's fleshy, petulant mouth.

His intellectual contribution consisted mainly in declaring that, in cases involving national security, the President has an inherent, unlimited power to use any means whatever, including break-ins and wiretapping, at his sole discretion. (This is a totally untenable position: even though a President _should_ have wide powers in regard to national security, and particularly in regard to surveillance, no government official may hold unlimited power in this country, in any issue, and the exercise of any power he holds must be clearly, carefully defined and delimited.) Ehrlichman asserted his sweeping generalization as a _principle_ - and got caught when one of the Senators asked him whether the President's power would include the right to murder. Ehrlichman answered that he did not know where to draw the line and shrugged it off by adding that he was not a constitutional lawyer. So much for the theoretician of the political party that claims to stand for freedom and individual rights.

But Ehrlichman showed a much greater interest, zeal and tenacity when he argued on another subject: he fought for the notion that exposing the private lives and personal weaknesses of candidates is a proper part of political campaigning. He confined his examples to alcoholism, but it was obvious that he meant sexual misbehavior as well. If the young pragmatists at the bottom of the pyramid had no idea of how to fight a battle of ideas, but hoped for leadership from the top, it was a dismal experience to see that the top was rocky, windswept and empty.

H.R. Haldeman completed the picture. He was regarded as a man of action, not of ideas - and he acted accordingly. He was a bit too cheery, he smiled a bit too often, he had the kind of face that used to be described as "wholesome and clean-cut," like a college cheerleader of the 1920s. His testimony was like his face: bland. He never referred to any ideological matters, in the carefree, almost righteous manner of a man who is said to have "his feet on the ground" and does not waste time on abstractions.

But one small incident made me wonder. Under the pressure of questioning about the campaign, Haldeman showed a touch of Magruder-like self-pity, complaining that the Democrats had indulged in many "dirty tricks," while the Republicans had been more restrained. And suddenly, sitting up, his eyes sparkling with authentic intensity, his voice acquiring the tone of a dedicated crusader, he declared that the Republicans had known some momentous secret - "the Fort Wayne incident" - but President Nixon had forbidden them ever to use it, and they never did. His manner suggested that the disclosure of the secret would have been disastrous for the Democrats - and there was a note of pride in his voice, suggesting the sadness and nobility of renunciation. It made me think that there was, perhaps, some important issue about which he cared profoundly - and I wondered why no one questioned him about it.

Next day, I learned from the newspapers what the Fort Wayne incident was. A woman in Fort Wayne had an illegitimate child whose father's name was listed as "George McGovern"; no one even knew whether it was Senator George McGovern or not. This "big secret" was, for me, the end of the Nixon Administration - i.e., of the hope that it would ever be able to offer anything of value or to achieve any intellectual stature. (No, I do not regret that I voted for Nixon, because I would vote for almost anyone against Senator McGovern or Senator Kennedy, but this is not saying much.)

The best witness of the hearings was the last - Henry E. Petersen, Assistant Attorney General - who gave the best characterization of the men involved in Watergate: "None of them acted innocent." I would apply it to more than their behavior in the campaign.

(To be continued.)

Ayn Rand

P.S. This <u>Letter</u> was written later than the date that appears on its heading.

OBJECTIVIST CALENDAR

We have been asked to announce that Phillip J. Smith will offer an acting workshop, open to beginning and intermediate students. The workshop will begin in the third week of September and will run for 14 weeks. For further information, contact Mr. Smith at 315 West 91st Street, New York, N.Y. 10024. Telephone: (212) 724-1117.

B.W.

The Ayn Rand Letter, published fortnightly by The Ayn Rand Letter, Inc., 183 Madison Avenue, New York, N.Y. 10016.
Contributing Editor: **Leonard Peikoff**; Subscription Director: **Elayne Kalberman**; Production Manager: **Barbara Weiss.**

Vol. II, No. 20 July 2, 1973

THE PRINCIPALS...

Part II

If the executive branch of the government presented a sorry picture at the Senate hearings, did the legislative branch do any better? If the Watergate affair was a national disgrace, was the antidote different in kind or only in degree? Let us take a look at the stature of the men on the other side of the committee table.

It is not wrong for a politician to seek to impress his audience: it is part of his profession. But in the midst of a solemn inquiry - with grandiloquent statements about this country's imperiled future, freedom, Constitution and rights, with lofty appeals to morality and pious invocations of justice - it is worse than wrong if the chief concern, superseding all others in the minds of the interrogators, is concern with their television close-ups.

Senator Sam J. Ervin Jr. (Democrat), the committee's Chairman, was the most obvious, but not the worst offender in this respect. He almost winked at the camera when it moved toward him; he did not purr - it was only the look on his face that suggested it. He acted like an old ham, worn out by the silence of years of touring the sticks, who suddenly hears himself applauded. He overdid it. He dragged in his entire repertoire, from Shakespeare to the Bible, he sputtered rustic jokes, he stammered thunderous maledictions, he basked, he rolled over, with one eye on the gallery and the other on the camera.

There were two embarrassing miscalculations in his performance. First, there is a type of humor which relies on a preposterous contrast, e.g., a beautiful woman referring to herself as "ugly"; it misfires when an ugly woman refers to herself as "ugly" - which is what happened whenever Senator Ervin referred to himself as "just a country lawyer." Second, jokes are appropriate on some occasions, but not when the occasion requires solemn dignity - and not over the body of a helpless victim subpoenaed to the rack, not even if the victim deserves it.

Senator Daniel K. Inouye (Democrat) appeared, at first, to be the most intelligent and dignified of the interrogators. He did not joke; he seldom smiled; he spoke briefly and to the point, in an unusually attractive voice that projected a kind of old-fashioned, patrician elegance. But when an aristocrat resorts to demagogic questions, the effect is sadder and worse than when a common rabble-rouser propounds them. For instance, Senator Inouye asked H.R. Haldeman whether he had erased any part of President Nixon's tapes. Since there was nothing in the evidence to indicate it, the only effect of the question was to plant in the minds of the audience (and of the press) a suspicion that could never be proved or disproved. Whatever the motives behind the question, a quest for truth was not one of them.

Senator Joseph M. Montoya (Democrat) was unable to focus long enough to remember the beginning of his question by the time he reached the end. He was unable to remember the testimony, and he kept holding the camera by means of long stretches of incoherent verbiage, delivering - in the aggressive tone of springing a bombshell - a question that had been asked and answered three or four times. Helplessness, as such, is not wicked; it becomes so when written all over a face in conjunction with belligerence, resentment, and a kind of pouting hostility. The grotesquely original part of Senator Montoya's performance was a question he repeated to witness after witness, to the effect that: How could anyone have been ignorant about the facts of Watergate when they had all been printed in the newspapers? - his tone of voice suggesting a kind of triumphantly self-righteous indignation, along with the belief that the truth of anything printed in the newspapers is beyond the realm of doubt. He asked it even of Assistant Attorney General Petersen - after Petersen had testified about the difficulties of establishing proof in criminal cases.

Senator Edward J. Gurney (Republican) seemed to be the lone dissenter on the committee. He did not lack courage, but he lacked ammunition - and hope - as if he had given up before he started. For instance, he tried to challenge Dean's testimony, but what did he pick on? He succeeded in proving that Dean had been inaccurate about the location of the Mayflower Coffee Shop.

Senator Herman E. Talmadge (Democrat) revealed nothing under the television camera, except a big grin and a heavy Southern accent. Perhaps, this was all he had to reveal.

Senator Lowell P. Weicker Jr. (Republican) revealed a great deal. He acted like a hatchet man in the service of the lowest-grade editorials of the leftist-liberal press. He used his on-camera time to make speeches on every standard item of their line. He screamed - literally screamed - at the witnesses and shook his finger at them in the manner of a district attorney in a grade-B movie melodrama, with as authentic a tone of righteous indignation. He was heavy, slumped and sprawling, but he shook all over: finger, arm, shoulders, voice and flesh. His acting was inept, but when he raised his face, with pale, blurred eyes and quivering jowls, the camera caught something real: such a profound, venomous, festering hatred that one had to turn away, with the feeling that he ought to be prosecuted for indecent exposure.

The worst - or most skillful - manipulator of the camera was Senator Howard H. Baker Jr. (Republican), the committee's Vice Chairman. His was a professional performance: it consisted in ignoring the camera too pointedly and achieving well-calculated "spontaneous" effects. His every gesture, pause and intonation were timed to project - in discrete installments - the attributes of a Madison-Avenue image of a young lawmaker: ingenuous openness, boyish earnestness, idealism, impartiality and depth. It was a solid act, a studied act, and an act aimed at showing that he had no act. For instance, would you regard the following as an expression of ingenuous unselfconsciousness? The camera moved in on him at the start of his turn to question a witness, and found him with his head bowed in thought and a pencil scratching the back of his ear, which lasted just the right number of seconds, while the hapless witness waited offscreen and the camera registered the portentous silence.

Senator Baker's "impartiality" was expressed by an obsequious courting of Senator Ervin, whom he addressed as "My Chairman" (in the manner of a French soldier addressing Napoleon as "Mon Empereur"), and by an insistent me-too-ing of Ervin's most partisan rulings, with compliments to "My Chairman's" fairness. Senator Baker's "boyish charm" was expressed by joking and bantering in the casual manner of a host letting his hair down at a small, private party. His "earnestness" was expressed by a sudden pause in the midst of an interrogation and a somber, silent stare at the more frightened of the younger witnesses, a stare held long enough to register on the witness and on the audience. His "idealism" was expressed by prying questions on the theme of morality, designed to elicit an abject concession of moral guilt, addressed to the younger, the more obviously vulnerable witnesses, but not addressed to men like Dean or Mitchell. His "depth" was expressed by the sudden introduction of an intense, personal plea, in some such words as: "Will you tell me, because I am really puzzled...because I really want to know..." - the tone of voice projecting a helpless groping for truth, followed by a question in the form of a remarkable flow of generalities suggesting some profound, philosophical concern, on some level above the mundane preoccupations of the moment, but actually saying nothing, like the gems of wisdom one finds in illustrated calendars.

Did the camera reveal anything beyond this act? Only the look in his eyes - which remained unchanged through theme and variations - the cold, shrewd, calculating look of a manipulator. Manipulator - to what end? The motive, the hidden power-lust, broke through once in a while, in the form of an unnecessary little speech drawled to many witnesses at the conclusion of his interrogation - seemingly, in the name of "fairness"; actually, as a threat, stressing his moment of power. The speech went something like this (I quote from memory): "Ah must tell you that Ah will take your testimony at face value until all the evidence is in, but then Ah will compare it to the testimony of other witnesses and then _Ah_ will judge." It is unfortunate that none of the victims was in a position to answer: "That's your tough luck, brother, not mine. _I_ know the truth."

Consider the fact that Senator Baker kept enunciating as leftist-liberal a line as Senator Ervin, yet that his, Baker's, voting record in the Senate is rightist-conservative; consider the fact that he has declared his (pragmatist) contempt for ideological consistency by stating, in an interview, that he disapproves of political "labels" - and you will realize that you are seeing a smoother, slyer, trickier Nixon.

Many commentators admit (and do not object to) the obvious fact that all these Senators are running their future campaigns from the green pasture of the committee table. Senator Baker is running - God help us! - for the office of President, or for the Presidential nomination on the Republican ticket. This means that he is after Mr. Nixon's job. And this raises the question: How does the ethical standard of "conflict of interest" apply to the Senate committee?

Suppose the president of a business corporation were in trouble, and the corporation appointed an investigating committee that included an ambitious young climber who had his eye on the president's job, while all the other members had special interests at stake, which took precedence over the task of discovering the truth. Would anyone regard such a committee as honorable, impartial and just? If not, then why are politicians judged by a different standard?

If all the members of the Nixon Administration are suspect because they have an interest in supporting Nixon, why should anyone trust men who have an interest in defeating him? What standard of objectivity decrees that the friends of the accused are prejudiced, but his enemies are not?

Many liberals defend the leftist demonstrators against complaints such as Magruder's, by declaring that the demonstrators broke the law _openly_, while the Watergate boys did it secretly. But it is an open question as to who is morally superior: those who practice an open, cynical, hooligan defiance of the law - or those who preserve some remnant of respect for morality, and practice their lawbreaking in secret. By the same token, who is more reprehensible: the men who are denounced for their hidden motives, such as authoritarian power-lust, unscrupulous ambition, "selfish" interests, partisan deceit, the sacrifice of moral principles for the sake of winning an election - or the men who denounce them, while practicing the same offenses for the same goal, in the open glare of a national television hookup?

But cynical amoralities of that size can seldom be perpetrated without the sanction of the victim. Once Mr. Nixon had impeached the integrity of the entire executive branch, by agreeing to have an "outside" prosecutor on the case and by accepting a political enemy as _impartial_, he cut the ground from under any potential defender on the Senate committee and gave a signal to the worst of Sam Ervin's boys that they could go ahead with an uncontested orgy.

The orgy was as ugly and fully as sadistic as the circus spectacles of ancient Rome - except that there were no lions and no Christians in the arena, only a bunch of seedy gladiators who had never learned how to fight.

To add insult to injury, Senator Ervin kept repeating that the hearings were not a court of law and were not bound by the same rules of evidence, that their purpose was not to condemn anyone, only "to discover the truth." But the rules of evidence binding a court are the best means men were able to devise for the purpose of discovering the truth. By what means, then, does the committee propose to discover it? Apart from undermining respect for legal procedure, Senator Ervin's statement raises the question: What is the actual purpose of the Watergate hearings?

Observe a significant precedent: an earlier television spectacular from Washington was the Army-McCarthy hearings, which took place in 1954 - at a time when there was a strong political trend to the right in this country. That trend was sidetracked by the election of Eisenhower, and defeated for a generation by the McCarthy hearings. The hearings were as confusing, messy, boring, overdetailed, inconclusive and one-sided as the present ones; and precisely for these reasons, they created a package-deal which the public was unable to untangle or define: the tag "McCarthyism," which was used thereafter to smear all rightists - and to discredit any serious ideological opposition to communism.

The Nixon landslide was a thunderous demonstration of a trend to the right. Hence, the Watergate hearings - for the purpose of creating a new tag, "Watergate," as an instrument of smearing and intimidation. The ideological victim, to be made intellectually disreputable this time, is patriotism and _concern with national security_ (it will be called "_excessive_ concern"). Senator Weicker admitted as much when he screamed at one of the witnesses, in regard to the question of national security: "This is what these hearings are all about!" No one picked him up on it.

Is there anything we can learn from this sordid spectacle? Yes, there is - as I shall discuss in my next _Letter_.

Ayn Rand

The Ayn Rand Letter, published fortnightly by The Ayn Rand Letter, Inc., 183 Madison Avenue, New York, N.Y. 10016.

Contributing Editor: **Leonard Peikoff**; Subscription Director: **Elayne Kalberman**; Production Manager: **Barbara Weiss.**

Vol. II, No. 21 July 16, 1973

...AND THE PRINCIPLES

In one of his philosophizing bits, during the Watergate hearings, Senator Howard H. Baker Jr. asked a very important question: What can we do to prevent the future occurrence of events such as Watergate?

It seems unlikely that he was looking for an answer, because he addressed the question to one of the youngest witnesses, who was least qualified to answer it. Groping for the safest, the most widely acceptable answer, the boy mumbled something about there being "too much money" in the re-election committee. Senator Baker let it go at that; apparently, the question had been merely rhetorical.

But there _is_ an answer - and it was illustrated, dramatized, virtually screamed by the entire progression of the Senate inquiry - only I doubt that Senator Baker or his colleagues would want to hear it.

The solution to any problem is implicit in the nature, i.e., the fundamental characteristics, of the problem. Assume that that question was asked of _you_ (because, in a certain sense, it _was_). Assume that you are the ultimate judge of events (because, in a certain sense, you _are_). Now ask yourself: Can _you_ judge the issues in the Watergate hearings? Can you determine who was lying and who was telling the truth, and to what extent, and on what specific points? Can you hold the total of the testimony in mind, including every detail - since it is particularly in regard to details that the witnesses gave different accounts? If you cannot do it from memory, would you be able to do it by studying the transcript? How long would it take you? How many volumes of the transcript would you be able to hold in mind before your memory and integrating capacity broke down? Would _you_ be able to determine the facts which the Senate committee is allegedly seeking: Who authorized the Watergate break-in and cover-up? What was done and by whom?

You would have to say that you cannot determine it, that you do not know, and worse: that the men involved in Watergate do not seem to know it, either. This gives you a clue to the nature of the problem.

The men involved in Watergate believed that they were carrying out a policy - but no one had set a policy and no one was able to define it. Most of them assumed that they were obeying orders - but no one had given them specific orders. Some of them thought that they had a free hand - but it was not free, and they found untraceable pressures countermanding their decisions. All of them seem responsible for everything in general - and no one seems responsible for anything in particular. All seem guilty collectively - and each claims innocence individually. But such a situation is, in fact, impossible. If men attempt to set it up and to function in such conditions, they can achieve nothing but self-destruction (which these men did). What was the nature of the setup? Undefined goals, undefined principles, undefined standards, undefined responsibility, undefined (and unlimited) power, unearned (and unlimited) wealth.

Liberal commentators are saying that the Nixon Administration was autocratic. In form (though not in essence, since the essence is the same), the opposite was true of the Nixon re-election committee; its setup was "democratic" in the exact sense in which this word is used by the sloppier kinds of welfare statists, socialists, "humanists," or New-Left communes: no one had authority, and everyone - power was diffuse and unspecified, each man (or clique) was free to take the initiative, to push his own schemes, to do his own thing - different people had different ideas and they resolved them <u>somehow</u>, by "democratic consensus" or compromise (or by some of them choosing not to know what others were doing).

Secrecy, stealth, and cliques jockeying for power are intrinsic in any setup of this kind. On the one hand, if power belongs to all, men dare not speak openly for fear of antagonizing others; on the other hand, if power belongs to none, men feel that it is theirs for the taking. Consequently, the general policy is not to persuade, but to put something over on one another. The sneaky evasiveness of the Watergate witnesses was not a manner they assumed for the benefit of the Senate committee, it was their normal manner of functioning. It was not aimed primarily at hiding their schemes from the press or the public, but from one another.

Since a group of men cannot act by indeterminate rules, yet action is required, anyone can put anything over on it. It offers a field day for manipulators or for anyone adept at fishing in muddy waters. Whether the source of the group's power, its nominally ultimate authority, is the King (as in an absolute monarchy) or "the people" (as in an unlimited democracy), the principle is the same: unlimited power - and its practical consequences are always the same. Neither of those authorities can rule a country personally; both have to delegate that unlimited power - either to court favorites or to skillful demagogues. (In a mixed economy, both elements are involved: political manipulators have to keep one eye on their boss, and the other on their "public image.")

John W. Dean 3d gave a graphic example of how one manipulates an absentee authority. The clandestine communications from Dean to McCord (via Caulfield, Ulasewicz, code names, and public phone booths) did not state explicitly that President Nixon had promised to give McCord executive clemency in exchange for his silence, only that the promise came "from way up on top." The man way up on top turned out to be Dean - who testified that he had not discussed the matter with Mr. Nixon, but had taken it upon himself to make that promise (on the basis, he alleged, of a similar promise made to another Watergate defendant - an allegation denied by Mr. Nixon and a number of witnesses).

Many witnesses testified that they had obeyed Dean (or Magruder or Mitchell or Ehrlichman or Haldeman) because of his position in the White House or his "closeness to the President." What were all those victims or suckers to do - in a situation ruled by unspecified power? They had no way of checking Dean's authority or his standing with the President, no way of knowing when or whether Dean spoke for the President or just for himself. They were afraid to trust Dean fully and afraid to defy him. They had to gamble on his unsupported word (or rather, on his veiled hints), and the stakes were high: for some of them, obedience meant the commission of crimes, such as perjury, destruction of evidence, illegal money-raising - and, in the case of McCord, a possible thirty-five-year prison sentence. So they complied, or passed the buck, or provided themselves with scapegoats - while Dean's maneuvering consisted in never telling the same story twice and never letting any of them know what he had told the others (which is one obvious reason why he could not put a report on his activities in writing).

Dean was merely the grossest, but not the only, manipulator in that group: most of them were playing the same game to various extents. No one initiated the cover-up, Dean testified, "it just happened." "It was fate," he said, in another passage of his testimony. This was true, as far as the manipulators' view of life was concerned. Cover-ups were their metaphysical necessity, to hide things was their automatized "instinct" - to hide from the world, from one another and, ultimately, from their distant boss, President Nixon, whose favor all of them were competing for, whose indeterminate views all of them were trying to guess, to satisfy, to anticipate, and to manipulate. (I have no opinion as to whether Mr. Nixon did or did not know anything about Watergate; it is a small matter compared to a much deeper default: his Pragmatism, the philosophy shared and exemplified by the re-election committee.)

Can you untangle this maze? Can you isolate individual ambitions, motives, influences, pressures, responsibilities, and con games? Can you judge anyone's guilt or innocence in a mess of this kind? Can you determine what ought to be corrected and what sort of law would correct it? Or do you turn away in disgust from the televised view of that complex chaos, feeling that a lifetime of study would not untangle it nor clean it up?

Now multiply the complexity of that chaos a thousandfold, then a thousandfold again - and you will have an approximate picture of the government of a mixed economy.

The Nixon re-election committee was a temporary organization, limited by a nominal goal (an election), supported by semi-voluntary financial contributions, and involving nothing but the personal ambitions and careers of a handful of men (who were unable to affect the outcome of the election). Try to project what is involved in the operations of a government that holds the power to control the economy of the whole country - which means: power to control the work, the career, the ambition, the achievement, the income, the property, the future of every citizen. What sort of pressures, schemes, intrigues, maneuvers and con games would this generate?

It is rumored that the Nixon re-election committee was torn by such clashes as the Haldeman-Ehrlichman faction versus the Mitchell faction, or Magruder versus Liddy, or Strachan versus Magruder, etc. - with future influence or promotion at stake. What is that compared to the clashes of business versus labor, or labor versus farmers, or producers versus consumers, or innovators versus ecologists - with survival at stake?

Whatever their motives, the men of the re-election committee were not moved by financial "greed." With millions of dollars in untraceable cash floating about, there is no evidence that anyone tried to line his own pockets (with the possible exception of Dean, who seems to have "borrowed" $15,000). Try to project the nature of the motives and the ferocity of the greed generated in people by a government that holds an unlimited power of taxation, disposes of an unlimited wealth and distributes it according to the machinations of any plausible or implausible pressure group. Would you be able to untangle those motives or the validity of the pressure groups' demands?

You have seen, within the span of the last few years, that controls breed more controls, and that the proliferation of controls breeds the proliferation of pressure groups. Today, you see political manipulators setting up new conflicts, such as ethnic minorities against the majority, the young against the old, the old against the middle, women against men, even welfare-recipients against the self-supporting. Openly and cynically, these new groups clamor for "a bigger slice of the pie" (which _you_ have to bake). If the Watergate affair is said to represent moral corruption, how would you describe the processes by which the government deals with all those claimants?

Would you be able to identify the motives and reasons behind any single piece of legislation? Could you determine what considerations moved every Congressman who voted for or against it? What lobbyists or fellow-Congressmen had approached him? What arguments had they offered? What had he been promised? What deals had been made? Had the inducements been material, such as a bribe, or spiritual, such as a commitment to deliver the vote at his next election, or both, such as an offer to support his pet legislation in exchange for his support of this one? Which pressure groups did he favor, and/or which were powerful in his home state? Whose interests could he or could he not afford to sacrifice? What did he know about the specific subject of that legislation? Had he read the bill or did he rely on the summary provided by his staff and, if so, what were their views? What was the degree of his knowledge, of his intelligence, of his integrity, of his independence? What was the firmness of his convictions (if any)? To what extent had his decision been influenced by such emotions as fear, guilt, self-doubt, vanity, envy, hatred?

If a public hearing were held to trace the causes of that one piece of legislation, it would uncover a vaster, vaguer, more tangled, more corrupt, more pernicious, and less identifiable maze of subterranean burrowings than the one uncovered in the Watergate hearings - and no one would be able to discover its starting point, to apportion responsibility, or to find the answers to the questions asked above, including the participants.

It is not a matter of personalities, nor of anyone's honesty or dishonesty. The corruption is inherent in the system: it is inherent in any situation in which men have to act without any goals, principles or standards to guide them. "The good of the country" is not a goal (unless one has a clear, objective definition of what is the good). "The public interest" is not a principle. (Observe that all pressure groups claim to represent "the public interest.") Someone's wish or "aspiration" is not a standard. You have heard every politician in every election proclaim his allegiance to those empty generalities. You have been wise enough not to believe his public utterances. What makes you believe that he has better principles in the privacy of his own mind and that, once elected, he will act on them? He hasn't and he can't.

In a controlled (or mixed) economy, a legislator's job consists in sacrificing some men to others. No matter what choice he makes, no choice of this kind can be morally justified (and never has been). Proceeding from an immoral base, no decision of his can be honest or dishonest, just or unjust - these concepts are inapplicable. He becomes, therefore, an easy target for the promptings of any pressure group, any lobbyist, any influence-peddler, any manipulator - he has no standards by which to judge or to resist them. You do not know what hidden powers drive him or what he is doing. Neither does he.

Now observe the results of such policies and their effect on the country. You have seen that Nixon's wage-price controls, imposed two years ago for the purpose of slowing down inflation, have accelerated it. You have seen that a shortage of soybeans, which you probably do not buy, has led to the shortage of most of the food items which you do buy and need. You have seen a demonstration of the fact that a country's economy is an integrated (and self-integrating) whole - and that the biggest computer would not be able to predict all the consequences of an edict controlling the price of milk, let alone an edict controlling the price, the costs, the sales, the amounts of wheat or beef or steel or oil or electricity. Can you hold in mind the total of a country's economy, including every detail of the interrelationships of every group, every profession, every kind of goods and services? Can you determine which controls are proper or improper, practical or impractical, beneficent or disastrous? If you cannot do it, what makes you assume that a politician can? In fact, there is no such thing as proper, practical or beneficent controls.

Like the Nixon re-election committee, the government of a mixed economy is a setup ruled by undefined goals, undefined principles, undefined standards, undefined responsibility, undefined (and unlimited) power, unearned (and unlimited) wealth. A country that accepts such conditions can achieve nothing but self-destruction, as the men of the re-election committee did. This is the lesson that comes loud and clear through the grimy mess of the Watergate hearings - a pictorial lesson that concretizes the senselessness, the pettiness, the futility, the chaos, and the depersonalized evil of a government swollen with a power no government can or should hold. (For a discussion of the proper functions of a government, I refer you to my book Capitalism: The Unknown Ideal.)

This is not, however, the lesson that the liberals are pounding and propounding today. The problem, they claim, does not lie in the system, but in men; the evil, they claim, is not arbitrary power, but those who exercise it; the power of the Presidency, they claim, is too great and should be switched to Congress. The crude double standard of the pragmatist-liberal doctrines is almost too obvious in this issue: it was the liberals who inflated the Presidency to its present, power-bloated, wholly unconstitutional size, during the decades of liberal Presidents; now, when the liberals have lost control of the White House, they demand the switching of power to Congress, which they hope to control by means of pressure groups. But a "redistribution" of power will not save a country ravaged by power - just as the switching of a cancer from one organ to another will not save the patient.

A "mixed" government is the only institution that grows not through its successes, but through its failures. Its advocates use every disaster to enlarge the power of the government that caused it. Today, the main circumstance that keeps politicians (more or less) in line is the fact that they still have to face the voters every few years. It is this restraint that the statists are now out to destroy. As a cure for the many abuses and corruptions of the electoral process (not all of them financial), the statists propose to give total power over elections to the abusers and the corrupters, i.e., the politicians. (It is not Big Business contributions that corrupt politicians, but the politicians' power to demand and extort such contributions, which works like a protection racket - as has been demonstrated recently in regard to both parties.)

The existence and rivalry of two parties, even such as they are, is the last protection of the (approximate) honesty of elections. It is obvious what sort of rigging would go on, if the government were given the power to finance elections. They call it "public financing," which means that you would be deprived of the right to decide which candidates you want to support, if any, and that the politicians would make that decision for you. But that power would be given to an "impartial, nonpartisan" commission, you are told? Impartial - like prosecutor Archibald Cox? Nonpartisan - like the Senate Watergate committee? In today's situation, you'd better pray for the survival of plain, old-fashioned grafters: when they vanish, you'll get a Robespierre or a Hitler, both of whom were anti-materialistic and incorruptible.

The solution, of course, is to eliminate both kinds of predators, material or spiritual, by eliminating their breeding ground: the government's power over the economy. No, it cannot be done overnight. But if you want to fight for that ultimate solution, Watergate provides you with intellectual ammunition: its lesson is the diametric opposite of the notions now being palmed off on the country by the statist-liberal establishment.

If you feel, as many people do, that such a battle would take too long and comes too late, there is one piece of advice I should like to give you: if you choose to resign yourself to the reign of an unchallenged evil, do so with your eyes open. Hold an image of the Watergate hearings in your mind and ask yourself what I asked you at the start of this discussion: Do you feel respect for the men on either side of the long committee table? To which of them would you care to surrender your freedom? To Senator Ervin? To Jeb Stuart Magruder? To John D. Ehrlichman? Whose judgment would you regard as superior to yours and competent to do a job which you can neither grasp nor judge nor define nor undertake: the impossible job of controlling this country's economy? The judgment of H.R. Haldeman? Of Frederick C. LaRue? Of Senator Montoya? Which of them would you entrust with the power to dispose of your life, your work, your income, and your children's future? Senator Baker? Senator Weicker? John W. Dean 3d?

If you hold Richard Nixon responsible for Watergate, as the absentee authority in whose name the men of the re-election committee were acting and whose favor they were scrambling to win, then - in relation to all the politicians of this country - _you_ are the absentee authority, it is in _your_ name that they are issuing their edicts, it is _your_ favor that they are scrambling to win (or wheedle or extort or manipulate) at election time. No, you cannot fight them by means of your one vote. But you can make yourself heard. It is your voice that they fear, when and if it is the voice of your mind, because their entire racket rests on the hope that you will not understand.

Do not hide behind the futile hope that the men you saw on television might be bigger in real life, that responsible government positions would raise their stature. In real life, they are smaller; today's government positions shrink them - for a reason stated by a great political thinker of the last century.

His statement was mentioned during the Watergate hearings, but no one paid much attention to it. Yet that statement is the real answer to Senator Baker's question: it indicates what must be eliminated in order to prevent the future occurrence of events such as Watergate (or such as the Watergate hearings).

That thinker was Lord Acton, who said: "Power tends to corrupt and absolute power corrupts absolutely."

Ayn Rand

OBJECTIVIST CALENDAR

On Sunday, October 21, Ayn Rand will give a talk on "Censorship: Local and Express," at The Ford Hall Forum in Boston. Time: 8 P.M. Place: Jordan Hall, 30 Gainsboro St. (Advance tickets are not available. On past occasions, the auditorium was filled to capacity, and many people had to be turned away. If you plan to attend, we suggest that you arrive at Jordan Hall far in advance of 7:30 P.M., when the doors open.)

The following starting dates have been scheduled for the tape lectures of Dr. Leonard Peikoff's courses. _Modern Philosophy: Kant to the Present_, Rockford, Ill., September 25, contact Dr. Fredrick Marler, (815) 397-4382 (days) or (815) 397-5083 (eves.). _Founders of Western Philosophy: Thales to Hume_, Rochester, N.Y., October 7, Harry Ladne, (716) 244-0873 (eves.).

B.W.

The Ayn Rand Letter, published fortnightly by The Ayn Rand Letter, Inc., 183 Madison Avenue, New York, N.Y. 10016.
Contributing Editor: **Leonard Peikoff;** Subscription Director: **Elayne Kalberman;** Production Manager: **Barbara Weiss.**

Vol. II, No. 22 July 30, 1973

PERRY MASON FINALLY LOSES

I do not like to make predictions about the success or failure of particular shows, because the irrationality of short-range reactions is incalculable. But it is safe to say that television's new "Perry Mason" is not long for this world - even today's world.

In an essay on "Bootleg Romanticism" (in my book The Romantic Manifesto), I wrote: "Art (including literature) is the barometer of a culture....If you find political issues too complex to diagnose, take a look at today's art: it will leave you no doubt in regard to the health or disease of our culture." To speak of current television shows as "art," is to stretch this concept out of bounds; but since such shows have pre-empted the spots once occupied by art, they acquire "social" (and diagnostic) significance. It is not merely the fact that they are bad, it is the particular nature of their badness that reveals which characteristics men are losing (or are intended to lose).

The new "Perry Mason" is not Romanticism; it is not Naturalism; it is not anything. It is merely boring. It is too inept to be called evil - except in the sense in which any product of pretentious mediocrity is evil. But it carries, unintentionally, a great - though futile - moral message: "Imitation doesn't pay." The message is futile because it will not deter the perceptual mentalities who know no method of mental functioning other than imitation. But the rest of us can observe a valuable psycho-epistemological lesson.

The source of art - and of man's need of art - is man's conceptual faculty (see "The Psycho-Epistemology of Art" in The Romantic Manifesto). In practical action, the hallmark of conceptual functioning is the ability to ask "Why?" about value-judgments, and to find the answer - which can be found only by means of identifying the essentials of the object one is judging. But this is beyond the power of a perceptual mentality. If it were asked: "This automobile is good - why?" - it would answer: "Because it has beautiful upholstery." A perceptual mentality is unable to distinguish the essential from the non-essential.

Bearing this in mind, let us consider what the makers of the new "Perry Mason" were trying to imitate.

The old "Perry Mason" (which is now billed as the real "Perry Mason") was a habit-forming experience. I was an addict; I saw most of the episodes two or three times, in various reruns, and never felt bored. The soul of the show was Raymond Burr. He gave such an inspired performance that it lifted, illuminated and imparted meaning to all the rest. His Perry Mason had one dominant characteristic: intelligence - and, as a consequence: firmness, self-confidence, moral certainty, and, as their consequence, dignity. These qualities are among the hardest to portray; they require esthetic absolutism - a single lapse makes them vanish. To appear authentic, they require the quiet steadiness of understatement; to appear natural, they require unself-consciousness. A hero is not conscious of being heroic: to him, it is just a matter of being himself. Raymond Burr achieved the unusual feat of faultlessly maintaining this kind of characterization through every episode, for nine years.

(The stress on intelligence was, apparently, the conscious intention behind the series, as indicated in the introductory shots: these show Perry Mason in a courtroom, studying a legal brief, frowning; then, suddenly, his face is hit by a "light-bulb" look - the look of grasping an idea.)

Burr's Perry Mason was a man of unusually active intelligence, a man whose mind never goes out of focus, whether he ponders a problem, or goes fishing, or jokes with Della Street, his charming, efficient secretary; a man of inexhaustible ingenuity, who risks his career on unconventional stunts - and wins, because he knows what he is doing; a man who does not solve problems by flashes of automatic omniscience, who works hard, who is often puzzled, but never helpless; a man who is passionately dedicated to justice (which he projects without ever saying a word about it); a man who keeps his head "when all about him are losing theirs" - and stands as an immovable rock of support for the fading strength and failing spirit of the helpless, the confused, the desperate victims of injustice.

It is obvious why such an image would have an overwhelming appeal today - and why people, millions of them, would cling to Perry Mason as desperately as the clients he saves on the TV screen. All of us today are victims of a gigantic injustice, which few can define or understand, all of us live under the pressure of an incomprehensible evil, which our public leaders seem to ignore and no one cares to explain, all of us feel that we need an indomitable defender - in a courtroom? no - in a much, much wider field.

This is the conceptual answer to the question: "'Perry Mason' was enormously popular - why?"

Before we switch channels, let me mention also that the old Perry Mason was shown, at times, attending his clients' parties, on which occasions his manner was the courteous, benevolent, but detached manner of an observer, as if he had much greater concerns on his mind.

Now let us take a look at the new "Perry Mason." (I missed the first episode, but saw the second and, as far as I am concerned, the last.) The show opens at a race track. A foolish, fluttering matron is prattling about horoscopes and fussing over some uncertainty as to whether her horse will be admitted to the race. The camera moves to a gangling, sloppy-postured, nondescript man entering the stands - escorting what looks like a mushroom with two stems, but turns out to be a girl in a mini-dress, crushed under a huge, hideous stovepipe hat. The man looks like a race-track tout; his face seems to blend with the background and is hard to remember: it is neither handsome nor ugly, neither grim nor friendly, neither young nor old; it does show some lines of age, but they seem premature because its expression suggests a perennial high-school - not college - student.

The matron rushes to meet him. "Perry Mason!" she cries. She adds, to the walking mushroom: "Hello, Miss Della Street" - then inquires about the fate of her horse. There was a bit of trouble, "but we fixed it!" he announces and practically winks at her, with a bashfully boastful grin. Whereupon the matron kisses him on the mouth.

Quite a bit later, we see him in his office. The potential client begging for his help, is a hysterical young woman who babbles incoherently and seems closer to psychosis than neurosis. He listens noncommittally and looks disturbed. "Excuse me a moment, please," is his first comment. Then he hurries to the anteroom, slumps, leaning for support with both hands on Miss Street's desk, and moans: "I don't know what to do!"

Then he mutters hesitantly: "Could you - " Miss Street completes his sentence: " - take her out to lunch?" in the maternal, patronizing tone of an adult wise to a child's tricks. The story goes on down from there.

In the courtroom, this alleged Perry Mason finds himself caught in some silly-sounding legalistic conflict, to the effect that he has to testify as a witness for the prosecution and, therefore, should not have undertaken this particular defendant's defense. He is told to approach the judge's bench - together with an incredible-looking creature that has a wizened, cadaverous face, a Hitler mustache, and no forehead, this being swallowed by the bangs of a hippie haircut, which creature turns out to be District Attorney Burger. Mason proceeds to explain, in a kind of part-pleading, part-apologetic, part-rancorous manner, that he accepted this case because he could not refuse the pleas of a sick, terrified, friendless woman who would not trust anyone else. He explained the legal situation to her, he states, but she insisted. "I don't know the answers," he declares. All this is delivered in the nasty tone of a small-time politician claiming altruism as his justification in a shady deal (a big-time politician would have done it more eloquently).

One has to see this mess in order fully to appreciate the skill, the ingenuity, the artistic achievement of the old "Perry Mason" scriptwriters. Some of their scripts were better than others, but here is what they were able to accomplish in the brief space of fifty minutes: clearly set up the conflicts of the future murder victim with a number of different characters - clearly convey his and their motivations - give a sharp characterization to each, in terms of essentials, so that each became a distinct personality, not to be confused with the others - lead events in a dramatic progression toward the murder - present the trial as an earnestly fought battle between Mason and Burger, involving a number of possible suspects - build a mounting suspense for the viewer, who is let in on the grounds for suspicion, and on the process by which Mason finally solves the case. Try to do it sometime - and you will realize what a feat those scriptwriters accomplished.

As to their dialogue, it was so simple and natural that I was inclined to take it for granted, until my husband said suddenly, one evening, as we were watching the old show: "Listen to how much they are saying how simply!" I focused specifically on the dialogue - and felt almost guilty for having overlooked its marvelously purposeful economy. _This_ was art of a high order. Remember it next time you hear some pretentious mediocrity sounding off on the notion that plot is an artificial "contrivance" and that detective stories are not "art."

Well, one thing can be said for certain: the script of the new "Perry Mason" was _not_ contrived. It was unintelligible. You could not tell what was happening or why, you could not tell one character from another, neither in action nor in appearance, and you could not care less. If I tell you that the motive of the murder turns out to be an astrologer's professional indignation at the fact that the villain had _faked_ a horoscope, you might not believe that this was offered seriously. But it was - and this gives you the flavor of the whole thing.

The final episode of the old "Perry Mason" was aired in 1966. It is hard to believe that the esthetic standards of the television (and movie) industry could deteriorate to such an extent in the span of seven years. The speed of our cultural disintegration is almost frightening. Since television or movie producers can hardly be regarded as original thinkers, their mental state is a good mirror of today's trends. By some ineffable osmosis of their own, the makers of the new "Perry Mason" sensed which human characteristics their masters - today's intellectuals - want men to lose: firmness, self-confidence, and any trace of a moral tone, as well as any touch of dignity. To say that the new Perry Mason is an anti-hero, would be to flatter the show: he is just a slob. It is the image of the *real* Perry Mason that today's cultural leaders want to eliminate from people's consciousness, as a vision, a hope, an inspiration, or even a possibility. So much for their view of man and for their concern with the education, the enlightenment, the happiness of "the people."

And so much for the claim that financial "greed" is the factor corrupting the producers of commercial entertainment. It is true that something like greed for the unearned would prompt imitators to pounce upon what they thought was a safe bet - a sensationally successful show - and to try to cash in on it. But their college-bred mentalities would render them incapable of equaling even the perceptiveness of a good forger: they would not know what they were imitating, nor why it had been successful. It is hard to say which is worse in this context: the fact that some men are capable of deliberately substituting trash for values, or the fact that their pupils - the graduates of today's schools and colleges, the products of Progressive education - *would not know the difference* and would not be able to produce, direct, write or act in anything resembling Romanticism, even on the popular level.

If you want to consider a broad integration, I would say that the new "Perry Mason" offers, unintentionally, its own refutation of Marxism: it demonstrates, in regard to art, what *Atlas Shrugged* demonstrated in regard to industry, specifically in the sequences dealing with the Twentieth Century Motor Company. One can expropriate the products of human intelligence; one will not be able to make them work.

To paraphrase a certain passage: "Ten years ago, the name 'Perry Mason' on a television series was as good as the karat mark on gold. I don't know what it was that the new producers thought, if they thought at all, but I suppose that like all social planners and like savages, they thought that this name was a magic stamp which did the trick by some sort of voodoo power and that it would make them rich, as it had made their predecessors. Well, when the viewers begin to see that everything Perry Mason stood for has been obliterated, the magic stamp will begin to work the other way around: people won't watch the show for free, if it is marked 'The New Perry Mason.'"

Ayn Rand

P.S. This *Letter* was written later than the date that appears on its heading.

OBJECTIVIST CALENDAR

Starting on October 28, the tape lectures of Leonard Peikoff's course, *Founders of Western Philosophy: Thales to Hume*, will be given in Providence, R.I. For further information, contact Bill Dawkins at (401) 943-0881 (eves.).

B.W.

The Ayn Rand Letter, published fortnightly by The Ayn Rand Letter, Inc., 183 Madison Avenue, New York, N.Y. 10016.

Contributing Editor: **Leonard Peikoff**; Subscription Director: **Elayne Kalberman**; Production Manager: **Barbara Weiss.**

Vol. II, No. 23 August 13, 1973

CENSORSHIP: LOCAL AND EXPRESS

I have been saying, for many years, that statism is winning by default - by the intellectual default of capitalism's alleged defenders; that freedom and capitalism have never had a firm, philosophical base; that today's conservatives share all the fundamental premises of today's liberals and thus have paved, and are still paving, the road to statism. I have also said repeatedly that the battle for freedom is primarily philosophical and cannot be won by any lesser means - because philosophy rules human existence, including politics.

But philosophy is a science that deals with the broadest abstractions and, therefore, many people do not know how to observe its influence in practice or how to grasp the process by which it affects the conditions of their daily life. A recent event, however, offers a clear, striking illustration of that process. It shows philosophy's influence in action, and reveals the essence (and the contradictions) of both the conservative and the liberal ideologies. This event is the decision of the Supreme Court in five recent "obscenity" cases.

In my *Letter* of November 20, 1972, I expressed hope in regard to the four men appointed to the Supreme Court by President Nixon, even though it was too early to tell the exact nature of their views. "But," I said, "if they live up to their enormous responsibility, we may forgive Mr. Nixon a great many of his defaults: the Supreme Court is the last remnant of a philosophical influence in this country." Today, less than a year later, the evidence is sufficient to indicate that there are no intellectual grounds left for forgiving Mr. Nixon.

Since inconsistent premises lead to inconsistent actions, it is not impossible that the present Supreme Court may make some liberating decisions. For instance, the Court made a great contribution to justice and to the protection of individual rights when it legalized abortion. I am not in agreement with all of the reasoning given in that decision, but I am in enthusiastic agreement with the result - i.e., with the recognition of a woman's right to her own body. But the Court's decision in regard to obscenity takes an opposite stand: it denies a man's (or a woman's) right to the exercise of his own mind - by establishing the legal and intellectual base of *censorship*.

Before proceeding to discuss that decision, I want to state, for the record, my own view of what is called "hard-core" pornography. I regard it as unspeakably disgusting. I have not read any of the books or seen any of the current movies belonging to that category, and I do not intend ever to read or see them. The descriptions provided in legal cases, as well as the "modern" touches in "soft-core" productions, are sufficient grounds on which to form an opinion. The reason of my opinion is the opposite of the usual one: I do not regard sex as evil - I regard it as good, as one of the most important aspects of human life, too important to be made the subject of public anatomical display. But the issue here is not one's view of sex. The issue is freedom of speech and of the press - i.e., the right to hold any view and to express it.

It is not very inspiring to fight for the freedom of the purveyors of pornography or their customers. But in the transition to statism, every infringement of human rights has begun with the suppression of a given right's least attractive practitioners. In this case, the disgusting nature of the offenders makes it a good test of one's loyalty to a principle.

In the five "obscenity" cases decided on June 21, 1973, the Court was divided five to four. In each case, the majority opinion was written by Chief Justice Burger, joined by Justices Blackmun, Powell, Rehnquist (all four appointed by Nixon) and Justice White (appointed by Kennedy); in each case, the dissenting opinion was written by Justice Brennan, joined by Justices Stewart and Marshall; Justice Douglas, in each case, wrote a separate dissenting opinion. The two most important cases are Miller v. California and Paris Adult Theater I v. Slaton.

The Miller case involves a man who was convicted in California of mailing unsolicited, sexually explicit material, which advertised pornographic books. It is in the Miller decision that Chief Justice Burger promulgated the new criteria for judging whether a given work is obscene or not. They are as follows:

"The basic guidelines for the trier of fact must be: (a) whether 'the average person, applying contemporary community standards' would find that the work, taken as a whole, appeals to the prurient interest...(b) whether the work depicts or describes, in a patently offensive way, sexual conduct specifically defined by the applicable state law, and (c) whether the work, taken as a whole, lacks serious literary, artistic, political, or scientific value."

These criteria are based on previous Supreme Court decisions, particularly on Roth v. United States, 1957. Nine years later, in the case of Memoirs v. Massachusetts, 1966, the Supreme Court introduced a new criterion: "A book cannot be proscribed unless it is found to be utterly without redeeming social value." This was bad enough, but the present decision emphatically rejects that particular notion and substitutes a horrendous criterion of its own: "whether the work, taken as a whole, lacks serious literary, artistic, political, or scientific value."

Morally, this criterion, as well as the rest of Chief Justice Burger's decision, taken as a whole, is a proclamation of collectivism - not so much political as specifically moral collectivism. The intellectual standard which is here set up to rule an individual's mind - to prescribe what an individual may write, publish, read or see - is the judgment of an average person applying community standards. Why? No reason is given - which means that the will of the collective is here taken for granted as the source, justification and criterion of value judgments.

What is a community? No definition is given - it may, therefore, be a state, a city, a neighborhood, or just the block you live on. What are community standards? No definition is given. In fact, the standards of a community, when and if they can be observed as such, as distinguished from the standards of its individual citizens, are a product of chance, lethargy, hypocrisy, second-handedness, indifference, fear, the manipulations of local busybodies or small-time power-lusters - and, occasionally, the traditional acceptance of some decent values inherited from some great mind of the past. But the great mind is now to be outlawed by the ruling of the Supreme Court.

Who is the average person? No definition is given. There is some indication that the term, in this context, means a person who is neither particularly susceptible or sensitive nor totally insensitive in regard to sex. But to find a sexually average person is a more preposterously impossible undertaking than to find the average representative of any other human characteristic - and, besides, this is not what the Court decision says. It says simply "average" - which, in an issue of judgment, means intellectually average: average in intelligence, in ability, in ideas, in feelings, in tastes, which means: a conformist or a nonentity. Any proposition concerned with establishing a human "average" necessarily eliminates the top and the bottom, i.e., the best and the worst. Thus the standards of a genius and the standards of a moron are automatically eliminated, suppressed or prohibited - and both are ordered to subordinate their own views to those of the average. Why is the average person to be granted so awesome a privilege? By reason of the fact that he possesses no special distinction. Nothing can justify such a notion, except the theory of collectivism, which is itself unjustifiable.

The Court's decision asserts repeatedly - just asserts - that this ruling applies only to hard-core pornography or obscenity, i.e., to certain ideas dealing with sex, not to any other kinds of ideas. Other kinds of ideas - it keeps asserting - are protected by the First Amendment, but ideas dealing with sex are not. Apart from the impossibility of drawing a line between these two categories (which we shall discuss later), this distinction is contradicted and invalidated right in the text of this same decision: the trial judges and juries are empowered to determine whether a work that contains sexual elements "lacks serious literary, artistic, political, or scientific value."

This means - and can mean nothing else - that the government is empowered to judge literary, artistic, political, and scientific values, and to permit or suppress certain works accordingly.

The alleged limits on that power, the conditions of when, where and by whom it may be exercised, are of no significance - once the principle that the government holds such a power has been established. The rest is only a matter of details - and of time. The present Supreme Court may seek to suppress only sexual materials; on the same basis (the will of the community), a future Court may suppress "undesirable" scientific discussions; still another Court may suppress political discussions (and a year later all discussions in all fields would be suppressed). The law functions by a process of deriving logical consequences from established precedents.

The "average person's community standards" criterion, was set up in the Roth case. But the Roth criterion of "utterly without redeeming social value" was too vague to be immediately dangerous - anything may be claimed to have some sort of "social value." So, logically, on the basis of that precedent, the present Court took the next step toward censorship. It gave to the government the power of entry into four specific intellectual fields, with the power to judge whether the values of works in these fields are serious or not.

"Serious" is an unserious standard. Who is to determine what is serious, to whom, and by what criterion? Since no definition is given, one must assume that the criterion to apply is the only one promulgated in those guidelines: what the average person would find serious. Do you care to contemplate the spectacle of the average person as the ultimate authority - the censor - in the field of literature? In the field of art? In the field of politics? In the field of science? An authority whose edict is to be imposed by force and is to determine what will be permitted or suppressed in all these fields? I submit that no pornographic movie can be as morally obscene as a prospect of this kind.

No first-rate talent in any of those fields will ever be willing to work by the intellectual standards and under the orders of any authority, even if it were an authority composed of the best brains in the world (who would not accept the job), let alone an authority consisting of "average persons." And the greater the talent, the less the willingness.

As to those who would be willing, observe the moral irony of the fact that they do exist today in large numbers and are generally despised: they are the hacks, the box-office chasers, who try to please what they think are the tastes - and the standards - of the public, for the sake of making money. Apparently, intellectual prostitution is evil, if done for a "selfish" motive - but noble, if accepted in selfless service to the "moral purity" of the community.

In another of the five "obscenity" cases (U.S. v. 12 200-Ft. Reels of Super 8mm. Film), but in a totally different context, Chief Justice Burger himself describes the danger created by the logical implications of a precedent: "The seductive plausibility of single steps in a chain of evolutionary development of a legal rule is often not perceived until a third, fourth or fifth 'logical' extension occurs. Each step, when taken, appeared a reasonable step in relation to that which preceded it, although the aggregate or end result is one that would never have been seriously considered in the first instance. This kind of gestative propensity calls for the 'line drawing' familiar in the judicial, as in the legislative process: 'thus far but not beyond.'"

I would argue that since a legal rule is a principle, the development of its logical consequences cannot be cut off, except by repealing the principle. But assuming that such a cutoff were possible, no line of any sort is drawn in the Miller decision: the community standards of average persons are explicitly declared to be a sovereign power over sexual matters and over the works that deal with sexual matters.

In the same Miller decision, Chief Justice Burger admits that no such line can be drawn. "Nothing in the First Amendment requires that a jury must consider hypothetical and unascertainable 'national standards' when attempting to determine whether certain materials are obscene as a matter of fact." He quotes Chief Justice Warren saying in an earlier case: "I believe that there is no provable 'national standard'....At all events, this Court has not been able to enunciate one, and it would be unreasonable to expect local courts to divine one."

By what means are local courts to divine a local one? Actually, the only provable standard of what constitutes obscenity would be an objective standard, philosophically proved and valid for all men. Such a standard cannot be defined or enforced in terms of law: it would require the formulation of an entire philosophic system; but even this would not grant anyone the right to enforce that standard on others. When the Court, however, speaks of a "provable national standard," it does not mean an objective standard; it substitutes the collective for the objective, and seeks to enunciate a standard held by all the average persons of the nation. Since even a guess at such a concept is patently impossible, the Court concludes that what is impossible (and improper) nationally, is permissible locally

- and, in effect, passes the buck to state legislatures, granting them the power to enforce arbitrary (unprovable) local standards.

Chief Justice Burger's arguments, in the Miller decision, are not very persuasive. "It is neither realistic nor constitutionally sound to read the First Amendment as requiring that the people of Maine or Mississippi accept public depiction of conduct found tolerable in Las Vegas, or New York City." I read the First Amendment as not requiring any person anywhere to accept any depiction he does not wish to read or see, but forbidding him to abridge the rights and freedom of those who do wish to read or see it.

In another argument against a national standard of what constitutes obscenity, the decision declares: "People in different States vary in their tastes and attitudes, and this diversity is not to be strangled by the absolutism of imposed uniformity." What about the absolutism of imposed uniformity within a state? What about the non-conformists in that state? What about communication between citizens of different states? What about the freedom of a national marketplace of ideas? No answers are given.

The following argument, offered in a footnote, is unworthy of a serious tribunal: "The mere fact juries may reach different conclusions as to the same material does not mean that constitutional rights are abridged. As this Court observed in Roth v. United States...'It is common experience that different juries may reach different results under any criminal statute. That is one of the consequences we accept under our jury system....'" In a criminal case, the jury's duty is only to determine whether a particular defendant committed the crime which is clearly and specifically defined by the statute. Under the new "obscenity" ruling, a jury is expected to determine whether the defendant committed an undefined crime and, simultaneously, to determine what that crime is.

Thus the Nixon Court's notion of censorship-sharing by diffusing it at random over the entire country, is as illusory as Nixon's notion of returning power to the states by means of revenue-sharing. While the public rides on the creaking train of local censorship, with delays, derailments and chaos at every whistle stop - the express of statism is flying full speed on an unobstructed track.

Four of the Justices who handed down the Miller decision, are regarded as conservatives; the fifth, Justice White, is regarded as middle-of-the-road. On the other hand, Justice Douglas is the most liberal or the most leftward-leaning member of the Court. Yet his dissent in the Miller case is an impassioned cry of protest and indignation. He rejects the notion that the First Amendment allows an implied exception in the case of obscenity. "I do not think it does and my views on the issue have been stated over and again." He declares: "Obscenity - which even we cannot define with precision - is a hodge-podge. To send men to jail for violating standards they cannot understand, construe, and apply is a monstrous thing to do in a Nation dedicated to fair trials and due process."

What about the antitrust laws, which are responsible for precisely this kind of monstrous thing? Justice Douglas does not mention them - but antitrust, as we shall see later, is a chicken that comes home to roost on both sides of this issue.

On the subject of censorship, however, Justice Douglas is eloquently consistent: "The idea that the First Amendment permits punishment for ideas that are 'offensive' to the particular judge or jury sitting in judgment is astounding. No greater leveler of speech or literature has ever been designed. To give the power to the censor, as we do today, is to make a sharp and radical break with the traditions of a free society. The First Amendment was not fashioned as a vehicle for dispensing tranquilizers to the people. Its prime function was to keep debate open to 'offensive' as well as to 'staid' people. The tendency throughout history has been to subdue the individual and to exalt the power of government. The use of the standard 'offensive' gives authority to government that cuts the very vitals out of the First Amendment. As is intimated by the Court's opinion, the materials before us may be garbage. But so is much of what is said in political campaigns, in the daily press, on TV or over the radio. By reason of the First Amendment - and solely because of it - speakers and publishers have not been threatened or subdued because their thoughts and ideas may be 'offensive' to some."

I can only say "Amen" to this statement.

Observe that such issues as the individual against the State are never mentioned in the Supreme Court's majority decision. It is Justice Douglas, the arch-liberal, who defends individual rights. It is the conservatives who speak as if the individual did not exist, as if the unit of social concern were the collective - the "community."

(To be continued.)

Ayn Rand

OBJECTIVIST CALENDAR

Ayn Rand's lecture on "Censorship: Local and Express" (to be given at The Ford Hall Forum in Boston on October 21), will be broadcast in New York City over radio station WNYC-AM (830 on the dial), on Friday, October 26, at 8:30 P.M. The lecture may also be broadcast in other cities; for further information, ask your local radio stations whether NPR (National Public Radio) has made the lecture available for broadcasting in your area.

Starting on November 3, the tape lectures of Leonard Peikoff's course, Modern Philosophy: Kant to the Present, will be given in West Lafayette, Ind. For further information, contact Dr. Richard Matula at (317) 463-3646 (eves.).

B.W.

The Ayn Rand Letter, published fortnightly by The Ayn Rand Letter, Inc., 183 Madison Avenue, New York, N.Y. 10016.

Contributing Editor: **Leonard Peikoff**; Subscription Director: **Elayne Kalberman**; Production Manager: **Barbara Weiss.**

Vol. II, No. 24 August 27, 1973

CENSORSHIP: LOCAL AND EXPRESS

Part II

A profound commitment to moral collectivism does not occur in a vacuum, as a causeless primary: it requires an epistemological foundation. The Supreme Court's majority decision in the case of Paris Adult Theater I v. Slaton reveals that foundation.

This case involves two movie theaters in Atlanta, Georgia, which exhibited allegedly obscene films, admitting only adults. The local trial court ruled that this was constitutionally permissible, but the Georgia Supreme Court reversed the decision - on the grounds that hard-core pornography is not protected by the First Amendment. Thus the issue before the U.S. Supreme Court was whether it is constitutional to abridge the freedom of consenting adults. The Court's majority decision said: "Yes."

Epistemologically, this decision is a proclamation of _non-objectivity_: it supports and defends explicitly the most evil of social phenomena: non-objective law.

The decision, written by Chief Justice Burger, declares: "we hold that there are legitimate state interests at stake in stemming the tide of commercialized obscenity...These include _the interest of the public in the quality of life and the total community environment_, the tone of commerce in the great city centers, and, possibly, the public safety itself." (Emphasis added.) Try to find a single issue or action that would be exempt from this kind of "legitimate" state interest.

Quoting a book by Professor Bickel, the decision declares: "A man may be entitled to read an obscene book in his room...But if he demands a right to obtain the books and pictures he wants in the market...then to grant him his right is to affect the world about the rest of us, and to impinge on other privacies.... what is commonly read and seen and heard and done intrudes upon us all, want it or not." Which human activity would be exempt from a declaration of this kind? And what advocate of a totalitarian dictatorship would not endorse that declaration?

Mr. Burger concedes that "there is no scientific data which conclusively demonstrates that exposure to obscene materials adversely affects men and women or their society." But he rejects this as an argument against the suppression of such materials. And there follows an avalanche of statements and of quotations from earlier Court decisions - all claiming (in terms broader than the issue of pornography) that _scientific knowledge_ and _conclusive proof_ are not required as a basis for legislation, that the State has the right to enact laws on the grounds of what does or might exist.

"Scientific data" (in the proper, literal sense of these words) means knowledge of reality, reached by a process of reason; and "conclusive demonstration" means that the content of a given proposition is proved to be a fact of reality. It is reason and reality that are here being removed as a limitation on the power of the State. It is the right to legislate on the basis of any assumption, any hypothesis, any guess, any feeling, any whim - on any grounds or none - that is here being conferred on the government.

"We do not demand of legislatures 'scientifically certain criteria of legislation,'" the decision affirms. "Although there is no conclusive proof of a connection between antisocial behavior and obscene material, the legislature of Georgia could quite reasonably determine that such a connection does or might exist. In deciding Roth, this Court implicitly accepted that a legislature could legitimately act on such a conclusion to protect 'the social interest in order and morality.'"

If the notion that something might be a threat to the "social interest," is sufficient to justify suppression, then the Nazi or the Soviet dictatorship is justified in exterminating anyone who, in its belief, might be a threat to the "social interest" of the Nazi or the Soviet "community."

Whatever theory of government such a notion represents, it is not the theory of America's Founding Fathers. Strangely enough, Chief Justice Burger seems to be aware of it, because he proceeds to call on a pre-American precedent. "From the beginning of civilized societies, legislators and judges have acted on various unprovable assumptions. Such assumptions underlie much lawful state regulation of commercial and business affairs."

This is pre-eminently true - and look at the results. Look at the history of all the governments in the world prior to the birth of the United States. Ours was the first government based on and strictly limited by a written document - the Constitution - which specifically forbids it to violate individual rights or to act on whim. The history of the atrocities perpetrated by all the other kinds of governments - unrestricted governments acting on unprovable assumptions - demonstrates the value and validity of the original political theory on which this country was built. Yet here is the Supreme Court citing all those bloody millennia of tyranny, as a precedent for us to follow.

If this seems inexplicable, the very next sentence of Mr. Burger's decision gives a clue to the reasons - and a violently clear demonstration of the role of precedent in the development of law. That next sentence seems to unleash a whirling storm of feathers, as chickens come flying home from every direction to roost on everyone's coop, perch or fence - in retribution for every evasion, compromise, injustice, and violation of rights perpetrated in past decades.

That next sentence is: "The same [a basis of unprovable assumptions] is true of the federal securities, antitrust laws and a host of other federal regulations."

Formally, I would have to say: "Oh, Mr. Chief Justice!" Informally, I want to say: "Oh, brother!"

"On the basis of these assumptions," Mr. Burger goes on, "both Congress and state legislatures have, for example, drastically restricted associational rights by adopting antitrust laws, and have strictly regulated public expression by issuers of and dealers in securities, profit sharing 'coupons,' and 'trading stamps,' commanding what they must and may not publish and announce....Understandably those who entertain an absolutist view of the First Amendment find it uncomfortable to explain why rights of association, speech, and press should be severely restrained in the marketplace of goods and money, but not in the marketplace of pornography."

On the collectivist premise, there is, of course, no answer. The only answer, in today's situation, is to check that premise and reject it - and start repealing all those catastrophically destructive violations of individual rights and of the Constitution. But this is not what the Court majority has decided. Forgetting his own warning about the "gestative propensity" of the judicial and legislative processes, Chief Justice Burger accepts the precedent as an irrevocable absolute and pushes the country many steps further toward the abyss of statism.

"Likewise," the decision continues, "when legislatures and administrators act to protect the physical environment from pollution and to preserve our resources of forests, streams and parks, they must act on such imponderables as the impact of a new highway near or through an existing park or wilderness area....Thus the Federal-Aid Highway Act of 1968...and the Department of Transportation Act of 1966...have been described by Mr. Justice Black as 'a solemn determination of the highest law-making body of this Nation that beauty and health-giving facilities of our parks are not to be taken away for public roads without hearings, fact-findings, and policy determinations under the supervision of a Cabinet officer....' The fact that a congressional directive reflects unprovable assumptions about what is good for the people, including imponderable aesthetic assumptions, is not a sufficient reason to find that statute unconstitutional."

Isn't it? If it is not, then _the imponderable aesthetic assumptions_ of government officials are entitled to invade the field of literature and art - as Mr. Burger's decision is inviting them to do.

The ugly hand of altruism slithers into the decision, in a passage that sideswipes the concept of free will. "We have just noted, for example, that neither the First Amendment nor 'free will' precludes States from having 'blue sky' laws to regulate what sellers of securities may write or publish about their wares. ...Such laws are to protect the weak, the uninformed, the unsuspecting, and the gullible from the exercise of their own volition." It is for this kind of purpose that the rest of us - who are not weak, uninformed, unsuspecting, and gullible - are to be _protected_ from _our_ volition and deprived of the right to exercise it. So much for the relation of altruism to rights and to freedom.

Here is another chicken flying home: "States are told by some that they must await a 'laissez-faire' market solution to the obscenity-pornography problem, paradoxically 'by people who have never otherwise had a kind word to say for laissez-faire,' particularly in solving urban, commercial, and environmental pollution problems."

The decision contains many other homing chickens of this kind - an entire barnyard of them - many more than I have space to quote. But these are sufficient to give you the nature, style and spirit of that ruling.

In his dissenting opinion, Justice Brennan, joined by Justices Stewart and Marshall, offers some good arguments to support the conclusion that censorship in regard to consenting adults is unconstitutional. But he wavers, hesitates to go that far, and tries to compromise, to strike "a better balance between the guarantee of free expression and the States' legitimate interests."

He concedes the notion that obscene material is not protected by the First Amendment, but expresses an anxious concern over the Court's failure to draw a clear line between protected and unprotected speech. He cites the chaotic, contradictory record of the Court's decisions in "obscenity" cases, but side-steps the issue by saying, in a footnote: "Whether or not a class of 'obscene' and thus entirely unprotected speech does exist, I am forced to conclude that the class is incapable of definition with sufficient clarity to withstand attack on vagueness grounds. Accordingly, it is on principles of the void-for-vagueness doctrine that this opinion exclusively relies."

Justice Brennan speaks eloquently about the danger of vague laws, and quotes Chief Justice Warren, who said that "the constitutional requirement of definiteness is violated by a criminal statute that fails to give a person of ordinary intelligence fair notice that his contemplated conduct is forbidden by the statute." But Justice Brennan does not mention the antitrust laws, which do just that. He states: "The resulting level of uncertainty is utterly intolerable, not alone because it makes 'bookselling...a hazardous profession,'...but as well because it invites arbitrary and erratic enforcement of the law." He deplores the fact that "obscenity" judgments are now made on "a case-by-case, sight-by-sight" basis. He observes that the Court has been struggling "to fend off legislative attempts 'to pass to the courts - and ultimately to the Supreme Court - the awesome task of making case by case at once the criminal and the constitutional law.'" But he does not mention the living hell of antitrust, the grim monument to law made case by case.

However, a greater respect for principles and a greater understanding of their consequences are revealed in Justice Brennan's dissenting opinion than in the majority decision. He declares that on the basis of that majority decision: "it is hard to see how state-ordered regimentation of our minds can ever be forestalled. For if a State may, in an effort to maintain or create a particular moral tone, prescribe what its citizens cannot read or cannot see, then it would seem to follow that in pursuit of that same objective a State could decree that its citizens must read certain books or must view certain films."

The best statement, however, is made again by Justice Douglas, who ends his forceful dissent with the words: "But our society - unlike most in the world - presupposes that freedom and liberty are in a frame of reference that make the individual, not government, the keeper of his tastes, beliefs, and ideas. That is the philosophy of the First Amendment; and it is the article of faith that sets us apart from most nations in the world."

I concur - except that it is not an "article of _faith_," but a _provable_, rational conviction.

(To be continued.)

Ayn Rand

The Ayn Rand Letter, published fortnightly by The Ayn Rand Letter, Inc., 183 Madison Avenue, New York, N.Y. 10016.
Contributing Editor: **Leonard Peikoff**; Subscription Director: **Elayne Kalberman**; Production Manager: **Barbara Weiss.**

Vol. II, No. 25 September 10, 1973

CENSORSHIP: LOCAL AND EXPRESS

Part III

In the life of a nation, the law plays the same role as a decision-making process of thought does in the life of an individual. An individual makes decisions by applying his basic premises to a specific choice - premises which he can change, but seldom does. The basic premises of a nation's laws are set by its dominant political philosophy and implemented by the courts, whose task is to determine the application of broad principles to specific cases; in this task, the equivalent of basic premises is precedent, which can be challenged, but seldom is.

How far a loosely worded piece of legislation can go in the role of precedent, is horrifyingly demonstrated by the Supreme Court's majority decision in another one of the five "obscenity" cases, U.S. v. Orito. This case involves a man charged with knowingly transporting obscene material by common carrier in interstate commerce.

The clause giving Congress the power to regulate interstate commerce is one of the major errors in the Constitution. That clause, more than any other, was the crack in the Constitution's foundation, the entering wedge of statism, which permitted the gradual establishment of the Welfare State. But I would venture to say that the framers of the Constitution could not have conceived of what that clause has now become. If, in writing it, one of their goals was to facilitate the flow of trade and prevent the establishment of trade barriers among the states, that clause has reached the opposite destination. You may now expect fifty different frontiers inside this country, with customs officials searching your luggage and pockets for books or magazines permitted in one state, but prohibited in another.

Chief Justice Burger's decision declares, quoting an earlier Court decision: "The motive and purpose of a regulation of interstate commerce are matters for the legislative judgment upon the exercise of which the Constitution places no restriction and over which the courts are given no control." Such an interpretation means that legislative judgment is given an absolute power, beyond the restraint of any principle, beyond the reach of any checks or balances. This is an outrageous instance of context-dropping: the Constitution, taken as a whole, *is* a fundamental restriction on the power of the government, whether in the legislative or in any other branch.

"It is sufficient to reiterate," Mr. Burger declares, "the well-settled principle that Congress may impose relevant conditions and requirements on those who use the channels of interstate commerce in order that those channels will not become the means of promoting or spreading evil, whether of a physical, moral or economic nature." As if this were not clear enough, a footnote is added: "Congress can certainly regulate interstate commerce to the extent of forbidding and punishing the use of such commerce as an agency to promote immorality, dishonesty, or the spread of any evil or harm to the people of other states from the state of origin." Immorality, evil and harm - by what standard?

The only rights which the five majority decisions leave you are the right to read and see what you wish in your own room, but not outside it - and the right to think whatever you please in the privacy of your own mind. But this is a right which even a totalitarian dictatorship is unable to suppress. (You are free to _think_ in Soviet Russia, but not to _act_ on your thinking.) Again, Justice Douglas's dissent is the only voice raised in desperate protest: "Our whole constitutional heritage rebels at the thought of giving government the power to control men's minds."

The division between the conservative and the liberal viewpoints in the opinions of the Supreme Court, is sharper and clearer than in less solemn writings or in purely political debates. By the nature of its task, the Supreme Court has to and does become the voice of philosophy.

The necessity to deal with principles makes the members of the Supreme Court seem archetypical of the ideas - almost, of the soul - of the two political camps they represent. They were not chosen as archetypes: in the undefined, indeterminate, contradictory chaos of political views loosely labeled "conservative" and "liberal," it would be impossible to choose an essential characteristic or a typical representative. Yet, as one reads the Supreme Court's opinions, the essential premises stand out with an oddly bright, revealing clarity - and one grasps that under all the lesser differences and inconsistencies of their followers, _these_ are the basic premises of one political camp or of the other. It is almost as if one were seeing not these antagonists' philosophy, but their sense of life.

The subject of the five "obscenity" cases was not obscenity as such - which is a marginal and inconsequential matter - but a much deeper issue: the sexual aspect of man's life. Sex is not a separate nor a purely physical attribute of a man's character: it involves a complex integration of all his fundamental values. So it is not astonishing that cases dealing with sex (even in its ugliest manifestations) would involve the influence of all the branches of philosophy. We have seen the influence of ethics, epistemology, politics, aesthetics (this last as the immediate victim of the debate). What about the fifth branch of philosophy, the basic one, the fundamental of the science of fundamentals: metaphysics? Its influence is revealed in - and explains - the inner contradictions of each camp. The metaphysical issue is their view of man's nature.

Both camps hold the same premise - _the mind-body dichotomy_ - but choose opposite sides of this lethal fallacy.

The conservatives want freedom to act in the material realm; they tend to oppose government control of production, of industry, of trade, of business, of physical goods, of material wealth. But they advocate government control of man's spirit, i.e., man's consciousness; they advocate the State's right to impose censorship, to determine moral values, to create and enforce a governmental establishment of morality, to rule the intellect. The liberals want freedom to act in the spiritual realm; they oppose censorship, they oppose government control of ideas, of the arts, of the press, of education (note their concern with "academic freedom"). But they advocate government control of material production, of business, of employment, of wages, of profits, of all physical property - they advocate it all the way down to total expropriation.

The conservatives see man as a body freely roaming the earth, building sand piles or factories - with an electronic computer inside his skull, controlled from Washington. The liberals see man as a soul freewheeling to the farthest reaches of the universe - but wearing chains from nose to toes when he crosses the street to buy a loaf of bread.

Yet it is the conservatives who are predominantly religionists, who proclaim the superiority of the soul over the body, who represent what I call the "mystics of spirit." And it is the liberals who are predominantly materialists, who regard man as an aggregate of meat, and who represent what I call the "mystics of muscle."

This is merely a paradox, not a contradiction: *each camp wants to control the realm it regards as metaphysically important; each grants freedom only to the activities it despises*. Observe that the conservatives insult and demean the rich or those who succeed in material production, regarding them as morally inferior - and that the liberals treat ideas as a cynical con game. "Control," to both camps, means the power to rule by physical force. Neither camp holds freedom as a value. The conservatives want to rule man's consciousness; the liberals, his body.

On that premise, neither camp has permitted itself to observe that force is a killer in both realms. The conservatives, frozen in their mystic dogmas, are paralyzed, terrified and impotent in the realm of ideas. The liberals, waiting for the unearned, are paralyzed, terrified and, frequently, incompetent in or hostile to the realm of material production (observe the ecology crusade).

Why do both camps cling to blind faith in the power of physical force? I quote from *Atlas Shrugged*: "Do you observe what human faculty that doctrine [the mind-body dichotomy] was designed to destroy? It was man's mind that had to be negated in order to make him fall apart." Both camps, conservatives and liberals alike, are united in their hatred of man's mind - i.e., of *reason*. The conservatives reject reason in favor of faith; the liberals, in favor of emotions. The conservatives are either lethargically indifferent to intellectual issues, or actively anti-intellectual. The liberals are smarter in this respect: they use intellectual weapons to destroy and negate the intellect (they call it "to redefine"). When men reject reason, they have no means left for dealing with one another - except brute, physical force.

I quote from *Atlas Shrugged*: "...the men you call materialists and spiritualists are only two halves of the same dissected human, forever seeking completion, but seeking it by swinging from the destruction of the flesh to the destruction of the soul and vice versa...seeking any refuge against reality, any form of escape from the mind." Since the two camps are only two sides of the same coin - the same *counterfeit* coin - they are now moving closer and closer together. Observe the fundamental similarity of their philosophical views: in metaphysics - the mind-body dichotomy; in epistemology - irrationalism; in ethics - altruism; in politics - statism.

The conservatives used to claim that they were loyal to tradition - while the liberals boasted of being "progressive." But observe that it is Chief Justice Burger, a conservative, who propounds a militant collectivism, and formulates general principles that stretch the power of the State way beyond the issue of pornography - and it is Justice Douglas, a liberal, who invokes "the traditions of a free society" and pleads for "our constitutional heritage."

If someone had said in 1890 that antitrust laws for the businessmen would, sooner or later, lead to censorship for the intellectuals, no one would have believed it. You can see it today. When Chief Justice Burger declares to the liberals that they cannot explain why rights "should be severely restrained in the marketplace of goods and money, but not in the marketplace of pornography," I am tempted to feel that it serves them right - except that all of us are the victims.

If this censorship ruling is not revoked, the next step will be more explicit: it will replace the words "marketplace of pornography" with the words "marketplace of ideas." This will serve as a precedent for the liberals, enabling them to determine which ideas _they_ wish to suppress - in the name of the "social interest" - when their turn comes. No one can win a contest of this kind - except the State.

I do not know how the conservative members of the Supreme Court can bear to look at the Jefferson Memorial in Washington, where his words are engraved in marble: "I have sworn...eternal hostility to every form of tyranny over the mind of man."

Permit me to add without presumptuousness: "So have I."

Ayn Rand

OBJECTIVIST CALENDAR

The broadcast of Ayn Rand's lecture, "Censorship: Local and Express," originally scheduled for October 26 in New York City, has been rescheduled for Saturday, November 10, 11 A.M.-1 P.M., over radio station WNYC-AM (830). We have also been informed that the lecture will be broadcast in Philadelphia on Sunday, November 25, at 8 P.M., over radio station WUHY-FM (90.9). As we go to press, these dates have been confirmed. However, changes in scheduling are possible, and it is advisable to check with the stations.

Beginning Tuesday, January 15, 1974, Leonard Peikoff will offer a ten-lecture course on _Introduction to Logic_.

The course covers the standard topics taught in introductory college courses in Aristotelian logic. It defines the basic principles and standards of valid reasoning, and discusses the most prevalent logical fallacies. It formalizes the steps by which one derives conclusions from premises; it provides the student with a methodology by which to evaluate his own thinking processes, and teaches him the art of proper argumentation.

Introduction to Logic will be given every week, on Tuesday evening at 7:30 P.M., from January 15 to March 19, at the Statler Hilton Hotel, 7th Ave. at 33rd St., New York City. Tuition is $50; registration is limited to 200 students. Brochures, including registration forms, will be sent, at the end of November, to _The Ayn Rand Letter_ subscribers in the New York Metropolitan area. For further information, write to Dr. Peikoff at P.O. Box 381, Forest Hills, N.Y. 11375.

In other cities, tapes of the lectures will be made available, to groups of ten persons or more, on a rental basis; inquiries should be addressed to Susan Ludel, 120 East 34th St., New York, N.Y. 10016.

B.W.

The Ayn Rand Letter, published fortnightly by The Ayn Rand Letter, Inc., 183 Madison Avenue, New York, N.Y. 10016.
Contributing Editor: **Leonard Peikoff**; Subscription Director: **Elayne Kalberman**; Production Manager: **Barbara Weiss.**

Vol. II, No. 26 September 24, 1973

THOUGHT CONTROL

In the first obscenity case brought before the Supreme Court of the State of New York since the U.S. Supreme Court ruling on this subject of June 21, 1973, Judge Abraham J. Gellinoff dismissed the case against the defendants and wrote a very interesting decision (August 14, 1973).

The defendants were the exhibitors of films claimed to be obscene by New York City authorities. The most significant part of Judge Gellinoff's decision was its conclusion: "...the films are, in this court's view, obscene. In the court's personal opinion, they are patently offensive.

"However, the Supreme Court has determined that 'obscenity is to be determined by applying "contemporary community standards"...not "national standards"'...

"Formerly, a court could determine national standards, based in part on prior trials of similar cases, and could judge a film merely on its content. But this is the first case of its kind since the Supreme Court decreed that community standards, not national standards, govern, and there is no evidence before the court, at this stage of the case, to enable the court to gauge the contemporary standards of this community. While the court knows its own standards, and believes it knows what the community standards should be, there are no facts presented before the court to enable it to say, with reasonable assurance, in advance of a full trial, what the trier of the facts will find the community standards actually to be."

If a conscientious judge cannot determine what the "community standards" are, who can? What would a judge accept as evidence of such standards? If he has to wait for a precedent, for a trier of the facts to determine these standards, _who_ is that trier to be and _how_ will he do it?

On November 27, 1973, the Appellate Division of the State Supreme Court reversed Judge Gellinoff's ruling and said in regard to the films: "The multiple and variegated ultimate acts of sexual perversion would have been regarded as 'obscene' by the community standards of Sodom and Gomorrah." This is undoubtedly true, but it is an attempt to invoke standards applicable to _all_ communities, national and international, contemporary and ancient (an attempt which the U.S. Supreme Court has invalidated), and it gives no clue to the method by which the particular "community standards" of New York City (or of Sodom and Gomorrah, for that matter) are to be established. The Appellate Division's ruling declared: "the average person in New York State, City or County would in all likelihood have concluded these pictures appealed to prurient interest." This is a guess about the average person's guess about the standards of other average persons in New York State. The decision decreed that the State's courts should "synthesize" these unnamed standards "by judicial construction" - which means, _arbitrarily_. There is no other way to determine the meaning of a term that denotes the non-existent, such as "community standards."

"Judicial construction" is one method of exercising arbitrary power. There is another - still more reprehensible in its actual meaning and potential consequences. The present U.S. Supreme Court's rulings do not describe that method explicitly. To find it, one must go back some fifteen years, to the Court's decision in the Roth case (1957).

The Roth case is, in large part, the foundation of all the subsequent Supreme Court decisions in regard to obscenity. It is interesting to note that the present rulings carry the practical application of the principles enunciated in Roth further toward censorship than did the Roth decision, but they do not discuss the principles: these are merely suggested implicitly, as if taken for granted and not open to critical examination.

(This is an example of the similarity in the working of legal precedents and of a man's basic premises: a bad premise may be available to a man's conscious awareness, at first; then, with each successive application to practice, the premise becomes automatized and is taken for granted, while its reasons or sources are forgotten and closed to re-examination; yet - unless he identifies and rejects it - that premise continues to direct the man's actions, and it works toward its ultimate logical consequences without his conscious knowledge or choice.)

The Roth decision, written by Justice Brennan, quotes with approval the trial judge's definition of obscenity: "The words 'obscene, lewd and lascivious' as used in the law, signify that form of immorality which has relation to sexual impurity and has a tendency to excite lustful _thoughts_." (Emphasis added by Justice Brennan.)

The decision states that the trial court "followed the proper standard" and "used the proper definition of obscenity." And, apparently as a clarification and as a guideline for other courts, the decision quotes the following passage from the Roth trial judge's instructions to the jury:

"...The test is not whether it would arouse sexual desires or sexual impure thoughts in those comprising a particular segment of the community, the young, the immature or the highly prudish or would leave another segment, the scientific or highly educated or the so-called worldly-wise and sophisticated indifferent and unmoved....

"The test in each case is the effect of the book, picture or publication considered as a whole, not upon any particular class, but upon all those whom it is likely to reach. In other words, you determine its impact upon the average person in the community. The books, pictures and circulars must be judged as a whole, in their entire context, and you are not to consider detached or separate portions in reaching a conclusion. You judge the circulars, pictures and publications which have been put in evidence by present-day standards of the community. You may ask yourselves does it offend the common conscience of the community by present-day standards....

"In this case, ladies and gentlemen of the jury, you and you alone are the exclusive judges of what the common conscience of the community is, and in determining that conscience you are to consider the community as a whole, young and old, educated and uneducated, the religious and the irreligious - men, women and children."

The formula: "you and you alone are the exclusive judges" is taken from the usual instructions to the jury in criminal cases, in which it reads: "you and you alone are the exclusive judges of the _facts_." Observe the horrendous enormity of the difference, when this formula is applied to intellectual issues.

"Facts," in a criminal case, means specified, defined, objectively perceivable, physical actions, such as murder or robbery. The rules of the jury's process of deliberation - what is relevant or not, what must be considered or ignored, what grounds are valid or invalid, even what degree of certainty is required - are determined by law, by the complex rules of legal evidence. The jury is not given carte blanche to determine something somehow; the judge is the guardian of the law, and it is his task to see that the jury abides by those legal rules; if it does not, he has the power to set aside its verdict. Moreover, the only thing submitted for the jury's decision is the particular facts of a particular case. The jury passes judgment on concretes, _not_ on abstractions: it does not write laws, it does not determine principles, its power ends with the case.

How are jurors to determine an issue such as "what the common conscience of the community is"? Most people are unable to identify, in clear, conceptual terms, what their own conscience is, i.e., their own moral convictions. Of those who can do so, very few (if any) are able to identify, with any degree of certainty, the conscience of others, of their own families, of their closest friends; in this respect, people often experience painful shocks of disappointment. Yet they are asked to judge the "common conscience of a community" - a floating abstraction which is not defined in any respect: neither what it _is_, nor what one may take it to be, nor the means of identifying it and judging it (nor even whether it exists).

There is no scientific method by which the "common conscience of a community" can be identified; there is no psychological method; there is no philosophical method. (A rational philosophy can demonstrate that that notion is a myth: "conscience" being a moral term, there is no such thing as a communal or collective morality, because there is no such thing as a communal or collective brain; a community is merely a number of individual citizens, the sum of whose moral standards cannot be computed.) Agreeing with and paraphrasing Judge Gellinoff, a conscientious, thinking man would have to say: "I know my own standards and I know what the community members' standards should be, but I do not (and cannot) know what the community standards are."

The trial judge in the Roth case was, apparently, aware of the intellectual problems involved: he did not instruct the jury to "identify" the community conscience, but to "_determine_" it - i.e., to issue an _edict_, an arbitrary pronouncement which, thereafter, is to be given the status of a proved fact and to be enforced by law. This means that twelve persons picked at random - regardless of their knowledge, intelligence, integrity, or moral character, regardless of _their_ "conscience" - are given the power to rule the most profoundly personal aspects of a man's life, and to force on him their own notions of morality (if any). To add insult to injury, it is not even the jurors' own views that are given such power, but worse: their guess about the views of others.

As a method of exercising arbitrary power, this is much worse than "judicial construction." The latter offers, at least, a pseudo-justification: the suggestion that legally trained minds are interpreting a difficult problem (which some judges try to do fairly, though it is impossible to do under non-objective laws). But an arbitrary pronouncement by a random jury implies and establishes three disastrous premises: 1. the collectivist notion that the will of the people (of the "community") is the source, the standard, and the ultimate authority in the field of morality; 2. the mystic notion that the jury is, somehow, an embodiment of the people's unlimited will (and thus the opposite of what a jury actually is: a practical device to obtain as objective a judgment as possible, limited by objective rules, in objectively defined cases); 3. an endorsement of the tendency toward the worst form of tyranny, which is fashionable today as the outgrowth of a mixed economy: the random endowment of private citizens with governmental power - i.e., the union of government and self-appointed, irresponsible private groups which were not elected by anyone, yet claim to represent the people or part of the people (e.g., Women's Lib).

The arbitrary power conferred on the jury by the Roth trial judge's instructions is all but explicit in the fact that the task he assigns to the jurors is a solid contradiction and, therefore, impossible: "in determining that conscience you are to consider the community as a whole, young and old, educated and uneducated, the religious and the irreligious - men, women and children." To consider them in what respect? In respect to the kind of _thoughts_ which a given "book, picture or publication" would arouse in them, specifically "lustful thoughts."

Since a man's views on sex are determined by the sum of his fundamental conscious and subconscious values, would the reaction of the young (who do not understand the subject) and of the old (who may have lost interest) be the same? Or of the educated (who may hold any number of false theories) and of the uneducated (who may regard sex as physicalistic brutality)? Or of the religious (who regard sex as sin) and of the irreligious (who may regard it as a great value)? Or of promiscuous men, of prudish women, and of uninformed children? The views and reactions of all these people will not merely be different, but diametrically opposed. Since no one can reconcile opposites, the Roth trial judge by-passed the problem by substituting force for justice, as all seekers of the impossible must do: let the jury issue an arbitrary edict and let it be enforced as the voice of the entire community. Why? Because the jury is the embodiment of the community's will. Such is the mystique of intellectual collectivization.

Morally, the most offensive part of this procedure is the fact that _you_, as an individual, are deprived of the right to express your own views, but a jury is given the right to determine what _your_ views are and to censor public expression accordingly, in _your_ name.

(To be continued.)

Ayn Rand

P.S. This _Letter_ was written later than the date that appears on its heading.

OBJECTIVIST CALENDAR

On Friday, November 2, Ayn Rand conducted a seminar in political philosophy for the New York City Urban Fellowship, a project affiliated with the Office of the Mayor of New York City; the project enables a group of outstanding college seniors and graduate students, selected from across the country, to study the workings of city government.

Starting on January 21, 1974, the tape lectures of Leonard Peikoff's course, _Modern Philosophy: Kant to the Present_, will be given in Atlanta. For further information, contact Dr. Bonar Newton at (404) 351-9096.

B.W.

The Ayn Rand Letter, published fortnightly by The Ayn Rand Letter, Inc., 183 Madison Avenue, New York, N.Y. 10016.

Contributing Editor: **Leonard Peikoff**; Subscription Director: **Elayne Kalberman**; Production Manager: **Barbara Weiss.**

Vol. III, No. 1 October 8, 1973

THOUGHT CONTROL

Part II

What is the purpose of the anti-obscenity legislation? The present Supreme Court decisions attempt to camouflage the issue by alleging that the purpose is to protect the nation from "antisocial" (i.e., criminal) actions. But the Supreme Court decision in the Roth case is more candid: it states clearly and openly that the purpose is not the control of action, but the control of thought.

In addition to the trial judge's definition of obscenity, the Roth decision quotes with approval a definition given in an earlier case, which holds material to be obscene if it has "a substantial tendency to deprave or corrupt its readers by inciting lascivious thoughts or arousing lustful desires." (Emphasis added by Justice Brennan.)

This is an unequivocal declaration and an official endorsement of the tenet that sex as such is evil.

Observe that that statement does not refer to some sorts of sexual aberrations or abuses; it does not refer to the conventional censure of extramarital sex; it makes the sweeping declaration that any "lustful," i.e., sexual, desire (presumably, even toward one's spouse) constitutes depravity and corruption.

Immediately following that quotation, the decision mentions the objection of those who hold that such rulings violate constitutional guarantees "because convictions may be had without proof either that obscene material will perceptibly create a clear and present danger of antisocial conduct, or will probably induce its recipients to such conduct." Justice Brennan disposes of this objection by declaring that "in light of our holding that obscenity is not [constitutionally] protected speech," it is unnecessary for the courts to consider such issues. In other words, the government's purpose in anti-obscenity cases is not to prohibit criminal conduct, but to prohibit thought - sexual thought.

"However," the decision continues, "sex and obscenity are not synonymous. Obscene material is material which deals with sex in a manner appealing to prurient interest" - and adds a footnote: "I.e., material having a tendency to excite lustful thoughts." The adjectives "prurient," "lustful," "lascivious," "lewd," etc. are repeated over and over again in court decisions in obscenity cases, as if these adjectives were clear, sufficient definitions. But if you want to make a linguistic experiment, look up the definitions of these adjectives in a good, unabridged dictionary. You will find yourself on a hopeless chase, being pushed from one word to another to another, in as bad an example of circularity as any which a class in freshman logic would teach you not to commit - and, buried somewhere along the way, as definition No. 2 or 3, you will find the words: "sexual desire."

Apparently, the Roth decision considers discussions of sex permissible (particularly, as it points out, "in art, literature and scientific works"), but prohibited if they appeal to sexual interest or arouse sexual desire. I submit that a work of art or literature which deals with sex without appealing to such interest, is guilty of lousy craftsmanship.

The attempt to prohibit thought - any kind of thought on any subject - is grotesquely futile. It is worse than grotesque in this country: it means that the Constitution guarantees us freedom of speech and of the press, but not freedom of thought.

To make matters still worse, the author of material claimed to be obscene is held responsible and punished not for his own thoughts, but _for the thoughts his work might arouse in others_. Who can tell what thoughts (or _feelings_) a book - on any subject - would arouse in a reader? Logically, it is possible to tell what thoughts a given book _should_ arouse - _if_ a reader is faultlessly logical. How many such readers are there today? And, for that matter, how many faultlessly logical authors? In a Kantian-Hegelian age, logic is the most unfashionable discipline. When men are trained to use words as meaningless sounds, as emotional grunts, or as tools of deception, who can tell which book will inspire whom to what?

Many people believe that the obscenity rulings apply only to pornography. But the Supreme Court has repeatedly admitted its inability to draw a line between pornography and other kinds of writing. And the Supreme Court does not deal with concretes - it deals with principles which establish legal policy. The principle of suppressing a book and punishing its author on the basis of the thoughts or feelings it might arouse in readers - is a monstrous notion, irreconcilable with the Constitution and with all constitutional guarantees. (Yet this notion is being voiced today outside the field of law and is being applied to issues other than pornography - as I shall discuss later.)

Justice Harlan, who dissented in part, states explicitly that the Roth majority decision attempts to prohibit thoughts. "Under the federal definition [of obscenity] it is enough if the jury finds that the book as a whole leads to certain thoughts. In California, the further inference must be drawn that such thoughts will have a substantive 'tendency to deprave or corrupt' - i.e., that the thoughts induced by the material will affect character and action." Justice Harlan points out that there is no proof of such a causal connection. He quotes from a document issued by the American Law Institute: "...regulation of thought or desire, unconnected with overt misbehavior, raises the most acute constitutional as well as practical difficulties." He declares: "The Federal Government has no business, whether under the postal or commerce power, to bar the sale of books because they might lead to any kind of 'thoughts.'"

But Justice Harlan undercuts his case and destroys the meaning of his dissent by granting this power to _state governments_. "Since the domain of sexual morality is pre-eminently a matter of state concern, this Court should be slow to interfere with state legislation calculated to protect that morality." And: "Congress has no substantive power over sexual morality. Such powers as the Federal Government has in this field...are not of the same nature as those possessed by the States, which bear direct responsibility for the protection of the local moral fabric."

The Supreme Court's best defender of intellectual freedom, in the Roth case as well as today, is Justice Douglas. His uncompromising dissent (with which Justice Black concurs) opens with the words: "When we sustain these convictions [of the defendants in the Roth case], we make the legality of a publication turn on the purity of thought which a book or tract instills in the mind of the reader. I do not think we can approve that standard and be faithful to the command of the First Amendment, which by its terms is a restraint on Congress and which by the Fourteenth is a restraint on the States."

He declares: "By these [California's] standards punishment is inflicted for thoughts provoked, not for overt acts nor antisocial conduct" - and insists that "speech to be punishable must have some relation to action which could be penalized by government." And: "To allow the State to step in and punish mere speech or publication that the judge or the jury thinks has an <u>undesirable</u> impact on thoughts but that is not shown to be a part of unlawful action is drastically to curtail the First Amendment."

Justice Douglas, properly, objects to the Roth trial judge's standard of defining obscenity, which he finds more inimical to freedom of expression than various other criteria. "The standard of what offends 'the common conscience of the community' conflicts, in my judgment, with the command of the First Amendment that 'Congress shall make no law...abridging the freedom of speech, or of the press.' Certainly that standard would not be an acceptable one if religion, economics, politics or philosophy were involved. How does it become a constitutional standard when literature treating with sex is concerned?" Further, he points out that "the test that suppresses a cheap tract today can suppress a literary gem tomorrow. All it need do is to incite a lascivious thought or arouse a lustful desire. The list of books that judges or juries can place in that category is endless."

These arguments are unanswerable. So is the following, for which I applaud Justice Douglas: "The tests by which these convictions were obtained require only the arousing of sexual thoughts. Yet the arousing of sexual thoughts and desires happens every day in normal life in dozens of ways. Nearly 30 years ago a questionnaire sent to college and normal school women graduates asked what things were most stimulating sexually. Of 409 replies, 9 said 'music'; 18 said 'pictures'; 29 said 'dancing'; 40 said 'drama'; 95 said 'books'; and 218 said 'man.'"

I would like to add that whenever a young man shaves or a young girl makes up her face, or either of them puts on attractive clothes, it is done for the implicit purpose of arousing sexual thoughts and desires - which does not mean the intention of rushing to bed with every stranger, but merely the wish to be admired, to receive a tacit acknowledgment of one's sexual value qua man or woman. This type of acknowledgment creates the heightened interest, the excitement, the color, the <u>personal</u> enjoyment in human relationships with the opposite sex. There is only one ideology that would condemn it - the ideology that opposes man's enjoyment of his life on earth and holds sex as such to be evil - the same ideology that is the source and cause of anti-obscenity censorship: religion.

For a discussion of the profound, metaphysical reasons of religion's antagonism to sex, I refer you to my article "Of Living Death" (<u>The Objectivist</u>, September-November 1968), which deals with the papal encyclical on contraception, "Of Human Life." Today, most people who profess to be religious, particularly in this country, do not share that condemnation of sex - but it is an ancient tradition which survives, consciously or subconsciously, even in the minds of many irreligious persons, because it is a logical consequence implicit in the basic causes and motives of any form of mysticism.

Justice Brennan's decision in the Roth case indicates the religious source of anti-obscenity legislation. Defending the tenet that obscenity is not protected by the First Amendment, Justice Brennan writes: "As early as 1712, Massachusetts made it criminal to publish 'any filthy, obscene, or profane song, pamphlet, libel or mock sermon' in imitation or mimicking of religious services. ...Thus, profanity and obscenity were related offenses."

Justice Douglas acknowledges this connection by saying: "I can understand (and at times even sympathize) with programs of civic groups and church groups to protect and defend the existing moral standards of the community. I can understand the motives of the Anthony Comstocks who would impose Victorian standards on the community." But he does not think that government "can become the sponsor of any of these movements" or that government "can throw its weight behind one school or another."

Some day, in a better, i.e., more philosophical age, someone will convince the Supreme Court that anti-obscenity legislation is unconstitutional because it represents an act explicitly forbidden by the Constitution: an establishment of religion - an attempt to enforce a purely religious doctrine.

The Supreme Court has been struggling from case to case, seeking to protect freedom of speech, but unable, apparently, to resist the perennial pressures clamoring for censorship. That struggle offers an important lesson on the consequences of clinging to or compromising with any irrational - i.e., indefinable, unprovable and indefensible - notion. The Roth decision explicitly admitted the intention to control thought, but still attempted to preserve a semblance of legal objectivity by demanding a <u>national</u> "community standard." The present Supreme Court gave up this attempt as impossible and opened the gates wide to the worst possible form of wanton, collectivist tyranny: judgment by <u>local</u> "community standards."

And, in order to justify the unjustifiable, in order to claim that the purpose of censorship is to prohibit "antisocial" actions, not thoughts, the conservative Chief Justice Burger was willing to propound a doctrine with a far more destructive potential than that of any smutty films or filthy post cards: the doctrine of a government's right to legislate on the basis of unprovable assumptions.

(To be continued.)

Ayn Rand

OBJECTIVIST CALENDAR

On Saturday, December 29, Ayn Rand will appear as one of the guests on Larry Cole's radio program in New York City. Station WRVR-FM (106.7), 10-11 A.M.

The following starting dates have been scheduled for the tape lectures of Dr. Leonard Peikoff's course, <u>Modern Philosophy: Kant to the Present</u>. Winnipeg, January 15 (contact Ellen Moore, 204-253-1630); Toronto, January 23 (Edmund West, 416-661-1777, after 8 P.M.).

B.W.

The Ayn Rand Letter, published fortnightly by The Ayn Rand Letter, Inc., 183 Madison Avenue, New York, N.Y. 10016.

Contributing Editor: **Leonard Peikoff**; Subscription Director: **Elayne Kalberman**; Production Manager: **Barbara Weiss.**

Vol. III, No. 2 October 22, 1973

THOUGHT CONTROL

Part III

The theoreticians of religion know that it is impossible to prohibit thought. They do not expect the ban on sexual thoughts to be obeyed. Their purpose is not to abolish such thoughts, but to induce guilt - and thus to undercut man's self-esteem.

The following small incident captures the essence of the religious censors' mentality. In the 1930s, the "self-censorship" office of the movie industry (known as the Hays Office or, later, the Johnson Office) went on one of its periodic crusades against sex in the movies. That office was run predominantly by a religious organization, the Purity League. The two foremost sex symbols of the period were Greta Garbo and Mae West, who embodied two diametrically opposite attitudes: Garbo projected an exquisitely spiritual, exalted, man-worshiping sexuality - Mae West offered an "earthy," eye-winking, hip-swinging, humorously vulgar image that verged on the obscene, projecting the silent invitation: "Come, one and all." A representative of the censorship office was quoted as saying: "We don't mind Mae West - she makes sex ludicrous. What we oppose is Greta Garbo - she makes it glamorous."

Use your own judgment on the question of whose goal is "to deprave or corrupt."

In this respect, modern hippies - with their insistence on personal ugliness or "natural," unglamorous appearance, their undifferentiated, "unisex" style of dressing, and their "uninhibited" freedom to copulate in public - are demonstrating one more aspect of their fundamental affinity with the conventional premises of mysticism: the view of sex as an animal function.

Today, it is the publicly flaunted, disgusting sexuality of hippie youths, of senile repressers, and of their panderers in books and movies, which drives people to support the religionists' clamor for censorship. This aspect of the issue is wider than religious influences: civilized men do not tolerate public displays of sub-animal sex. Many people regard a public representation of sexual intercourse as disgusting - not because sex is evil, but precisely because it is a value, an exception-making value that requires privacy. Censorship, however, is not the solution: resorting to censorship is like cutting a man's head off in order to cure a cold.

Only one aspect of sex is a legitimate field for legislation: the protection of minors and of unconsenting adults. Apart from criminal actions (such as rape), this aspect includes the need to protect people from being confronted with sights they regard as loathsome. (A corollary of the freedom to see and hear, is the freedom not to look or listen.) Legal restraints on certain types of public displays, such as posters or window displays, are proper - but this is an issue of procedure, of <u>etiquette</u>, not of morality.

No one has the right to do whatever he pleases on a public street (nor would he have such a right on a privately owned street). The police power to maintain order among pedestrians or to control traffic is a procedural, not a substantive, power. A traffic policeman enforces rules of <u>how</u> to drive (in order to avoid clashes or collisions), but cannot tell you <u>where</u> to go. Similarly, the rights of those who seek pornography would not be infringed by rules protecting the rights of those who find pornography offensive - e.g., sexually explicit posters may properly be forbidden in public places; warning signs, such as "For Adults Only," may properly be required of private places which are open to the public. This protects the unconsenting, and has nothing to do with censorship, i.e., with prohibiting thought or speech.

Religious influences are not the only villain behind the censorship legislation; there is another one: the social school of morality, exemplified by John Stuart Mill. Mill rejected the concept of individual rights and replaced it with the notion that the "public good" is the sole justification of individual freedom. (Society, he argued, has the power to enslave or destroy its exceptional men, but it should <u>permit</u> them to be free, because it benefits from their efforts.) Among the many defaults of the conservatives in the past hundred years, the most shameful one, perhaps, is the fact that they accepted John Stuart Mill as a defender of capitalism.

Mill's influence is spread all over the Supreme Court decision in the Roth case, as well as over the recent "obscenity" decisions.

"...implicit in the history of the First Amendment," writes Justice Brennan in the Roth decision, "is the rejection of obscenity as utterly without redeeming social importance." He quotes from an earlier Court decision: "It has been well observed that such [lewd and obscene] utterances are no essential part of any exposition of ideas, and are of such slight social value as a step to truth that any benefit that may be derived from them is clearly outweighed by the social interest in order and morality..."

Quoting from another earlier Court decision, Justice Brennan writes: "Freedom of discussion, if it would fulfill its historic function in this nation, must embrace <u>all issues about which information is needed or appropriate to enable the members of society to cope with the exigencies of their period</u>." (Emphasis added by Justice Brennan.) How many "members of society" must need that information before a free discussion is permitted? Two men? A hundred men? A majority? And what about the rights of the man who discovers and provides that needed information?

"The fundamental freedoms of speech and press," Justice Brennan continues on his own, "have contributed greatly to the development and well-being of our free society and are indispensable to its continued growth." True enough - but this is only a secondary consequence, <u>not</u> a moral justification.

The moral justification is the "development and well-being" and rights of those who contribute the knowledge indispensable to growth. But they are not mentioned or considered.

Justice Douglas, the Court's best defender of intellectual freedom, offers the worst justification: "As recently stated by two of our outstanding authorities on obscenity, 'The danger of influencing a change in the current moral standards of the community, or of shocking or offending readers, or of stimulating sex thoughts or desires apart from objective conduct, can never justify the losses to society that result from interference with literary freedom.'" What about the losses to - and the rights of - the writers? No answer is possible in J.S. Mill's parasitical, "consumerist" swamp.

The extent to which Mill's influence is accepted as an automatized absolute in modern thinking, is demonstrated by the following curious passage. In the Roth decision, Justice Brennan states: "The protection given speech and press was fashioned to assure unfettered interchange of ideas for the bringing about of political and social changes desired by the people." This narrow, collectivistic interpretation does not sound like the Founding Fathers' view of freedom. Now read the quotation which comes immediately after Justice Brennan's words, and ask yourself whether it says what he claims it does: "This objective was made explicit as early as 1774 in a letter of the Continental Congress to the inhabitants of Quebec:

"'The last right we shall mention, regards the freedom of the press. The importance of this consists, besides the advancement of truth, science, morality, and arts in general, in its diffusion of liberal sentiments on the administration of Government, its ready communication of thoughts between subjects, and its consequential promotion of union among them, whereby oppressive officers are shamed or intimidated, into more honourable and just modes of conducting affairs.'"

The purpose of the Constitution was to protect individual rights, i.e., the freedom of man's mind - not to implement "the people's" whims. Man's right to pursue "truth, science, morality, and arts in general," is the validation of the freedom of the press - not mere politics and not the people's desires, particularly not any unspecified desires for "political and social changes." The political element in that quotation is specified: it is opposition to tyranny, to "oppressive officers" of the government.

If Justice Brennan had been aware of distorting the meaning of that quotation, he would not have been likely to include its full text. Apparently, he did not see the difference. The terrible aspect of Mill's influence is the fact that his followers become unable to consider great values - such as truth, science, morality, art - apart from and without the permission of "the people's desires."

In the Miller decision, Chief Justice Burger quotes Justice Brennan's statement - but omits the text of the 1774 quotation. (Such is the process of the "gestative propensity" of precedent.)

In the Paris Adult Theater I decision, Chief Justice Burger rejects "the proposition that conduct involving consenting adults only is always beyond state regulation" - and cites as supporting evidence Mill's On Liberty.

The first social consequences of the Burger Court decisions came swiftly and predictably. By banning one type of indecent exposure, the Court liberated some others. On June 27, 1973, a certain publication hailed the decisions by printing a piece that was as bad an act of undressing in public as one would hope not to see. The piece begins by describing the issue as the Supreme Court's "ongoing effort to set standards when a powerful element of society believes there should be no standards." This means that unless moral standards are imposed on a nation _by force_, it will have no standards - and that anyone opposing censorship is amoral.

The piece defines the battle as follows: "On one side are the proponents of the traditional culture, as we have called them, the bedrock Americans. On the other side are what we have called the cosmopolitan Americans, numerically smaller but immensely powerful because they are articulate, leisured and _entirely persuaded of the righteousness of their beliefs_." (Emphasis added.) It is obvious that this means: the people versus the intellectuals - and it is also obvious why the author(s) of the piece chose to hide his meaning behind such shabby definitions by non-essentials. If he spoke openly, he would have to admit that the American people are not "proponents of the traditional culture" - and that the advocates of "tradition" are neither popular nor intellectual.

The above sounds like the usual voice of the conservatives, but to what ideology would you ascribe the following? "But the debate after all is not over whether it is wise to ban pornography, but over whether majorities can be prevented from banning it through their duly constituted governments. Surely arguments for setting aside majority rule ought to be serious ones." _Unlimited_ majority rule? Over intellectual-moral issues? _This_ - as "bedrock" Americanism?

"On a more practical level, take the problem of definition. Laws against obscenity cannot be enforced, it is argued, because the term simply cannot be defined..." the piece declares - and dismisses the problem by proclaiming that "any definition [on any subject] will include an element of the arbitrary..."

Further, in a more appeasing mood: "...there is something appealing in the vision of a society without inhibiting social codes. Tolerating the exploitation of sex, it can persuasively be argued, is a small price to pay to maximize human choice. Yet we think there is a more enduring truth in the contrary view that _any society must set some standards_; that even if it cannot effectively ban pornography, for example, _it has to express a view of right and wrong_." (Emphases added.) Translated from mush into English, this means that society must issue edicts on "right and wrong," i.e., establish a government-imposed code of morality - and "express" it at the point of a gun. (The rulers of Soviet Russia are more open and honest about policies of this kind.)

This is bad enough, but the piece sinks still lower. "With enough will, these two visions of society can be more or less reconciled in any number of ways....The first step toward consensus, it seems to us, is for the cosmopolitan Americans to recognize that their case is not nearly as strong as they tend to assume, that the issue is not entirely one-sided, and that perhaps after all some degree of compromise would not spell the end of civilization."

This means: let us prohibit both Greta Garbo and Mae West - and compromise on Betty Grable.

Now who do you think published that piece? No, it is not the ghost of Fiorello LaGuardia, the New Dealer who declared, in the flush of the 1940 Presidential election victory, that freedom consists in obeying the will of the majority. It is not the ghost of Wittgenstein cackling that there is no such thing as precise definitions. It is not the ghost of Lenin nor of Torquemada. It is that alleged champion of businessmen and free enterprise - _The Wall Street Journal_.

(Dear New Left Activists [if any of you happen to see this _Letter_]: If, on the grounds of that piece, you conclude that capitalism is a contemptible, hypocritical system, and this moves you further to the Left, you would be right - except that it is not capitalism that those boys are after.)

Observe, incidentally, the extent to which those conservatives resent the liberals' confidence in "the righteousness of their beliefs." What is the motive - and the goal - of anyone who pleads that the most important thing is "to recognize that one's case is not nearly as strong as one tends to assume"? See the opening paragraph of this _Letter_.

The liberals' moral confidence is merely apparent, but it is bedrock real compared to the shivering gelatin of dogmatism and Pragmatism that drives the conservatives. While the voice of Wall Street scorns definitions and prattles about "majority rule," the leftists put it into practice by pouncing on the logical implications of a definition when they hear one.

In _The New York Times_ of November 16, 1973, in a column entitled "The Shockley Case," Tom Wicker offers a startling example of it. He discusses - and condemns - the current campaign of some student organizations to prevent Dr. William Shockley from speaking on college campuses. Shockley is a physicist who turned into a crusader on genetics. His views are outrageous: he alleges that blacks are congenitally inferior, a conclusion he reached on so dubious, arbitrary, unscientific a basis as I.Q. tests. But, as Wicker points out, Shockley's views are not the issue: the issue is whether he has the _right_ to speak.

In my _Letter_ of August 13, 1973, I wrote: "It is not very inspiring to fight for the freedom of the purveyors of pornography or their customers. But in the transition to statism, every infringement of human rights has begun with the suppression of a given right's least attractive practitioners." This new target of suppression is even less inspiring or attractive. But his case demonstrates the speed with which the suppression of pornography leads to the suppression of ideas.

Tom Wicker identifies the essence of the issue: "Unsound and even noxious views can be suppressed only if there is some power that can suppress _any_ view..." (_This_ is the power which the Burger decisions have granted to the worst elements of any local community.)

Wicker's discussion centers on an incident at Staten Island Community College, whose president invited Shockley to speak. This raised "campus and community opposition...which may take the form of active efforts to prevent Dr. Shockley from being heard....Joan Bodden, a student senator and Progressive Labor party member, thinks...that Dr. Shockley's appearance at S.I.C.C. is part of a 'national movement of racism in the universities,' sponsored by 'the ruling class.'" (Are these views morally superior to Shockley's?)

And: "Helen Bracey, another student senator, invokes the Supreme Court's recent decision that 'community standards' could govern what she called 'moral standards.' 'We the students are the local community,' Miss Bracey said, asserting that they found the Shockley views on race 'obscene and immoral.'"

That this little female saw what The Wall Street Journal missed, does not astonish me. But what I do wonder about is: Didn't the Supreme Court majority see it?

Ayn Rand

P.S. This Letter was written later than the date that appears on its heading.

OBJECTIVIST CALENDAR

A reminder: The opening lecture of Leonard Peikoff's course, Introduction to Logic, will be given on Tuesday, January 15, 7:30 P.M., at the Statler Hilton Hotel, 7th Ave. and 33rd St., New York City. Visitor's admission is $6.00.

Starting on February 3, the tape lectures of Leonard Peikoff's course, Modern Philosophy: Kant to the Present, will be given in Providence, R.I. For further information, contact Bill Dawkins at (401) 943-0881 (eves.).

We have been asked to announce that the Association for Romantic Representational Art will sponsor an exhibit presenting the work of twenty painters, sculptors and draftsmen, including Joan Mitchell Blumenthal and Frank O'Connor. The exhibition will take place at the Manufacturers Hanover Bank, 401 Madison Avenue at 47th Street, New York City, and will be open to the public Monday through Friday, from 9:00 A.M. to 3:00 P.M., February 4 through February 15.

The Association is headed by Ira Barkoff, Anthony Antonios and Joan Mitchell Blumenthal. Its goal is to present - in a variety of personal styles - that category of art which may be described as selective realism, i.e., which is neither photographic nor non-objective.

B.W.

The Ayn Rand Letter, published fortnightly by The Ayn Rand Letter, Inc., 183 Madison Avenue, New York, N.Y. 10016.
Contributing Editor: **Leonard Peikoff**; Subscription Director: **Elayne Kalberman**; Production Manager: **Barbara Weiss.**

Vol. III, No. 3 November 5, 1973

THE ENERGY CRISIS

Many readers have been asking whether I intended to write about the energy crisis. I would be tempted to answer: "I already have" - but they anticipate me by adding that things are "just as in Atlas Shrugged." Well, so they are. What I suggest is that you tell it to the country at large or to as much of it as you can reach. I don't like having to repeat: "I told you so" - but the occasions that require it are becoming more and more frequent.

Speaking impersonally, however, there are a few things I can add - for instance, about the difference between fiction and real life. In real life, there is no Ellis Wyatt. There are only bits of him, scattered among many men, like sparks which flicker only when the men are doing their work, and which they struggle to extinguish the rest of the time. If there was an Ellis Wyatt among them, he vanished silently long ago.

Had he stayed a few years longer, he would have had to become like the men you see today, the men who spend their time in Washington, begging permissions, instructions and favors from shoddy economists in cushy governmental jobs, no two of whom have the same notions or give the same orders - fighting lawsuits and injunctions - making extorted campaign contributions to politicians, who do not keep their promises, and taking the blame for the spread of corruption - apologizing, for their success, for their profits, for their ability to produce oil, to Congressional committees, to the press, to the media, to the "independent" gas stations, to the consumers, to the ecologists, to the sea gulls of Santa Barbara and the caribou of Alaska. One cannot accept such conditions for long without acquiring that type of mentality. The most naturalistic character in Atlas Shrugged is Dr. Robert Stadler.

In real life, there is no single, sudden blow that makes it clear to the country, in the glare of Wyatt's burning oil fields, that the oil industry has been killed. What there is, instead, is such a long, slow, tortuous agony of strangulation that neither the country nor the victims can grasp it. And you would be bored to death reading about all its creeping details.

The oil industry is being destroyed by a bombardment of paper - of governmental rules, regulations, directives, edicts, commands - any one of which is as intelligible and exciting as the small print in an insurance policy. You would not be able to read it or integrate it - no one can. But that bombardment is more effective than other kinds of air raids: it blasts your power stations, extinguishes your lights, freezes your homes, stops your motors, locks your factories, wipes out your jobs, and leaves a barren land on which nothing will grow again for generations, because what it paralyzes is your brain; there are no shelters against it and no antiaircraft guns - the heavier the bombing, the more of it the victims will demand. But, today, it is only fiction that will tell you that words on paper can be a deadly weapon, and that the munitions-makers are in the philosophy departments of the universities. In real life, they tell you that ideas are impotent.

The most eloquent clue to the nature of the energy crisis is the fact that people are asking: "_Is_ there an energy crisis or not?" - and that no one gives a clear answer.

You have seen the Watergate hearings on television. As I have suggested, multiply the chaos of those hearings over and over again, and you will have some idea of what it means to do business in a controlled economy. It is controlled by everyone and anyone, and no one: by dozens of government departments, agencies, bureaus, commissions, committees, by hundreds of pressure groups, with their lobbyists, their publicists, their special interests, their manipulators, their climbers. As indicated on television, none of the bureaucrats knows or cares to know what the others are doing. Each of them is clinging ferociously to his own square foot of territory and scrambling to enlarge it, flaunting his power, throwing his weight about, making decisions, and passing the buck when necessary.

There is always a scapegoat: the industrialist, who may be sent to jail by one government agency for obeying the orders of another. Integration - of plans, activities, knowledge, thought - is forbidden by the nature of the politicians' game. Their deliberately cultivated, evasive, concrete-bound, range-of-the-moment level of perception would make a retarded five-year-old look like a genius of abstract thinking. And, on the basis of such perception, they issue orders to an industry that functions in terms of decades and deals with the entire globe.

(Yet this unspeakable chaos is the country's only protection today. If the controls were centralized in the hands of a single, omnipotent "planning" authority - as the statists are frantically urging us to do - the destruction would be swift and final. As witness, Soviet Russia - which, after half a century, is unable to feed her population.)

The result of our present economic system is that the men who do the work - in this case, the oil industry - know the state of their production at a given moment, but do not know what edict will shatter them next month or next year. The government officials do not know the state of the industry they are controlling - nor what edict they will feel like issuing next week. The Arab oil embargo was not the cause of the energy crisis in this country: it was merely the straw that showed that the camel's back was broken.

The immediately visible problem is what _The New York Times_ calls the "Oil Refinery Gap." (December 9, 1973.) "Insufficient refining capacity is a bottleneck that will leave the nation short of gasoline, home heating fuel and other petroleum products, even if the Arab oil embargo is lifted....Not one new refinery is being built in the United States today. And some companies that had decided to increase refining capacity are now reconsidering their plans.

"The dearth of refinery construction has been attributed by the oil companies to import restrictions on crude oil in the face of declining domestic production and growing American dependence on foreign petroleum supplies. Low prices for petroleum products and environmental restrictions also inhibited construction, industry spokesmen have said....A refinery is a costly undertaking. More than $200-million may be needed to build one capable of handling 150,000 barrels of crude oil a day. Without assured long-term supplies of crude oil, no company is likely to build one."

What long-term assurance can the oil industry count on today? Nixon's promises? The declarations of his economic advisers? Or the whim of some Arab sheik? "It takes about three years from drawing board to completion of a major refinery," states the Times. In today's situation, who can foresee what will happen in three months, let alone three years? As to the causes of "declining domestic production and growing American dependence on foreign petroleum supplies," the Times story does not discuss them.

According to "The 1972 Joint Association Survey of the U.S. Oil and Gas Producing Industry," 26,443 wells were drilled in the United States in that year; 40% of them were dry. The average cost of drilling a well was $106,424; the total cost of all those wells was $2.814 billion. How long can men continue to take this kind of gamble, when they have no chance to win? The government's policy, in this respect, is like the theologians' doctrine which claims that if a man is sinful, the fault is his - but if he is virtuous, the credit belongs to God. Similarly, if an investor loses his money on dry holes, the loss is his - but if he discovers a gusher, his profits are eroded by taxes, surtaxes, excess-profit taxes, windfall-profit taxes, etc., whose amounts he has no way of guessing before he ventures out. At best, he will not be left enough to enlarge production, to drill new wells, to look for new fields, or to supply a rising demand. The costs of discovering and developing new sources of oil are increasing every year, while the profits are shrinking.

There are abundant, untouched oil resources in this country, but they are difficult and expensive to reach - so taxes and controls have made them unreachable. There is enough coal in this country to supply all our energy needs for several centuries - but taxes, controls and ecologists have all but wrecked the coal mining industry, and a long period of time will be needed to revive it. Price controls have wrecked the natural gas industry, stopping exploration for new domestic fields; at present, we import increasing amounts of natural gas from Algeria, at prices substantially above the price permitted to domestic producers; and one item of Nixon's "brilliant" foreign policy proposes that we develop the natural gas resources of Siberia in order to be able to buy its gas. Since you have seen the results of depending on Arab sheiks for a supply of energy, how would you like having to depend on Soviet Russia?

The oil industry had foreseen the approach of a crisis; it has been pleading with Washington for years, begging for a change of policy in order to avert a disaster. Its pleas were ignored - or shunted from one agency to another, without any answer; no one would commit himself to accept or reject its recommendations. But we all remember the tirades of Presidential candidate George McGovern denouncing the "unfair burden of taxation" and demanding the closing of "tax loopholes," with special emphasis on the oil depletion allowance.

The suddenness of the government's announcement of an energy crisis - without warning, at the approach of winter, with the plea to lower your thermostats, and the pious, shopworn demand for sacrifices - has an element of unreality, incredibility and indecency. Any question one asks about it (and any current explanation) makes things worse. The alleged excuse for it was the Arab oil embargo. But, if so, how could the government have let things go that far? How could it have let the economy, the well-being and the survival of the country hang by a thread which any camel could snap off? This excuse, however, was dropped pretty swiftly - inasmuch as Arabian oil represents only 5% of our total energy supply. Then what was the reason?

Many people are saying that the sudden crisis was manufactured by Nixon's clique, in order to distract public attention from Watergate. This may be true or not, it is as good or as bad a reason as any, and it does not matter which - because, if the government has the power to do it, what position are we in? Other people fear that blaming the crisis on the Arab embargo will arouse a wave of anti-Semitism - and they believe that the crisis is a means of preparing an excuse for selling Israel down the river. That, too, is possible. What is certain is that people will go on groping for explanations, because any explanation, no matter how vicious, is preferable to the staggering irrationality of the fact that there is no specific explanation, that we are caught in a machine driven by blind chance and blinder pressures, and that we have no way of checking the stories, no way of knowing the truth, no way of ever finding out - just as we shall never find out the causes of Watergate, and for the same reason.

There is no "natural" or geological crisis; there is an enormous political one. It is in the nature of a mixed economy that its policies are rationally inexplicable, that there are no identifiable causes, no accountable initiators, no ascertainable villains - and that you are losing your jobs, giving up your automobiles, catching pneumonia in unheated bedrooms, not because some giant evildoers are plotting your destruction, but because some seedy hack wanted an unearned salary, and some crummy professor wanted an undeserved prestige, and some measly shyster wanted a chance to fish in muddy laws, and none of them cared to or could watch the state of the country's economy, and the sum of such termite aspirations has eaten through the pillars of the structure so that one kick from a sheik was sufficient to make it crumble.

Since this is real life, I will not quote fiction, but will paraphrase it: "Take a look at your political system, now, while you still have a choice - and if you choose to perish, do so with full knowledge of how cheaply how small an enemy has claimed your life."

(To be continued.)

Ayn Rand

P.S. This Letter was written later than the date that appears on its heading.

OBJECTIVIST CALENDAR

Starting on February 26, the tape lectures of Leonard Peikoff's course, Modern Philosophy: Kant to the Present, will be given in Chicago. For further information, contact Dr. Douglas Mayfield, (312) 649-3232 (days) or (312) 787-9836 (eves.).

Please note the following change of address. Hereafter, inquiries and correspondence pertaining to any of Leonard Peikoff's tape courses should be sent to Barbara Weiss, P.O. Box 95, Murray Hill Station, New York, N.Y. 10016.

B.W.

The Ayn Rand Letter, published fortnightly by The Ayn Rand Letter, Inc., 183 Madison Avenue, New York, N.Y. 10016.

Contributing Editor: **Leonard Peikoff**; Subscription Director: **Elayne Kalberman**; Production Manager: **Barbara Weiss.**

Vol. III, No. 4 November 19, 1973

THE ENERGY CRISIS

Part II

Of all the alleged, rumored and whispered explanations, the most outrageous one blames the energy crisis on its foremost victim: the oil industry.

Resorting to the methods of the John Birch Society, the liberals are spreading the notion that the crisis was caused by a _conspiracy_ - that the big oil companies conspired to raise the price of oil, in greedy pursuit of selfish profit. This technique appeals to (or hopes for) three elements in the public's psychology: paranoid fear, which makes "conspiracy" plausible; envy, which sees "greed" as the root of any achievement; and altruism, which damns anyone who profits. But, this time, the rabble-rousing slogans launched by the demagogues of the turn of the century, are directed at an industry chained by the government.

At first, the attack on the oil industry came as a hissing whisper from the kinds of totalitarian statists who would blame anything on businessmen, by conditioned reflex. But, encountering no _moral_ opposition or indignation, the attack grew louder and bolder. Among the liberals or "moderate" statists, the initial response to the crisis was only an automatically immediate demand for _rationing_ - as if rationing, like snake oil, were the cure for anything and everything. Then, as it became clear that the crisis was a gigantic, government-caused breakdown of the mixed economy, the "moderates" joined the totalitarians, blaming the oil industry, demanding more controls, scrambling to cash in on the emergency, and revealing their own motives.

A typical exponent of the liberal "stance" is Walter W. Heller, who was chairman of the Presidential Council of Economic Advisers in the Kennedy and Johnson Administrations. At a news conference reported in _The New York Times_ (December 28, 1973), Mr. Heller warned that, in consequence of the energy shortage, "the United States was in for a 'fairly profound change' in its way of life" - and he endorsed the government's contingency plan for gasoline rationing. "He had earlier called for immediate rationing; but, he said today, his original recommendation had been based on Government estimates of a 3.2 million-barrel-a-day fuel shortfall in early 1974. Washington officials now speak instead of a 1.2 million-barrel supply gap. Mr. Heller said that 'we don't want _rationing just for the discipline of it_; but we ought to at least hedge our bets.'" (Emphasis added.)

Observe with what irresponsible ease a former economic planner jumps at the opportunity to paralyze the economy and deprive you of freedom - without even pausing to ascertain the facts. As to the notion that a government decree brings "discipline" to the people, what political system(s) does it remind you of?

"The Government's newly proposed excise tax on crude production, said Mr. Heller, 'is a very deceptive kind of proposal and relatively weak-kneed.' It would give most of the benefits of a price increase to the companies, not to the Government, Mr. Heller said." A weak-kneed government, according to Mr. Heller, is one that leaves benefits in the pockets of the producers who earned them; a strong government, like a gangster, would have the guts to grab all the benefits for itself - in the name of fighting "hoggishness" (a term Mr. Heller applies to the American people, referring to "their energy hoggish ways").

Mr. Heller is an economist, publicized as an expert; if you assume that he must have some serious, scientific reasons for his pronouncements, the following should disabuse you: "Instead [of the weak-kneed proposal], he proposed a 10-cent excise tax on gasoline at the pump, with the revenues used to help the poor."

At a time when, after years of inadequate profits, the oil industry is financially unable to develop new sources of energy - when the airlines are cutting their schedules and laying off one of the most competent, most highly trained groups of men, the men able daily to carry a life-or-death responsibility, the airplane pilots, who can find no other work - when gas-station operators, truckers, taxi drivers, home builders suddenly find their means of livelihood slashed off - when automobile companies are tottering, and utility companies are cringing under an axe, and thousands upon thousands of skilled workers are losing their jobs, and inflation is eating away the wages of the rest - if, at such a time, a man wants to raise taxes and prices in order "to help the poor," he is not motivated by compassion. It is only the unchallenged obscenity of altruism that can blind anyone to the nature of his motive and of the "profound change" in the American way of life he is so eager to bring about.

In startling contrast to most of the oil industry's timid, floundering attempts at self-defense, a letter to the Editor of the Times tells the story straight (January 9, 1974). It was written by Anthony F. Mauriello, Executive Director, New York State Petroleum Council. "...it has been the Government which - more than any other agent - has been the cause of the energy shortfall Americans are now experiencing. The Government has repeatedly and consistently hobbled, in every conceivable way, the petroleum industry's efforts to explore for and produce the oil and gas this nation - and its citizens - need for economic, military and political security. And, having effectively hobbled the industry, voices are now raised in ever-increasing stridency, crying, 'See, they're not drilling. It must be a conspiracy! Let's take them over.'

"But it is not the petroleum industry that has:

"For more than half a decade delayed plans to build a pipeline to bring the approximately ten billion barrels of North Slope oil discoveries south through Alaska for transshipment to refineries.

"Delayed lease sales of Federal offshore tracts...

"Refused, despite frequent industry assertions of the pressing need, to establish sound national energy policies, policies recognizing the essentiality of energy production.

"Imposed a fuel penalty of some 380,000 barrels a day (at 42 gallons to the barrel) of gasoline, 365 days a year, through emission controls on automobiles, while hampering the search for replacement crude oil reserves.

"Raised the industry's tax burden by more than $500 million a year - roughly the cost of drilling 5,000 oil and gas wells - in the face of an obvious need to increase, not decrease, drilling operations.

"Imposed - for more than two decades - artificially low prices on natural gas sold in interstate commerce, an act which drove investment interest from new field exploration and development.

"Anyone wishing to know the facts has but to look at the public record - to Congressional and agency actions (or, in many cases, inactions)..."

If there were a crusader, in or out of Congress, a man dedicated to seeking the truth, this last is what he would demand and undertake. He would demand a public inquiry - a televised Congressional hearing - into the role of the government in the events that led to the energy crisis, including the actions of all the governmental agencies involved, with all their policy makers, advisers, economists, recommendations and reasons.

Who cares about Watergate and about which politicians were spying on one another? Who cares whether Mr. Nixon filed proper income tax returns, whether he was entitled to landscape gardening at San Clemente, whether $100,000 was stashed in Bebe Rebozo's safe? What does it matter compared to the catastrophe facing the livelihood, the lifeblood, and the life of the country? What did the equivalents of John W. Dean and Jeb Stuart Magruder do to bring about this catastrophe? Who was responsible - the businessmen or the bureaucrats? Who is to be punished (by heavier chains) or rewarded (by greater power)? Which element in the mixture of our crashing economy should now be liberated or restricted? These are the things the American people have the right to know - if that empty slogan is to have any meaning.

If some ambitious politician wanted to make a name for himself, a public hearing of that kind would be his passport to immortality. But there is no such person today, and no such courage. The exact opposite is being done - by an ambitious politician. I regret that it is Senator Henry M. Jackson. I had held some hope that he would develop into a man of stature, on the basis of his stand on foreign policy. But his activity on the domestic front has wiped it out. He is engaged - openly and brazenly - in an ideological cover-up that makes Watergate look like a two-bit prank.

By the mere fact of leading a Congressional investigation focused one-sidedly on the oil industry, he is covering up the role of government and proclaiming the industry guilty, guilty ahead of inquiry, guilty by nature - he is exposing or accomplishing nothing, but he is lynching the usual scapegoat and throwing fodder to the rabble who would howl (he hopes): "It's all the fault of big business!"

This is low enough, but it is not the lowest. The lowest public posture in regard to the energy crisis was assumed by another leader. With uncanny, unfailing regularity, whenever an issue requires a moral stand, Mr. Richard Nixon falls flat on his face.

On January 19, 1974, Mr. Nixon delivered a nationwide radio address on the energy situation. No, he did not say that the oil industry was responsible for the crisis; what he did, instead, was as follows: after an opening of perfunctory bromides - about the success of energy conservation measures, such as year-round daylight-saving time, and the federal government cutting its energy consumption by 20 percent, and these steps proving the government's determination "to meet the problem head-on" - Mr. Nixon came to life, which, in his style, means a tensely emphatic tone of gentle fist-pounding, and declared: "Now let me turn directly to the tough questions which are now being asked by millions of concerned Americans. First, will the big oil companies be allowed to make huge profits from the shortage? Will they reap the benefits of your personal sacrifices? My feelings on this question could not be stronger. The sacrifices made by the American people in the energy crisis must be for the benefit of all the people and not for the benefit of big business."

Is this the first question in the minds of millions of Americans? Not the question of whether their jobs, homes, cars, savings, and standard of living will survive - but whether the big oil companies will make "huge profits"? Are "concerned Americans" concerned not about rising, but about making sure that everybody falls? Is envy the dominant emotion of the American people, and hatred of "big business" their driving motive? If so, why the landslide vote for Mr. Nixon? Mr. McGovern appealed to such feelings much more convincingly.

"Your sacrifices," Mr. Nixon went on, "must mean that jobs can be preserved, that schools can stay open, that homes will be heated. They must not mean that a few get rich at the expense and sacrifice of the many." As an alleged defender of free enterprise, Mr. Nixon should know that businessmen cannot get rich at the expense and sacrifice of the people - that there is only one group of men who can do so: the bureaucrats of a controlled economy (and the recipients of their favors) - that if jobs, schools and homes are to be preserved, it is their creator, industry, that must be preserved. If he does not know it, under what false pretenses has he won two Presidential elections?

"I pledge to you," Mr. Nixon declared, "that I shall do everything in my power to prevent the big oil companies and other major energy producers from making an unconscionable profit out of this crisis. Too many Americans have sacrificed too much to allow that to happen. That is why I shall urge the Congress...to act immediately on the windfall profits tax that I requested last month. This tax would require that windfall profits either be turned over to the Government or be invested in the development of new supplies, supplies that will be vitally needed in the years ahead. [What does Mr. Nixon think - or want us to think - that oil companies do with their profits?] Private profiteering at the expense of public sacrifice must never be tolerated in a free country." But public profiteering at the expense of private sacrifice is okay?

Mr. Nixon went right on: "Another question many people are asking, to put it bluntly, is whether there is really an energy shortage at all. If so, how serious is it? I am just as interested as you are in getting at the truth in this matter." (As interested as he was in "getting at the truth" of Watergate?) The President of a mixed economy cannot know every detail of the operations of his regulatory agencies; but he is the policy maker and he has to know, in general terms, the state of every aspect of the economy they meddle with; at the very least, he has to know whether a crucial industry is approaching disaster. But Mr. Nixon did not know it. If so, in whose name and by what authority have all those government regulators been choking the oil industry all these years?

Philosophical issues cannot be determined by legislation and, properly, are not part of impeachment proceedings. If they were, it is for this speech - not for Watergate - that Mr. Nixon would deserve to be impeached.

Part of Mr. Nixon's just deserts came almost immediately - in the form of a frenzied editorial in the Times (January 21, 1974). Denouncing Mr. Nixon's tax proposals as "window dressing," the editorial screamed: "Quite apart from the Administration's determination to label this a windfall-profits tax for public relations reasons [Whose public? McGovern's?], it is a mere slap on the wrist to the oil industry....the oil companies would almost certainly figure out ways of recapturing the bulk of those 'windfall' tax payments by increasing their drilling operations and capital expenditures..."

At a time when the nation needs the oil industry desperately, the Times does not want the industry to be merely slapped on the wrist - it wants it to be battered black-and-blue. You know which work of fiction told you that the altruists' method of dealing with mankind consists in unleashing hatred, insults, threats, punishment and martyrdom on those whom men need most. Here is a real-life example of it. The Times editorial was not concerned with the energy crisis; it was not concerned with an increase in drilling operations, if the oil industry were to profit; its sole concern was with drumming up an opportunity to tax, tax, tax businessmen out of existence.

(Actually, Mr. Nixon's proposal would not benefit the oil industry. It is merely an attempt to sneak the government's claws deeper into the oil industry's investment policies and to gain control of the disposal of its profits.)

The behavior of most oil industry executives - as displayed on television and in full-page ads - projects a childish, hopeless, impotent bewilderment. Those allegedly powerful tycoons, the heads of multi-billion-dollar corporations - who have always been contemptuous of ideas, preferring to be "practical" - now find themselves helplessly at the mercy of any committee, any tabloid journalist, leftist disk jockey, or statist ward heeler. For years, businessmen have shunned ideological battles, believing that it is safer and easier to deal with politicians than with political principles - i.e., easier to pay off the protection racket of sundry government officials than to defend capitalism. They are now facing the consequences.

The Wall Street Journal typifies most businessmen's intellectual policy. In a front-page article - eloquently entitled "Sticks and Stones..." - the Journal tried to reassure the oil industry about the future (January 25, 1974). The article did not discuss political issues, ideas, principles or even facts; it discussed men. It suggested that the industry may, perhaps, stave off some totally destructive legislation "with help from strategically placed congressional allies and from a fairly friendly Nixon administration." In the manner of poor relatives speculating about the intentions of their rich benefactor, the article searched for hopeful signs among the opinions of various political authorities. For instance: "'You don't really think Wilbur Mills and Russell Long are going to castrate the oil industry, do you?' asks one lawmaker..."

After a column-and-a-half of this sort of stuff - including a hopeful mention of the fact that one of Ralph Nader's lieutenants is not very optimistic about a real crackdown on the oil industry - the article concluded as follows: "This isn't to say the administration won't take some steps designed to displease the petroleum people. ...However, in the key areas of taxation, antitrust policy and regulatory requirements, the administration's position and the oil industry's remain very similar. This is a genuine concern to some high-ranking officials of an administration already tarred by the Watergate scandals. 'Our biggest problem is to do what's right and not look like we're in bed with the oil companies,' says a high official in the Federal Energy Office. 'I'm not sure how long we'll be able to walk that tightrope.'"

The American people are not anti-business, particularly not today. To the best of their knowledge (however inadequate), the majority are in favor of free enterprise. But if they hear business defenders such as The Wall Street Journal, and if such "conservative" leaders as President Nixon and Senator Jackson keep telling them that the businessmen's pursuit of profits is the cause of all our troubles, do not blame the people if they come to believe it. If they do, it will not be Ralph Nader or The New York Times that will have persuaded them.

(The statists, so far, have not found a way to blame businessmen for the disgraceful foreign policy of this country and of Western Europe - a policy of international altruism, dictated by liberals for over fifty years, which has brought the entire Western world to the position of a colony ruled by Arab sheiks.)

As to the solution of the oil crisis, I asked Alan Greenspan, the distinguished economic analyst, what would happen if the government lifted all taxes and controls from the oil industry and signed a (credible) contract to the effect that no new ones would be imposed for, say, ten years. He laughed and said: "We would have oil spurting from under our feet."

As things stand today, the country's most urgent need is to observe who has been profiteering on every public disaster. The remedy offered for the scandal of Watergate, a scandal perpetrated by politicians, is more power to the politicians: the power to finance and control elections. The remedy offered for the oil shortage, caused by politicians, is more power to the politicians: the power to expropriate the oil industry. Those who observe it, will realize that the demagogues' spook of "financial greed as the root of all evil" is a cover to deflect attention from a real and deadly motive: power-lust.

Why do people fail to observe it? Because the oil crisis is merely a large-scale symptom of a much more profound disaster: a crisis of *intellectual energy*. The filling stations of the universities have dried up long ago and have been peddling a stale, corrosive mix that paralyzes the brains of the nation. If you want to fight pollution, start with the philosophy departments; and if you want to refuel - well, look for new sources of energy.

Ayn Rand

P.S. This *Letter* was written later than the date that appears on its heading.

OBJECTIVIST CALENDAR

On Wednesday, March 6, Ayn Rand will address the graduating class of the United States Military Academy at West Point. Her subject: "Philosophy: Who Needs It." The lecture is not open to the public.

The following starting dates have been scheduled for the tape lectures of Dr. Leonard Peikoff's course, *Introduction to Logic*: Boston, March 1 (contact Frank Peseckis, 617-261-2491, eves.); Washington, D.C., March 6 (Wayne Martin, 301-552-3856, eves.); Minneapolis, March 6 (Jane Kettleson, 612-777-0391, eves.); Cleveland, March 10 (Lesley Dunn, 216-423-3147, eves.); Nuernberg, West Germany, March 12 (Gerald Salchert, Elsa-Brandstroemstr. 6, Nuernberg; phone: 0911-61-31-89, eves.).

We have been asked to announce that reproductions of paintings and drawings by Joan Mitchell Blumenthal, José Manuel Capuletti, Frank O'Connor and Ilona Royce Smithkin, are available from Sures Art Enterprises, Ltd. For descriptive brochures, write to SAE, Ltd., P.O. Box 207, Silver Spring, Md. 20907.

B.W.

The Ayn Rand Letter, published fortnightly by The Ayn Rand Letter, Inc., 183 Madison Avenue, New York, N.Y. 10016.

Contributing Editor: **Leonard Peikoff**; Subscription Director: **Elayne Kalberman**; Production Manager: **Barbara Weiss.**

Vol. III, No. 5 December 3, 1973

This issue of my Letter features our guest correspondent and Contributing Editor, Dr. Leonard Peikoff. It offers an excerpt from his forthcoming book, The Ominous Parallels, to be published by Weybright & Talley, Inc. For an earlier excerpt, as well as a brief summary of the book's thesis, see the December 4 and 18, 1972, issues of this Letter.

The present excerpt, from the chapter "Philosophy and America," is of special interest and importance to my readers, on two counts. 1. It deals with a subject which is all but obliterated today: the philosophic foundations of this country. While everyone seems to concede that the United States is different, in some unspecified manner, from all other countries, the deliberate obfuscation of its intellectual roots now permits any and every group to seek a cover of respectability by attaching the tag of "Americanism" to their own ideologies, most of which are diametrical opposites of the philosophy of the Founding Fathers.

In the 1930s, the Communist Party claimed that "Communism is twentieth-century Americanism." Modern conservatives claim that this country was based on religious faith and that a belief in God is the precondition of a free society. A Presidential candidate, George McGovern, claimed that the "American Dream" was an egalitarian Welfare State, in which material support is guaranteed to some men at the expense of others, and none is permitted to rise above a level set by the government. Today, observe the mean little obscenity of the fact that the coupons for the proposed gas-rationing plan bear a picture of George Washington.

Tradition as such is not a proof of an idea's truth or falsehood; anyone is free to challenge any tradition. What is reprehensible is the attempt not to challenge, but to distort - to smuggle one's notions into people's minds by misrepresenting a tradition that deserves the respect it has earned. What was the original philosophy that gave birth to the United States of America?

2. One of the questions I hear very often is: "If America's original philosophy was so good and so successful, if it gave rise to such spectacular achievements, *why* was it discarded?"

These are the two questions which Dr. Peikoff answers. In the grand-scale context of the history of ideas, his summary presents the essentials of America's philosophic base - and the cracks or missing elements that permitted its eventual destruction.

(We have omitted the footnote references for quoted material; these will appear in the book.)

Ayn Rand

AMERICA'S PHILOSOPHIC ORIGIN

By Leonard Peikoff

Since the golden age of Greece, there has been only one era of reason in twenty-three centuries of Western philosophy. It was during this era's final decades that the United States of America was created as an independent nation. This is the key to the country - to its nature, its development, and its uniqueness: the United States is _the nation of the Enlightenment_.

The progression of European thought from Aquinas through Locke and Newton, represents more than four hundred years of stumbling, tortuous, prodigious effort to secularize the Western mind, i.e., to liberate man from the medieval shackles. It was the build-up toward a climax: the eighteenth century, the _Age of Enlightenment_. For the first time in modern history, an authentic respect for reason became the mark of an entire culture; the trend that had been implicit in the centuries-long crusade of a handful of innovators, now swept the West explicitly, reaching and inspiring educated men in every field. Reason, for so long the wave of the future, had become the animating force of the present. For the first time since the high point of classical civilization, thinkers regarded the acceptance of reason as _uncontroversial_. They regarded the exercise of man's intellect not as a sin to be proscribed, or as a handmaiden to be tolerated, or even as a breath-taking discovery to be treated gingerly - but as _virtue_, as the norm, the to-be-expected....

In the early decades of the eighteenth century, the European Enlightenment came to America, gradually becoming the dominant philosophic power.

In every area of thought, the American Enlightenment represents a profound reversal of the Puritans' philosophic priorities. Confidence in the power of man, replaced dependence on the grace of God - and that rare intellectual orientation emerged, the key to the Enlightenment approach in every branch of philosophy: _secularism without skepticism_.

In metaphysics, this meant a fundamental change in emphasis: from God to this world, the world of particulars in which men live, the realm of _nature_. For centuries of medievalism, nature had been regarded as a shadowy, transitory reflection of a transcendent dimension representing true reality. Now, whatever the vestigial concessions to the earlier mentality, the operative conviction seizing men's mind was that nature is an autonomous realm - solid, eternal, _real_ in its own right. For centuries, nature had been regarded as a realm of miracles manipulated by a personal deity, a realm whose significance lay in the clues it offered to the purpose and plan of its author. Now, the operative conviction was that nature is a realm governed by _scientific laws_, which permit no miracles and which are intelligible without reference to the supernatural. Now, when men looked at nature, they saw not erratic intervention from beyond (nor inexplicable chance nor Heraclitean flux), but order, stability, "eternal and immutable" principles - i.e., the reign of absolute, impersonal cause and effect.

In such a universe, the fundamental epistemological principle was the sovereignty of human reason. For centuries, men had sought primary truth in revelation, submitting docilely to the alleged deliverances of supernatural authority, or - later - had sought a compromise between the domain of the secular intellect and the domain of faith. Now, the animating conviction was that the rational mind is man's _only_ means of knowledge. Faith, revelation, mystic insight, the whole apparatus of Christian dogmas, mysteries, sacraments, etc. - these the spokesmen of the Enlightenment swept aside as the futile legacy of a primitive past. _Reason the Only Oracle of Man_, Ethan Allen titled his work, expressing the widespread viewpoint. "Fix reason firmly in her seat," writes Jefferson to a nephew, "and call to her tribunal every fact, every opinion. Question with boldness even the existence of a God; because, if there is one, he must more approve of the homage of reason, than that of blindfolded fear."

Reason - according to the characteristic Enlightenment conception - is a faculty which acquires knowledge by derivation from the evidence of the senses; there are no divinely inspired, innate ideas. It is a faculty which, properly employed, can discover explanatory principles in every field, and achieve _certainty_ in regard to them. Since these principles, it was held, are absolute truths stating facts of reality, they are binding on every man, whatever his feelings or nationality; i.e., knowledge is _objective_. It was not heavenly illumination or skeptical doubt or subjective emotion that the Enlightenment mind extolled ("enthusiasm," i.e., irrational passion, was regarded as the cardinal epistemological sin), it was the exercise of the fact-seeking _intellect_ - logical, deliberate, dispassionate, potent.

The consequence of this view of reason was the legendary epistemological self-confidence of the period - the conviction that there are no limits to the triumphant advance of science, of human knowledge, of human progress. "The strength of the human understanding is incalculable, its keenness of discernment would ultimately penetrate into every part of nature, were it permitted to operate with uncontrouled and unqualified freedom," writes Elihu Palmer, a militant American spokesman of the period. "...it has hitherto been deemed a crime to think," he states; but at last, men have escaped from the "long and doleful night" of Christian rule, with its "frenzy," its "religious fanaticism," its "mad enthusiasm"; at last, men have grasped "the unlimited power of human reason" - "Reason, which every kind of supernatural Theology abhors - Reason, which is the glory of our nature..." Now, "a full scope must be given to the operation of intellectual powers, and man must feel an unqualified confidence in his own energies."

A being who has discovered "the glory of his nature" cannot regard himself as a chunk of depravity whose duty is self-abasing obedience to supernatural commandments. After centuries of medieval wallowing in Original Sin and the ethics of unquestioning submissiveness, a widespread wave of _moral_ self-confidence now swept the West, reflecting and complementing man's new epistemological self-confidence. Just as there are no limits to man's knowledge, many thinkers held, so there are no limits to man's moral improvement. If man is not yet perfect, they held, he is at least perfectible: just as there are objective, natural laws in science, so there are objective, natural laws in ethics - and man is capable of discovering such laws, and of acting in accordance with them; he is capable not only of using his intellect, but also of _living_ by its guidance (this, at least, was the Enlightenment's ethical program and promise).

Whatever the vacillations or doubts of particular thinkers, the dominant trend represented a new vision and estimate of man: man as a self-sufficient, rational being and, therefore, as basically good, as potentially noble, as a value.

For centuries, the dominant moralists had said that man must not seek his ultimate fulfillment on earth; that he must renounce the pleasures of this life - whether as a flesh-mortifying ascetic or as an abstemious toiler - for the sake of God, salvation, and the life to come. With the new view of reality and of man, this could no longer be taken seriously. Now, a new concept of the good moved insistently to the forefront of men's mind: the purpose of life, it was held, is to live, to live in this world and to enjoy it. Men refused to wait any longer: they wanted to achieve happiness - now, here, and as an end in itself.

For centuries, whatever their concern with the individual soul, the medievals had derogated - or failed to discover - the individual man. In philosophy, the Platonizing Christians had denied his reality; in practice, the feudal system had (by implication) treated the group - the rigidly defined caste, the guild, etc. - as the operative social unit. Then, in post-medieval Europe, a dawning appreciation of the individual had appeared, in two different forms, in the Renaissance and the Reformation movements. Now, particularly in America, that generalized appreciation became a specific, ruling conviction.

Metaphysically - thinkers held - since reality is this world of particulars, the individual is fully real. Epistemologically and ethically, since reason is an attribute of the individual, the potency and value of man the rational being, means the potency and value of the individual who exercises his reason. Thus, when the Enlightenment upheld the pursuit of happiness, the meaning (Christian contradictions aside for the moment) was: the pursuit by each man of his own happiness, to be gained by his own independent efforts - by self-reliance and self-development, leading to self-respect and self-made worldly success.

The leaders of the American Enlightenment did not reject the idea of the supernatural completely; characteristically, they were deists, who believed that God exists as nature's remote, impersonal creator, and as the original source of natural law; but, they held, having performed these functions, God thereafter retires into the role of a passive, disinterested spectator. This view (along with the continuing belief in an afterlife) is a remnant of medievalism, but, in terms of its operative influence on the period, it is in the nature of a vestigial afterthought, which diminishes the role and power of religion in men's lives. The threat to "Divine religion," observed one concerned preacher at the time, was "the indifference which prevails" and the "ridicule"; mankind, he noted, are in "great danger of being laughed out of religion..."

The result of the Enlightenment ideas and attitudes, in every branch of philosophy, was a surging sense of liberation. "We have it in our power to begin the world over again," says Thomas Paine. "A situation, similar to the present, hath not happened since the days of Noah until now. The birthday of a new world is at hand..."

The father of this new world was a single philosopher: Aristotle. On countless issues, Aristotle's views differ from those of the Enlightenment. But, in terms of broad fundamentals, the philosophy of Aristotle is the philosophy of the Enlightenment. The primacy of this world; the lawfulness and intelligibility of nature; the reality of particulars and, therefore, of individuals; the sovereignty and power of man's secular reason; the rejection of innate ideas; the non-supernaturalist affirmation of certainty, objectivity, absolutes; the uplifted view of man and of the human potential; the value placed on intellectual self-development as a means to self-fulfillment and personal happiness on earth - the sum of it is Aristotelian, specifically Aristotelian, as against the mysticism of the Platonic tradition and the self-proclaimed bankruptcy of the skeptical tradition. If the key to the Enlightenment is secularism without skepticism, this means: the key is Aristotle.

In the deepest philosophic sense, it is Aristotle who laid the foundation of the United States of America. The nation of the Enlightenment is the nation of Aristotelianism.

Aristotle provided the foundation, but he did not know how to implement it politically. In the modern world - under the influence of the pervasive new spirit - a succession of thinkers developed a new conception of the nature of government. The most important of these men, the one with the greatest direct influence on America, was John Locke. The political philosophy Locke bequeathed to the Founding Fathers was the social implementation of the regnant Aristotelianism; it became the base of the new nation's distinctive institutions.

Throughout history, the state had been regarded, implicitly or explicitly, as the ruler of the individual - as a sovereign authority (with or without supernatural mandate), an authority logically antecedent to the citizen, and to which he must submit. The Founding Fathers challenged this primordial notion. They started with the premise of the _primacy and sovereignty of the individual_. The individual, they held, logically precedes the group or the institution of government. Whether or not any social organization exists, each man possesses certain _individual rights_. And "among these are Life, Liberty and the pursuit of Happiness" - or, in the words of a New Hampshire state document, "among which are the enjoying and defending life and liberty; acquiring, possessing, and protecting property; and in a word, of seeking and obtaining happiness."

These rights were regarded not as a disparate collection, but as a unity, expressing a single fundamental right. Man's rights, declares Samuel Adams, often termed the father of the American Revolution, "are evident branches of, rather than deductions from, the duty of self-preservation, commonly called the first law of nature." Man's rights are _natural_, i.e., their warrant is the laws of reality, not any arbitrary human decision; and they are _inalienable_, i.e., absolutes not subject to renunciation, revocation or infringement by any person or group. Rights, affirms John Dickinson, "are not annexed to us by parchments and seals....They are born with us; exist with us; and cannot be taken from us by any human power without taking our lives. In short, they are founded on the immutable maxims of reason and justice."

And "to secure these rights, Governments are instituted among Men, deriving their just powers from the consent of the governed..." The powers of government are, therefore, _limited_, not merely de facto or by default, but on principle: government is forbidden to infringe man's rights. It is forbidden because, in Adams's words, "the grand end of civil government, from the very nature of its institution, is for the support, protection, and defence of those very rights..."

On this view, the state is the servant of the individual; it is not a sovereign possessing primary authority, but an agent possessing only delegated authority pursuant to the voluntary decision of the citizens, charged by them with a specific practical function - and subject to dissolution and reconstruction if it trespasses outside its assigned purview. Far from being the ruler of man, the state - in the American conception - exists to _prevent_ the division of men into rulers and ruled, i.e., to enable the individual, in Adams's words, "to be free from any superior power on earth, and not to be under the will or legislative authority of man, but only to have the law of nature for his rule."

(To be continued.)

OBJECTIVIST CALENDAR

The following starting dates have been scheduled for the tape lectures of Dr. Leonard Peikoff's courses. _Introduction to Logic_. Hartford, Conn., March 7 (contact Brian Bambrough, 203-429-1535); St. Louis, April 6 (Fulton Huxtable, 314-291-7130, eves. and wkends.). _Modern Philosophy: Kant to the Present_. Webster, N.Y., March 10 (John Krehling, 716-872-2287, eves.).

B.W.

The Ayn Rand Letter, published fortnightly by The Ayn Rand Letter, Inc., 183 Madison Avenue, New York, N.Y. 10016.
Contributing Editor: **Leonard Peikoff**; Subscription Director: **Elayne Kalberman**; Production Manager: **Barbara Weiss.**

Vol. III, No. 6 December 17, 1973

AMERICA'S PHILOSOPHIC ORIGIN

Part II

By Leonard Peikoff

"I have sworn upon the altar of God, eternal hostility against every form of tyranny over the mind of man."

Jefferson - and the other Founding Fathers - meant it. They did not confine their efforts to the battle against theocracy and monarchy; they fought - on the same grounds, invoking the same principle of individual rights - against *democracy*, i.e., the system of unlimited majority rule. They recognized that the cause of freedom is not advanced by the multiplication of despots, and they did not propose to substitute the tyranny of a mob for that of a handful of autocrats.

We must bear in mind, says Jefferson, that the will of the majority "to be rightful, must be reasonable; that the minority possess their equal rights, which equal laws must protect, and to violate which would be oppression." In a pure democracy, writes Madison in a famous passage of *The Federalist*, "there is nothing to check the inducements to sacrifice the weaker party or an obnoxious individual. Hence it is that such democracies have ever been spectacles of turbulence and contention; have ever been found incompatible with personal security or the rights of property; and have in general been as short in their lives as they have been violent in their deaths."

When the framers of the American republic spoke of "the people," they did not mean a collectivist entity one part of which was authorized to consume the rest. They meant a sum of individuals, each of whom - whether strong or weak, rich or poor - retains his inviolate guarantee of individual rights. "It is agreed," says John Adams, "that 'the end of all government is the good and ease of the people, in a secure enjoyment of their rights, without oppression'; but it must be remembered, that the rich are *people* as well as the poor; that they have rights as well as others; that they have as clear and as sacred a right to their large property as others have to theirs which is smaller; that oppression to them is as possible and as wicked as to others."

The genius of the Founding Fathers was their ability not only to grasp the revolutionary political ideas of the period, but to devise a means of implementing those ideas in practice, i.e., of translating them from the realm of philosophic abstraction into that of socio-political reality. By defining in detail the division of powers within the government, and the ruling procedures, including the brilliant mechanism of checks and balances, they established a system whose operation and integrity were independent, so far as possible, of the moral character or personal ambition of any of its temporary officials - a system impervious, so far as possible, to subversion by an aspiring statist or by the public mood of the moment.

The heroism of the Founding Fathers was that they recognized an unprecedented opportunity, the chance to create a country of individual liberty for the first time in history - and staked everything on their judgment: the new nation, and their own lives, fortunes, and sacred honor. If liberty requires the principled recognition and practical implementation of man's individual rights, then Lord Acton, the famous student of liberty, spoke the truth when he said: liberty "was that which _was not_, until the last quarter of the eighteenth century in Pennsylvania."

The American approach to politics, however, rested on the basic philosophy of the Enlightenment - above all, on its view of _reason_ and its view of _values_, i.e., its epistemology and its ethics. And in regard to basic philosophy, the Americans of the revolutionary era were counting on Europe.

There was no American attempt to give systematic, comprehensive statement to the ideas of the Enlightenment mind, and little concern with the technical issues involved in their defense. The American thinkers functioned within an intellectual atmosphere largely taken for granted as incontestable, made of generalized emphases and tendencies absorbed from Europe - an atmosphere whose elements were invoked as and when necessary, in no particular order, in the course of countless letters, pamphlets, essays, etc. It was an era dominated by men of action, philosophically minded but eager to apply in political practice the abstract principles they had learned; men who assumed - insofar as they raised the question at all - that the ultimate validation and philosophic base of their principles had already been established beyond challenge by the thinkers of Europe.

The Americans were counting on what did not exist. There was no such base in Europe. In every fundamental area, the thought of the European Enlightenment was filled with unanswered questions, torn by contradictions - and eminently vulnerable to challenge.

In epistemology, the European champions of the intellect had been unable to formulate a tenable view of the nature of reason and, therefore, to validate their proclaimed confidence in its powers. As a result, from the beginning of the eighteenth century (and even earlier), the philosophy advocating reason was in the process of gradual, but accelerating, disintegration.

John Locke - widely regarded during the Enlightenment as Europe's leading philosopher, taken as the definitive spokesman for reason and the new science - is a representative case in point. The philosophy of this spokesman is a contradictory mixture, part Aristotelian, part Christian, part Cartesian, part skeptic - in short, an eclectic shambles all but openly inviting any Berkeley or Hume in the vicinity to rip it into shreds. The philosopher taken as the defender of nature, could not establish its reality; the philosopher taken as the defender of scientific law, could not validate the concept of causality, held that basic causes are outside man's power to grasp, and stated explicitly that a "science of bodies" (i.e., a science of material entities) is impossible; the philosopher taken as the champion of the senses, was promulgating every doctrine necessary to invalidate them; the philosopher taken as the spokesman for the unlimited, self-confident power of the human mind, was proclaiming (in effect) that the field open to human cognition is a precarious island surrounded by a sea of the uncertain, the subjective, the unintelligible, the unknowable.

When the men of the Enlightenment counted on Locke (and his equivalents) as their intellectual defender, they were counting on a philosophy of reason so profoundly undercut as to be in process of self-destructing.

The same destruction was occurring in Europe in the field of ethics. Although Locke and many others had held out the promise of a rational, demonstrative science of ethics, none of them delivered on this promise; none could produce or define such an ethics. Meanwhile, European voices, rising and growing louder, were declaring that the principles of ethics are ultimately based not on reason, but on *feeling*.

James Wilson, one of the most distinguished legal philosophers of the American Enlightenment, a man who signed both the Declaration of Independence and the Constitution, expresses this view clearly. Reflecting the influence of Hume (and others), Wilson declares: "The *ultimate* ends of human actions, can never, in any case, be accounted for by reason. They recommend themselves entirely to the sentiments and affections of men, without dependence on the intellectual faculties." Morality, he states, derives from man's "moral sense" or "instincts" or "conscience." As to the validation of this faculty's pronouncements, "I can only say, I *feel* that such is my duty. Here investigation must stop..." Jefferson, among others, held similar views. But, regardless of who formally agreed or disagreed with Wilson on this issue, the fact is that he spoke for all of them: no American did identify the basis of a rational, scientific ethics; all - admittedly or not - were relying for ethical guidance on what they *felt* to be moral.

And what did they feel? What they inherited from their mentors, i.e., the mixture they absorbed from the European Enlightenment: the mixture endorsing Aristotelian, egoist self-assertion - and Christian, self-denying "love"; with moral superiority awarded to the latter.

In America, the egoist element was more pronounced and went deeper than in Europe. It was embedded, implicitly, in the foundations of the country: it was presupposed by the new, individualist system, which stressed the right of each man to the preservation of his own life and the pursuit of his own happiness. But the Americans did not identify the ethical issue in such terms. The general tenor of their (unsystematic) ethical statements, the dominant sentiment voiced during the period, is captured in a few brief extracts from Jefferson.

The philosophers of the ancient world, he writes, were "really great" in defining "precepts related chiefly to ourselves...[but] in developing our duties to others, they were short and defective." They did not advocate "charity and love to our fellow men" or "benevolence [to] the whole family of mankind." It was Jesus who left man the principles of "the most perfect and sublime" ethics - the ethics of "universal philanthropy, not only to kindred and friends, to neighbors and countrymen, but to all mankind" - the ethics which recognizes that there is "implanted in our breasts a love of others, a sense of duty to them, a moral instinct, in short, which prompts us irresistibly to feel and to succor their distresses..."

The Americans were political revolutionaries, but not *ethical* revolutionaries. Whatever their partial (and largely implicit) acceptance of the principle of ethical egoism, they remained *explicitly* within the standard European tradition, avowing their primary allegiance to a moral code stressing utilitarian service and social duty. Such was the American conflict: an impassioned politics presupposing one kind of ethics, within a cultural atmosphere professing the sublimity of an opposite kind of ethics.

The signs of the conflict, and of the toll it exacted from the distinctively American political approach, were evident at the beginning - in Jefferson's proposal for free public education; in Paine's advocacy of a variety of governmental welfare functions; in Franklin's view that an individual has no right to his "superfluous" property, which the public may dispose of as it chooses, "whenever the Welfare of the Publick shall demand such Disposition"; etc.

The American Enlightenment (like the European) came to an abrupt end. "Its ideas were soon repudiated or corrupted," writes Herbert Schneider, "its plans for the future were buried, and there followed on its heels a thorough and passionate reaction against its ideals and assumptions."

It was a reaction prepared for by the Enlightenment itself, by its own philosophical deficiencies, by the seeds it had nourished and allowed to sprout - the seeds of an irrationalism it was not equipped to combat and an altruism it predominantly endorsed. Philosophically, America was born a profound anomaly: a solid political structure, erected on a tottering base.

The Founding Fathers did not know that the era in which they lived and fought and planned, was on the threshold of yielding to its antipode. They did not know that they had snatched a country from the jaws of history at the last possible moment. They did not know that, even as they struggled to bring the new nation into existence, its philosophical gravediggers were already at work, cashing in on the period's contradictions: in the very decade in which the Founding Fathers were publishing their momentous documents, Kant was publishing *his*.

Symbolically, this is America's philosophical conflict, running through all the years of its subsequent history: the Declaration of Independence, with everything it presupposes, against the *Critique of Pure Reason*, with everything to which it leads.

POSTSCRIPT

I would like to call Dr. Peikoff's essay to the particular attention of two groups, both of whom believe that the solution of this country's problems requires not new philosophical thinking, but merely an uncritical return to the unsolved contradictions of the past. These groups are: 1. The conservatives, who believe that capitalism can stand on a base of mysticism and altruism. 2. The businessmen, who believe that philosophy has no practical influence - as taught by *their* philosophy, Pragmatism.

Ayn Rand

OBJECTIVIST CALENDAR

The following starting dates have been scheduled for the tape lectures of Dr. Leonard Peikoff's course, *Introduction to Logic*: Lake Oswego, Oreg., March 31 (contact Joyce Lee, 503-636-4268, eves.); Phoenix, April 3 (Dennis Wilson, 602-956-7678, eves.); Calgary, Alberta, Canada, April 8 (Al Kincius, 403-264-5254).

B.W.

The Ayn Rand Letter, published fortnightly by The Ayn Rand Letter, Inc., 183 Madison Avenue, New York, N.Y. 10016.

Contributing Editor: **Leonard Peikoff**; Subscription Director: **Elayne Kalberman**; Production Manager: **Barbara Weiss.**

Vol. III, No. 7 December 31, 1973

PHILOSOPHY: WHO NEEDS IT

(An address given to the graduating class of the United States Military Academy at West Point on March 6, 1974.)

Since I am a fiction writer, let us start with a short short story. Suppose that you are an astronaut whose spaceship gets out of control and crashes on an unknown planet. When you regain consciousness and find that you are not hurt badly, the first three questions in your mind would be: Where am I? How can I discover it? What should I do?

You see unfamiliar vegetation outside, and there is air to breathe; the sunlight seems paler than you remember it and colder. You turn to look at the sky, but stop. You are struck by a sudden feeling: if you don't look, you won't have to know that you are, perhaps, too far from the earth and no return is possible; so long as you don't know it, you are free to believe what you wish - and you experience a foggy, pleasant, but somehow guilty, kind of hope.

You turn to your instruments: they may be damaged, you don't know how seriously. But you stop, struck by a sudden fear: how can you trust these instruments? How can you be sure that they won't mislead you? How can you know whether they will work in a different world? You turn away from the instruments.

Now you begin to wonder why you have no desire to do anything. It seems so much safer just to wait for something to turn up somehow; it is better, you tell yourself, not to rock the spaceship. Far in the distance, you see some sort of living creatures approaching; you don't know whether they are human, but they walk on two feet. *They*, you decide, will tell you what to do.

You are never heard from again.

This is fantasy, you say? You would not act like that and no astronaut ever would? Perhaps not. But this is the way most men live their lives, here, on earth.

Most men spend their days struggling to evade three questions, the answers to which underlie man's every thought, feeling and action, whether he is consciously aware of it or not: Where am I? How do I know it? What should I do?

By the time they are old enough to understand these questions, men believe that they know the answers. Where am I? Say, in New York City. How do I know it? It's self-evident. What should I do? Here, they are not too sure - but the usual answer is: whatever everybody does. The only trouble seems to be that they are not very active, not very confident, not very happy - and they experience, at times, a causeless fear and an undefined guilt, which they cannot explain or get rid of.

They have never discovered the fact that the trouble comes from the three unanswered questions - and that there is only one science that can answer them: _philosophy_.

Philosophy studies the _fundamental_ nature of existence, of man, and of man's relationship to existence. As against the special sciences, which deal only with particular aspects, philosophy deals with those aspects of the universe which pertain to everything that exists. In the realm of cognition, the special sciences are the trees, but philosophy is the soil which makes the forest possible.

Philosophy would not tell you, for instance, whether you are in New York City or in Zanzibar (though it would give you the means to find out). But here is what it _would_ tell you: Are you in a universe which is ruled by natural laws and, therefore, is stable, firm, absolute - and knowable? Or are you in an incomprehensible chaos, a realm of inexplicable miracles, an unpredictable, unknowable flux, which your mind is impotent to grasp? Are the things you see around you real - or are they only an illusion? Do they exist independent of any observer - or are they created by the observer? Are they the object or the subject of man's consciousness? Are they _what they are_ - or can they be changed by a mere act of your consciousness, such as a wish?

The nature of your actions - and of your ambition - will be different, according to which set of answers you come to accept. These answers are the province of _metaphysics_ - the study of existence as such or, in Aristotle's words, of "being qua being" - the basic branch of philosophy.

No matter what conclusions you reach, you will be confronted by the necessity to answer another, _corollary_ question: How do I know it? Since man is not omniscient or infallible, you have to discover what you can claim as knowledge and how to _prove_ the validity of your conclusions. Does man acquire knowledge by a process of reason - or by sudden revelation from a supernatural power? Is reason a faculty that identifies and integrates the material provided by man's senses - or is it fed by innate ideas, implanted in man's mind before he was born? Is reason competent to perceive reality - or does man possess some other cognitive faculty which is superior to reason? Can man achieve certainty - or is he doomed to perpetual doubt?

The extent of your self-confidence - and of your success - will be different, according to which set of answers you accept. These answers are the province of _epistemology_, the theory of knowledge, which studies man's means of cognition.

These two branches are the theoretical foundation of philosophy. The third branch - _ethics_ - may be regarded as its technology. Ethics does not apply to everything that exists, only to man, but it applies to every aspect of man's life: his character, his actions, his values, his relationship to all of existence. Ethics, or morality, defines a code of values to guide man's choices and actions - the choices and actions that determine the course of his life.

Just as the astronaut in my story did not know what he should do, because he refused to know where he was and how to discover it, so you cannot know what you should do until you know the nature of the universe you deal with, the nature of your means of cognition - and your own nature. Before you come to ethics, you must answer the questions posed by metaphysics and epistemology: Is man a rational being, able to deal with reality - or is he a helplessly blind misfit, a chip buffeted by the universal flux? Are achievement and enjoyment possible to man on earth - or is he doomed to failure and disaster? Depending on the answers, you can proceed to consider the questions posed by ethics: What is good or evil for man - and why? Should man's primary concern be a quest for joy - or an escape from suffering? Should man hold self-fulfillment - or self-destruction - as the goal of his life? Should man pursue his values - or should he place the interests of others above his own? Should man seek happiness - or self-sacrifice?

I do not have to point out the different consequences of these two sets of answers. You can see them everywhere - within you and around you.

The answers given by ethics determine how man should treat other men, and this determines the fourth branch of philosophy: politics, which defines the principles of a proper social system. As an example of philosophy's function, political philosophy will not tell you how much rationed gas you should be given and on which day of the week - it will tell you whether the government has the right to impose any rationing on anything.

The fifth and last branch of philosophy is esthetics, the study of art, which is based on metaphysics, epistemology and ethics. Art deals with the needs - the refueling - of man's consciousness.

Now some of you might say, as many people do: "Aw, I never think in such abstract terms - I want to deal with concrete, particular, real-life problems - what do I need philosophy for?" My answer is: In order to be able to deal with concrete, particular, real-life problems - i.e., in order to be able to live on earth.

You might claim - as most people do - that you have never been influenced by philosophy. I will ask you to check that claim. Have you ever thought or said the following? "Don't be so sure - nobody can be certain of anything." You got that notion from David Hume (and many, many others), even though you might never have heard of him. Or: "This may be good in theory, but it doesn't work in practice." You got that from Plato. Or: "That was a rotten thing to do, but it's only human, nobody is perfect in this world." You got it from Augustine. Or: "It may be true for you, but it's not true for me." You got it from William James. Or: "I couldn't help it! Nobody can help anything he does." You got it from Hegel. Or: "I can't prove it, but I feel that it's true." You got it from Kant. Or: "It's logical, but logic has nothing to do with reality." You got it from Kant. Or: "It's evil, because it's selfish." You got it from Kant. Have you heard the modern activists say: "Act first, think afterward"? They got it from John Dewey.

Some people might answer: "Sure, I've said those things at different times, but I don't have to believe that stuff all of the time. It may have been true yesterday, but it's not true today." They got it from Hegel. They might say: "Consistency is the hobgoblin of little minds." They got it from a very little mind, Emerson. They might say: "But can't one compromise and borrow different ideas from different philosophies according to the expediency of the moment?" They got it from Richard Nixon - who got it from William James.

Now ask yourself: if you are not interested in abstract ideas, why do you (and all men) feel compelled to use them? The fact is that abstract ideas are conceptual integrations which subsume an incalculable number of concretes - and that without abstract ideas you would not be able to deal with concrete, particular, real-life problems. You would be in the position of a newborn infant, to whom every object is a unique, unprecedented phenomenon. The difference between his mental state and yours lies in the number of conceptual integrations your mind has performed.

You have no choice about the necessity to integrate your observations, your experiences, your knowledge into abstract ideas, i.e., into principles. Your only choice is whether these principles are true or false, whether they represent your conscious, rational convictions - or a grab-bag of notions snatched at random, whose sources, validity, context and consequences you do not know, notions which, more often than not, you would drop like a hot potato if you knew.

But the principles you accept (consciously or subconsciously) may clash with or contradict one another; they, too, have to be integrated. What integrates them? Philosophy. A philosophic system is an integrated view of existence. As a human being, you have no choice about the fact that you need a philosophy. Your only choice is whether you define your philosophy by a conscious, rational, disciplined process of thought and scrupulously logical deliberation - or let your subconscious accumulate a junk heap of unwarranted conclusions, false generalizations, undefined contradictions, undigested slogans, unidentified wishes, doubts and fears, thrown together by chance, but integrated by your subconscious into a kind of mongrel philosophy and fused into a single, solid weight: *self-doubt*, like a ball and chain in the place where your mind's wings should have grown.

You might say, as many people do, that it is not easy always to act on abstract principles. No, it is not easy. But how much harder is it, to have to act on them without knowing what they are?

Your subconscious is like a computer - more complex a computer than men can build - and its main function is the integration of your ideas. Who programs it? Your conscious mind. If you default, if you don't reach any firm convictions, your subconscious is programmed by chance - and you deliver yourself into the power of ideas you do not know you have accepted. But one way or the other, your computer gives you print-outs, daily and hourly, in the form of *emotions* - which are lightning-like estimates of the things around you, calculated according to your values. If you programmed your computer by conscious thinking, you know the nature of your values and emotions. If you didn't, you don't.

(To be continued.)

Ayn Rand

The Ayn Rand Letter, published fortnightly by The Ayn Rand Letter, Inc., 183 Madison Avenue, New York, N.Y. 10016.
Contributing Editor: **Leonard Peikoff**; Subscription Director: **Elayne Kalberman**; Production Manager: **Barbara Weiss.**

Vol. III, No. 8 January 14, 1974

PHILOSOPHY: WHO NEEDS IT

(An address given to the graduating class of the United States Military Academy at West Point on March 6, 1974.)

Part II

Many people, particularly today, claim that man cannot live by logic alone, that there's the emotional element of his nature to consider, and that they rely on the guidance of their emotions. Well, so did the astronaut in my story. The joke is on him - and on them: man's values and emotions are determined by his fundamental view of life. The ultimate programmer of his subconscious is philosophy - the science which, according to the emotionalists, is impotent to affect or penetrate the murky mysteries of their feelings.

The quality of a computer's output is determined by the quality of its input. If your subconscious is programmed by chance, its output will have a corresponding character. You have probably heard the computer operators' eloquent term "gigo" - which means: "Garbage in, garbage out." The same formula applies to the relationship between a man's thinking and his emotions.

A man who is run by emotions is like a man who is run by a computer whose print-outs he cannot read. He does not know whether its programming is true or false, right or wrong, whether it's set to lead him to success or destruction, whether it serves his goals or those of some evil, unknowable power. He is blind on two fronts: blind to the world around him and to his own inner world, unable to grasp reality or his own motives, and he is in chronic terror of both. Emotions are not tools of cognition. The men who are not interested in philosophy need it most urgently: they are most helplessly in its power.

The men who are not interested in philosophy absorb its principles from the cultural atmosphere around them - from schools, colleges, books, magazines, newspapers, movies, television, etc. Who sets the tone of a culture? A small handful of men: the philosophers. Others follow their lead, either by conviction or by default. For some two hundred years, under the influence of Immanuel Kant, the dominant trend of philosophy has been directed to a single goal: the destruction of man's mind, of his confidence in the power of reason. Today, we are seeing the climax of that trend.

When men abandon reason, they find not only that their emotions cannot guide them, but that they can experience no emotions save one: terror. The spread of drug addiction among young people brought up on today's intellectual fashions, demonstrates the unbearable inner state of men who are deprived of their means of cognition and who seek escape from reality - from the terror of their impotence to deal with existence. Observe these young people's dread of independence and their frantic desire to "belong," to attach themselves to some group, clique or gang. Most of them have never heard of philosophy, but they sense that they need some fundamental answers to questions they dare not ask - and they hope that the tribe will tell them *how to live*. They are ready to be taken over by any witch doctor, guru, or dictator. One of the most dangerous things a man can do is to surrender his *moral* autonomy to others: like the astronaut in my story, he does not know whether they are human, even though they walk on two feet.

Now you may ask: If philosophy can be that evil, why should one study it? Particularly, why should one study the philosophical theories which are blatantly false, make no sense, and bear no relation to real life?

My answer is: In self-protection - and in defense of truth, justice, freedom, and any value you ever held or may ever hold.

Not all philosophies are evil, though too many of them are, particularly in modern history. On the other hand, at the root of every civilized achievement, such as science, technology, progress, freedom - at the root of every value we enjoy today, including the birth of this country - you will find the achievement of *one man*, who lived over two thousand years ago: Aristotle.

If you feel nothing but boredom when reading the virtually unintelligible theories of *some* philosophers, you have my deepest sympathy. But if you brush them aside, saying: "Why should I study that stuff when I *know* it's nonsense?" - you are mistaken. It *is* nonsense, but you *don't* know it - not so long as you go on accepting all their conclusions, all the vicious catch phrases generated by those philosophers. And not so long as you are unable to *refute* them.

That nonsense deals with the most crucial, the life-or-death issues of man's existence. At the root of every significant philosophic theory, there is a legitimate issue - in the sense that there is an authentic need of man's consciousness, which some theories struggle to clarify and others struggle to obfuscate, to corrupt, to prevent man from ever discovering. The battle of philosophers is a battle for man's mind. If you do not understand their theories, you are vulnerable to the worst among them.

The best way to study philosophy is to approach it as one approaches a detective story: follow every trail, clue and implication, in order to discover who is a murderer and who is a hero. The criterion of detection is two questions: Why? and How? If a given tenet seems to be true - why? If another tenet seems to be false - why? and how is it being put over? You will not find all the answers immediately, but you will acquire an invaluable characteristic: the ability to think in terms of essentials.

Nothing is given to man automatically, neither knowledge, nor self-confidence, nor inner serenity, nor the right way to use his mind. Every value he needs or wants has to be discovered, learned and acquired - even the proper posture of his body. In this context, I want to say that I have always admired the posture of West Point graduates, a posture that projects man in proud, disciplined control of his body. Well, philosophical training gives man the proper *intellectual* posture - a proud, disciplined control of his mind.

In your own profession, in military science, you know the importance of keeping track of the enemy's weapons, strategy and tactics - and of being prepared to counter them. The same is true in philosophy: you have to understand the enemy's ideas and be prepared to refute them, you have to know his basic arguments and be able to blast them.

In physical warfare, you would not send your men into a booby trap: you would make every effort to discover its location. Well, Kant's system is the biggest and most intricate booby trap in the history of philosophy - but it's so full of holes that once you grasp its gimmick, you can defuse it without any trouble and walk forward over it in perfect safety. And, once it is defused, the lesser Kantians - the lower ranks of his army, the philosophical sergeants, buck privates, and mercenaries of today - will fall of their own weightlessness, by chain reaction.

There is a special reason why you, the future leaders of the United States Army, need to be philosophically armed today. You are the target of a special attack by the Kantian-Hegelian-collectivist establishment that dominates our cultural institutions at present. You are the army of the last semi-free country left on earth, yet you are accused of being a tool of imperialism - and "imperialism" is the name given to the foreign policy of this country, which has never engaged in military conquest and has never profited from the two world wars, which she did not initiate, but entered and won. (It was, incidentally, a foolishly overgenerous policy, which made this country waste her wealth on helping both her allies and her former enemies.) Something called "the military-industrial complex" - which is a myth or worse - is being blamed for all of this country's troubles. Bloody college hoodlums scream demands that R.O.T.C. units be banned from college campuses. Our defense budget is being attacked, denounced and undercut by people who claim that financial priority should be given to ecological rose gardens and to classes in esthetic self-expression for the residents of the slums.

Some of you may be bewildered by this campaign and may be wondering, in good faith, what errors you committed to bring it about. If so, it is urgently important for you to understand the nature of the enemy. You are attacked, not for any errors or flaws, but for your virtues. You are denounced, not for any weaknesses, but for your strength and your competence. You are penalized for being the protectors of the United States. On a lower level of the same issue, a similar kind of campaign is conducted against the police force. Those who seek to destroy this country, seek to disarm it - intellectually and physically. But it is not a mere political issue; politics is not the cause, but the last consequence of philosophical ideas. It is not a communist conspiracy, though some communists may be involved - as maggots cashing in on a disaster they had no power to originate. The motive of the destroyers is not love for communism, but hatred for America. Why hatred? Because America is the living refutation of a Kantian universe.

Today's mawkish concern with and compassion for the feeble, the flawed, the suffering, the guilty, is a cover for the profoundly Kantian hatred of the innocent, the strong, the able, the successful, the virtuous, the confident, the happy. A philosophy out to destroy man's mind is necessarily a philosophy of hatred for man, for man's life, and for every human value. Hatred of the good for being the good, is the hallmark of the twentieth century. *This* is the enemy you are facing.

A battle of this kind requires special weapons. It has to be fought with a full understanding of your cause, a full confidence in yourself, and the fullest certainty of the *moral* rightness of both. Only philosophy can provide you with these weapons.

The assignment I gave myself for tonight is not to sell you on my philosophy, but on philosophy as such. I have, however, been speaking implicitly of my philosophy in every sentence - since none of us and no statement can escape from philosophical premises. What is my selfish interest in the matter? I am confident enough to think that if you accept the importance of philosophy and the task of examining it critically, it is my philosophy that you will come to accept. Formally, I call it Objectivism, but informally I call it a philosophy for living on earth. You will find an explicit presentation of it in my books, particularly in Atlas Shrugged.

In conclusion, allow me to speak in personal terms. This evening means a great deal to me. I feel deeply honored by the opportunity to address you. I can say - not as a patriotic bromide, but with full knowledge of the necessary metaphysical, epistemological, ethical, political and esthetic roots - that the United States of America is the greatest, the noblest and, in its original founding principles, the only moral country in the history of the world. There is a kind of quiet radiance associated in my mind with the name West Point - because you have preserved the spirit of those original founding principles and you are their symbol. There were contradictions and omissions in those principles, and there may be in yours - but I am speaking of the essentials. There may be individuals in your history who did not live up to your highest standards - as there are in every institution - since no institution and no social system can guarantee the automatic perfection of all its members; this depends on an individual's free will. I am speaking of your standards. You have preserved three qualities of character which were typical at the time of America's birth, but are virtually non-existent today: earnestness - dedication - a sense of honor. Honor is self-esteem made visible in action.

You have chosen to risk your lives for the defense of this country. I will not insult you by saying that you are dedicated to selfless service - it is not a virtue in my morality. In my morality, the defense of one's country means that a man is personally unwilling to live as the conquered slave of any enemy, foreign or domestic. This is an enormous virtue. Some of you may not be consciously aware of it. I want to help you to realize it.

The army of a free country has a great responsibility: the right to use force, but not as an instrument of compulsion and brute conquest - as the armies of other countries have done in their histories - only as an instrument of a free nation's self-defense, which means: the defense of man's individual rights. The principle of using force only in retaliation against those who initiate its use, is the principle of subordinating might to right. The highest integrity and sense of honor are required for such a task. No other army in the world has achieved it. You have.

West Point has given America a long line of heroes, known and unknown. You, this year's graduates, have a glorious tradition to carry on - which I admire profoundly, not because it is a tradition, but because it is glorious.

Since I came from a country guilty of the worst tyranny on earth, I am particularly able to appreciate the meaning, the greatness and the supreme value of that which you are defending. So, in my own name and in the name of many people who think as I do, I want to say, to all the men of West Point, past, present and future: Thank you.

Ayn Rand

The Ayn Rand Letter, published fortnightly by The Ayn Rand Letter, Inc., 183 Madison Avenue, New York, N.Y. 10016.

Contributing Editor: **Leonard Peikoff**; Subscription Director: **Elayne Kalberman**; Production Manager: **Barbara Weiss.**

Vol. III, No. 9 January 28, 1974

PHILOSOPHICAL DETECTION

My last two Letters were devoted to a brief presentation of an enormous subject: "Philosophy: Who Needs It." I covered the essentials, but a more detailed discussion of certain points will be helpful to those who wish to study philosophy (particularly today, because philosophy has been abolished by the two currently fashionable schools, Linguistic Analysis and Existentialism).

I said that the best way to study philosophy is to approach it as one approaches a detective story. A detective seeks to discover the truth about a crime. A philosophical detective must seek to determine the truth or falsehood of an abstract system and thus discover whether he is dealing with a great achievement or an intellectual crime. A detective knows what to look for, or what clues to regard as significant. A philosophical detective must remember that all human knowledge has a hierarchical structure; he must learn to distinguish the fundamental from the derivative, and in judging a given philosopher's system, he must look - first and above all else - at its fundamentals. If the foundation does not hold, neither will anything else.

In philosophy, the fundamentals are metaphysics and epistemology. On the basis of a knowable universe and of a rational faculty's competence to grasp it, you can define man's proper ethics, politics and esthetics. (And if you make an error, you retain the means and the frame of reference necessary to correct it.) But what will you accomplish if you advocate honesty in ethics, while telling men that there is no such thing as truth, fact or reality? What will you do if you advocate political freedom on the grounds that you feel it is good, and find yourself confronting an ambitious thug who declares that he feels quite differently?

The layman's error, in regard to philosophy, is the tendency to accept consequences while ignoring their causes - to take the end result of a long sequence of thought as the given and to regard it as "self-evident" or as an irreducible primary, while negating its preconditions. Examples can be seen all around us, particularly in politics. There are liberals who want to preserve individual freedom while denying its source: individual rights. There are religious conservatives who claim to advocate capitalism while attacking its root: reason. There are sundry "libertarians" who plagiarize the Objectivist theory of politics, while rejecting the metaphysics, epistemology and ethics on which it rests. That attitude, of course, is not confined to philosophy: its simplest example is the people who scream that they need more gas and that the oil industry should be taxed out of existence.

As a philosophical detective, you must remember that nothing is self-evident except the material of sensory perception - and that an irreducible primary is a fact which cannot be analyzed (i.e., broken into components) or derived from antecedent facts. You must examine your own convictions and any idea or theory you study, by asking: Is this an irreducible primary - and, if not, what does it depend on? You must ask the same question about any answer you obtain, until you do come to an irreducible primary: if a given idea contradicts a primary, the idea is false. This process will lead you to the field of metaphysics and epistemology - and you will discover in what way every aspect of man's knowledge depends on that field and stands or falls with it.

There is an old fable which I read in Russian (I do not know whether it exists in English). A pig comes upon an oak tree, devours the acorns strewn on the ground and, when his belly is full, starts digging the soil to undercut the oak tree's roots. A bird perched on a high branch upbraids him, saying: "If you could lift your snoot, you would discover that the acorns grow on this tree."

In order to avoid that pig's role in the forest of the intellect, one must know and protect the metaphysical-epistemological tree that produces the acorns of one's convictions, goals and desires. And, conversely, one must not gobble up any brightly colored fruit one finds, without bothering to discover that it comes from a deadly yew tree. If laymen did no more than learn to identify the nature of such fruit and stop munching it or passing it around, they would stop being the victims and the unwary transmission belts of philosophical poison. But a minimal grasp of philosophy is required in order to do it.

If an intelligent and honest layman were to translate his implicit, common-sense rationality (which he takes for granted) into explicit philosophical premises, he would hold that the world he perceives is real (existence exists), that things are what they are (the Law of Identity), that reason is the only means of gaining knowledge and logic is the method of using reason. Assuming this base, let me give you an example of what a philosophical detective would do with some of the catch phrases I cited in my preceding <u>Letters</u>.

"It may be true for you, but it's not true for me." What is the meaning of the concept "truth"? Truth is the recognition of reality. (This is known as the correspondence theory of truth.) The same thing cannot be true and untrue at the same time and in the same respect. That catch phrase, therefore, means: a. that the Law of Identity is invalid; b. that there is no objectively perceivable reality, only some indeterminate flux which is nothing in particular, i.e., that there is no reality (in which case, there can be no such thing as truth); or c. that the two debaters perceive two different universes (in which case, no debate is possible). (The purpose of the catch phrase is the destruction of objectivity.)

"Don't be so sure - nobody can be certain of anything." Bertrand Russell's gibberish to the contrary notwithstanding, that pronouncement includes itself; therefore, one cannot be sure that one cannot be sure of anything. The pronouncement means that no knowledge of any kind is possible to man, i.e., that man is not conscious. Furthermore, if one tried to accept that catch phrase, one would find that its second part contradicts its first: if nobody can be certain of anything, then everybody can be certain of everything he pleases - since it cannot be refuted, and he can claim he is not certain he is certain (which is the purpose of that notion).

"This may be good in theory, but it doesn't work in practice." What is a theory? It is a set of abstract principles purporting to be either a correct description of reality or a set of guidelines for man's actions. Correspondence to reality is the standard of value by which one estimates a theory. If a theory is inapplicable to reality, by what standard can it be estimated as "good"? If one were to accept that notion, it would mean: a. that the activity of man's mind is unrelated to reality; b. that the purpose of thinking is neither to acquire knowledge nor to guide man's actions. (The purpose of that catch phrase is to invalidate man's conceptual faculty.)

"It's logical, but logic has nothing to do with reality." Logic is the art or skill of non-contradictory identification. Logic has a single law, the Law of Identity, and its various corollaries. If logic has nothing to do with reality, it means that the Law of Identity is inapplicable to reality. If so, then: a. things are not what they are; b. things can be and not be at the same time, in the same respect, i.e., reality is made up of contradictions. If so, by what means did anyone discover it? By illogical means. (This last is for sure.) The purpose of that notion is crudely obvious. Its actual meaning is not: "Logic has nothing to do with reality," but: "I, the speaker, have nothing to do with logic (or with reality)." When people use that catch phrase, they mean either: "It's logical, but I don't choose to be logical" or: "It's logical, but people are not logical, they don't think - and I intend to pander to their irrationality."

This is a clue to the kind of error (or epistemological sloppiness) that permits the spread of such catch phrases. Most people use them in regard to some concrete, particular instance and are not aware of the fact that they are uttering a devastating metaphysical generalization. When they say: "It may be true for you, but it's not true for me," they usually mean some optional matter of taste, involving some minor value-judgment. The meaning they intend to convey is closer to: "You may like it, but I don't." The unchallenged idea that value-preferences and emotions are unaccountable primaries, is at the root of their statement. And, in defense of their failure of introspection, they are recklessly willing to wipe the universe out of existence.

When people hear the catch phrase: "It may have been true yesterday, but it's not true today," they usually think of man-made issues or customs, such as: "Men fought duels yesterday, but not today" or: "Women wore hoop skirts yesterday, but not today" or: "We're not in the horse-and-buggy age any longer." The proponents of that catch phrase are seldom innocent, and the examples they give are usually of the above kind. So their victims - who have never discovered the difference between the metaphysical and the man-made - find themselves, in helpless bewilderment, unable to refute such conclusions as: "Freedom was a value yesterday, but not today" or: "Work was a human necessity yesterday, but not today" or: "Reason was valid yesterday, but not today."

Now observe the method I used to analyze those catch phrases. You must attach clear, specific meanings to words, i.e., be able to identify their referents in reality. This is a precondition, without which neither critical judgment nor thinking of any kind is possible. All philosophical con games count on your using words as vague approximations. You must not take a catch phrase - or any abstract statement - as if it were approximate. Take it literally. Don't translate it, don't glamorize it, don't make the mistake of thinking, as many people do: "Oh, nobody could possibly mean this!" and then proceed to endow it with some whitewashed meaning of your own. Take it straight, for what it _does_ say and mean.

Instead of dismissing the catch phrase, _accept_ it - for a few brief moments. Tell yourself, in effect: "If I were to accept it as true, what would follow?" This is the best way of unmasking any philosophical fraud. The old saying of plain con men holds true for intellectual ones: "You can't cheat an honest man." Intellectual honesty consists in taking ideas seriously. To take ideas seriously means that you intend to live by, to _practice_, any idea you accept as true. Philosophy provides man with a comprehensive view of life. In order to evaluate it properly, ask yourself what a given theory, if accepted, would do to a human life, starting with your own.

Most people would be astonished by this method. They think that abstract thinking must be "impersonal" - which means that ideas must hold no personal meaning, value or importance to the thinker. This notion rests on the premise that a personal interest is an agent of distortion. But "personal" does not mean "non-objective"; it depends on the kind of person you are. If your thinking is determined by your emotions, then you will not be able to judge anything, personally or impersonally. But if you are the kind of person who knows that reality is not your enemy, that truth and knowledge are of crucial, personal, selfish importance to you and to your own life - then, the more passionately personal the thinking, the clearer and truer.

Would you be willing and able to act, daily and consistently, on the belief that reality is an illusion? That the things you see around you, do not exist? That it makes no difference whether you drive your car down a road or over the edge of an abyss - whether you eat or starve - whether you save the life of a person you love or push him into a blazing fire? It is particularly important to apply this test to any moral theory. Would you be willing and able to act on the belief that altruism is a moral ideal? That you must sacrifice everything - everything you love, seek, own, or desire, including your life - for the benefit of any and every stranger?

Do not evade such issues by means of self-abasement - by saying: "Maybe reality is unreal, but I'm not wise enough to transcend my low-grade, materialistic bondage" or: "Yes, altruism is an ideal, but I'm not good enough to practice it." Self-abasement is not an answer - and it is not a license to apply to others the precepts from which you exempt yourself; it is merely a trap set by the very philosophers you are trying to judge. They have spent a prodigious effort to teach you to assume an unearned guilt. Once you assume it, you pronounce your mind incompetent to judge, you renounce morality, integrity and thought, and you condemn yourself to the gray fog of the approximate, the uncertain, the uninspiring, the flameless, through which most men drag their lives - which is the purpose of that trap.

The acceptance of unearned guilt is a major cause of philosophical passivity. There are other causes - and other kinds of guilt which are earned.

(To be continued.)

Ayn Rand

OBJECTIVIST CALENDAR

On Tuesday, April 30, Ayn Rand will appear on "Day at Night," an interview program on WNET-TV (Channel 13), at 11:30 P.M., in New York City. This program is syndicated in many other cities, on different dates; for information, contact your local public TV station.

The following starting dates have been scheduled for Dr. Leonard Peikoff's taped courses. Introduction to Logic. Eugene, Oreg., April 14 (contact Joyce H. Lee, 503-636-4268, eves.); Atlanta, May 6 (Dr. Bonar Newton, 404-351-9096). Founders of Western Philosophy: Thales to Hume. San Diego, April 17 (Anton Rosenlund, 714-297-1990 or 714-296-2277); San Antonio, April 20 (Dr. Lee Brooks, 512-684-7565, eves.).

B.W.

The Ayn Rand Letter, published fortnightly by The Ayn Rand Letter, Inc., 183 Madison Avenue, New York, N.Y. 10016.

Contributing Editor: **Leonard Peikoff**; Subscription Director: **Elayne Kalberman**; Production Manager: **Barbara Weiss.**

Vol. III, No. 10 February 11, 1974

PHILOSOPHICAL DETECTION

Part II

A major source of men's earned guilt in regard to philosophy - as well as in regard to their own minds and lives - is failure of introspection. Specifically, it is the failure to identify the nature and causes of their emotions.

An emotion as such tells you nothing about reality, beyond the fact that something makes you feel something. Without a ruthlessly honest commitment to introspection - to the conceptual identification of your inner states - you will not discover what you feel, what arouses the feeling, and whether your feeling is an appropriate response to the facts of reality, or a mistaken response, or a vicious illusion produced by years of self-deception. The men who scorn or dread introspection take their inner states for granted, as an irreducible and irresistible primary, and let their emotions determine their actions. This means that they choose to act without knowing the context (reality), the causes (motives), and the consequences (goals) of their actions.

The field of extrospection is based on two cardinal questions: "What do I know?" and "How do I know it?" In the field of introspection, the two guiding questions are: "What do I feel?" and "Why do I feel it?"

Most men can give themselves only some primitively superficial answers - and they spend their lives struggling with incomprehensible inner conflicts, alternately repressing their emotions and indulging in emotional fits, regretting it, losing control again, rebelling against the mystery of their inner chaos, trying to unravel it, giving up, deciding to feel nothing - and feeling the growing pressure of fear, guilt, self-doubt, which makes the answers progressively harder to find.

Since an emotion is experienced as an immediate primary, but is, in fact, a complex, derivative sum, it permits men to practice one of the ugliest of psychological phenomena: rationalization. Rationalization is a cover-up, a process of providing one's emotions with a false identity, of giving them spurious explanations and justifications - in order to hide one's motives, not just from others, but primarily from oneself. The price of rationalizing is the hampering, the distortion and, ultimately, the destruction of one's cognitive faculty. Rationalization is a process not of perceiving reality, but of attempting to make reality fit one's emotions.

Philosophical catch phrases are handy means of rationalization. They are quoted, repeated and perpetuated in order to justify feelings which men are unwilling to admit.

"Nobody can be certain of anything" is a rationalization for a feeling of envy and hatred toward those who _are_ certain. "It may be true for you, but it's not true for me" is a rationalization for one's inability and unwillingness to prove the validity of one's contentions. "Nobody is perfect in this world" is a rationalization for the desire to continue indulging in one's imperfections, i.e., the desire to escape morality. "Nobody can help anything he does" is a rationalization for the escape from moral responsibility. "It may have been true yesterday, but it's not true today" is a rationalization for the desire to get away with contradictions. "Logic has nothing to do with reality" is a crude rationalization for a desire to subordinate reality to one's whims.

"I can't prove it, but I _feel_ that it's true" is more than a rationalization: it is a description of the process of rationalizing. Men do not accept a catch phrase by a process of thought, they seize upon a catch phrase - _any_ catch phrase - because it fits their emotions. Such men do not judge the truth of a statement by its correspondence to reality - they judge reality by its correspondence to their feelings.

If, in the course of philosophical detection, you find yourself, at times, stopped by the indignantly bewildered question: "How could anyone arrive at such nonsense?" - you will begin to understand it when you discover that _evil philosophies are systems of rationalization_.

The nonsense is never accidental, if you observe what subjects it deals with. The elaborate structures in which it is presented are never purposeless. You may find a grim proof of reality's power in the fact that the most virulently rabid irrationalist senses the derivative nature of emotions and will not proclaim their primacy, their sovereign causelessness, but will seek to justify them as responses to reality - and if reality contradicts them, he will invent another reality of which they are the humble reflectors, not the rulers.

In modern history, the philosophy of Kant is a systematic rationalization of every major psychological vice. The metaphysical inferiority of this world (as a "phenomenal" world of mere "appearances"), is a rationalization for the hatred of reality. The notion that reason is unable to perceive reality and deals only with "appearances," is a rationalization for the hatred of reason; it is also a rationalization for a profound kind of epistemological egalitarianism which reduces reason to equality with the futile puttering of "idealistic" dreamers. The metaphysical superiority of the "noumenal" world, is a rationalization for the supremacy of emotions, which are thus given the power to know the unknowable by ineffable means.

The complaint that man can perceive things only through his own consciousness, not through any other kinds of consciousnesses, is a rationalization for the most profound type of second-handedness ever confessed in print: it is the whine of a man tortured by perpetual concern with what others think and by inability to decide which others he should conform to. The wish to perceive "things in themselves" unprocessed by any consciousness, is a rationalization for the wish to escape the effort and responsibility of cognition - by means of the automatic omniscience a whim-worshiper ascribes to his emotions. The moral imperative of the duty to sacrifice oneself to duty, a sacrifice without beneficiaries, is a gross rationalization for the image (and soul) of an austere, ascetic monk who winks at you with an obscenely sadistic pleasure - the pleasure of breaking man's spirit, ambition, success, self-esteem, and enjoyment of life on earth. Et cetera. These are just some of the highlights.

Observe that the history of philosophy reproduces - in slow motion, on a macrocosmic screen - the workings of ideas in an individual man's mind. A man who has accepted false premises is free to reject them, but until and unless he does, they do not lie still in his mind, they grow without his conscious participation and reach their ultimate logical conclusions. A similar process takes place in a culture: if the false premises of an influential philosopher are not challenged, generations of his followers - acting as the culture's subconscious - milk them down to their ultimate consequences.

Since Kant substituted the collective for the objective (in the form of "categories" collectively creating a "phenomenal" world), the next step was the philosophy of Hegel - which is a rationalization for subjectivism, for the power-lust of an ambitious elite who would create a "noumenal," non-material world (by means of establishing the brute force of an absolute state in the "phenomenal," material one). Since those outside the elite could not be counted upon to obey or accept such a future, the next side step was Pragmatism - which is a rationalization for the concrete-bound, range-of-the-moment, anti-conceptual mentalities that long for liberation from principles and future.

Today, there is the philosophy of Linguistic Analysis - which is a rationalization for men who are able to focus on single words, but unable to integrate them into sentences, paragraphs or philosophical systems, yet who wish to be philosophers. And there is the philosophy of Existentialism - which discards the politeness of rationalization, takes Kant straight, and proclaims the supremacy of emotions in an unknowable, incomprehensible, inexplicable, nauseating non-world.

Observe that, in spite of their differences, altruism is the untouched, unchallenged common denominator in the ethics of all these philosophies. It is the single richest source of rationalizations. A morality that cannot be practiced is an unlimited cover for any practice. Altruism is the rationalization for the mass slaughter in Soviet Russia - for the legalized looting in the welfare state - for the power-lust of politicians seeking to serve the "common good" - for the concept of a "common good" - for envy, hatred, malice, brutality - for the arson, robbery, highjacking, kidnapping, murder perpetrated by the selfless advocates of sundry collectivist causes - for sacrifice and more sacrifice and an infinity of sacrificial victims. When a theory achieves nothing but the opposite of its alleged goals, yet its advocates remain undeterred, you may be certain that it is not a conviction or an "ideal," but a rationalization.

Philosophical rationalizations are not always easy to detect. Some of them are so complex that an innocent man may be taken in and paralyzed by intellectual confusion. At their first encounter with modern philosophy, many people make the mistake of dropping it and running, with the thought: "I know it's false, but I can't prove it. I know something's wrong there, but I can't waste my time and effort trying to untangle it." Here is the danger of such a policy: you might forget all about Kant's "categories" and his "noumenal" world, but some day, under the pressure of facing some painfully difficult choice, when you feel tempted to evade the responsibility or to make a dishonest decision, when you need all of your inner strength, confidence and courage, you will find yourself thinking: "How do I know what's true? Nobody knows it. Nobody can be certain of anything." *This* is all Kant wanted of you.

A thinker like Kant does not want you to agree with him: all he wants is that you give him the benefit of the doubt. He knows that your own subconscious does the rest. What he dreads is your conscious mind: once you understand the meaning of his theories, they lose their power to threaten you, like a Halloween mask in bright sunlight.

One further suggestion: if you undertake the task of philosophical detection, drop the dangerous little catch phrase which advises you to keep an "open mind." This is a very ambiguous term - as demonstrated by a man who once accused a famous politician of having "a wide open mind." That term is an anti-concept: it is usually taken to mean an objective, unbiased approach to ideas, but it is used as a call for perpetual skepticism, for holding no firm convictions and granting plausibility to anything. A "closed mind" is usually taken to mean the attitude of a man impervious to ideas, arguments, facts and logic, who clings stubbornly to some mixture of unwarranted assumptions, fashionable catch phrases, tribal prejudices - and emotions. But this is not a "closed" mind, it is a *passive* one. It is a mind that has dispensed with (or never acquired) the practice of thinking or judging, and feels threatened by any request to consider anything.

What objectivity and the study of philosophy require is not an "open mind," but an *active mind* - a mind able and eagerly willing to examine ideas, but to examine them *critically*. An active mind does not grant equal status to truth and falsehood; it does not remain floating forever in a stagnant vacuum of neutrality and uncertainty; by assuming the responsibility of judgment, it reaches firm convictions and holds to them. Since it is able to prove its convictions, an active mind achieves an unassailable certainty in confrontations with assailants - a certainty untainted by spots of blind faith, approximation, evasion and fear.

If you keep an active mind, you will discover (assuming that you started with common-sense rationality) that every challenge you examine will strengthen your convictions, that the conscious, reasoned rejection of false theories will help you to clarify and amplify the true ones, that your ideological enemies will make you invulnerable by providing countless demonstrations of their own impotence.

No, you will not have to keep your mind eternally open to the task of examining every new variant of the same old falsehoods. You will discover that they are variants of attacks on certain philosophical essentials - and that the entire, gigantic battle of philosophy (and of human history) revolves around the upholding or the destruction of these essentials. You will learn to recognize at a glance a given theory's stand on these essentials, and to reject the attacks without lengthy consideration - because you will know (and will be able to *prove*) in what way any given attack, old or new, is made of contradictions and "stolen concepts."

I will list these essentials for your future reference. But do not attempt the shortcut of accepting them on faith (or as semi-grasped approximations and floating abstractions). That would be a fundamental contradiction and it would not work.

The essentials are: in metaphysics, the Law of Identity - in epistemology, the supremacy of reason - in ethics, rational egoism - in politics, individual rights (i.e., capitalism) - in esthetics, metaphysical values.

If you reach the day when these essentials become your absolutes, you will have entered Atlantis - at least, psychologically; which is a precondition of the possibility ever to enter it existentially.

Ayn Rand

A REPORT

Many readers have written to us asking about the response to Ayn Rand's lecture at West Point. They are interested, they said, because they regard West Point as an institution representing the original premises of this country.

Miss Rand's lecture, sponsored by the English Department, had been intended for the graduating class (about 400), as part of the senior-year philosophy course. With military punctuality, the audience assembled - 1200 people, including row after row of gray-uniformed cadets, a great many faculty members (all of whom are military officers), and some civilians; when Miss Rand reached the podium, they greeted her with a standing ovation. Throughout the talk, attentive silence alternated with bursts of laughter or applause, at appropriate points. At the end, after her solemn tribute to the Army of the United States, as Miss Rand raised her hand in a military salute, the audience rose in a body, offering a longer, more tumultuous ovation.

After a brief question period, during which Miss Rand's answers on political and philosophical subjects evoked stormy cheers, a reception was held in another building. The place was jammed with cadets struggling to break a path to Miss Rand, bombarding her with questions. A distinguished colonel, a senior faculty member, told me: "Usually these receptions consist of a handful of people seated in a corner. I've never seen anything like this."

As we were leaving, I overheard an exchange between Miss Rand and the head of the Point's philosophy program. "Did I sell the cadets on philosophy to your satisfaction?" she asked. "You did more," he said. "You satisfied me qua philosophy teacher, qua colonel, and qua man."

Since our return to New York, we have received reports of unusual philosophic ferment among the cadets, including heated discussions in class and out. We have received a request for 100 copies of the Letters containing the lecture, to be distributed to students and teachers who wish to study it.

The most eloquent evidence of the response is the following: West Point has asked (and received) permission to reprint "Philosophy: Who Needs It" in a new philosophy textbook which the English Department is publishing for this fall's classes. The editors are placing Ayn Rand's lecture at the beginning of the book - to serve as our future officers' introduction to the subject of philosophy.

Leonard Peikoff

OBJECTIVIST CALENDAR

The following starting dates were scheduled for the taped lectures of Dr. Leonard Peikoff's course, Introduction to Logic: Denver, May 23 (contact Robert Gifford, 303-751-8052); Montreal, June 13 (Christian David Sweeny, 514-484-8094).

B.W.

The Ayn Rand Letter, published fortnightly by The Ayn Rand Letter, Inc., 183 Madison Avenue, New York, N.Y. 10016.

Contributing Editor: **Leonard Peikoff**; Subscription Director: **Elayne Kalberman**; Production Manager: **Barbara Weiss.**

Vol. III, No. 11 February 25, 1974

"IDEAS V. GOODS"

In the 1930s, Isabel Paterson (author of The God of the Machine) used to say to me: "If you hear some bad collectivistic notions, chances are that they came from liberals. But if you hear or read something outrageously, god-awfully collectivistic, you may be sure that the author is a conservative."

In this respect, things have not changed much since the 1930s, except that the pronouncements of both sides have become cruder and more obvious. The liberals are riding the puddles left by the spent tide of the collectivist philosophy. The conservatives, who share all their basic premises, are trying to dispense with philosophy. Some liberals go as far as one can go, though most of them still mumble something about individual rights. But most conservatives drop such old-fashioned concerns and manage to gallop ahead of the enemy toward the enemy's goal.

In my Letters on "Censorship: Local and Express" (August 13-September 10, 1973), I discussed the fact that Chief Justice Burger, a conservative, used government controls of business (e.g., antitrust) as precedent and justification for imposing censorship on the expression of ideas (allegedly only in the field of pornography); the liberal Justices dissented, properly, in the name of individual rights, but did not (and could not) answer Burger in regard to the violation of the rights of businessmen. I wrote: "When Chief Justice Burger declares to the liberals that they cannot explain why rights 'should be severely restrained in the marketplace of goods and money, but not in the marketplace of pornography,' I am tempted to feel that it serves them right - except that all of us are the victims. If this censorship ruling is not revoked, the next step will be more explicit: it will replace the words 'marketplace of pornography' with the words 'marketplace of ideas.'"

We did not have long to wait. Under the title "Ideas v. Goods," a story in Time magazine (January 14, 1974) shows how and by whom the road for that next step is being paved.

According to the story, Professor Ronald H. Coase of the University of Chicago, a British economist, is advocating government control of the press. "He suggests that federal regulation of the press would be appropriate on social and economic principle. In a scholarly paper given before a recent New York City seminar, Coase...challeng[ed] the special status of the American press and assault[ed] the philosophical validity of its chief protector, the First Amendment."

The hallmark of the _unphilosophical_ mind is its indiscriminate mixture of floating abstractions and momentary concretes, without the ability (or the need) to tie the first to reality, and the second to principles. "Neither in his paper nor in informal remarks did Coase specify what kind of regulation he had in mind. Rather, he talked of a 'real law that would actually regulate what people say.' He believes that the 'market for ideas,' to which journalism belongs, is economically motivated, like the market for goods, and therefore as fit for public regulation as railroads or drug companies. 'I do not believe that this distinction between the market for goods and the market for ideas is valid,' he declared."

This much is true: that distinction is _not_ valid. It is a product of the mystics' mind-body dichotomy, which holds that ideas belong to some higher, "spiritual" dimension of reality, while goods belong to an inferior, material dimension: this earth. But, in reality, there is only one reality; man is an integrated entity of mind and body, and neither can survive without the other. Man's mind (his _ideas_) is as crucially necessary to the production of goods as the translation into a material form (into speech or print) is to the development of ideas. (See _Atlas Shrugged_.) This is not, however, the way Mr. Coase sees it.

Observe the curious justification he offers for advocating control of the press. If _Time_ reports it correctly, his justification is the fact that the market for ideas is "_economically motivated_." This means that an economic motivation as such is unworthy, reprehensible or evil, that it deserves no respect and those who act on it deserve no freedom. Since an "economic motivation" is a desire to be paid for one's work, i.e., a desire to earn a living (on any scale, great or modest), this means that Mr. Coase denies a man's right to support his own life and regards a man's work as the property of others (of "society"), to be disposed of as they see fit. This means that Mr. Coase regards man's survival (and everything it requires) as a contemptible activity of this vulgar, material earth, an activity to which man is not entitled and which must be curbed, restricted, controlled by the government.

Mr. Coase goes beyond the liberals' usual double standard, which differentiates a desire for profits from a desire for wages, even though both _do_ represent an economic motivation. He cashes in on this particular dichotomy, as the intellectually appropriate nemesis of those who attack the profit-makers, but champion the wage-earners. He damns them all. And he damns all forms of trade, i.e., all free markets, whether of goods or of ideas.

"Coase challenged two assumptions that, he says, have created the distinction in public policy: 1) that consumers are able to distinguish good ideas from bad on their own, though they need help in choosing among competing goods; and 2) that publishers and broadcasters deserve laissez-faire treatment while other entrepreneurs do not. He sees journalists as salesmen of products. Hence there is no reason to believe that 'producers who are found to be so unscrupulous in their behavior in other markets can be trusted to act in the public interest whether they publish or work for the New York _Times_, the Chicago _Tribune_ or CBS.'"

This is an excellent example of what happens to the thought processes of an unphilosophical mind. Care to count, as an exercise in philosophical detection, how many assumptions this sort of challenger has left unchallenged?

1. That consumers are the ultimate idol of any society, the "final causation" of all its efforts. 2. That the needs of the consumers constitute "the public interest" and are the standard by which one judges the value of all human activity. 3. That service to the consumers is the only moral justification and proper motivation of a man's life. 4. That all rights inhere in the consumers, while the producers have none. 5. That "laissez-faire treatment" is a privilege which has to be "deserved." 6. That the non-commercial, the unearned, the unpaid-for, the given-or-thrown-away, might have some merit, but to classify men as "salesmen" is to brand them as malefactors. 7. That producers of material goods have been <u>proved</u> to be so unscrupulous that they cannot be trusted in any field. 8. That material success requires unscrupulousness, that dishonesty is practical, that competition in a free market is won by the purveyors of shoddy goods and services, and that there is no such thing as an honest product honestly sold. 9. That the omnipotent consumers are congenitally incapable of distinguishing the good from the bad, either among material goods or among ideas. 10. That it is unnecessary to explain who would be qualified, and by what criterion, to protect the consumers from their freedom of choice, for their own good - i.e., which people would be empowered to regulate which other people's speech. It is necessary only to demand "a real law."

Care to integrate all these assumptions - and many, many others - into one concept? It is a concept which Mr. Coase, on the evidence, would be incapable of challenging: <u>altruism</u>.

Now observe the motivation (and the triviality) of an unphilosophical mind. Observe the depth at which it stops, i.e., what issues it regards as fundamental enough to justify so awesome a proposal as the erection of the ultimate capstone of a totalitarian dictatorship: government control of speech and press. "Coase seems to find little virtue in any form of journalism ('It deals with sensation and scandal, things that can be made entertaining or amusing'). He depicts the press collectively as a self-serving purveyor of misinformation. While journalists presume a high moral standard for others, they are willing to publish material drawn from 'stolen' documents....Coase finds it paradoxical that, historically, liberal journalists and intellectuals have urged further Government control in other fields while they use the First Amendment to deny such interference in the ideas markets. His explanation: the press trades profitably in the ideas market but cloaks its purpose in 'a mantle of virtue.'"

This means that to "trade profitably" is a shameful purpose which has to be hidden under some "mantle of virtue" - virtue having nothing to do with profit or trade. (Do you remember who said that if you seek to benefit by it, your action has no moral import? Do you recognize Kant's influence?) This means that to offer people a value, whether goods or ideas, for which they are willing to pay, is a vice - but to force the unwanted down their throats and minds at the point of a gun, is a virtue.

Wouldn't you suppose that notions of this kind are (or should be) propagated by a confirmed totalitarian statist or, at the least, by some liberal of the New Left variety? "Coase, 63, is no admirer of Orwellian Big Brothers. A British subject who has taught in the U.S. since 1951, he favors Barry Goldwater among politicians and has a low opinion of Government's ability to regulate anything properly. Ideally, he is against any public intervention in private enterprise. But that caveat is irrelevant to his thesis."

This is what happens to men - to all those "practical," cynical, hard-headed realists - who discard ideals and philosophy.

When one discards ideals, the fact that a given policy (such as government controls) is evil, does not constitute a reason for rejecting it. On the contrary, such an estimate serves as an incentive to adopt and expand that policy: to a cynic's mind, that which is evil, is potent and practical.

When one discards philosophy, one accepts the world "as it is" - as it is made by other people - and one does not challenge the _fundamental_ premises of current beliefs: one loses the capacity to perceive fundamentals. The fact that a given policy (such as government controls) has been proved, over and over again, to be a devastating failure, does not constitute a reason for abolishing it: an unphilosophical mind has no means to conceive of an alternative. Taking the man-made as the metaphysical, such a mind merely struggles to seize "a slice of the pie" by devising some controls of its own.

Transposed to another field, this sort of mind and policy would produce the figure of a doctor who snaps resentfully that to look for the cause of an epidemic would take too long, and advises - in the name of justice - that the disease be spread to other cities. For years, the conservatives did not object to the outrageous injustice of antitrust legislation imposed on businessmen; instead, they have been advocating the extension of antitrust to labor unions. The proposal to combat today's ills (which are the result of government controls) by giving the government the power to control the press, is a shocking but logical development of that policy.

If principles are not the motivation of the conservatives' policy, what is? The _Time_ story offers a clue. The state of today's press is not good; it is not, however, as bad as Mr. Coase alleges. But even if it were, consider the degree of blinding hatred a man would have to feel against the press in order to be eager to chain it at the price of giving up the freedom of the mind (his own included), without being able to see that those he hates, whoever they are, would be the first commissars of the censorship bureau.

Better than any other example, the _Time_ story captures and conveys the _smell_ of the conservatives' style: the stale odor of rancorous anti-intellectuality, concrete-bound stubbornness, shifting murk, evasion, appeasement, compromise - and, ultimately, nothing but a festering hostility.

Apparently disturbed by Mr. Coase's proposal, _Time_ attempts to answer him, but does not do much better. Nowhere in its alleged refutation does it mention the words "the _right_ to freedom of speech," nor even the word "rights." It relies exclusively on empirical observations, tradition, and the public good - e.g., "...the Coase theory ignores more than 200 years of American experience ..." and "Despite its lapses and excesses, an unfettered press provides a unique check on powerful institutions that need constant scrutiny." And: "If direct competition among newspapers has declined, the public still has a choice of ideamongers: the surviving papers, a variety of magazines, an assortment of network and independent broadcasters. Further, there is a small but healthy trend among newsmen toward self-examination and criticism. None of these factors promise perfection. But the Coase theory, if ever put into practice, is a prescription for impotence." This sounds like a Freudian slip. _Whose_ impotence? The individual's? The people's? Or the press's?

If this is the best defense that can be offered for the freedom of the press - if hostility and power-lust are the motivating forces of the two adversaries on such an issue - any aspiring censor can feel safe in the knowledge that he will have no serious opposition to contend with.

Do not wonder why capitalism is losing ground or what powerful enemy is destroying it - or why one can expect nothing but betrayal from those alleged anti-statists who propose to save it without the help of philosophy.

Ayn Rand

OBJECTIVIST CALENDAR

We have been asked to announce that Allan Blumenthal will offer a twelve-lecture course on MUSIC: theory, history and performance.

The course deals with the nature of music - its structure, forms, components, and technical vocabulary - its development, rise and fall, from ancient Greece to the present - its meaning in human life. The lectures offer the student an overview of the problems and achievements of a great art, and a fuller understanding of his own response to music. The course will be illustrated throughout by live and recorded demonstrations.

The lectures will be given every week, on Tuesday, at 7:30 P.M., from September 17 to December 17, 1974 (excluding October 22 and November 19), at the Statler Hilton Hotel, 7th Avenue at 33rd Street, New York City. Tuition is $75.00. Brochures, including registration forms, will be sent shortly to The Ayn Rand Letter subscribers in the New York Metropolitan area. For further information, write to Dr. Allan Blumenthal at P.O. Box 381, Forest Hills, N.Y. 11375.

In other cities, tapes of the lectures will be made available, on a rental basis, to groups of ten persons or more. Inquiries should be addressed to Barbara Weiss, P.O. Box 95, Murray Hill Station, New York, N.Y. 10016.

The following starting dates have been scheduled for Dr. Leonard Peikoff's taped courses. Introduction to Logic. Cavalier, N.D., July 11 (contact John Page, 701-265-4254, 10-11 P.M.). Modern Philosophy: Kant to the Present. St. Louis, August 18 (Fulton Huxtable, 314-291-7130, evenings, or 314-862-2420, days).

B.W.

The Ayn Rand Letter, published fortnightly by The Ayn Rand Letter, Inc., 183 Madison Avenue, New York, N.Y. 10016.
Contributing Editor: **Leonard Peikoff**; Subscription Director: **Elayne Kalberman**; Production Manager: **Barbara Weiss.**

Vol. III, No. 12 March 11, 1974

MORAL INFLATION

"Inflation" is defined in the dictionary as "undue expansion or increase of the currency of a country, esp. by the issuing of paper money not redeemable in specie." (Random House Dictionary.) It is interesting to note that the word "inflated" is defined as "distended with air or gas; swollen."

This last is not a coincidence: in regard to social issues, "inflation" does not mean growth, enlargement or expansion, it means an "undue" - or improper or fraudulent - expansion. The expansion of a country's currency (which, incidentally, cannot be perpetrated by private citizens, only by the government) consists in palming off, as values, a stream of paper backed by nothing but promises (or hot air) and getting actual values, the citizens' goods or services, in return - until the country's wealth is drained. A similar activity, in private performance, is the passing of checks on a non-existent bank account. But, in private performance, this is regarded as a crime - and most people understand why such an activity cannot last for long.

Today, people are beginning to understand that the government's account is overdrawn, that a piece of paper is not the equivalent of a gold coin, or an automobile, or a loaf of bread - and that if you attempt to falsify monetary values, you do not achieve abundance, you merely debase the currency and go bankrupt.

The same is true of all values, material or spiritual. If a country's professed moral values are false, it may survive and stumble on for a while (not too happily) so long as and to the extent that those values are ignored in practice. But if you attempt to put such values into wide circulation, if you infuse them into a country's practical politics and saturate its culture, you set in motion a process of moral inflation: the more a country pursues those values, the greater its moral lethargy; the more you accelerate the printing presses of the spirit, the worse the drain on the country's moral energy; you do not achieve a reign of virtue, you merely debase morality and drive the public into a state of bitterly cynical despair.

But this type of inflation is more complex and harder for people to understand than the economic one, particularly since the first is the basic cause of the second. It is in the name of altruism - of self-sacrificial help to others - that the ravages of government spending have been perpetrated, in every country that tried such policies; without the belief that self-immolation is their moral duty, the victims would not have stood for it. Today, we are witnessing the burst of the balloon of altruism, which was being inflated for centuries, yet our public leaders keep cursing the sins of ambition, ability and selfishness as the cause of our plight, and demanding more sacrifices as the cure.

Of late, the liberals have begun to join the conservatives in voicing an anxious concern about the moral deterioration of this country. Both groups have their own scapegoats, usually political, whom they blame for "setting a bad example," for "permissiveness," etc. But politicians do not - and cannot - determine the moral character of a country: the government is the product, not the cause, of a nation's moral standards. If these standards are false, the government cashes in on them and accelerates the country's destruction. A country's moral tone is set by its intellectuals. This is true even in dictatorships, if their docile hacks can be called intellectual: observe the importance a dictatorship attaches to ideological propaganda, which perpetuates the evil notions that brought it to power.

The average man lacks the time, the interest and, in most cases, the independence to formulate a moral philosophy of his own. He picks his moral guidance, as best he can, from the cultural atmosphère of his time - as a rule, subconsciously. When there is a profound rift between the people and the intellectuals - as there is in this country - the average man can neither follow the leaders nor hold out indefinitely: he gives up.

What moral guidance is he offered today? The price which modern intellectuals are paying for their anti-conceptual, range-of-the-moment, pragmatist (or existentialist) notions is their moral impotence, their inability to grasp the meaning of their own actions. If any of them are sincere in their concern about this country's moral twilight - and I believe that some of them are - they have no capacity to see that _they_ are its cause, that they are blaming their victim, the people, for their own default, and that whenever one of them tries to appeal to morality, he is merely contributing to the country's demoralization.

For example, consider the liberals' indignant assertions that the American people are cynical or morally corrupt because they are indifferent to the Watergate scandals. Under any code of morality, a double standard is regarded as a vicious injustice. It is hard to defend Mr. Nixon, but it is impossible to applaud the prosecution of lesser malfeasances when much greater ones have been committed with impunity by the political party now conducting the prosecution, and have been covered up by the silence of the very clique now accusing the people of being morally indifferent. How long will an average man preserve his moral stature under a daily barrage of accusations of that kind, before he concludes that immorality consists, not in evildoing, but in getting caught?

What is he offered on the other side? There was a conservative group that advocated "Fairness to the President" in some rather well-reasoned newspaper ads. But if he joined it, he would find himself squirming with embarrassment when he saw, on television, the result and climax of that campaign: a bunch of neat-looking, young hippies with homemade placards, _praying_ for Mr. Nixon on the steps of the Capitol. How long will that average man preserve the conviction that fairness is practical?

If the religionist wing of conservatism is futile, the secular one is, perhaps, worse. The religionists preach the morality of altruism, knowing that the liberals and the extreme left are its much more consistent practitioners, but hoping - since consistency is a requirement of reason, not of faith - that a miracle will wipe out that fact. The secular conservatives solve the contradiction by discarding morality altogether, by surrendering it to the enemy and declaring that social-political-economic problems are _amoral_.

A small example of this viewpoint, on the popular level, is offered by a conservative columnist of _The New York Times_. Let me preface it by saying that I have no opinion on the subject of "no-fault insurance," because I do not know the legal issues involved in automobile accidents. But the moral implications of that slogan, which make me feel uneasy, are precisely the ones that the _Times_ columnist acclaims. In a piece entitled "The No-Fault Society" (February 4, 1974), he extols the possibilities of what his title indicates; his manner is humorous, but he is only half-kidding. "What might happen if we were to apply the no-fault principle to other matters in our lives?" he asks, and cites, as an example, the energy crisis, which he describes as "a national orgy of oily recrimination" among various political groups. "In a no-fault society, all this irrelevant fault finding would give way to factfinding and solution finding: oilmen, politicians and consumers of energy would stop fishing for carp and start providing incentives for new supplies and reductions of demand."

How does one engage in "fact-finding" if, in fact, a disaster occurs through someone's fault? Would the "solution finding" consist in placing the burden of the disaster's consequences equally on the guilty and the innocent? How would one bring the guilty party to correct his fault? In the name of what? If the energy crisis was caused by the government's regulations (or, for that matter, by the oilmen's "greed," or by the consumers' "overindulgence," or by the Arab sheiks' international blackmail), what would no-faultfinding consist in? Apparently, in saying: "Please, boys, change your policy. We know that you mean well and that your motives are pure, but your policy is impractical." If they answer: "We're getting away with it," you say: "You'll suffer in the long run." They answer: "In the long run, we'll all be dead." You say: "But you're ruining us!" They answer: "So what?" What are you going to say at this point? "It's unfair"? That would be a moral judgment.

The worst fault of these amoralists - who regard moral concerns as naive - is their abysmal naiveté: they seem to believe that practicality, and the knowledge of what is practical, and long-range vision (i.e., a rational grasp of reality, respect for facts, devotion to truth) have nothing to do with morality and do not represent the rarest of virtues; that these characteristics are innate, instinctual and dominant in all people, that nobody seeks evil goals, and that human atrocities are merely the products of errors. Since it is not likely that anyone could hold such a belief past the age of five, one must ask oneself what unimaginable fear of moral judgment could prompt men to maintain an illusion of that kind.

The column offers an indication: "But there are dangers, of course [in "a no-fault way of life"]: without blame, there is no shame, and without an abiding sense of guilt, no purifying conscience to become our guide." An inspiring notion, isn't it? If, on hearing that the purpose of morality is to induce shame and guilt, an average young man declares: "Then to hell with morality!" - could you blame him? That column would not be worth discussing if it were not for the fact that it presents, in crudely explicit terms, a theory preached by many prominent conservative economists.

If that average young man withstands such theories and resists the temptation to drop out of school (he is constantly told that a diploma would bring him a better job), another Times essay might get him. Written by a different author and entitled "Keeping Cool in Alaska" (December 28, 1973), this one discusses the Alaskan aborigines' resistance to the civilizing influence of outsiders, to "acculturation." "They have, of course, paid dearly [for their resistance], in a low standard of living, a frighteningly high infant-mortality rate, inferior health care and a high rate of illiteracy. But theirs is a freedom that white men might well envy. I began to understand it back in 1965, as a reporter in southeastern Alaska, when a man representing a pulpmill spoke to the local chamber of commerce on what was wrong with the Indians." The man explained that the area had a lot of unemployed Indians, that they all signed on and proved to be excellent workers. "'But in two or three months, when those Indians had a little more money than they needed, they quit - went off to hunt and fish!' he said, still struck by the incredibility of it all. 'And then, three or four months later when they were broke, they came back and wanted to work for us again! Now, what we've got to teach these people is that they have to work an eight-hour day, a five-day week and a 50-week year.' I wondered then just who had the right philosophy, the pulpmill man or the Indians? Today I believe that the Indians are wiser."

If the average young man then chucks the discipline of schooling, picks up a guitar and goes off to search for wisdom - and for food in garbage cans along the way - would one blame him? If he is a little brighter than average, he might realize that it's no use struggling for success in business, because he would be expected to provide jobs for the unemployed anywhere on earth and to keep that pulpmill running, somehow, until those superior beings felt like coming back to work.

He might even remember reading that when Charles E. Wilson said: "What's good for the country is good for General Motors and vice versa" (which, in a free-market economy, would be true), a howl of indignation about "selfishness" went up from the commentators. But nobody protested when one of the "little people," a working woman, was recently asked by a reporter whether she had lost confidence in all politicians, and answered as follows: "Not really, because I try to find out what a politician stands for. If he has been supported by big business in his campaigns and his votes favor that view, that's a tip-off. I do research to find out whether a politician is likely to put *me* first." (*Daily News*, May 30, 1974; emphasis added.)

If, stumbling down a dark, frozen road, that young man sees the lights of a city skyline in the foggy distance and, for a brief moment, feels a desperate stab of love and pride for his country, a UPI dispatch (December 20, 1973) would cut it off. "The Senate adopted a resolution today calling for observance of a National Day of Humiliation, Fasting and Prayer on April 30. The resolution was introduced by Sen. Mark O. Hatfield, R. Ore., and adopted by voice vote and with no debate or opposition. The resolution says that because of the nation's failings, it 'behooves us to humble ourselves before Almighty God, to confess our national sins and to pray for clemency and forgiveness.'...In a Senate speech, Hatfield said: 'We witness a country torn apart with division and lacking the spiritual foundation which would restore its vision and purpose. We, as a people, through our own acquiescence to corruption and waste, have helped to create a moral abyss that produces a disdain for honesty and humility in high levels of national leadership.'"

This, I submit, is the bottom of the abyss.

(To be continued.)

Ayn Rand

OBJECTIVIST CALENDAR

The following starting dates have been scheduled for Dr. Leonard Peikoff's taped courses. *Modern Philosophy: Kant to the Present*. Fairfield Heights, N.S.W., Australia, August 2 (contact R.E. Barros, 604-1333, days). *Introduction to Logic*. West Lafayette, Ind., September 14 (Richard Matula, 317-463-3646, eves.). *Founders of Western Philosophy: Thales to Hume*. Calgary, Alberta, Canada, September 16 (Al Kincius, 403-264-5254).

B.W.

The Ayn Rand Letter, published fortnightly by The Ayn Rand Letter, Inc., 183 Madison Avenue, New York, N.Y. 10016.

Contributing Editor: **Leonard Peikoff**; Subscription Director: **Elayne Kalberman**; Production Manager: **Barbara Weiss.**

Vol. III, No. 13 March 25, 1974

MORAL INFLATION

Part II

Here are some of the things that men had to evade in order to think up a moral atrocity such as a "National Day of Humiliation."

Self-abasement is the antithesis of morality. If a man has acted immorally, but regrets it and wants to atone for it, it is not self-abasement that prompts him, but some remnant of love for moral values - and it is not self-abasement that he expresses, but a longing to regain his self-esteem. Humility is not a recognition of one's failings, but a rejection of morality. "I am no good" is a statement that may be uttered only in the past tense. To say: "I am no good" is to declare: "- and I never intend to be any better."

One can feel nothing but mistrust, disgust and contempt for a man who spits in his own face. To drag others along into the same degradation and spit in the face of one's own country, is as base an affront to morality as can be imagined. Yet this has been the policy of American intellectuals for many decades. That it is now adopted by a Senator and approved "with no debate or opposition" by the U.S. Senate, is a measure of the extent to which moral proclamations and moral *principles* are not taken seriously by today's public leaders.

One may disapprove of one's country's policies, one may disagree with most or with all of its citizens, one may seek to change, reform or improve particular laws, conditions or trends; and if one finds an entire country so evil that it deserves damnation, one must leave it. But to stay here and to damn this country - *this country*! - on such phony, trashy allegations as "acquiescence[?] to corruption and waste[!!]" is to step out of any moral bounds.

What effect did the sponsors of that resolution expect it to have on the American people?

There still are people in this country who lost loved ones in World War I. There are more people who carry the unhealed wounds of World War II, of Korea, of Vietnam. There are the disabled, the crippled, the mangled of those wars' battlefields. No one has ever told them why they had to fight nor what their sacrifices accomplished; it was certainly not "to make the world safe for democracy" - look at that world now. The American people have borne it all, trusting their leaders, hoping that someone knew the purpose of that ghastly devastation. The United States gained nothing from those wars, except the growing burden of paying reparations to the whole world - the kind of burden that used to be imposed on a defeated nation.

People have borne patiently the unending drain of their wealth, their effort, their standard of living - first, to help the unemployed of the New Deal era, then the war allies, then the former enemies, and now the unemployables of the entire globe. People have seen and read enough to know the subhuman squalor of human existence in other countries and the atrocities to which men submit. In their innocent, foolishly overgenerous benevolence, the American people have been willing to help, knowing that <u>theirs</u> is the greatest country on this ravaged earth, a blessed oasis in a desert of bloody savagery.

Then to hear a proclamation of their country's self-abasement - in this day of raucously chauvinistic boasting, when every racist tribe in every backyard of the globe, from Albania to Uganda, is proclaiming the uniquely sanctified value of the non-achievements of its non-culture - to hear that they, the American people, have not done enough and that their reward is a "National Day of Humiliation," is more than human beings should be asked to bear or understand. If, under a leadership of this kind, people are losing respect for morality and crumbling into cynicism, bitterness, helpless anger, or blind hatred - can one blame them?

Yet the altruist morality dictates such policies to the nation's leaders. Even though altruism declares that "it is more blessed to give than to receive," it does not work that way in practice. The givers are never blessed; the more they give, the more is demanded of them; complaints, reproaches and insults are the only response they get for practicing altruism's virtues (or for their <u>actual</u> virtues). Altruism cannot permit a recognition of virtue; it cannot permit self-esteem or moral innocence. Guilt is altruism's stock in trade, and the inducing of guilt is its only means of self-perpetuation. If the giver is not kept under a torrent of degrading, demeaning accusations, he might take a look around and put an end to the self-sacrificing.

Altruists are concerned only with those who suffer - not with those who provide relief from suffering, not even enough to care whether they are able to survive. When no actual suffering can be found, the altruists are compelled to invent or manufacture it. Observe their admission that, compared to the rest of the world, people do not suffer from real poverty in this country - they suffer from <u>relative</u> poverty (i.e., from envy). Observe that with the inflation of altruism into a government policy - with public cash and legislative favors pouring upon the pressure groups of newly minted sufferers - the proper, basic functions of the government are crumbling, corroded by neglect and "lack of funds"(!). Yet these are the functions required for the survival of the givers, who carry all the rest on their shoulders and are the greatest victims of altruistic exploitation: the middle class.

These basic functions are: the police, the law courts, the military. (These represent the only moral justification for the existence of a government: the protection of individual rights, i.e., the protection of individual citizens from the initiators of physical force.) What is the state of these governmental functions today?

Observe the conditions of an average American's existence. He has lost the most rudimentary form of protection: the safety of city streets. He is in danger on his way to work in the morning, and on his way home; he is in danger if he steps out of the house after dark; his family are in danger if they go shopping, visiting, or walking in a public park. They dare not ride the subway, yet they are threatened with the loss of their safest transportation: their car. Criminal attacks are a daily occurrence, any time, any place: purse-snatching, mugging, burglary, rape, murder. The police are helpless: they have been brought close to impotence by impossible rules, which protect the "rights" of the criminals. The policemen struggle on as best they can, but they admit bitterly that there is little they can do: they risk their lives to arrest a thug, but the courts set him free.

The average man cannot seek redress in court, whether in criminal or civil matters: he cannot afford it. The cost, the length of time required, and the unpredictable outcome of non-objective laws, have made him give up the hope of appealing to justice, whether he suffers from a neighbor's petty chiseling or from some major violation of his rights. He has grown stoically - or cynically - indifferent: he knows (or senses) that the main violator is the government, that no muggers can deprive him of the sums which the government seizes at income-tax time.

The moral inflation leaves him unprotected against the financial inflation: he works harder and harder (often in the form of "moonlighting"), but his real income is shrinking, he is not rising in the world, he is not getting anywhere, he is running on a hopeless treadmill. Try to tell his wife - in the midst of her desperate struggle to provide the family with decent meals, which they can't afford - that she must bear "humiliation" for the sin of "waste"!

Just as these people sense that today's leadership does not regard them as worth protecting, so they sense that their country, too, is regarded as not worth defending. The military services have survived, so far - in the midst of an unrelenting campaign of attacks, vilifications, and demands that the defense budget be cut (even though welfare projects, not defense, consume the largest share of the national budget).

To add insult to the American people's injury, The New York Times published an editorial (May 25, 1972), entitled "Retreat on Rights," which said: "The Supreme Court decisions permitting criminal convictions by less than unanimous juries and narrowing witnesses' immunity against self-incrimination are disquieting in their practical effects but, even more, as portents of things to come.

"In the United States and other free countries, the drift of history in this century has been toward strengthening the power of government and diminishing the liberties of the individual. One of the few countervailing pressures has been the libertarian tendency of the Supreme Court to construe the Bill of Rights and the Fourteenth Amendment broadly in behalf of accused individuals, racial and religious minorities, the impoverished and ignorant, and political radicals and dissenters. The Court's new majority bloc made up mostly of Nixon appointees may be bringing that tendency to an end." After discussing the possible consequences of the Supreme Court decision - such as: "Prosecutors will find it easier to get convictions in cases which now end in hung juries" - the editorial urges the country to hope that the effects will not prove "destructive of individual rights."

This means that we must fight the world's drift toward statism by protecting the individual rights of criminals.

(Don't remind me that an accused person is not necessarily a criminal and that he must be protected against unjust accusations. The rights of the accused are not a primary - they are a consequence derived from a man's inalienable, individual rights. A consequence cannot survive the destruction of its cause. What good will it do you to be protected in the rare emergency of a false arrest, if you are treated as the rightless subject of an unlimited government in your daily life?)

A mawkish sentimentality toward criminals, coupled with a brutal cruelty toward innocent citizens, is not a new phenomenon. In my review of The Language of Dissent by Lowell B. Mason (The Objectivist Newsletter, August 1963), I wrote: "Mr. Mason makes a profoundly important observation: whenever a country's criminal laws are more lenient than its civil laws, it means that the country is accepting the basic principle of statism and is moving toward a totalitarian state. (Such a trend means that crimes against individuals are regarded as negligible, while the collectivist concept of 'Crimes against the State' becomes paramount and supersedes all rights.) In Soviet Russia, he points out, criminals were treated 'with tolerance and circumspection. On the other hand, those accused of violating the state's political and economic commands were sentenced to death or exiled to Siberia without any semblance of trial as we know the word here in America.'"

Now observe the odd assortment of individuals whose rights and liberties are singled out by the Times editorial for special protection. "Racial and religious minorities," as well as "political radicals and dissenters," should find it offensive to be lumped with "the impoverished and ignorant" and the (probably) criminal. The obvious question is: What about the rights and liberties of the honest, the educated, the self-supporting, the majority? The answer is that the assortment is dictated by and represents a confession of altruism's essence: it is only suffering, weakness, failure, default - real or imaginary, spiritual or material or numerical or moral - that entitle men to rights, liberties and public concern; happiness, strength, success, virtue do not.

In a cultural atmosphere of this sort, who can find any inspiration or desire to preserve his moral integrity? The signs of moral deterioration are all around us. But, to the great credit of this country, most people, so far, have not given up.

(To be continued.)

Ayn Rand

OBJECTIVIST CALENDAR

Starting on September 15, the taped lectures of Dr. Leonard Peikoff's course, Introduction to Logic, will be given in Boston. For further information, contact Frank Peseckis, (617) 261-2491 (after September 3).

B.W.

The Ayn Rand Letter, published fortnightly by The Ayn Rand Letter, Inc., 183 Madison Avenue, New York, N.Y. 10016.
Contributing Editor: Leonard Peikoff; Subscription Director: Elayne Kalberman; Production Manager: Barbara Weiss.

Vol. III, No. 14 April 8, 1974

MORAL INFLATION

Part III

The ideologues of altruism have miscalculated in regard to this country. Materially, they have obtained more than they could hope to extort from any other, poorer nation. Spiritually, they have failed: they mistook generosity for guilt; the guilt-infection did not take hold. Men who live on an earned income are not likely to accept an unearned guilt.

Since the inflation of altruism has not breached the American people's basic self-esteem, the altruists are now trying to revive the grotesque, anti-moral absurdity of original sin - i.e., of prenatal guilt - in a secular form. Having failed to induce personal guilt, they are struggling to induce *racial* guilt - by proclaiming that people must suffer and pay for the (alleged) sins of their fathers.

This prehistorical notion requires more than the destruction of morality. It requires the obliteration of all the concepts which centuries of growing civilization struggled to identify: reason, individualism, personal integrity (and *person*), volition, choice, responsibility, language, understanding, and human communication.

The inversion of all standards - the propagation of racism as anti-racist, of injustice as just, of immorality as moral, and the reasoning behind it, which is worse than the offenses - is flagrantly evident in the policy of preferential treatment for minorities (i.e., racial quotas) in employment and education. (See my essay on "Racism" in *The Virtue of Selfishness*.) If there is a quicker way to destroy people than by preaching brotherly love while spreading blind, interracial hatred, you name it.

The most eloquent example of that policy is the DeFunis case.

In 1971, Marco DeFunis, Jr., a Phi Beta Kappa, *magna cum laude* graduate of the University of Washington in Seattle, was denied admission to the University's Law School. The school accepted 275 out of 1600 applicants (for an eventual class of 150). They were chosen mainly on the basis of special tests which purported to give a student's "Predicted First Year Average," estimating his ability to succeed in law school - and, in part, on the basis of various other considerations. Four racial minority groups - Black, Chicano, American Indian, and Filipino - were singled out for preferential treatment; their applications were processed separately and differently from all the others. I quote from

Justice Douglas's opinion in a subsequent Supreme Court decision: "Thirty-seven minority applicants were admitted under this procedure. Of these, 36 had Predicted First Year Averages below DeFunis' 76.23, and 30 had averages below 74.5, and thus would ordinarily have been summarily rejected by the Chairman....What places this case in a special category is the fact that the school did not choose one set of criteria but two, and then determined which to apply to a given applicant on the basis of his race."

DeFunis sued the University of Washington, claiming that he was a victim of "reverse discrimination," that his constitutional rights had been violated and he had been denied the Fourteenth Amendment guarantee of "equal protection of the laws." The Washington trial court upheld his claim and ordered the school to admit him. The school complied, but appealed. The Washington Supreme Court reversed the decision. DeFunis took the case to the U.S. Supreme Court, obtaining a stay which permitted him to attend the Law School until the final disposition of his case.

The case aroused intense public controversy. Various groups and organizations filed friend-of-the-court briefs, supporting DeFunis or opposing him - a greater number of briefs than in any other case in recent history. It was clear to both sides that a crucially important *moral* issue was at stake. The Court announced its decision on April 23, 1974. By that time, DeFunis was completing his last term at the Law School, and the school had agreed to let him graduate, regardless of the Court's decision. This permitted the Supreme Court to avoid judgment on the issue.

It was the Court's *conservative* majority that took advantage of a legal technicality and - in a brief, unsigned opinion - declared the case to be moot, since DeFunis's rights were not affected any longer. The four liberal Justices dissented, objecting to the avoidance of the constitutional issues. Justice Douglas wrote a separate, dissenting opinion of an extremely confusing, inconclusive nature. The moral question was left unanswered.

What is of special significance to this country's public morale and morality, is the kind of argumentation that this case brought forth in advance of the Supreme Court's ruling.

The brief of the B'nai B'rith Anti-Defamation League, filed in support of DeFunis, states: "If the Constitution prohibits exclusion of blacks and other minorities on racial grounds, it cannot permit the exclusion of whites on racial grounds....discrimination on the basis of race is illegal, immoral, unconstitutional, inherently wrong and destructive of democratic society....A racial quota is a device for establishing a status, a caste, determining superiority or inferiority for a class measured by race without regard to individual merit."

This, of course, is unanswerable. The advocates of racial quotas do not attempt to answer it; they ignore it, or worse: they declare that their goal is to end racial discrimination eventually by means of practicing it temporarily. (This is borrowed from the methodology of Marxism, which claims that we can bring the state to wither away eventually by means of establishing a totalitarian dictatorship temporarily. In neither case are we given any indication of *how* such a trick is to be accomplished.)

An article eloquently entitled "Discriminating to end discrimination" (*The*

New York Times Magazine, April 14, 1974) presents a good cross section of arguments offered by both sides of the issue. "Advocates of affirmative action [i.e., of preferential treatment] like to compare the racial situation in America to two runners, one of whom has had his legs shackled for 200 years....Removing the shackles doesn't make the two instantly equal in ability to compete. The previously shackled runner has to be given some advantage in order to compete effectively until he gets his legs into condition." (How? By shackling the fast runner, lowering the standards, and slowing down everyone's running? No answer is given. But it must be mentioned that many intelligent blacks regard this type of argument as a racist insult, which it is.)

The article quotes a woman attorney for some anti-DeFunis groups, who said: "It is now well understood, however, that our society cannot be completely color-blind in the short term if we are to have a color-blind society in the long term." She "argues that a racial classification can only be presumed unconstitutional if it disadvantages a group subject to a history of discrimination or held down by special disabilities. She contends that the 14th Amendment was meant to help powerless, oppressed minorities, and that the white majority needs no such help." (This is altruism superseding and rewriting the Constitution: if you have no special disabilities, you have no rights and no protection of the laws.)

The University of Washington, according to the article, "concedes that some white students may be excluded from law school because of the affirmative-action program, but it maintains that its program is 'necessary' to achieve an 'overriding purpose' - i.e., to increase the number of minority lawyers in the state and the nation...And, the university notes, had it not been for the nation's history of racial discrimination, white students would have had far more students to compete with than they do now."

This type of argument, which modern intellectuals permit themselves to use with growing frequency, is a measure of their growing distance from reality: it consists in changing one factor of a complex situation and assuming that all the rest would remain unchanged. In fact, if racial discrimination hampered the intellectual development of black students, the absence of such discrimination would not have brought more competition to white students, but less: it would have created more universities to satisfy a greater demand (assuming a free economy).

But if projected potentialities are to be equated with actuality, if "might have been" is to be the equivalent of "was," then I submit the following argument: If my grandfather had come to this country and if he had gone into the oil business, he would have given stiff competition to Nelson A. Rockefeller's grandfather and, therefore, Mr. Rockefeller would not be as rich as he is today and, therefore, I demand my constitutional right to half of Mr. Rockefeller's money.

Absurd? Not by today's standards. The grossness of such absurdity did not prevent the broadcast of an editorial which declared: "WCBS Radio endorses the argument of the University of Washington Law School - had it not been for the nation's history of racial discrimination, white students would have far more students to compete with than they do today. Affirmative-action programs that give preference to qualified minorities over more qualified whites may seem unjust, but that injustice pales beside the monstrosities of two centuries of segregation." (May 1, 1974.)

Dr. Alvin Lashinsky, Vice President of the Jewish Rights Council, who broadcast a reply to that editorial, sounded like a welcome voice of sanity: "We utterly condemn what appears to us to be a call by WCBS for retribution - to have children pay for acts their grandfathers committed, and for innocents of other minorities to also suffer only because their skin is white....Excellence of our professions has always been achieved by high standards and the only way to give minorities self-respect is by improving the ability of the poorly qualified through remedial education beforehand, otherwise the finished product may be a poorly qualified physician or lawyer or a poorly skilled surgeon or even a semi-literate clerk or secretary. Does anyone, WCBS or the minorities, really want this?" (May 3, 1974.)

The answer is: Yes - as far as the ideologues of altruism are concerned - that is precisely what they want. They do not want to lift the poorly qualified, but to tear down the competent; they do not want to help the weak, but to destroy the strong. How many of them would admit such motives, even to themselves, I do not know. Observe that the WCBS editorial did not dare openly to demand the rejection of the qualified in favor of the unqualified; it fudged, it spoke of "qualified minorities" versus "more qualified whites," making it a matter of degree - which does not make the injustice any the less vicious.

While the altruists proclaim that the financially or racially handicapped are their chief concern, none of them noticed the fact that DeFunis was doubly handicapped. The admission requirements at the University of Washington Law School (as at most universities) are highly arbitrary: apart from scholastic achievement, the committee considers such factors as "recommendations" from prominent persons or groups (i.e., pull) and a student's "extra-curricular and community activities" (i.e., altruism). "Community activities" are a luxury which DeFunis could not have afforded: his "extra-curricular activity" consisted in working his way through college. And if the persecution suffered by a student's ancestors is grounds for giving him special advantages, DeFunis belongs to the racial minority that suffered the longest, most horrendous record of persecution in history: he is Jewish. So much for the sincerity of the altruists' motives.

Now consider the moral import of their arguments. Observe that the common denominator of their claims is the total absence of the concept of a person. An individual and a group are regarded as interchangeable - and it is instructive to observe the switching. A group can be "shackled for 200 years," an individual cannot - but it is individuals who collect reparations, not the group as a whole. A group, the white majority, must pay for their ancestors' racial discrimination, it is alleged - but it is white individuals who pay, by being denied job and education opportunities, not the group as a whole. It is, allegedly, an "overriding purpose" to increase the number of minority lawyers in the nation - but minority lawyers are individuals, and what is being "overridden"? The rights of other individuals, who are white.

The crass indifference of all such tribal profiteers to the reality of an individual human life, is their most vicious and shocking characteristic. An individual human life is a brief and fragile period of time. If the goal of "reverse discrimination" is a color-blind society in some indeterminate future, what good will it do to DeFunis (and to thousands like him), who is denied a professional education in the brief, irreplaceable years of his youth and finds his plans, his future, his life-course wrecked? Who has the right to do this to him? For the sake of what? For the alleged future benefit of society, i.e., of a large majority of people? But it is for the sake of a minority that he has been sacrificed.

There is no such thing as a collective guilt. A country may be held responsible for the actions of its government and it may be guilty of an evil (such as starting a war) - but then it is a public, not a private, matter and the entire country has to bear the burden of paying reparations for it. The notion of random individuals paying for the sins of an entire country, is an unspeakable modern atrocity.

This country has no guilt to atone for in regard to its black citizens. Certainly, slavery was an enormous evil. But a country that fought a civil war to abolish slavery, has atoned for it on such a scale that to talk about racial quotas in addition, is grotesque. However, it is not for injustices committed by the government that the modern racists are demanding reparations, but for racial prejudice - i.e., for the personal views of private citizens. How can an individual be held responsible for the views of others, whom he has no power to control, who may be his intellectual enemies, whose views may be the opposite of his own? What can make him responsible for them? The answer we hear is: The fact that his skin is of the same color as theirs. If this is not an obliteration of morality, of intellectual integrity, of individual rights, of the freedom of man's mind (and, incidentally, of the First Amendment), you take it from here; I can't - it turns my stomach.

What I am able to discuss is the ancient notion of paying for the sins of one's fathers, and the effect of this notion on morality. Suppose a man leads a decent, responsible life financially: he works hard, lives within his means, plans his future accordingly, and always pays his debts; then, suddenly, he is confronted with a demand that he pay a debt of his father's, contracted before he was born - and he is given to understand that other demands will be sprung on him, for the debts of his grandfather, his great-grandfather, etc. Would he accept it? Would he remain decent, conscientious and hard-working? Or would he blow his savings on one drunken orgy, then drift at the whim of the moment, mooching and chiseling as best he can?

The same is true in the realm of morality. Morality is inseparable from personal choice and personal responsibility. If a man lives conscientiously according to a set of moral principles, then hears that his moral rectitude does not depend on his actions, but on the actions of his ancestors, he will not remain moral for long. He will let himself slide into that cynical, senseless, hopeless gray bog which is today's culture, where floating shapes scowl at him menacingly and hoarse voices screech about "affirmative action."

No, men are not evil by nature - and when evil ideas take over a culture, two factors are responsible: the absence of good ideas, and force. Just as financial inflation is caused by the government, so is moral inflation. The government is destroying the people's morality by many forms of injustice, which include such things as forcing racial quotas on schools and business concerns. As the Times Magazine article explains in regard to the DeFunis case: "H.E.W. [Department of Health, Education and Welfare] was leaning hard on the university for alleged noncompliance with affirmative action in campus hiring. The university, like 2,500 other institutions of higher learning in the United States, holds Government grants and contracts and thus is required by Federal law to institute 'goals and timetables' for hiring more women and minorities on its faculty." (So much for the notion of the government granting subsidies to education without strings attached, i.e., without affecting the schools' intellectual freedom.)

The next time you hear a politician deplore the moral decline of this country, remember (and, perhaps, remind him) that if one wants to preserve a nation's morality, one must set up conditions of existence in which moral behavior is rewarded, not punished - and that this cannot be done on an altruist basis: after centuries of moral inflation, the balloon of altruism has burst.

Ayn Rand

P.S. This _Letter_ was written later than the date that appears on its heading.

OBJECTIVIST CALENDAR

On Sunday, October 20, Ayn Rand will give a talk at The Ford Hall Forum in Boston. Time: 8 P.M. Place (new location): Alumni Hall, Northeastern University, 360 Huntington Ave. The title of the talk will be announced later. (Advance tickets are not available. On past occasions, the auditorium was filled to capacity, and many people had to be turned away. If you plan to attend, we suggest that you arrive at Alumni Hall far in advance of 7:30 P.M., when the doors open.)

The following starting dates have been scheduled for Dr. Leonard Peikoff's taped courses. _Founders of Western Philosophy: Thales to Hume_. Nashville, September 18 (contact R. Paul Drake, 615-322-4465, after 7:30 P.M.). _Introduction to Logic_. South Chicago, September 29, and North Chicago, October 3 (Dr. Douglas Mayfield, 312-649-4400, days or 312-787-9836, eves.); Toronto, October 2 (Edmund West, 416-661-1777, after 8 P.M.); Providence, October 5 (Bill Dawkins, 401-331-4346, eves.).

Correction: The course that will begin in Boston on September 15 is _Founders of Western Philosophy: Thales to Hume_ (Frank Peseckis, 617-261-2491, after September 3).

A reminder: The opening lecture of Allan Blumenthal's course, _Music: Theory, History and Performance_, will be given on Tuesday, September 17, 7:30 P.M., at the Statler Hilton Hotel, 7th Ave. at 33rd St., New York City. Visitors may attend this lecture, space permitting; admission is $7.50.

B.W.

The Ayn Rand Letter, published fortnightly by The Ayn Rand Letter, Inc., 183 Madison Avenue, New York, N.Y. 10016.

Contributing Editor: **Leonard Peikoff**; Subscription Director: **Elayne Kalberman**; Production Manager: **Barbara Weiss.**

Vol. III, No. 15 April 22, 1974

IDEAS V. MEN

In my Letter of February 25, 1974, under the title "Ideas v. Goods," I discussed a Time magazine story about a lecture by Professor Ronald H. Coase, advocating government control of the press. Thereafter, I received several interesting letters on the subject. They may be summarized by two representative excerpts:

Declaring that I have made "a disastrous error," one letter says: "The error consisted in trusting the veracity of Time's account of the talk...Time's account was disgracefully inaccurate, and in fact represented Coase's thesis as having been precisely the opposite of what it was."

The other letter says: "Your article on Coase was brilliant....I have the text of his speech - it is far more evil than the Time summary."

This great a difference of opinion about the same story, was intriguing. So I read the full text of Mr. Coase's lecture, which was published in the May 1974 issue of The American Economic Review, under the title "The Market for Goods and the Market for Ideas." The lecture was originally delivered at a meeting of the American Economic Association, as part of a discussion devoted to "The Economics of the First Amendment."

Of the two letters I quoted, the second one is right. If the Time summary erred at all, it erred on the side of kindness to Mr. Coase: it imparted dignity to his lecture by presenting it as if it were the forthright advocacy of a specific viewpoint. But it wasn't. The reporter got the message, however; what he omitted was the deviousness of the form.

Mr. Coase did not say that *he* favors government control of the press. He structured his talk in the form of a question mark, as if he were merely presenting an issue raised by others, to be mulled over and resolved by others - while *his* part was confined to piling up the kind of evidence that could lead to only one conclusion: the one reached by the Time reporter.

Mr. Coase states his thesis as follows: "What is the general view that I will be examining? It is that, in the market for goods, government regulation is desirable whereas, in the market for ideas, government regulation is undesirable and should be strictly limited." He challenges this "ambivalence" and states (later): "I do not believe that this distinction between the market for goods and the market for ideas is valid. There is no fundamental difference between these two markets and, in deciding on public policy with regard to them, we need to take into account the same considerations."

If this is his thesis, how does Mr. Coase proceed to discuss it? Presumably for the sake of argument, he accepts all the arguments advocating government regulation of the market for goods, or he takes such arguments as an unchallenged given, and applies them to the market for ideas. Does he do it facetiously? No, in dead earnest. Does he reduce those arguments to absurdity? No, he makes them sound plausibly and easily applicable to the market for ideas. Does he use that method to dramatize the impracticality or the evil of government regulation? No, he suggests that such regulation would be more desirable in the market for ideas than in the market for goods.

Mr. Coase begins his attack on the dichotomy, not by defending the market for goods, but by denouncing "the peculiar status of the market for ideas." He seems to regard the importance which men attach to the freedom of the mind as inexplicable, and seeks for an explanation. He quotes from an article by Aaron Director, who quotes a statement by Justice William O. Douglas in a Supreme Court opinion: "free speech, free press, free exercise of religion are placed separate and apart; they are above and beyond the police power; they are not subject to regulation in the manner of factories, slums, apartment houses, production of oil and the like." Mr. Coase's own comment on this quotation is: "a statement which is no doubt intended as an interpretation of the First Amendment, but which obviously embodies a point of view not dependent on constitutional considerations." (?!)

"Director remarks of the attachment to free speech that it is 'the only area where *laissez-faire* is still respectable.' Why should this be so? In part, this may be due to the fact that belief in a free market in ideas does not have the same roots as belief in the value of free trade in goods. To quote Director again: 'The free market as a desirable method of organizing the intellectual life of the community was urged long before it was advocated as a desirable method of organizing its economic life. The advantage of free exchange of ideas was recognized before that of the voluntary exchange of goods and services in competitive markets.'" Mr. Coase seems to regard this as a historical accident or a matter of tradition. He does not see or mention the fact that the demand for freedom of ideas *had to* precede freedom of trade, that without the heroic struggle of those who fought for a free market in ideas, no such thing as a free market in goods would or could have been discovered.

That he does not see it, is indicated in his next paragraph: "For most people in most countries (and perhaps in all countries), the provision of food, clothing, and shelter is a good deal more important than the provision of the 'right ideas,' even if it is assumed that we know what they are." Obviously, Mr. Coase does not know and does not care to know what they are - nor does he care to observe that the food, clothing and shelter of most people in all countries depend on certain philosophical ideas and vanish when those ideas vanish. It is not on the basis of *Time*'s alleged "inaccuracy" that I accuse the conservatives of anti-intellectuality.

"...the difference in view about the role of government in these two markets," Mr. Coase goes on, "is really quite extraordinary and demands an explanation. It is not enough merely to say that the government should be excluded from a sphere of activity because it is vital to the functioning of our society....The paradox is that government intervention which is so harmful in the one sphere becomes beneficial in the other....What is the explanation for the paradox?"

And now, his manner implying the approach of the new, the startling, the daringly original ("Director's gentle nature does not allow him to do more than hint at it...I would put the point more bluntly"), Mr. Coase reveals the notion he regards as sufficiently explanatory: "The market for ideas is the market in which the intellectual conducts his trade. The explanation of the paradox is self-interest and self-esteem. Self-esteem leads the intellectuals to magnify the importance of their own market. That others should be regulated seems natural, particularly as many of the intellectuals see themselves as doing the regulating. But self-interest combines with self-esteem to ensure that, while others are regulated, regulation should not apply to them. And so it is possible to live with these contradictory views about the role of government in these two markets. It is the conclusion that matters. It may not be a nice explanation, but I can think of no other for this strange situation."

Observe that an alleged defender of capitalism regards self-interest as a base motive, and uses the word "self-esteem" as a pejorative term.

What follows is columns and columns devoted to denouncing the sins of the American and British press, some of which is true, some too trivial to bother about, all of it held together by an intense hostility and prefaced by the statement: "If we examine the actions and views of the press, they are consistent in only one respect: they are always consistent with the self-interest of the press." (I wish this were true; if it were, New York City would still have eight newspapers, instead of the present three; five of them committed suicide by advocating or compromising with the public policies that killed them.) If the purpose of Mr. Coase's talk was to fight government control of business by showing that the extension of such control to the press would be a calamity, can that purpose be achieved by presenting the press as so irresponsible and unscrupulous that an innocent bystander would begin to wish for government control?

But the issue goes deeper than that. Mr. Coase's hostility is not directed merely at modern journalists: it is directed at man's mind as such and at the mind's demand for freedom. A revolting sequence, which Time generously omitted, begins with: "There has surely never been a more high-minded scholar than John Milton. As his Areopagitica 'for the liberty of unlicensed printing' is probably the most celebrated defense of the doctrine of freedom of the press ever written, it seemed to me that it would be worthwhile to examine the nature of his argument for a free press." He quotes from Milton: "Give me the liberty to know, to utter, and to argue freely according to conscience, above all liberties" - and he quotes a series of other passages from Milton, which are beautiful, eloquent and unanswerable.

Mr. Coase's answer is: "In the formation of Milton's views, self-interest may perhaps have played a part, but there can be little doubt that his argument embodies a good deal of intellectual pride..." There follows Mr. Coase's sarcastic, inaccurate paraphrase of Milton's arguments: "The writer is a learned man, diligent and trustworthy. The licenser [censor] would be ignorant, incompetent, and basely motivated, perhaps 'younger' and 'inferior in judgment.' The common man always chooses truth as against falsehood" - and Mr. Coase's conclusion: "The picture is a little too one-sided to be wholly convincing."

No, Mr. Coase does not say that he favors government regulation of the press. He merely suggests that in all the history of thought, from a great classic on down, no valid argument for a free press has ever been offered.

As to Mr. Coase's view of man and of man's nature: "In all markets, producers have some reasons for being honest and some for being dishonest; consumers have some information but are not fully informed or even able to digest the information they have; regulators commonly wish to do a good job, and though often incompetent and subject to the influence of special interests, they act like this because, like all of us, they are human beings whose strongest motives are not the highest." (E.g., such low-grade motives as self-interest, self-esteem and intellectual pride.)

In case any listener missed the implications of his foggier statements, Mr. Coase permits himself an explicit one: "My argument is that we should use the same approach for all markets when deciding on public policy. In fact, if we do this and use for the market for ideas the same approach which has commended itself to economists for the market for goods, it is apparent that the case for government intervention in the market for ideas is much stronger than it is, in general, in the market for goods."

To prove this, Mr. Coase lists a number of examples, applying to the market for ideas the arguments used by economists to justify government intervention in the market for goods. He succeeds: granting the unchallenged premises of the arguments, the list is a veritable arsenal for statists. E.g.: "Or consider the question of consumer ignorance which is commonly thought to be a justification for government intervention. It is hard to believe that the general public is in a better position to evaluate competing views on economic and social policy than to choose between different kinds of food. [This particular bit of argumentation was picked up and mentioned, without rebuttal, by the three press reports that I have read.] Yet there is support for regulation in the one case but not in the other."

In the concluding paragraph of his lecture, Mr. Coase states that "there remains the question of which policies would be, in fact, the most appropriate. ...I do not believe that we will be able to form a judgment in which we can have any confidence unless we abandon the present ambivalence about the performance of government in the two markets and adopt a more consistent view. We have to decide whether the government is as incompetent as is generally assumed in the market for ideas, in which case we would want to decrease government intervention in the market for goods, or whether it is as efficient as it is generally assumed to be in the market for goods, in which case we would want to increase government regulation in the market for ideas. Of course, one could adopt an intermediate position - a government neither as incompetent and base as assumed in the one market nor as efficient and virtuous as assumed in the other. In this case, *we ought to reduce the amount of government regulation in the market for goods and might want to increase government intervention in the market for ideas*. I look forward to learning which of these alternative views will be espoused by my colleagues in the economics profession." (Emphasis added.)

Can there be any doubt as to which of these alternative views will be espoused by most of Mr. Coase's colleagues on the basis of his lecture? Men committed to statism will not be stopped by the fear of propounding a logical contradiction; but if they choose to be consistent, they will leap at the opportunity to extend government regulation to the market for ideas - particularly since Mr. Coase has provided them with the ammunition by formulating all the arguments they need, in terms of their own premises.

The tone of the lecture gives the impression that Mr. Coase does not care about the issue one way or the other: it is the tone of a speaker taking pleasure, not in presenting his topic, but in outwitting his audience. The lecture is not an open advocacy: it is a futile *threat*. It says to the liberals, in effect: If you don't let up on the controls of business, we conservatives will turn the tables on you and introduce government controls of the press. Such escalation of controls has been the policy of conservatives in regard to antitrust laws, labor legislation, the military draft, taxation, the "negative income tax," etc.

Mr. Coase does not seem to understand that the statist liberals would be delighted to let him do their dirty work for them and that they would be first to pounce upon the jobs of censors - as has been the case in every other instance of conservatives trying to cash in on the liberals' premises. Nor does he seem to see that at a time like the present, in the face of statism's triumphant advance, one does not play games, parlor tricks, or rhetorical in-jokes with an issue such as freedom of the press.

If the liberation of the market for goods was Mr. Coase's purpose, why didn't he reverse his method? Why didn't he take the best arguments for the freedom of the market of ideas and demonstrate that they apply to the market of goods? Think of how different the impact of his lecture would have been. But Mr. Coase is contemptuous of the arguments for the freedom of the market of ideas.

It is interesting to note that *The Wall Street Journal* (January 11, 1974) came to the defense of Mr. Coase against the critique of his lecture in *Time* magazine. "...it seems to us that *Time* entirely missed the point of the professor's thesis, which is that there should be no distinction 'between the market for goods and the market for ideas.'" (*Time* did not miss the thesis: they saw through it.) And: "While we don't subscribe to the professor's undiluted brand of laissez faire [this is in reference to his reputation], and see a usefulness to society in libel laws and pure food and drug acts, we see merit of another sort in the Coase thesis. It's not really a long step to argue that just as consumers need government help in choosing among competing goods, they need assistance in choosing between good ideas and bad. Given the hypothetical situation of a United States that controls every facet of economic life but that of the press, who can doubt that the press too would fall like a feeble domino?" The rest of the piece goes the same way, substituting threats for principles.

By contrast, *The New York Times*'s report on the same lecture was like a breath of fresh air (December 23, 1973). It was written by Leonard Silk, who is, I believe, a liberal. "In a sense, the First Amendment is the finest and perhaps the last flower of the liberal revolutions of the 17th and 18th centuries. Economists, like other intellectuals, cling to it as a defense against tyranny." When I read that paragraph, I felt as if I were emerging from a dank cave where concrete-bound children whimper about the "good" or the "bad" character of government officials, to a hillside where adults are still able to deal with abstractions and to remember the concept "tyranny." It was not an unblemished hillside, there were patches of dangerous fog - such as the contention that newspapermen and broadcasters "still insist upon their *unique* right to freedom from government regulation" (emphasis added) - but what a relief it was to hear a man say that government controls represent *tyranny*, and not a matter of efficient or inefficient functioning!

The worst error of the non-totalitarian liberals is their failure to understand that material production depends on man's mind and requires freedom, just as intellectual production does. But, at least, they retain some (implicit) inkling of the existence of a faculty such as the mind - as against the sort of conservatives who propose to save freedom by seeking an explanation for the "incomprehensible" importance which men attach to the freedom of ideas (and finding the explanation in human "imperfections," such as intellectual pride).

This brings us to the common denominator uniting Mr. Coase, *The Wall Street Journal*, and those readers who wrote to me in defense of Mr. Coase.

As I have pointed out many times, those who discard abstractions and principles, i.e., philosophy, discard the conceptual level of their consciousness; they confine themselves to the perceptual level, are able to deal only with immediate concretes, and are compelled to substitute men for ideas. Hence the preposterous spectacle of a scholarly economist who, denying the importance of ideas, offers the childish, cracker-barrel notion of conceit and material greed as the motive power of men's struggle for intellectual freedom throughout history; and, denying the relevance of morality to economics, resorts to the crudest kind of conventional morality, takes for granted that self-interest is evil, and presents the issue of government controls as a matter of the personal honesty or dishonesty, the good or bad character of government officials.

The same kind of problem affected the listeners who were taken in by his lecture. They did not focus on the speech, but on the speaker: since he was known as a defender of free enterprise, they assumed that anything he said was in defense of freedom. They listened selectively, in snatches, trusting the superior knowledge of the "leader," hearing only what they wanted to hear, ignoring the rest. This means that they were listening emotionally - and, in this respect, the speech did give them what they wanted: it fed their smoldering hostility toward the liberal-dominated press, and this made them feel certain that they had heard a defense of free enterprise. But emotions are not tools of cognition, and negative emotions less so than any others. It has been said that the enemies of our enemies are not necessarily our friends. But this is an abstract statement, which the unphilosophical mentality can neither grasp nor remember.

There is, however, a valuable lesson in Mr. Coase's lecture for those young people who, being desperately anxious to fight statism, are willing to form a united front with any of its alleged opponents. That lecture might help them to see why there is no way to fight a political or economic battle while by-passing philosophy, why there is no shortcut, no escape from fundamental principles - and why an indiscriminate activism will not merely fail, but will hasten the victory of the enemy.

Ayn Rand

OBJECTIVIST CALENDAR

Starting on October 29, the taped lectures of Dr. Leonard Peikoff's course, Introduction to Logic, will be given in Winnipeg. For further information, contact Ellen Moore, (204) 253-1630.

B.W.

The Ayn Rand Letter, published fortnightly by The Ayn Rand Letter, Inc., 183 Madison Avenue, New York, N.Y. 10016.

Contributing Editor: **Leonard Peikoff**; Subscription Director: **Elayne Kalberman**; Production Manager: **Barbara Weiss.**

Vol. III, No. 16 May 6, 1974

Philosophy, today, is a dead science, like one of those dead towns that can still be found in the West: a single street, leading nowhere, with gusts of wind and sand whistling through the empty eye sockets of broken windows, flapping the shreds of an awning against a crumbling doorway, battering the rotted, paintless walls, erasing the last of the letters that had once been signs announcing a general store or a saloon, the signs of human activity, life and hope - and, in the distance, the black hole of an abandoned gold mine.

Like that dead town, philosophy, in its present state, has only a historical interest to offer - a record of what men had thought once, since they do not engage in that activity any longer. The vast majority of philosophy's present representatives are only random derelicts who seek refuge in those abandoned ruins on a rainy night and then drift on, leaving nothing behind but an occasional empty beer can.

For most people today, the cardinal problem is confusion: they are unable to understand one another, or their cultural leaders, or their government's policies, or the direction in which this country is moving - or what is the matter with the whole world and how it got that way. Life is becoming too complex and too precarious, they cry, to worry about philosophical theories, which are of no practical consequence and have no power to affect human existence.

Those who want to recapture a glimmer of understanding, should read the following excerpt from Dr. Leonard Peikoff's forthcoming book, The Ominous Parallels, to be published by Weybright and Talley, Inc. (We have omitted the footnote references for quoted material; these will appear in the book.) This excerpt is a theoretical presentation of the philosophy of pragmatism; it reads like a journalistic report on the mental state of today's leaders - like a frightening dissection, diagnosis and explanation of current newspaper headlines.

Do you hear it said that men don't think? Read what their thinkers have taught them. Do you hear it said that ideas are impotent? See whether you recognize the ideas that hang like a gray smog over today's cultural wastelands. Do you hear it said that men cannot be consistent? Observe with what rigid consistency they have carried out the commandments of the philosophy they absorbed. Do you hear it said that nobody wants to die for an ideal? Observe that those who say it are dying for the most vicious of notions.

In my Letter of January 14, 1974, I wrote: "The men who are not interested in philosophy need it most urgently: they are most helplessly in its power." Such men should realize that their lives are not in the power of living malefactors any longer, but in the power of ghosts - the ghosts that wail in the wind of the abandoned town they killed.

Ayn Rand

PRAGMATISM VERSUS AMERICA

By Leonard Peikoff

The original American system of government - capitalism - continued to function through most of the nineteenth century. No matter how hampered and, progressively, contradicted, the system was sustained by the remnants of the Enlightenment heritage still embedded in the American mind. Those remnants could not, however, hold out indefinitely: the philosophy of the Enlightenment, which gave birth to the United States, had never had a proper foundation or defense, and was profoundly undercut by the unremitting attacks of the nineteenth-century intellectuals. By the end of the century, the American system was hanging by a thread - which was promptly cut. A new philosophy swept the intellectuals and then the country.

This philosophy was _pragmatism_, its leading exponents were William James and John Dewey, and its message to a nation on the threshold of abandoning the fundamental principles of the Founding Fathers, was: There are no principles.

Pragmatism represents a continuation of the central ideas of Kant and Hegel - with an added twist of its own. Pragmatism is _German metaphysical idealism_, given an _activist_ development.

Kant and Hegel had launched a massive attack on the concept of external, independent reality. Such a reality, said Kant, is unknowable; no, said Hegel, it is non-existent. The nature of thought, both concluded, must be radically reconceived: it is not the function of thought to grasp the facts of a universe which exists independent of mind.

Pragmatism agrees. The mind, Dewey insists, is _not_ a "spectator"; knowledge - any kind of knowledge, whether in science or in ethics - is _not_ "a disclosure of reality, of reality prior to and independent of knowing..."; it is not "a revelation of antecedent existences or Being." "The business of thought," he says, "is not to conform to or reproduce the characters already possessed by objects..."

The business of thought, Kant had said, is to construct, out of the data it receives, a universe of its own making - the physical (phenomenal) world. The business of thought (the Absolute thought), Hegel had said, is to produce a universe out of itself, by its own operations. The essence of mind, both concluded, is not to be a perceiver of reality, but to be the _creator_ of reality. This is the heart of German idealism - and this is the heart of the pragmatist metaphysics.

Men, the pragmatists allow, do receive some kind of data on which their thought operates. These data, however - which the pragmatists call "experience" - do not represent a firm, "antecedent" reality to be identified by man, but an unformed, amorphous material to be shaped, molded, _changed_ by man. The function of thought is not to "spectate," but - to use Dewey's term - actively to "reconstruct" this material, i.e., to impose a specific character on it, and thereby to bring a definite reality into existence.

Reality, the pragmatists state, is not "fixed and complete in itself"; it is not "ready-made"; in itself, it is "unfinished," "plastic," "in the making," "malleable," "problematic," "indeterminate." Hegel, therefore, is wrong on this point: apart from thought, according to pragmatism, there _is_ some sort of realm. Kant, however, is wrong also: this realm is not definite but unknowable - it is not anything specific. In itself, reality is a spread of something - _without identity_; something - which is nothing in particular.

The spread, on this view, is not infinitely malleable. Sometimes, the pragmatists observe, the data man receives prove intractable, and man fails in his attempted "reconstruction" of reality. _Why_ this should be - how it is possible for nothing-in-particular to be recalcitrant - pragmatism does not say. (Any explanation would have to refer to the "antecedent" nature of reality, a concept which pragmatism rejects.) _When_ success or failure in reshaping reality will occur, no one - according to pragmatism - can know in advance. In each situation, all one can do is try and see. Thought is "experimental," the pragmatists state - and the essence of the experiment is the attempt to discover whether, in any particular case, the malleable material will or will not yield to man's demands.

Kant and Hegel, each in his own way, had imposed certain limitations on the operation of the mind, holding that, although mind is the creator of reality, the mind nevertheless has its own inner nature and fixed principles of functioning, which it has to obey. Pragmatism disagrees. Dispensing with all "rigidity," all principles, all necessary laws, whether of reality or of the mind, the pragmatists proclaim the final climax of the idealist view: human beings, they hold, are free to select their own thought processes and patterns, in accordance with their own unrestricted choice; they are free to "experiment" with any form or method of thought which they can imagine or concoct - and, therefore, they are free to attempt to create whatever reality they choose, no holds barred.

Is there anything to function as a guide to men in their selection of a pattern of thought? Yes, answers pragmatism, the guide is: the demands of _action_. Human thought, on this view, is nothing but a practical "tool," an "instrument" to facilitate human action, and its content is to be judged, not by reference to reality (or to any laws of its own), but by the criterion applicable to any tool: Does it satisfy the purposes for which it was created? Does it "work"?

In the normal course of affairs, the pragmatists elaborate, men do not - and need not - think; they merely act - by habit, by routine, by unthinking impulse. But, in certain situations, the malleable material of reality suddenly asserts itself, and habit proves inadequate: men are unable to achieve their goals, their action is blocked by obstacles, and they begin to experience frustration, tension, trouble, doubt, "dis-ease." This, according to pragmatism, is when men should resort to the "instrument" of thought. And the goal of the thought is to "reconstruct" the situation so as to escape the trouble, alleviate the tension, remove the obstacles, and resume the normal process of unimpeded (and unthinking) action.

Toward this end, the mind formulates an "idea" - which is, according to Dewey, simply a "plan to _act_ in a certain way as the way to arrive at the clearing up of a specific situation." If the plan, when acted on, removes the frustration; if the reshaping of reality succeeds; if, in Dewey's words, "existences, following upon the action rearrange or readjust themselves in the way the idea intends" - then the idea is true, pragmatically true; if not, then the idea is (pragmatically) false. The ruling epistemological standard, therefore, is consequences in action. "[An idea's] active, dynamic function is the all-important thing about it," writes Dewey, "and in the quality of activity induced by it lies all its truth and falsity."

Since consequences in action determine truth (and since the success of man's "experiments" to reshape reality cannot be predicted), the truth of an idea, according to pragmatism, cannot be known in advance of action. The pragmatist does not expect to know, prior to taking an action, whether or not his "plan" will "work." He accepts, in Dewey's words, "the fundamental idea that we know only after we have acted and in consequences of the outcome of action."

Aristotle (and the Enlightenment shaped by his philosophy) had held that reality exists prior to and independent of human thought - and that human thought precedes human action; man, he held, must first grasp the appropriate facts and laws of reality; on this basis, he can then set the goals and determine the course of his action. Pragmatism represents a total reversal of this progression. For the pragmatist, the order is: man acts; he invents forms of thought to satisfy the needs of his action; reality adapts itself accordingly (except when, inexplicably, it resists). First, action - second, thought - third, reality.

On such a view, there is nothing (in thought or reality) to impose any fixed pattern on the course of human action. Men's actions, according to pragmatism, are subject to perpetual change, in every respect, as and when men so decide - and, therefore, so is thought, so is truth, so is reality. Men not only make reality, on this view; they make it and then, when the demands of their action change in character, they remake it according to a new pattern, until, suddenly blocked and "dis-eased," they discard that pattern and "experiment" with a new model, and so on without end.

In the whirling Heraclitean flux which is the pragmatist's universe, there are no absolutes. There are no facts, no fixed laws of logic, no certainty, no objectivity.

There are no facts - only provisional "hypotheses" which, for the moment, facilitate human action. There are no fixed laws of logic - only subjective, mutable, pragmatic "conventions," without any basis in reality. (Aristotle's logic, Dewey remarks, worked so well for earlier cultures that it is now overdue for a replacement.) There is no certainty - the very quest for it, says Dewey, is a fundamental aberration, a "perversion." There is no objectivity - the object is created by the thought and action of the subject. The only question for a pragmatist in this latter regard is: what form of subjectivism to adopt? If reality is created by men - by _which_ men? If truth is that which works satisfactorily in fulfilling the demands of action - _whose_ action? _whose_ satisfaction? works - for _whom_?

William James - characteristically, although not consistently - adopts the personal version of subjectivism. Human actions and purposes, he observes, vary from individual to individual - and, therefore, so does truth. To be true, states James, "means for that individual to work satisfactorily for him; and the working and the satisfaction, since they vary from case to case, admit of no universal description." "...the 'same' predication," writes the pragmatist F.C.S. Schiller, "may be 'true' for me and 'false' for you if our purposes are different."

John Dewey, typifying the dominant wing within the movement, rejects this Jamesian approach; his _social_ version of pragmatist subjectivism represents a more faithful adherence to the ideas of Hegel (whose avowed disciple Dewey had been in the early years of his career). There is, according to Dewey, no such thing as an autonomous individual: human intelligence, he holds, is fundamentally conditioned by the collective thinking of society; the mind is not a "private" phenomenon, it is a social phenomenon. On this view, the pragmatist "reconstructor" of reality is not the individual, but society. Pragmatic truth, accordingly, is that which works - for the group; truth, like thought, is "public"; truth is those hypotheses which facilitate the actions and purposes of the community at large. In Dewey's philosophy, the concept of "public service" is fundamental not merely to ethics: it becomes the ruling standard in epistemology and metaphysics. (Following the practice of Kant and Hegel, Dewey denies that he is a subjectivist; equating the "objective" with the "collective," he insists that his social subjectivism is a defense of objectivity.)

As to ethics: on what, according to pragmatism, are man's value-judgments to be based?

On subjective feeling, answers James, on arbitrary desire or demand, whatever its content. "Any desire," he writes in one of his earlier essays, "is imperative to the extent of its amount; it *makes* itself valid by the fact that it exists at all." Hence, "*the essence of good is simply to satisfy demand*. The demand may be for anything under the sun."

Not so, declares Dewey. Before men act on a desire, he says, they must first evaluate the means required to implement it, and the consequences that will (probably) flow from acting on it. What standard is to guide this evaluation? There are no absolutes, answers Dewey; in each particular situation, in each bout of ethical "dis-ease," men are to evaluate the particular desire at issue, by reference to whatever values they do not choose to question at the time - although any one of these values may be questioned and discarded in the next situation. The test of a desire is its compatibility not with reality, but with the rest of men's desires of the moment. The operative standard, therefore, is feeling. In this way, despite his disclaimers, Dewey's ethical position reduces to that of James. (Dewey regards his version of the pragmatist ethics as the method of being "intelligent," "scientific" and "objective" in regard to value-judgments.)

When pragmatists claim action as the philosophic primary, the deeper meaning of their claim is: *feeling* is the primary, the metaphysical bulwark on which the pragmatist universe is built, the irreducible, all-controlling factor, which determines action, and thus thought, and thus reality. At the core of the pragmatist universe is emotion - raw, unreasoned, blind; or, in the traditional, romanticist terminology, "will."

Qua idealist, pragmatism is an outgrowth of Kant and Hegel; qua activist, it is an outgrowth of the nineteenth-century romanticist tradition, fully accepting that tradition's subjectivism, its anti-intellectualism, its blatant, voluntarist irrationalism. The typical romanticist, however, dismissed reason openly, in favor of feelings. Pragmatism goes one step further: it urges the same dismissal, and calls it a new view of reason.

By itself, as a distinctive theory, the pragmatist ethics is contentless: it urges men to pursue "practicality," but refrains from specifying any "rigid" set of values that could serve to define the concept. As a result, pragmatists - despite their repudiation of all systems and codes of morality - are compelled, if they are to implement their ethical approach at all, to accept and apply in some (usually eclectic) form the value codes formulated by other, non-pragmatist moralists.

The dominant, virtually the only, moral code advocated by modern intellectuals in Europe and in America, is some variant of altruism. This, accordingly, is what the American pragmatists (especially those of the "social" school) routinely accept and preach. Typically, they do not crusade for it (there are no absolutes), or even adhere to it systematically (there is no system); they merely take it for granted as unquestionable, whenever they feel like it - which, given their Kantian-Hegelian schooling, is 90% (or more) of the time.

At one point in his earlier years, however, William James went so far as to elevate the altruist approach into a formal principle: "Since everything which is demanded is by that fact a good," he writes, "must not the guiding principle for ethical philosophy (since all demands conjointly cannot be satisfied in this poor world) be simply to satisfy at all times as many demands as we can [i.e., as many arbitrary demands of as many people as we can]?" This, despite its "rigidity," is the best formulation of the content of American pragmatist ethics, insofar as the latter is capable of fixed formulation. In practice, American pragmatism emerges as a version of Utilitarianism, though without the traditional Utilitarians' commitment to happiness as the absolute value-standard. It is a Utilitarianism whose motto is not: "the greatest happiness of the greatest number," but: "the greatest whims of the greatest number."

(To be continued.)

OBJECTIVIST CALENDAR

The title of Ayn Rand's talk at The Ford Hall Forum in Boston, on October 20, will be: "Egalitarianism and Inflation."

Starting on October 13, the taped lectures of Dr. Leonard Peikoff's course, Modern Philosophy: Kant to the Present, will be given in the San Antonio-Austin area. For further information, contact Dr. Lee Brooks, (512) 684-7565 (eves.).

We have been asked to announce that on Friday, October 11, Joan Mitchell Blumenthal will give a lecture at Hunter College, under the auspices of Hunter College Students of Objectivism. Title: "How Paintings Work." Time: 7:30 P.M. Place: Hunter High School Auditorium, Lexington Ave. between 68th and 69th Sts., New York City. For further information, call Robin Stark, (914) 969-2027 (eves.).

B.W.

The Ayn Rand Letter, published fortnightly by The Ayn Rand Letter, Inc., 183 Madison Avenue, New York, N.Y. 10016.
Contributing Editor: **Leonard Peikoff**; Subscription Director: **Elayne Kalberman**; Production Manager: **Barbara Weiss.**

Vol. III, No. 17 May 20, 1974

PRAGMATISM VERSUS AMERICA

Part II

By Leonard Peikoff

The two points central to the pragmatist ethics are: a formal rejection of all fixed standards - and an unquestioning absorption of the prevailing standards. The same two points constitute the pragmatist approach to politics, which, developed most influentially by Dewey, became the philosophy of the Progressive movement in this country (and of most of its liberal descendants down to the present day).

On the one hand, pragmatism presents itself, politically, as opposed to "rigidity," to "dogma," to "extremes" of any kind, whether capitalist or socialist; it avows that it is relativist, "moderate," "flexible," "experimental." The function of political thought, like that of all thought - says Dewey - is not to formulate general principles for the guidance of human action, but to deal pragmatically with particular social frustrations in a particular situation at a particular time, as and when such occasions arise. Pragmatism, he says, rejects "all social system-making and programs of fixed ends"; it holds that "Wholesale creeds and all-inclusive ideals are impotent in the face of actual situations..." There is, he says, "no antecedent universal proposition" to enable men to decide whether "the functions of a state should be limited or should be expanded." In each concrete case, these functions are to be "experimentally determined."

As in ethics, however, so in politics: the pragmatist is compelled, in practice, to employ some kind of standard to evaluate the results of his social "experiments" - a standard which, given his own self-imposed default, he necessarily absorbs from other, non-pragmatist trend-setters. Dewey virtually admits it, when he declares that "the genuine work of the intellectual class at any period" is not to originate standards or ideals, but "to detect and make articulate the nascent movements of their time" - which means: to take over and propagate whatever standards and ideals have already been launched by earlier intellectuals.

The "nascent movement" when Dewey wrote, the political principle imported from Germany and proliferating in all directions, was: <u>collectivism</u>.

The Enlightenment, states Dewey, is wrong. The traditional liberals (these include Locke and the Founding Fathers) are wrong in their "rigid doctrine of natural rights inherent in individuals independent of social organization." They are wrong in their "conception of natural law as supreme over positive [i.e., state-made] law..." They are wrong in championing "the primacy of the individual over the state..." They are wrong in holding that the individual possessed antecedent "liberties of thought and action...which it was the sole business of the state to safeguard." They are wrong in believing that an expanding government is "the great enemy of individual liberty..." All these ideas, Dewey remarks, were "relevant" once, but none are "immutable truths good at all times and places" - and today, he claims, these "negative" ideas are outdated. Today, we must abandon the Enlightenment's "peculiar idea of personal liberty": "atomistic individualism," laissez-faire capitalism, the concern with private profit and "pecuniary aims," the "regime of individual initiative and enterprise conducted for private gain" - all of it, now, must be discarded.

We must get away from the distinctively American system, says Dewey, because, at root, we must "get away from the inherent conception of the individual as an isolated and independent unit." "The idea of a natural individual in his isolation possessed of full-fledged wants, of energies to be expended according to his own volition, and of a ready-made faculty of foresight and prudent calculation is as much a fiction in psychology as the doctrine of the individual in possession of antecedent political rights is one in politics."

Intelligence, says Dewey, is not "an individual possession"; it is "a social asset and is clothed with a function as public as is its origin..." Hence, "property and reward" are not "intrinsically individual"; since the minds of scientists and industrialists are a collectively created social resource, so is the wealth these minds have made possible. What America needs now, Dewey concludes, is "organized action in behalf of the social interest," "organized planning" of the economy - in short, "some kind of socialism."

He does not, says Dewey, wish to be "dogmatic" in regard to details, but there is, he suggests in several places, a useful model for Americans to emulate. He does not accept the philosophy or tactics of the authors of this model, he is a liberal and a democrat, Dewey insists, but, he states, it is nevertheless true that if Americans were to undertake to implement the pragmatist vision of a planned society, it "would signify that we had entered constructively and voluntarily upon the road which Soviet Russia is traveling with so much attendant destruction and coercion."

He advocates "real liberty" for man, says Dewey, and true opportunity for personal development. He does not reject individualism, he says - only the concepts of an independent individual and of individual rights. (He calls this theory a "new individualism.")

The process of spreading a philosophy by means of free discussion among thinking adults, is long and complex. From Plato to the present, it has been the dream of certain philosophers and social planners to circumvent this process, and, instead, to inject a controversial ideology directly into the plastic, unformed minds of children - by means of seizing a country's educational system and turning it into a vehicle for indoctrination. In this way, one may capture an entire generation, and thus, shortly, a country, without intellectual resistance, in a single _coup d'école_.

Rarely, if ever, has a free nation capitulated to this kind of demand as rapidly, as extensively, as abjectly, as America did. When the country surrendered its educational institutions - in countless forms, direct and indirect, public and private, from nursery school on up - to the legion of Progressive educators spawned, above all, by Dewey, it formally delivered its youth into the hands of the philosophy of pragmatism, to be "reconstructed" according to the pragmatist image of man. It was a development which, in a few decades, created a new intellectual establishment in America: it was the inauguration, in the country of the Enlightenment, of the formal reign of Kant and Hegel, not merely among a handful of intellectuals, but among the leaders of American life in every field.

The goal of the Progressive indoctrinators was not, however, to impose a specific system of ideas on the student, but to destroy his capacity to hold _any_ firm ideas, on any subject.

The theory of Progressive education begins with an all-out assault on the traditional, reality-oriented, intellect-oriented approach to education. For the pragmatist, education is not a process in which knowledge of "antecedent" reality, already accumulated and logically organized by men, is transmitted to the minds of their young. The function of education, writes Dewey, is not to communicate "a ready-made universe of knowledge"; a school is not primarily a place to learn "intellectual lessons"; the "staple of the curriculum" is not to be academic subject matter, not "facts, laws, information," not "various bodies of external fact labeled geography, arithmetic, grammar, etc." The traditional approach was satisfactory, says Dewey, given the traditional assumptions, which are now outdated: "mind was supposed to get its filling by direct contact with the world..." - and men supposed that primary importance was to be ascribed to "the intellectual aspect of our natures..."

According to the Progressives, education is to be not subject-centered, but child-centered. ("We don't teach history, we teach Johnny.") Education is to be "relevant," relevant to the "real interests" of the child - above all, to his interest in "self-expression." His "self," in this context, is his "instincts" and his "spontaneous impulses"; their natural "expression" is: action.

For pragmatism, the child (like the man he fathers) is not primarily a thinking being, but an acting being. He does not learn primarily by "listening" or by reading - he "learns by doing." Since he has not been taught "ready-made" knowledge, his classroom "doings" are to be "experimental." Like the pragmatist man, he learns to resort to thought as a "practical instrument" to enable him to escape the obstacles of the moment, whenever these, inexplicably, occur - and then drops the "instrument" when things are "working" again, as determined by his feelings. Since action is inherently concrete, the child's "doings" are centered around disconnected "projects," which cut across all the lines of traditional academic subjects, but dip briefly - without systematic order or principled organization - into whichever subjects the teacher (or the class) feels are "relevant" to the project of the moment.

Such random bits of information as the child does manage to absorb by this method are not, the Progressives insist, to be presented or accepted as certainties. Above all, the teacher (and the pupils) must not be "authoritarian," but "tentative" and "flexible."

Except on one point. Since group demands, according to Dewey, have metaphysical primacy, the function of the school is not to develop a reality-spirit, or an intellectual spirit, but a "social spirit." Since "mind cannot be regarded as an individual, monopolistic possession," the function of the school is to be a trustbuster: to recondition any aspiring "monopolist" of this kind, i.e., any intellectually independent student, by training him, in Dewey's words, "to share in the social consciousness," i.e., to submit his mind to the demands of the group. The fundamental goal of education, writes Dewey, "is the development of a spirit of social co-operation and community life..."; the goal is to foster the child's "social capacity" - by, among other things, "saturating him with the spirit of service..."

Despite their relativism, the Progressives do feature one absolute, one certainty, one iron thread on which the child's various "doings" and "projects" are strung: *society*, and the imperative of conforming to it. "Life-adjustment," for this movement, means "community-adjustment." The school is to be centered on the child - and the child is to be centered on the collective. This is the "new individualism" translated into the field of education.

And this is still another reason why the child should not concentrate on facts and truths in his years at school: "The mere absorbing of facts and truths," writes Dewey, "is so exclusively individual an affair that it tends very naturally to pass into selfishness. There is no obvious social motive for the acquirement of mere learning, there is no clear social gain in success thereat." In the Progressive school, the child learns something transcending facts, truths and selfishness; the modern Johnny may not be able to read - or add, or spell, or think - but he does learn to serve, to serve others, to adapt to others, to obey their spokesmen. He does not absorb "a ready-made universe of knowledge"; instead, he absorbs a "ready-made," pragmatist contempt for knowledge (and for reason), combined with a "ready-made," "practical" philosophy: altruism, collectivism, statism.

For the most part, the American intellectuals who accepted the philosophy of pragmatism were under few illusions in regard to its meaning or consequences. This was not true, however, of the general public - businessmen included. The American public were led to embrace the pragmatist philosophy not because of its actual, theoretical content (of which they were, and remain, largely ignorant), but because of the method by which that content was presented to them: *in its terminology and promises*, pragmatism is a philosophy calculated to appeal specifically to an American audience.

The method, perfected especially by the Deweyites, consists in describing the philosophy in reverse: the pragmatists adopt the traditional language of science and philosophy, they flaunt the long-established, value-laden words which name the ideas deeply admired by most Americans - and they do it while discarding, and even *inverting*, the meaning of such language. Thus they pose as champions of the very ideas which their own philosophy systematically attacks and repudiates.

The American public, descendants of the era of Enlightenment, wanted a philosophy of this world; dismissing supernaturalism and religion, the Deweyites stress "nature" - and then construe the term as meaning a flux without identity, to be molded by the desires of the group. The Americans wanted a philosophy based on reason; the Deweyites stress "scientific method" and "intelligence" - then, in the name of these, propound a skeptic-voluntarist irrationalism which denies the mind's capacity to grasp reality, abstract principles, or fixed, causal laws. The Americans wanted a philosophy based on facts; the pragmatists stress "experience" - and deny that it yields information about facts. The Americans had little sympathy for self-indulgent wallowing in emotion; the Deweyites denounce "subjectivism" and "sentimentalism" - while raising feelings to a position of philosophic primacy. The Americans admired human self-confidence; the pragmatists stress man's "power" - not his power to know, but to create, reality.

The Americans wanted a morality relevant to life; so do they, say the pragmatists - and disseminate a nihilistic amoralism. The Americans admired individualism; so do they, say the Deweyites - a "new" kind of individualism, which teaches social conformity as the fundamental imperative. The Americans, unbound by agelong traditions, scornful of passive ancestor-worship, were open to new ideas; in every branch of philosophy, the pragmatists stress "experiment," "novelty," "progress" - and offer a rehash of traditional theories culminating in the oldest politics of all: statism. The Americans were unable to stomach the overt mysticism of the post-Kantian Germanic axis in philosophy; the pragmatists present themselves as the exponents of a distinctively "American" philosophic approach - which consists in enshrining the basic premises of such Germanism, while rejecting every fundamental idea, from metaphysics to politics, on which this country was founded. Above all, the Americans wanted ideas to be good for something on earth, to have tangible, practical significance; and, above all, the pragmatists stress "practicality" - which, according to their teachings, consists in action divorced from thought and reality.

The pragmatists stress the "cash value" of ideas. But the Americans did not know the "cash value" of the pragmatist ideas they were buying. They did not know that pragmatism could not deliver on its promise of this-worldly success because, at root, it is a philosophy which does not believe in this - or any - world.

When the Americans flocked to pragmatism, they believed that they were joining a battle to advance <u>their</u> essential view of reality and of life. They did not know that they were being marched in the opposite direction, that the battle had been calculated for a diametrically opposite purpose - or that the enemy they were being pushed to destroy was: themselves.

POSTSCRIPT

The theory of pragmatism, and its practical consequences - which we have to live with and fight against, today - may help you to concretize two issues:

1. The power of philosophy. Even though the American public accepted pragmatism with good intentions and under false pretenses, it is not their good intentions and incoherent hopes that unwary people helped to spread and to put into practice, but the literal meaning of the vicious theories they had never taken seriously nor cared fully to grasp.

2. The importance of a clear, rigidly <u>precise</u> understanding of the philosophical ideas you profess to accept. A superficial glance, a smattering, an approximation, a reliance on a pleasant feeling are disastrous in this realm. You would not sign a contract to buy an automobile on such a basis or written in such terms. A contract to buy philosophical convictions requires much more stringent language: the forfeit is your life.

If you want a current example, consider the following. The biggest mystery of Watergate is not what Richard Nixon did, but what he thought. No enemy could have destroyed him as thoroughly as he destroyed himself: consistently, systematically, he undercut his own case with every successive public statement he made and every step he took, until there was nothing left of him or to him. Yet he was known as a "smart" politician, a clever manipulator, not a man of thought, but of action. Moral issues apart, what happened to his purely practical judgment?

There is a paragraph in the first part of Dr. Peikoff's article, which answers this question. Reading it, I had an eerie feeling, as if a psychologist were describing the nature of Mr. Nixon's thought-processes - yet that paragraph was written over two years ago, about a philosophy originated in the past century:

> In the normal course of affairs, the pragmatists elaborate, men do not - and need not - think; they merely act - by habit, by routine, by unthinking impulse. But, in certain situations, the malleable material of reality suddenly asserts itself, and habit proves inadequate: men are unable to achieve their goals, their action is blocked by obstacles, and they begin to experience frustration, tension, trouble, doubt, "dis-ease." This, according to pragmatism, is when men should resort to the "instrument" of thought. And the goal of the thought is to "reconstruct" the situation so as to escape the trouble, alleviate the tension, remove the obstacles, and resume the normal process of unimpeded (and unthinking) action.

Mr. Nixon's desperate, contradictory, incomprehensible actions were aimed at "reconstructing" the situation (even though it is unlikely that he had ever heard of this particular metaphysical prescription). But the malleable material of reality stubbornly refused to let itself be reconstructed.

This, dear readers, is an example of philosophy's power - of what a particular philosophic theory, pragmatism, did to its most consistent practitioner.

Ayn Rand

OBJECTIVIST CALENDAR

Starting on November 1, the taped lectures of Dr. Leonard Peikoff's course, Founders of Western Philosophy: Thales to Hume, will be given in Minneapolis. For further information, contact Jane Kettleson at (612) 633-4085 (evenings).

B.W.

The Ayn Rand Letter, published fortnightly by The Ayn Rand Letter, Inc., 183 Madison Avenue, New York, N.Y. 10016.

Contributing Editor: **Leonard Peikoff**; Subscription Director: **Elayne Kalberman**; Production Manager: **Barbara Weiss.**

Vol. III, No. 18 June 3, 1974

EGALITARIANISM AND INFLATION

The classic example of vicious irresponsibility is the story of Emperor Nero who fiddled, or sang poetry, while Rome burned. An example of similar behavior may be seen today in a less dramatic form. There is nothing imperial about the actors, they are not one single bloated monster, but a swarm of undernourished professors, there is nothing resembling poetry, even bad poetry, in the sounds they make, except for pretentiousness - but they are prancing around the fire and, while chanting that they want to help, are pouring paper refuse on the flames. They are those amorphous intellectuals who are preaching egalitarianism to a leaderless country on the brink of an unprecedented disaster.

Egalitarianism is so evil - and so silly - a doctrine that it deserves no serious study or discussion. But that doctrine has a certain diagnostic value: it is the open confession of the hidden disease that has been eating away the insides of civilization for two centuries (or longer) under many disguises and cover-ups. Like the half-witted member of a family struggling to preserve a reputable front, egalitarianism has escaped from a dark closet and is screaming to the world that the motive of its compassionate, "humanitarian," altruistic, collectivist brothers is not the desire to help the poor, but to destroy the competent. The motive is hatred of the good for being the good - a hatred focused specifically on the fountainhead of all goods, spiritual or material: the men of ability.

The mental process underlying the egalitarians' hope to achieve their goal, consists of three steps: 1. they believe that that which they refuse to identify, does not exist; 2. therefore, human ability does not exist; and 3. therefore, they are free to devise social schemes which would obliterate this non-existent. Of special significance to the present discussion is the egalitarians' defiance of the law of causality: their demand for equal results from unequal causes - or equal rewards for unequal performance.

As an example, I shall quote from a review by Bennett M. Berger, professor of sociology at the University of California, San Diego (The New York Times Book Review, January 6, 1974). The review discusses a book entitled More Equality by Herbert Gans. I have not read and do not intend to read that book: it is the reviewer's own notions that are particularly interesting and revealing. "[Herbert Gans] makes it clear from the start," writes Mr. Berger, "that he's not talking about equality of opportunity, which almost nobody seems to be against any more, but about equality of 'results,' what used to be called 'equality of condition.'... What he cares most about is reducing inequalities of income, wealth and political power...More equality could be achieved, according to Gans, by income redistribution (mostly through a version of the Credit Income Tax) and by decentralizations of power ranging from more equality in hierarchical organizations (e.g., corporations and universities) to a kind of 'community control' that would provide to those minorities most victimized by inequality some insulation against being consistently outvoted by the relatively affluent majorities of the larger political constituencies."

If being consistently _outvoted_ is a social injustice, what about big businessmen, who are the smallest minority and would always be consistently outvoted by other groups? Mr. Berger does not say, but since he consistently equates economic power with political power, and seems to believe that money can buy anything, one can guess what his answer would be. And, in any case, he is not an admirer of "democracy."

Mr. Berger reveals some of his motivation when he describes Herbert Gans as a "policy scientist" who suffers from a certain "malaise." "Part of this malaise is a nightmare in which 'the policy scientist' - not _poorly_ prepared, but _in full possession_ of the facts, reasons and plans he needs to promote persuasively the changes he advocates... - is frustrated, defeated, humiliated by Congressional committees and executive staffs politically beholden to the constituencies and the patrons who keep them in office." In other words: they did not let him have his way.

Lest you think it is only material wealth that Mr. Berger is out to destroy, consider the following: "Decentralization of power, for example, doesn't necessarily produce more equality...Even the direct democracy of the New England town meeting... does very little to rid the local political community of the excessive influence exercised by the more educated, the more articulate, the more politically hip." This means that the educated and the ignorant, the articulate and the incoherent, the politically active and the passive or inert should have an equal influence and an equal power over everyone's life. There is only one instrument that can create an equality of this kind: a gun.

Mr. Berger stresses that he agrees with Mr. Gans's egalitarian goal, but he doubts that it can be achieved by the open advocacy of more equality. And, with remarkably open cynicism, Mr. Berger suggests "another strategy": "The advocacy of equality inevitably comes into conflict with other liberal values, such as individualism and achievement. But...the advocacy of 'citizenship' does not, and the history of democracy is a history of political struggles to win more and more 'rights' for more and more people to bring ever larger proportions of the population to fully functioning citizenship....in the 20th century there have been struggles to remove racial and sexual impediments...to win rights to decent housing, medical care, education - all on the grounds not of 'equality,' but on the grounds that they are necessary conditions for citizens, equal by definition, to exercise their responsibility to govern themselves. Who knows what 'rights' lie over the horizon: a right to orgasm, to feel beautiful? I think these will make people better citizens." In other words, he suggests that egalitarian goals can be achieved by blowing up the term "citizenship" into a totalitarian concept, i.e., a concept embracing all of life.

If Mr. Berger is that open in advising the setting up of an ideological booby trap, who are the boobs he expects to catch? The underendowed? The general public? Or the intellectuals, whom he tempts with such bait as "a right to orgasm" in exchange for forgetting individualism and achievement? I hope your guess is as good as mine.

I will not argue against egalitarian doctrines by defending individualism, achievement, and the men of ability - not after writing _Atlas Shrugged_. I will let reality speak for me - it usually does.

Under the heading of "Allende's Legacy," an article in _The Wall Street Journal_ (April 19, 1974) offers some concrete, real-life examples of what happens when income, wealth and power are distributed equally among all men, regardless of their competence, character, knowledge, achievement, or brains.

"By the time the military acted to overthrow the Allende government, prices had soared more than 1,000% in two years and were climbing at the rate of 3% a day at the very end. The national treasury was practically empty." The socialist government had seized a number of American-owned industrial firms. The new military government invited the American managements to come back. Most of them accepted.

Among them was the Dow Chemical Company, which owned a plastics plant in Chile. Bob G. Caldwell, Dow's director of operations for South America, came with a technical team to inspect the remains of their plant. "'What we found was unbelievable to us,' he recalls. 'The plant was still operable, but in another six months we wouldn't have had any plant at all. They never checked anything. We found valves that hadn't been maintained leaking corrosive chemicals that would have eventually eaten away practically everything.'...Worse yet, the highly inflammable chemicals handled at the plant were in imminent danger of blowing up. 'Safety went to pot,' Mr. Caldwell says. 'The fire-sprinkler system was disconnected and the valves taken away for some other use outside. Then they were smoking in the most dangerous areas. They told us, "You didn't have any fires while you were here before, so it must not be as dangerous as you said."'"

I submit that the mentality represented by this last sentence, a mentality capable of functioning in this manner, is the loathsomely evil root of all human evils.

Apparently, some mentalities in the new Chilean government belong to the same category: they have the same range and scope, but the consequences of <u>their</u> actions are not so immediately perceivable, though not much farther away. In order to avoid labor disputes, the new government has frozen all labor contracts in the form and on the terms established under the Allende regime. For example, the Dow Company's contract includes a "requirement that all the plant's plastic scrap be given to the union, which then sells it. 'We hope to get that one changed,' a company official says, 'because it's a clear incentive to produce almost nothing but scrap.'"

Then there is the case of a big Santiago textile firm. "Its contract with 1,300 workers virtually guarantees bankruptcy. The textile firm's employes get a certain amount of cloth free as part of their wages and can buy unlimited quantities at a 37% discount; at those prices the firm loses money. Under President Allende the workers sold the cloth on the black market at huge profits, and it was an important factor in assuring their backing for the Allende government."

How long can a company - or a country, or mankind - survive under a policy of this sort? Most people today do not see the answer, but some do. Material shortages are the consequence of another, much more profound shortage, which is created by egalitarian governments and ignored by the public - until it is too late. "Chile's experiment with Marxism has also left the country with a shortage of engineers and technicians that could reach serious proportions. Thousands of them left during the Allende regime. Despite incentives offered by the junta, they haven't been coming back, and many more key people continue to leave for higher-paying jobs abroad....'Here in Chile [says a business executive] we must get used to the fact that good people must be paid well.'"

But here in the United States, we are told to get used to the idea that they must not.

There is no such thing as "good people," cries Professor Berger - or Professor

Gans, or Professor Rawls - and if some are good, it's because they're exploiting those who aren't. There is no such thing as "key people," says Professor Berger, we're all equal by definition. No, says Professor Rawls, some were born with unfair advantages, such as intelligence, and should be made to atone for it to those who weren't. We want more equality, says Professor Gans, so that those who devise sprinkler systems and those who smoke around inflammable chemicals would have equal pay, equal influence, and an equal voice in the community control of science and production.

The term "brain drain" is known the world over: it names a problem which various governments are beginning to recognize, and are trying to solve by chaining the men of ability to their homelands - yet social theoreticians see no connection between intelligence and production. The best among men are running - from every corner and slave-pen of the globe - running in search of freedom. Their refusal to cooperate with slave drivers is the noblest moral action they could take - and, incidentally, the greatest service they could render mankind - but they don't know it. No voices are raised anywhere in their honor, in acknowledgment of their value, in recognition of their importance. Those whose job it is to know - those who profess concern with the plight of the world - look on and say nothing. The intellectuals turn their eyes away, refusing to know - the practical men do know, but keep silent.

One can't blame the dazed brutes of Chile, who swoop down on an industrial plant and cavort at a black-market fiesta, for not understanding that the plant cannot run at a loss - if their social superiors tell them that they are entitled to more equality. One can't blame savages for not understanding that everything has its price, and what they steal, seize or extort today will be paid for by their own starvation tomorrow - if their social superiors, in management offices, in university classrooms, in newspaper columns, in parliamentary halls, are afraid to tell them.

What are all those people counting on? If a Chilean factory goes bankrupt, the equalizers will find another factory to loot. If that other factory starts crumbling, it will get a loan from the bank. If the bank has no money, it will get a loan from the government. If the government has no money, it will get a loan from a foreign government. If no foreign government has any money, all of them will get a loan from the United States.

What they don't know - and neither does this country - is that the United States is broke.

Justice does exist in the world, whether people choose to practice it or not. The men of ability are being avenged. The avenger is reality. Its weapon is slow, silent, invisible, and men perceive it only by its consequences - by the gutted ruins and the moans of agony it leaves in its wake. The name of the weapon is: inflation.

(To be continued.)

Ayn Rand

The Ayn Rand Letter, published fortnightly by The Ayn Rand Letter, Inc., 183 Madison Avenue, New York, N.Y. 10016.

Contributing Editor: **Leonard Peikoff**; Subscription Director: **Elayne Kalberman**; Production Manager: **Barbara Weiss.**

Vol. III, No. 19 June 17, 1974

EGALITARIANISM AND INFLATION

Part II

Inflation is a man-made scourge, made possible by the fact that most men do not understand it. It is a crime committed on so large a scale that its size is its protection: the integrating capacity of the victims' minds breaks down before the magnitude - and the seeming complexity - of the crime, which permits it to be committed openly, in public. For centuries, inflation has been wrecking one country after another, yet men learn nothing, offer no resistance, and perish - not like animals driven to slaughter, but worse: like animals stampeding in search of a butcher.

If I told you that the precondition of inflation is psycho-epistemological - that inflation is hidden under perceptual illusions created by broken conceptual links - you would not understand me. That is what I propose to explain and to prove.

Let us start at the beginning. Observe the fact that, as a human being, you are compelled by nature to eat at least once a day. In a modern American city, this is not a major problem. You can carry your sustenance in your pocket - in the form of a few coins. You can give it no thought, you can skip meals, and, when you're hungry, you can grab a sandwich or open a can of food - which, you believe, will always be there.

But project what the necessity to eat would mean in nature, i.e., if you were alone in a primeval wilderness. Hunger, nature's ultimatum, would make demands on you daily, but the satisfaction of the demands would not be available immediately: the satisfaction takes time - and tools. It takes time to hunt and to make your weapons. You have other needs as well. You need clothing - it takes time to kill a leopard and to get its skin. You need shelter - it takes time to build a hut, and food to sustain you while you're building it. The satisfaction of your daily physical needs would absorb all of your time. Observe that time is the price of your survival, and that it has to be paid in advance.

Would it make any difference if there were ten of you, instead of one? If there were a hundred of you? A thousand? A hundred thousand? Do not let the numbers confuse you: in regard to nature, the facts will remain inexorably the same. Socially, the large numbers may enable some men to enslave others and to live without effort, but unless a sufficient number of men are able to hunt, all of you will perish and so will your rulers.

The issue becomes much clearer when you discover agriculture. You can survive more safely and comfortably by planting seeds and collecting a harvest months later - on condition that you comply with two absolutes of nature: you must save enough of your harvest to feed you until the next harvest, and, above all, you must save enough seeds to plant your next harvest. You may run short on your own food, you may have to skimp and go half-hungry, but, under penalty of death, you do not touch your stock seed; if you do, you're through.

Agriculture is the first step toward civilization, because it requires a significant advance in men's conceptual development: it requires that they grasp two cardinal concepts which the perceptual, concrete-bound mentality of the hunters could not grasp fully: time and savings. Once you grasp these, you have grasped the three essentials of human survival: time-savings-production. You have grasped the fact that production is not a matter confined to the immediate moment, but a continuous process, and that production is fueled by previous production. The concept of "stock seed" unites the three essentials and applies not merely to agriculture, but much, much more widely: to all forms of productive work. Anything above the level of a savage's precarious, hand-to-mouth existence requires savings. Savings buy time.

If you live on a self-sustaining farm, you save your grain: you need the saved harvest of your good years to carry you through the bad ones; you need your saved seed to expand your production - to plant a larger field. The safer your supply of food, the more time it buys for the upkeep or improvement of the other things you need: your clothing, your shelter, your water well, your livestock and, above all, your tools, such as your plow. You make a gigantic step forward when you discover that you can trade with other farmers, which leads you all to the discovery of the road to an advanced civilization: the division of labor. Let us say that there are a hundred of you; each learns to specialize in the production of some goods needed by all, and you trade your products by direct barter. All of you become more expert at your tasks - therefore, more productive - therefore, your time brings you better returns.

On a self-sustaining farm, your savings consisted mainly of stored grain and foodstuffs; but grain and foodstuffs are perishable and cannot be kept for long, so you ate what you could not save; your time-range was limited. Now, your horizon has been pushed immeasurably farther. You don't have to expand the storage of your food: you can trade your grain for some commodity which will keep longer, and which you can trade for food when you need it. But which commodity? It is thus that you arrive at the next gigantic discovery: you devise a tool of exchange - money.

Money is the tool of men who have reached a high level of productivity and a long-range control over their lives. Money is not merely a tool of exchange: much more importantly, it is a tool of saving, which permits delayed consumption and buys time for future production. To fulfill this requirement, money has to be some material commodity which is imperishable, rare, homogeneous, easily stored, not subject to wide fluctuations of value, and always in demand among those you trade with. This leads you to the decision to use gold as money. Gold money is a tangible value in itself and a token of wealth actually produced. When you accept a gold coin in payment for your goods, you actually deliver the goods to the buyer; the transaction is as safe as simple barter. When you store your savings in the form of gold coins, they represent the goods which you have actually produced and which have gone to buy time for other producers, who will keep the productive process going, so that you'll be able to trade your coins for goods any time you wish.

Now project what would happen to your community of a hundred hard-working, prosperous, forward-moving people, if one man were allowed to trade on your market, not by means of gold, but by means of paper - i.e., if he paid you, not with a material commodity, not with goods he had actually produced, but merely with a promissory note on his future production. This man takes your goods, but does not use them to support his own production; he does not produce at all - he merely consumes the goods. Then, he pays you higher prices for more goods - again in promissory notes - assuring you that he is your best customer, who expands your market.

Then, one day, a struggling young farmer, who suffered from a bad flood, wants to buy some grain from you, but your price has risen and you haven't much grain to spare, so he goes bankrupt. Then, the dairy farmer, to whom he owed money, raises the price of milk to make up for the loss - and the truck farmer, who needs the milk, gives up buying the eggs he had always bought - and the poultry farmer kills some of his chickens, which he can't afford to feed - and the alfalfa grower, who can't afford the higher price of eggs, sells some of his stock seed and cuts down on his planting - and the dairy farmer can't afford the higher price of alfalfa, so he cancels his order to the blacksmith - and you want to buy the new plow you had been saving for, but the blacksmith has gone bankrupt. Then all of you present the promissory notes to your "best customer," and you discover that they were promissory notes not on <u>his</u> future production, but on <u>yours</u> - only you have nothing left to produce with. Your land is there, your structures are there, but there is no food to sustain you through the coming winter, and no stock seed to plant.

Would it make any difference if that community consisted of a thousand farmers? A hundred thousand? A million? Two hundred and eleven million? The entire globe? No matter how widely you spread the blight, no matter what variety of products and what incalculable complexity of deals become involved, <u>this</u>, dear readers, is the cause, the pattern, and the outcome of inflation.

There is only one institution that can arrogate to itself the power legally to trade by means of rubber checks: the government. And it is the only institution that can mortgage your future without your knowledge or consent: government securities (and paper money) are promissory notes on future tax receipts, i.e., on your future production.

Now project the mentality of a savage, who can grasp nothing but the concretes of the immediate moment, and who finds himself transported into the midst of a modern, industrial civilization. If he is an intelligent savage, he will acquire a smattering of knowledge, but there are two concepts he will not be able to grasp: "credit" and "market."

He observes that people get food, clothes, and all sorts of objects simply by presenting pieces of paper called checks - and he observes that skyscrapers and gigantic factories spring out of the ground at the command of very rich men, whose bookkeepers keep switching magic figures from the ledgers of one to those of another and another and another. This seems to be done faster than he can follow, so he concludes that <u>speed</u> is the secret of the magic power of paper - and that everyone will work and produce and prosper, so long as those checks are passed from hand to hand fast enough. If that savage breaks into print with his discovery, he will find that he has been anticipated by John Maynard Keynes.

Then the savage observes that the department stores are full of wonderful goods, but people do not seem to buy them. "Why is that?" he asks a floorwalker. "We don't have enough of a market," the floorwalker tells him. "What is that?" he asks. "Well," his new teacher answers, "goods are produced for people to consume, it's the consumers that make the world go 'round, but we don't have enough consumers." "Is that so?" says the savage, his eyes flashing with the fire of a new idea. Next day, he obtains a check from a big educational foundation, he hires a plane, he flies away - and comes back, a while later, bringing his entire naked, barefoot tribe along. "You don't know how good they are at consuming," he tells his friend, the floorwalker, "and there's plenty more where these came from. Pretty soon you'll get a raise in pay." But the store, pretty soon, goes bankrupt.

The poor savage is unable to understand it to this day - because he had made sure that many, many people agreed with his idea, among them many noble tribal chiefs, such as Governor Romney, who sang incantations to "consumerism," and warrior Nader, who fought for the consumers' rights, and big business chieftains who recited formulas about serving the consumers, and chiefs who sat in Congress, and chiefs in the White House, and chiefs in every government in Europe, and many more professors than he could count.

Perhaps it is harder for us to understand that the mentality of that savage has been ruling Western civilization for almost a century.

Trained in college to believe that to look beyond the immediate moment - to look for causes or to foresee consequences - is impossible, modern men have developed context-dropping as their normal method of cognition. Observing a bad, small-town shopkeeper, the kind who is doomed to fail, they believe - as he does - that lack of customers is his only problem; and that the question of the goods he sells, or _where these goods come from_, has nothing to do with it. The goods, they believe, are here and will always be here. Therefore, they conclude, the consumer - not the producer - is the motor of an economy. Let us extend credit, i.e., our savings, to the consumers - they advise - in order to expand the market for our goods.

But, in fact, consumers _qua consumers_ are not part of anyone's market; qua consumers, they are _irrelevant_ to economics. Nature does not grant anyone an innate title of "consumer"; it is a title that has to be earned - by production. Only _producers_ constitute a market - only men who trade products or services for products or services. In the role of producers, they represent a market's "supply"; in the role of consumers, they represent a market's "demand." The law of supply and demand has an implicit subclause: that it involves the same people in both capacities. When this subclause is forgotten, ignored or evaded - you get the economic situation of today.

A successful producer can support many people, e.g., his children, by delegating to them his market power of consumer. Can that capacity be unlimited? How many men would you be able to feed on a self-sustaining farm? In more primitive times, farmers used to raise large families in order to obtain farm labor, i.e., productive help. How many _non-productive_ people could you support by your own effort? If the number were unlimited, if demand became greater than supply - if demand were turned into a _command_, as it is today - you would have to use and exhaust your stock seed. _This_ is the process now going on in this country.

There is only one institution that could bring it about: the government - with the help of a vicious doctrine that serves as a cover-up: altruism. The visible profiteers of altruism - the welfare recipients - are part victims, part window dressing for the statist policies of the government. But no government could have gotten away with it, if people had grasped the other concept which the savage was unable to grasp: the concept of "credit."

(To be continued.)

Ayn Rand

The Ayn Rand Letter, published fortnightly by The Ayn Rand Letter, Inc., 183 Madison Avenue, New York, N.Y. 10016.
Contributing Editor: **Leonard Peikoff**; Subscription Director: **Elayne Kalberman**; Production Manager: **Barbara Weiss.**

Vol. III, No. 20 July 1, 1974

EGALITARIANISM AND INFLATION

Part III

If you understand the function of stock seed - of savings - in a primitive farm community, apply the same principle to a complex, industrial economy.

Wealth represents goods which have been produced, but not consumed. What would a man do with his wealth in terms of direct barter? Let us say a successful shoe manufacturer wants to enlarge his production. His wealth consists of shoes; he trades some shoes for the things he needs as a consumer, but he saves a large number of shoes and trades them for building materials, machinery and labor to build a new factory - and another large number of shoes, for raw materials and for the labor he will employ to manufacture more shoes. Money facilitates this trading, but does not change its nature. All the physical goods and services he needs for his project must actually exist and be available for trade - just as his payment for them must actually exist in the form of physical goods (in this case, shoes). An exchange of paper money (or even of gold coins) would not do any good to any of the parties involved, if the physical things they needed were not there and could not be obtained in exchange for the money.

If a man does not consume his goods at once, but saves them for the future, whether he wants to enlarge his production or to live on his savings (which he holds in the form of money) - in either case, he is counting on the fact that he will be able to exchange his money for the things he needs, when and as he needs them. This means that he is relying on a continuous process of production - which requires an uninterrupted flow of goods saved to fuel further and further production. This flow is "investment capital," the stock seed of industry. When a rich man lends money to others, what he lends to them is the goods which he has not consumed.

This is the meaning of the concept "investment." If you have wondered how one can start producing, when nature requires time paid in advance, this is the beneficent process that enables men to do it: a successful man lends his goods to a promising beginner (or to any reputable producer) - in exchange for the payment of interest. The payment is for the risk he is taking: nature does not guarantee man's success, neither on a farm nor in a factory. If the venture fails, it means that the goods have been consumed without a productive return, so the investor loses his money; if the venture succeeds, the producer pays the interest out of the new goods, the profits, which the investment enabled him to make.

Observe, and bear in mind above all else, that this process applies only to financing the needs of production, not of consumption - and that its success rests on the investor's judgment of men's productive ability, not on his compassion for their feelings, hopes or dreams.

Such is the meaning of the term "credit." In all its countless variations and applications, "credit" means money, i.e., unconsumed goods, loaned by one productive person (or group) to another, to be repaid out of future production. Even the credit extended for a consumption purpose, such as the purchase of an automobile, is based on the productive record and prospects of the borrower. Credit is not - as the savage believed - a magic piece of paper that reverses cause and effect, and transforms consumption into a source of production.

Consumption is the final, not the efficient, cause of production. The efficient cause is savings, which can be said to represent the opposite of consumption: they represent unconsumed goods. Consumption is the end of production, and a dead end, as far as the productive process is concerned. The worker who produces so little that he consumes everything he earns, carries his own weight economically, but contributes nothing to future production. The worker who has a modest savings account, and the millionaire who invests a fortune (and all the men in between), are those who finance the future. The man who consumes without producing is a parasite, whether he is a welfare recipient or a rich playboy.

An industrial economy is enormously complex: it involves calculations of time, of motion, of credit, and long sequences of interlocking contractual exchanges. This complexity is the system's great virtue and the source of its vulnerability. The vulnerability is psycho-epistemological. No human mind and no computer - and no planner - can grasp the complexity in every detail. Even to grasp the principles that rule it, is a major feat of abstraction. This is where the conceptual links of men's integrating capacity break down: most people are unable to grasp the working of their hometown's economy, let alone the country's or the world's. Under the influence of today's mind-shrinking, anti-conceptual education, most people tend to see economic problems in terms of immediate concretes: of their paychecks, their landlords, and the corner grocery store. The most disastrous loss - which broke their tie to reality - is the loss of the concept that money stands for existing, but unconsumed goods.

The system's complexity serves, occasionally, as a temporary cover for the operations of some shady characters. You have all heard of some manipulator who does not work, but lives in luxury by obtaining a loan, which he repays by obtaining another loan elsewhere, which he repays by obtaining another loan, etc. You know that his policy can't go on forever, that it catches up with him eventually and he crashes. But what if that manipulator is the government?

The government is not a productive enterprise. It produces nothing. In respect to its legitimate functions - which are the police, the army, the law courts - it performs a service needed by a productive economy. When a government steps beyond these functions, it becomes an economy's destroyer.

The government has no source of revenue, except the taxes paid by the producers. To free itself - for a while - from the limits set by reality, the government initiates a credit con game on a scale which the private manipulator could not dream of. It borrows money from you today, which is to be repaid with money it will borrow from you tomorrow, which is to be repaid with money it will borrow from you day after tomorrow, and so on. This is known as "deficit financing." It is made possible by the fact that the government cuts the connection between goods and money. It issues paper money, which is used as a claim check on actually existing goods - but that money is not backed by any goods, it is not backed by gold, it is backed by nothing. It is a promissory note issued to you in exchange for your goods, to be paid by you (in the form of taxes) out of your future production.

Where does your money go? Anywhere and nowhere. First, it goes to establish an altruistic excuse and window dressing for the rest: to establish a system of subsidized consumption - a "welfare" class of men who consume without producing - a growing dead end, imposed on a shrinking production. Then the money goes to subsidize any pressure group at the expense of any other - to buy their votes - to finance any project conceived at the whim of any bureaucrat or of his friends - to pay for the failure of that project, to start another, etc. The welfare recipients are not the worst part of the producers' burden. The worst part are the bureaucrats - the government officials who are given the power to regulate production. They are not merely unproductive consumers: their job consists in making it harder and harder and, ultimately, impossible for the producers to produce. (Most of them are men whose ultimate goal is to place all producers in the position of welfare recipients.)

While the government struggles to save one crumbling enterprise at the expense of the crumbling of another, it accelerates the process of juggling debts, switching losses, piling loans on loans, mortgaging the future and the future's future. As things grow worse, the government protects itself not by contracting this process, but by expanding it. The process becomes global: it involves foreign aid, and unpaid loans to foreign governments, and subsidies to other welfare states, and subsidies to the United Nations, and subsidies to the World Bank, and subsidies to foreign producers, and credits to foreign consumers to enable them to consume our goods - while, simultaneously, the American producers, who are paying for it all, are left without protection, and their properties are seized by any sheik in any pesthole of the globe, and the wealth they have created, as well as their energy, is turned against them, as, for example, in the case of Middle Eastern oil.

Do you think a spending orgy of this kind could be paid for out of current production? No, the situation is much worse than that. <u>The government is consuming this country's stock seed</u> - the stock seed of industrial production: investment capital, i.e., the savings needed to keep production going. These savings were not paper, but actual goods. Under all the complexities of private credit, the economy was kept going by the fact that, in one form or another, in one place or another, somewhere within it, actual material goods existed to back its financial transactions. It kept going long after that protection was breached. Today, the goods are almost gone.

A piece of paper will not feed you, when there is no bread to eat. It will not build a factory, when there are no steel girders to buy. It will not make shoes, when there is no leather, no machines, no fuel. You have heard it said that today's economy is afflicted by sudden, unpredictable shortages of various commodities. These are the advance symptoms of what is to come.

You have heard economists say that they are puzzled by the nature of today's problem: they are unable to understand why inflation is accompanied by recession - which is contrary to their Keynesian doctrines; and they have coined a ridiculous name for it: "stagflation." Their theories ignore the fact that money can function only so long as it represents actual goods - and that at a certain stage of inflating the money supply, the government begins to consume a nation's investment capital, thus making production impossible.

The value of the total tangible assets of the United States at present, was estimated - in terms of 1968 dollars - at 3.1 trillion dollars. If government spending continues, that incredible wealth will not save you. You may be left with all the magnificent skyscrapers, the giant factories, the rich farmlands - but without fuel, without electricity, without transportation, without steel, without paper, without seeds to plant the next harvest.

If that time comes, the government will declare explicitly the premise on which it has been acting implicitly: that its only "capital asset" is you. Since you will not be able to work any longer, the government will take over and will make you work - on a slope descending to sub-industrial production. The only substitute for technological energy is the muscular labor of slaves. This is the way an economic collapse leads to dictatorship - as it did in Germany and in Russia. And if anyone thinks that government planning is a solution to the problems of human survival, observe that after half a century of total dictatorship, Soviet Russia is begging for American wheat and for American industrial "know-how."

A dictatorship would find it impossible to rule this country in the foreseeable future. What is possible is the blind chaos of a civil war.

It is at a time like this, in the face of an approaching economic collapse, that the intellectuals are preaching egalitarian notions. When the curtailment of government spending is imperative, they demand more welfare projects. When the need for men of productive ability is desperate, they demand more equality for the incompetents. When the country needs the accumulation of capital, they demand that we soak the rich. When the country needs more savings, they demand a "redistribution of income." They demand more jobs and less profits - more jobs and fewer factories - more jobs and no fuel, no oil, no coal, no "pollution" - but, above all, more goods for free to more consumers, no matter what happens to jobs, to factories, or to producers.

The results of their Keynesian economics are wrecking every industrial country, but they refuse to question their basic assumptions. The examples of Soviet Russia, of Nazi Germany, of Red China, of Marxist Chile, of socialist England are multiplying around them, but they refuse to see and to learn. Today, production is the world's most urgent need, and the threat of starvation is spreading through the globe; the intellectuals know the only economic system that can and did produce unlimited abundance, but they give it no thought and keep silent about it, as if it had never existed. It is almost irrelevant to blame them for their default at the task of intellectual leadership: the smallness of their stature is overwhelming.

Is there any hope for the future of this country? Yes, there is. This country has one asset left: the matchless productive ability of its people. If, and to the extent that, this ability is liberated, we might still have a chance to avoid a collapse. We cannot expect to reach the ideal overnight, but we must at least reveal its name. We must reveal to this country the secret which all those posturing intellectuals of any political denomination, who clamor for openness and truth, are trying so hard to cover up: that the name of that miraculous productive system is Capitalism.

As to such things as taxes and the rebuilding of a country, I will say that in his goals, if not his methods, the best economist in Atlas Shrugged was Ragnar Danneskjöld.

Ayn Rand

OBJECTIVIST CALENDAR

Starting on November 21, the taped lectures of Dr. Leonard Peikoff's course, Modern Philosophy: Kant to the Present, will be given in Montreal. For further information, contact Ferial Balassiano at (514) 739-2631 (8 A.M.-8 P.M.). B.W.

The Ayn Rand Letter, published fortnightly by The Ayn Rand Letter, Inc., 183 Madison Avenue, New York, N.Y. 10016.

Contributing Editor: **Leonard Peikoff**; Subscription Director: **Elayne Kalberman**; Production Manager: **Barbara Weiss.**

Vol. III, No. 21 July 15, 1974

THE INVERTED MORAL PRIORITIES

A widespread ignorance of a crucial economic issue is apparent in most discussions of today's problems: it is ignorance on the part of the public, evasion on the part of most economists, and crude demagoguery on the part of certain politicians. The issue is the function of wealth in an industrial economy.

Most people seem to believe that wealth is primarily an object of consumption - that the rich spend all or most of their money on personal luxury. Even if this were true, it would be their inalienable right - but it does not happen to be true. The percentage of income which men spend on consumption, stands in inverse ratio to the amount of their wealth. The percentage which the rich spend on personal consumption is so small that it is of no significance to a country's economy. The money of the rich is invested in production; it is an indispensable part of the stock seed that makes production possible.

Even the most primitive forms of production require an investment of time and sustenance (i.e., of unconsumed goods), to enable men to produce. The higher a society's industrial development, the more expensive the tools required to put men to work (and the greater the productivity of their labor). Some years ago, it took an investment of $5,000 per worker to create jobs in industry; I have no exact figures for the present time, but the investment is now much higher. Deferred consumption (i.e., savings) on a gigantic scale is required to keep industrial production going. Savings pay for machines which enable men to produce in a day an amount of goods they would not be able to produce by hand in a year (if at all). This enables the workers in turn to defer consumption and to save some of their income for their future needs or goals. The hallmark of an industrial society is its members' distance from a hand-to-mouth mode of living; the greater this distance, the greater men's progress.

The major part of this country's stock seed is not the fortunes of the rich (who are a small minority), but the savings of the middle class - i.e., of responsible men who have the ability to grasp the concept "future" and to deposit one dollar (or more) into a bank account. A man of this type saves money for his own future, but the bank invests his money in productive enterprises; thus, the goods he did not consume today, are available to him when he needs them tomorrow - and, in the meantime, these goods serve as fuel for the country's productive process.

Except for short periods of unforeseeable emergency, a rational person cannot stand living hand-to-mouth. No matter what his income, he saves some part of it, large or small - because he knows that his life is not confined to the immediate moment, that he has to plan ahead, and that savings are his means of control over his life: savings are his badge of independence and his door to the future - if he is to have a future.

Project fully and concretely what a hand-to-mouth existence would be like. Assume that you have a job which takes care of your immediate physical needs (food, clothing and shelter), but nothing more: you consume everything you earn. Without the possibility of saving, you would live in a state of chronic terror: terror of losing your job and terror of sudden illness. (Never mind unemployment insurance and Medicaid: insurance is a form of saving, and compulsory savings leave you at the mercy of the government.) Could you look for a better job? No - because you have no reserves to carry you a single day. Could you go to school to learn a new skill? No - because this takes savings. Could you plan to buy a car? No - this takes savings. Could you plan to buy a home of your own? No - this takes an enormous amount of savings over a long period of time. Could you plan an unusual vacation, such as a trip to Europe? No, nor any kind of vacation - a vacation takes savings. Could you go to a movie, a theater, a concert? No - this takes savings. Could you buy a book, a phonograph record, a print for your bare walls? No - these take savings. If you have a family, could you send your children through college? No - this takes a small fortune in savings. If you are single, could you get married? No - you have no way to increase your income. If you are an aspiring young writer or artist, could you hold a job, and skimp and go hungry and deny yourself everything - in order to buy time to write or paint? Forget it.

Would you care to go on living in such conditions? Since you are a person able to read, the answer is: No. Yet this is the state to which today's intellectual leaders (who are led by the egalitarians) wish to reduce you.

There is an old saying: "Time is money," which is true enough in an efficient, productive, free society. Today, the urgent thing to realize is that <u>money is time</u>. Money is the goods which <u>you</u> produced, but did not consume; what your deferred consumption buys for you is time to achieve your goals. Bear this in mind when you consider what inflation is doing to <u>your</u> savings.

Let us suppose that you have $1,000 in a savings account. If the current rate of inflation is 10% (it is actually higher), you lose $100 a year - the government is robbing you of that amount, as surely as if it took the bills out of your pocket. Are you permitted to write that loss off on your tax return? No - the government is pretending that the loss did not occur. But the bank pays you, say, 5% interest, i.e., $50 a year - does this make up for half of your loss? No - because the government regards bank interest as "unearned income," and taxes you on it (the amount of the tax depends on your income bracket). Are there any public voices - in this age of "social conscience" - protesting against so vicious an injustice? No.

"Stripped of its academic jargon, the welfare state is nothing more than a mechanism by which governments confiscate the wealth of the productive members of a society to support a wide variety of welfare schemes." (Alan Greenspan, "Gold and Economic Freedom," in my book <u>Capitalism: The Unknown Ideal</u>.) The major part of this country's wealth belongs to the middle class. The middle class is the heart, the lifeblood, the energy source of a free, industrial economy, i.e., of capitalism; it did not and cannot exist under any other system; it is the product of upward mobility, incompatible with frozen social castes. Do not ask, therefore, for whom the bell of inflation is tolling; it tolls for <u>you</u>. It is not at the destruction of a handful of the rich that inflation is aimed (the rich are mostly in the vanguard of the destroyers), but at the middle class. It is the middle class that was wiped out in the German inflation; and the cannibalistic society that permitted it to happen, got what it deserved: Hitler.

Inflation is a symptom of the terminal stage of that social disease which is a mixed economy. A mixed economy (as I have said many, many times) is an invalid, unstable, unworkable system which leads to one of two endings: either a return to freedom or a collapse into dictatorship. In the face of an approaching disaster, what is the attitude of most of our public leaders? Politics as usual, evasion as usual, moral cowardice as usual.

In view of what they hear from the experts, the people cannot be blamed for their ignorance and their helpless confusion. If an average housewife struggles with her incomprehensibly shrinking budget and sees a tycoon in a resplendent limousine, she might well think that just one of his diamond cuff links would solve all her problems. She has no way of knowing that if all the personal luxuries of all the tycoons were expropriated, it would not feed her family - and millions of other, similar families - for one week; and that the entire country would starve on the first morning of the week to follow. (This is what happened in Chile.) How would she know it, if all the voices she hears are telling her that we must soak the rich?

No one tells her that higher taxes imposed on the rich (and the semi-rich) will not come out of their consumption expenditures, but out of their investment capital (i.e., their savings); that such taxes will mean less investment, i.e., less production, fewer jobs, higher prices for scarcer goods; and that by the time the rich have to lower their standard of living, hers will be gone, along with *her* savings and her husband's job - and no power in the world (no *economic* power) will be able to revive the dead industries (there will be no such power left).

Since the men who know it keep silent, they leave the field open to swarms of political demagogues, who cash in on that housewife's despair and bewilderment. They provide her with a scapegoat, the usual one, the easiest to set up: the businessman. When she hears denunciations of "windfall" profits (or "exorbitant" profits, or "unfair" profits), she does not know how to determine what this means, what the size of profits "should" be - and she does not suspect that the demagogues do not know it, either (because no one can determine it, except the free market). It merely confirms her consumption-oriented view of wealth and suggests that she is the victim of somebody's "greed" - which nurtures her ugliest emotions. No one tells her that the businessmen's *profits* are the only protection of her home, her family, her life - and that if the erosion of profits were to force businessmen out of production altogether, the only alternative would be a "non-profit" industry run by the government; what *this* would mean to the people has been demonstrated amply and conclusively in Soviet Russia.

These are the things which the public urgently needs to know today, but is not being told. The better kinds of politicians do not indulge in business-baiting demagoguery, but they do not fight it; they are afraid to fight it; they merely struggle to appease the demagogues. So do most economists and most businessmen. What do they all fear?

The televised summit conference on inflation gave a clue to the answer. It presented a sorry spectacle of this country's intellectual leadership - and a startling dramatization of the fundamental problem: today's inverted moral priorities.

The representatives of the men who are of greatest importance to this country's production and are most needed today - the businessmen - were quiet, earnest, undemanding, and concerned (a little too selflessly) with the state of the economy as a whole.

The representatives of the men next in importance to production - organized labor - were louder and more self-assertive; but, with the exception of a few demagogues, they assumed the responsibility of concern with national problems.

The representatives of the men who contribute nothing - the welfare recipients, the professional consumerists, the non-producers, the objects of public charity - were the loudest, the most aggressive, the most self-righteously arrogant and hostile. They made demands, displaying the kind of conventional "selfishness" - the greedy, grasping, grabbing kind - which is usually ascribed to a rich magnate, in leftist cartoons. They shouted, screamed, hissed accusations and commands in the tone of conquerors delivering ultimatums to their cowed, vanquished serfs. Their message, in effect, was that the needs of the non-producers are a first mortgage on the nation and must be met regardless of what happens to the rest of the country. How? They scorned the necessity to think of an answer. The answer was loudly implicit in their manner: Somehow.

Acting as if _need_ conferred on their clients a special privilege, superseding reality - as if the _needy_ had rights denied to the rest of mankind - they flaunted the consumption-oriented, range-of-the-moment, hand-to-mouth mentality that sees economics in terms of hunger, not of production, seeks "fairness" in terms of equalizing the hunger, and stands ready to devour the rest of the country (_this_ country, where - according to their own leaders - poverty is not absolute, but "relative").

Nobody (with a very few exceptions) answered them or protested at that conference. Why did the reputable politicians, the economists, the businessmen keep silent in the face of outrageous abuse? Why did they allow the deadly, illiterate nonsense to proliferate without opposition? Why did they listen respectfully, apologetically, "compassionately," and promise more help to egalitarian savages? There is only one power that could paralyze the country's leaders, a power more potent than the power of money, of professional knowledge, even of political force: the power of morality. _This_ was what the inverted morality of altruism accomplished, _this_ was the kind of moral cowardice, intellectual disintegration, professional dishonesty, and patriotic default it led to in practice, at a time of national emergency.

There is a group of economists who deserved it: the so-called "conservatives" who claim that economics has nothing to do with morality.

Ayn Rand

P.S. This _Letter_ was written later than the date that appears on its heading.

OBJECTIVIST CALENDAR

We have been asked to announce that on Friday, December 13, Dr. George Reisman will give a lecture at Hunter College, under the auspices of Hunter College Students of Objectivism. Title: "Capitalism: The Cure for Racism." Time: 7:30 P.M. Place: Hunter High School Auditorium, Lexington Ave. between 68th and 69th Sts., New York City. For further information, call Robin Stark, (914) 969-2027 (eves.).

B.W.

The Ayn Rand Letter, published fortnightly by The Ayn Rand Letter, Inc., 183 Madison Avenue, New York, N.Y. 10016.

Contributing Editor: **Leonard Peikoff**; Subscription Director: **Elayne Kalberman**; Production Manager: **Barbara Weiss.**

Vol. III, No. 22 July 29, 1974

HUNGER AND FREEDOM

I hope that my last four Letters have helped you to see the cannibalistic nature of altruism in action and the extent to which it is devouring this country. But you have not yet heard the whole story.

At a time like the present - when this country is threatened with economic collapse under the burden of supporting millions of non-productive citizens, and the heavier burden of the parasites-on-parasitism: the welfare-state bureaucracy - a new campaign is being sneaked up on us, softly, tentatively, but insistently: a campaign to load us with the responsibility of feeding the whole world.

No, that campaign does not mean it symbolically or allegorically or oratorically, or in the form of aspirational mush - but literally, officially, permanently, by law and by force. (I do not know which is more evil in this context: those who believe that that mush *is* an idealistic aspiration or those who cash in on it. I am inclined to say: the former.)

An interesting trial balloon was sent up in a column by Anthony Lewis, entitled "The Politics of Hunger" (*The New York Times*, October 24, 1974). It is particularly interesting (and revealing) in its implications, which the columnist, apparently, did not see and does not consider.

In its own journalistic terms, the column is honestly factual: it presents the problem clearly and offers no solution (except in murky hints). It starts with: "On the current trends of population and food production, according to international experts, by 1985 the poor countries of the world would need 85 million tons of grain a year from outside. In a year of bad harvests, the need could be 100 million tons, or even more." And: "Before the problem of moving that much food, there are the questions of how to grow it and pay for it. At today's prices, 100 million tons of cereals would cost something approaching $20 billion. Haiti and Bangladesh and the thirty other food-short countries will not have the foreign exchange to pay for it. Who will?" This, properly, is the first question to ask. (The column does not answer it.)

"That is the scale of the issues facing the World Food Conference in Rome starting Nov. 5. Public discussion of the food problem understandably tends to focus on immediate matters, such as the amount of American aid to hold off imminent mass starvation in south Asia. But the conference is meant to take a longer view, and <u>that means dealing with the most fundamental issues of population, resources and the wealth of nations</u>." (Emphasis added.) It sure does. (No such issues were raised at that conference.)

Mr. Lewis indicates that "State Department officials preparing for the conference seem modestly hopeful of agreed progress in defining the problems" - and lists some of the points they "sketch." One such point reads: "There must be intensified international efforts to increase food production in the less developed countries, for example by scientific improvements in tropical agriculture."

"Scientific improvement" means <u>technology</u>. How would they reconcile it with the world-wide assault on science and technology by ecological crusaders, who demand a return to "unspoiled" nature? Those starving populations are certainly living in the midst of "unspoiled," untouched nature. Which fundamental goal are the world-planners going to pursue: production or ecology? And how will the scientists function in countries where science is banned, reason is a hated enemy, and the crudest mystic superstitions rule the people's lives, traditions and rudimentary culture? What self-respecting scientist would want to work in such conditions - and why should he? Neither the column nor, I am sure, the State Department answers any of these questions.

The paragraph continues: "But for the foreseeable future there will be dependence on imports from a handful of surplus countries, primarily the U.S., Canada, Australia, Argentina and the Common Market." Ask yourself: What do these countries (with one exception) have in common? Two paragraphs later, Mr. Lewis says that the American delegates expect another conference after the one in Rome, "a negotiating conference among the major grain-exporting countries and the big consistent importers: India, Pakistan, Bangladesh, Japan, the Soviet Union and China." What do <u>these</u> countries (also with one exception) have in common?

The column offers some vague hints about someone's proposal to establish world grain reserves, and to agree on "who should contribute how much... in what would amount to an international system of national reserves." (?) There is even an indication of what is the immediate, "practical" goal behind that food conference and what sort of deadly game is being played. "Secretary Kissinger is said by his associates to see the food issue now as a crucial example of the new interdependence of nations."

The game, apparently, is to trick the Arabs into some sort of One-World Economic Order which would enable us to barter our grain for their oil (if they don't outsmart us). And <u>this</u> is the sort of lofty purpose for which somebody is willing to sell America's soul, her sovereignty, her freedom, and <u>your</u> standard of living. The alleged justification is global need, compassion, altruism. To pragmatists of this kind, altruism is the window dressing, the bait that lures the victims to slaughter.

(This is an interesting example of today's alliance between the "practical" men and the intellectuals - an alliance based on mutual contempt, with each side believing that it is using the other. The "practical" men are willing to adopt any currently fashionable ideology in exchange for some material advantage of the moment. The intellectuals are willing to support any "practical" policy that leads toward their own long-range, ideological goals. In this case, the "practical" men want oil; the intellectuals want One World.)

Mr. Lewis seems to see a little further than the "practical" diplomats. He seems to take altruism seriously - and he is pressing for the logical consequences of such international schemes. His concluding paragraph states: "All of the thought on reserve mechanisms, hard as it is, *only touches the surface of the world food problem. Underneath there is the question of money* - the need for the less developed countries to have enough of it so the U.S. and others can go all-out in food production for them. Aid can hardly make a dent in that need. *In the long run there must be real transfers of purchasing power*, and that in turn raises the whole question of the oil producers and their responsibility as well as ours." (Emphasis added.)

And this in turn raises the whole question of what is purchasing power and whether it can be "transferred."

In my *Letters* on "Egalitarianism and Inflation," I said that money cannot function as money, i.e., as a medium of exchange, unless it is backed by actual, *unconsumed* goods. Mr. Lewis's last paragraph is a nice bit of evidence to support my contention. If money does not have to be backed by goods, why do the less developed countries need it so badly? Why can't their governments print more paper currency? Why are the U.S. and others unable to go all-out in food production, without receiving any payment for it? Why doesn't the need - the desperate need - of the consumers endow them with purchasing power?

Obviously, purchasing power is an attribute of producers, not of consumers. Purchasing power is a consequence of production: it is the power of possessing goods which one can trade for other goods. A "*purchase*" is an exchange of goods (or services) for goods (or services). Any other form of transferring goods from one person to another may belong to many different categories of transactions, but it is *not a purchase*. It may be a gift, a loan, an inheritance, a handout, a fraud, a theft, a robbery, a burglary, an expropriation. In regard to services, however (omitting temporary or occasional acts of friendship, in which the payment is the friend's value), there is only one alternative to trading: unpaid services, i.e., slavery.

How can you "transfer purchasing power" to people who are unwilling or unable to produce? You can transfer your goods to them without payment - by means of one of the transactions listed above - but if you then receive from them the goods which you produced, in payment for the goods which you are now producing, this cannot be designated as a "purchase" even by the sloppiest of today's linguistic usage. And even if we all agreed so to designate it, how long would we be able to continue producing under a system of that kind? How would we accumulate the stock seed of production, i.e., unconsumed goods?

If you are sick (as I am) of hearing such accusations as "Americans represent only 6% of the world population, but consume 54% of its natural resources," ask the accusers: "How can 6% of the world population feed 94% of it?" (This is the ultimate intention of all international-feeding schemes.)

But the real question goes deeper than that. The real question lies in those "most fundamental issues of population, resources and the wealth of nations" which Mr. Lewis mentioned, but did not discuss. Why are some nations wealthy and others not? Why do some nations produce abundance and others starve? The answer, strangely enough, is contained (implicitly) in Mr. Lewis's column - and one can see it, without any further research, if one accepts his facts as facts (which they are).

Let us go back to the two groups of countries he lists. The "handful of [grain] surplus countries [are] primarily the U.S., Canada, Australia, Argentina and the Common Market." The "big consistent [grain] importers [are] India, Pakistan, Bangladesh, Japan, the Soviet Union and China." The surplus countries are semi-free economies, with a century of greater freedom behind them and, in various degrees, some traditional remnants and memories of freedom. (The exception is Argentina, a semi-dictatorship in bad economic shape, but traditionally an agricultural country.) The grain importers, which live under a chronic threat of hunger, are socialist and communist dictatorships. (The exception is Japan, which, however, has never been a free country, and which is geographically unable to develop its agriculture to any significant extent.)

The relevance of two of Mr. Lewis's "fundamental issues" breaks down in the light of his own lists. "Population" and "resources" do not determine "the wealth of nations." The countries of Europe's Common Market are as densely populated as most of the countries on the hunger list. Russia has greater natural resources than the U.S., but they are untouched and unused.

It is the presence of Russia on the hunger list that blasts all modern economic theories out of the realm of serious consideration. Under the inept government of the Czars and with the most primitive methods of agriculture, Russia was a major grain exporter. The unusually fertile soil of the Ukraine alone was (and is) capable of feeding the entire world. Whatever natural conditions are required for growing wheat, Russia had (and has) them in overabundance. That Russia should now be on a list of hungry, wheat-begging importers, is the most damning indictment of a collectivist economy that reality can offer us.

The simple, metaphysical fact - which no man-made wishes or edicts can alter - is that individual freedom is the precondition of human productivity and, therefore, of abundance, and, therefore, of the wealth of nations. The history of mankind bears witness to this fact - particularly, the prosperity-explosion of the nineteenth century (the century dominated by capitalism), as against the millennia of stagnant misery under every variant of "democratically" or autocratically controlled economy.

(If you hear it said that that prosperity was caused by an abundance of natural resources, which are now exhausted, remember that similar allegations and dire warnings were voiced by statists from the beginning of the Industrial Revolution, and that they were prompted by the same motives. Furthermore, at the turn of this century, there were voices claiming that all possible forms of industrial production had been discovered and we could expect nothing but general decline. This was said before the invention of the electric light bulb, the automobile, the airplane, the telephone, the telegraph, the movies, radio, television, atomic motors, spaceships, etc.)

The simple, metaphysical fact is that man by nature is not equipped to survive "in nature." His mind is his basic tool of survival, and his mind creates three life-supporting achievements: science, technology, industrial production. Without these, he cannot wrest sufficient sustenance from nature to fill his immediate, physical needs. In the pre-industrial era, population control was accomplished by starvation: a periodic famine, every twenty years, wiped out the surplus population, which the handplows and handlooms of Europe were unable to feed. The famines were assisted by periodic wars, which tribal rulers waged in order to loot one another's precarious sustenance. The famines (and the world wars) stopped with the coming of the Industrial Revolution - and, in the nineteenth century, the population of Europe rose by over 300%.

Today, as freedom vanishes from an ever larger area of the globe, famine is coming back - mass famine killing off the millions of human beings whom controlled economies are unable to feed.

In the face of a spectacle of this kind, what are we to think of those alleged humanitarians who plead with us for help and compassion, screaming that the horror of mass starvation supersedes all selfish, political concerns? Does it?

If a self-respecting American industrialist were to declare that he cannot and will not help the starving, because his productive capacity is not unlimited and he has no desire to descend to a Haitian's standard of living - it is easy to imagine the howls of indignation we would hear from today's intellectuals. Why are they practicing a double standard? Why do they scream that the needs of the hungry supersede our lives, freedom, future, and all values - _except_ their hatred of capitalism? Why do they ask us to sacrifice everything - while they refuse to sacrifice their power-lust or their mental lethargy long enough to discover the cure, _the only cure_, of global starvation?

While you consider these questions, consider also the following facts: contemporary history has demonstrated that the lives of the people, of the broad masses, have not been improved under any collectivist system, but have been reduced to hopeless misery. But there have been profiteers under every such system: the ruling bureaucracy - the parasites-on-parasitism - the wretched handful of pretentious mediocrities who, unable to compete on a free market, extort an unearned "prestige" and a luxurious living from "the sores of the poor and the blood of the rich."

These are the men who would let mankind starve, but will not relinquish their power - these are the men to whom the world is being sacrificed - these, not the poor brutes of Russia, China or India who are perishing because the last of their meager earnings has been plundered to support the nuclear armaments of their rulers.

It is to these rulers that we are now asked to sacrifice the last, best hope on earth: the United States of America.

Such is the nature of altruism.

Ayn Rand

P.S. This *Letter* was written later than the date that appears on its heading.

OBJECTIVIST CALENDAR

The following starting dates have been scheduled for the taped lectures of Allan Blumenthal's course, *Music: Theory, History and Performance*. St. Louis, January 19 (contact Fulton Huxtable, 314-291-7130); Toronto, January 21 (Edmund West, 416-661-1777, after 8 P.M.); Winnipeg, January 21 (Ellen Moore, 204-253-1630); West Lafayette, January 26 (Richard Matula, 317-463-3646, evenings).

B.W.

The Ayn Rand Letter, published fortnightly by The Ayn Rand Letter, Inc., 183 Madison Avenue, New York, N.Y. 10016.
Contributing Editor: **Leonard Peikoff**; Subscription Director: **Elayne Kalberman**; Production Manager: **Barbara Weiss.**

Vol. III, No. 23 August 12, 1974

CASHING IN ON HUNGER

If you want to observe the mechanics of an ideological campaign, Mr. Anthony Lewis offers a good example. As I indicated in my last Letter, Mr. Lewis started his campaign with a trial balloon on the issue of world hunger, in a column which reported the facts and merely hinted at solutions (The New York Times, October 24, 1974). The next step was a column entitled "Making A Difference" (Times, November 14, 1974), which stated explicitly the purpose behind the veiled hints.

To be exact, the column did not state, but screamed its purpose so crudely and angrily that one suspects that the trial balloon did not go over too well. The purpose was to push, force or wheedle the United States into assuming the burden of feeding the whole world. That purpose is not new: it is a bromide of altruism periodically dusted off and touted. But it is instructive to observe the nature of Mr. Lewis's arguments.

The column plugs a plan offered by "Oxfam-America, an affiliate of the International Relief Agency" which "suggests that Americans go without food for 24 hours next Thursday, Nov. 21 [i.e., a week before Thanksgiving]....The proposal is that money not spent on food next Thursday be sent to Oxfam," which would use it "to help farmers and villagers around the world raise their own food."

Mr. Lewis sees "a larger significance" in that idea. "It is a way for Americans to become aware of what is reality for hundreds of millions of people in the world." Addressing, apparently, the lowest kinds of today's concrete-bound, anti-conceptual mentalities, Mr. Lewis calls this "an opening to consciousness." (A consciousness that needs such an "opening" would be a consciousness aware of nothing but immediate sensations; if so, it might feel that its belly is empty, but would not be able to draw any further conclusions: conclusions require concepts.)

In order to make us aware of the reality of a starving world, it is the awareness of the reality of America that Mr. Lewis wants us to lose. Thanksgiving is a typically American holiday. In spite of its religious form (giving thanks to God for a good harvest), its essential, secular meaning is a celebration of successful production. It is a producers' holiday. The lavish meal is a symbol of the fact that abundant consumption is the result and reward of production. Abundance is (or was and ought to be) America's pride - just as it is the pride of American parents that their children need never know starvation. This is the pride which Mr. Lewis, as an altruist, seeks to demolish by urging Americans to experience hunger in conjunction with the holiday of abundance.

To plead his case, the altruist pulls an astonishing switch, and turns - of all things - into an individualist. "A premise of our democracy is that individual action can make a difference - that one man's conscience can change a country. Neither Jefferson nor Thoreau thought Americans should wait for governments to tell them what to do. It would be grotesque in the extreme if we abandoned individual initiative at a time when the world is facing fundamental change and the United States Government is so indifferent or so slow in its response."

Neither Jefferson nor Thoreau (this last in spite of his many faults) thought Americans should defy the government for the sake of becoming free to practice self-immolation. The "right to self-sacrifice" was not one of the rights that Jefferson listed in the Declaration of Independence and fought for. It would, indeed, be grotesque in the extreme if we abandoned individual initiative in such realms as our thinking, our values, our work, the control of our lives, the enjoyment of our liberty, the pursuit of our happiness - but preserved it in the realm of becoming a sacrificial animal. It is grotesque to advocate such a notion at a time when the "fundamental change" facing the world is the extinction of all individual initiative. But altruists have never been too fastidious about the nature of their arguments.

Here is a glimpse of altruist economics. "If we cut back our appetite for meat, we could in time release large amounts of grain for human instead of animal consumption. If we changed our policy on fertilizer to encourage instead of discourage its export, we would save money as well as lives. A ton of fertilizer in Bangladesh will grow more than twice as much additional grain as the same ton on a heavily fertilized field in Iowa. Helping others to grow their own food will actually reduce inflationary pressure on American food supplies."

If we cut back our appetite for meat, we would release large numbers of Americans to join the growing ranks of the unemployed. Cattle farmers would go bankrupt, then meat packers, canners, butchers, restaurant owners, leather manufacturers, innumerable allied industries, and the employees of all these enterprises. For those who did not cut back their appetite, and for growing children who need solid nourishment, the price of meat would skyrocket out of reach. The list of bankruptcies would include those Iowa farmers who would not be able to survive, with their harvests shrinking for lack of the fertilizer that had been shipped to Bangladesh. Are these the conditions that would "reduce inflationary pressure on American food supplies"?

The argument from intimidation appears in the form of Mr. Lewis's predictions about the future. "Not only on food but on all that goes into the standard of life, the miserable of the earth will be demanding change in _the grotesque inequality that now prevails. They will in effect be insisting that rich countries use less of the world's resources._ And they will be able to press for that change with something stronger than _appeals to justice_." (Emphases added.)

To call American abundance a "grotesque inequality," to brush aside the source and cause of that abundance - the tremendous effort, the heroic struggle, the unremitting work, the intelligence, the ambition (and the _freedom_) of millions of men that transformed an empty wilderness into a land of unprecedented abundance - to ascribe that magnificent achievement to the use of "the world's resources," is to utter a grotesque obscenity. To call it an appeal to _justice_ is the ultimate touch of cynical effrontery.

Since I take ideas seriously, I have to express moral indignation - but, simultaneously, I know that indignation is beside the point. The switches and contradictions of his arguments suggest that Mr. Lewis does not intend to be taken seriously. In this respect, he offers a valuable demonstration of the modern method of writing - valuable, because it is cruder and clearer than today's average.

Have you ever wondered how modern intellectuals are able to write at all, if they accept the notions that reality is unknowable, reason is impotent, words refer to nothing, and ideas are arbitrary constructs? Mr. Lewis indicates the answer: they do not try to communicate ideas, but to manipulate emotions, they do not count on people to read, but to skim, and they scatter emotional bait indiscriminately, in the hope that the skimmers will get hooked by one sort of emotion or another - compassion, or hatred, or collective guilt, or "individualistic" defiance, or fear, any sort of fear - anything that would push them toward the writer's wish: to induce self-sacrifice somehow and anyhow.

This method does not work too well. A public battered by a daily avalanche of irrationality, will skim that column and forget it, as one more item added to the readers' growing store of contempt for the printed word. But consider what sort of sediment remains in people's minds and what it contributes to our cultural atmosphere.

Who is pushing campaigns of this kind? Mr. Lewis indicates one source. "A second report to the Club of Rome on world resources and growth, 'Mankind at the Turning Point,' has just been published. Its authors...say industrialized countries must stop 'further overdevelopment' and limit their own use of finite resources, in order to help others find a way out of poverty." Then follows the threat (from the same report): "'Unless this lesson is learned in time, there will be a thousand desperadoes terrorizing those who are now rich, and eventually nuclear blackmail and terror will paralyze further orderly development.' In short, self-interest requires Americans and the other fortunate of the earth to make do with less." (In shorter short, this means: self-interest requires self-sacrifice. This is the old gimmick of altruism: the beggar with a tin cup in one hand and a gun in the other - a beggar who snarls: "Have pity on me, or I'll bash your head in!")

In fact, self-interest requires Americans - at all times and, particularly, in today's economic crisis - _not_ to make do with less, but to decide to have more and more, and to _earn_ it, i.e., to _produce_ it. Neither wealth nor prosperity nor even minimal security (nor any other kind of value) can be achieved by abstinence, passivity, privation, renunciation and resignation; it can be achieved only by ambition, the ambition to improve one's life, and by greater and ever greater productiveness. (Saving one's money for one's own goals is not abstinence, since it expands one's future rewards; "deferred consumption" is not renounced consumption.)

The various mystics to the contrary notwithstanding, it is _material_ ambition that America needs today, but is losing. The danger signs, new to this country, are all around us: passivity, lethargy, indifference, lack of pride in one's work, lack of vision beyond the immediate moment. These are the various stages of that willingness to "make do with less" which culminates in the swinish indignity of hippies living off garbage cans.

The causes of our economic decadence are obvious: growing government controls and mystic-altruist-collectivist influences have all but destroyed personal ambition by closing most doors and undercutting all incentives. The leitmotif of today's culture - hatred of the good for being the good - has been put into practice in the form of legislation that penalizes success for being success. This has all but paralyzed the best men and the best within all men - not merely the men of productive genius, but the good average workers (who lose money by earning a raise and hitting a higher tax bracket). When our gross national product is falling, when we desperately need men of productive ability, our legislators are prattling about "equalizing sacrifices," not liberating production, and about "fairness" to the poor, not *justice* to the productive. *That* is the difference made by hundreds or thousands of columns such as "Making A Difference."

If some altruist should still ask you why the sacrifice of an American's meal to feed a man in Bangladesh will not work (and, if practiced widely enough, will merely lead to the starvation of both givers and receivers) - tell him that reality is too clean to permit it to work, and that man is not a cannibalistic species.

Can the victims of starvation be helped in a non-sacrificial way? This is the question which an altruist will not ask you, because the actual fate of those victims is not his concern; the victims are merely a means to his end: the destruction and enslavement of the successful. The proof of altruism's motive lies in the fact that altruists do not want to hear the answer to that question.

The answer is that the only way to help the victims of starvation, is to teach them the only way of life that enables men to produce and to prosper, i.e., capitalism. But when the direct, "civilized" beneficiaries of capitalism do not know its meaning or its philosophic base, when they spend their time denouncing it, hobbling it, crippling it, and apologizing for it to the bloodiest looters on earth, one cannot expect them to teach anything to the victims of the global looters' governments.

In this connection, and by way of contrast to Mr. Lewis, I want to quote another - much brighter - contemporary voice: Reverend Ike. He is a black evangelist and a curiously fascinating TV personality, who has attracted an enormous following. I do not know what his philosophy actually is, but what he says on the air about man's right to the enjoyment of life on earth sets him apart from this age of global whining. *The New York Times Magazine* (March 9, 1975) quotes Reverend Ike as saying: "The best thing you can do for the poor is not to be one of them. And if you must do something, teach the poor how to do something for themselves. If you give a man a fish, you feed him for a day; teach him how to fish, and you feed him forever."

Ayn Rand

P.S. In my *Letter* on "The Inverted Moral Priorities" (Vol. III, No. 21), I wrote: "The higher a society's industrial development, the more expensive the tools required to put men to work (and the greater the productivity of their labor). Some years ago, it took an investment of $5,000 per worker to create jobs in industry; I have no exact figures for the present time, but the investment is now much higher."

Professor C. Lowell Harriss of the Economics Department of Columbia University has graciously sent me some recent figures on this subject, which I want my readers to see.

"Capital invested per production worker in manufacturing [average for all manufacturing]: 1939 - $5,188. 1949 - $8,089. 1959 - $17,528. 1963 - $20,426. 1970 - $37,079." Source: National Industrial Conference Board; Treasury Department; U.S. Department of Labor, Bureau of Labor Statistics; and Tax Foundation computations.

(This *Letter* was written later than the date that appears on its heading.)

This is to say a personal "thank you" to the readers who sent so many kind letters and cards during my recent illness. I regret that I cannot answer your messages individually, but I want each of you to know how much I appreciate your thoughtfulness and concern.

I am happy to tell you that the operation was a complete success and that I am now fully recovered.

In view of the lengthy delay in our publication schedule, I am presently working out a change of format for the *Letter*; I will inform you about it in the near future. Meanwhile, thank you for your patience and courtesy during all of that difficult period.

Ayn Rand

OBJECTIVIST CALENDAR

The following starting dates have been scheduled for taped lecture courses. Although these courses began during the period when the *Letter*'s publication schedule was interrupted, they are still in progress.

Leonard Peikoff's *Modern Philosophy: Kant to the Present*. Calgary, Alberta, Canada, January 27 (contact Al Kincius, 403-264-5254); Nashville, February 5 (R. Paul Drake, 615-322-4465, after 7:30 P.M.). Dr. Peikoff's *Introduction to Logic*. Dallas, February 19 (Harry Knickerbocker, 214-691-5645, eves.); Rochester, N.Y., March 16 (Paul Westrich, 716-247-7782); San Antonio-Austin area, March 16 (Lee Brooks, 512-684-7565, eves.).

Allan Blumenthal's *Music: Theory, History and Performance*. Boston, February 21 (Frank Peseckis, 617-261-2491, eves.); Rockford, Ill., February 24 (Fredrick

Marler, 815-397-5083, eves.); Denver, February 27 (Robert Gifford, 303-751-8052); Portland, Oreg., March 8 and Eugene, Oreg., March 23 (Joyce Hoberg Lee, 503-636-4268, eves.); Washington, D.C.-Maryland area, March 18 and Washington, D.C.-Virginia area, March 30 (Jack Crawford II, 301-422-9165, Monday-Wednesday, 6-10 P.M.); Cleveland, March 31 (Lesley Dunn, 216-423-3147, eves.).

We have been asked to announce that on Friday, April 18, Dr. Allan Gotthelf (Visiting Assistant Professor of Philosophy, Swarthmore College) will give a lecture at Hunter College, under the auspices of Hunter College Students of Objectivism. Title: "Love and Metaphysics: Aristotelian vs. Platonic." Time: 7:30 P.M. Place: Roosevelt House, 47-49 East 65th Street, New York City. For further information, call Robin Stark, (914) 969-2027 (eves.).

B.W.

The Ayn Rand Letter, published fortnightly by The Ayn Rand Letter, Inc., 183 Madison Avenue, New York, N.Y. 10016.
Contributing Editor: **Leonard Peikoff**; Subscription Director: **Elayne Kalberman**; Production Manager: **Barbara Weiss.**

Vol. III, No. 24 August 26, 1974

THE LESSONS OF VIETNAM

The televised scenes of South Vietnam's sudden collapse at Da Nang seemed oddly familiar to me; they had a faded, distant quality of déjà vu. The scenes of people in hopeless flight, the panic, the despair, the frantic struggle for a foothold on the last plane or ship leaving a doomed land, with everything left behind and nothing ahead - people running into a void outside history, as if squeezed off the face of the earth - I had seen it all before. It took me a moment and a shock of sadness to realize where I had seen it: this was the Russian population fleeing before the advance of the Red Army in the civil war of 1918-21.

The newscaster's voice said that fleeing South Vietnamese soldiers had seized control of an American rescue ship and had proceeded to rob, rape and murder refugees, their own countrymen. I felt indignation, disgust, disappointment - and, again, a faint touch of familiarity. The shock was more painful, this time, when I realized that _this_ was an example of the ignominious amorality of the so-called political right.

Let me hasten to say that individual brutes exist in any army and cannot be taken as representative of an entire people; that the atrocities committed by those particular South Vietnamese would not even be reported if and when committed by the North Vietnamese, since such atrocities represent the official, ideological policy of North Vietnam; that South Vietnam does _not_ represent the political right nor the political anything. Granting all this, it is still true that if a group of soldiers attack their own countrymen, in the midst of a national disaster, it means that attackers and victims have no values in common, not even the solidarity of primitive tribalism, that they have nothing to uphold or defend militarily, that they do not know what they are fighting for. And, in today's world, there is no one to tell them.

I was in my early teens during the Russian civil war. I lived in a small town that changed hands many times. (See _We the Living_; that part of the story is autobiographical.) When it was occupied by the White Army, I almost longed for the return of the Red Army, and vice versa. There was not much difference between them in practice, but there was in theory. The Red Army stood for totalitarian dictatorship and rule by terror. The White Army stood for nothing; repeat: _nothing_. In answer to the monstrous evil they were fighting, the Whites found nothing better to proclaim than the dustiest, smelliest bromides of the time: we must fight, they said, for Holy Mother Russia, for faith and tradition.

I wondered, even in those years, which is morally worse: evil - or the appeasement of evil, the cowardly evasion that leaves an evil unnamed, unanswered and unchallenged. I was inclined to think that the second is worse, because it makes the first possible. I am certain of it today. But in the years of my adolescence, I did not know how rare a virtue intellectual integrity (i.e., the *non-evasion* of reality) actually is. So I kept waiting for some person or group among the Whites to come out with a real political manifesto that would explain and proclaim *why* one must fight against communism and *what* one must fight for. I knew even then that the "what" was freedom, *individual* freedom, and (a concept alien to Russia) *individual rights*.

I knew that man is *not* a slave of the state; I knew that man's right to his own life (and, therefore, to freedom) has to be upheld with as great and proud a sense of moral righteousness, as any idea could ever deserve; I knew that nothing less would do - and that without such a stand the anti-Reds were doomed. But I thought that this was self-evident, that the whole civilized world knew it, and that there surely existed some minds able to communicate this knowledge to Russia, which was perishing for lack of it. I waited through the years of the civil war. Nothing resembling that manifesto was ever uttered by anyone.

In a passive, indifferent way, the majority of the Russian people were behind the White Army: they were not *for* the Whites, but merely *against* the Reds; they feared the Reds' atrocities. I knew that the Reds' deepest atrocity was intellectual, that the thing which had to be fought - and *defeated* - was their *ideas*. But no one answered them. The country's passivity turned to hopeless lethargy, as people gave up. The Reds had an incentive, the promise of nationwide looting; they had the leadership and the semidiscipline of a criminal gang; they had an allegedly intellectual program and an allegedly moral justification. The Whites had icons. The Reds won.

I learned a great deal in the years since. I learned that the concept of individual rights is far, far from self-evident, that most of the world does not grasp it, that the United States grasped it only for a brief historical moment and is now in the process of losing the memory. I learned that the civilized world is being destroyed by its dominant schools of philosophy - by irrationalism, altruism, collectivism - and, specifically, that altruism is the tear gas that defeats resistance, by reducing men to crying and vomiting.

The hardest thing to learn (the most difficult one to believe) was the fact that the so-called political rightists in this country - the alleged defenders of freedom (i.e., of capitalism) - were as vague, as empty and as futile as the leaders of the White Army (more shamefully so, since they had a much, much greater knowledge to evade). For years, the intellectual posture of America's political leaders has been a long, pleading, appeasing, self-abasing whine of apology for this country's greatness - an apology addressed to every advocate or perpetrator of collectivism's horrors and failures anywhere on earth.

But even American politicians had some sort of stature when compared to their intellectual mentors, those (to me, still incredible) bipeds who - unable to find a moral justification for man's life and happiness - attempted to defend freedom on the grounds of altruism (of the "public good"), or on the grounds of faith in the supernatural, or on the grounds of brushing the issue aside and proclaiming that morality is irrelevant to economics (i.e., to man's life and livelihood).

(At a certain point, in recent years, I realized with astonishment that the kind of voice and manifesto I had been waiting for, was my own. No, this is not a boast; it is an admission of a sort I don't like to make: a complaint. [I don't like self-pity.] I did not want, intend or expect to be the only philosophical defender of man's rights, in the country of man's rights. But if I am, I am. And, dear reader, if I am giving you the kind of intellectual ammunition [and inspiration] I had so desperately waited to hear in my youth, I'm glad. I can say that I know how you feel.)

No country could stand for long on the kind of moral erosion that the altruists and amoralists of the right had done their best to aid and abet. The war in Vietnam was the result and dramatization of that erosion. The military collapse of South Vietnam was preceded by the philosophical collapse of the United States some decades earlier.

It was a shameful war - not for the reasons which leftists and sundry friends of North Vietnam are proclaiming, but for the exactly opposite reasons: shameful, because it was a war which the U.S. had no <u>selfish</u> reason to fight, because it served no national interest, because we had nothing to gain from it, because the lives and the heroism of thousands of American soldiers (and the billions of American wealth) were sacrificed in pure compliance with the ethics of altruism, i.e., selflessly and senselessly.

In compliance with epistemological irrationalism, it was a war and a non-war at the same time. It was a modern monstrosity called a "no win" war, in which the American forces were not permitted to act, but only to react: they were to "contain" the enemy, but not to beat him.

In compliance with modern politics, the war was allegedly intended to save South Vietnam from communism, but the proclaimed purpose of the war was not to protect freedom or individual rights, it was not to establish capitalism or any particular social system - it was to uphold the South Vietnamese right to "national self-determination," i.e., the right to vote themselves into any sort of system (including communism, as American propagandists kept proclaiming).

The right to vote is a <u>consequence</u>, not a primary cause, of a free social system - and its value depends on the constitutional structure implementing and strictly delimiting the voters' power; unlimited majority rule is an instance of the principle of tyranny. Outside the context of a free society, who would want to die for the right to vote? Yet <u>that</u> is what the American soldiers were asked to die for - not even for their own vote, but to secure that privilege for the South Vietnamese, who had no other rights and no knowledge of rights or freedom.

Picking up the liberals' discarded old slogan of World War I days - "the self-determination of nations" - the American conservatives were trying to hide the American system, <u>capitalism</u>, under some sort of collectivistic cover. And it is not capitalism that most of them were (and are) advocating, it was a mixed economy. Who would want to die for a mixed economy?

In compliance with a Hegelian sort of "A is non-A" metaphysics, both sides kept contradicting their professed beliefs. Soviet Russia, who regards men as the property and fodder of the state, did not send soldiers to North Vietnam (she could not trust them to fight, so she sent only military supplies). The United States, whose foundation is the supremacy of man's right to life, sent soldiers to die in South Vietnam. Soviet Russia, the philosophical apostle of materialism, won the war in Vietnam by spiritual, i.e., moral-intellectual, means: the

North Vietnamese and the Vietcong were thoroughly indoctrinated with the notion of the righteousness of their cause. The United States - whose modern leadership scorns materialism and professes to be moved by purely spiritual beliefs (mystical-religious on the right, tribalist and anti-industrial on the left) - abstained from proclaiming any moral principles or any principles whatever, and relied on an abundance of material supplies to fight the war, an abundance of planes, bombs and guns in the hands of men who had no idea of why they should use them.

The savagely primitive farmers of North Vietnam had an incentive, the promise of looting the richer, industrialized South; they had the leadership and the semidiscipline of a criminal gang; they had an allegedly intellectual program, Marxism, and an allegedly moral justification: altruism, the sacrifice of all to some "higher" cause. The South Vietnamese had nothing but some mixed-economy echoes of the same altruism. The North Vietnamese won.

As a rule, there is an ugly period of gloating among the winners and of bitter buck-passing among the losers, following a war. But I do not know of a historical precedent for the spectacle displayed by American intellectuals: an explosion of gloating over America's "defeat," of proclaiming America's "weakness," of denouncing America's "guilt," of glorifying and glamorizing the enemy, of pelting America with insults, accusations, humiliations - like an orgy of spitting at their own country's face.

When a national catastrophe, such as the U.S. involvement in Vietnam, has no generally known reason and no clearly perceivable cause, one may find leads to some contributory causes by observing who profits from the catastrophe. The intellectuals are the profiteers on the Vietnam war. They are of so miserably small a stature that it would be impossible to suspect them of causing the disaster. They are not lions, but jackals. (The lion who avenged himself for too long a neglect, was philosophy, which left the U.S. vulnerable to the jackals.) What are the suspicious paw-prints of a scavenger pack?

Observe the double-standard switch of the anti-concept of "isolationism." The same intellectual groups (and even some of the same aging individuals) who coined that anti-concept in World War II - and used it to denounce any patriotic opponent of America's self-immolation - the same groups who screamed that it was our duty to save the world (when the enemy was Germany or Italy or fascism), are now rabid isolationists who denounce any U.S. concern with countries fighting for freedom, when the enemy is communism and Soviet Russia.

The catch phrase of these new isolationists is a shabby little equivocation to the effect that "other countries are not ours to lose" - e.g., we did not lose South Vietnam (or China, or Hungary, or Czechoslovakia), because it was not ours to lose - i.e., the fate of other countries is none of our business. This means: other countries are not ours to judge, to deal with, to trade with, or to help. (Unless it is help with no strings attached, i.e., help without moral judgment, political appraisal, or even humanitarian concern about the results - as demanded by Laos, when it threw out a U.S. aid agency, but wanted the U.S. money turned over to the Laotian government.)

The purpose of this new isolationism is to play on the American people's legitimate weariness, confusion and anger over Vietnam, in the hope of making the U.S. government afraid to become involved in another foreign war of any kind. This would paralyze the U.S. in the conduct of any foreign policy not agreeable to Soviet Russia. The first intended victim of the new isolationism will probably be Israel - if the "anti-war" efforts of the new isolationists succeed. (Israel and Taiwan are the two countries that need and deserve U.S. help - not in the name of international altruism, but by reason of actual U.S. national interests in the Mediterranean and the Pacific.)

To oppose the spread of communism, is a worthy goal. But one cannot oppose it in jungle villages while surrendering civilized countries - and one cannot oppose it by hiding from the world the nature and the moral meaning of communism's only opposite and enemy: capitalism. To use America's phony involvement in Vietnam as a scarecrow to keep us away from the real, the essential centers of the fight against communism - _this_ is the current gimmick or policy of the neo-isolationists.

(To be continued.)

Ayn Rand

P.S. This _Letter_ was written in May 1975.

This is to announce that _The Ayn Rand Letter_ will shortly be changed from a fortnightly to a monthly publication.

Miss Rand has found that it is impossible for her to complete a philosophical article every two weeks. Any time-requiring event in her life, professional or personal, has proved to be incompatible with that type of deadline.

The new schedule will begin after Miss Rand finishes the third full year of the _Letter_, i.e., Volume III, Number 26. Beginning with Volume IV, the _Letter_ will be issued twelve times a year, on a monthly basis.

The note which you will find enclosed, will tell you about the effect of this change on your present subscription, and about our new rates.

Thank you for your interest in this publication.

Leonard Peikoff

OBJECTIVIST CALENDAR

The following starting dates have been scheduled for the taped lectures of Allan Blumenthal's course, _Music: Theory, History and Performance_. Richardson, Texas, mid-June (contact Katherine Kroeger, 214-235-8938, 6-10 P.M.); Los Angeles, July 8 (Michael Berliner, 213-474-0173, after 5 P.M., from June 12 on).

We have been asked to announce that reproductions of paintings and drawings by Joan Mitchell Blumenthal, José Manuel Capuletti, Frank O'Connor and Ilona Royce Smithkin, are still available from Sures Art Enterprises, Ltd. For descriptive brochures and current prices, write to SAE, Ltd., P.O. Box 207, Silver Spring, Maryland 20907.

B.W.

The Ayn Rand Letter, published fortnightly by The Ayn Rand Letter, Inc., 183 Madison Avenue, New York, N.Y. 10016.

Contributing Editor: **Leonard Peikoff**; Subscription Director: **Elayne Kalberman**; Production Manager: **Barbara Weiss.**

Vol. III, No. 25 September 9, 1974

THE LESSONS OF VIETNAM

Part II

Observe the frame-up staged against America's military power.

One of the methods used by statists to destroy capitalism, consists in establishing controls that tie a given industry hand and foot, making it unable to solve its problems, then declaring that freedom has failed and stronger controls are necessary. A similar frame-up is now being perpetrated against America's military power. It is claimed that the U.S. forces were defeated - _in a war they had never been allowed to fight_. They were defeated, it is claimed - two years after their withdrawal from Vietnam. The ignominious collapse of the South Vietnamese, when left on their own, is being acclaimed as an American _military_ failure.

There is no doubt that America's entire involvement in Vietnam is a failure unworthy of a great power. It is a _moral_ failure, a diplomatic failure, a political failure, a philosophical failure - the failure of American politicians and of their intellectual advisers. But to regard it as a _military_ failure is worse than outrageous, when you consider the heroic performance of Americans in a war they should never have had to fight. If there are men or groups with a vested interest in creating an impression of America's _military weakness_, use your own judgment as to their nature and goals.

Now observe the moral bankruptcy of the "humanitarians." After decades of ever louder protestations of compassionate concern with every possible form of suffering - the suffering of the poor, the young, the old, the female, the black, the brown, the Indian, the sick, the weak, the illiterate, the retarded, the criminal, the psychotic - after such a barrage of pleas and threats, of saccharine and blood, that one could be tempted, in protest, to hate babies and kittens, the altruists have suddenly shut up before an unprecedented atrocity of historic scale: the murder of a city, the evacuation of Phnom Penh.

A horde of savages that would make Attila look civilized by comparison, has given the world a perfect concretization of three abstractions, which civilized men have taken with too foggy a tolerance: collectivism, which regards individual lives as of no value - the rule of force, which implements the whims of the subhuman - ecology as a social principle, which condemns cities, culture, industry, technology, the intellect, and advocates men's return to "nature," to the state of grunting subanimals digging the soil with their bare hands.

Since the Khmer Rouge are peasants who feel hatred for cities, the inhabitants of Phnom Penh - its entire population without exceptions - were ordered to march out of the city and to go on marching until they reached uninhabited countryside, where they were to start farming on their own, without knowledge, tools or seed. This order applied to everyone: young and old, rich and poor, men, women and children, the well and the ill, even the crippled and, according to a news report, even the hospital patients who had just had their legs amputated. Everyone was ordered to walk. They walked.

This is all we know. There have been no further reports on the fate of that evacuation. After a few shocked remarks, there were no protests from our media or from those liberal altruists who cry over the victims of "relative poverty" in America. The liberals had been minimizing or ridiculing the conservatives' fear that a "blood bath" would follow a communist victory. If human suffering concerned them at all, one would expect the altruists to scream their heads off against an atrocity which is worse than a blood bath: a mass execution by long-drawn-out torture. But the altruists have shut their traps. So have the altruists of Europe. There has been no significant protest from the hundreds of world organizations devoted to the relief of suffering, including that contemptible citadel of global hypocrisy, the U.N.

The best commentary on Phnom Penh, of those I have read, was "Get Out of Town" by William Safire, a conservative (The New York Times, May 12, 1975). "In all human history nothing has taken place quite like the emptying of Phnom Penh. Sennacherib destroyed Babylon, the Romans sacked Carthage, and Hitler's bombers leveled Guernica, but in every case the attacker was destroying a particular city, not the idea of a city itself....A city is civilization; civilization is diversity and creativity, which needs personal freedom; Communism is by its nature anti-city, anti-civilization, anti-freedom. The Khmer Rouge understand this; too many Americans do not."

To go from the horrendous to the grotesque, consider the Mayaguez incident. I hasten to say that were it not for the proper and highly moral action taken by President Ford, the consequences of that incident could have been more horrendous than Phnom Penh. That a small band of those same Cambodian savages dared seize an unarmed American ship, was such an affront to America (and to civilization) that the collapse of international law would have followed, if President Ford had not acted as he did. To borrow Senator Goldwater's very appropriate phrase, every "half-assed nation" would have felt free to attack the U.S. - which would have meant world rule by terrorist gangs.

We shall never know whether the seizure of the Mayaguez was a deliberate provocation to test what the global communist scum could get away with - or the spontaneous feat of a local gang drunk with power and acting more royalist than their kings. But this does not concern us: in either case, when a foreign country initiates the use of armed force against us, it is our moral obligation to answer by force - as promptly and unequivocally as is necessary to make it clear that the matter is non-negotiable.

Believe it or not, some American intellectuals (and some politicians) objected to President Ford's action. Mr. Anthony Lewis went so far as to declare it was America that was "a bully among nations, acting without consultation, without concern for facts or principle." (The Times, May 19, 1975.) His principle (and filthy accusations) rests on the fact that "we allowed less than a day and a half for a response from the untried and isolated government of a shattered country." After which, he struggles to prove that part of the U.S. bombing of a Cambodian airport "could only have been punitive in purpose." (I hope so.)

This is international altruism gone wild. It demands that the U.S. give up self-defense in order to make allowances for an "untried government." (This means, I suppose, that we should wait until that government has gained experience in attacking us.) If those Cambodian brutes were so ignorant as to permit themselves an attack on a U.S. ship, the more reason to use force in answer, in order to teach them caution in the future; force is the only language that totalitarian brutes understand.

An interesting appraisal of the Mayaguez incident was given by C.L. Sulzberger, a liberal, who hailed President Ford's action in a column entitled "Just What The Doctor Ordered." (The Times, May 17, 1975.) Since Mr. Sulzberger's columns deal mainly with the reactions of other countries to U.S. foreign policy, his enthusiasm in this instance is significant, revealing, and almost pathetic: it shows the extent of the dismal, gray hopelessness previously conveyed by our international diplomacy. "Small as the incident may later seem in history, a polluting stain is being erased from the previous American image of lassitude, uncertainty and pessimism. This is a matter of world ideological concern as well as strategic balances because too many democracies are sick....Now a new vibrancy creeps into the picture."

Mr. Sulzberger explains: "The internationally renowned 'American tempo' and productivity still lag and the work ethic with its emphasis on speed and efficiency - whether prompted by puritanism or by the capitalistic profit motive - has certainly undergone visible and withering change. In this uncertain age American flabbiness is...harmful to the United States." In the absence of American leadership, Mr. Sulzberger concludes, many Western countries were left adrift. "Now Gerald Ford seems to have put an end to that sad phase. Abruptly he has shown Americans and the world that he knows how to get where he wishes to go. Hopefully, he also possesses a good sense of direction."

Nobody respects an altruist, neither in private life nor in international affairs. An altruist is a person who keeps sacrificing himself and his values, which means: sacrificing his friends to his enemies, his allies to his antagonists, his interests to any cry for help, his strength to anyone's weakness, his convictions to anyone's wishes, the truth to any lie, the good to any evil. How would you tell an altruist's treacherously unpredictable policy from that of a cowardly milquetoast? And what difference would it make to his victims? A man practicing such a policy would be mistrusted and despised by everyone, including the profiteers on his "generosity" - yet this is the policy which the U.S. has come as close to practicing as any nation ever could. And if foreign countries are now cheering the sight of a giant, the U.S., standing up to a flea, Cambodia, it is the (momentary) defeat of altruism that they are cheering unknowingly, it is America's liberation from altruism's flabbiness, it is America's declaration to all the fleas of the world that the world is not to perish as a meal for fleas.

The American people's reaction to the Mayaguez incident was a great - and tragic - demonstration of America's sense of life. Great, because when the news broke out, the letters and wires received at the White House ran - ten to one - in support of President Ford's intention to use military force against Cambodia. The American people - battered by disillusionment over a senseless war and by vicious pro-enemy, anti-war propaganda - could have had an excuse to fear and oppose the potential risk of another war in the same geographical area. But they did not. They understood the principle involved; they were willing to fight, but not to accept an affront. (Which, incidentally, is the only way to avoid a war, but not many leaders said so.) This grasp of principles, when the chips are down, this proudly rebellious independence in the face of lies and threats, is what defeats the calculations of the manipulators, foreign or domestic, who attempt to con the American people.

The tragedy lies in the fact that these American characteristics can come into play only when the chips are down. A sense of life cannot foresee or prevent a catastrophe; it cannot save people from moving toward a disaster by single, gradual steps. Foresight and prevention are the task of conscious thought and knowledge, i.e., of political philosophy. In regard to a nation, they are the task of the intellectuals.

Just as Russia collapsed through the philosophical bankruptcy of its anticommunists, so did China - so did every rebellion against communist rule, in Hungary, in Czechoslovakia, in Poland - so did, does and will every attempt to hold out a mixed economy (and/or socialism!) as an alternative to communism worth fighting and dying for. The greatest intellectual crime today is that of the alleged "rightists" in this country: with reason, reality and (potentially) an overwhelming majority of the American people on their side, they are afraid to assume the responsibility of a moral crusade for America's values - i.e., for capitalism (with everything this necessitates). Observe the extent to which the tear gas of altruism is making them squirm. But unless men are brave enough to ventilate this country's moral atmosphere, they have no chance. For a nation, as for a man, a Declaration of Independence implies a declaration of self-esteem. Neither can stand without the other.

Much as I admire President Ford's conduct in the Mayaguez incident, there are many aspects of his policies with which I do not agree. The relevant one here is his appeal to leave Vietnam behind us and to avoid "recriminations" over that war. The lessons of Vietnam, he claims, have been learned. Have they?

What - and who - got us into that war? Why? For what reason and purpose? How did a war advocated and begun by the liberals (mainly by Presidents Kennedy and Johnson) become the conservatives' war? Isn't a moral obscenity such as a "no win" war unconstitutional - as a violation of the soldiers' right to life - since it turns soldiers into cannon fodder?

These are just a few of the questions to which the country has no clear answers. The Vietnam war is one of the most disastrous foreign-policy failures in U.S. history. We spent two years investigating everything connected with seven burglars sent by a bunch of politicians to bug the headquarters of another bunch of politicians. What was that compared to the enormity of Vietnam? We kept hearing, and are still hearing, that Watergate represented a threat to our rights, our freedom, our social system, and our Constitution. What was Vietnam?

Shouldn't there be an investigation of the U.S. involvement in Vietnam, wider, deeper and more thorough than the investigation of Watergate - with nationally televised Congressional hearings, with dozens of famous witnesses, with daily headlines, editorials, debates, etc.? The purpose? To discover the causes in order to avoid the recurrence (or the continuation) of the policies that led to Vietnam.

Such an investigation would not be likely to uncover any crimes other than intellectual ones - but try to imagine the magnitude of those! Intellectual crimes cannot - and need not - be punished by law: the only punishment required is exposure. But who would conduct such an inquiry? Who would be able to ask the right questions, and integrate the answers, and point out the contradictions, and hammer at the evasions, and bring out the fundamental issues? Obviously, this is not a task for politicians, it is a task for theoretical thinkers, for intellectuals, for philosophers. But today they are the men who were responsible for the kind of thinking that was responsible for our involvement in Vietnam...

This is the reason why no such investigation can or will be held today. And this is the all-inclusive lesson to be learned from Vietnam.

Ayn Rand

P.S. This Letter was written in May 1975.

The Ayn Rand Letter, published fortnightly by The Ayn Rand Letter, Inc., 183 Madison Avenue, New York, N.Y. 10016.

Contributing Editor: **Leonard Peikoff**; Subscription Director: **Elayne Kalberman**; Production Manager: **Barbara Weiss.**

Vol. III, No. 26 September 23, 1974

FROM MY "FUTURE FILE"

This Letter was written over a period of about fifteen years.

I keep a file of notes for my future work, many of which are passages I have cut out of my various articles in the past. I have cut them chiefly for lack of space, and I save them for more detailed discussion in the future.

But I realized that although I intend to write further on some of these subjects, it is very unlikely that I will write again on others. Yet I do want to express these particular thoughts - so I decided to publish them in their original form, as self-contained excerpts. Square brackets indicate additions I have written for the present issue.

News Events

There is no proper solution for the war in Vietnam: it is a war we should never have entered. We are caught in a trap: it is senseless to continue, and it is now impossible to withdraw - impossible and unspeakable, for the following reasons. Soviet Russia has been preparing for a showdown war with the West, from as far back as the twenties; this is part of her declared, official doctrine; and her only hope of winning in such a war is the constantly reiterated claim that the Western "proletariat" will not let their governments fight against Soviet Russia. Khrushchev repeated that claim during his visit to the United States.

The Western "proletariat," i.e., the people, have not fulfilled that hope, but the Western intellectuals have. This is the motive behind the small, but very noisy minority of Vietniks in this country, whether they know it individually or not: to give the world the impression that the American people will not fight against Soviet Russia. If the United States were now to withdraw from Vietnam, it would be a confirmation and a surrender, a declaration of our debilitated impotence. It could unleash an unobstructed flood of communism on the world, and a nuclear war - since it would encourage the Soviet thugs, doped by their own stooges and their own propaganda, to believe that America would not fight. (Cut from "The Wreckage of the Consensus." Written in 1967. See the paperback edition of my book Capitalism: The Unknown Ideal.)

[I hope that our foreign policy will be clear and forceful enough to forestall such an impression.]

* * * * *

Observe the stressed insistence of modern intellectuals on the virtue of "flexibility" as opposed to "ideological dogmatism." By "dogmatism," they do not mean merely faith in mystical doctrines, but adherence to rationally demonstrated principles as well (they make no distinction between these two). It is to prepare them for decisions such as the present one [on wage-price controls] that the notion of pragmatist "flexibility" was devised. What it actually means is that men may permit their wishes or whims to be inflexible, in the hope that a flexible reality will adjust to them. But reality is not flexible; neither is men's need of a livelihood; neither are the requirements of a productive economy.

As to the effect of Pragmatism on personal integrity, on credibility, and on public confidence, the best summary was given by James Reston in a discussion of another, earlier turnabout of Mr. Nixon's policy: the attempted rapprochement with Red China. (The New York Times, September 3, 1971.) "The problem here in Tokyo and to a lesser extent in Peking after all this is that officials don't quite know what to expect next. Maybe the Democrats and even the 'regular' Republicans are in the same boat. They recognize the problems and even admire the President's willingness to reverse and even defy his past policies and principles, but they are left without much confidence about where we all go from here....Mr. Nixon has demonstrated his flexibility and his pragmatism, but where will this lead next month or next year?" (Cut from "The Moratorium on Brains." This Letter, October 25-November 8, 1971.)

Psychology

The intellectuals' standard complaint against this country - that it is materialistic, anti-intellectual, and treats them unfairly - is an obvious rationalization. There is no country on earth where the intellectuals receive higher remuneration for their services, have greater opportunities, and are given more authentic (often undeserved) respect. But this is not what they want: what they want is authority - arbitrary authority over uncritically obedient, helplessly awed subjects - a thing this country will never give to anyone. There are no such subjects in this country, beyond a handful of specially conditioned college students. (Cut from "A Preview," Part III. This Letter, August 28, 1972.)

* * * * *

The effort that the men of that category [the men of a perceptual mentality] dread is mental, not physical. Their desire is to escape from a firm, objective, absolute, unforgiving reality - a reality that has no compassion for a mind that feels like slipping out of focus. It is the desire to substitute the absolutism of a dictator for the much more firm absolutism of nature.

The very aspect of a dictatorship which makes the man of reason, the man of a conceptual mentality, prefer to die rather than live at the mercy of some ruler's whims, is the aspect that appeals to the perceptual mentalities: the capricious, arbitrary, unpredictable nature of a ruler gives them the universe they want, where nothing is certain or firm, where they may be destroyed at whim, but may also have a chance to beg forgiveness, and a chance to get away with their whims - where they may get away with a lifetime of unfocused stupor, where their ideas, values, motions, work and food will be obtained, not by choice, but by obedience.

That is the soul and the ideals of the men who have won their chance to destroy the world by means of being called "impractical idealists." (Cut from "For the New Intellectual." Written in 1960. See my book of the same title.)

* * * * *

What men need to learn is that their subconscious is a computer, programmed by their minds, which generates their emotions, that it is a needed computer on their journey through life, but that the task of their minds is to control and correct it in accordance with the facts they observe as they move forward.

There was one incident in the journey of Apollo 11 that stands as an immortal symbol of this issue. In the last moments before the lunar landing, Commander Armstrong observed that the spacecraft's overworked computer was directing it toward a crash in a crater filled with rocks. He had ninety seconds in which to take over and to select a better place for landing. He did.

Most people have longer than that to correct their course when their mind observes that the misprogrammed computer of their emotions is directing them toward a crash. But - in consequence of their modern training - most of them choose to crash. (Cut from "Apollo 11." *The Objectivist*, September 1969.)

Ethics

There is nothing so naive as cynicism. A cynic is one who believes that men are innately depraved, that irrationality and cowardice are their basic characteristics, that fear is the most potent of human incentives - and, therefore, that the most practical method of dealing with men is to count on their stupidity, appeal to their knavery, and keep them in constant terror.

In private life, this belief creates a criminal; in politics, it creates a statist. But, contrary to the cynic's belief, crime and statism do not pay.

A criminal might thrive on human vices, but is reduced to impotence when he comes up against the fact that "you can't cheat an honest man." A statist might ride to power by dispensing promises, threats and handouts to the seekers of the unearned - but he finds himself impotent in a national emergency, because the language, methods and policies which were successful with parasites, do not work when the country needs producers. (A note written in 1961.)

* * * * *

"Productive work" does not mean the blind performance of the motions of some job. It means the conscious, rational pursuit of a *productive career*. In popular usage, the term "career" is applied only to the more ambitious types of work; but, in fact, it applies to *all* work: it denotes a man's attitude toward his work.

The difference between a career-man and a job-holder is as follows: a career-man regards his work as constant progress, as a constant upward motion from one achievement to another, higher one, driven by the constant expansion of his mind, his knowledge, his ability, his creative ingenuity, never stopping to stagnate on any level. A job-holder regards his work as a punishment imposed on him by the incomprehensible malevolence of reality or of society, which, somehow, does not let him exist without effort; so his policy is to go through the least amount of motions demanded of him by somebody and to stay put in any job or drift off to another, wherever chance, circumstances or relatives might happen to push him.

In this sense, a man of limited ability who rises by his own purposeful effort from unskilled laborer to shop-foreman, is a career-man in the proper, ethical meaning of the word - while an intelligent man who stagnates in the role of a company president, using one-tenth of his potential ability, is a mere job-holder. And so is a parasite posturing in a job too big for his ability. It is not the degree of a man's ability that is ethically relevant in this issue, but the full, purposeful use of his ability. (Cut from "The Objectivist Ethics." Written in 1961. See my book The Virtue of Selfishness.)

* * * * *

Let me relate two incidents out of many in my own experience that helped me to identify the nature of the Argument from Intimidation.

The first was a private discussion in which I was presenting my political ideas. My opponent exclaimed indignantly, in rebuttal: "I've never heard of such a thing!" "Well, you're hearing it now," I said. This had some peculiar effect on him, out of proportion to the meaning of my words; it was as if I had cut the ground from under his feet; he argued half-heartedly a little longer, then gave up.

It was not till much later that I understood what it was that he had been telegraphing by the second-hander's code: "Since no one else has said such a thing before, who are you to say it?" My answer told him who I was: it rejected any second-hand sanction and demanded that he focus on the facts of reality. On such terms, he was unable to argue or to think.

The second incident took place when I was working in Hollywood. A literary agent approached me with an offer from a major studio that wanted me to write a novel for one of their stars, on a theme and subject of their own choice, a novel that would be published first as a book, then made into a movie. I answered that I don't write novels to order. He said, in an oddly resentful, accusatory manner: "Many good writers are doing it." I answered cheerfully: "Then I guess I'm not a good writer." Again, this had some peculiar, disproportionate, ground-cutting effect on him; he argued half-heartedly a little longer, then gave up.

Later, I grasped what he had been signaling between the lines. He was threatening me with the fact that good writers do not share my attitude. What my answer told him was: "If such are their values, then I do not care to be regarded as good by their standards." He had no further arguments to offer. (Cut from "The Argument from Intimidation." Written in 1964. See The Virtue of Selfishness.)

Politics

There is still another sense in which capitalism may be said to achieve "the common good." Since the good is objective, it has to be defined in terms of abstract principles covering a wide variety of concretes; it is up to every individual to apply these principles to the particular goals and problems of his own life. It is only such principles that can provide a [proper] common bond among men; men can agree on a principle without necessarily agreeing on the choice of concretes. For instance, men can agree that one should work, without prescribing any man's particular choice of work.

It is only with abstract principles that a social system may properly be concerned. A social system cannot force a particular good on a man nor can it force him to seek the good: it can only maintain conditions of existence which leave him free to seek it. A government cannot live a man's life, it can only protect his freedom. It cannot prescribe concretes, it cannot tell a man how to work, what to produce, what to buy, what to say, what to write, what values to seek, what form of happiness to pursue - it can only uphold the principle of his right to make such choices.

It is in this sense that "the common good" or "the public interest" lies not in what men do when they are free, but in the fact that they are free. (Cut from "What Is Capitalism?" Written in 1965. See Capitalism: The Unknown Ideal.)

* * * * *

Property rights and the right of free trade are man's only "economic rights" (they are, in fact, political rights). There can be no such thing as "an economic bill of rights." But observe that its advocates are the vociferous enemies of and have all but destroyed those two authentic rights.

Political rights pertain to the organization of a society, to the establishment of a social system, a government, and a legal code. As such, they are validated by reference to the facts of reality: to man's nature and to the metaphysical conditions of his life on earth - and they establish basic principles for the creation of a rational, morally defensible society, i.e., a society appropriate to the requirements of man's survival.

But the concept of "economic rights" is a mystics' flight from reality. It is an attempt to extort from some men (from the ablest and most productive) a security which is metaphysically impossible: the security of a guaranteed, automatic, effortless, unearned survival. Glance back at that Democratic Party platform [of 1960] and observe such eloquent touches as "the right to enjoy good health" and "the right to adequate protection from the economic fears of old age, sickness, accidents and unemployment." It is an attempt to change the nature of the universe by bureaucratic edict, by the power of the coercive mechanism of the absolutist state, by the omnipotent power of a gun - and by the grace of those nameless victims who are to perish in that attempt and whose existence must never be acknowledged. It is an attempt to gain freedom from reality - from nature, from reason, logic, thought, effort or work. But there is no such thing as freedom from reality. (Cut from "Man's Rights." Written in 1963. See The Virtue of Selfishness.)

* * * * *

A businessman's success depends on his intelligence, his knowledge, his productive ability, his economic judgment - and on the voluntary agreement of all those he deals with: his customers, his suppliers, his employees, his creditors or investors. A bureaucrat's success depends on his political pull. A businessman cannot force you to buy his product; if he makes a mistake, he suffers the consequences; if he fails, he takes the loss. A bureaucrat forces you to obey his decisions, whether you agree with him or not - and the more advanced the stage of a country's statism, the wider and more discretionary the powers wielded by a bureaucrat. If he makes a mistake, you suffer the consequences; if he fails, he passes the loss on to you, in the form of heavier taxes.

A businessman cannot force you to work for him or to accept the wages he offers; you are free to seek employment elsewhere and to accept a better offer, if you can find it. (Remember, in this context, that jobs do not exist "in nature," that they do not grow on trees, that someone has to create the job you need, and that that someone, the businessman, will go out of business if he pays you more than the market permits him to pay you.) A bureaucrat can force you to work for him, when he achieves the totalitarian power he seeks; he can force you to accept any payment he offers - or none, as witness the forced labor camps in the countries of full statism. (Cut from "America's Persecuted Minority: Big Business." Lecture at The Ford Hall Forum, Boston, December 17, 1961. See Capitalism: The Unknown Ideal.)

* * * * *

Some of you may believe that some things are more important than freedom, justice or human rights - for instance, the seizure of unearned material wealth, or the power to distribute the goods one has not produced, or charity to some at the price of the immolation of others. Most of today's intellectuals believe that these things justify statism. But if such is their belief, why do they choose to disguise it by using the concepts and terms of a political theory which is the opposite of their own? They should not talk about "_freedom_ from want" when they mean: "_privilege_ to loot" - or about "a _just_ distribution of goods" when they mean: "a _demand_ for an unearned share of the goods produced by others" - or about "the _right_ to a minimum livelihood" when they mean: "the chance to _enslave_ those who will provide it." "Freedom," "justice" and "rights" are concepts that belong to the political-economic system of laissez-faire capitalism. (Cut from the same lecture.)

Epistemology

With the collapse of philosophy in the twentieth century, science has been left in the state of an expedition that has lost its leader and its way in the jungle of the unknown, with the members of the disintegrating team - from assistants to secretaries to mess boys to weight-carriers - scattering through the jungle in any random direction, each going blindly through the motions of inquiry, turning over rocks, scratching tree-bark, counting raindrops, with no knowledge of what he is looking for, what to do if he finds it, or what may be properly taken as knowledge. (Cut from "What Is Capitalism?" Written in 1965. See _Capitalism: The Unknown Ideal_.)

Esthetics

Have you noticed the proliferation of trashy science-fiction movies dealing with the same preposterous theme: the stealthy takeover of this earth by some evil creatures from outer space, in the form of giant insects, conscious vegetables, or shapeless sponges growing at uncheckable speed? These stories are true, in the way that ancient myths were true - as an attempt of primitive men to express an inexplicable fear by projecting an emotional equivalent: by inventing some mysterious phenomenon, such as a supernatural monster, which they had no power to identify; the phenomenon was fantasy, the emotion it evoked was real. (Cut from "The Establishing of an Establishment." This _Letter_, May 8-22, 1972.)

[Modern men sense that some terrible evil is taking over the world, an evil which is more frightening, more insidious, and less tangible than flying saucers: irrationalism. As evidence, I offer the movies in which a character stares at the face of another, of his wife or child or closest friend, trying to guess whether an evil force has taken over the body of his loved one. _This_ is a good dramatization of the emotion a man would experience at the sudden, wanton, incomprehensible irrationality of another man.]

Ayn Rand

P.S. This _Letter_ was published in June 1975.

The Ayn Rand Letter, published fortnightly by The Ayn Rand Letter, Inc., 183 Madison Avenue, New York, N.Y. 10016.

Contributing Editor: **Leonard Peikoff**; Subscription Director: **Elayne Kalberman**; Production Manager: **Barbara Weiss.**

Vol. IV, No. 1 October 1975

FROM THE HORSE'S MOUTH

While recovering from my illness, I had a chance to catch up on some reading I had wanted to do for a long time. Opening one interesting book, I almost leaped out of bed. I read some statements which shocked me much more profoundly than any of today's pronouncements in the news magazines or on the Op-Ed page of The New York Times. I had been reporting on some of those journalistic writings occasionally, as a warning against the kinds of intellectual dangers (and booby traps) they represented. But they looked like cheap little graffiti compared to the sweep of wholesale destruction presented in a few sentences of that book.

Just as, at the end of Atlas Shrugged, Francisco saw a radiant future contained in a few words, so I saw the long, dismal, slithering disintegration of the twentieth century held implicitly in a few sentences. I wanted to scream a warning, but it was too late: that book had been published in 1898. Written by Friedrich Paulsen, it is entitled Immanuel Kant: His Life and Doctrine.

Professor Paulsen is a devoted Kantian; but, judging by his style of writing, he is an honest commentator - in the sense that he does not try to disguise what he is saying: "There are three attitudes of the mind towards reality which lay claim to truth, - Religion, Philosophy, and Science....In general, philosophy occupies an intermediate place between science and religion....The history of philosophy shows that its task consists simply in mediating between science and religion. It seeks to unite knowledge and faith, and in this way to restore the unity of the mental life....As in the case of the individual, it mediates between the head and the heart, so in society it prevents science and religion from becoming entirely strange and indifferent to each other, and hinders also the mental life of the people from being split up into a faith-hating science and a science-hating faith or superstition." (New York, Ungar, 1963, pp. 1-2.)

This means that science and mystic fantasies are equally valid as methods of gaining knowledge; that reason and feelings - the worst kinds of feelings: fear, cowardice, self-abnegation - have equal value as tools of cognition; and that philosophy, "the love of wisdom," is a contemptible middle-of-the-roader whose task is to seek a compromise - a détente - between truth and falsehood.

Professor Paulsen's statement is an accurate presentation of Kant's attitude, but it is not Kant that shocked me, it is Paulsen. Philosophic system-builders, such as Kant, set the trends of a nation's culture (for good or evil), but it is the average practitioners who serve as a barometer of a trend's success or failure. What shocked me was the fact that a modest commentator would start his book with a statement of that kind. I thought (no, hoped) that in the nineteenth century a man upholding the cognitive pretensions of religion to an equal footing with science, would have been laughed off any serious lectern. I was mistaken. Here was Professor Paulsen casually proclaiming - in the nineteenth century - that philosophy is the handmaiden of theology.

Existentially (i.e., in regard to conditions of living, scale of achievement, and rapidity of progress), the nineteenth century was the best in Western history. Philosophically, it was one of the worst. People thought they had entered an era of inexhaustible radiance; but it was merely the sunset of Aristotle's influence, which the philosophers were extinguishing. If you have felt an occasional touch of wistful envy at the thought that there was a time when men went to the opening of a new play, and what they saw was not Hair or Grease, but Cyrano de Bergerac, which opened in 1897 - take a wider look. I wish that, borrowing from Victor Hugo's Notre Dame de Paris, someone had pointed to the Paulsen book, then to the play, and said: "This will kill that." But there was no such person.

I do not mean to imply that the Paulsen book had so fateful an influence; I am citing the book as a symptom, not a cause. The cause and the influence were Kant's. Paulsen merely demonstrates how thoroughly that malignancy had spread through Western culture at the dawn of the twentieth century.

The conflict between knowledge and faith, Paulsen explains, "has extended through the entire history of human thought" (p. 4) and Kant's great achievement, he claims, consisted in reconciling them. "...the critical [Kantian] philosophy solves the old problem of the relation of knowledge and faith. Kant is convinced that by properly fixing the limits of each he has succeeded in furnishing a basis for an honorable and enduring peace between them. Indeed, the significance and vitality of his philosophy will rest principally upon this....it is [his philosophy's] enduring merit to have drawn for the first time, with a firm hand and in clear outline, the dividing line between knowledge and faith. This gives to knowledge what belongs to it, - the entire world of phenomena for free investigation; it conserves, on the other hand, to faith its eternal right to the interpretation of life and of the world from the standpoint of value." (P. 6.)

This means that the ancient mind-body dichotomy - which the rise of science had been healing slowly, as men were learning how to live on earth - was revived by Kant, and man was split in two, not with old daggers, but with a meat-ax. It means that Kant gave to science the entire material world (which, however, was to be regarded as unreal), and left ("conserved") one thing to faith: morality. If you are not entirely certain of which side would win in a division of that kind, look around you today.

Material objects as such have neither value nor disvalue; they acquire value-significance only in regard to a living being - particularly, in regard to serving or hindering man's goals. Man's goals and values are determined by his moral code. The Kantian division allows man's reason to conquer the material world, but eliminates reason from the choice of the goals for which material achievements are to be used. Man's goals, actions, choices and values - according to Kant - are to be determined irrationally, i.e., by faith.

In fact, man needs morality in order to discover the right way to live on earth. In Kant's system, morality is severed from any concern with man's existence. In fact, man's every problem, goal or desire involves the material world. In Kant's system, morality has nothing to do with this world, nor with reason, nor with science, but comes - via feelings - from another, unknowable, "noumenal" dimension.

If you share the error prevalent among modern businessmen, and tend to believe that nonsense such as Kant's is merely a verbal pastime for mentally unemployed academicians, that it is too preposterous to be of any practical consequence - look again at the opening quotation from Professor Paulsen's book. Yes, it is nonsense and vicious nonsense - but, by grace of the above attitude, it has conquered the world.

There is more than one way of accepting and spreading a philosophic theory. The guiltiest group, which has contributed the most to the victory of Kantianism, is the group that professes to despise it: the scientists. Adopting one variant or another of Logical Positivism (a Kantian offshoot), they rejected Kant's noumenal dimension, but agreed that the material world is unreal, that reality is unknowable, and that science does not deal with facts, but with constructs. They rejected any concern with morality, agreeing that morality is beyond the power of reason or science and must be surrendered to subjective whims.

Now observe the breach between the physical sciences and the humanities. Although the progress of theoretical science is slowing down (by reason of a flawed epistemology, among other things), the momentum of the Aristotelian past is so great that science is still moving forward, while the humanities are bankrupt. Spatially, science is reaching beyond the solar system - while, temporally, the humanities are sliding back into the primeval ooze. Science is landing men on the moon and monitoring radio emissions from other galaxies - while astrology is the growing fashion here on earth; while courses in astrology and black magic are given in colleges; while horoscopes are sent galloping over the airwaves of a great scientific achievement, television.

Scientists are willing to produce nuclear weapons for the thugs who rule Soviet Russia - just as they were willing to produce military rockets for the thugs who ruled Nazi Germany. There was a story in the press that during the first test of an atom bomb in New Mexico, Robert Oppenheimer, head of the Los Alamos group who had produced the bomb, carried a four-leaf clover in his pocket. More recently, there was the story of Edgar Mitchell, an astronaut who conducted ESP experiments on his way to the moon. There was the story of a space scientist who is a believer in occultism and black magic.

Such is the "honorable and enduring peace" between knowledge and faith, achieved by the Kantian philosophy.

Now what if one of those men gained political power and had to consider the question of whether to unleash a nuclear war? As a Kantian, he would have to make his decision, not on the grounds of reason, knowledge and facts, but on the urgings of faith, i.e., of feelings, i.e., on whim.

There are many examples of Kantianism ravaging the field of today's politics in slower, but equally lethal, ways. Observe the farce of inflation versus "compassion." The policies of welfare statism have brought this country (and the whole civilized world) to the edge of economic bankruptcy, the forerunner of which is inflation - yet pressure groups are demanding larger and larger handouts to the nonproductive, and screaming that their opponents lack "compassion." Compassion as such cannot grow a blade of grass, let alone of wheat. Of what use is the "compassion" of a man (or a country) who is broke - i.e., who has consumed his resources, is unable to produce, and has nothing to give away?

If you cannot understand how anyone can evade reality to such an extent, you have not understood Kantianism. "Compassion" is a moral term, and moral issues - to the thoroughly Kantianized intellectuals - are independent of material reality. The task of morality - they believe - is to make demands, with which the world of material "phenomena" has to comply; and, since that material world is unreal, its problems or shortages cannot affect the success of moral goals, which are dictated by the "noumenal" real reality.

Dear businessmen, why do you worry about a half-percent of interest on a loan or investment - when <u>your</u> money supports the schools where those notions are taught to your children?

No, most people do not know Kant's theories, nor care. What they do know is that their teachers and intellectual leaders have some deep, tricky justification - the trickier, the better - for the net result of all such theories, which the average person welcomes: "Be rational, except when you don't feel like it."

Note the motivation of those who accepted the grotesque irrationality of Kant's system in the first place - as declared by his admirer, Professor Paulsen: "There is indeed no doubt that the great influence which Kant exerted upon his age was due just to the fact that he appeared as a deliverer from unendurable suspense. The old view regarding the claims of the feelings and the understanding on reality had been more and more called in question during the second half of the eighteenth century....Science seemed to demand the renunciation of the old faith. On the other hand, the heart still clung to it....Kant showed a way of escape from the dilemma. His philosophy made it possible to be at once a candid thinker and an honest man of faith. For that, thousands of hearts have thanked him with passionate devotion." (Pp. 6-7; emphasis added - no other comment is necessary.)

Philosophy is a necessity for a rational being: philosophy is the foundation of science, the organizer of man's mind, the integrator of his knowledge, the programmer of his subconscious, the selector of his values. To set philosophy against reason, i.e., against man's power of cognition, to turn philosophy into an apologist for and a protector of superstition - is such a crime against humanity that no modern atrocities can equal it: it is the cause of modern atrocities.

If Paulsen is representative of the nineteenth century, the twentieth never had a chance. But if men grasp the source of their destruction - if they dedicate themselves to the greatest of all crusades: a crusade for the absolutism of reason - the twenty-first century will have a chance once more.

Ayn Rand

OBJECTIVIST CALENDAR

The following starting dates have been scheduled for taped lecture courses (some of these courses have already begun).

Allan Blumenthal's Music: Theory, History and Performance. Calgary, Alberta, Canada, Sept. 15 (contact Al Kincius, 403-264-5254); Hartford, Oct. 21 (Brian Bambrough, 203-563-7902).

Leonard Peikoff's Modern Philosophy: Kant to the Present. Boston, Sept. 26 (Roger Burkhart, 617-253-1000, Dorm Line 5-6178, after 7 P.M.); Minneapolis, Oct. 17 (Jane Kettleson, 612-633-4085, eves.). Founders of Western Philosophy: Thales to Hume. West Lafayette, Ind., Oct. 19 (Richard Matula, 317-463-3646, eves.); St. Louis, Oct. 17 (Fulton Huxtable, 314-291-7130). Dr. Peikoff's Introduction to Logic. Kansas City, Oct. 19 and Cape Girardeau, Mo., Nov. 2 (Fulton Huxtable, 314-291-2539, call collect); Lafayette, Cal., Oct. 26 (Raymond Cole, 415-653-2323, weekdays or 415-283-2778, eves. and weekends).

B.W.

The Ayn Rand Letter, published fortnightly by The Ayn Rand Letter, Inc., 183 Madison Avenue, New York, N.Y. 10016.

Contributing Editor: **Leonard Peikoff**; Subscription Director: **Elayne Kalberman**; Production Manager: **Barbara Weiss.**

Vol. IV, No. 2 November-December 1975

A LAST SURVEY

Part I

This is to tell you, regretfully, that I am discontinuing the publication of The Ayn Rand Letter after these last two issues.

I say "regretfully" because I am sorry to disappoint the readers who have supported this publication, and its predecessors, for so many years. That is why I wanted to make this announcement personally and to tell you my reasons. But first, I want to thank all of you for your interest, your support, and your patience in this last, very difficult year.

My illness was not the cause of my decision, but it did contribute to the cause - by giving me time to reconsider certain issues. There are many aspects of the Letter's publication which I will miss and regret, but, for me personally, the decision to close it, was something of a relief.

There are three reasons for my decision.

1. I had hoped that I could learn to write the Letter fast enough to be able to combine it with working on a book. I have tried it. It took me four years to convince myself that it cannot be done or, at least, that I cannot do it. I thought that it was merely a matter of automatizing the process of writing an article. But my second reason showed me that I was mistaken.

2. My purpose in writing articles was to discuss the application of Objectivism to modern events - i.e., to explain today's trends by identifying their philosophical roots and meaning, and to present the Objectivist alternative. In this respect, reality has proved too cooperative: so many trends are going the way I predicted they would (only more crudely and viciously so) that I find myself in the "untitled" predicament over and over again. Most of you will remember that I wrote "An Untitled Letter" once (January 29, 1973). Its first paragraph read: "The most appropriate title for this discussion would be 'I told you so.' But since that would be in somewhat dubious taste, I shall leave this Letter untitled." I am tired of saying "I told you so" indirectly. It would be better for someone else to observe it.

My criterion in selecting the subjects I discussed was: the subject's philosophical importance, which had to be demonstrable, but not too obvious. Today, the issues are becoming so crudely obvious that those who do not see them, cannot be helped by any discussion. Time and again, I have found that the basic evil behind today's ugliest phenomena is altruism. Well, I told you so. I have been telling you so since We The Living, which was published in 1936. Those who still pretend that they can save freedom and individual rights without challenging altruism, are outside my power of persuasion (and, I suspect, outside any sort of persuasion, i.e., outside the field of ideas).

Today's disasters are concrete manifestations of one or more of three fundamental abstractions: mysticism, altruism, collectivism. I have discussed such manifestations in many of their current forms, so that the method or pattern of identifying, understanding and opposing them should be clear to you by now. You should be able to recognize them in their next appearance or latest fashion, which will vary endlessly in form, but not in essence. In this respect, I have given you the intellectual ammunition required.

As far as I am concerned, I do not care to go on analyzing and denouncing the same indecencies of the same irrationalism. I enjoy writing only so long as I say something I have not said before. For me, every article has to involve some new identification, big or small, not only new to my readers, but new to me. I cannot bear merely to repeat myself. In the last two years, watching the gray monotony of the culture's disintegration, I saw that the time was approaching when I would have to report on the same kinds of phenomena over and over again. I began to feel as if I would have to become a journalist. Casting no aspersions on that once honorable and always badly needed profession, a journalist is what I most emphatically am not.

This is why I was unable to automatize the process of writing an article. What I was asking of myself was a contradiction: one automatizes the known, one cannot automatize the new.

3. The state of today's culture is so low that I do not care to spend my time watching and discussing it. I am haunted by a quotation from Nietzsche: "It is not my function to be a fly swatter." The evils destroying modern civilization are enormous, but their representatives, agents and carriers are too small to contemplate. This is an illustration of the fact that evil is not "single and big, [it is] many and smutty and small" (<u>The Fountainhead</u>) - or that evil is a default.

Perhaps the last cultural fad one could still argue against was Karl Marx. But Freud - or Rawls? To argue against such persons is to grant them a premise they spend all of their effort disproving: that reason is involved in their theories. (One may discuss those people only long enough to expose the specific nature of their irrationality. Some excellent work is being done in this field, notably by Professor George Walsh in regard to Rawls's "theory of justice.")

You will probably want to ask about my future plans. I intend to return, full time, to my primary work: writing books. I have two books in mind, but I have not yet decided which I will do first.

Now I want to give you a brief indication of the kinds of issues that are coming up, on which you might want to know my views.

1. The Presidential election of 1976. I urge you, as emphatically as I can, <u>not</u> to support the candidacy of Ronald Reagan. I urge you not to work for or advocate his nomination, and not to vote for him. My reasons are as follows: Mr. Reagan is not a champion of capitalism, but a <u>conservative</u> in the worst sense of that word - i.e., an advocate of a mixed economy with government controls slanted in favor of business rather than labor (which, philosophically, is as untenable a position as one could choose - see Fred Kinnan in <u>Atlas Shrugged</u>, pp. 541-2). This description applies in various degrees to most Republican politicians, but most of them preserve some respect for the rights of the individual. Mr. Reagan does not: he opposes the right to abortion.

Not every wrong idea is an indication of a fundamental philosophical evil in a person's convictions; the anti-abortion stand _is_ such an indication. There is no room for an error of knowledge in this issue and no venal excuse: the anti-abortion stand is horrifying _because_ it is non-venal - because no one has anything to gain from it and, therefore, its motive is pure ill will toward mankind.

Never mind the vicious nonsense of claiming that an embryo has a "right to life." A piece of protoplasm has no rights - and no life in the human sense of the term. One may argue about the later stages of a pregnancy, but the essential issue concerns only the first three months. To equate a _potential_ with an _actual_, is vicious; to advocate the sacrifice of the latter to the former, is unspeakable.

One method of destroying a concept is by diluting its meaning. Observe that by ascribing rights to the unborn, i.e., the nonliving, the anti-abortionists obliterate the rights of the living: the right of young people to set the course of their own lives. The task of raising a child is a tremendous, lifelong responsibility, which no one should undertake unwittingly or unwillingly. Procreation is not a duty: human beings are not stock-farm animals. For conscientious persons, an unwanted pregnancy is a disaster; to oppose its termination is to advocate sacrifice, not for the sake of anyone's benefit, but for the sake of misery qua misery, for the sake of forbidding happiness and fulfillment to living human beings.

A man who takes it upon himself to prescribe how others should dispose of their own lives - and who seeks to condemn them by law, i.e., _by force_, to the drudgery of an unchosen, lifelong servitude (which, more often than not, is beyond their economic means or capacity) - such a man has no right to pose as a defender of rights. A man with so little concern or respect for the rights of the individual, cannot and will not be a champion of freedom or of capitalism. (For a full discussion of the issue of birth control, see my article "Of Living Death.")

Some people say that Mr. Reagan does not mean his anti-abortion stand, that he adopted it merely to buy the votes of a certain pressure group. If true, this makes his position more reprehensible still. Even if all modern politicians have to compromise on some issues, a certain fastidiousness is required of them when they are choosing _what_ to give in on and _to whom_.

If, which is very doubtful, Mr. Reagan gets the Republican nomination, there is only one group of people that could make it necessary to vote for him: the Democrats - by nominating some equivalent of Senator McGovern, such as Senator Kennedy.

In today's political situation, a positive statement about any candidate is valid only at the time it is made, since no one can tell whose policy may change to what or when. Up to the present (and, I hope, in the future), I support the candidacy of President Ford. I disagree with his policies in very many respects, but he deserves great credit for his fight against government spending and for his attempt to cut down on government controls. Obviously, he is an honest man who shows no symptoms of power-lust and no desire to run everyone's life. This is an unusual value in today's politics.

Many things could be said on the negative side, but the major one is President Ford's foreign policy, including détente and the rest of the mess he inherited. The worst heirloom is Mr. Kissinger; but it looks as if, in the last three years, Mr. Kissinger was given enough rope to demonstrate the exact nature of the "practicality" of his, not policy, but range-of-the-moment manipulations.

President Ford's recent cabinet shuffle was not an enlargement, but a shrinking of Mr. Kissinger's influence. Most of the press, however, misinterpreted it as a Kissinger victory - and this (as well as the trip to China) was probably the reason why President Ford's popularity fell in the polls taken since. People are getting wise to the fact that Metternichean amorality is not a good import on American soil.

(To be continued.)

Ayn Rand

Full refunds for the unexpired portion of all paid subscriptions to The Ayn Rand Letter will be mailed out to our readers within the next two months.

Elayne Kalberman

OBJECTIVIST CALENDAR

On Wednesday, January 28, 1976, Ayn Rand will participate in a forum sponsored by the National Town Meeting's Bicentennial Series. The other participant will be Senator Walter F. Mondale. Time: 10:30-11:30 A.M. Place: Eisenhower Theatre, Kennedy Center, Washington, D.C. Topic: "The Limits of Government." Admission to the program is free. (The National Town Meeting forums are broadcast nationwide by National Public Radio. For the date of Miss Rand's appearance on the broadcast, check with your local Public Radio Station.)

On Sunday, April 11, 1976, Ayn Rand will give a talk at The Ford Hall Forum in Boston. The topic will be announced at a later date, in the Forum program. Time: 8 P.M. Place: Alumni Hall, Northeastern University, 360 Huntington Avenue. Advance tickets are available only to members of the Forum. (On past occasions, the auditorium was filled to capacity, and many people had to be turned away. If you plan to attend, we suggest that you arrive at Alumni Hall far in advance of 7:30 P.M., when the doors open.)

Starting on January 23, 1976, the taped lectures of Allan Blumenthal's course, Music: Theory, History and Performance, will be given in Minneapolis. For further information, contact Jane Kettleson at (612) 633-4085 (eves.).

A Dutch edition of Ayn Rand's Capitalism: The Unknown Ideal has just been published in Holland by Uitgeverij Luitingh B.V. Publishers. This is the first translation of a nonfiction work by Miss Rand.

B.W.

The Ayn Rand Letter, published fortnightly by The Ayn Rand Letter, Inc., 183 Madison Avenue, New York, N.Y. 10016.

Contributing Editor: **Leonard Peikoff**; Subscription Director: **Elayne Kalberman**; Production Manager: **Barbara Weiss.**

Vol. IV, No. 3 January-February 1976

A LAST SURVEY

Part II

2. Today's political trend. There can be no doubt that this country is turning to the right. Observe the nationwide rejection of the various state bond issues, i.e., of government spending, in the last elections. This was another confirmation of my trust in the common sense of the American people, who have rejected statism every time they had a clear-cut opportunity to do so.

But the people are helpless without intellectual leadership. It is too late for cheap, shopworn slogans. The world is being destroyed by the wrong philosophy - and only the right philosophy, which provides a fully consistent stand, can save it.

To rush into politics on an intellectual shoestring, to posture as a champion of freedom, to get into power by cashing in on the people's hope and despair, then to offer them, for inspiration and guidance, nothing better than the old religion-family-tradition stuff - the stuff that has lost the world to communism - is so dark a betrayal that those guilty of it deserve what they get. They do not merely lose, they disillusion the people, they discredit the ideas of a free society and thus assist the victory of statism. So much for today's conservatives, "Libertarians," and sundry third- fourth- or tenth-party organizers.

3. The progress of Objectivism. On July 19, 1975, *The New Republic* published a cheap little column or editorial entitled "The Ayn Rand Factor." It began by stating: "I keep running across bits and pieces of Ayn Rand in Mr. Ford's speeches." This would be wonderful, and the world would be in a much, much better condition if this were true, but it is not true. The rest of the column was devoted to disproving its own contention.

An old smear technique consists in quoting an adversary's least significant statements, in order to make it appear that he has said nothing better. That column quoted President Ford on such stuff as: "over a period of 90 years we have erected a massive federal regulatory structure" and ascribed *this* remark to my influence. Anyone who has ever read anything I have written, knows that no Ayn Rand is needed to arrive at observations of that kind.

I am not an admirer of President Ford's speechwriters, but they have given him better material than that, notably some strong, clear-cut statements in support of individual rights, which I would be happy to take credit for, if I had any influence in the matter, which I do not have. Apparently, the columnist was afraid to quote those statements and afraid to mention the essentials of my philosophy (such as individualism), so he engaged in a sort of compound misrepresentation of President Ford, of Alan Greenspan, and of me.

I laughed when I read that column, because the columnist's fear was obvious. I said to my friends: "If he thinks there's an 'Ayn Rand factor' around, let him think it." Today, I am beginning to wonder whether there might not be an "Ayn Rand factor" in the world, though not in the way he meant it.

A story in The New York Times (March 22, 1974) discussed a growing opposition to the welfare state in the Scandinavian countries. In Denmark "a party formed solely in opposition to the welfare state received nearly half a million votes in its first campaign and became the second largest in Parliament. A similar party, equally new, jolted Norwegian politics last September by capturing 108,000 votes and four parliamentary seats." The founder of that Norwegian party, Anders Lange, "claims American inspiration. 'You can say our principle is that of Ayn Rand and Milton Friedman,' he explained. 'They are leaders in our economic philosophy.'"

I have virtually nothing in common with Mr. Friedman, whom I do not regard as an advocate of capitalism - but I could not resent that kind of confusion at that kind of distance, when much greater confusions exist in our own country, so the story pleased me.

A story on Margaret Thatcher, the new leader of the British Conservative party (The New York Times Magazine, June 1, 1975), stated that her "'think tank' of intellectuals" is studying and popularizing "the theories of" - and there followed a hodgepodge of so-called rightist names, ending on "Ayn Rand." I did not pay much attention to that story - but, later, I was told privately that my ideas actually do have an influence on Mrs. Thatcher's group.

The story that gave significance to the preceding ones appeared in The New York Times on December 15, 1975. It was a brief profile of Malcolm Fraser, the new Prime Minister of Australia, who defeated the welfare-statist Labor Party by the biggest landslide in Australian history. I was delighted with the results of that election, but as I reached for the profile, I couldn't help wondering what disappointing stuff I would have to read. Instead, I read the following:

"All of this [Mr. Fraser's activity] is directed to his single-minded pursuit of a conservative political philosophy that is best summarized by that of his favorite author, Ayn Rand. His favorite book is the Rand novel, 'Atlas Shrugged,' a saga of a welfare state run wild."

Dear readers, ideas do work, they do reach the minds of the wise and honest. No, I am not saying that Mr. Fraser is necessarily an Objectivist: a great many disagreements and/or errors are possible in the practical implementation of a philosophy. What is great about this story is the fact that Mr. Fraser stated openly that he agrees with Atlas Shrugged - and he not merely won an election, but won it by an unprecedented landslide. Apparently, the Australian people were ready to hear the truth, and Malcolm Fraser was able to convey it. No, this does not mean a guaranteed future of freedom for Australia. But it does mean a great opportunity (and the only kind of opportunity) to achieve it.

Once, years ago, I said that the progress of my career reminded me of the progress of Howard Roark in The Fountainhead. Today, the progress of my philosophy is following the same pattern: "It was as if an underground stream flowed through the [world] and broke out in sudden springs that shot to the surface at random, in unpredictable places." I do not know how many of these springs will remain and, eventually, grow into rivers, or how many will turn muddy and dry up. But in the case of these last, others will rise to take their place. Such is the history of the progress of innovations.

Now to turn from a world scale back to our own activities and to the present. The Objectivist Calendar in this Letter lists the kinds of activities that will be of interest to my readers - as far in advance as the information available permits.

I call your particular attention to Leonard Peikoff's lecture course on The Philosophy of Objectivism. This course does not start until September, but it is to be a memorable event. It will be a systematic presentation of my philosophy, from metaphysics through esthetics, intended for informed students of Objectivism, given by a teacher who has demonstrated a matchless ability to present ideas clearly and dramatically. Until or unless I write a comprehensive treatise on my philosophy, Dr. Peikoff's course is the only authorized presentation of the entire theoretical structure of Objectivism, i.e., the only one that I know of my own knowledge to be fully accurate.

I regret that the closing of the Letter will not permit me to present further excerpts from Dr. Peikoff's book The Ominous Parallels (to be published by Weybright & Talley, Inc.). I cannot tell you the book's publication date, because Dr. Peikoff has not yet completed the manuscript, but I have read it much further than the excerpts we have published - and my informal report to you is: Oh, boy! I thought I knew the subject, but that book has taught me something about the influence of philosophy on a country's culture.

The Objectivist Book Service will be closed eventually, but it will remain open for a while. If there are pamphlets or back issues which you wanted or intended to buy, now is the time to get them, because the stock will not be reprinted.

Among current books, I recommend to your attention a very interesting work, Steel Titan: The Life of Charles M. Schwab (Oxford University Press) by Robert Hessen. Dr. Hessen, a former contributor to The Objectivist, is a historian who teaches at Stanford University and is a Research Fellow at the Hoover Institute. Steel Titan is the first biography of Charles Schwab (1862-1939), who was one of the last great American industrialists. It is a comprehensive presentation, focused primarily on Schwab's business career, describing the struggles, the problems, and the achievements of the man who rose from day laborer to first president of U.S. Steel, and then to founder of Bethlehem Steel.

Schwab's life could be entitled "An American Tragedy" with much more justice than the trashy novel which bears that title. Reading Steel Titan, one sees, in microcosm, the tragedy of late-nineteenth-century America: unprecedented industrial achievements created in philosophical silence. Like most of his fellow industrialists, Schwab was a genius in production and a deaf-mute in philosophy - with the emphasis on "mute." He liked to make public speeches, but had no idea of the intellectual foundations or justification of business or of politics. This made him vulnerable to the most vicious charges and attacks of leftist intellectuals and politicians, who pursued him throughout his life. He did not know how to defend himself - and there were no effective voices to defend him.

This issue is not Dr. Hessen's theme: he has written a factual biography, meticulously researched and thoroughly documented, presenting Schwab's virtues as well as his flaws, including his conventional, often unattractive, personal life. But the facts speak for themselves. I urge you not to miss Appendix B, which is subtitled "The Genealogy of an Historical Myth: The Armor Scandal of 1894." It offers a brief and devastating picture of how misrepresentations are perpetuated by American historians.

(The list price of *Steel Titan* is $14.95; available from The Objectivist Book Service at $13.50.)

In regard to our future activities, we have received so many letters urging us to continue publishing the Objectivist Calendar in some form that we are now considering the possibility of offering such a service. The tentative plan is to issue bulletins, for a nominal fee, on an irregular basis, as the news warrants. The news would cover activities such as lectures, courses, books, television and radio appearances, my views on political candidates, etc. If you would be interested in subscribing to such a service, please send a post card to that effect to Barbara Weiss, c/o *The Ayn Rand Letter*, 183 Madison Avenue, New York, N.Y. 10016. It is understood that such a post card does not represent any obligation on your part.

If you wish to keep in touch with us, please keep your name on our mailing list by notifying us (at the above address) of any future change in your address.

Thank you for the very nice letters you wrote me about the closing of this *Letter*. I truly appreciate your understanding.

With my best wishes to all of you, I will say good-by and good premises -

Ayn Rand

Full refunds for the unexpired portion of all paid subscriptions to *The Ayn Rand Letter* will be mailed out to our readers by the end of February.

Elayne Kalberman

OBJECTIVIST CALENDAR

As we announced in our last Calendar, Miss Rand will be speaking at The Ford Hall Forum in Boston on Sunday, April 11. The Forum has asked us to make the following statement: They will not accept new memberships after March 15, and memberships will not be sold at the door on the night of Miss Rand's lecture. The Forum has arranged to provide a second room, near Alumni Hall, to handle the overflow crowd;

people seated in this room will not be able to see Miss Rand, but they will be able to hear her lecture and the question-and-answer period.

Beginning Tuesday, September 14, Leonard Peikoff will offer a twelve-lecture course in New York City on _The Philosophy of Objectivism_. The lectures will be given on Tuesday evenings, at 7:30 P.M., from September 14 through December 21 (omitting October 19, November 2 and November 30). Place: Statler Hilton Hotel, Broadway and 33rd Street. Brochures, including registration forms, will be sent next July to individuals in the New York Metropolitan area who are now on our mailing list. Further information can be obtained, after July, from Flora Reekstin, P.O. Box 533, Richmond Hill, N.Y. 11418.

Next year, tapes of the lectures will be made available in other cities to groups of ten persons or more, on a rental basis. Inquiries may be sent, late this fall, to Barbara Weiss, P.O. Box 95, Murray Hill Station, New York, N.Y. 10016.

The following taped lecture courses are currently available to groups of ten persons or more, on a rental basis. Leonard Peikoff's _Founders of Western Philosophy: Thales to Hume_ (12 lectures), _Modern Philosophy: Kant to the Present_ (12 lectures), _Introduction to Logic_ (10 lectures). Allan Blumenthal's _Music: Theory, History and Performance_ (12 lectures). For further information, contact Barbara Weiss, P.O. Box 95, Murray Hill Station, New York, N.Y. 10016.

The following starting dates have been scheduled for taped lecture courses. Leonard Peikoff's _Modern Philosophy: Kant to the Present_. West Lafayette, Ind., February 8 (contact Richard Matula, 317-463-3646, eves.); Indianapolis, March 6 (Richard Matula, 317-259-1902, eves. except Tues.). Dr. Peikoff's _Founders of Western Philosophy: Thales to Hume_. Calgary, Alberta, Canada, February 23 (Al Kincius, 403-264-5254). Allan Blumenthal's _Music: Theory, History and Performance_. Montreal, February 25 (Ferial Balassiano, 514-739-2631 or 514-935-8666); Lafayette, Cal., February 29 (Raymond Cole, 415-284-4193).

Joan Mitchell Blumenthal is planning to resume her Monday evening Life Drawing Classes in New York City on April 5. Those interested should contact her through Dr. Blumenthal's office at (212) PL 2-2162 after March 1.

A full-color reproduction of _The Conductor_, a painting by Joan Mitchell Blumenthal, is available from Sures Art Enterprises, Ltd. The painting portrays a young musician in casual dress, prepared for rehearsal. The background is dark; strong, warm light emphasizes his profile, hands, and baton. For information about _The Conductor_ and other reproductions, write to SAE, Ltd., P.O. Box 207, Silver Spring, Md. 20907.

We have been asked to announce that Dr. George Reisman is planning to offer a nine-lecture course on _Inflation and Price Controls_, tentatively scheduled to begin in New York City in late March or early April. For information about the course, and about possible tape rentals in other cities, write to Dr. Reisman at 420 East 72nd Street, New York, N.Y. 10021.

The Ayn Rand Letter, published fortnightly by The Ayn Rand Letter, Inc., 183 Madison Avenue, New York, N.Y. 10016.

Contributing Editor: **Leonard Peikoff**; Subscription Director: **Elayne Kalberman**; Production Manager: **Barbara Weiss.**

www.ingramcontent.com/pod-product-compliance
Lightning Source LLC
LaVergne TN
LVHW061236100826
845148LV00008B/966

* 9 7 9 8 9 8 6 2 7 0 3 7 1 *